EXAM✓PREP

ACT
2007 Edition

Susan Ludwig

ACT Exam Prep 2007 Edition

International Standard Book Number: 0-7897-3616-0

Printed in the United States of America

First Printing: December 2006

10   09   08   07   06   4   3   2   1

Trademarks

All terms mentioned in this book that are known to be trademarks or service marks have been appropriately capitalized. Que Publishing cannot attest to the accuracy of this information. Use of a term in this book should not be regarded as affecting the validity of any trademark or service mark.

The ACT Assessment is a registered trademark of ACT, Inc., which does not sponsor or endorse this product.

Warning and Disclaimer

Every effort has been made to make this book as complete and as accurate as possible, but no warranty or fitness is implied. The information provided is on an "as is" basis. The authors and the publisher shall have neither liability nor responsibility to any person or entity with respect to any loss or damages arising from the information contained in this book or from the use of the CD or programs accompanying it.

Library of Congress Cataloging-in-Publication data is on file.

Bulk Sales

Que Publishing offers excellent discounts on this book when ordered in quantity for bulk purchases or special sales. For more information, please contact

U.S. Corporate and Government Sales

1-800-382-3419

corpsales@pearsontechgroup.com

For sales outside the U.S., please contact

International Sales

international@pearsoned.com

ASSOCIATE PUBLISHER
David Dusthimer

ACQUISITIONS EDITOR
Betsy Brown

DEVELOPMENT EDITOR
Jill Batistick

MANAGING EDITOR
Patrick Kanouse

PROJECT EDITOR
Seth Kerney

COPY EDITOR
Margaret Berson

INDEXER
Angie Bess

PROOFREADER
Audrey Doyle

TECHNICAL EDITORS
Nina Metzner
Molly Forster

PUBLISHING COORDINATOR
Cindy Teeters

MULTIMEDIA DEVELOPER
Dan Scherf

BOOK DESIGNER
Gary Adair

Contents at a Glance

Introduction   1

Part I: Exam Preparation

CHAPTER 1   Introduction to the ACT Exam   5

CHAPTER 2   The English Test   23

CHAPTER 3   The Reading Test   81

CHAPTER 4   The Writing Test   119

CHAPTER 5   The Mathematics Test   153

CHAPTER 6   The Science Reasoning Test   261

Part II: Practice Exams

FF   Fast Facts   295

CHAPTER 7   Practice Exam 1   303

CHAPTER 8   Answers to Practice Exam 1   385

CHAPTER 9   Practice Exam 2   429

CHAPTER 10   Answers to Practice Exam 2   501

Part III: Appendixes

APPENDIX A   Glossary   535

APPENDIX B   Additional Resources   549

Index   551

Table of Contents

Introduction **1**

   What ACT Exam Prep Is Designed to Do 1

   What ACT Exam Prep Will Not Do 1

   About This Book 1

Part I: Exam Preparation

CHAPTER 1:
Introduction to the ACT Exam **5**

   About the ACT Test 5

      Are You Ready? 6

      Put Yourself to the Test 7

      Assessing Your Exam Readiness 8

   A Personalized Study Plan 9

      Setting Up a Schedule 10

      Structuring Your Study Sessions 11

   Registering for the Test 12

   Keep These Valuable Test-Taking Tips in Mind 14

   What to Expect on Test Day 16

   How to Interpret Your Scores 18

   How the Test Scores Are Used 19

   What Colleges Are Looking For 20

      Most Competitive Schools 20

      Highly Competitive Schools 21

      Very Competitive Schools 21

      Moderately Competitive Schools 21

      Less, or Minimally, Competitive Schools 21

   Where Do You Go from Here? 22

CHAPTER 2:
The English Test **23**

   What to Expect on the ACT English Test 23

      The Test Format 23

      The Passage 24

      The Directions 24

      The Plan 25

   Understanding Punctuation 26

      Apostrophe 26

      Colon 29

Comma 31

Dash 37

Exclamation Point 38

Parentheses 39

Period 40

Question Mark 41

Quotation Marks 42

Semicolon 44

Understanding Basic Grammar and Usage 46

Parts of Speech 46

Subject-Verb Agreement 50

Pronoun-Antecedent Agreement 58

Coordinating Conjunctions 60

Subordinating Conjunctions 61

Sentence Structure 63

Checking for Fragments 63

Revising Run-ons 64

Finding the Main Idea 66

Organization of Sentences in Paragraphs and Passages 68

Sentence and Paragraph Style 70

Sentence Style 71

Paragraph Style 71

Ensuring Consistent Tone and Correct Word Choice 72

Consistent Tone 72

Correct Word Choice 73

Sample ACT English Test Questions 75

Answers to Sample ACT English Questions 78

CHAPTER 3:
The Reading Test **81**

What to Expect on the ACT Reading Test 81

On the Test 81

Directions 81

The Content Areas 82

Preparing for the Reading Test 83

Passage Questions 86

Prose Fiction 89

Working with a Sample Passage 90

Working with Sample Questions 91

Social Science 93

Working with a Sample Passage 95

Working with Sample Questions 96

Humanities 98

   Working with a Sample Passage 99

   Working with Sample Questions 100

Natural Science 102

   Working with a Sample Passage 103

   Working with Sample Questions 104

Sample Exam Prep Passages and Questions 106

   Passage 1 Text 106

   Passage 1 Questions 107

   Passage 2 Text 109

   Passage 2 Questions 110

   Suggested Underlining for Passages 1 and 2 112

   Correct Answers for Passages 1 and 2 115

CHAPTER 4:
The Writing Test **119**

Preparing for the ACT Writing Test 120

   Read Good-Quality Material 120

   Practice Free-Writing 121

   The Actual Directions for the Writing Test 123

   An Explanation of the Actual Directions for the Writing Test 124

The Writing Process: The System You Will Use to Write Your Essay 125

   Step 1: Prewriting 126

   Step 2: Drafting 130

   Step 3: Revising 136

   Sample Prompt 139

How Your Essay Is Scored 140

Practice, Practice, Practice: The Best Way to Improve Your Essay Writing 141

   Practice Finding Opposing Viewpoints 142

   Practice Writing Introductions 145

Challenge Exercises 147

   Challenge Exercise #1 147

   Challenge Exercise #2 147

   Challenge Exercise Essay Responses 148

CHAPTER 5:
The Mathematics Test **153**

The Basic Structure of the Mathematics Test 153

Pre-Algebra and Elementary Algebra 155

   Understanding and Working with Different Number Types 155

   Absolute Value 161

Scientific Notation 163

Properties 164

Roots and Powers 167

Bases and Exponents 170

Factors and Multiples 173

Arithmetic and Geometric Sequences 180

Fractions, Decimals, and Percents 183

Rate Problems 196

Functions 197

Probability 199

Ratio, Proportion, Mean, Median, Mode 203

Algebraic Expressions 209

Solving Linear Equations 220

Solving for a Variable in Terms of Other Variables 221

Solving Systems of Linear Equations 222

Solving Operations with Matrices 224

Solving Inequalities and Inequalities with Absolute Values 225

Intermediate Algebra and Coordinate Graphing 227

Intermediate Algebra 227

Coordinate Graphing 230

Plane Geometry/Trigonometry 236

Plane Geometry 236

Basic Trigonometric Functions 249

Sample Exam Prep Questions and Answers 256

Questions 256

Answers 259

CHAPTER 6:
The Science Reasoning Test **261**

The Basic Structure of the Seven Reading Passages 261

The Passage Text 262

The Data Section 263

The Questions Themselves 263

The Specific Structure of the Three Types of Reading Passages 265

Data Representation 266

Research Summaries 273

Opposing Viewpoints 282

Challenge Questions 284

Challenge Question Answers with Explanations 291

Part II: Practice Exams

Fast Facts **295**

    English 295

    Mathematics 296

        Pre-Algebra and Elementary Algebra 296

        Intermediate Algebra and Coordinate Graphing 298

        Plane Geometry and Trigonometry 299

    Writing 300

    Science 300

CHAPTER 7:
Practice Exam 1 . . . . **303**

    ACT English Assessment 304

        Passage I 304

        Passage II 308

        Passage III 312

        Passage IV 316

        Passage V 321

    ACT Reading Assessment 327

        Passage I: Prose Fiction 327

        Passage II: Social Science 331

        Passage III: Humanities 334

        Passage IV: Natural Science 337

    Math Test 340

    Science Reasoning Test 362

        Passage I, Questions 1–6 362

        Passage II, Questions 7–11 364

        Passage III, Questions 12–17 366

        Passage IV, Questions 18–23 370

        Passage V, Questions 24–28 372

        Passage VI, Questions 29–35 378

        Passage VII, Questions 36–40 380

    ACT Writing Assessment 384

CHAPTER 8:
Answers to Practice Exam 1 . . . . **385**

    English 385

    Reading 394

    Math 400

    Science Reasoning 417

    Scoring Your Sample Test 426

CHAPTER 9:
Practice Exam 2 . . . . **429**

English Test 430

Passage I 430

Passage II 435

Passage III 440

Passage IV 445

Passage V 449

Reading Test 454

Passage I: Prose Fiction 454

Passage II: Social Science 457

Passage III: Humanities 460

Passage IV: Natural Science 463

Math Test 466

Science Reasoning Test 484

Passage I (Questions 1–5) 484

Passage II (Questions 6–12) 486

Passage III (Questions 13–17) 488

Passage IV (Questions 18–23) 490

Passage V (Questions 24–29) 493

Passage VI (Questions 30–34) 495

Passage VII (Questions 35–40) 497

Writing Test 500

CHAPTER 10:
Answers to Practice Exam 2 . . . . **501**

English 501

Reading 510

Math 515

Science 526

Scoring Your Sample Test 531

Part III: Appendixes

APPENDIX A:
Glossary **535**

APPENDIX B:
Additional Resources **549**

English 549

Reading 549

Writing 549

Math 550

Science 550

General ACT Preparation 550

Index **551**

About the Author

Susan French Ludwig is an author of *Exam Cram ACT* and is the author of *Score Higher on the ACT*, both from Que Publishing. She has served as a curriculum designer, textbook writer, tutor, adult education instructor, book author, and author of numerous articles in varied areas of education. She earned her M. A. in education from Pennsylvania State University.

Susan currently works on the community college level, coordinating a National Science Foundation grant created to bring more students into the math, science, technology, and engineering disciplines.

Dedication

To my mother, Carmen B. French

Acknowledgments

Thanks to Betsy Brown and Lynn Haller for their help and guidance.

We Want to Hear from You!

As the reader of this book, *you* are our most important critic and commentator. We value your opinion and want to know what we're doing right, what we could do better, what areas you'd like to see us publish in, and any other words of wisdom you're willing to pass our way.

As an associate publisher for Que Publishing, I welcome your comments. You can email or write me directly to let me know what you did or didn't like about this book—as well as what we can do to make our books better.

Please note that I cannot help you with technical problems related to the topic of this book. We do have a User Services group, however, where I will forward specific technical questions related to the book.

When you write, please be sure to include this book's title and author as well as your name, email address, and phone number. I will carefully review your comments and share them with the author and editors who worked on the book.

Email: scorehigher@pearsoned.com

Mail: David Dusthimer
         Associate Publisher
         Que Publishing
         800 East 96th Street
         Indianapolis, IN 46240 USA

Reader Services

Visit our website and register this book at www.examcram.com/register for convenient access to any updates, downloads, or errata that might be available for this book.

Introduction

Congratulations! You have chosen one of the most detailed and comprehensive ACT study guides on the market today. As you know, taking the ACT Assessment is an important early step in your college planning. In the weeks and months ahead, you will review and prepare for the test—let this wide-ranging book serve as your primary guide. You can think of *ACT Exam Prep* as a tool for doing your best on the assessment. Within these pages, you will find all of the information you need to register and plan for the test, and review and reinforce your understanding of each subject area (English, reading, math, science, and optionally, writing).

What *ACT Exam Prep* Is Designed to Do

This book is designed to be used as a review for the components of the subject areas found on the ACT Assessment. Some students will want to take one of the sample tests at the end of this book prior to beginning to prepare for the ACT. The results of that sample test will pinpoint particular strong and weak areas to help you plan test preparation time.

By systematically reading through each chapter of the book and working through the challenge questions, then taking a practice test under test conditions and reviewing your responses with the correct answers when you have completed the practice test, you will be adequately prepared to do your personal best on the ACT.

What *ACT Exam Prep* Will Not Do

If you do not have a solid understanding of any of the parts of the test, do not depend on this book to teach you. You may want to consider working with a private tutor, talking with your guidance counselor or subject area teachers at your high school, and possibly postponing taking the test until you have received adequate remediation in the areas where you need it. The ACT test covers a vast scope of material. Make sure you are at your test-taking best before attempting it.

About This Book

It is recommended that you work through *ACT Exam Prep* from beginning to end to ensure that you get the most benefit from it. Don't skip portions because you think you know certain material already. You will want to at least skim those parts of the book for any topics with which you are unfamiliar. Make sure you stress the areas where the Self-Assessment indicated you need reinforcement and review before taking the test.

The bulk of *ACT Exam Prep* follows this chapter structure:

▶ A discussion of what to expect on the test

▶ Tips, alerts, and notes concerning that subject area of the test

▶ A narrative of the components making up that subject area

▶ Challenge questions related to the material found on the test

▶ Correct answers and explanations for the challenge questions

There are a few other elements that you should note:

▶ **Sample tests**—The sample tests in Chapters 7 and 9 (with the answer keys in Chapters 8 and 10) are a very close approximation of the types of questions you are likely to encounter on the ACT Assessment that you take.

▶ **Answer keys**—The answer keys provide the correct responses to the sample test questions and include explanations of the correct and incorrect responses.

▶ **Glossary**—The glossary is an alphabetical listing of the important terms used in this book.

▶ **The CD**—The CD provides additional practice items, passages, and test questions for you to review. Remember, though, that the ACT is a paper-and-pencil test. Don't get overly comfortable reading and typing in your responses on the computer. You'll get a test booklet and answer sheet, as well as some scratch paper for taking your actual test.

To ensure that you get the most you can out of this book, you will want to plan adequate time to review and study for the ACT test. Spend the bulk of the days and weeks before the test focused on your review and practice. Instead of watching television, surfing the Internet, or listening to music, spend your time reading, reviewing, and preparing. It may not sound like a whole lot of fun right now, but you will find that the time you invest now is time well spent. You'll never regret that you did all you could to attain your personal best score on the ACT.

TIP

Some students wonder whether they should be taking the ACT or the SAT test. As you probably know, the SAT is also a college admissions test and is accepted by most colleges and universities in the United States. Deciding which of the two tests you should take is completely up to you, your guidance counselor, and your parents or other family members. You can find out more information about the SAT test at www.collegeboard.com.

P A R T I
Exam Preparation

Chapter 1 Introduction to the ACT Exam

Chapter 2 The English Test

Chapter 3 The Reading Test

Chapter 4 The Writing Test

Chapter 5 The Mathematics Test

Chapter 6 The Science Reasoning Test

1

Introduction to the ACT Exam

This chapter is designed to help you understand what the ACT test is all about and what to expect in each subject area.

About the ACT Test

As you probably already know, the ACT Assessment is a national college admissions examination. The ACT Assessment is accepted by almost every college and university in the country, and the scores on the test are used by admissions departments to help make their decisions about accepting students. Scores on the ACT are also used by colleges to help them with students' course placement, for academic advising, and for certain scholarships and student loans. If you are planning to pursue further education after high school, you will probably need to take the ACT test and strive to do your personal best in every subject area.

The ACT Assessment consists of five subtests, and the material presented on the test is what you have learned up until your junior year of high school. The test will measure your ability in the subject areas of English, reading, mathematics, and science, and there is an optional test in writing.

TIP

> Some colleges require the writing test and others do not, although most schools will accept and assess scores from the writing test even if they do not require it. Check with the schools to which you plan to apply to find out their requirements. You can often find this information on individual college websites under "Admission Requirements" and you can also obtain it by calling the schools' Admissions Office.

After you have finished reading and working through *ACT Exam Prep*, the sample tests at the end of the book will provide you with a reasonably accurate post-preparation assessment of your knowledge of each subject area. Some students may choose to take one of the two sample tests before they begin working with the material in this book. In that way, they are able to identify the subject areas where they may need extra time to prepare.

TIP

> After you complete each sample test and compare your responses to the correct ones, remember that reviewing the correct responses and their accompanying explanations can provide further reinforcement of the material. In other words, know why you got a particular question wrong.

Table 1.1 gives an overview of the general format of the ACT, what is included in each subject area test, and how much time is allotted for each section. In the chapters that follow, you will learn more details about what is included in each subject area's test and how you can best utilize the time allotted for each test section.

TABLE 1.1   Overview of the ACT Exam

Test	Subsets Evaluated
English test: 75 questions, 45 minutes	Usage/mechanics: 40 questions Rhetorical skills: 35 questions (Strategy, organization, style)
Math test: 60 questions, 60 minutes	Elementary algebra: 24 questions Intermediate algebra and coordinate geometry: 18 questions Plane geometry and trigonometry: 18 questions
Reading test: 40 questions, 35 minutes	Arts/literature: 20 questions Social studies/sciences: 20 questions
Science Reasoning test: 40 questions, 35 minutes	Data representation: 15 questions Research summaries: 18 questions Conflicting viewpoints: 7 questions
Writing test (optional): 1 writing prompt, 30 minutes	One essay responding to the prompt

Are You Ready?

You may wonder what the best time would be for you to take the ACT. Some students take the test early in their junior year, and a few wait until they are seniors in high school. As mentioned earlier in this chapter, the material presented on the test is what you have learned up until your junior year of high school, so you are in prime testing shape anytime in your junior or senior year. When is the ideal time, though? Probably when you are a junior in high school, in either February or April. Taking it then gives you a chance to take the test again if you feel that you want to.

Here are the qualities of the ideal ACT Assessment candidate. Think about how each of them relates to you. The candidate will

> ▶ Be a high school junior or senior

> ▶ Be in the top half of his or her class academically

> ▶ Have prepared extensively for the test

> ▶ Have a serious commitment to achieve his or her personal best on the test

> ▶ Have read and understood the directions for each subject area on the ACT test

That's the *ideal* candidate. If you see yourself as fitting most of the listed criteria, the odds are in your favor that you will do well on this test.

Think of the aspects that you have control over right now: You can still prepare extensively for the test and have a serious commitment to achieve your best on the test. You can still ensure that you read and understand the directions for each subject area on the test. So most of the criteria needed to do well on the ACT are still under your control. Keep in mind constantly that the more you prepare for it, the better you will ultimately do on the ACT Assessment. You are directly responsible for your test score.

Put Yourself to the Test

Assessing your readiness to take the ACT is a sensible beginning for your test preparation. To figure out where to begin, though, take some time to think about how you would respond to each question in the subsections that follow. Take an honest look at yourself and your abilities, and gauge the skills and information you have already mastered in each subject area assessed on the ACT. When you take a self-assessment like this, you are better prepared to make a plan outlining how you will concentrate your study and test preparation time, which is probably limited.

The questions that follow are designed to help you assess your strengths and weaknesses on the material presented in each area of the ACT Assessment. There are no right or wrong responses to these questions, so answer each of them honestly.

The English Subject Area

1. Are you able to spot errors in sentence and paragraph style?

2. When you read a sentence, is it readily apparent to you whether the subject and verb agree?

3. Can you differentiate between a fragment and a complete sentence?

4. In your own writing, do you generally follow the rules for correct punctuation, including the rules related to commas, colons, semicolons, quotation marks, parentheses, dashes, and other common punctuation marks?

The Mathematics Subject Area

1. Do you understand how fractions work? Are you able to add, subtract, multiply, divide, and otherwise work with fractions with relative ease?

2. Are you able to work with basic algebraic functions? Can you plug numbers into the Pythagorean theorem and calculate an answer?

3. Are you able to find the area of a circle, square, rectangle, and triangle, and do other basic geometry problems? Do you know the formulas for basic geometry calculations? Can you work comfortably with those formulas?

4. Can you calculate percents and work with percentages of a number?

5. Can you find probability as it is presented in various types of story problems?

The Reading Subject Area

1. Are you comfortable reading somewhat lengthy passages and responding to questions about them?

2. Do you usually understand what you have read?

3. Are you able to read a passage efficiently without going back and rereading portions of it?

4. Can you quickly discern the main idea of an article or passage?

The Science Reasoning Subject Area

1. Are you comfortable deciphering scientific information?

2. Are you able to find ways to make sense of the information and data on tables and graphs?

3. Are you familiar with how a hypothesis is formed and tested?

The Writing Test

1. Can you efficiently outline, draft, revise, and write on a subject you have just been assigned?

2. Are you able to quickly proofread your own work for errors in style, punctuation, spelling, form, and grammar?

Assessing Your Exam Readiness

You should have answered "Yes" to most if not all of the questions on the self-assessments in the previous sections. All of the information you are asked about in those sections is presented in some form on the ACT Assessment, and there is no way to cut corners if you aren't familiar with all of the subject matter.

If you answered "No" to any of the questions, ask yourself whether you will be able to learn the necessary content in the time you have before the test. Read those questions again. Think about whether you may need remediation before you take the test. Don't hesitate to seek additional help from guidance counselors or teachers if you find yourself weak in a particular subject area. Most are happy to help.

If you don't know the basics of geometry, for example, it will be extremely difficult to get comfortable with the fundamentals in the same period that you are practicing other subject material for the test. Weak writing skills may be difficult to hone if you don't have adequate time and a good mentor. You may want to discuss your particular situation with a teacher, guidance counselor, or adult family member before moving forward. Often intense private tutoring in the weeks prior to the test will help a student who needs more than just practice and a good refresher before this type of test. Be honest with yourself, though. Additional preparation prior to taking the test *at a later date* might be the best thing to enhance your score.

You may want to use one of the practice tests at the back of this book as a pretest. A pretest is generally taken before doing any studying or preparing—it is taken "cold." This is probably the best indicator of your preparation needs. If you decide to take one sample test now, plan to take it under strict test conditions, that is, with a minimum of distractions, with supplies (for example, some pencils, a calculator, some scrap paper) at hand, and with a watch or a proctor (a family member or friend) to time each section. If you can, have a friend, teacher, or family member who is in the know read and discuss your essay response with you.

Another pretesting strategy is to work with just a sampling of questions from each subject area. If you don't want to spend time now taking an entire test, take half of the English test, one passage of the reading test, the middle 20 questions on the math test, and the first two passages on the science test. Take the writing test only if you have someone available to read your essay and comment on it for you.

Both of the preceding strategies are effective ways to find the parts of the test that you may need to spend additional time with and to confirm your readiness in the other subject areas. Taking a second practice test after you have worked through this guide is a good way for you to chart your progression and see your elevated level of test readiness.

A Personalized Study Plan

After you've assessed your readiness for the ACT Assessment, think about the amount of time you will be able to set aside to prepare for the test. You will maximize your review and study time if you create a study plan schedule right away, before you even begin to read and work through this study guide.

Part of your plan will be to decide when you should take the ACT. Look on the ACT website (www.actstudent.org) to find out the next scheduled test dates, and then pinpoint the date when you will actually take the ACT Assessment. Generally, the test is given in February, April, June, September, October, and December; however, it is not given in all locations in each of the listed months. You will want to enter your city and state into the website's "Test Date" locator, or check a printed copy of the registration materials to see whether it is offered when and where you hope to take it. You should plan to take the test early enough so that you are able to retake it if you are not entirely satisfied with your score.

TIP

For many students, planning to take the test more than once serves to alleviate many of their fears about their scores. On the other hand, there are a variety of reasons some students might get only one opportunity to take the ACT. These reasons include having the test site far from their home, having to work on the weekends, or being unable to afford to take the test more than once. If you anticipate having just one opportunity to take the test, ensure that you have practiced and reviewed adequately so that you get your personal best score.

In the subject areas covered on the test (English, reading, math, science, and the optional writing test), you are probably already aware of your strong and weak areas. Depending on how much preparation time you have available prior to the test, you will probably want to study and review your weaker areas first.

> **NOTE**
>
> Some students wonder whether they should gather a group of classmates or friends to work together to study and review for the ACT test. This is not usually the most effective way to prepare for the test. Most students have definite strong and weak subject areas for this test and will plan their study time accordingly. Working with one person for part of your study time may work well if that study mate plans to concentrate on the same areas you feel you need to work on.

Setting Up a Schedule

Ideally you are not picking up *ACT Exam Prep* two weeks before you are taking the actual test. If you are, you will need to spend as much time as you can reviewing this material. A four- to six-week preparation time is more realistic for fully preparing for the test.

Reading articles from a variety of sources, writing well-organized essays about different subjects, and going over the types of math problems you have worked on in your classes are all ways to prepare yourself for the ACT Assessment. Preparing for this test means familiarizing yourself with the subject areas and the types of questions you will encounter on the actual test.

> **NOTE**
>
> You won't be memorizing material for this test. You will need to know strategies to respond to the questions.

Make your preparation time consistent, serious, and worthwhile by working in an area free of distractions. Strive to do the best you can and use your practice time wisely.

Set up a weekly schedule of regular times that you plan to set aside exclusively to work through this book. To set up this type of schedule, think about your typical weekly activities and commitments, and then map out times when you will be able to review and study. Stick to your schedule. Make sure your plans are attainable; if you create a master plan that is too ambitious, you'll find yourself getting discouraged and losing interest.

Your plan may look something like Table 1.2, with some days marked as "No time" because of your prior commitments, work schedule, or other activities. Other days have carefully figured times when you will be available to work on ACT-related preparation and study. Remember: Make a schedule that you can and will stick to, and don't allow yourself to make excuses not to follow it. Display the schedule somewhere where your family members can see it too. If you take the time to explain your plan to them, your family members can be helpful in ensuring that you have adequate study time and will also know that these are the times you have set aside. They will know that, as much as possible, you don't want to be sidetracked by phone calls from friends or other distractions.

TABLE 1.2   Sample Four-Week Preparation Time Schedule

Week of	Monday	Tuesday	Wednesday	Thursday	Friday	Saturday	Sunday
Jan. 4	4:00-6:00pm	No time	4:00-6:00pm	6:00-8:30pm	4:00-5:30pm	9:00-1:00pm	No time
Jan. 11	7:30-9:00pm	No time	4:00-6:00pm	7:30-9:00pm	No time	9:00-1:00pm	1:00-5:00pm
Jan. 18	7:30-9:00pm	No time	4:30-8:00pm	6:00-8:30pm	7:30-9:00pm	9:00-1:00pm	8:00-9:30am
Jan. 25	7:30-9:00pm	6:00-8:30pm	No time	6:00-8:30pm	7:30-9:00pm	7:00-10:00am	7:30-9:00pm

It also may help to plan to reward yourself, even if only in a small way, for following through with your scheduled study time. For some students, a reward could be watching a favorite TV show; for others, it could mean renting a movie they have wanted to see; some may find playing a game for an hour on the computer to be a good reward; still others may think that spending an afternoon out with a friend is fun. For you a reward could be a warm brownie straight from the oven. Think about what makes you happy, and plan a celebratory reward after each practice week.

Structuring Your Study Sessions

To get the most of the time you have to study, consider making a list of the subject areas (English, reading, math, science, writing) in the order in which you will want to work on them. Either work through each subject area in as many practice sessions as it takes, or plan to spend each study session on a different subject area on your list. This rotation method may maximize your time. As you work through the book, ensure that you understand and practice all of the concepts mentioned in each chapter. Spend additional time practicing the specific skills that are still trouble spots.

Consider asking a teacher or guidance counselor at your school for additional supplemental aids (for example, textbooks and worksheets) that offer even more practice in the specific topics for which you need extra work.

Additionally, reading articles from a variety of sources, writing well-organized essays about different subjects, going over the types of math problems you have worked on in your classes, and analyzing charts and graphs from scientific journals are all good ways to prepare yourself for the ACT Assessment. Looking through math textbooks and materials from high school math classes you have already taken may provide some additional information and practice on these skills.

It's a good idea to use any time at all, even if it is impromptu and unscheduled, prior to your test date to continue to *practice, practice, practice*. Retake a test from the back of this book. Consider carefully the correct responses to the questions that you didn't answer correctly. Continue this pattern of testing, evaluation, study, and retesting. Keep your eye on your ultimate goal: doing your personal best on the ACT test.

Registering for the Test

Look into registering for the ACT at least two months before you plan to take the test. Registration deadlines are approximately a month before the scheduled date of the test. The ACT Assessment is given primarily on Saturdays in the months of February, April, June, September, October, and December at hundreds of locations nationwide. Even though you may have taken the PLAN (the pre-ACT test) at a particular testing location, the ACT test may not be offered there. Ensure that the location where you hope to take the test is an actual ACT testing center and that the test is given there and on that date. This information is available on the ACT website.

Note, too, that not all states offer the ACT Assessment each of the six months, and the states offering September test dates are especially limited. Check the ACT website (www.actstudent.org) before making any plans so that you can be sure the test is offered when and where you would like to take it.

The quickest and easiest way to register for the test is to go directly to the ACT website (www.actstudent.org) and follow the links to sign up online. Using this method will require a credit card. If you would rather submit a check or if you don't have Internet access, you will want to register through the postal mail using a paper registration form. You can obtain this registration form at the guidance department of your local high school (whether or not you are enrolled there) or by calling ACT directly at 319-337-1270 and requesting that a registration form be sent to you.

EXAM ALERT

Find out whether the schools to which you plan to apply require you to take the ACT Plus Writing portion of the ACT as an admissions requirement. If so, make sure you register for that part of the ACT Assessment, too. See Chapter 4 of this book for further information.

The basic ACT Assessment costs $29 if registration is completed before the posted deadline. The writing test, called ACT Plus Writing, costs an additional $14. The late registration charge of $17 can be avoided in almost all instances by registering within the timeframe parameters provided on the ACT website. Check these out now.

NOTE

A limited number of fee waivers are available for students who qualify for financial assistance. You will want to look into this early if you believe it applies to you. Refer to the ACT website (www.actstudent.org) for further information.

TIP

Don't procrastinate about registering for the ACT test. Instead, do this well in advance of the date you plan to take it. Choose a test date that is at least two months prior to the college application deadlines for the schools to which you may want to apply. Keep in mind that it can take up to two months for the schools to which you are applying to receive your scores.

CAUTION

If for religious reasons you are unable to take the ACT Assessment on one of the regularly scheduled Saturday dates, or if you live in a remote area and have difficulty traveling to a testing center, you may request to take the test on one of the limited Sunday or Monday dates. The ACT website (www.actstudent.org) has detailed information concerning the restrictions for taking the test on one of these alternate days. You will want to look into alternate day plans early if this type of situation applies to you.

TIP

If you have special needs that call for accommodations of any kind, be sure you alert ACT at the time you register. The ACT website (www.actstudent.org) has further information about the types of accommodations testing centers are able to provide. You will want to investigate this early if it applies to you.

Some students with Individual Education Plans (IEP) or 504 Plans may need to submit a form to that effect to receive necessary accommodations for taking the test. Check with your guidance counselor or with ACT for further information. As with all other test-related situations, make sure you do this early so that all of your needs can be taken care of.

When you register for the test, you will have the opportunity to request that copies of your scores be sent directly to up to four schools to which you are interested in applying. These four schools' reports are included with the registration fee for the test. Additional schools over the first four may be added for a fee of $7 per school.

Some students feel more comfortable waiting until they have actually seen their scores before sending them out to their chosen schools. ACT charges $7 per school to send reports after the test. These reports are sent to the school within one week of your request. For a $13 fee, ACT will send scores out within one day of a request.

If you decide to retake the test after your original date, you may choose which testing date's scores you want sent out. Only you and those close to you know the best plan for sending your scores to the colleges and universities you are interested in. Talk this over with your guidance counselor or an adult family member to help you decide which option is right for you. There are good arguments for each choice.

TIP

ACT research shows that the majority of students who took the ACT more than once attained a higher score on their second try.

Keep These Valuable Test-Taking Tips in Mind

To maximize their scores on the ACT test, it is likely that most students will need all the review time they can fit into their schedules in the days and weeks before the test. In addition to reading, reviewing, and preparing, here are some procedures and ideas that can help you do your personal best on the ACT test:

> **NOTE**
>
> The English, reading, math, and science subject tests on the ACT comprise only multiple-choice questions. That means the correct answer is there, right in front of you, at all times.

▶ **Never leave a question blank**—There is no penalty for guessing on the ACT, so you should make sure that you mark a bubble for an answer for every question. If you are unsure of an answer, make a tiny mark on the answer sheet after you mark your best guess. Try to save at least a minute at the end of a test section to check answers of questions you did not get to. If it is impossible for you to return to some questions, you will still have an answer filled in for each question.

> **TIP**
>
> It's important that you keep in mind that the ACT Assessment does not penalize you for guessing. In other words, no points are subtracted from your score for wrong answers. This means that you should *never* leave a question unanswered, even if you have to choose an answer randomly. However, it's always best to use the process of elimination to make an educated guess if you can.

▶ **Reduce anxiety**—Plan to take the ACT early enough in your high school career so that you can take the test again if you are not happy with your score. Also, set a realistic personal goal for yourself. For example, answering about 45 of the 60 questions correctly on the math section produces a score of 27. You don't need to answer every question correctly to get a good score.

> **TIP**
>
> The questions on the ACT test are not arranged in order of difficulty. Don't dismay if you run through a patch of questions you consider tough to answer. There may be easier ones on the way.

▶ **Wear a watch**—Don't spend too much time on one question. Although you may know this already, when you're facing a complicated word problem or an intense science passage, it's easy to ignore this important strategy. Remind yourself often that good time management is essential to success on the test.

▶ **Work on the easiest questions first**—The best way to make sure that you use your time wisely is to answer all the questions that are easiest for you first. You will know right away whether a question is difficult—you will find yourself reading it more than once and still being unsure of what is being asked. Remember: Those questions that you find difficult are worth the same number of points as the easy questions. Don't spend three minutes figuring out a hard question when you could have answered three easy questions during the same time period.

▶ **Just get the answer and move on**—Think creatively to find the solution to each question in the shortest amount of time that you are able. When appropriate, plug in each of the answer choices to find the correct answer. No one cares what method you used to get the answer.

▶ **Make your best smart guess**—Knowing what an answer can't be makes for smart guessing. If you are able to eliminate some of the wrong answer choices, the probability that you will guess the correct answer is higher.

▶ **Give the question what it's asking for**—The ACT test writers fill the answer choices with distracters—wrong answers that they know will be chosen by students as likely errors. Take ample time before you read through the answer choices to make sure that you know what the question is actually asking you. Pay careful attention to words such as "not" in the question stem. It is likely that the answer choices will include a response that would be correct if "not" weren't in the question.

▶ **Check periodically to see that the number on your answer sheet matches the number of the question you are working on**—Nothing is more of a time-waster and stress-producer than discovering that the answer key and the question you are working on don't match up. Everyone has probably had this happen to them at least once in their life, though. To ensure that this doesn't happen, some students prefer to mark answers in groups, such as three at a time. Others simply stop and check at the end of each answer column. Don't wait until you realize you are marking the wrong question's response to go back and check. Instead, periodically ensure that the question number matches the number on the answer sheet.

▶ **Reduce other activities near the test date**—Most high school students are busier than ever before. Make sure you give your planned ACT test date the respect it deserves by keeping to your study schedule and limiting your other activities a few days before the test. It takes stamina to feel alert during a test of this length.

▶ **Be as prepared as possible**—Know the directions and the format of each test section ahead of time. Follow the guidelines in this book to complete a study plan. Work to strengthen any weak areas. You'll feel more confident if you know what to expect. Know that on test day, you will be doing your personal best.

What to Expect on Test Day

Most regularly scheduled ACT Assessment tests begin at 8:00 a.m. Plan in advance to be at the test center at least half an hour prior to the test.

If you are not sure exactly where the test center is located, obtain accurate directions in advance of the test day. If necessary, drive to the center a day or two prior to the test, and make note of how much time you will need to allot the morning of the test. Don't rely on directions you may obtain from mapping sites online—check for yourself. It is unnecessary to be stressed about arrival time on the actual test day. Ensure that you have a reliable ride if you are not driving yourself to the testing site. Gas up your car, locate a calculator, have your pencils sharpened. In short, don't leave anything to chance.

> **NOTE**
>
> The ACT is made up of 215 multiple-choice questions, and with breaks between subject areas, the test takes approximately 3-1/2 hours to complete. Add half an hour if you are taking the ACT Plus Writing test.

When you arrive at the test center the morning of the test, you will be asked to show your admission ticket (which will be mailed to you a few weeks after you register) as well as "acceptable identification" to be admitted.

> **TIP**
>
> Don't panic if you have not received an admission ticket in the mail or if you lose your ticket prior to the test. If you haven't received your ticket 10 days before the test, call ACT at 319-337-1270. If you lose your admission ticket, call immediately.

The identification you will be asked to present with your admission ticket ensures that you are who you say you are. ACT works to ensure that its testing procedures leave no room for fraud. Those who check identification at each testing center are given stringent rules that they must follow, without exception. Ensure that you have acceptable identification with you when you arrive to take the test.

"Acceptable" identification for the ACT test is one of the following:

▶ **A current photo ID**—Provided it contains both your name and a current photograph, acceptable identification is one of the following: your driver's license, your passport, your school ID, or your work ID.

▶ **A recently published photograph**—Your photograph needs to have been published in a newspaper or a high school yearbook, and both your first and last names must appear and be captioned underneath the photo.

▶ **A school letter or a transcript**—Make plans to obtain this form of ID a few weeks before the test. The official letter must be on school letterhead and must include your name and a full physical description, with your height, weight, age, gender, race, and hair and eye color. Alternatively, the letter can include a recent photograph with the school seal affixed and a school administrator's signature across a portion of the photograph.

▶ **A notarized statement with your photo**—If you are home-schooled or are otherwise unable to obtain an official letter on a school letterhead, you may obtain and use a notarized statement with your photo. You'll need to sign a statement in ink in the presence of the notary and ensure that the notary's stamp or seal is affixed to a portion of the photo.

These forms of identification are not considered acceptable for ACT test purposes:

▶ A learner's permit

▶ A Social Security card

▶ A library card

▶ A birth certificate

TIP

Just like finding the location of the test center in advance of the test, obtaining the proper identification well before the test day is absolutely essential. Keep in mind that ACT does not issue refunds, even if you are turned away from the test for lack of acceptable identification.

Check the ACT website (www.actstudent.org) and the materials you will be sent after registering to ensure that you have proper identification prior to the day of the test. Testing officials will not permit you to take the test if you do not have a required form of identification—and students are turned away at every testing station for that reason. Don't be one of them.

NOTE

In especially bad weather, the ACT test is usually cancelled. If you wake up on test day and wonder whether the weather will affect your test, listen to the local radio or television station. You will hear whether the test is cancelled at your test center. If it is not cancelled but you think the weather conditions are too dangerous to travel, don't even try to get there.

Expect to be notified by mail if your test was cancelled due to inclement weather. You will be given an alternate test date. This rescheduled date will also be posted on the ACT website by the Thursday after your original planned test date. Also, you can call ACT Test Administration (319-337-1510).

If you did not travel to the test center because of severe weather, but the test center remained open, call ACT Registration (319-337-1270) during the week after the test date to find out how you can reschedule the test.

Remember to bring with you a supply of sharpened #2 pencils with erasers on test day. You will also want to make sure you have a calculator to use during the mathematics test. If you forget to bring your own calculator, you will not be permitted to share with another student, and you may not let another student use your calculator even when you are finished with it. Also, remember to wear a watch on test day. You will be asked to turn off your cell phone, so don't rely on using that as your clock. You will need to keep close track of time and pace yourself as you work through the parts of the test.

NOTE

If you wake up ill on test day morning and decide that you are unable to take the test, you will need to follow the instructions on the back of your admission ticket. You will have to pay a fee to secure a new test date. Check the website (www.actstudent.org) or call ACT (319-337-1270) for specific information about what to do if you miss the test.

Exam Day Checklist

Gather these important items in one location at least the day before the test:

▶ Your admission ticket

▶ Your proper identification

▶ A calculator

▶ At least four sharpened #2 pencils with erasers

▶ A watch

After all the students have been checked in to the test center, the ACT Assessment will begin. For each subject area test, the test administrator will tell you the present time and the time limit in which the section test needs to be completed. Check your watch and keep track of how long you have to complete each test. After the first two subject area tests, you can expect to be given a short break.

Now is when your preparation and review will pay off. You will take the test and feel confident in your abilities.

NOTE

Occasionally a student is unable to complete the test; he or she may feel ill or otherwise not competent enough to finish the test. In the unfortunate event that this happens to you on test day, make sure you tell the test proctor right away that your test should not be scored. Don't wait until after you leave the test center to attempt to make this request because by then it will be too late. Remember that you can reregister and retake the test on a later date if you need or want to.

How to Interpret Your Scores

Approximately four to seven weeks after the date you take the test, you will receive a score report in the mail from ACT. This report will list your composite, or overall score, and your scaled scores for each of the four tests. The scaled scores will fall between 1 and 36. Of course, the higher your score, the better. The report will also give a percentile for each scaled score, which tells you how many other students (in percentage form) received scores that were the same as or lower than yours. In addition, you will receive subscores for the content areas of English, mathematics, and reading. If you look at your report and observe that the subscores don't seem to add to the scaled score for each content area, don't panic. The test administrators have a special process they use to create your scaled scores. This process allows for comparison among many versions of the ACT.

NOTE

Although your composite, or total score, on the ACT is the magic number you will be most interested in, the score report will include detailed scores for all of the subject area tests (English, reading, math, and science). You will receive a score from 1 to 36 on each subject area.

Note that the optional writing test is scored separately and is reported as a score of 1 to 12. If you take the writing test, you will receive a Combined English Writing Test score (from 1 to 36) that includes both the English and writing tests. You can find additional information about the writing test score in Chapter 4 of *ACT Exam Prep*.

Your composite score is the average of each of the four subject area tests (the optional writing test is not included in figuring the composite), and it is rounded to the nearest whole number.

TIP

You can view your scores online too. If you simply can't wait for your report to arrive in the mail, you can view your scores by going to the ACT Student website (www.actstudent.org) and clicking the "Early Scores" link. Your scores will be available approximately 10 days after you have taken the test. For an $8 fee, you can see how you have done on the test. Scores viewed online can't be sent anywhere, though, and if you print the score from your computer it won't be considered "official."

Note that once you receive your scores in the mail, you can view them online at any time at no cost.

How the Test Scores Are Used

As you read earlier in this chapter, the ACT Assessment is universally accepted by almost all colleges and universities nationwide. Students' ACT scores provide schools with necessary and reliable information about the students' likelihood for success as they pursue coursework and an undergraduate degree at the institution. Colleges and universities use ACT scores as one component in their admissions decisions.

Scores from the ACT Assessment are a composite of all four subject areas (and the written test, if taken) and are measured in scaled scores ranging from 1 to 36. According to ACT, half of all ACT test takers score from 17 to 23 on the test, and the national average score is 20. It is interesting to note that a score of 20 on this test means that a student got only a bit more than half of the questions correct.

Check with the colleges and universities to which you plan to apply to find out each of their ACT cut-off scores. You will find that many competitive schools will not admit students who have scored less than a 22 on the test, and some highly selective schools demand a score above that for admission. Be realistic. Set your sights on schools to which you have a reasonable chance of being admitted with your present grades, class rank, and anticipated ACT Assessment score. Keep in mind that tough admissions policies are in place to help ensure an individual student's success in each school—you likely won't be admitted to a school that you would not be able to do well in.

TIP

If your GPA, ACT test scores, and other admissions criteria don't fit a school's standards, there is a good reason you won't be admitted to that school. All colleges and universities want their students to succeed in their studies. A school with very competitive standards will have rigorous coursework that will be at a scope and pace that some students will find daunting. Your goal should be to be admitted to the school where you will be able to do well, not to be in over your head.

What Colleges Are Looking For

All colleges and universities have general standards for admission. Most criteria include a student's secondary school grade point average; class ranking; admission test scores; and often extracurricular activities, sports, and clubs. Each admissions component is important, and rarely does one criterion stand alone. Attaining even a terrific score on the ACT test won't guarantee a student will be considered for admission at a particular school if his or her GPA and class ranking aren't equally good. On the flip side, though, a low score (below 17) on the ACT may prevent you from being admitted to some schools.

TIP

There are many fine schools throughout the country for which the only admissions standard is a high school diploma. Most community colleges require an ACT test score for placement purposes, but a student's score is not part of their admissions criteria. You will want to talk with parents, older siblings or family members, guidance counselors, and teachers at your high school to help you decide which schools you should apply to.

For admissions purposes, colleges and universities are ranked according to how competitive their admissions standards are. These rankings are typically described as Most Competitive, Highly Competitive, Very Competitive, Moderately Competitive, and Less or Minimally Competitive, as explained in the following sections.

Most Competitive Schools

Schools in this category have the most stringent admissions standards. Although every school differs in what it is looking for, generally students admitted to schools in this category have an A (4.0) average, are in the top 5% of their high school graduating class, and have an ACT composite score of 29 or above.

One *Most Competitive* school is Duke University, located in Durham, North Carolina. This school has approximately 1,650 students in each freshman class, and its School of Arts & Sciences requires an ACT score in the range of 29–34. Its Engineering School's ACT requirements are in the range of 31–34.

Duke mentions on its website (www.duke.edu) that it has no minimum standardized test score or class rank. Admission is generally contingent on the combination of test scores, class rank, activities, leadership, and other school admissions criteria.

Highly Competitive Schools

Schools in the Highly Competitive category generally enroll students with at least a B+ (3.6) average and who fall into the top 25% to 30% of their high school graduating class. ACT composite scores usually need to be 27 or 28.

DePauw University in Greencastle, Indiana, is a *Highly Competitive* school. DePauw is a private, liberal arts university, and each freshman class contains close to 700 students.

A recent freshman class had median ACT scores of 27, a high school class rank of approximately 90%, and a median GPA of 3.69 (www.depauw.edu).

Very Competitive Schools

Most students enrolling in these Very Competitive schools generally have a B (3.0) average, are in the top 35% to 50% of their high school graduating class, and have an ACT composite score of at least 26.

American University in Washington, D.C., is a *Very Competitive* school. Fifty-two percent of a recent freshman class were in the top 10% of their high school graduating class. The average ACT composite score was 28, with 26–30 the range of scores of accepted students. There are about 5,700 undergraduate students at the school (www.american.edu).

Moderately Competitive Schools

Most schools in the Moderately Competitive category generally consider students in the top 50% to 65% of their high school class and with a C+ or C (2.0) high school average. The ACT composite score for these schools is generally 21–23.

Florida Gulf Coast University in Fort Myers, Florida, is a *Moderately Competitive* school. ACT composite scores averaged 22 in a recent freshman class, with students' median GPA at 3.3. The school has close to 3,000 undergraduate students (www.fgcu.edu).

Less, or Minimally, Competitive Schools

Less Competitive schools generally accept the students with ACT scores below 21 and with varying high school grades.

Franklin Pierce College in Rindge, New Hampshire, is one example of a *Less Competitive* school. Students are evaluated for admission on an individual basis (www.fpc.edu).

> **TIP**
>
> Don't count yourself out of the running if your ACT scores aren't up to the standards a certain school sets. Remember that schools weigh all information they obtain about each student.

> **TIP**
>
> Don't make the mistake of thinking that a school with lower admissions standards is not a "good" school. All accredited colleges and universities in the United States are fine schools; your dilemma is to find the school that you are most comfortable with and that will help you work toward your career goals.

Ask your guidance counselor and family members for assistance in helping you decide which schools you will ultimately apply to. There are many fine schools in all admissions categories.

Where Do You Go from Here?

By now, you should have a good general idea about what to expect on the ACT test. You will need to begin your test preparation right away:

- ▶ Explore and become familiar with the www.actstudent.org website.
- ▶ Plan a date to take the test. Make sure that it is given at the test center most convenient to you.
- ▶ Find out the registration deadline for that test date.
- ▶ Register online or on a paper registration form, or plan to register in advance of the deadline.
- ▶ Make a mental note to keep an eye out for your admission ticket.
- ▶ Take the Self-Assessment in this chapter.
- ▶ Chart out your plan of study.
- ▶ Consider taking the first of the two sample tests at the back of this book.
- ▶ Analyze your answers.
- ▶ Think about which subject areas should be getting the bulk of your study time.
- ▶ Get to work!

The English Test

The English test encompasses a variety and assortment of ways to verify your understanding of many aspects of English. You will want to review all of the information presented here to refresh your understanding of the parts of English that you may consider to be "automatic" in your reading and your writing.

What to Expect on the ACT English Test

The ACT English test is an assessment of test takers' knowledge of the conventions of standard written English. That means that the test is designed to see what you know about punctuation, grammar and usage, and sentence structure. The test also measures your understanding of strategy, organization, and paragraph and passage style—these are known as "rhetorical skills" on the test. As you read through this chapter, you will see that most, if not all, of what is presented on the test is information that you have already been working with throughout the past five or more years.

> **TIP**
>
> The English test will not assess your spelling aptitude, or ask you to define vocabulary words.

The Test Format

To assess all of the areas contained under the "English" umbrella, ACT will present you with five reading passages of varying lengths. Each passage is accompanied by 15 multiple-choice test questions embedded with its passage. There are a total of 75 questions on this portion of the ACT test.

You are allotted 45 minutes to finish this part of the ACT test, which means that you have about 30 seconds to answer each question. Throughout this chapter, you will learn some procedures developed to save time as you work through the passages and the questions on the test. If you spend a few minutes now reading and thinking about the directions for this section, then reviewing the information that follows and familiarizing yourself with the types of questions you will see on the test, you will find that 45 minutes is plenty of time to complete this part of the ACT.

The Passage

Running along the left column of each test page is the reading passage, with its accompanying questions arranged in a column to the right.

The reading passages contain underlined and numbered words and phrases, as well as some boxed numerals. These numbered identifiers refer to the questions. To work through the test, you will first read a passage. Then you will answer each of the five questions associated with it by darkening the corresponding oval on your answer sheet, and moving on to the next passage. Each question will have five answer choices, with the letters A through D (or F through J) identifying them. Choice "A" or "F" generally offers the response, "No Change." You will choose letter A or F if you find that the word, phrase, or sentence is correct as it is written on the test.

TIP

Some students think twice about choosing the answer "No Change" on the test. They mistakenly believe that something has to be incorrect in every question presented, and they don't like to make "No Change" their response. Don't be afraid to choose "No Change" if you find that the word, phrase, or sentence is correct as it is.

The Directions

Just as in the other subject areas on the ACT, the directions and the format of the English test will not change from test to test. You will appreciate this fact as you prepare for the test, because it means that you can read and review the ACT English test's directions now. Then on test day, you will already be completely familiar with what you will be asked to do, so you will be able to skip over the directions or just read them very quickly and get right to work. You won't spend any of the precious 45 minutes allotted for the test on thinking about what you are going to have to do on this portion of the test.

The actual test directions will be similar to the wording shown in the following sidebar. Read and think about them now.

Directions for the Test

Within the five passages below are 75 underlined words and phrases in context, and questions about the passages. Most of these underlined sections question its structure, expression, style, punctuation, or word usage.

The test also includes questions about entire paragraphs and the passage as a whole. These questions are identified by a digit enclosed in a box.

For each question, select which of the five choices is the best response, and darken the appropriate oval on your answer sheet. If you consider the original version to be the best, choose letter A or F: NO CHANGE.

The Plan

As you read through the passages presented in the actual ACT English test, you will want to use a formula similar to this one to maximize your time:

1. You already know what the directions say, so breeze right past them and begin skimming the first passage. Don't be afraid to make notes in your test booklet if you find there's anything you want to jot down.

2. After you have finished skimming the passage, reread the sentence that contains the first underlined word or phrase and then go to the question related to that underlined word or phrase.

3. Ask yourself what you are being asked in the question. Is the question asking you to assess a sentence's punctuation, the placement of a word within a sentence, or something else?

    Remember to use only the information contained within the passage. If you happen to disagree with what it is saying or do not particularly like what the passage is talking about, don't dwell on it. You are just being asked to respond to English questions, not to engage in a debate over content.

4. Before looking at the response choices, decide what you think the correct answer could be.

5. Check to see whether your response is one of those offered within the answer choices. If it is, shade in that oval on the answer sheet and move on to the next question.

6. If you don't see your response offered, take each provided answer and substitute it for the underlined word or phrase. (This will take time, which is why it is essential that you attempt to come up with your own answer first.) See which of the responses seems to make the most sense. You may be able to cross out a few—or at least one—of the answer choices that you know to be incorrect. Then consider each remaining answer in order to make the best choice.

7. If you are unsure of the meaning of a word, use context clues—words before and after the word you are wondering about—to figure out an approximate meaning of the word. If the word has nothing to do with a question being asked, don't spend any time trying to figure out what it means.

8. Remind yourself that you have to work at a consistent and brisk pace. With 45 minutes total time on the English test, you will have about 9 minutes to work on each of the five passages. Don't spend too much time on one question or one passage, or you will find that you have no time for the questions that fall at the end of the test.

9. If you are stumped on the response to a question, circle it in the test booklet and go back to it later. Put a light pencil dot beside that test number, one that you can see but that doesn't detract from the answer sheet. Go back to the question later if you have time. If you find that you are running out of time overall, pick an answer at random. Don't leave any responses blank.

> **TIP**
>
> Remember that the ACT does not penalize you for inaccurate responses; it gives you credit for responses that are correct. If you are particularly stymied between two responses, pick one and move on.

Understanding Punctuation

You can anticipate seeing about 10 of the 45 questions on the English test that will ask about some type of punctuation. A wide variety of questions fall under the "punctuation" heading—these can include determining whether the marks of punctuation that are already in place are correct or if they should be changed, or whether some particular punctuation marks should be added to a sentence or phrase.

You will probably find that the questions relating to punctuation will be a cinch for you to complete if you review and are familiar with how each of the common marks of punctuation works. Keep in mind that you will not be asked to actually name any marks of punctuation; the questions here will concentrate only on the correct usage of the punctuation marks.

The following section explains the standard marks of punctuation that you may be asked about on the test and gives you some examples of how each of these can be used.

Apostrophe

An *apostrophe* looks like this: '. It can be used in two ways, as discussed in the following sections.

To Form Contractions

First, an apostrophe can be used to show where letters have been left out of a *contraction* (two words that are joined together to make one word). For example, the contraction *can't* is made up of the words *can* and *not*. In that contraction, you can see that the letters *n* and *o* have been left out. To show this omission, an apostrophe is added at the point of the missing letters, in this case, between the *n* and the *t*.

Here are some examples of contractions. Think about what letters the apostrophe is taking the place of in these contractions:

> don't (do not)
>
> shouldn't (should not)
>
> they're (they are)
>
> wasn't (was not)
>
> don't (do not)
>
> won't (will not)

To Show Possession

An apostrophe and an *s* also can be added to a noun to show possession. *Possession* means that someone or something owns or has something, or that something belongs to someone.

You can indicate possession for a singular noun, as shown in the following examples:

Mike's bicycle (the bicycle belonging to Mike)

the bird's nest (the nest belonging to ONE bird)

the girl's earring (the earring belonging to the girl)

the table's leg (the leg belonging to a table)

the sky's color (the color of the sky)

Note that when a singular ends with an *s* or an *s* sound, just add an apostrophe to show possession:

Susan Jones' hat (the hat of Susan Jones)

You can also indicate possession for a plural noun. Plural possession is formed by adding the apostrophe after the plural noun is formed, as shown in the following examples:

the players' locker room (the locker room belonging to ALL the players)

my parents' idea (the idea of BOTH my parents)

If the noun is already in its plural form, add an apostrophe-s:

The women's club

The children's playground

So, the *boy's toys* indicates the toys belonging to just one boy, but the *boys' toys* refers to toys belonging to more than one boy. Pay close attention to where the apostrophe is placed when you answer these types of questions on the test.

Practicing Plural Possessive

As some students find plural possession particularly tricky, take a few minutes to write the correct form of possession for each of the following phrases:

1. The bed belonging to the three pups   *The pups' bed.*

2. The clubhouse belonging to the boys   *The boys' clubhouse.*

3. A song written by the children   *The children's song.*

4. A mess made by two kittens   *The kittens' mess.*

5. A game played by more than one man   *The men's game.*

Correct answers:

1. The pups' bed

2. The boys' clubhouse

3. The children's song

4. The kittens' mess

5. A men's game

Make sure that the noun is in the correct (singular or plural) form and then add the apostrophe and the letter *s*. Forming possession in any other order will usually cause the word to be incorrect.

The Special Circumstance of Its/It's

It is important to note that the contraction *it's* always means *it is*. *It's* never shows possession. *The bird broke its beak* is correct. *The bird broke it's beak* is not correct. It is very common to see *its* and *it's* misused in standard written English.

Read through and think about these correct forms of the words *its/it's*:

> *It's* a snowy day. (We can substitute *it is*.)
>
> I'm thinking that *it's* a fine day to play football. (We can substitute *it is*.)
>
> Please keep the dog in *its* room because *it's* a problem to try to get it back there. (We cannot substitute *it is* for the first example, but later in the sentence we are able to substitute *it is* successfully.)
>
> *Its* problem is mainly that it likes to play with anyone it sees. (We cannot substitute *it is*.)

TIP

To test whether *it's/its* is being used correctly, ask yourself whether the words *it is* can be substituted. If they can, *it's* is correct. If *it is* cannot be substituted, *its* is correct.

Using It's and Its

Try these examples by deciding whether *it's* or *its* belongs in the blank in each sentence.

1. Jeff will be deciding whether ___*it's*___ worth it for him to drive all the way to the meeting.
2. The car lost ___*its*___ right headlight in the crash, but ___*it's*___ fortunate that nothing else was damaged.
3. ___*It's*___ a long show, so ___*it's*___ probably wise to grab a drink and a snack before you go in.
4. He always thinks ___*it's*___ annoying that there aren't enough parking spaces in the school lot.
5. Mack told me that ___*it's*___ probable that my old television will soon lose ___*its*___ capability to pick up a signal.

Correct answers:

1. Jeff will be deciding whether *it's (it is)* worth it for him to drive all the way to the meeting.
2. The car lost *its* right headlight in the crash, but *it's (it is)* fortunate that nothing else was damaged.
3. *It's (it is)* a long show, so *it's* probably wise to grab a drink and a snack before you go in.
4. He always thinks *it's (it is)* annoying that there aren't enough parking spaces in the school lot.
5. Mack told me that *it's (it is)* probable that my old television will soon lose *its* capability to pick up a signal.

The Special Circumstance of Your/You're

The words *your* and *you're* are never interchangeable. *You're* always means *you are*. *Your* means *belonging to you*. Check out the following examples:

You're my brother. (You are my brother.)

This is your coat.

TIP

To test whether *your/you're* is being used correctly, ask yourself whether the words *you are* can be substituted. If they can, *you're* is correct. If *you are* cannot be substituted, *your* is correct.

Using Your and You're

Try these examples by deciding whether *your* or *you're* belongs in the blank in each sentence.

1. _____ friend is starting to act as if she's _____ girlfriend.

2. I can tell that _____ just kidding about wanting to leave the party now.

3. What did _____ parents say about the scrape on the car?

4. I think _____ going to find out _____ grade on the math test tomorrow.

5. _____ horse seems to be limping. What are _____ plans to get it some help?

Correct answers:

1. *Your* friend is starting to act as if she's *your* girlfriend.

2. I can tell that *you're (you are)* just kidding about wanting to leave the party now.

3. What did *your* parents say about the scrape on the car?

4. I think *you're (you are)* going to find out *your* grade on the math test tomorrow.

5. *Your* horse seems to be limping. What are *your* plans to get it some help?

Colon

A *colon* looks like this: :.

It can be used in a variety of situations, as discussed in the following sections.

Setting up a List

When setting up a list, you place the colon after a clause that can stand by itself. It separates that clause from the list that follows it, as in the following example:

The cleaning team includes three men: Joseph, Mike, and Ben.

Notice that the clause before the colon, "the cleaning team includes three men," can stand by itself. Read how the sentence looks without the colon:

The cleaning team includes three men Joseph, Mike, and Ben.

You can see that the men's names blend right into the rest of the sentence and it is difficult to figure out exactly what the true meaning of the sentence may be.

Setting up a Quote

You can set up a quote with a colon. The colon would then separate the independent clause from the quote, like so:

My father repeated a quote from Patrick Henry: "Give me liberty or give me death!"

There was a huge sign in front of us: "No Trespassing."

Note that in both instances, the independent clause can stand by itself and does not need what comes after the colon to make the sentence whole. In the first example, the actual quote from Patrick Henry is not needed to make a complete thought. Similarly, in the second sentence, the words from the sign are not needed to make a complete thought.

If the second sentence had said, *There was a huge sign in front of us that said, "No Trespassing,"* the first part of the sentence is no longer an independent clause. It is referring to a specific sign (*There was a huge sign in front of us that said*). The clause cannot stand by itself and needs a comma, not a colon, to separate itself from the actual sign words.

> **TIP**
>
> In this example, a colon cannot be used:
>
> *The cleaning team includes Joseph, Mike, and Ben.*
>
> The phrase "the cleaning team includes" cannot stand by itself. It is not an independent clause.

Using Colons

Work with these examples by deciding whether a colon, a comma, or no further punctuation mark belongs in the underlined portion of each sentence.

1. I read several good books over <u>vacation</u> The *Da Vinci Code, Wuthering Heights,* and *Breakfast at Tiffany's.*

2. The brochure says to bring specific items to <u>camp a</u> flashlight, a small radio, and a pocketknife.

3. I have two favorite <u>songs</u> "New York, New York" and "Hey Jude."

4. Office hours are only <u>on Tuesday</u>, Wednesday, and Friday this week.

Correct answers:

1. *I read several good books over vacation:* The Da Vinci Code, Wuthering Heights, *and* Breakfast at Tiffany's.

   The independent clause *I read several good books over vacation* can stand by itself. A colon is needed to separate the names of the books from the clause.

2. *The brochure says to bring specific items to camp: a flashlight, a small radio, and a pocketknife.*

   The independent clause *The brochure says to bring specific items to camp* can stand by itself. A colon is needed to separate the list of items from the clause.

3. *I have two favorite songs: "New York, New York" and "Hey Jude."*

   The independent clause *I have two favorite songs* can stand by itself. A colon is needed to separate the names of the two songs from the clause.

4. *Office hours are only on Tuesday, Wednesday, and Friday this week.*

   Office hours are only on is not an independent clause. The clause *Office hours are only on* cannot stand by itself because it does not contain one complete idea. It needs to be joined with the other words in the sentence and a comma is not necessary here.

Comma

A *comma* looks like this: ,.

It can be used in a variety of ways, as discussed in the following sections.

To Set off a Nonessential Phrase

A comma can be used to set off a phrase that further explains the word the phrase is talking about:

> *Her house, the first one on the street, will be easy for all of the partygoers to find.*

All of the information that is enclosed within the comma is nonessential. It can be removed and the sentence will still make sense. (*Her house will be easy for all of the partygoers to find.*)

Here are some additional examples of this use for the comma:

> *The baseball, the one Babe Ruth hit into the stands, is in a museum in his home town.*
>
> *The storm, which knocked out power in our entire town, completely scared both my dog and my little sister.*
>
> *The player's injury, a broken right arm, will cause her to miss the entire rest of the season.*

Note that in each sentence, the phrase included within the commas helps to further explain the subject of the sentence. If the phrase is removed from the sentence, though, the rest of the sentence still makes sense.

To Set off Additional Information

Similar to the previous section's example, a comma can be used to set off added information that can be removed from the sentence:

> *My sister, who has a broken leg, needs a ride to the library.*
>
> *His new song, written in just one day, will be played on the radio tomorrow.*
>
> *The movie, which the critics didn't like, ended up being sold out.*

We can remove each phrase or clause set aside by commas and the sentence will still make sense:

My sister needs a ride to the library.

His new song will be played on the radio tomorrow.

The movie ended up being sold out.

Using Commas

Insert commas in the appropriate places in each of the following sentences.

1. Jack's new apartment, near where his old one was located, will be a better place for him to live.

2. The new carpeting, meticulously picked out by my mother, already has a stain near the sofa.

3. The store, which was completely destroyed by the recent flood, will close next week.

4. Your pitching, which I know you have worked on all summer, has greatly improved since last year.

5. This book, signed by the author, is worth much more than its face value.

Correct answers:

1. *Jack's new apartment, near where his old one was located, will be a better place for him to live.*

   We can remove the phrase within the comma and the sentence still makes sense:

   Jack's new apartment will be a better place for him to live.

2. *The new carpeting, meticulously picked out by my mother, already has a stain near the sofa.*

   We can remove the phrase within the comma and the sentence still makes sense:

   The new carpeting already has a stain near the sofa.

3. *The store, which was completely destroyed by the recent flood, will close next week.*

   We can remove the phrase within the comma and the sentence still makes sense:

   The store will close next week.

4. *Your pitching, which I know you have worked on all summer, has greatly improved since last year.*

   We can remove the phrase within the comma and the sentence still makes sense:

   Your pitching has greatly improved since last year.

5. *This book, signed by the author, is worth much more than its face value.*

   We can remove the phrase within the comma and the sentence still makes sense:

   This book is worth much more than its face value.

To Join Independent Clauses

A comma should be used with a conjunction to join two independent clauses. Independent clauses can stand by themselves, and each one is a complete thought:

The ice cream melted, but she didn't get any on her coat.

I usually like yogurt, but this kind does not taste very good.

The shirt was on sale, so there were only a few left.

In each of these sentences, the two clauses can stand alone. To see this, you'll have to remove the conjunction between the clauses:

The ice cream melted.

She didn't get any on her coat.

I usually like yogurt.

This kind does not taste very good.

The shirt was on sale.

There were only a few left.

Note that the comma belongs before the conjunction, and the conjunction is the word that is joining the two phrases.

Joining Two Phrases

Read the following examples and add the comma before the conjunction. If you are unsure of where to put the comma, separate the two independent clauses from each other, and you will find the conjunction. The comma will go right before the conjunction.

1. I hope to go to your party, but I am having a tooth pulled that morning.

2. Our teacher has assigned homework, but it is a review of what we did last week.

3. The park is fun to visit, but today it is too cold outside.

4. We didn't get our newspaper delivered, so she bought a copy at the store.

5. It's nice to see you again, but I can't remember your name.

Correct answers:

1. *I hope to go to your party, but I am having a tooth pulled that morning.*

   The two independent clauses are *I hope to go to your party* and *I am having a tooth pulled that morning.* The conjunction here is the word *but.*

2. *Our teacher has assigned homework, but it is a review of what we did last week.*

   The two independent clauses are *Our teacher has assigned homework* and *It is a review of what we did last week.* The conjunction here is the word *but.*

3. *The park is fun to visit, but today it is too cold outside.*

   The two independent clauses are *The park is fun to visit* and *Today it is too cold outside.* The conjunction here is the word *but.*

4. *We didn't get our newspaper delivered, so she bought a copy at the store.*

   The two independent clauses are *We didn't get our newspaper delivered* and *She bought a copy at the store.* The conjunction here is the word *so.*

5. *It's nice to see you again, but I can't remember your name.*

   The two independent clauses are *It's nice to see you again* and *I can't remember your name.* The conjunction here is the word *but.*

To Set off an Introductory Phrase

A comma is also used to set off an introductory phrase in a sentence:

> *Afraid of falling, I walked slowly down the steps.*
>
> *Jumping from the diving board, he held his nose.*
>
> *Sizing up the situation quickly, he dialed the police.*

These introductory phrases are not independent clauses, which means that they are not able to stand by themselves: *Afraid of falling*, for example, gives additional information about the rest of the sentence. This phrase must be set off with a comma so that the reader does not get confused. If this sentence didn't include the comma, *Afraid of falling I walked slowly down the steps*, it might be difficult to know exactly what the writer means.

Using Introductory Phrases

Add the comma to the following sentences, all of which include an introductory phrase. Make sure your comma is placed at the end of the introductory phrase.

1. Despite his stubbed toe, Marco still ran in the cross-country state finals.

2. Buttoning her coat Melissa stepped out into the cold.

3. Even though he loved pizza, Jorge didn't have anything to eat at the party.

4. Except for Marge, everyone has already completed his or her shift chores.

5. Despite the fact that he slept late this morning, Jerry was still tired all day at school.

Correct answers:

1. *Despite his stubbed toe, Marco still ran in the cross-country state finals.*

2. *Buttoning her coat, Melissa stepped out into the cold.*

3. *Even though he loved pizza, Jorge didn't have anything to eat at the party.*

4. *Except for Marge, everyone has already completed his or her shift chores.*

5. *Despite the fact that he slept late this morning, Jerry was still tired all day at school.*

> **TIP**
>
> If you are unsure where the comma goes in these types of sentences, remember that if you can remove the introductory phrase from the sentence and have the sentence still be correct, you need to set it off with a comma.
>
> For example, remove the phrase from the first sentence and you will be left with this: *Marco still ran in the cross-country finals.* The sentence still makes sense.

To Set off a Series

A comma is also used to set off a series of adjectives, nouns, or verbs:

> *His car is a loud, slow, and very old vehicle.*
>
> *We had sandwiches, pickles, soda, and cake at the party.*
>
> *We need to run to the store, return the video, pick up Aunt Jean, and meet at the theater.*

The last adjective in a series or list (for example, in the first sentence in the preceding examples, *very old*) is not followed by a comma. This adjective simply attaches itself to the noun that the entire list is talking about *(vehicle)*. Similarly, the last noun in the series (for example, in the second sentence in the preceding examples, *cake*) does not have a comma after it.

Sometimes the list may include items or names that belong in pairs. Make sure you add the comma after the pair, which should be treated as a set:

> *Al plans to invite Mike and Sue, Tori and Blake, Dawn and Jerome, and Eli and Mary to the show.*

> *Acceptable color choices for the uniforms are red and blue, yellow and blue, red and green, and solid blue.*

Using Serial Commas

Add commas in the correct place in each of the following sentences.

1. You should probably bring a hat gloves two pairs of pants and at least four pairs of socks along with your ice skates.

2. Good gift choices for Marty include a new calculator a briefcase a watch or a gift card for his favorite restaurant.

3. Countries that Trina has visited include France Canada Mexico Puerto Rico and Spain.

4. His favorite television shows tend to be on channels 2 5 7 and 9.

5. Ice cream flavors available today are vanilla chocolate strawberry and chocolate chip.

Correct answers:

1. *You should probably bring a hat, gloves, two pairs of pants, and at least four pairs of socks, along with your ice skates.*

   If you placed the commas in any incorrect places, reread the list of items that "you should probably bring" and place a comma after each word or phrase that identifies the item(s):

   > *hat*

   > *gloves*

   > *two pairs of pants*

   > *at least four pairs of socks*

2. *Good gift choices for Marty include a new calculator, a briefcase, a watch, or a gift card for his favorite restaurant.*

   The list here is:

   > *a new calculator*

   > *a briefcase*

   > *a watch*

   > *a gift card for his favorite restaurant*

3. *Countries that Trina has visited include France, Canada, Mexico, Puerto Rico, and Spain.*

   The list of countries here is:

   France

   Canada

   Mexico

   Puerto Rico

   Spain

4. *His favorite television shows tend to be on channels 2, 5, 7, and 9.*

   The list of channels is:

   2

   5

   7

   9

5. *Ice cream flavors available today are vanilla, chocolate, strawberry, and chocolate chip.*

   The list of ice cream flavors here is:

   vanilla

   chocolate

   strawberry

   chocolate chip

To Enclose the Name of a Person

A comma is also used to enclose the name of a person to whom you are speaking or writing directly:

> *Sandra said she might be here late, Maria, so I don't think you should call her.*
>
> *The doctor is ready to see you, Mr. Vazquez, so please step into this room.*
>
> *The lightning scares the puppy, Jennifer, so please stay in this room if it begins raining.*

You can see that in these sentences, the person's name enclosed in commas can be removed and the sentence will still make sense:

> *She said she might be here late, so I don't think you should call her.*
>
> *The doctor is ready to see you, so please step into this room.*
>
> *The lightning scares the puppy, so please stay in this room if it begins raining.*

Using Commas with Names

Now add the commas in the sentences that follow.

1. Eddie your bicycle is in the driveway and not locked.

2. I can't practice today Coach Ernie because I have a dental appointment.

3. Watch out for the glass on the ground Luke because I don't want you to cut yourself.

4. Eat all of your dinner little Mitch and then you can have a piece of cake.

5. Please help me carry these books Cousin Tina and then we can get something to drink.

Correct answers:

1. *Eddie, your bicycle is in the driveway and not locked.*

   Take "Eddie" out of the sentence and it still makes sense:

   Your bicycle is in the driveway and not locked.

2. *I can't practice today, Coach Ernie, because I have a dental appointment.*

   Take "Coach Ernie" out of the sentence and it still makes sense:

   I can't practice today because I have a dental appointment.

3. *Watch out for the glass on the ground, Luke, because I don't want you to cut yourself.*

   Take "Luke" out of the sentence and it still makes sense:

   Watch out for the glass on the road because I don't want you to cut yourself.

4. *Eat all of your dinner, little Mitch, and then you can have a piece of cake.*

   Take "little Mitch" out of the sentence and it still makes sense:

   Eat all of your dinner and then you can have a piece of cake.

5. *Please help me carry these books, Cousin Tina, and then we can get something to drink.*

   Take "Cousin Tina" out of the sentence and it still makes sense:

   Please help me carry these books and then we can get something to drink.

Dash

A *dash* looks like this: —.

As you might guess, it has a variety of uses, as discussed in the following sections.

For Emphasis

It is often used to emphasize a part of a sentence that can be segregated from the rest of the sentence.

> **TIP**
>
> If you encounter a question on the test where you are asked about a dash, there will not be any confusion about whether a dash or a comma should be used in the correct answer. Only one of those choices (either a comma or a dash) will be given.

The weather is so unpredictable lately—glance outside right now—that I think we should plan to have the party indoors.

My new car—which cost me $20,000—already needs to be serviced.

The movie—which is rated "R"—is not appropriate for high school students.

To Interrupt a Thought

A dash can also be used to interrupt a thought.

My uncle—who really is a great guy—forgot to pick me up at school.

Dinner—which is being prepared tonight by Sally—will be served at 7:00 p.m.

The school—which was named in honor of astronaut John Glenn—is at the end of this street.

Using Dashes

Decide where the dashes belong in each of these sentences.

1. My first time sky diving which I actually thought would be my last was only two months ago.
2. Her newborn baby definitely the most beautiful baby I have ever seen is now home from the hospital.
3. The frozen lake not completely ready for skating is at the end of that street.
4. Gerry's older brother whom he hasn't seen in over a year should be home from Japan this week sometime.
5. Her grandmother who lived to be 102 went for a 20-minute walk every day for years.

Correct answers:

1. *My first time sky diving—which I actually thought would be my last—was only two months ago.*
2. *Her newborn baby—definitely the most beautiful baby I have ever seen—is now home from the hospital.*
3. *The frozen lake—not completely ready for skating—is at the end of that street.*
4. *Gerry's older brother—whom he hasn't seen in over a year—should be home from Japan this week sometime.*
5. *Her grandmother—who lived to be 102—went for a 20-minute walk every day for years.*

To add dashes successfully, reread each sentence slowly and listen for a phrase that needs to be isolated from the rest of the sentence.

Exclamation Point

An *exclamation point* looks like this: !.

It is used to show that a word, phrase, or sentence is emphasized, that is, that it is very important. Exclamation points are often used at the end of commands when strong emotion is being conveyed. When a sentence with an exclamation point is read aloud, it is read with surprise or strong emotion:

I can't find my daughter!

Fire!

Look out below!

Exclamation points should not be overused and should be saved for instances when they are truly necessary. An exclamation point should not be used when a word, phrase, or sentence should not be emphasized in context. For example, the exclamation point in *I drew this picture!* is probably not necessary. A period would work fine here, unless the speaker is a three-year-old child who is exclaiming about his or her artistic talents to a parent or teacher.

Using Exclamation Points

Decide which sentence in this paragraph most deserves an exclamation point instead of a period.

The town was pretty much desolate, save for the squirrels running along the ground and the birds chirping as they flew from tree to tree. Jerome knew all his friends would be out of town this weekend, but he didn't realize the entire town would be at the State Football Finals. He kicked a stone as hard as he could. Wendy. He knew that beautiful and fun Wendy would be home. He also knew that her girl-friends would be out of town too.

Correct answer:

The one-word sentence "Wendy" needs an exclamation mark here. When this sentence has emotion associated with it, that part of the story takes on a more serious slant.

Parentheses

Parentheses looks like this: ( ).

They are used to enclose words or phrases that need to appear in the sentence or paragraph, but are not to be emphasized as much as the rest of the sentence or paragraph:

Her brother (a senior at Harvard) is planning to look for a job after the summer.

He needs some new clothes (for interviews) so he will save money from his lifeguard job.

The board members (Martin Drake, Allan Ross, and Pam Tyler) will meet next week to discuss those and other issues.

While the parking lot is being repaved (scheduled to be completed on Wednesday), please ensure that you do not park in fire zones or in places that are clearly marked "No Parking."

TIP

In some instances, the material enclosed in parentheses could also be set off by commas.

Sometimes parentheses will enclose entire sentences. Ensure that the material in the parentheses actually belongs there. Ask yourself whether it is part of the paragraph, or whether it is extra, or inside information that may be necessary or interesting for the reader to know. For example:

> *He worked in New York City for most of his life, and commuted on the Long Island Railroad every weekday. (Back then, the railroad was heated poorly and air conditioning was nonexistent. Today, the railroad cars are as comfortable as riding in a regular automobile.) He worked for the same company for 35 years and when he retired last week, he said that what he would miss most was the predictable routine of his day.*

In this paragraph, the information within the parentheses is not necessary; however, it adds some interesting information to the rest of the paragraph.

Using Parentheses

Add parentheses to enclose words or phrases in the following sentences.

1. Juan's mother is out of town Dallas, then Houston for the next two weeks.

2. Carlos may change his major chemistry next semester.

3. We will drive halfway probably to Evanston on the first leg of our trip.

4. Don't forget to take extra batteries you'll need them and also some bottled water.

5. Eve was sick last week strep throat and yesterday bad cold.

Correct answers:

1. *Juan's mother is out of town (Dallas, then Houston) for the next two weeks.*

2. *Carlos may change his major (chemistry) next semester.*

3. *We will drive halfway (probably to Evanston) on the first leg of our trip.*

4. *Don't forget to take extra batteries (you'll need them) and also some bottled water.*

5. *Eve was sick last week (strep throat) and yesterday (bad cold).*

Period

A *period* looks like this: .. A period is used at the end of a sentence:

> *My cat seems to have run away.*
>
> *He made a bad decision when he rode his bike in the snow.*
>
> *This isn't the correct way to play this game.*

A period is sometimes wrongly used to end a phrase or fragment that is not a sentence. For example:

> *The hot sun.*
>
> *Green grass.*
>
> *Beautiful weather.*

Each of these phrases is a fragment and does not make a statement. It is not a complete idea. Make sure that any fragments on the test do not have a period at the end.

On the other hand, you may encounter words or short sentences with a period that actually are correct because they do state a full idea:

> *Stop.*
>
> *She's here.*

Identifying Fragments

Decide whether each group of words is a complete thought, by stating whether each is a sentence or a fragment.

1. A beautiful sunset.

2. Jeff's winning catch saved the game.

3. Marty likes Jill.

4. Running to the store to get eggs.

5. Her new apartment

Correct answers:

1. *A beautiful sunset* (fragment)

   This doesn't include a verb; it is only a subject.

2. *Jeff's winning catch saved the game* (sentence)

   This is a complete thought with a subject and verb.

3. *Marty likes Jill* (sentence)

   This is a complete thought with a subject and verb.

4. *Running to the store to get eggs* (fragment)

   There is no subject in this sentence.

5. *Her new apartment* (fragment)

   A fragment has only a subject and no verb, as is shown here.

Don't assume that because a group of words is short, it is not a complete sentence. Note that the short sentences in the preceding examples are a complete thought. Read through each group of words and think about whether it is a complete thought.

Question Mark

A *question mark* looks like this: ?.

A question mark is used only at the end of a sentence that asks a question:

> *Do you know whether Marco will be joining us?*
>
> *Is this really the type of weather you like best?*

Question marks are not used at the end of a sentence when the sentence does not ask a question. If a character wonders or thinks about something, such a sentence is a statement and does not mean that a question is being asked:

Terry wants to see the new movie. I think she knows it is playing right in town.

The following sentence is a statement:

Mrs. Marshall wants to know when the party begins.

To turn it into a question, the writer would have to revise it:

When does the party begin? Mrs. Marshall wants to know.

Using Question Marks

Decide whether each sentence here needs a question mark or a period at the end.

1. I think Marty said he would be here at eight

2. Albany is the capital of New York, isn't it

3. Did he say the test would be tomorrow

4. Some people may think this ride is too scary

5. I wonder if it will rain later today

Correct answers:

1. *I think Marty said he would be here at eight.*

   This is a statement and needs a period at the end.

2. *Albany is the capital of New York, isn't it?*

   This sentence asks a question (isn't it).

3. *Did he say the test would be tomorrow?*

   This sentence asks a question, whether the test would be tomorrow.

4. *Some people may think this ride is too scary.*

   This sentence does not ask a question, so it simply needs a period at the end.

5. *I wonder if it will rain later today.*

   This sentence does not ask a question. Wondering about something is not questioning it.

Quotation Marks

Quotation marks come in pairs and look like this: " ". Quotation marks are used to set off text that represents quoted or spoken language. Only words that are actually included in the quote are enclosed in quotation marks:

"I'm using the car tonight," my brother said. "Where are my keys?" he asked.

Punctuation that is used at the end of the quotation goes inside the quotation marks:

> *"What's for dinner?" Mary asked.*

When the speaker is identified before the quote, a comma is placed before the quote:

> *John asked, "Who will be riding in my car?"*

When the speaker is identified after the quote, place a period at the end:

> *"Will you be staying for the entire meeting?" Mom asked.*

When the speaker's name interrupts the quote, set it off with commas:

> *"It won't be too long," Jack said, "because I measured the wood twice."*

When the speaker's name comes between two complete sentences of dialogue, separate the two sentences with a period:

> *"I don't like working late hours," Don said. "I have trouble waking up for school in the morning."*

Begin a new paragraph each time the speaker changes:

> *"I really should be leaving," Jessie said.*
>
> *"Oh, you can stay another ten minutes," Gail said. "Your parents won't even know."*

Using Quotation Marks

Add quotation marks where they belong in the following sentences.

1. Joanna sighed, I am never sure how to get to my aunt's new house.

2. Bill, Tom, and Zach stood by the gym door. I'm not going in first, Zach told his friends.

3. Do you think school will be cancelled today? Marie asked.

4. Years earlier, my grandfather had told me this day might come. Keep your head clear and your eyes and ears open, he had warned me.

5. I hope to see all of you at the concert tonight Mrs. Carpenter said as she left the room.

Correct answers:

1. *Joanna sighed, "I am never sure how to get to my aunt's new house."*

   The exact words that Joanna says, "I am never sure how to get to my aunt's new house," are enclosed in quotation marks. Note that the period at the end of that sentence is also enclosed by the end quote.

2. *Bill, Tom, and Zach stood by the gym door. "I'm not going in first," Zach told his friends.*

   Zach says, "I'm not going in first," so this is enclosed by the quotes. Note that a period does not end this quoted sentence, but a comma (enclosed by the end quote mark) is necessary.

3. *"Do you think school will be cancelled today?" Marie asked.*

   Because there is a question mark at the end of the sentence uttered by Marie, there is no need for an additional comma to separate her words from the rest of the sentence. Note that the quotation marks must enclose the question mark. Also, since the statement "Marie asked" is not a question, a question mark does not belong at the end of the complete sentence.

4. *Years earlier, my grandfather had told me this day might come. "Keep your head clear and your eyes and ears open," he had warned me.*

   The quote in the second sentence has a comma to separate it from the rest of the sentence.

5. *"I hope to see all of you at the concert tonight," Mrs. Carpenter said as she left the room.*

   A comma is needed after Mrs. Carpenter's words to separate them from the rest of the sentence.

Only enclose words actually uttered by the person speaking. For example, quotation marks don't belong in the sentence *John told me that "he doesn't like the lunch selections today."* Quotation marks are not used for paraphrased words.

TIP

Pay attention to where the quotation marks are placed in short stories, articles, and books that you read. Look for commas that enclose the quotes.

Semicolon

A *semicolon* looks like this: ;. A semicolon can be used in two ways, as shown in the following sections.

To Organize a List

You can use the semicolon to organize a potentially confusing list, as shown in the following examples:

> *Expected at the movie premiere are: Terry Perkins, Los Angeles, California; Manuel Park, Buffalo, New York; and Paul Trent, Ft. Lauderdale, Florida.*
>
> *High scores for the Tiny Tot Bowling Championship were: Mark Smyth, 78; Donald Barry, 77; and Diana Blank, 70.*
>
> *The dinner orders are: Pizza, 10 orders; Cheeseburger, 8 orders; Vegetable Lasagna, 5 orders; and Salad Bar, 5 orders.*

Commas separate the individual items and semicolons separate groups of items.

To Separate Clauses

You can use a semicolon to separate closely related independent clauses. Note that these clauses can stand alone and can be correctly written as separate sentences too.

> *I like playing softball; I hope the new team is formed soon.*
>
> *Mr. Smith is very ill; we may want to see if he needs anything.*
>
> *Twenty students came to the game; we won a school spirit award.*

Using Commas and Semicolons

Read the following sentences and add commas and semicolons where needed.

1. We had some high scores in the game: Malcolm Smith 41 Evan George 56 Dewayne Clark 55 Joseph Martins 49 and Jean Yoder 57

2. Screening appointments are this Thursday afternoon for the following members: Pat Cross 2:15 Thomas Anderson 2:30 Derek Smith 2:45 Amber Collins 3:00 and Terry Oslow 3:15

3. This is one of my favorite movies *Jaws* is my other.

4. The times for all track team members improved: Alison 4:33 Elizabeth 4:10 Gina 4:20 and Andrea 4:15.

5. Three students will give their oral reports at the Open House: James Haller George Washington Carver Mindy Ross Susan B. Anthony and Gwen Holmes Thomas Jefferson.

Correct answers:

1. *We had some high scores in the game: Malcolm Smith, 41; Evan George, 56; Dewayne Clark, 55; Joseph Martins, 49; and Jean Yoder, 57.*

   A comma goes after each person's full name and a semicolon goes after each score.

2. *Screening appointments are this Thursday afternoon for the following members: Pat Cross, 2:15; Thomas Anderson, 2:30; Derek Smith, 2:45; Amber Collins, 3:00; and Terry Oslow, 3:15.*

   A comma goes after each person's full name and a semicolon goes after each appointment time.

3. *This is one of my favorite movies;* Jaws *is my other.*

   A comma goes after each student's name and a semicolon goes after the film's title.

4. *The times for all track team members improved: Alison, 4:33; Elizabeth, 4:10; Gina, 4:20; and Andrea, 4:15.*

   A comma goes after each student's name and a semicolon goes after each time.

5. *Three students will give their oral reports at the Open House: James Haller, George Washington Carver; Mindy Ross, Susan B. Anthony; and Gwen Holmes, Thomas Jefferson.*

   A comma goes after each student's full name and a semicolon goes after each report subject.

Don't use a semicolon where a comma belongs. In each of the following sentences, a comma should be used instead of the semicolon because one of the clauses in each line is a dependent clause:

> *Although my brother is a good singer, his band is too loud.*
>
> *Despite the bad weather, we still had a good time.*
>
> *Even though we each had a ticket, there were no seats available at the concert.*

Reviewing Additional Resources

Reread and review the explanations of the marks of punctuation, and pay attention to all punctuation in the essays, articles, and books that you read between now and the time you take the ACT test.

For more explanation of the mechanics of punctuation marks, you may want to read through Strunk and White's *The Elements of Style*, or Vincent Hopper's *Elements of English* (see Appendix B for more information about these and other helpful books).

Understanding Basic Grammar and Usage

You will need to have a clear understanding of basic grammar and usage for this test. It is likely that you are a bit rusty with some parts of grammar and can benefit from a full-scale review of parts of speech and other aspects of grammar.

You can expect approximately a dozen of the questions on the test to target your knowledge of the following areas: the parts of speech, subject-verb agreement, pronoun-antecedent agreement, and coordinating and subordinating conjunctions. Although it is probable that you know most of these rules and ideas fairly well already, take some time to examine and review components of basic grammar and usage in the sections that follow.

Parts of Speech

Let's first review some of the parts of speech you are likely to be familiar with and briefly discuss how each of these types of words is commonly used in a sentence.

Noun

A *noun* is a word that names a person, a place, or a thing:

The table already has two plates and some napkins.

In this sentence, the words *table*, *plates*, and *napkins* are all nouns because these words name things.

A triangle has three sides.

In this sentence, the words *triangle* and *sides* are both nouns.

Finding Nouns

Find the nouns in each of these sentences.

1. The suitcase was left in the hall by the door.

2. The boy won't ask a question with his brother in the room.

3. The truck drove through a puddle and got water and mud on my pants.

4. Jane's eyeglasses broke into two pieces.

5. A flag is flying on the flagpole near our school.

Correct answers:

1. The <u>suitcase</u> was left in the <u>hall</u> by the <u>door</u>.

2. The <u>boy</u> won't ask a <u>question</u> with his <u>brother</u> in the <u>room</u>.

3. The <u>truck</u> drove through a <u>puddle</u> and got <u>water</u> and <u>mud</u> on my <u>pants</u>.

4. <u>Jane's</u> <u>eyeglasses</u> broke into two <u>pieces</u>.

5. A <u>flag</u> is flying on the <u>flagpole</u> near our <u>school</u>.

Pronoun

A *pronoun* is a word that is used in place of a noun. Usually the noun (called the pronoun's *antecedent)* was used previously in the sentence or paragraph. The words *I, he, she, it, we, you, they,* and *one* are commonly used pronouns. Whenever the word *noun* is used to describe a concept in this chapter, you can substitute the word *pronoun* too. For our purposes, pronouns and nouns do pretty much the same job in a sentence.

In the sentence,

> Ms. Carpenter says that she doesn't feel well today.

the word *she* is a *pronoun.* In this sentence, *she* is taking the place of *Ms. Carpenter.*

If the pronoun were not used in that sentence, it would read:

> *Ms. Carpenter* says that *Ms. Carpenter* doesn't feel well today.

This sounds awkward and is the main reason pronouns are used in speaking and writing.

Working with Pronouns

Change one noun in each of these sentences to a pronoun.

1. The letter fell near the table.
2. Canada is situated north of the United States.
3. That hat can't be purchased in this store.
4. Mike and John like to volunteer at the youth center.
5. The mouse simply can't be caught.

Correct answers:

1. *The letter fell near the table.*

   It fell near the table. OR The letter fell near it.

2. *Canada is situated north of the United States.*

   Canada is situated north of it. OR It is situated north of the United States.

3. *That hat can't be purchased in this store.*

   That hat can't be purchased in this store. OR It can't be purchased in this store.

4. *Mike and John like to volunteer at the youth center.*

   They like to volunteer at the youth center. OR Mike and John like to volunteer at the youth center.

5. *The mouse simply can't be caught.*

   It simply can't be caught.

Verb

A *verb* is a word that tells the action of a noun (or a pronoun). It tells what a noun (or a pronoun) in a sentence is doing. *Run, walk, breathe, laugh, sit, fall*, and *look* are all examples of the thousands of verbs in the English language.

In the sentence, "I danced for hours at Tina's party," *danced* is a verb telling what *I* (the pronoun) did.

Be aware that the forms of the verb *to be* are also verbs: *am, is, are, was, were*. In the sentence "He is here this week," *is* is the verb.

Finding Verbs

Find the verb in each of the following sentences.

1. The storm destroyed the entire new development on Morris Street.
2. The commuters rushed to the waiting train.
3. Daryl questioned the principal about the new attendance policy.
4. I will read that tomorrow.
5. Tim should have been ready to go at 6:00 a.m.

Correct answers:

1. The storm <u>destroyed</u> the entire new development on Morris Street.
2. The commuters <u>rushed</u> to the waiting train.
3. Daryl <u>questioned</u> the principal about the new attendance policy.
4. I <u>will read</u> that tomorrow.
5. Tim <u>should have been ready</u> to go at 6:00 a.m.

Adjective

An *adjective* is a word that describes or tells more about a noun or pronoun. Adjectives often, but not always, appear right before the noun or pronoun in a sentence.

Jackie's kind mother is permitting lucky me to go to the pool with them.

In this sentence, the words *kind* and *lucky* are adjectives. These words modify, or describe, the nouns in the sentence.

Adding Adjectives

Add an adjective before a noun in the following sentences, as appropriate.

1. The baby is sleeping in his crib.
2. Will you buy a car in the next few months?
3. That athlete comes into the restaurant once a week.
4. His brother likes to play games.
5. The musician has an album due this week.

Correct answers:

Note that the adjectives are suggestions. Your responses will differ.

1. *The baby is sleeping in his crib.*

    The <u>newborn</u> baby is sleeping in his <u>tiny</u> crib.

2. *Will you buy a car in the next few months?*

    Will you buy a <u>new</u> car in the next few months?

3. *That athlete comes into the restaurant once a week.*

    That <u>famous</u> athlete comes into the <u>Italian</u> restaurant once a week.

4. *His brother likes to play games.*

    His <u>older</u> brother likes to play <u>card</u> games.

5. *The musician has an album due this week.*

    The <u>rock</u> musician has a <u>new</u> album due this week.

Adverb

An *adverb* is a word that describes or tells more about a verb, an adjective, or another adverb. For example, in the sentence "She nervously twirled her hair," *nervously* is an adverb that describes how she twirled her hair (*twirled* is the verb). Most (but not all) adverbs end in *-ly* and appear in a sentence near the word they are modifying (talking about). Some examples of adverbs that don't end in *-ly*:

> He drives a *very* fast car.

> Ride *faster* if you hope to get there on time.

Identifying and Using Adverbs

Identify the adverb in each of the following sentences.

1. Michael ran quickly out of the burning building.

2. The birds chirp loudly pretty much every morning.

Add an adverb to each of the following sentences.

3. We exited the trail and went to our car.

4. I can tell that he is nervous because he is walking to the door.

5. The computer processes the data as soon as we are able to enter it.

Correct answers:

1. *Michael ran <u>quickly</u> out of the burning building.*

    Quickly describes how Michael ran out of the burning building.

2. *The birds chirp <u>loudly</u> pretty much every morning.*

    Loudly describes how the birds chirp pretty much every morning.

3. *We exited the trail and went to our car.*

 We <u>slowly</u> exited the trail and went to our car.

4. *I can tell that he is nervous because he is walking to the door.*

 I can tell that he is nervous because he is <u>slowly</u> walking to the door.

5. *The computer processes the data as soon as we are able to enter it.*

 The computer processes the data <u>instantly</u> as soon as we are able to enter it.

EXAM ALERT

Remember, you won't be asked to identify or name any parts of speech on the ACT English test, but you do need to have an understanding of these concepts and how the parts of speech are used.

Subject-Verb Agreement

Subject-verb agreement is an important grammar rule that is nowhere near as technical or intimidating as it may sound at first. It simply means that the word or phrase forming the subject of the sentence must agree in number with the verb. You are probably doing this automatically as you write and speak anyway. You never say, "I *wants* to borrow your car." You say, "I <u>want</u> to borrow your car."

TIP

The noun that makes up the simple subject must agree with the verb that follows it. A simple subject is the subject of a sentence without its modifiers, those words and phrases that are used to describe or tell more about something. It can be one word, more than one word, or an entire phrase.

In the sentence "This pen leaks ink," we know that *pen* is the simple subject and that it is singular. *Leaks* is the verb that tells what the pen is doing. The subject (*pen*) and the verb (*leaks*) are the same number—that is, they agree. The sentence is correct.

Consider these subject and verb tenses:

> *The pen leaks.*
> *The pen(s) leaked.*
> *The pen has leaked before. BUT The pens have leaked before.*
> *The pen(s) will leak.*

If the sentence instead had read, "This pen leak ink," we would see that the singular subject (*pen*) and the verb (*leak*) don't agree; they are not both using the same number.

Similarly, in the sentence "These pens leaks ink," when we again match the simple subject (*pens*) with the verb (*leaks*), we realize right away that the subject and the verb don't agree. The sentence is incorrect.

Subject-Verb Agreement for Simple Subjects

When a test question asks you to decide whether the subject and verb in a particular sentence are in agreement, use this formula:

1. First, read the sentence.

2. Underline the simple subject (the noun or nouns that appear in the subject— without any of the adjectives that may describe them).

3. Underline the verb (or verb phrase) that is telling what that noun or nouns did, does, or will do. Now read the noun and verb to yourself and think about whether they are in agreement. This whole process will take you just a few seconds.

Here's an example of how the formula is actually used with a sentence:

Sentence: Joe's puppy like to play outdoors.

1. Underline the simple subject:

   Joe's <u>puppy</u> like to play outdoors.

   Don't underline *Joe's* here. That word is a possessive noun, but not the subject in this sentence.

   Don't underline *outdoors* here. That word is an adverb.

2. Underline the verb that is telling what the noun or nouns did, does, or will do:

   Joe's <u>puppy</u> <u>like</u> to play outdoors.

3. Now read the noun and verb to yourself and think about whether they are in agreement:

   puppy like to play

   We can tell that the subject and verb are not in agreement in this sentence. The sentence should correctly read:

   Joe's puppy likes to play outdoors.

Building Subject-Verb Agreement

Use the formula you just learned to test whether each of these sentences' subjects and verbs agree.

1. The car's overhead light works fine.

2. The experiment seeks to find the freezing point for that liquid.

3. The weather forecaster may predict a sunny day.

4. The flower arrangement look great on that shelf.

5. The professors like to meet in the early afternoon.

Correct answers:

1. *The car's overhead light works fine.*

   Subject: *light* (note that the words *car's* and *overhead* describe *light*)

   Verb: *works*

   Subject-Verb Agreement: *light works*

   The sentence is correct.

2. *The experiment seeks to find the freezing point for that liquid.*

   Subject: *experiment*

   Verb: *seeks*

   Subject-Verb Agreement: *experiment seeks*

   The sentence is correct.

3. *The weather forecaster may predict a sunny day.*

   Subject: *forecaster* (note that the word *weather* describes *forecaster*)

   Verb: *may predict* (make sure both parts of the verb phrase are included here, or you may come up with an incorrect conclusion about subject/verb agreement in this sentence)

   Subject-Verb Agreement: *forecaster may predict*

   The sentence is correct.

4. *The flower arrangement look great on that shelf.*

   Subject: *arrangement* (*flower* describes the arrangement)

   Verb: *look*

   Subject-Verb Agreement: *arrangement look*

   The sentence is not correct. The sentence should say: The flower arrangement *looks* great on that shelf.

5. *The professors like to meet in the early afternoon.*

   Subject: *professors*

   Verb: *like*

   Subject-Verb Agreement: *professors like*

   The sentence is correct.

Subject-Verb Agreement for Compound Subjects

When you are checking for subject-verb agreement, you will sometimes come across long subjects in a sentence:

> *His brother, his sister, his best friend, and his grandfather will all make the trip to the beach.*

These types of subjects are called *compound subjects* because there is more than one subject to the sentence. For compound subjects, it is often easier to work with the sentence if you change the long subject to a pronoun (a simple subject). Thus, in the preceding sentence example, the entire string of nouns could be replaced by the word *they*. The sentence then becomes:

> *They will all make the trip to the beach.*

You can see that changing the long subject to a one-word pronoun does not affect the meaning of the sentence at all. It does make the sentence easier to work with, though. This procedure becomes almost necessary to accurately assess subject-verb agreement in sentences.

In the sentence "My dog, my cat, my surfboard, and my girlfriend doesn't fit into my sports car," the subject is *My dog, my cat, my surfboard, and my girlfriend.* We can shorten this subject to the pronoun *They* for the purposes of checking subject-verb agreement. The sentence then becomes: *They doesn't fit into my sports car.*

You can see right away then that the words that make up the subject (condensed to *they* in this case) and the verb (*doesn't*) don't agree. If we had left the subject as the long list of words it originally was, we might have tried to make the final noun in the subject, *my girlfriend*, agree with the verb *doesn't*. Your response to that question might have been incorrect.

> **TIP**
>
> Make sure that the verb agrees with the subject and not the prepositional phrase that follows it. *The carton of eggs is on the table* is correct because it is one *carton* of eggs. *The set of kitchen knives isn't in this bag* is correct because it is one set.

> **TIP**
>
> Don't take any chances. Always change compound subjects to a pronoun when checking for subject-verb agreement on the test.

Working with Compound Subjects

Try these examples of sentences with compound subjects. Shorten each compound subject before you compare it with the verb.

1. The dog, the parrot, and the new kitten requires too much attention from me these days.

2. His brother, his father, and his best friend all hope that Glen qualifies for the competition.

3. Flour, sugar, butter, and, of course, chocolate chips is included in the recipe.

4. The trucks' cargo and parts of a car are all over the highway.

5. The police officer and his dog is standing right by the front door.

Correct answers:

1. *The dog, the parrot, and the new kitten requires too much attention from me these days.*

   Shorten the compound subject: *The dog, the parrot, and the new kitten = They*

   Identify the verb: *requires*

   Subject/verb: *they requires*

   The sentence is not correct. The sentence should read: *The dog, the parrot, and the new kitten require too much attention from me these days.*

2. *His brother, his father, and his best friend all hope that Glen qualifies for the competition.*

   Shorten the compound subject: *His brother, his father, and his best friend = They*

   Identify the verb: *hope*

   Subject/verb: *they hope*

   The sentence is correct.

3. *Flour, sugar, butter, and, of course, chocolate chips is included in the recipe.*

   Shorten the compound subject: *Flour, sugar, butter, and, of course, chocolate chips = They*

   Identify the verb: *is*

   Subject/verb: *they is*

   The sentence is not correct. The sentence should read: *Flour, sugar, butter, and, of course, chocolate chips are included in the recipe.*

4. *The trucks' cargo and parts of a car are all over the highway.*

   Shorten the compound subject: *The trucks' cargo and parts of a car = They*

   Identify the verb: *are*

   Subject/verb: *They are*

   The sentence is correct.

5. *The police officer and his dog is standing right by the front door.*

   Shorten the compound subject: *The police officer and his dog = They*

   Identify the verb: *is*

   Subject/verb: *they is*

   The sentence is not correct. The sentence should read: *The police officer and his dog are standing right by the front door.*

Subject-Verb Agreement for Sentences That Begin with a Phrase or Clause

Another situation you may encounter on the test is the presence of a phrase or clause at the beginning of the sentence. You may think for a moment that this is the subject of the sentence.

For example, consider this sentence:

Expected at the ceremony later today is Clint Downing, Mercedes Gomez, Mark Smith, and Grace Lee.

Many students may read this sentence and mistakenly think that the subject and verb are in agreement. A simple check will reveal that this is not so. To do this, first disregard the clause that begins the sentence and identify the subject in the sentence.

The subject is a list of four names:

Clint Downing, Mercedes Gomez, Mark Smith, Grace Lee

As you read earlier, it is best to change a longer subject like this one to a pronoun. In this case, change the subject to the pronoun *they*.

Now, look for the verb in the sentence. In this case it is a form of the verb to be: *is*.

Put the pronoun together with the verb and you will see that it is not correct:

They is

The verb here should be changed to *are* to have the subject and verb agree.

Reviewing Subject-Verb Agreement

Now look at the following sentences. Find and underline the simple subject and then the verb or verb phrase. Decide whether there is subject-verb agreement in each sentence. If there isn't, write the correct verb beside the sentence to make the sentence correct.

1. Timmy and his sister both have a present to give you.

2. Marline, Abe, Tessa, and Julio like to meet on Wednesdays.

3. My club has one meeting left this year.

4. Coach Brown and the entire team is going to the dinner.

Correct answers:

1. *Timmy and his sister both have a present to give you.*

   Shorten the compound subject: *Timmy and his sister = They*

   Verb: *have*

   Subject/verb: *They have*

   The sentence is correct.

2. Marline, Abe, Tessa, and Julio like to meet on Wednesdays.

   Shorten the compound subject: *Marline, Abe, Tessa, and Julio = They*

   Verb: *like*

   Subject/verb: *They like*

   The sentence is correct.

3. *My club has one meeting left this year.*

   Subject: *club*

   Verb: *has*

   Subject/verb: *club has*

   The sentence is correct.

4. *Coach Brown and the entire team is going to the dinner.*

   Shorten the compound subject: *Coach Brown and the entire team = They*

   Verb: *is going*

   Subject/verb: *They is going*

   The sentence is not correct. The sentence should read: *Coach Brown and the entire team are going to the dinner.*

Problematic Subject-Verb Agreement Situations

The sometimes-confusing words listed in Table 2.1 are *always* considered to be singular, and should take verbs accordingly. You will find that in some sentences, the words may not sound as if they are singular. Don't let this fool you. The words must be treated as singular subjects.

TABLE 2.1   Words Always Treated As Singular

anything	anybody	anyone	either
everything	everybody	everyone	neither
something	somebody	someone	each
nothing	nobody	no one	

For example, the sentence "Everybody must take their keys to the office" is incorrect. As we see in Table 2.1, the word *Everybody* is always considered to be singular. The sentence should correctly be written as: "Everybody must take his keys to the office," or "Everybody must take her keys to the office."

Similarly, "Anyone with a ticket should take his or her seat" is correct. "Anyone with a ticket should take their seat" is not. *Anyone* is singular. (Note that the words "with a ticket" are describing more about *anyone*.) Always think of these words as just talking about one person, place, or thing, and you won't have a problem with the verb that follows it.

When assessing whether the subject and verb agree, it may be easier to substitute *he* or *she* in any sentence where any of these words appear. For example, in the preceding sample sentences, you can substitute the singular pronoun:

She must take her keys to the office.

She should take her seat.

In this way, subject/verb agreement can be easily and accurately accessed.

Examining Subject-Verb Agreement

Determine whether the following sentences have correct subject/verb agreement.

1. Somebody is trying to take over our club.

2. Neither Jamal nor Mickey are going to the meeting tomorrow.

3. Either he or she is going to win this race.

4. Each are responsible for one of these projects.

5. Anybody is able to use one of the extra tickets.

Correct answers:

1. *Somebody is trying to take over our club.*

   Subject: *Somebody*

   Change to a singular subject: *He*

   Verb: *is*

   Subject/verb: *He is*

   The sentence is correct.

2. *Neither Jamal nor Mickey are going to the meeting tomorrow.*

   Subject: *Neither Jamal nor Mickey*

   Change to a singular subject: *He*

   Verb: *are*

   Subject/verb: *He are*

   The sentence is not correct. The sentence should read: *Neither Jamal nor Mickey is going to the meeting tomorrow.*

3. *Either he or she is going to win this race.*

   Subject: *Either he or she*

   Change to a singular subject: *He*

   Verb: *is*

   Subject/verb: *He is*

   The sentence is correct.

4. *Each are responsible for one of these projects.*

   Subject: *Each*

   Change to a singular subject: *She*

   Verb: *is*

   Subject/verb: *She is*

   The sentence is not correct. The sentence should read: *Each is responsible for one of these projects.*

   5. *Anybody is able to use one of the extra tickets.*

   Subject: *Anybody*

   Change to a singular subject: *She*

   Verb: *is*

   Subject/verb: *She is*

   The sentence is correct.

Pronoun-Antecedent Agreement

As you reviewed earlier in this chapter, pronouns (*I, he, she, it, we, you, they,* and *them*) are used in place of nouns in our speech and in our writing. Instead of saying, "Mr. Clark went to the ball game and Mr. Clark watched Mr. Clark's favorite team win," we use pronouns. That sentence then becomes "Mr. Clark went to the ball game and *he* watched *his* favorite team win." In the new sentence, "Mr. Clark" is the *antecedent*—the noun that *he* is talking about. It is a rule in English that all pronouns in a sentence, and even in the entire paragraph, agree with their antecedent—the original person, place, or thing that they are replacing. If they do not, it is often impossible to understand the meaning of the sentence or the paragraph.

Use this chart for clarification:

	Singular	Plural
First Person	I	We
Second Person	You	You
Third Person	He, she, it	They

Of course, some pronouns have been used so often in their incorrect form that they may even sound correct to you. You may be surprised to learn that both of these sentences are incorrect:

   Jennifer and me will be late this morning.

   Anna has saved a place for you and I.

Whenever the words *I* or *me* are joined with another noun in a sentence, you will need to perform a simple test to see whether the pronoun is being used correctly. To do this, first, circle *I* or *me* in the sentence. Delete the other nouns and whatever may be attached with it using the word *and* or commas.

For example, in the sentence "Jennifer and me will be late this morning," circle the word *me* and cross out the words *Jennifer and.* Now read the sentence again and think about whether it is still correct:

   Me will be late this morning.

You can see right away that the sentence is not correct. You need to change *me* to *I.* The sentence should correctly read: *Jennifer and I will be late this morning.*

Now check the second sentence. If you remove the words *you and*, the sentence reads: *Anna has saved a place for I.* You can tell immediately that the sentence is incorrect. The word *me* needs to be substituted for *I*:

> *Anna has saved a place for you and me.*

Practicing Pronoun-Antecedent Agreement

Practice pronoun-antecedent agreement by ensuring that these sentences are correct.

1. The review of *Underneath the Starry Sky* was favorable. He cited the writer's depth and style.

2. When a person wants to learn a new skill, sometimes you have to find a good teacher.

3. If anybody wants a slice of pizza, they had better get over here now.

4. In our company, anyone being interviewed needs a recommendation from their supervisor.

5. Each of the interview subjects sent his resume in last week.

Correct answers:

1. *The review of* Underneath the Starry Sky *was favorable. He cited the writer's depth and style.*

   Pronoun: *he*

   Antecedent: *The review*

   This sentence is incorrect. A review is not a "he." It should correctly read: *The review of* Underneath the Starry Sky *was favorable. It cited the writer's depth and style.*

2. *When a person wants to learn a new skill, sometimes you have to find a good teacher.*

   Pronoun: *you*

   Antecedent: *a person*

   This sentence is incorrect. The noun *a person* should be replaced by a second person pronoun (*you*).

3. *If anybody wants a slice of pizza, they had better get over here now.*

   Pronoun: *they*

   Antecedent: *anybody*

   This sentence is incorrect. As you'll recall from Table 2.1, the word *anybody* should always be treated as singular. The pronoun must then be *he* or *she*. The sentence should correctly read: *If anybody wants a slice of pizza, she had better get over here now.* OR *If anybody wants a slice of pizza, he had better get over here now.*

4. *In our company, anyone being interviewed needs a recommendation from their supervisor.*

   Pronoun: *their*

   Antecedent: *anyone*

   This sentence is incorrect. As you'll recall from Table 2.1, the word *anyone* should always be treated as singular. The pronoun then must be *his* or *her*. The sentence should correctly read: *In our company, anyone being interviewed needs a recommendation from his supervisor.* OR *In our company, anyone being interviewed needs a recommendation from her supervisor.*

5. *Each of the interview subjects sent his resume in last week.*

Pronoun: *his*

Antecedent: *each*

This sentence is correct. Each is singular, and *his* is the correct form. Note that the sentence could also correctly read: *Each of the interview subjects sent her resume in last week.*

Promise yourself right now that when you encounter these types of questions on the test, you won't trust your instinct. From these examples, you can probably see that some words, phrases, and sentences may sound correct when they actually are grammatically incorrect. Make sure that you remove the words surrounding *you*, *me*, and/or *I* to check for the sentence's correctness.

Coordinating Conjunctions

Coordinating conjunctions are small words that are used to connect other words, phrases, and clauses in a sentence. Some examples of coordinating conjunctions include the following words:

and, or, so, but, for, yet, nor

One job of coordinating conjunctions is to join two main clauses that should be emphasized equally. Here's an example:

He likes baseball, so he will get tickets to the game this weekend.

You can see that the clauses on both sides of the coordinating conjunction are independent clauses; that is, they can stand alone:

He likes baseball.
He will get tickets to the game this weekend.

As you work with this concept, remember that whenever a coordinating conjunction connects two independent clauses, a comma is required between the clauses. The comma belongs directly before the coordinating conjunction.

I like playing the piano, but I really don't practice enough.

The clauses on either side of the conjunction (*but*) are independent clauses. They both are of equal value in the sentence.

My son enjoys going to the movies, yet he can never give me a good summary of what he sees.

The comma is joining the first clause, *My son enjoys going to the movies*, with the second clause, *He can never give me a good summary of what he sees*. A comma is required before the coordinating conjunction, *yet*, in this sentence.

TIP

It may be easier on the test to circle the coordinating conjunction, and then add the comma right before it.

Working with Coordinating Conjunctions

Think about where the comma should be paired with a conjunction in each of these sentences.

1. Michael likes this costume but he liked the other costume too.
2. My sister has never caught a fish yet she tries every time we go to the lake.
3. Tony's car is very old yet it starts and runs without problems.
4. Jenny doubts she will go to the dinner party so later today she will bring the salad she promised.
5. The water is filled with sea creatures but Amanda still wants to jump in and look around.

Correct answers:

1. *Michael likes this costume but he liked the other costume too.*

   Coordinating conjunction: *but*

   The comma goes before *but*, so the correct sentence should read: *Michael likes this costume, but he liked the other costume too.*

2. *My sister has never caught a fish yet she tries every time we go to the lake.*

   Coordinating conjunction: *yet*

   The comma goes before *yet*, so the correct sentence should read: *My sister has never caught a fish, yet she tries every time we go to the lake.*

3. *Tony's car is very old yet it starts and runs without problems.*

   Coordinating conjunction: *yet*

   The comma goes before *yet*, so the correct sentence should read: *Tony's car is very old, yet it starts and runs without problems.*

4. *Jenny doubts she will go to the dinner party so later today she will bring the salad she promised.*

   Coordinating conjunction: *so*

   The comma goes before *so*, so the correct sentence should read: *Jenny doubts she will go to the dinner party, so later today she will bring the salad she promised.*

5. *The water is filled with sea creatures but Amanda still wants to jump in and look around.*

   Coordinating conjunction: *but*

   The comma goes before *but*, so the correct sentence should read: *The water is filled with sea creatures, but Amanda still wants to jump in and look around.*

TIP

Remember that you will not have to identify and name a coordinating conjunction on the ACT English test, but you will have to recognize that the comma belongs before it.

Subordinating Conjunctions

A *subordinating conjunction* is a word that joins a dependent clause and an independent clause. Many words are subordinating conjunctions, as follows:

after, although, as, because, before, even if, even though, if, in order that, once, provided that, rather than, so, than, that, though, unless, until, when, whenever, where, whereas, whether, while, why

Subordinating conjunctions are used to begin subordinate clauses, which are clauses that cannot stand by themselves; subordinate clauses require a comma right after they appear in a sentence. For example, read this sentence:

Although we were all very tired we still decided to go to the movies together.

The conjunction *although* begins the subordinate clause, "Although we were all very tired." This clause cannot stand by itself because it is not a complete thought. We need to put a comma directly after that clause. The sentence should look like this:

Although we were all very tired, we still decided to go to the movies together.

Look at this example:

Even if we win our game tonight we still won't be in the championship this season.

The subordinating conjunction *even if* begins the subordinate clause, "Even if we win our game tonight." This phrase cannot stand by itself. We must put a comma after this phrase, and it belongs after the word *tonight*, the last word of the subordinate clause. The sentence should look like this:

Even if we win our game tonight, we still won't be in the championship this season.

Subordinate clauses can also appear at the end of a sentence: Here are two examples:

Don't talk to John until he has had his coffee.
Mara is going home because she has a test tomorrow.

No punctuation is needed for these end-of-sentence subordinate clauses.

Working with Subordinating Conjunctions

Decide where the comma would go in each of these sentences.

1. *Although he enjoys playing the flute he doesn't want to be in the school band.*

   Subordinating conjunction: *although*

   Subordinate clause: *although he enjoys playing the flute*

   The sentence should correctly read: *Although he enjoys playing the flute, he doesn't want to be in the school band.*

2. *Unless you are able to get someone else Ms. Olsen will plan to speak at the meeting.*

   Subordinating conjunction: *unless*

   Subordinate clause: *unless you are able to get someone else*

   The sentence should correctly read: *Unless you are able to get someone else, Ms. Olsen will speak at the meeting.*

3. *Rather than pull the tooth the dentist wants to see if it falls out by itself.*

   Subordinating conjunction: *rather than*

   Subordinate clause: *rather than pull the tooth*

   The sentence should correctly read: *Rather than pull the tooth, the dentist wants to see if it falls out by itself.*

4. *Despite what you have read in that magazine you will still need to increase your training if you want to run in the finals.*

   Subordinating conjunction: *despite*

   Subordinate clause: *despite what you have read in that magazine*

   The sentence should correctly read: *Despite what you have read in that magazine, you will still need to increase your training if you want to run in the finals.*

5. *Regardless of your plans you should still be setting money aside for next year.*

   Subordinating conjunction: *regardless of*

   Subordinate clause: *regardless of your plans*

   The sentence should correctly read: *Regardless of your plans, you should still be setting money aside for next year.*

EXAM ALERT

You won't be asked to identify subordinate conjunctions on the English test, but you will need to be able to recognize them and ensure that there is a comma directly after each subordinating clause.

If you see a subordinating conjunction on the test, immediately look to see whether there is a comma after the subordinate clause. Remember that subordinate clauses appearing at the end of a sentence don't require a comma.

Sentence Structure

Typically 12 test questions have to do with sentence structure—that is, the logical sequence of ideas in a paragraph or passage. The goal with these types of questions is for you to create the best possible paragraph or passage by ordering the sentences in the sequence that seems to make the most sense.

Test questions may appear in one of two formats. Both formats are discussed in the following sections.

Checking for Fragments

You may be asked to consider a sentence or a part of a sentence and decide whether it conveys a complete thought. As you reviewed earlier in this chapter, phrases or clauses that aren't a complete thought are called *fragments*. Because of their placement in a passage, some fragments may appear to be sentences, as does the underlined portion in the following example:

> *I spent extra time wrapping my boyfriend's gift. <u>Wanting George to know that I really cared about him.</u>*

You can probably figure out what the author of these sentences is trying to say; however, the second sentence isn't a sentence at all. The clause is a fragment.

If you read the clause without benefit of the sentence preceding it, you can tell that it really doesn't contain a complete thought:

> *Wanting George to know that I really cared about him.*

The sentence can be corrected in a few ways, for example:

> *Wanting George to know that I really cared about him, I spent extra time wrapping my boyfriend's gift.*
>
> *I spent extra time wrapping my boyfriend's gift. I wanted George to know that I really cared about him.*
>
> *I spent extra time wrapping my boyfriend's gift because I wanted George to know that I really cared about him.*

Here is another example. The fragment here is embedded into a paragraph, making it a bit more difficult to see that it does not contain a complete thought:

> *Henry didn't like taking the dog for a walk alone, but he didn't tell anyone that. He knew his big brothers would laugh and call him a baby. The truth was that if Sarge saw a person, another dog, or even a squirrel, he ran. It was easy for the leash to slip right out of Henry's hands. You see. Henry was a daydreamer. He never paid much attention to what he was actually engaged in. He enjoyed thinking about what he could be doing. His dream was to fly to the moon.*

The fragment in this paragraph is "You see." Correctly punctuated, that part of the paragraph should read as follows: "You see, Henry was a daydreamer." Pay careful attention to sentence structure throughout the entire English test.

Revising Run-ons

You might be asked to revise a run-on sentence on the test. A run-on sentence is actually more than one sentence; it consists of two sentences that are run together without punctuation. Here's an example:

> *Renee likes the new restaurant in town it's not open on Mondays, though.*

You may be able to tell that this sentence is actually two sentences. If you read it aloud, you can hear that it even sounds as if it is two sentences. The sentence needs to be made into more than one sentence, or some form of punctuation is needed to make the sentence correct and readable.

One way the sentence could be revised is like this:

> *Renee likes the new restaurant in town. It's not open on Mondays, though.*

The sentences are now easy to read and both of them make sense.

The run-on sentence could also be revised to read like this:

Renee likes the new restaurant in town, but it is not open on Mondays.

The sentence can also be revised by using a semicolon, like this:

Renee likes the new restaurant in town; it is not open on Mondays.

It can also be revised by having it begin with a subordinating conjunction, like this:

Although Renee likes the new restaurant in town, it is not open on Mondays.

Make sure that you are able to spot these types of sentences within a paragraph.

Identifying Run-ons

Read each sentence. If the sentence is a run-on sentence, rewrite it in a way that is correct.

1. My elderly mother enjoys those lazy Saturdays when her sister Andrea comes to visit.

2. Jon could not find time to do his studying this means he will have to stay home from football practice today.

3. The sailboat looks as if it is tipped over too much on one side you should come over here.

4. I'm thinking of taking chemistry, world geography, precalculus, and American literature next year.

5. John hopes to qualify for the summer program, and he is working to get his application completed.

Correct answers:

1. *My elderly mother enjoys those lazy Saturdays when her sister Andrea comes to visit.*

   This sentence is not a run-on sentence and its punctuation is correct as is.

2. *Jon could not find time to do his studying this means he will have to stay home from football practice today.*

   This is a run-on sentence. It could be written correctly like this:

   Jon could not find time to do his studying. This means he will have to stay home from football practice today.

   As Jon could not find time to do his studying, he will have to stay home from football practice today.

3. *The sailboat looks as if it is tipped over too much on one side you should come over here.*

   This is a run-on sentence. It could be written correctly like this:

   The sailboat looks as if it is tipped over too much on one side. You should come over here.

   You should come over here because the sailboat looks as if it is tipped over too much on one side.

4. *I'm thinking of taking chemistry, world geography, precalculus, and American literature next year.*

   This sentence is not a run-on sentence and its punctuation is correct as is.

5. *John hopes to qualify for the summer program, and he is working to get his application completed.*

   This sentence is not a run-on sentence and its punctuation is correct as is.

Finding the Main Idea

Two or three questions on the ACT English test will ask you about the main idea of the paragraph or passage, about the purpose of the paragraph or passage, or about the audience to whom the writer is directing the passage. The main idea is the central thought or the message of the story, essay, article, or other written work. It is what the piece is about.

In most paragraphs, articles, and essays, the main idea is stated at the beginning of the passage. An author does this so that the rest of the piece can be spent exploring that main idea or giving more details about it.

The following list contains tips that will help you navigate questions about the main idea of a passage:

1. If you are unsure of the main idea of a paragraph, reread its first sentence. Read the next sentence if the first one is more of an introductory sentence:

   Your parents. Your siblings. Your boyfriend or girlfriend. Relationships: These links are the cornerstone of both your business and personal life. The stronger you can make each of your relationships, the more lucrative are the fruits of the connection for both parties. Indeed, careful nurturing of your relationships can turn acquaintances into friends, prospects into customers, and customers into loyal patrons of your business.

   In the preceding paragraph, you would have to read more than just the first sentence to figure out that the main idea is relationships. Don't be afraid to read on to find the main idea of the paragraph. Sometimes sentences appearing at the beginning of a paragraph are there to hook the reader. The writer doesn't get into the gist of the paragraph until a few sentences later.

> **TIP**
>
> If you are unsure of the point of the article, reread its first paragraph.

2. Often the concluding paragraph or sentence wraps up the entire piece and restates the main idea. If you are unable to find or confirm the main idea by the first sentence or paragraph, reread the final sentence in the paragraph, or the final paragraph in a longer piece.

3. After reading the story, essay, or article, ask yourself: "What point is the author trying to make here?" Your response to this question should be one sentence, for example:

   It's dangerous to swim without a lifeguard or buddy.

   Washing one's hands can prevent most common winter illnesses.

   Even newborn babies benefit from social interaction.

Test questions about the main idea will come in a variety of formats; for example:

What is the theme of this passage?

What is the author telling us in this passage?

What is this passage mainly about?

You will need to quickly skim the paragraph or passage as you think about what each question asks.

TIP

Do not spend time thinking about details (for example, dates, names, places) as you skim through the passage.

Identifying the Main Idea

Read this first sample excerpt from a passage and then consider the question that follows.

The outcomes of World War I and the Great Depression were perhaps the most significant factors contributing to the Second World War. World power and influence changed after each of these two events, and the combined effect proved devastating. Indeed, Europe had been the center of industry and capital for the world. The war caused severe damage and destruction to huge areas on the European continent. Europe was not able to readily get back on its feet after this devastation. Rebuilding was both time-consuming and expensive.

Question: Suppose the assignment the writer was responding to had asked her to discuss what happened to the continent of Europe as a result of World War I. From what you have read of it, would this passage probably accomplish that goal?

A. No, the passage discusses the causes of World War II.

B. No, the passage talks about Europe's problems rebuilding.

C. Yes, the passage talks about what happened to Europe as a result of World War I.

D. Yes, the passage mentions this as a factor that contributed to World War II.

Correct answer:

The correct answer is A. The passage's topic sentence tells the main idea: "The outcomes of World War I and the Great Depression were perhaps the most significant factors contributing to the Second World War." This sentence clearly tells us that the rest of the passage will explain more about the factors leading up to World War II. Europe's problems as a result of World War I are secondary here.

Read this second passage:

Most people find the idea of staying in good shape to be an important one, but actually implementing the changes needed to do so is more difficult. A good number of people start each year on a healthy, promising note. They vow to limit the amount of junk food they eat, cut down on sugar, consume less soda, and eat healthy foods. They decide that snacking between meals will decline in the year ahead. They also schedule, either mentally or on paper, regular times to walk, jog, run, or go to the gym. In short, their initial intentions are excellent ones.

The main idea of this passage is:

A. Most people know that they have to stay in good shape.

B. Most people agree that staying in shape is important, but they don't always have time.

C. Most people don't eat healthy foods.

D. Most people go to the gym or do other exercise every day.

Correct answer:

The correct response is A. The passage's topic sentence states the main idea: "Most people find the idea of staying in good shape to be an important one, but actually implementing the changes needed to do so is more difficult."

TIP

As you read articles in newspapers and magazines in preparation for the test, ask yourself what the paragraph, passage, or article is about. Make the process automatic—find the main idea in every paragraph and article you read.

Organization of Sentences in Paragraphs and Passages

Approximately a dozen questions on the ACT English test have to do with the organization of sentences, paragraphs, and passages. In this case, *organization* means the way a paragraph or passage is laid out. Topic sentences begin a piece, supporting details follow, and the passage, article, or essay ends with a concluding statement or paragraph. This conclusion will often restate the main idea and tie up the entire reading.

Some questions you encounter will involve reorganizing sentences within a paragraph so that the paragraph reads in a more logical fashion. Reorganizing will make the paragraph more understandable to the reader.

TIP

A topic sentence is usually the first sentence of a paragraph. The topic sentence tells the reader what the paragraph will be about.

To respond to these types of test questions, you will read through the sentences and look first for a topic sentence to begin the paragraph. Pencil in the number "1" on top of that sentence. Then you will find a concluding sentence to end the paragraph. Then you'll make sure that the other sentences fall into what seems to be a logical sequence. It's a good idea to pencil in a "2" and a "3" above these sentences after you have determined in which order each should fall.

Ordering Sentences in a Paragraph, Part I

The following article excerpt is an example. Read through the sentences and find a topic sentence. Note that sentence number. Then look for supporting details and note these sentence numbers. Finally, identify the sentence that is the paragraph's conclusion.

(1) Initially he was nervous because he knew nothing about growing asparagus. (2) Those chores ended up being packing the asparagus to ship, organizing the shipping containers, distributing drinks and snacks to the field workers, and answering the phone in the main office. (3) He was told by Farmer Thomas that most of the more experienced workers handle the actual farming of the vegetable and that Jack would do other chores. (4) Jack worked at Thomas Asparagus Farm this summer.

Reorder the sentences in the paragraph so that it begins with a topic sentence and the other sentences flow in sequence.

A. 4, 1, 3, 2

B. 2, 1, 4, 3

C. 4, 2, 1, 3

D. 1, 3, 2, 4

Correct answer:

The correct answer is A. "Jack worked at Thomas Asparagus Farm this summer" tells what the rest of the paragraph will be about. The concluding sentence begins with "Those chores ended up being...," which can be a clue that the sentence will summarize the paragraph. The two sentences in the middle of the paragraph: "Initially he was nervous because he knew nothing about growing asparagus. He was told by Farmer Thomas that most of the more experienced workers handle the actual farming of the vegetable and that Jack would do other chores," follow in logical sequence.

TIP

You can often eliminate potential responses by finding the topic sentence and seeing which answer choices include that sentence number first. You already know that you won't be using the other response choices.

In this example, you would know right away that choice A is the correct response, mainly because it is the only one given with sentence 2 as the topic sentence, coming first in the paragraph. Look for this shortcut as you work through these types of questions. You will save time that can ultimately be used for tougher questions.

Ordering Sentences in a Paragraph, Part II

Now try rearranging the following excerpt into the correct order. Remember to look for the topic sentence first.

(1) From that time on, bananas were part of the regular diet in the Caribbean. (2) It may surprise many people to know that bananas have been around for over 2,000 years; indeed, parts of Spain have had bananas growing for what seems like forever. (3) In the 1500s, Spanish explorers traveled to the New World, bringing banana roots with them. (4) They must have known that if they found good soil and decided to stay, they would want bananas to eat.

Reorder the sentences in the paragraph so that it begins with a topic sentence and the other sentences flow in sequence.

A. 3, 4, 1, 2

B. 3, 2, 1, 4

C. 1, 4, 2, 3

D. 2, 3, 4, 1

Correct answer:

The correct response is D. Sentence 2, "It may surprise many people to know that bananas have been around for over 2,000 years; indeed, parts of Spain have had bananas growing for what seems like forever," is the topic or introductory sentence here. The sentences that follow (3 and 4), "In the 1500s, Spanish explorers traveled to the New World, bringing banana roots with them. They must have known that if they found good soil and decided to stay, they would want bananas to eat," back up that main idea, and sentence 1, "From that time on, bananas were part of the regular diet in the Caribbean," concludes the passage excerpt.

Ordering Sentences in a Paragraph, Part III

Now try this one.

(1) The beaches were crowded with people, completely unlike Key West, which we visited last year. (2) We visited Ft. Lauderdale, Florida, for a week this winter. (3) We still had a great time, though. (4) Truth be told, living in upstate New York, any time spent in Florida in winter is welcome.

Reorder the sentences in the paragraph so that it begins with a topic sentence and the other sentences flow in sequence.

A. 2, 1, 3, 4

B. 1, 2, 3, 4

C. 4, 2, 1, 3

D. 2, 1, 4, 3

Correct answer:

The correct answer is A. Sentence 2, "We visited Ft. Lauderdale, Florida, for a week this winter," is the topic sentence, and it tells what the paragraph will be about. Sentence 1, "The beaches were crowded with people, completely unlike Key West, which we visited last year," further describes the topic sentence. Sentence 3, "We still had a great time, though," completes that description. Sentence 4, "Truth be told, living in upstate New York, any time spent in Florida in winter is welcome," concludes the paragraph.

Sentence and Paragraph Style

Approximately 12 questions on the ACT English test have to do with sentence and paragraph style. Questions in this section may involve asking you to reorder a sentence or a paragraph so that its style is more logical. *Style* means choosing the word that is most effective for the sentence or paragraph, or removing a word that is redundant.

TIP

Something that is *redundant* has already been said.

Sentence Style

In the sentence "The two twins both wore the same color shirts," the words *two* and *twins* are redundant. The word *two* should be deleted from the sentence. Similarly, in the sentence "She voted 'yes' affirmatively," both *yes* and *affirmatively* mean the same thing. The sentence should be changed to "She voted affirmatively," or "She voted 'yes.'"

The sentence "Slowly I watched my great-grandmother walk to the front door" would be reordered as "I watched my grandmother slowly walk to the front door." We can't "slowly watch" anything, so the way the sentence is originally written is unclear.

Paragraph Style

Correct paragraph style means that the paragraph is coherent and relates to one main idea. Paragraphs should not include excess words or sentences, to include an overuse of adjectives. Words within a paragraph should flow together well and paragraphs should generally not include slang words or phrases. Paragraphs should be as casual or formal as the entire piece.

The following paragraph's style is too wordy and has too casual a tone:

> Our trip to huge and sometimes intimidating New York City was a blast. We checked out the unbelievably tall Empire State Building. I really liked scooting along Fifth Avenue and checked out some of the big places there. My brother begged for us to go to Yankee Stadium, so we finally said we would go there. Sheesh, we had to take a long subway trip all the way into the Bronx. No fun at all, but it was good to see the game.

The paragraph works better when adjectives are removed and the style is made a bit more formal:

> Our trip to New York City was fun. We visited the Empire State Building. I especially enjoyed walking along Fifth Avenue and going into some of the department stores. My brother insisted we visit Yankee Stadium. I didn't realize we would have to take a subway train all the way to the Bronx. I don't think he did either, but I am glad that we were able to see the Yankees play.

You'll be offered suggested sentences and paragraph answer choices when you respond to these questions.

Revising for Style

Revise these sentences so that each makes more sense, contains no redundant words, and has a clear meaning.

1. Hannah is her two parents' only child.

2. Her happy smile tells us that she is glad that she visited the exhibit.

3. The boys silently spoke to each other, ensuring that they were not bothering anyone.

4. We loudly yelled the team cheer aloud to the audience.

Correct answers:

1. *Hannah is her two parents' only child.*

   "Two parents" is redundant, so the sentence should correctly read: *Hannah is her parents' only child.*

2. *Her happy smile tells us that she is glad that she visited the exhibit.*

   A "happy smile" is redundant, so the sentence should be reworded: *Her happy face tells us that she is glad that she visited the exhibit.* OR *Her huge smile tells us that she is glad that she visited the exhibit.*

3. *The boys silently spoke to each other, ensuring that they were not bothering anyone.*

   The boys can't "silently" speak, so this sentence should be reworded: *The boys quietly spoke to each other, ensuring that they were not bothering anyone.* OR *The boys whispered to each other, ensuring that they were not bothering anyone.* OR *The boys almost silently spoke, ensuring that they were not bothering anyone.*

4. *We loudly yelled the team cheer aloud to the audience.*

   The words "loudly" and "aloud" are redundant as they are used here, so the sentence could be revised like this: *We loudly yelled the team cheer to the audience.* OR *We yelled the team cheer aloud to the audience.*

Ensuring Consistent Tone and Correct Word Choice

Pay close attention to both the tone and word choice in the sentences and paragraphs you read. These both need to be consistent throughout the piece.

Consistent Tone

You will need to ensure that the words and phrases highlighted in test questions take the same tone as the rest of the paragraph and passage. That means that the words in a passage need to be as serious or as casual as the paragraph dictates. Don't use casual language or slang when the passage is formal or serious in tone. For example, this paragraph is written in a serious tone:

Generally, homework is assigned to review and reinforce the concepts that have been taught during the day. The teacher is then able to assess whether the students have a good understanding and recall of what has been taught that day. Occasionally, a teacher will learn from students' homework struggles that a particular concept needs more classroom time.

We would not add this as the next sentence:

This is a drag for a teacher.

The word *drag* is thought of as both casual and slang. The following sentence, however, is parallel in tone and language to the rest of the paragraph and would be a good concluding sentence in this case:

A teacher will then allot additional class time for further review.

Idioms, expressions, and phrases where the meaning isn't obvious to the reader should not be used in any type of serious or formal writing. For example, expressions and phrases such as *dog-tired*, *leave you holding the bag*, *kick the bucket*, and *to and fro* should be left for more casual writing, not the type found on the ACT English test.

Correct Word Choice

The words *to*, *two*, and *too* are often used incorrectly. Remember that *to* means that something is intended for, identifies a direction, or tells how far something is reaching:

This present will be given to Coach Brown.
Jeanne hopes to make it to Topeka by noon.
This rope will reach from the boat to the dock.

Too means *also*:

I believe that Dr. Costello will be speaking too.

Two means "more than one":

We have two reasons to drive rather than fly.

The words *there*, *they're*, and *their* are also often used incorrectly. Keep in mind that *there* means "in that place":

She hopes to build her new home there in a few years.

Their means "belonging to them":

Sitting out at the dock is their new yacht.

They're means "they are":

They're throwing a party for most of the class.

Who and Whom

These words provide many students with unnecessary headaches. Remember that *who* is the subject form of this pronoun. *Whom* is the object form.

Who is working on the experiment?

She had two brothers whom she had not seen in years.

To test whether who or whom should be used in a sentence, remove the word and substitute *he* or *him*. You may have to rework the order of the sentence.

If *he* works correctly in the sentence, *who* should be used. If *him* works correctly, *whom* should be used. For example:

Who is working on this experiment? He is working on this experiment. (*who* is correct here)

She had two brothers whom she had not seen in years. She had not seen them in year. (*whom* is correct here)

Using the Appropriate Tone and Words

Revise these sentences so that the tone and word choice are appropriate. If the sentence is correct as presented, don't do anything to change it.

1. We observed numerous cases of smaller animals of this species being overpowered by predators. It is unfortunate that these little guys can't defend themselves.

2. Unbeknownst to the captain, the sail became untied from the mast, causing the vessel to list quickly from one side to the other. Soon, though, pandemonium reigned. One woman screamed at the jerkiness of the boat's movements, undoubtedly frustrated by the constant and severe movements.

Sample revisions:

1. (a) *Many times we saw small animals being attacked by predators. It saddened us that the small beings couldn't protect themselves.*

   (b) *While we were in the jungle, we saw many small animals being attacked by larger ones. Although the small animals are prey, it's too bad they aren't able to protect themselves.*

2. (a) *The captain didn't realize that the sail became untied and the boat shifted from one side to the other. Things quickly got out of hand, with one woman screaming loudly and causing panic among the others.*

   (b) *The captain didn't see the sail as it untied itself from the mast. The boat was then able to move jerkily from one side to the other. The passengers became upset and scared, and one woman's scream seemed to scare those on board even more.*

Sample ACT English Test Questions

The sample passages that follow consist of underlined words and phrases in context, or questions about the passages. Most of these underlined sections contain errors in structure, expression, style, punctuation, or word usage.

The test also includes questions about entire paragraphs and the passage as a whole. These questions are identified by a number in a box.

For each question, select which of the four choices is the best answer. If you consider the original version to be the best, choose answer A or F: NO CHANGE.

You might want to read each passage through before answering the questions based on it.

1. Swimmers should ensure that the open water is not dangerously cold before they attempt a swim. It is important for winter swimmers to wear <u>wet suits</u> to keep their internal temperature stable. A swim cap will work to prevent hypothermia. (Some swimmers will even wear two.)

   (A.) NO CHANGE

   (B.) a wet suit

   (C.) wet suit's

   (D.) wet suits'

2. <u>Although it is better than not swimming at all an indoor pool doesn't substitute completely for the open water.</u> Triathletes should consider swimming in the open water at some time during the winter months, keeping in mind that the cooler water temperatures of the winter months are typical of many triathlon situations.

   (F.) NO CHANGE

   (G.) Although it is better than not swimming at all, an indoor pool doesn't substitute completely for the open water.

   (H.) Although it is better than not swimming at all an indoor pool, doesn't substitute completely for the open water.

   (J.) Although, it is better than not swimming at all. An indoor pool doesn't substitute completely for the open water.

3. If it is possible, get a group together to plan a regular open-water swim once a week or every other week. Swim even if it is colder than you are accustomed to. <u>Don't compromise your health and safety though get out of the water if you are feeling at all uncomfortable.</u> Just as in the warmer months, remember to drink lots of water during your winter workout. Most athletes won't realize they are thirsty during this time of year, but dehydration is still a very real concern in the winter.

   (A.) NO CHANGE

   (B.) Don't compromise your health and safety, though! Get out of the water if you are feeling at all uncomfortable.

   (C.) Don't compromise your health and safety, though; get out of the water if you are feeling at all uncomfortable!

   (D.) Don't compromise your health, and safety, though; get out of the water if you are feeling at all uncomfortable.

4. It was late 1947 and in the United States, <u>President Harry Truman was enjoying its first term.</u> World War II had been over for almost two years.

   (F.) NO CHANGE

   (G.) President Harry Truman was enjoying it's first term.

   (H.) President Harry Truman was enjoying his first term.

   (J.) President: Harry Truman, was enjoying his first term.

5. On the other side of the world in the country of Burma, there was excitement. Ne Win was putting the final revisions on legislation for Burma to gain independence from England. Ne Win had been born in Burma. <u>He had made it his lifes work to drive the British from his country, so it could be a free and democratic nation.</u>

   (A.) NO CHANGE

   (B.) He had made it his lives work to drive the British from his country so that it could be a free and democratic nation.

   (C.) He had made it his life's work to drive the British from his country so that it could be a free, and democratic nation.

   (D.) He had made it his life's work to drive the British from his country so that it could be a free and democratic nation.

6. Years of tireless work had gotten him to this point. The people of Burma saw Ne Win as an icon, indeed, as Burma's national hero. <u>The country would soon be free and independent, thanks to Ne Win's work and vision.</u> Genuine love was apparent between the people of Burma and their leader.

   (F.) NO CHANGE

   (G.) The country would soon be free, and independent, thanks to Ne Win's work and vision.

   (H.) The country would soon be free and independent thanks, to Ne Win's work and vision.

   (J.) The country would soon be: free and independent, thanks to Ne Win's work and vision.

7. Love was also apparent between Ne Win and his very young daughter, Aung San Suu Kyi. Daw Suu, as the girl was known, was just two years old, but it was probable that she could sense the excitement in her house that July day 60 years ago. Just as surely as there was excitement, in one day there was terrible sadness. <u>On July 19, just six months before Burma would gain its independence from Britain, Ne Win was assassinated.</u>

   (A.) NO CHANGE

   (B.) On July 19 just six months before Burma would gain it's independence from Britain, Ne Win was assassinated.

   (C.) On July 19 just six months before Burma would gain its independence from Britain, Ne Win was assassinated.

   (D.) On July 19, just six months before Burma would gain his independence from Britain, Ne Win was assassinated.

8. At that time and at her young age, Daw Suu knew nothing about the troubled past of her country. She would eventually become a student of its history, though. <u>Burma, who in the present day is called Myanmar, has had disputes and disruptions for most of its long history.</u>

   (F.) NO CHANGE

   (G.) Burma who in the present day, is called Myanmar, has had disputes and disruptions for most of its long history.

   (H.) Burma, what in the present day is called Myanmar, has had disputes and disruptions for most of its long history.

   (J.) Burma, in the present day called Myanmar, has had disputes and disruptions for most of its long history.

Answers to Sample ACT English Questions

1. **Answer A, NO CHANGE, is correct.** The noun *swimmers* is plural and *wet suits* is also plural.

   Answer C, *wet suit's*, is not correct. The apostrophe implies that the wet suit possesses something. This would be correct if we were talking about the *wet suit's zipper*, for example.

   Answer D, *wet suits'*, is not correct. The apostrophe implies that more than one wet suit possesses something. This answer would be correct if we were talking about many wet suits' zippers, for example.

2. **Answer G is correct.** The phrase "Although it is better than not swimming at all" begins with a subordinate conjunction, and it is a subordinate clause. A subordinate clause at the beginning of a sentence must be separated from the rest of the sentence by a comma.

   Answer F, NO CHANGE, is not correct.

   Answer H is not correct. The subordinate clause does not include the words *an indoor pool*. If you remove that entire phrase, including those three words, from the sentence, you can see that it no longer makes sense.

   Answer J is not correct. The comma is placed after the subordinate conjunction, not after the entire phrase. There is a period after the subordinate clause. A comma belongs there and not after the word *Although*.

3. **Answer B is correct.** The exclamation point is used to separate the two clauses into two sentences here.

   Answer A, NO CHANGE, is not correct. A semicolon or punctuation break is needed here to join two closely related independent clauses.

   Answer C is not correct. Again, this statement does not need the emphasis of an exclamation point.

   Answer D is not correct. The comma after *health* is not necessary because there is not a list or series here, just two words.

4. **Answer H, *President Harry Truman was enjoying his first term*, is correct.** The pronoun *his* refers to Harry Truman.

   Answer F is not correct.

   Answer G is not correct. *It's* is a contracted form of the words *it is*.

   Answer J is not correct. There is no reason for a colon after the word *President*.

5. **Answer D is correct.** The possessive form of the word *life* is necessary to make this sentence correct.

   Answer A, NO CHANGE, is not correct.

   Answer B is not correct. *Lives* is plural, and the subject of the sentence had only one life.

   Answer C is not correct. The comma after *free* is not necessary because *and democratic nation* is not an independent clause and the words describing *nation* are not a list.

6. **Answer F, NO CHANGE, is correct.**

   Answer G is not correct. The words *and independent* are not an independent clause, so should not be enclosed by commas.

   Answer H is not correct. The comma after *thanks* joins it with the phrase preceding it, rather than with *Ne Win's work and vision,* where it belongs.

   Answer J is not correct. Based on the words that follow it, the colon after *be* is not necessary.

7. **Answer A, NO CHANGE, is correct.**

   Answer B is not correct. *It's* is a contracted form of *it is*. An apostrophe after the letter *t* is not necessary.

   Answer C is not correct. A comma is needed to segregate the entire independent clause, *just six months before Burma would gain its independence,* from the rest of the sentence. Note that this is a nonessential clause. It can be taken out of the sentence and the sentence still makes sense: *On July 19 Ne Win was assassinated.*

   Answer D is not correct. The pronoun *his* is not correct here, as it refers to Burma, not Ne Win.

8. **Answer J is correct.** The clause within commas is a nonessential clause.

   Answer F, NO CHANGE, is not correct.

   Answer G is not correct. The words *"is called Myanmar"* are not an essential clause and should not be enclosed in commas.

   Answer H is not correct. The word *what* is not correctly used to refer to Burma.

CHAPTER THREE

The Reading Test

What to Expect on the ACT Reading Test

Some students say that they find the reading test to be the least problematic portion of the ACT test. That may be because the test involves reading passages and answering questions based on those passages. If you prepare well for the reading test by using the tips and ideas in this chapter, you will probably find yourself among those who find the reading test a cinch.

Think of the ACT Reading test as an assessment of how efficiently you read and how well you understand and recall what you have read. You can prepare yourself for the type of reading and the questions you will encounter on this test, so make sure you take the time to be fully ready on test day.

On the Test

On this portion of the test, you will be presented with four reading passages. Each passage is typically approximately 750 words in length, and is followed immediately by 10 multiple-choice questions relating directly to the material just encountered.

Although the reading portion of the ACT Assessment seems as though it should allot students the most time to complete, it actually allows test takers the least time. You will have 35 minutes to read each of the four passages and answer the 40 accompanying questions.

Most students do find that this is a reasonable amount of time to complete the reading test. You will need to wear a watch, though, and make sure that you ration eight minutes for each passage and its 10 questions. This is where your pretest reading practice to improve your speed and comprehension will come in handy.

In the pages that follow, you will learn tips for reading the passages and answering the questions accurately and efficiently.

Directions

As with the other subject areas on the ACT, it is important for you to be familiar with the directions for the reading test well before you arrive at the test site. You will not want to waste any of your 35 minutes of test time reading and thinking about the directions.

Read and consider the reading test instructions that follow now. Note that as with the other sections of the test, the actual test directions may not use the identical wording you see here but the guidance that they will give you will be the same. You may want to briefly scan them as you begin the test to refresh your memory, but rest assured that they will be the same as those shown here.

Read and think about the test directions now.

Basic Instructions for the ACT Reading Test

On this test, you will have 35 minutes to read four passages and answer 40 questions (10 questions pertaining to each passage). Each set of 10 questions appears directly under the passage it refers to. You should select the answer choice that best answers the question. There is no time limit for work on individual passages, so you can move freely between the passages and refer to them as often as you'd like.

The directions are telling you that you can move through the passages in any order and at your own pace, that you can go back to a passage if you need to, and that you can refer to details within each passage as you respond to the questions. In short, you are pretty much on your own with the reading test—you will simply read passages and answer questions for 35 minutes.

The Content Areas

The passages on the test are about a variety of subjects, but there are four content or subject areas that the passages will be based on:

- ▶ Prose Fiction
- ▶ Social Science
- ▶ Humanities
- ▶ Natural Science

The function of the subject area passages is to assess your comprehension of a wide assortment of types of passages. Although passages may appear in any order on the test, they are most typically arranged in the sequence shown here. Some students believe that the passages on the test are arranged in order of their difficulty, with the easiest passage appearing first and the more difficult passages following, but this may not be true of your personal experience. You may find Social Science passages to be of personal interest and to be generally easy to read and work with, for example, and other students may find it difficult to identify character traits in the Prose Fiction passage. Later in this chapter, you will learn more about the composition of each subject area.

As you read through each passage, you will notice numbers appearing along the left side of the text. These numbers offer a running count of the lines of each passage's text and may be referred to within a question (for example, "In Line 5 of this passage, …"). Because of this numbering system, you can easily glance back at the passage and figure out which sentence, word, or phrase the question is asking about. It's best to ignore these numbers until you are called upon to use them.

EXAM ALERT

Students who are unable to complete the ACT Reading test in the time allotted most often say that they knew they were spending too much time rereading one particular passage or one specific question early in the test.

Manage your time well and move away from a passage or question with which you are not comfortable. Place a light pencil dot or other marking on the answer sheet margin beside those questions you may want to return to later.

Come back to these after you've completed the other passages and questions.

TIP

Keep in mind that although some subject area passages may seem easier for you than others, most test takers find it most efficient to simply work through the ACT Reading test passages in the order each is presented.

It doesn't seem to save time to skip around, and it can cause confusion on the answer sheet.

Preparing for the Reading Test

Probably the most effective way to prepare yourself for the reading test is to read constantly from an array of articles and texts and from many different sources. You will need to become even more familiar than you already are with different types of writing, different genres of writing, and different sources of writing. It is important that you are comfortable with and not intimidated by any type of reading regardless of the level to which it is written, its subject area, or your interest in the topic. So practice reading good-quality newspaper, magazine, and journal articles. You can find these at your school or public library, at bookstores, or through your teachers or guidance counselors at school. Explain that you are trying to read a variety of types of literature to prepare for this test, and invite your teachers to share material they think might be appropriate.

Reading Speed

As you do outside reading in preparation for the test, and when you eventually work through the actual test passages, remember to try to read quickly, but not so fast that you don't know what you are reading. Think about what the passage is about. Don't try to memorize details and facts but instead underline these as you come across them in your reading. You may or may not be asked about everything that you underline, but it is easier to find these details later if they are highlighted in some way.

TIP

The main idea of an article or passage is its central thought or message. One way to find the main idea of a passage is to ask yourself this question as you are reading:

What is the author trying to tell me?

Your one-sentence answer is the passage's main idea.

As you read, concentrate just on what you are reading. Read in a place where there are few outside distractions or noise. The actual testing conditions will be quiet and conducive to total focus.

As you read more and different types of writing, strive to increase your speed without losing your grasp of what the article is about. It is probable that the reading that you have done for your high school classes involved paying close attention to names, dates, cities, states, and other important details. You may have even trained yourself to stop and read these types of important details slowly and carefully. Remind yourself, though, that with this type of reading, you will need to avoid getting bogged down with any of those details you encounter. There is never any need to memorize any of the details that you come across. This is not to say that these details aren't important, though. In the pages that follow, you will read about ways to underline the important parts of what you read so that you can quickly find them later, in response to a question.

Vocabulary Words

Don't simply skip over unfamiliar words in your preparatory before-test reading. If you encounter words that you don't immediately know the meaning of, stop. Use the context of the sentence or paragraph to help you figure out each word's meaning.

You will be asked to tell what vocabulary words in the test passages mean, so you will want to be accustomed to using context clues to help you infer approximate meanings.

Summarizing Text

As you practice for the test and read articles, essays, stories, or other types of writing, spend approximately five minutes writing down information about the passage. Attempt to write just from your memory:

> A summary of what you have read: *Write approximately 30–50 words that summarize the article, essay, story, or other piece of writing that you have just read.*
>
> For nonfiction: *State the main idea of the passage.*
>
> For fiction: *State the plot, main character, two personality characteristics of the main character, and the conflict in the story.*

This type of quick writing forces you to really think about what you have read and decide what is important. As you read more and more in preparation for this subject area of the test, you will find that your summary writing and note taking on the passages become almost automatic.

TIP

Knowing the main idea of each nonfiction passage is important because it is almost always asked about in some format as a question on the test. You can usually find the main idea within the first paragraph or within the last paragraph as part of the conclusion.

TIP

Don't get involved with details within the passage. Read them, underline them, and move on.

Test Time

Remember these important ideas as you work through the passages in the reading section of the ACT Assessment:

1. **Don't skip any passages.**

   Read the passage and then answer the questions. Don't skip over the passage and begin with the questions, as some students are tempted to do. It may seem as though you can answer some questions without reading the passage, but your response is not likely to be correct. All of the questions are tied to the reading and are designed to be closely linked to the passage that precedes them.

2. **Watch for signal words.**

   As you read, look for signal words and phrases. These may be indicators of a detail to follow. Remember to recognize subordinating conjunctions from the English test (for example, *but*, *however*) as signals of an important fact following. Underline these facts as they may be referred to in the questions that follow.

Signal Words to Look For

These words show that a contrast follows:

- ► Except
- ► Nevertheless
- ► On the other hand
- ► But

For example: The weather was excellent, *but* the explorers still got lost.

These words show that a conclusion follows:

- ► Therefore
- ► In summary

For example: *In summary*, the apartments being built will be rented within two months' time.

These words back up the conclusion:

- ► Since
- ► Because of

For example: The experiment can still be considered a success *since* the hypothesis was proven to be true.

These words tell that the same thought or the same idea restated in a different way follows:

▶ Furthermore

▶ Indeed

For example: None of the buses would start; *furthermore*, none of the mechanics had shown up for work that day.

3. **Think about the main idea.**

Concentrate on the beginning and ending paragraphs in each passage as probable places to locate the main idea of the entire piece. Keep in mind that the first sentence of an article or passage may be intended to hook the reader ("Who hasn't wanted to throw an alarm clock across the room?"), so you might have to read beyond that to find the main idea.

4. **Wear a watch.**

Even if you don't ordinarily wear one, a watch is a big help in staying within time constraints on the test.

Pace yourself as you read the passages and work on the questions, allotting no more than eight minutes to reading and working on the questions for each passage.

5. **You may know the answer.**

After you read the passage and as you read each question, decide whether you know the answer before even considering the offered responses. If the answer you thought of is listed as a response choice, fill in the answer sheet and move on.

Although you shouldn't spend too much time on one question and should mark it and go back to it later, it is best to try to eliminate at least a few of the potential responses before moving away from the question. If you don't, when you eventually do go back to these difficult questions, you will have to spend time refreshing your memory completely about what each was about.

6. **Don't waste time.**

Force yourself to mark and move away from any question that you know is stumping you.

Passage Questions

Be aware that the questions on the test are not intended to be tied to information or details that you may already know. Some of the questions will ask you directly about stated passage information, and others will ask you to think about what you have read and make predictions, conclusions, implications, or speculations about it. Always use the information from the passage or that can be inferred from the passage to respond to the questions.

The reading test assumes...

TIP

> The reading test assumes that you, the reader, have no prior knowledge of the material presented in each passage. This means that you can answer all questions based on what you have just read, and it is not necessary to know anything about the subject before you read a particular passage. Keep this in mind as you read and answer the questions, and don't let any information that you already know about an individual subject affect your response.
>
> For example, if you are reading about fruit flies and the passage mentions that the fruit fly lives for three weeks, and you know that a fruit fly actually lives longer than that, use the information contained in the passage.

Here are the types of questions you can expect to see on the test. Each group of 10 questions will have some of these types of questions, but not all types of questions will necessarily be in each 10-question group. This listing is meant to give you an idea of the scope of questions you will encounter on this part of the test.

You will encounter questions that

▶ **Ask you to identify specific facts and details that are contained in the passage**

Hint: This is where underlining will be especially useful. You should highlight the details asked about in these types of questions so that they are quick and easy for you to find.

Question example: According to the passage, by increasing the amount of time a runner trains, she will:

▶ **Ask you to ascertain the meanings of words from the passage**

Hint: You may be familiar with the word cited and know its meaning without going through the answer choices. If you aren't familiar with the word, find it by reading the sentence again, considering the words, phrases, and sentences surrounding this word, and thinking about whether you are familiar with a form of the word. Then you will be able to get a good idea of its meaning.

Question example: As used in line 13, the word "vain" most nearly means:

▶ **Ask you to identify cause-and-effect relationships**

Hint: Think about what and why something will happen in the story or passage. Ask yourself: Why would the character do this? What will happen if she does? What will happen if this is done? What could happen if something else happens?

Question example: In lines 36 and 37, the author states that the man who forges this type of friendship is confident in himself. This is because:

▶ **Ask you to make analogies and comparisons**

Hint: Locate the area in the passage that the question refers to. If you're unable to quickly figure out the question response on your own, look at the answer choices and refer to the passage to eliminate some answers.

Question example: The author uses all of the following comparisons in the story EXCEPT:

▶ **Ask you to draw inferences from ideas within the passage**

Hint: Think about the question and what is stated within the passage. Decide which answer choice works best. If one answer choice doesn't stand out, eliminate the responses you know to be wrong.

Question example: The author would most likely agree with the statement that…

▶ **Ask you to understand the characters and character development**

Hint: Think about each character's personality and traits, and try to quickly figure out the answer without looking at the choices. If your answer isn't among the choices, decide which answer choice is the most reasonable.

Question example: Linda's main reason for returning the money seems to be:

▶ **Ask you to identify the main idea of the passage or a part of the passage**

Hint: If you aren't sure of the main idea after reading the passage, reread the first few lines of the first paragraph and the first few lines of the final paragraph. If the question asks about the main idea of a particular paragraph, reread that paragraph's first sentence. If this sentence doesn't offer a clue, read the following sentence and the concluding sentence.

Question example: The main purpose of the last paragraph is for:

▶ **Ask you to identify the author's point of view or the tone the author uses**

Hint: Think about the author's attitude toward the subject she is writing about. Ask yourself to describe the tone of the passage in a short phrase. Look at the answer choices to see whether a form of your short phrase is included there. Otherwise, consider each answer choice and eliminate those that you don't agree with.

Question example: The narrator's tone can best be described as:

Use these steps to help you answer the questions presented to you on this test:

▶ Read the first question.

▶ Before looking at the answer choices, think of your response to the question.

▶ Look through the answer choices to see whether your answer is one of the choices.

▶ If your answer appears as one of the choices, choose it and move on.

▶ If it is not given as a choice, look at each answer.

▶ Eliminate answers that you know to be incorrect.

▶ If you've got one choice left, trust that this is the correct answer.

▶ If you have more than one choice remaining, decide between those responses.

▶ If you are stumped, circle the question and come back to it later.

Prose Fiction

The Prose Fiction passage is the only subject area on the reading test appearing in the fiction genre. On most versions of the reading tests, this passage appears first.

The Prose Fiction passage is approximately 750 words in length, and may be an excerpt from a novel, a complete short story, or a portion of a longer story. The style of writing in the passage will be typical of other types of fiction writing you have encountered in your high school classes.

As you read the Prose Fiction passage, think about the characters, the setting, the conflict, and how the main character fits into the story. Notice all of the characters and what they are doing, what the author is telling you about each of them, what is actually happening in the piece, and what emotions the characters are showing, telling, or implying. Most of the Prose Fiction passages focus on one person or character or tell the story from one person's point of view.

A sample portion of a Prose Fiction passage follows (note that this is a short excerpt and is only about one-third the length of a typical reading test passage). As you read it, pay close attention to the style of writing and the passage's plot, character development, mood, style, and overall tone:

Line   The drive was arduous. Mom didn't say much of anything for a few hours. Then she started to tell me about Manuel, and the fun they had growing up. I had sat through this story more than a few times before, and I was painfully aware that she generally talked about her brother only when she was already depressed or sad. I knew that talk of
(5)   Manuel doesn't bode well for the immediate future, and that the more intensely she discussed her brother and her childhood, the more seriously unhappy she was at the moment.

     It wasn't really necessary for me to say much. She just talked as she drove. She told me about how she and Manuel had collected baseball cards as children, and how they
(10)   formed a singing group when they were 9 and 10 years old, and how they sang rock-and-roll songs at family parties and on the holidays. She mentioned that many people used to think they were twins because they looked so much alike. She was a year older, but they were both the same height for a long time.

     I remember quite a bit about Uncle Manuel. He lived in California, but he was
(15)   often at our home outside Chicago when I was growing up. He'd stay in the spare bedroom and have dinner with us after being in the city all day. He'd toss me up in the air and catch me, and I still have about five of the fifty-cent pieces that he would give me each time he came over.

The entire time you are reading the passage, you need to be processing the information within it. For example, in this short sample portion of a Prose Fiction passage, there are details that you know and that you don't know. Here are some examples:
You do know:

▶ The narrator and his or her mother are driving somewhere.

▶ The mother is intent on talking about her brother.

▶ Something about this discussion is making the mother sad.

You don't know:

▶ Whether the narrator is a male or a female

▶ The age of the narrator

▶ Where the mother and narrator are going

▶ Why talk of Manuel seems to upset the mother

Few of these ideas are explicitly mentioned within the passage; each is implied or can be inferred from what is actually stated by the writer.

Working with a Sample Passage

You should expect to find a mixture of types of questions following the Prose Fiction passage. Some of the questions will assess your knowledge of the meaning of words in context, some will ask you to draw inferences, and others will want you to speculate, or predict, what will happen next in the story or tell what a particular character is likely to do next.

It is often helpful to quickly underline, circle, or otherwise highlight certain words and phrases as you read through the passage. This may make it quicker for you to locate information to respond to the questions, but underlining is certainly not mandatory. If it works for you, hone the skill so that it becomes second nature for test day.

For example, in the passage excerpt you just read, you may want to underline as shown here so that you will be able to refer to these parts of the passage later:

Line   The drive was arduous. Mom didn't say much of anything for a few hours. Then she started to tell me about Manuel, and the fun they had growing up. I had sat through this story more than a few times before, and I was painfully aware that she generally talked about her brother only when she was already depressed or sad. I knew that talk of
(5)   Manuel doesn't bode well for the immediate future, and that the more intensely she discussed her brother and her childhood, the more seriously unhappy she was at the moment.

    It wasn't really necessary for me to say much. She just talked as she drove. She told me about how she and Manuel had collected baseball cards as children, and how they
(10) formed a singing group when they were 9 and 10 years old, and how they sang rock-and-roll songs at family parties and on the holidays. She mentioned that many people used to think they were twins because they looked so much alike. She was a year older, but they were both the same height for a long time.

    I remember quite a bit about Uncle Manuel. He lived in California, but he was
(15) often at our home outside Chicago when I was growing up. He'd stay in the spare bedroom and have dinner with us after being in the city all day. He'd toss me up in the air and catch me, and I still have about five of the fifty-cent pieces that he would give me each time he came over.

Working with Sample Questions

The three questions that follow are typical of the types of questions you may see following the fiction passage on the actual test. This test is not assessing your memorization skills; refer to the passage as you attempt to answer these.

1. As it is used in Line 1 of the passage, what does *arduous* most nearly mean?

    (A) unplanned

    (B) simple

    (C) smooth

    (D) difficult

2. This passage is probably excerpted from:

    (E) a mystery story

    (F) a memoir

    (G) a journal article

    (H) a work of historical fiction

3. It is likely that the narrator will eventually:

    (A) talk about his or her day at school

    (B) attempt to be humorous

    (C) invite us to take pity on the mother

    (D) discuss where they are going

Correct answers:

1. **The correct answer is D.**

   The word *arduous* means *grueling* or *strenuous*. If you had been in doubt about which word to choose, you could have read the next sentence or two and then attempted to replace *arduous* with each of the suggested words offered as answers, like this:

   A. The drive was *unplanned*. Mom didn't say much of anything for a few hours. Then she started to tell me about <u>Manuel</u>, and the fun they had growing up. I had sat through this story more than a few times before, and I was painfully aware that she generally talked about her brother only when she was <u>already depressed</u> or sad.

   "Unplanned" may be a possible response, until you read on and see that the trip being unplanned doesn't seem to have anything to do with what follows in the paragraph. This answer choice should <u>not</u> be eliminated yet.

   B. The drive was *simple*. Mom didn't say much of anything for a few hours. Then she started to tell me about <u>Manuel</u>, and the fun they had growing up. I had sat through this story more than a few times before, and I was painfully aware that she generally talked about her brother only when she was <u>already depressed</u> or sad.

   Nothing in the paragraph emphasizes that the drive was "simple." The writer would have likely given examples of the simplicity of the trip, which are not present in the sentences following. This answer choice can be eliminated.

   C. The drive was *smooth*. Mom didn't say much of anything for a few hours. Then she started to tell me about <u>Manuel</u>, and the fun they had growing up. I had sat through this story more than a few times before, and I was painfully aware that she generally talked about her brother only when she was <u>already depressed</u> or sad.

   Referring to the drive as "smooth" doesn't add anything to our understanding of the passage. The sentences that follow don't back up a smooth drive. This answer choice can be eliminated.

   D. The drive was *difficult*. Mom didn't say much of anything for a few hours. Then she started to tell me about <u>Manuel</u>, and the fun they had growing up. I had sat through this story more than a few times before, and I was painfully aware that she generally talked about her brother only when she was <u>already depressed</u> or sad.

   This seems like the likely answer choice. The sentences following the word seem to describe an almost uncomfortable drive. This answer choice should not be eliminated.

   You are left with choice A and choice D. Choice D seems to be a better fit, as it describes more of what the rest of the paragraph details. The author never refers to the *unplanned* nature of the drive, so it is unlikely that this choice is correct.

2. **The correct answer is F.**

The narrator seems to be recalling a scene from his or her life. Nothing at this point in the reading would indicate that there is a mystery to this story. A journal article will always take a more serious and academic tone than this passage (do not confuse a "journal article" with the more casual "journal entry," which this could possibly be). Also, you can tell that this passage is written in the present day and could not be historical fiction.

3. **The correct answer is D.**

The narrator is in the car going somewhere with his or her mother, and it is likely that their destination will have to be discussed later in the passage.

You would not expect the narrator to go back and talk about school, as all indications so far show that school doesn't seem to apply in this story. From the part of the passage you have read so far, you can already tell that you are not expected to take pity on the mother. From the narrator's tone in the passage, the narrator clearly does not. There is no reason to think that the narrator will become humorous in the passage.

Social Science

The Social Science portion of the reading test is a broad subject area that can include any type of reading under the umbrella of social science. The reading passage may describe a person, place, or event, but it is always based on reality (that is, it is nonfiction and fact based).

> **TIP**
>
> Social science is usually defined as the study of human society and of individual relationships in society. Areas usually falling under the umbrella of social science include sociology, psychology, economics, political science, anthropology, and history.

Some passages in this section will be historical and laden with facts. Some will give the writer's view on a particular issue; others will be about groups of people or observations the writer has had about someone, something, or someplace.

> **TIP**
>
> No passages here are intended to inflame or annoy you as the reader, and you will find no intended controversial viewpoints either. Attempt to set your own personal feelings aside as you read through these passages and simply concentrate on what the author is telling you.

As you read this and all nonfiction passages on the reading test, pay close attention to facts as they are presented. Be aware of details such as dates, names, events, and time order that are embedded within the text. Remember: Don't even try to memorize any of these important components, but instead quickly underline, circle, or otherwise efficiently highlight them for possible later reference.

TIP

Err on the side of underlining too much information in the text rather than not underlining enough. If a word or phrase seems important, highlight it and don't give it a second thought. Don't spend too much time thinking about what to underline, though. Each second of your test-taking time is valuable.

To get an idea of the type of passage you'll encounter under the Social Science heading, read this short sample excerpt from a passage. This passage excerpt is short—about a third as long as the typical test passage—and is intended here to show you the type of information contained within this subject area.

Line　　　　It was 1947, and in the United States, Harry Truman was enjoying his first term as president. World War II had been over for nearly two years. On the other side of the world, in Burma, there was exhilaration of another type. Ne Win was putting the finishing touches on his plans to achieve independence from Great Britain. Ne Win had

(5)　　been born in Burma and had made it his life's work to extricate the British from his country so that it could be a free and democratic nation. Years of tireless work had gotten him to this point, and the people of Burma saw Ne Win as an icon—Burma's national hero. Indeed, the country would soon be free and independent, thanks to Ne Win's work and vision. Genuine love was perceptible between the people of Burma and

(10)　　their leader.

　　　　Love was also apparent between Ne Win and his toddler daughter, Aung San Suu Kyi. Daw Sui, as she was known, was a mere two years old, but it was likely that she could sense the enthusiasm in her dwelling that July day 60 years ago.

　　　　Just as certainly as there was enthusiasm, quickly there was even more sadness than

(15)　　the small country could fathom. On July 19, just six months before Burma would gain its independence from Britain, Ne Win was assassinated.

You can probably see already that this passage is filled with details and important ideas, in contrast to the Prose Fiction passage that you just read. As you read these types of detail-laden nonfiction passages, you will want to underline all of the facts and information you read and that you will likely be asked about later.

TIP

Keep in mind that you probably won't ever use all the information you highlight, but when you move your eyes down your underlined passage, you will find that it is easier to find important information if it somehow stands out.

Working with a Sample Passage

You'll find questions in this section about finding the main idea of a passage, determining the meaning of words within context, drawing inferences, identifying the author's point of view, recognizing cause-and-effect relationships, and making comparisons.

If you didn't do it when you first read the passage, reread the passage excerpt and underline the words, sentences, and phrases that you want to be able to find quickly when responding to questions. Remember: As you read, if you consider a word, phrase, or sentence to be of importance, underline it. Don't spend any time wondering whether what you are underlining is important enough to highlight. Just underline and move on.

Compare what you have underlined with what is highlighted here. Note that there are no right or wrong words or phrases to underline, but most of what you see in the following example should be noted on your passage excerpt too.

Line   It was 1947, and in the United States, Harry Truman was enjoying his first term as president. World War II had been over for nearly two years. On the other side of the world, in Burma, there was exhilaration of another type. Ne Win was putting the finishing touches on his plans to achieve independence from Great Britain. Ne Win had

(5)   been born in Burma and had made it his life's work to extricate the British from his country so that it could be a free and democratic nation. Years of tireless work had gotten him to this point, and the people of Burma saw Ne Win as an icon—Burma's national hero. Indeed, the country would soon be free and independent, thanks to Ne Win's work and vision. Genuine love was perceptible between the people of Burma and

(10) their leader.
     Love was also apparent between Ne Win and his toddler daughter, Aung San Suu Kyi. Daw Sui, as she was known, was a mere two years old, but it was likely that she could sense the enthusiasm in her dwelling that July day 60 years ago.
     Just as certainly as there was enthusiasm, quickly there was even more sadness than

(15) the small country could fathom. On July 19, just six months before Burma would gain its independence from Britain, Ne Win was assassinated.

Here's the rationale behind why each of these words and phrases is underlined:

- ▶ *1947*: the year discussed in this part of the passage, which may be referred to in a question

- ▶ *Burma*: the country that is the subject of this passage excerpt

- ▶ *Ne Win*: the leader of Burma

- ▶ *independence from Great Britain*: Ne Win and Burma's goal

- ▶ *born in Burma*: shows that Ne Win is a native of this country

- ▶ *Burma's national hero*: cites his importance to the country

- ▶ *their leader*: describes Ne Win

▶ *Aung San Suu Kyi*: Ne Win's daughter

▶ *Daw Sui*: Aung San Suu Kyi's more familiar name

▶ *two years old*: Daw Sui's age at the time of this passage excerpt

▶ *July 19*: date Ne Win is killed

▶ *just six months*: when Burma would have achieved its plans for independence

These words and phrases are now clearly visible when you begin working on questions related to the passage.

Working with Sample Questions

Questions for this passage excerpt may include those that are similar to the following. As you work through and respond to the questions, allow your eyes to lock on the parts of the passage that you've underlined, as they may contain information to help you respond to the questions.

Now answer these sample questions, which are representative of the types of questions you may encounter on this part of the test.

1. As it is used in Line 3, the word *exhilaration* most nearly means:

    (A) ambivalence

    (B) exaggeration

    (C) lethargy

    (D) ebullience

2. It can be inferred from the passage that:

    (E) Someone from Great Britain killed Ne Win.

    (F) Burma quickly replaced Ne Win with a comparable leader.

    (G) Daw Sui is still living in Burma.

    (H) Burma was shocked at its loss.

3. July 19 is remembered by those in Burma primarily because:

    (A) It was six months before they were to gain independence from Britain.

    (B) It was the day Ne Win was assassinated.

    (C) It was the date Burma gained its independence.

    (D) It marked the end of World War II.

Correct answers:

1. **The correct answer is D.**

   If you didn't know the meaning of *exhilaration*, you can infer from the passage that the word has something to do with happiness. With this in mind, answer choice B can be eliminated, as *exaggerated* and *exhilaration* do not have anything at all to do with each other. We can also eliminate answer choice C, as *lethargy* means slow (*lethargic*). We are then left with *ambivalence* and *ebullience*. If you don't know the meaning of *ebullience* or *ebullient*, you should consider the meaning of *ambivalence*. To be *ambivalent* is to be unsure or undecided.

   If you substitute each answer choice in place of the word *exhilaration*, you may be able to eliminate some responses:

   A. It was 1947, and in the United States, Harry Truman was enjoying his first term as president. World War II had been over for nearly two years. On the other side of the world, in Burma, there was *ambivalence* of another type.

   "Ambivalence" doesn't work here because the sentence above it doesn't discuss the U. S. being undecided or unsure about anything.

   B. ...there was *exaggeration* of another type.

   The passage doesn't mention any type of exaggeration, so "exaggeration of another type" isn't appropriate here.

   C. ...there was *lethargy* of another type.

   There isn't any lethargy mentioned in the beginning of the passage, so this is likely not the correct answer.

   D. ...there was *ebullience* of another type.

   Even if you aren't entirely certain of the meaning of "ebullience," you have eliminated the rest of the responses.

2. **The correct answer is H.**

   (E) Someone from Great Britain killed Ne Win.

   (F) Burma quickly replaced Ne Win with a comparable leader.

   (G) Daw Sui is still living in Burma.

   (H) Burma was shocked at its loss

   Choice E cannot be correct. From the passage excerpt, we are not able to ascertain whether Ne Win's assassin was British or from somewhere else.

   Choice F cannot be inferred from the passage excerpt, so it is not a correct choice. Burma may or may not have immediately replaced Ne Win, but there is no way to infer either response from the passage excerpt.

Choice G is not correct. We don't know from the reading whether Daw Sui is still living in Burma. (Some students may be aware of Aung San Suu Kyi and know that she has been living under house arrest in what is now Myanmar, but this can't be inferred from the information within the passage.)

3. The correct answer is B.

The last line of the passage reads, "On July 19, just six months before Burma would gain its independence from Britain, Ne Win was assassinated." This phrase is suggested as one to underline in the passage.

> **TIP**
>
> Usually only about a third of the 10 questions are directly answered by information within the passage. The remaining questions will ask you to make logical assumptions or inferences based on what you have read.

> **TIP**
>
> Don't spend any time at all arguing silently to yourself about whether a particular year listed in a passage is accurate, or if a person's name is spelled correctly.
>
> Take the information stated in the passage as the truth and work with it.

Humanities

The Humanities subject area will include a passage relating to culture and the arts, possibly including the theater, film, radio, television, and other segments fitting underneath the general "arts" umbrella.

As with the other nonfiction areas on the test, you will find questions here asking you to infer the meaning of certain words in the passage, identify the author's point of view, and find the main idea of the passage. Remember that thinking beyond what is stated in the passage, really thinking about what the question is asking, is very important here.

Read this short excerpt from the type of passage you might find in the Humanities section. (Note that this passage excerpt is only about a third as long as the typical test passage.)

As you read, practice underlining important details that you may need to refer to when you answer questions:

Line   Filmmaker George Williams traveled to rural Illinois to record the story of a literal change of life. His 60-minute documentary recounts the saga of the Dornings, a Midwest quartet of a family who are intent on turning back the hands of time and living a more primitive type of existence than is typical of our present modern times. Charles

(5)   lives with his wife, Polly, and children Russell, age 10, and Bethany, age 6.

      Three years ago, Charles Dorning sold his family's modest home, his car, and his and his family's personal belongings. In the wooded area on the acreage behind what

was once his house, his kin now live in a wooden abode most nearly described as a makeshift log cabin. It's a one-room shack, though, with both a well and an outhouse in
(10)   the backyard. Their home has no electricity, so there was no air conditioning to ward off the oppressive heat that is typical of August in this area of the country. During the school year, the children are home-schooled by their parents.

At various times throughout the documentary, each of the Dornings is interviewed individually. Out of earshot of each other, the family members give their individual
(15)   opinions about their lifestyle. Young Russell's comments about his family and his home are heartbreaking at times. He recounts a weekend visit last year to a cousin's home 500 miles away, when the family gathered to honor a family member who had recently died. Russell tells of his amazement at the modern frills his cousin, Marco, lives with and enjoys. Although he seems to appreciate his family's simple way of life, Russell's heart
(20)   seems torn by some of the activities and conveniences he recalls from his visit.

Working with a Sample Passage

Using the highlighting technique described in the subject areas we have already discussed, the underlined excerpt would look similar to what follows. Your own underlined work should look close to this:

Filmmaker George Williams traveled to rural Illinois to record the story of a literal change of life. His 60-minute documentary recounts the saga of the Dornings, a Midwest quartet of a family who are intent on turning back the hands of time and living a more primitive type of existence than is typical of our present modern times. Charles lives with his wife, Polly, and children Russell, age 10, and Bethany, age 6.

Three years ago, Charles Dorning sold his family's modest home, his car, and his and his family's personal belongings. In the wooded area on the acreage behind what was once his house, his kin now live in a wooden abode most nearly described as a makeshift log cabin. It's a one-room shack, though, with both a well and an outhouse in the backyard. Their home has no electricity, so there was no air conditioning to ward off the oppressive heat that is typical of August in this area of the country. During the school year, the children are home-schooled by their parents.

At various times throughout the documentary, each of the Dornings is interviewed individually. Out of earshot of each other, the family members give their individual opinions about their lifestyle. Young Russell's comments about his family and his home are heartbreaking at times. He recounts a weekend visit last year to a cousin's home 500 miles away, when the family gathered to honor a family member who had recently died. Russell tells of his amazement at the modern frills his cousin, Marco, lives with and enjoys. Although he seems to appreciate his family's simple way of life, Russell's heart seems torn by some of the activities and conveniences he recalls from his visit.

Here is why each of the words and phrases are underlined in the passage excerpt:

▶ *rural Illinois*: where the documentary takes place

▶ *Midwest quartet*: tells how many people are in the family

- *three years ago*: tells when the passage takes place

- *wooded area on the acreage behind…house*: tells where the family lives now

- *makeshift log cabin*: describes where the family lives

- *one-room shack*: gives more information about where the family is living now

- *well, outhouse*: tell the conditions under which the family is presently living

- *no electricity, no air conditioning*: give more information about the family's life, imply that it is very warm and that the narrator is uncomfortable

- *August*: tells when this passage is taking place

- *cousin's home 500 miles away*: tells where the cousin lives

- *Marco*: Russell's cousin's name

Remember that the words and phrases you choose to underline may differ from what was underlined here. Underlining is a simple tool to help you quickly locate information within a passage.

Working with Sample Questions

Refer to the passage excerpt to respond to the sample questions that follow.

1. It can be inferred from the passage that the Dornings:

  (A) are a fictional family

  (B) will soon go back to a modern way of living

  (C) enjoy the attention they are getting

  (D) have not watched television in years

2. As it is used in Line 11 in the passage, what does the word *oppressive* most nearly mean?

  (E) overwhelming

  (F) impenetrable

  (G) insignificant

  (H) magnified

3. Charles Dorning can best be described as:

  (A) egocentric

  (B) eccentric

  (C) foolish

  (D) modernistic

Correct answers:

1. **The correct answer is D.**

   The Dornings have no electricity, so it can be inferred that they haven't watched television since they have lived in the log cabin.

   Response A cannot be correct. The passage states that the Dornings are part of a documentary. This infers that they are an actual family.

   Response B states that the Dornings will soon go back to a modern way of living. Nothing within the passage excerpt indicates that after three years of living their primitive type of life they would go back to their former lifestyle.

   Response C is not correct, as nothing within the passage makes the reader believe or infer that the family is enjoying (or not enjoying) the attention they are getting from their appearance in the documentary.

2. **The correct answer is E.**

   From the passage, we can infer that the heat is bothering the narrator and that air conditioning is needed. The heat must be great.

   Answer F, *impenetrable*, means *impassable*.

   Answer G, *insignificant*, means *not important*.

   Answer H, *magnified*, means *made larger*.

   If each response is inserted in place of *oppressive* in the sentence, the correct response becomes easier to see:

   Their home has no electricity, so there was no air conditioning to ward off the *overwhelming* heat that is typical of August in this area of the country.

   Their home has no electricity, so there was no air conditioning to ward off the *impenetrable* heat that is typical of August in this area of the country.

   Heat is neither penetrable nor impenetrable.

   Their home has no electricity, so there was no air conditioning to ward off the *insignificant* heat that is typical of August in this area of the country.

   The heat is mentioned as being significant.

   Their home has no electricity, so there was no air conditioning to ward off the *magnified* heat that is typical of August in this area of the country.

   The heat is not made larger in any way.

3. **The correct answer is B.** Dorning acts odd and unconventional, some of the characteristics of an eccentric person.

   Answer A is not correct. Dorning does not give indications of being *selfish* (egocentric).

   Answer C is not correct, as he doesn't act *foolish* (stupid).

Answer D is not correct. *Modernistic* means that someone or something is ahead of his time. You may believe that Charles Dorning is a foolish or a selfish man to give up his modern possessions, but your opinion should not be the basis for the answer.

Natural Science

The Natural Science passage may be about natural history, physics, zoology, botany, or chemistry and is usually in the form of an original article, passage, report, or other writing from a natural scientist.

The passage will usually contain some statements of fact, statistics, and data. You will find that it is written in the serious tone typical of a journal-type report. Pay attention to and consider underlining facts and theories as you read, but don't memorize anything. It is advantageous to underline facts and details here, as they will possibly blend into each other and be difficult to locate to respond to questions.

As with the Social Science and Humanities passage areas, you will find questions here about determining the meaning of words through context, drawing inferences, identifying the author's point of view, and finding the main idea of the passage. Remember that just like the other subject areas, all the information discussed in the question is only what you will learn from reading the passage and is not dependent on what you may already know from previous reading on a particular subject.

What follows is a short sample excerpt of the type of passage you would expect to find in the Natural Science part of the test. Note that this is only about a quarter of the length of an actual test passage.

As you read this excerpt, underline those details that you find important.

Line   The study was conducted under controlled laboratory conditions and spanned three months. The subjects were male and the group of 30 participants ranged in age from 18 to 49, with the median age 32. The primary criterion for participants in this study was reporting a consistent daily intake of more than five cups of coffee or tea, or
(5)   more than five cans of caffeinated soft drink.
        Those subjects who adopted what is commonly known as the "cold turkey" method of caffeine withdrawal had the most serious symptoms. A majority (17) reported experiencing these symptoms within 24 hours of their last ingestion of their favored caffeinated drink. Twelve patients endured headaches, which ranged from moderate to
(10)   what some categorized as severe. Many of those in the study (15) reported being especially irritable in the 36 to 48 hours after removing caffeine from their diet. Other indications and complaints ranged from feeling sleepy, nauseous, and unable to concentrate, to a lack of motivation, and muscle ache.

Working with a Sample Passage

The highlighted passage might appear like this (note that your passage might have additional items underlined):

The study was conducted under <u>controlled</u> laboratory conditions and spanned <u>three months</u>. The subjects were <u>male</u> and the group of <u>30 participants</u> ranged in age from <u>18 to 49</u>, with the median age <u>32</u>. The primary criterion for participants in this study was reporting a consistent daily intake of more than <u>five cups of coffee or tea, or more than five cans of caffeinated soft drink</u>.

Those subjects who adopted what is commonly known as the "<u>cold turkey</u>" method of caffeine withdrawal had the most serious symptoms. A majority (17) reported experiencing these symptoms <u>within 24 hours</u> of their last ingestion of their favored caffeinated drink. <u>Twelve patients endured headaches</u> which ranged from moderate to what some categorized as severe. Many of those in the study (15) reported being <u>especially irritable</u> in the 36 to 48 hours after removing caffeine from their diet. Other indications and complaints ranged from feeling sleepy, nauseous, and unable to concentrate, to a lack of motivation, and muscle ache.

Here are the reasons each of these words and phrases were underlined in the passage excerpt. Remember, you may or may not have underlined all of these, and you may have chosen to underline others that don't appear here.

▶ *controlled*: describes the type of experiment conditions

▶ *three months*: the length of the study

▶ *male*: tells participants' sex

▶ *30 participants*: number of participants

▶ *18 to 49*: age range

▶ *32:* median age

▶ *five cups of coffee or tea, or more than five cans of caffeinated soft drink*: criteria for participating in the study

▶ *cold turkey*: the method used to kick the caffeine habit

▶ *within 24 hours*: length of time before symptoms were experienced

▶ *Twelve patients endured headaches*: a result of eliminating caffeine

▶ *especially irritable*: a result of eliminating caffeine

Working with Sample Questions

Here are some questions that could follow the entire 750-word passage.

1. According to the passage, how many of the subjects reported experiencing excess irritability after giving up caffeine?

   (A) 15

   (B) 20

   (C) 25

   (D) 30

2. Related follow-up research with the study participants would most importantly look into whether the subjects:

   (E) went back to drinking caffeine

   (F) found the researchers to be amiable

   (G) influenced colleagues to cut down on caffeine intake

   (H) traveled long distances to take part in the study

3. As it is used in the passage, "cold turkey" probably most nearly means:

   (A) drinking only cold caffeinated drinks

   (B) not drinking any cold caffeinated drinks

   (C) giving up caffeinated drinks slowly

   (D) giving up caffeinated drinks abruptly

Correct answers:

1. **The correct response is A.**

   According to the passage (and what was underlined in the highlighted version), 15 of the subjects reported excess irritability from caffeine withdrawal. Because the total number of subjects in the study is 30 (refer again to the second sentence in the first paragraph), this is the correct response. You can see then that the other responses offered are incorrect.

2. **The correct response is A.**

   According to the passage, the study was mainly about cutting down on caffeine consumption. Researchers would most likely be interested in whether the participants themselves were drinking caffeine products after the study was over.

3. **The correct response is D.**

   According to the passage, the participants removed caffeine from their diet.

TIP

Remember that all the answers to all the questions presented appear somewhere within the passage or can be inferred from the information within the passage.

TIP

Don't choose an answer just because you know it to be factually true; choose it because it relates directly to the passage you have just read.

Sample Exam Prep Passages and Questions

Read each test-length passage that follows. Attempt to keep your reading and question-answering time to the eight minutes you'll ration yourself for each actual test passage and its related questions. As you read, you may want to underline words and phrases that you will refer to and quickly find later. (You'll find a suggested-underlining answer key for each passage later in this section.)

Then answer the questions accompanying each passage. Compare your responses to those in the *Correct Answers* section. If you find that your answer is incorrect, read the explanations to find out why.

Passage 1 Text

A New Day

Line   Today, just like every other morning, I pressed the wall switch to open the garage door, and then I jumped into the van to wait for Andy. He had to be at wrestling practice extra early this morning, and the clock inside the van read that it was still 15 minutes until it would even be 6:00 a.m.

(5)   I started the van to warm it up. Last weekend, we had reset the clocks back an hour, so I now sat in almost complete darkness, save for the lights on the dashboard. This darkness convinced me to close my eyes for the few minutes that it would take for Andy to come out to the van.

     Mentally, I went over my day: go to work, pick up the dry cleaning, buy a birthday
(10)   present for the party Willie was going to tomorrow, pick up the boys at school, take Mikey to his piano lesson, pick up my new glasses at the eye center. With luck, I'd be able to catch the news on late-night TV. I decided I had better write all this stuff down.

     I'm not sure how long I had nodded off, seat-belted into my driver's seat, when I felt the van door open and Andy suddenly beside me. He nudged me, and in my now-
(15)   robotic trance, I reached up on the van's visor and felt for the button that would open the garage door. Andy and I didn't say even one word to each other. We never spoke in the morning. We really didn't have anything to say to each other. Listening until the garage door motor finished humming, I put the van into reverse. Andy put on his seat belt, tilted his head back, and began his own nap.

(20)   I felt resistance as I backed up, but in my still-confused haziness, I actually attempted to accelerate the engine, push harder as it were. It probably took five seconds for me to realize that I was driving full force right into the now-closed garage door. I glanced at Andy. He had woken up and was staring at my face. He didn't seem to understand what was happening and I felt as though I were an actress in a movie. Surely this
(25)   was not going on. Certainly I was still asleep. Someone please wake me up. This was all just a sick dream.

     It wasn't, though. I cursed under my breath as I jumped out of the van to assess the damage. The vehicle, built like a tank it seems, appeared fine. From where I stood in the interior of the garage, the automatic door did not look too bad, but when I asked Andy
(30)   to press the button on the wall of the garage to open it, the door refused to budge.

I noticed that my voice shook a bit as I asked, then ordered Andy to open the opposite garage door and I ran out into the still-dark morning. The damaged garage door bulged out like a very uncomfortable, pregnant wall, and I quickly assessed that the door could never possibly open on its own. Using all my strength to push the door into
(35) some semblance of its former flat likeness, I willed it to get rid of its now-distasteful profile. If I pushed on the giant wood bump on the door extremely hard, it would straighten up just a slight bit, and at my cue, Andy would push the door-opening button. I calculated that the door would inch up a full 3 inches each time we did this.

It took a full half hour to get the door to open enough to get the van out. My body
(40) was tired and I was sweating a bit. I knew my son was frustrated. The occasional early-morning wrestling practice is mandatory and was starting in just 10 minutes. I wondered to myself if I had exacerbated my back problem from six months ago.

The drive to school was normally a little less than a half hour. I drove in silence, my day's list now a jumble in my head. I pulled into the school parking lot and Andy
(45) jumped out of the van. "Things can only get better from here!" he told me, smiling now. I drove back home and called in sick at work. I called Ray's Garage Door Service, and escaped into the world of daytime TV. It took Ray's only an hour to arrive at my house, and just 10 minutes to decide that a brand-new garage door was needed.

Passage 1 Questions

1. As it is used in Line 7, *save* most nearly means:

    (A) to collect

    (B) in addition to

    (C) except for

    (D) to prevent from harm

2. According to the passage, what initially caused the problem?

    (F) The door was already open when the button was pressed.

    (G) The door wasn't working correctly.

    (H) The car was backing out too fast.

    (J) The switch for the door malfunctioned.

3. Andy's actions can best be described as:

    (A) deflecting blame

    (B) undermining efforts

    (C) emphasizing the problem

    (D) willing to assist

4. From the tone of the passage, it is probable that the narrator is:

   (F) exaggerating

   (G) summarizing

   (H) recounting

   (J) embellishing

5. From what is learned in the passage, the narrator's personality can best be described as:

   (A) explosive

   (B) unpredictable

   (C) victimized

   (D) sensible

6. The main purpose of the first paragraph of this passage is to:

   (F) introduce the situation

   (G) summarize the main parts of the passage

   (H) establish the conflict

   (J) provide character description

7. The narrator would most likely agree with which of the following statements?

   (A) Two heads are better than one.

   (B) Some days you wake up on the wrong side of the bed.

   (C) A penny saved is a penny earned.

   (D) Don't put off until tomorrow what you can do today.

8. In Line 33, the garage door is being compared with:

   (F) an expectant woman

   (G) a heavy sheet of wood

   (H) a disobedient child

   (J) an inert rock

9. The narrator surmises that if the door switch is pressed while pressure is exerted on the door:

   (A) The car will move.

   (B) The door will quickly become unstuck.

   (C) The door will inch up.

   (D) The car will be free of the door.

10. It can be inferred from the story that the narrator:

   (F) spent part of the day relaxing

   (G) would not be able to pay for the new door

   (H) often calls in sick at work

   (J) isn't happy with her life

Passage 2 Text

STEM Careers

In the next decade, many jobs and careers in the STEM (science, technology, engineering, and math) disciplines will be lacking adequately trained workers. Truth be told,
most major industries have been concerned for years that the number of high school
students making a STEM discipline their major in college is dwindling. The govern-
(5)   ment is taking notice of this declining interest too. Indeed, a federally commissioned
study by the Rand Corporation last year noted that "knowledgeable sources…have
voiced fears that this [STEM] workforce is aging and may soon face a dwindling job
pool."

     What's going on? Although it's difficult to pinpoint the exact causes for the
(10) seeming exodus from the STEM disciplines, we do know of a few reasons students are
shying away from these areas. Traditionally, careers in the STEM fields have had some
stereotypes, or generalities, attached. Students going into science careers, for example,
would typically have premed as their goal, aspiring to be medical doctors. Other careers
in science were never thought of as particularly popular, and there were few role models,
(15) especially for girls in science fields. Engineering students have long been thought of as
both creative and artistic (although engineers themselves are thought of as having
breast-pocket shirt protectors with an ample supply of pens available). Seldom would the
non-doodler express interest in or be recruited to a career in civil engineering.
Technology and math majors have traditionally been thought of as nerds, so those
(20) students who are interested in their social lives probably wouldn't be flaunting their
graphing calculators. Further, traditionally girls have never thought of entering STEM
fields in the way boys do. If premed wasn't an option, girls would consider nursing but
rarely a career in marine biology, geology, or astronomy.

     Regardless of the reasons, though, some huge initiatives are attempting to get a
(25) handle on this imminent problem. After intense research, NASA concluded that if they
were successful in interesting even a handful of students early in their school career,
they'd likely have them hooked on space technology for the long term. NASA Explorer
Schools is a relatively new program designed to inform and excite elementary grade
students in math and science. After a pilot group of 50 schools, 50 new schools are
(30) added to the program each year. Budding NASA scientists and engineers are in the
making, with NASA-sponsored scholarships helping these students pay for college.

     To inform and interest more students about what engineering is all about, Project
Lead the Way (PLTW), a national nonprofit organization, has developed an engineering
program for middle and high schools. School districts purchase the curriculum and

(35) PLTW rigorously trains teachers who will implement the program in their schools. Juniors and seniors who have been part of PLTW in high schools around the country are likely to be welcomed into the engineering school at the college of their choice at graduation.

Countless other initiatives are also in place. The National Science Foundation, for
(40) instance, recently awarded a five-year STEM grant to a large community college in Iowa; the grant was specifically intended to increase the number of students going into STEM majors. Byproducts of that grant are STEM academies in high school, high-interest summer "bridge" courses in science and math to excite non-STEM majors, job shadowing, mentoring, and professional development workshops for teachers and guid-
(45) ance counselors.

What can schools do? Teachers and guidance counselors can be aware of and read up on this national problem. Become knowledgeable about the types of STEM careers students in your area can pursue. Target students who do well in math and/or science, but haven't necessarily expressed a strong interest to major in those fields in college. Pay
(50) particular attention to students who are not necessarily top tier or enrolled in AP classes, but are strong in those subjects.

Arrange for appropriate employers to host a small group of students so that they can learn more about careers in these fields. Invite professionals in an assortment of jobs in STEM fields to talk with the students and discuss what they do. Work hard to ensure
(55) that the decrease in students going into STEM fields is stemmed.

Passage 2 Questions

11. The main idea of this passage is:

(A) High school students are entering the wrong fields in college.

(B) Some companies will eventually go out of business if they do not get an increase in qualified workers.

(C) Students should be encouraged to get involved in STEM fields.

(D) STEM fields are difficult for students to major in.

12. The likely target audience for this passage is:

(F) high school students

(G) college admissions officers

(H) textbook publishers

(J) high school staff

13. As it is used in Line 24, *initiatives* most nearly means:

    (A) inertia

    (B) steps

    (C) pretension

    (D) apathy

14. What is the desired result of the situation discussed in the passage?

    (F) an increase in the number of high school students entering STEM disciplines in college

    (G) higher salaries for those in the STEM fields

    (H) more rigorous high school science, engineering, math, and technology classes

    (J) more physicians in those areas of the country with the highest need

15. What is the main idea of the final paragraph of this passage?

    (A) The number of students going into the STEM fields is declining.

    (B) There are ways schools can work to stop the decline of students into the STEM fields.

    (C) Most people enjoy talking about their career choice.

    (D) School staff aren't working hard enough to circumvent this problem.

16. According to the passage, one reason for the decrease in students in the STEM fields is:

    (F) stereotypes regarding the careers

    (G) indifferent instructors and administrators

    (H) curriculum that isn't relevant

    (J) a lack of job openings in these fields

17. It can be inferred from the passage that if certain measures aren't undertaken:

    (A) The space program will become stagnant.

    (B) Some jobs will continue to be unfilled.

    (C) Salaries in STEM careers will decline.

    (D) The nation's workforce will protest.

18. It is probable that high-interest summer bridge courses are mainly designed to:

    (F) increase students' grade point average

    (G) enable students to amass credits over the summer

    (H) provide student peers in these subject areas

    (J) interest more students in the STEM fields

19. It can be inferred from the passage that:

    (A) Employers are concerned about filling certain jobs.

    (B) Careers in STEM fields are high-paying.

    (C) Students are not working hard enough in high schools.

    (D) Guidance counselors are largely to blame for the decline of students going into STEM fields.

20. The author's tone is this passage is mainly:

    (F) irrational

    (G) sarcastic

    (H) biased

    (J) objective

Suggested Underlining for Passages 1 and 2

Passage 1

A New Day

Line   Today, just like every other morning, I pressed the wall switch to open the garage door, and then I jumped into the van to wait for Andy. He had to be at wrestling practice extra early this morning, and the clock inside the van read that it was still 15 minutes until it would even be 6:00 a.m.

(5)   I started the van to warm it up. Last weekend, we had reset the clocks back an hour, so I now sat in almost complete darkness, save for the lights on the dashboard. This darkness convinced me to close my eyes for the few minutes that it would take for Andy to come out to the van.

    Mentally, I went over my day: go to work, pick up the dry cleaning, buy a birthday

(10)   present for the party Willie was going to tomorrow, pick up the boys at school, take Mikey to his piano lesson, pick up my new glasses at the eye center. With luck, I'd be able to catch the news on late-night TV. I decided I had better write all this stuff down.

    I'm not sure how long I had nodded off, seat-belted into my driver's seat, when I felt the van door open and Andy suddenly beside me. He nudged me, and in my now-

(15)   robotic trance, I reached up on the van's visor and felt for the button that would open

the garage door. Andy and I didn't say even one word to each other. We never spoke in the morning. We really didn't have anything to say to each other. Listening until the garage door motor finished humming, I put the van into reverse. Andy put on his seat belt, tilted his head back, and began his own nap.

(20)   I felt resistance as I backed up, but in my still-confused haziness, I actually attempted to accelerate the engine, push harder as it were. It probably took five seconds for me to realize that I was driving full force right into the now-closed garage door. I glanced at Andy. He had woken up and was staring at my face. He didn't seem to understand what was happening and I felt as though I were an actress in a movie. Surely this

(25) was not going on. Certainly I was still asleep. Someone please wake me up. This was all just a sick dream.

It wasn't, though. I cursed under my breath as I jumped out of the van to assess the damage. The vehicle, built like a tank it seems, appeared fine. From where I stood in the interior of the garage, the automatic door did not look too bad, but when I asked Andy

(30) to press the button on the wall of the garage to open it, the door refused to budge.

I noticed that my voice shook a bit as I asked, then ordered Andy to open the opposite garage door and I ran out into the still-dark morning. The damaged garage door bulged out like a very uncomfortable, pregnant wall, and I quickly assessed that the door could never possibly open on its own. Using all my strength to push the door into

(35) some semblance of its former flat likeness, I willed it to get rid of its now-distasteful profile. If I pushed on the giant wood bump on the door extremely hard, it would straighten up just a slight bit, and at my cue, Andy would push the door-opening button. I calculated that the door would inch up a full 3 inches each time we did this.

It took a full half hour to get the door to open enough to get the van out. My body

(40) was tired and I was sweating a bit. I knew my son was frustrated. The occasional early-morning wrestling practice is mandatory and was starting in just 10 minutes. I wondered to myself if I had exacerbated my back problem from six months ago.

The drive to school was normally a little less than a half hour. I drove in silence, my day's list now a jumble in my head. I pulled into the school parking lot and Andy

(45) jumped out of the van. "Things can only get better from here!" he told me, smiling now. I drove back home and called in sick at work. I called Ray's Garage Door Service, and escaped into the world of daytime TV. It took Ray's only an hour to arrive at my house, and just 10 minutes to decide that a brand-new garage door was needed.

Passage 2

STEM Careers

Line   In the next decade, many jobs and careers in the STEM (science, technology, engineering, and math) disciplines will be lacking adequately trained workers. Truth be told, most major industries have been concerned for years that the number of high school students making a STEM discipline their major in college is dwindling. The govern-

(5) ment is taking notice of this declining interest too. Indeed, a federally commissioned study by the Rand Corporation last year noted that "knowledgeable sources…have voiced fears that this [STEM] workforce is aging and may soon face a dwindling job pool."

(10)   What's going on? Although it's difficult to pinpoint the exact causes for the seeming exodus from the STEM disciplines, we do know of a few <u>reasons</u> students are shying away from these areas. Traditionally, <u>careers in the STEM fields have had some stereotypes, or generalities, attached</u>. Students going into science careers, for example, would typically have premed as their goal, aspiring to be medical doctors. Other careers in science were never thought of as particularly popular, and there were few role models,

(15)   especially for girls in science fields. <u>Engineering students have long been thought of as both creative and artistic</u> (although engineers themselves are thought of as having breast-pocket shirt protectors with an ample supply of pens available). Seldom would the non-doodler express interest in or be recruited to a career in civil engineering. Technology and math majors have traditionally been thought of as nerds, so those

(20)   students who are interested in their social lives probably wouldn't be flaunting their graphing calculators. Further, traditionally <u>girls have never thought of entering STEM fields in the way boys do</u>. If premed wasn't an option, girls would consider nursing but rarely a career in marine biology, geology, or astronomy.

Regardless of the reasons, though, some huge initiatives are attempting to get a

(25)   handle on this imminent problem. After intense research, NASA concluded that if they were successful in interesting even a handful of students early in their school career, they'd likely have them hooked on space technology for the long term. <u>NASA Explorer Schools</u> is a relatively new program <u>designed to inform</u> and excite <u>elementary grade students in math and science</u>. After a pilot group of 50 schools, 50 new schools are

(30)   added to the program each year. Budding NASA scientists and engineers are in the making, with <u>NASA-sponsored scholarships</u> helping these students pay for college.

To inform and interest more students about what <u>engineering is all about</u>, <u>Project Lead the Way (PLTW)</u>, a national nonprofit organization, has developed an engineering program for middle and high schools. School districts purchase the curriculum and

(35)   PLTW rigorously trains teachers who will implement the program in their schools. Juniors and seniors who have been part of PLTW in high schools around the country are likely to be welcomed into the engineering school at the college of their choice at graduation.

Countless other initiatives are also in place. The <u>National Science Foundation</u>, for

(40)   instance, recently awarded a <u>five-year STEM grant</u> to a large community college in Iowa; the grant was specifically intended to increase the number of students going into STEM majors. Byproducts of that grant are <u>STEM academies in high school</u>, high-interest <u>summer "bridge" courses in science and math to excite non-STEM majors, job shadowing, mentoring, and professional development workshops for teachers and guid-</u>

(45)   <u>ance counselors</u>.

What can schools do? <u>Teachers and guidance counselors</u> can be <u>aware of</u> and <u>read up</u> on this national problem. Become <u>knowledgeable</u> about the types of STEM <u>careers</u> students in your area can pursue. <u>Target students</u> who do well in math and/or science, but haven't necessarily expressed a strong interest in majoring in those fields in college.

(50)   <u>Pay</u> particular <u>attention</u> to students who are not necessarily top tier or enrolled in AP classes, but are strong in those subjects.

Arrange for appropriate <u>employers to host</u> a small group of students so that they can learn more about careers in these fields. <u>Invite professionals</u> in an assortment of jobs in STEM fields to talk with the students and discuss what they do. Work hard to ensure

(55)   that the decrease in students going into STEM fields is stemmed.

Correct Answers for Passages 1 and 2

1. **The correct answer is C.**

   Although the most familiar definition for the word *save* means "to prevent from harm," in this passage, *save* is used in this way: "...so I now sat in complete darkness, *save* for the lights on the dashboard," and means that the dashboard lights are the only illumination that the narrator has at that time. If you had substituted the other answer choices in place of *save* in this sentence, only "except for" would have retained the meaning of the sentence.

2. **The correct answer is F.**

   In Line 1, the passage states that "I pressed the wall switch to open the garage door...". Three paragraphs later, in Line 15, the passage states, "...and felt for the button that would open the garage door ...Listening until the garage door motor finished humming...". The door and its switch clearly work correctly; however, the door was opened and closed within a few minutes.

3. **The correct answer is D.**

   Andy helps to get the car out of the garage, making him a willing helper. He doesn't do anything to suggest that he is undermining these efforts or to emphasize the problem. There is no reference to blame in the passage.

4. **The correct answer is H.**

   The passage is not written as a summary; it gives details about what happened that morning. The narrator seems to be telling the story as it happened, and there doesn't seem to be exaggeration or embellishment in her words.

5. **The correct answer is D.**

   The narrator of the passage seems to act in a sensible way throughout the event. All steps undertaken after the car hit the garage door seemed to be logical. The narrator doesn't act in an explosive manner; we didn't read that the narrator was screaming or complaining loudly. The narrator also doesn't act in an unpredictable manner. Everything seems to occur in a step-by-step fashion. Nowhere in the passage does the narrator complain about being a victim. It seems understood that what happened was an accident.

6. **The correct answer is F.**

   The paragraph discusses what the narrator is doing and plans to do next. Answer G cannot be correct as the paragraph doesn't summarize the passage nor does it establish the conflict in the passage (Answer H). There is no description of the characters in this paragraph, so Answer J cannot be correct.

7. **The correct answer is B.**

The passage describes an unfortunate start to the narrator's day, so Answer B is the most appropriate here. Answer A implies that the characters in the passage had to brainstorm what they would do to solve their problem, and clearly the narrator is the one who figured out how to get the garage door back up. Answer C doesn't apply to this passage. Answer D is not correct, as there was never any decision about whether the van could stay put until the next day—Andy needed to get to wrestling practice.

8. **The correct answer is F.**

The garage door is described as being "like a very uncomfortable, pregnant wall." Answer G is not correct because there is no reference to a heavy sheet of wood in the passage, nor does the writer describe the door as being "like a disobedient child" (Answer H) or an "inert rock" (Answer J) anywhere within these cited lines.

9. **The correct answer is C.**

The narrator mentions that the door moves up about 3 inches each time the switch is pressed as the door is nudged up. Answer A is not correct because this scenario has nothing to do with the car's movement. Answer B is not correct because the narrator mentions that the process is a slow one, and takes a full half hour. Answer D is not correct because the car and the door are never stuck together.

10. **The correct answer is F.**

The narrator seems to be overwhelmed with the early events of the day and after calling in sick likely spent part of the day relaxing. Nothing in the passage indicates that the narrator worried about paying for the new door. The narrator doesn't mention calling in sick to work prior to this incident, and there is no reason to think she is unhappy with her life.

11. **The correct answer is C.**

The article doesn't suggest that any fields are "wrong," so Answer A is incorrect. Answer B, although it can possibly be inferred from the reading, is not a main idea of the passage. Answer D may be some students' opinion, but it is not the main idea of the passage.

12. **The correct answer is J.**

The article may appeal to high school students, college admissions officers, and textbook publishers, but it gives suggestions for ways high school teachers, administrators, and guidance counselors can interest students in the STEM fields.

13. **The correct answer is B.**

Initiatives are steps, beginnings. *Inertia* means inactive, resistant to motion. *Pretension* is a claim to something, a false appearance, and *apathy* means lack of interest, uncaring. If you are unable to figure out the meaning of *initiatives* from context clues, try substituting each word in the sentence.

14. The correct answer is F.

The passage emphasizes that there is a need to increase the number of students entering the STEM fields as majors in college. The other responses are details that support this idea.

15. The correct answer is B.

The main idea of the entire passage is Answer A, but this question asks for the main idea of just the last paragraph. Answer C is one detail that can be inferred from the last paragraph in the passage, and Answer D is an opinion some readers may have after reading the passage.

16. The correct answer is F.

In the second paragraph in the passage the author mentions that stereotypes about certain STEM careers may keep some students from pursuing them. The passage does not mention indifferent staff and instructors (Answer G), or curriculum that isn't relevant (Answer H). Answer J is not correct—employers have plenty of job openings in the STEM fields, and many of these jobs will not be filled because there are not enough qualified applicants.

17. The correct answer is B.

The passage discusses ways to interest students in careers in the STEM fields and the measures being taken to get students involved in engineering (Project Lead the Way) and NASA. It can be inferred that if these measures were not undertaken, certain jobs would not be filled. Answer A is not correct because there is nothing in the paragraph to suggest that the space program will become stagnant because some of the important jobs are not filled. Answer C is not correct because if there is a need for people to fill certain jobs, salaries may rise, not decline. Answer D is not correct because there is no reason for the nation's workforce to protest anything having to do with what is discussed in this article.

18. The correct answer is J.

The courses are described as being high-interest, and it can be inferred that these are designed to spark an interest in students who may not have STEM in mind as a college major. Answer F is not correct because grade point average is not mentioned here. Answer G is not correct because the passage doesn't discuss students' desire to amass credits over the summer, and Answer H is not correct because there is no discussion of whether having peers with interest in the STEM fields will be of benefit to increasing students' overall interest.

19. The correct answer is A.

The passage mentions that some employers are finding ways to recruit students and it can be inferred that the employers are concerned about filling jobs. Nothing in the passage indicates that STEM jobs are necessarily high-paying, nor is there any reason to believe that students are not working hard enough in high school. Guidance counselors have nothing to do with the decline of students going into these fields; they are mentioned as being part of the solution, though.

20. **The correct answer is J.**

The author's tone does not seem to be influenced by his or her emotions, meaning that it is written objectively. *Irrational* means "without reason," or "lacking sound judgment." This is not true of this passage. There is no *sarcasm* in the passage and it doesn't seem to be *biased* in its attempt to tell the story.

CHAPTER FOUR

The Writing Test

Some students welcome and some students dread the newest section of the ACT Assessment—the writing test. Officially called the ACT Plus Writing test, the writing test measures your ability to create and hone an essay in a relatively short period of time and on a topic you won't be aware of in advance. Thinking about and forming ideas quickly, writing well, and working systematically and efficiently will serve you well on this portion of the ACT Assessment.

The ACT writing test may not be required by all of the colleges and universities to which you apply. As mentioned in this book's introduction, you will need to check with your favored schools and see what their policy is concerning this part of the test. You can often find this information on a school's website, under "Admissions" or "Application Procedures," or you can obtain it by calling or emailing the admissions office of the schools to which you plan to apply.

If you are confident in your writing abilities, you might want to take the writing test even if it is not required by your school or schools. Most colleges and universities will look at your score on this part of the test regardless of whether they require it.

Students who elect to take the ACT Plus Writing test begin the test after they have completed the ACT Assessment. If you decide to take this test, you'll receive a short break and will be directed to return to the testing room to take this portion of the test.

TIP

> The cost of the writing test is not included in the basic ACT registration fee. As mentioned in this book's Introduction, the basic test fee is $29; taking the writing portion of the test costs an additional $14.

The information included here is designed to give you a good idea of what to expect on the ACT writing test and how to best prepare yourself for taking the test.

Preparing for the ACT Writing Test

Here are some good strategies for preparing for the writing test.

Read Good-Quality Material

There are different ways to get ready for the writing test. The preparatory reading of high-quality magazines and periodicals you have been doing to prepare for the ACT reading test will also serve you well on this part of the test. Reading good writing helps your own writing improve. You will come to recognize how an opening sentence hooks the reader, how an article or essay is organized, how transitions are used effectively, and how a conclusion is intended to summarize and tie up the entire piece. You will also come to know which writing simply makes sense and sounds good to you.

TIP

High-quality magazines and periodicals include the following:

▶ Magazines—*The New Yorker, The Atlantic Monthly, Harpers, National Geographic*

▶ Newspapers—*The New York Times, The Wall Street Journal, The Washington Post, The Chicago Tribune*

Your public library should have a subscription to at least one or two of these magazines and periodicals, or will be able to obtain back issues from an interlibrary loan system.

Look in particular at the editorial page in newspapers. Whether you agree or disagree with what is being said, it is important to notice how these opinion pieces are composed. You will want to read with an eye for how these are put together, paying extra attention to the introductory, or the first, sentence or sentences of an essay. Notice how the beginning of the work serves to hook the reader. Look at how the conclusion sums up the entire piece. Pay attention to the particular words and phrases the writer used. Think about whether the piece is written in a style that holds your interest, or whether it is flat or boring. Ask yourself why this is so and what you would change about what you have just read.

As you read, pay close attention to the particular words the writer uses, how sentences and articles are organized, the tone of the writer, and how the writer's opinion or the main idea of the piece is first stated and then expanded upon in different types of articles and writing. Think about how some articles hold your interest, whereas others seem to be written for a more specialized audience of which you may not be a member. You'll want your writing to be of interest to those who read it, no matter what subject you may be writing about.

Regardless of how well you believe you write, you will need to practice your essay writing skills to prepare for this test. You will have to think, plan, and write relatively quickly here because the writing test requires you to complete your essay in a half hour's time. The time is divided between reading the directions (which you will do now), prewriting your essay, drafting it, and then rereading it to ensure that you have said everything you want to say and that it all makes sense.

Practice Free-Writing

Forming ideas quickly is crucial to writing this type of test essay. You don't have the luxury of brainstorming many ideas and thinking of the possibilities of writing about each. Instead, you will have to make quick decisions about what you will write about, and then write.

Practicing free-writing is important as you prepare for the writing test. *Free-writing* means writing on a particular subject, right off the top of your head. To do this well, just start with the first reasonable idea that pops into your head when you are presented with a topic.

You will need to be able to quickly think of ideas about any topic presented to you. On the test, the topics will be presented such that you will have to give a viewpoint or opinion on a particular topic. If you are able to brainstorm ideas about that topic, you will find that the actual essay writing will go quickly and efficiently.

In the following sections, we'll look at an easy topic on which to free-write; then we'll look at one that is a bit more difficult.

An Easy Free-Writing Exercise

For example, if you are given the topic "the importance of exercise," what do you think of? Jot down the ideas that pop into your head when you think about why exercise is important. Spend just 60 seconds brainstorming and writing down ideas.

If you brainstormed on this topic, you probably came up with ideas such as these:

- ▶ Keeps the body healthy
- ▶ Keeps weight in check
- ▶ Is good for stress control
- ▶ Makes people feel good in many ways
- ▶ Wards off some kinds of illnesses
- ▶ Can make the rest of the day more enjoyable

A Difficult Free-Writing Exercise

It may have been simple for you to come up with ideas to respond to the prompt in the preceding section. Not all writing topics are that easy, though. Often you will be asked to write about subjects and topics that will require you to use creative thinking. In such cases, you will have to really brainstorm to think of ideas to write about.

For example, consider this prompt:

> Dogs should be permitted in U.S. grocery stores, just as they are in many European countries. Do you agree or disagree? Give reasons to back up your opinion.

This topic is potentially difficult to write about. You may initially balk about the thought of having animals in grocery stores, but you have to be able to provide reasons why the practice may seem wrong to you. On the other hand, if you agree with permitting dogs in grocery stores, you will have to be able to provide some reasons that you feel this way.

Brainstorm for a moment to think of reasons that dogs *should* be permitted in U.S. grocery stores. You needn't have visited Europe to understand what the prompt is about. The idea is probably strange to you, so write down anything sensible that comes into your head. Spend about 60 seconds thinking of ideas.

If you agree with the idea of permitting dogs in grocery stores, you may have come up with ideas similar to the following ones:

▶ It's good for dogs to get out of the house.

▶ Dogs sometimes wait in cars in the parking lot, and that seems cruel.

▶ Dogs would not get into any trouble in a grocery store, so it isn't such a big deal.

▶ Dogs would be with their owners, so they would be under control.

▶ Owners of aggressive dogs could be asked to remove the dogs from the store.

▶ Not everyone would want to bring their dog to the store, so it would not be overrun with the animals.

If you disagree with the idea of permitting dogs in grocery stores, you may have come up with ideas such as these:

▶ Dogs are unclean animals and don't belong in a food store.

▶ Some people are uncomfortable around dogs and should not have to put up with them while out shopping.

▶ Dogs can get aggressive and unpredictable if they are nervous.

▶ Dogs will bark and this annoys many people.

▶ There is always an alternative to bringing a dog into a grocery store.

A List of Sample Free-Writing Topics

In the days and weeks ahead, and as your study and preparation time permits, choose topics from the list that follows and practice thinking about ideas for the topics. Don't do them all at once. Do two or three of them at a time, just jotting down phrases and ideas as they pop into your head.

Later in this chapter we will discuss the format for putting together an essay, but this exercise is designed to help you feel at ease when writing about anything.

TIP

When you practice writing for the test, use lined paper and pen or pencil as you will do on the actual test. Handwrite your draft and your essay—don't use a computer at any time to type up your work as you practice. If you do, you may falsely believe that you are a quicker writer than you actually will be under strict test conditions. Plus, you won't have a spell-checker or grammar checker to fall back on when you take the writing test.

▶ What frightens you most

▶ Someone you would like to meet in person

▶ Interesting careers

▶ A celebrity you admire

▶ Something you do especially well

▶ What you wish you were better at

▶ A strong person you know

▶ Your feelings about your hometown

▶ Your dream car

▶ Something kind you have done lately

▶ What you like most about yourself

▶ A sport you wish you were good at

▶ A time when you would have to lie

▶ A popular vacation spot you wouldn't enjoy visiting

▶ Someone you would like to interview

▶ A time when you were embarrassed

▶ A way to show friendship

▶ A difficult decision you have made

The Actual Directions for the Writing Test

As with the other parts of the ACT Assessment, it is important for you to already be completely familiar with this test section's instructions prior to the morning you take the test. Reading directions takes up valuable time, and you won't want to waste a second on this essay test.

Spend some time now reading and thinking about the instructions for the ACT writing test. Keep in mind that just as with the other areas of the test, the wording here may be a bit different from what you see on the actual test you take, but the fundamental parts of the directions will never change from test to test.

You will see the following directions located directly before the writing prompt on the test:

Directions

This is a test of your writing skills. You will have thirty (30) minutes to write an essay in English. Before you begin planning and writing your essay, read the writing prompt carefully to understand exactly what you are being asked to do. Your essay will be evaluated on the evidence it provides of your ability to express judgments by taking a position on the issue in the writing prompt; to maintain a focus on the topic throughout the essay; to develop a position by using logical reasoning and by supporting your ideas; to organize ideas in a logical way; and to use language clearly and effectively according to the conventions of standard written English.

You may use the unlined pages in this test booklet to plan your essay. These pages will not be scored. You must write your essay in pencil on the lined pages in the answer folder. Your writing on those lined pages will be scored. You may not need all the lined pages, but to ensure that you have enough room to finish, do NOT skip lines. You may write corrections or additions neatly between the lines of your essay, but do NOT write in the margins of the lined pages. Illegible essays cannot be scored, so you must write (or print) clearly.

If you finish before time is called, you may review your work. Lay down your pencil immediately when time is called.

You will see the following directions located inside the test booklet, right before your essay-writing prompt:

Please write an essay in response to the topic below. During the 30 minutes permitted, develop your thoughts clearly and effectively. Try to include relevant examples and specific evidence to support your view. A plain, natural style is best. Your essay's length is up to you, but quality should take precedence over quantity. Be sure to write only on the assigned topic.

An Explanation of the Actual Directions for the Writing Test

You may have questions about specific parts of the test directions. The following list explains some of those parts. The bulleted paragraphs are the actual test instructions; the paragraphs in italics are my explanations.

▶ Please write an essay in response to the topic below.

You will be given a topic paragraph and, at the end, will be asked to write about it.

▶ During the 30 minutes permitted, develop your thoughts clearly and effectively.

"Clearly and effectively" means that the reader should understand exactly what you are talking about, and should understand the viewpoints that you are writing about.

▶ Try to include relevant examples and specific evidence to support your view.

When you make a statement, try to back it up with an incident or real-world example. If you are writing, for example, that "the voting age should be lowered to 16 because most people are intelligent enough at that age to be able to form an opinion of whom they would want to vote for," you could add, "Jack, my brother's best friend in high school, reads more newspapers and books than many adults I know and is probably more in-the-know about the world than some of his college professors. Yet Jack is not able to vote, and my Aunt Wilma, who doesn't even know the name of the president of the United States, is welcomed to the voting booth."

▶ A plain, natural style is best.

Don't attempt to puff up your writing with words you don't normally use. Sound like yourself, not how you think an English professor would sound. You're a high school student, and that is the caliber of writing that is expected on this part of the test.

▶ Your essay's length is up to you, but quality should take precedence over quantity.

Length is not important here. None of the scoring criteria has to do with the essay's word count. Just ensure that you answer the question and don't add sentences and paragraphs in an attempt to impress the scorers.

▶ Be sure to write only on the assigned topic.

Don't veer off course. Reread the writing prompt if you become confused about what is actually being asked. Remind yourself as you are writing to support the position you are taking on the topic.

NOTE

A long essay is not necessarily a good essay. Essays on this test can span from 300 to 1,000 words or more. You choose the length you feel is needed to write well on your topic. Don't think a long essay impresses the scorers. Essay quality and format are what is important here. Be confident in your abilities. Don't write just to increase word count.

The Writing Process: The System You Will Use to Write Your Essay

To write a good essay in the 30 minutes allotted, you will be using the same tried-and-true writing process you probably originally learned in elementary school, and may still be using as your formula to write well. You may call it by another name, but the writing process generally comprises prewriting, drafting, revising, and finally, completing your essay.

As you know, with most types of writing the entire writing process takes days, weeks, or even months to complete. All magazine and newspaper drafts are revised more than once, and in an attempt to make them the best work possible, they are often read and revised by several people. Magazine articles often take weeks to completely draft, and then they often go through a series of many complete revisions before finally being published. Newspapers have shorter time frames, but news articles are still drafted, revised, and published within hours, rather than the minutes you will have here to complete your work.

Unfortunately, you don't have the luxury of time or an assortment of eyes to revise your work for the writing test—you will have to think fast to form your ideas and write well, and be confident in what you are writing about so that you aren't tempted to go back and change anything. You will have to have an organized plan to write.

The Writing Process

Prewriting: Thinking of ideas, outlining, jotting down notes, planning your essay

Drafting: Writing a first draft of a piece

Revising: Rereading your draft and making notes on what needs to be changed, rewriting the draft with those changes, and then considering your final copy

In the following subsections, we'll review these step in detail. Then we'll work through an example that takes all the steps into account. The steps will assume that the following text is your prompt:

> The city where you live is considering converting an old and unused movie theater into a teen center. The new teen center would have pool tables, Ping-Pong tables, arcade games, and a concession stand and would be designed to keep the city's teens off the streets and out of trouble at night.
>
> Many residents of the city are not happy with the idea. These people say that teens will get into even more trouble in the teen center, or that there will be insufficient supervision because no city employees will want to work the late hours required. They also say it will cost too much money to renovate the movie theater, and they wonder aloud where this money will come from. Many parents say that teens should be hanging out at the city's basketball complex or that they should be at home studying.
>
> Argue in favor of or against the teen center.

Step 1: Prewriting

Prewriting means to think about, brainstorm, outline, or write down ideas you will use to craft your essay. Prewriting is an essential part of essay writing and you won't be able to write a cohesive essay without spending at least a few minutes of your half hour thinking of ideas and jotting them down.

NOTE

Brainstorm literally means "a sudden clever plan or idea." For our purposes, it means to write down all of the ideas you can think of.

At this point, your task is to consider the viewpoint that you will take in your essay. That means you will think of your opinion, or view, of the subject. Any prompt that you are presented with on this test will ask you to take a side and write about it. Each writing prompt will be written in such a way that there are at least two viewpoints, or angles, for you to consider as you plan and write your essay. You will need to identify those viewpoints right away.

TIP

The actual question you are being asked to respond to may be different from what you expect after reading the passage, so make no assumptions about what you are being asked: Read the prompt and think about it. Don't try to cut any corners there.

Outlining the Essay

Outlining before beginning your writing is crucial—don't skip it. Outlining provides the basic components of your essay and allows you the words you will need to build upon. Writing without an outline, especially within the short period of time you will have for creating this essay, produces text that is poorly organized, is often repetitive, and always requires extensive revision. You simply won't have the leisure of that kind of writing here. Don't skip the outline!

TIP

An *outline* is a brief plan for your essay. Successful essay writers always outline before writing their essays.

With just a half hour to create and complete the entire essay, there is simply no time for long ponderings or trying to figure out the perfect way to approach your essay writing. Naturally you want to write the best essay you can, but it is important that you complete the essay in the time parameters given. That means you won't be able to write a long and detailed outline here—instead you will need to get right to work and create a usable table to outline the major parts of your essay. The quickest way to begin this is to draw a line down the center of your scrap paper to create two columns:

Now think of the two points of view that could be taken to respond to the prompt you just read. In this case, the essay prompt says:

Argue in favor of or against the teen center.

First, create a short heading for each column so that you won't forget what you are writing about. Keep in mind that this is your prewriting scrap paper. Your headings need to make sense only to you, so don't waste time writing long, wordy ones unless you need them to help you remember what you are writing about.

Here is what your prewriting paper would look like:

In Favor	Not in Favor

Brainstorming Viewpoints

The viewpoints should be easy for you to identify: being *in favor of* the teen center and being *not in favor of (against)* the teen center. In the left column, you will jot down points of view that are in favor of the teen center; in the column on the right, you will write some opposite or opposing viewpoints.

The ideas in each column will serve as the basic skeleton of your essay. To come up with ideas to write under each heading, you may want to start by putting yourself briefly in the place of someone who lives in the town and is in favor of the teen center. Brainstorm two or three viewpoints that someone who wants the teen center in town would use as their reasons. Ask yourself questions such as these:

Why do I want the teen center?

What will the teen center do for the town?

Why does it matter to me that the teen center is opened in town?

Write each answer in the "In Favor" column. Don't stop to think about whether each reason is terrific, whether you can think of a "better" one, or whether it may sound silly. Just write down each idea in the table and move on.

You won't need a long list of reasons in your table to write your essay, and you do not want to take more than 5 minutes for this part of your prewriting. Write at least three viewpoints on your paper right now. Don't take more than a few minutes to write the reasons on the table. Keep the 30-minute essay-writing time constraint in mind as you work through each part of the writing process.

Here's how your scrap paper might look after writing some ideas in the "In Favor" column. You may have these or other ideas on your own table. It doesn't matter as long as you were able to think of at least three ideas:

In Favor
Can never get a good basketball game going.
Need a fun place to hang out.
Basketball complex is closed some nights.

Now complete the second column, "Not in Favor," on your draft sheet by jotting down some possible opposing ideas. To come up with opposing ideas quickly, simply think to yourself, "Why might someone *not* want the teen center?" If you found it helpful as you did for the first column, you may want to imagine yourself as a teen who does not want the teen center in town.

To help yourself to come up with ideas quickly, ask questions such as these:

What are your reasons for not wanting the teen center?

What's so bad about a new teen center?

What problems might occur if there is a new teen center?

Here's how the right column might look after you have filled it in:

Not in Favor
Some teens will get into trouble regardless of supervision.
Some teens will be intimidated to go to a teen center.
It would be expensive to renovate it. Where would the money come from?

NOTE

Some students have trouble thinking of ideas as they prewrite. They simply can't come up with enough thoughts to complete a table or outline and then begin their draft. If you find yourself unable to brainstorm ideas and opinions, it may be because you question whether your ideas are "good" enough for an ACT essay. Pretty much any ideas that you list in your prewriting column are appropriate for this type of essay, as long as you are able to back up your statements with details or explanations. The essay scorers are not looking for the winning essay; they are looking for a well-written essay that responds to the essay prompt. Feel confident. If you feel that you are weak in brainstorming, spend adequate time practicing this skill as you prepare for the test.

Figuring Out Your Angle

Now that you have your prewriting, or essay planning, complete, take a moment or two to look at and assess both columns.

In Favor	Not in Favor
Can never get a good basketball game going.	Some teens will get into trouble regardless of supervision.
Need a fun place to hang out.	Some teens may be intimidated to go to a teen center.
Some teens will get into trouble regardless of supervision.	It would be expensive to renovate it. Where would the money come from?

Your goal now is to decide which of the two viewpoints you will want to take as your focus for writing the essay. Often this will be the viewpoint for which you have written the most phrases or ideas, or the one you feel most comfortable talking about. It is probably the column that was the quickest and easiest for you to write. Keep in mind that it really doesn't matter which viewpoint you favor as you write your essay; it's important that you choose one. Put an *X* or a star next to the column you have chosen and prepare to write. Do that now. This will be the main stance you will take for your essay.

You are now finished with the super-quick and condensed prewriting phase. Next you will move on to actually drafting your essay.

TIP

It does not matter whether the stance you take reflects your true feelings or views about an issue, an event, or a person you have been asked to write about. No one will interview you later to confirm your opinion. Style and organization, or what you write and how you write it, are most important here.

Step 2: Drafting

Now that you have your ideas on paper and have chosen the stance you will take in your essay, you're ready to move to the next phase of the writing process, the drafting phase.

Here is where you will gather all your ideas together and write your essay. This stage must also be done in a quick and condensed manner, as time is still at a premium.

> **TIP**
>
> Keep in mind that your essay is meant to respond to the question in the essay prompt. Reread the prompt as often as necessary to remind yourself of this important fact. Also, keep your outline table close by as you write. Stick to what you planned to write about. Don't change paths at all as you write. There is no time to veer from your original plan.

If you took 3 minutes to read the essay prompt, and then 5 minutes to do your outlining, you have 22 of the 30 minutes remaining to actually draft your essay. That's plenty of time. Let's get to work!

Creating an Introduction

The first step in the "condensed" drafting stage is to create an *introduction*: an opening sentence or sentences stating your viewpoint and showing that you understand what the essay topic is asking you to write about. Even though the description here may make you think otherwise, your introduction does not have to be complex. However, you probably will need to go back and quickly scan the original writing prompt to help you develop your introductory sentence.

> **NOTE**
>
> We will use a *linear approach* to write the essay. This means we will be starting with the introduction and working through the draft to the summary. Although there are many ways to construct an essay, this approach tends to work best with the short period of time provided for this essay.

When you take the actual writing test, you will have the prompt permanently open on your desk or table in front of you so that you can refer to it whenever you want to. For now, it is reprinted here so that you don't have to turn back to it.

> The city where you live is considering converting an old and unused movie theater into a teen center. The new teen center would have pool tables, Ping-Pong tables, arcade games, and a concession stand and would be designed to keep the city's teens off the streets and out of trouble at night.
>
> Many residents of the city are not happy with the idea. These people say that teens will get into even more trouble in the teen center, or that there will be insufficient supervision because no city employees will want to work the late hours required. They also say it will cost too much money to renovate the movie theater, and they wonder aloud where this money will come from. Many parents say that teens should be hanging out at the city's basketball complex, or that they should be at home studying.
>
> Argue in favor of or against the teen center.

Your first step is to write an introduction. This introduction is an essay's attention-grabber. Although it can include an anecdote or some interesting information about the topic, it's probably best to begin this type of essay with a summary of the prompt to show your understanding of the task. It's important to restate the prompt somewhere within the beginning of your essay.

Ensure that you don't begin your essay with phrases such as "I think" or "I agree." These openings are generally considered to be weak. Similarly, some students begin an essay by telling the reader what they plan to write about. Avoid doing that. Writing opening sentences or essay introductions that begin "In this essay I will explain" or "I am going to tell you about" is not good writing style. Let your writing tell the story for you.

To write the introduction for this essay, you'll need to reread the question included with the prompt. In this case, that question is, "Argue in favor of or against the teen center." So you are being asked to argue whether the town needs or doesn't need a new teen center.

TIP

Consider the audience for your essay to be adults and teens of your age. That means you should write your essay as though you were trying to interest a group of people of mixed ages in what you are saying. There is no need for sophisticated or flowery language here, unless that is how you usually speak. The readers of your essay will not be impressed by complicated words or phrases, and your score on the essay won't be affected by these types of embellishments. Put your own personal stamp on your essay by making sure it sounds like you. Trust your own writing.

The introduction to your essay should reiterate the issue in your own words. The introduction could be general, such as:

Bayport has some problems to work out if it is ever to come to an agreement about a new teen center.

or this:

Bayport may want to look to nearby Franklyn City as it tries to figure out whether a new teen center is warranted.

In each example, the teen center is mentioned and the issue is alluded to.

TIP

Even though no town or city name was mentioned in the prompt, it is fine in this case to give the city a fictional (or even a real) name and then use it throughout your essay. It can make it easier to write about a place or a person when you are able to refer to it by a name.

Your introduction could also be a general statement of your viewpoint. For example:

Bayport needs a teen center, and the old movie theater is a perfect place to put it. Some people may question why we need a new teen center, though. There are a few reasons.

The opposite viewpoint would also work fine as an opening sentence:

> Bayport's tentative plans to create a new teen center should stay just that: plans. The city does not need to spend another cent on renovating facilities in the area.

TIP

> If you are unable to figure out a way to begin your essay, imagine yourself standing in front of a group of your classmates who know nothing about the teen-center controversy. You will have to quickly make them aware of what is going on and then give your opinion. If you think of yourself saying the words, it is often easy to just write them down as a springboard to your essay.

In each example, the teen center is mentioned and the idea that there are opposing viewpoints to the proposed teen center is brought out.

Another way you can write an introduction to your essay and take the "not-in-favor" stance is like this:

> Mayberry has been discussing a new teen center for years. Now some city officials are pressing the idea of converting the movie theater on Locust Street into a center. For a variety of reasons, this is not a very wise plan.

That introduction expresses the idea that there is a problem with the teen-center plan.

Look at your outlining table and think about the stance you decided to take with this essay. Then take a moment and write your own opening sentence or sentences to introduce your essay. Find a way to restate the problem presented in the essay. Make sure that you choose a stance you can support; it can be similar to either the "in favor" or "not in favor" example. These introductory sentences should clearly show your understanding of the question being asked.

NOTE

> Do not write anything other than an essay to respond to the prompt. Using clever or unique ideas, such as an email format, a newspaper announcement or article, or a letter to a friend, in an attempt to impress scorers will backfire. Instead, your work will likely not even be scored. Your response must be in the form of an essay.

Adding the Body Paragraphs

Now that you have written your introduction, you will add the body—the main portion—of your essay. As you write this main part of your essay, keep in mind that you are trying to confirm what the reader may have already been thinking about a topic (based on your introductory paragraph) and then adding your own twist to it. With that in mind, try to include your reader in the essay as much as you can. Talk about ideas that may be familiar to the reader so that he or she is able to identify with the viewpoint you are taking even if he or she does not agree with it. Adding your own clarification of that viewpoint is especially important here.

> **NOTE**
>
> Getting the reader involved with your essay means that you mention points that are familiar to everyone. When you discuss not being able to get into a basketball game, most readers will know what you are talking about and may have had similar experiences. If you write on too narrow an idea, such as discussing how the present teen center is also used for after-school care, you may not hook or interest as many readers. Keep it general and interesting.

To begin to write the body of your essay, simply write each idea from your chosen side of the viewpoint columns and then further explain each one by writing a brief explanation and details below it.

Suppose you starred the "In Favor" column as your main viewpoint and you plan to write about being in support of the teen-center idea. The first comment written in the table is, "Can never get a good basketball game going." Underneath your introductory sentence or sentences, write a full sentence stating this viewpoint in your essay and then add a sentence or two to explain it, like this:

> Bayport needs a teen center in the city and the old movie theater is a perfect place to put it. Some people may question why we need a new teen center, though. There are a few reasons.
>
> We can never get a good basketball game going. The same guys end up on one team, and they never let anyone else play on their team. For the past six or nine months, the opposing basketball team has been made up of another tight group of people who rarely let anyone else play on their team. Younger players and girls have an especially hard time getting into a game. It really isn't a teen center at all; it's a private club ruled by those two basketball teams.

With this approach you have nearly completed the first paragraph of the body of the essay. Now you can move on to the next comment: "Need a fun place to hang out."

> **NOTE**
>
> *Transition* words are the cement that holds sentences together. They help readers connect ideas in your essay and make your essay flow as smoothly as possible.
>
> Use transition words when you move from general to specific ideas, or from one idea to another. Transition words can join two short sentences or ideas and they serve to keep your essay flowing.
>
> Here are some words that help you transition from one thought to another:
>
> | | | |
> |---|---|---|
> | ▶ also | ▶ furthermore | ▶ next |
> | ▶ as a result | ▶ however | ▶ on the other hand |
> | ▶ besides | ▶ in addition | ▶ so |
> | ▶ consequently | ▶ in other words | ▶ still |
> | ▶ finally | ▶ in conclusion | ▶ that is |
> | ▶ first | ▶ in fact | ▶ therefore |
> | ▶ for example | ▶ later | ▶ thus |
> | ▶ for instance | ▶ likewise | |
> | ▶ further | ▶ meanwhile | |

You'll need to add a sentence or two to transition, or move, from the first comment to this next one. For example:

> We probably wouldn't mind that we can't get into a basketball game if the center itself were an enjoyable place to hang out. It's not. There is literally nothing to do there if you're not involved with playing in or watching a basketball game. Consequently, we teens really need a place to go where there are a variety of things to do.

Now add more detail to that comment:

> Video games, Ping-Pong tables, a television, and other fun additions would be nice to have.

Write another few sentences that complete the idea regarding additional activities:

> The new teen center would appeal to teens with a variety of interests, or just those who want to sit around and chat with their friends. It would be an ideal meeting place.

> **NOTE**
>
> Don't hesitate to add your own personal information and opinions if they are relevant to the essay. Talking about your own experience can add more detail to your essay. For example, mentioning a particular teen center that you have visited in another town and what made that center notable might enhance a part of your essay.

Now transition to your next comment: "Basketball complex is closed some nights." Transition to this comment by writing a sentence that ties in with the last sentence of the preceding example. For instance:

> No nights would be off limits as they are now. The basketball complex is closed two nights a week, and it would be terrific to be able to look forward to going to the center every night if we wanted to. It's doubtful that anyone I know would actually be there seven days a week, but at least the option for some socializing and fun would be open to us.

By further explaining why you think having a teen center that is open every night would be beneficial to teens in your community, you have completed three paragraphs that offer support for your opening statement.

Writing the Conclusion

Now it's time to tie up all the ideas and thoughts in your essay with a concluding statement that summarizes your opening and your supporting ideas.

> **TIP**
>
> The *conclusion* of an essay sums up everything you have said and provides closure to the essay. The best conclusions will review the essay's main points and then offer your opinion.

For this essay, an example of a conclusion or summary could be something such as this:

> I hope the idea for a new teen center is approved and they renovate the theater quickly. I want to be able to use it before I graduate from high school.

or this:

> I'm happy that the adults in the city have concerns about the activities of teens in the area. A new teen center seems to be an idea whose time has come. I am eager to see what happens next.

Your conclusion can be anywhere from one to three or sometimes more sentences.

Taking a Look at Your Draft Essay

You have now completed a draft of your essay. Here is a version of the complete essay that we just wrote together:

> Bayport needs a teen center in the city, and the old movie theater is a perfect place to put it. Some people may question why we need a new teen center, though. There are a few reasons.
>
> We can never get a good basketball game going. The same guys end up on one team, and they never let anyone else play on their team. For the past six or nine months, the opposing basketball team has been made up of another tight group of people who rarely let anyone else play on their team. Younger players and girls have an especially hard time getting into a game. It really isn't a teen center at all; it's a private club ruled by those two basketball teams.
>
> We probably wouldn't mind that we can't get into a basketball game if the center itself were an enjoyable place to hang out. It's not. There is literally nothing to do there if you're not involved with playing in or watching a basketball game. Consequently, we teens really need a place to go where there are a variety of things to do. Video games, Ping-Pong tables, a television, and other fun additions would be nice to have.
>
> The new teen center would appeal to teens with a variety of interests, or just those who want to sit around and chat with their friends. It would be an ideal meeting place. No nights would be off limits as they are now. The basketball complex is closed two nights a week, and it would be terrific to be able to look forward to going to the center every night if we wanted to. It's doubtful that anyone I know would actually be there seven days a week, but at least the option for some socializing and fun would be open to us.
>
> I'm happy that the adults in the city have concerns about the activities of teens in the area. A new teen center seems to be an idea whose time has come. I am eager to see what happens next.

Step 3: Revising

Revising an essay serves to polish it to a finished product. True revision involves pulling the essay apart, analyzing each sentence, reordering some paragraphs, and changing words to ones that more accurately bring out what you are trying to say. After a good revision, the essay is in the best shape it can be in. Often, revising an essay takes hours or days. A writer may want to revise an essay, put it away for a period of time, and then go back and reread it to find other places where the flow of words isn't what he or she is truly happy with.

It is unfortunate that you can't give the revision stage of your essay writing the time it truly deserves. Usually the revision stage is a big and time-consuming deal: rereading, changing sentences around, deleting some sentences, often reviewing and helping to revise a peer's work. There simply isn't much time left, though. Glance at your watch before you begin this stage and make a mental note of how much time you have to reread your essay. You probably spent about 15 minutes putting together the draft of your essay. That means you probably have about 5–7 minutes remaining. You will want to use this time wisely.

In this revision phase, you will make sure your essay makes sense, is grammatically correct, and does not contain spelling errors, at least as much as you can ascertain. As you can probably surmise, you won't be rewriting or recopying your work because there won't be enough time. You won't want to be crossing out or editing too much of your work. However, you will not be penalized for using editing marks or for crossing out a few words and rewriting them to correct spelling or grammar errors.

To revise, read your draft slowly by saying each word to yourself. Think about whether the sentences and ideas make sense and whether they flow together well. Be sure that to the best of your knowledge, all of the spelling, grammar, and punctuation are correct, that sentences flow well, that there are no fragments or extra-long sentences, and that you have tied it all up again at the end. Ensure that you feel confident about everything you have written.

Use the proofreading checklist in the following sidebar as you read over and revise your work.

Proofreading Checklist

As you consider your final draft, check your work against these criteria:

Believable: *Is my essay convincing to the reader?*

On Topic: *Do I stay on the topic?*

Neat: *Is my writing legible?*

Understandable: *Are my points and opinions clear to the reader?*

Spelling: *Are all words spelled correctly?*

Streamlined: *Have I transitioned from one idea to the next and from one viewpoint to the next?*

Punctuation: *Are all sentences punctuated correctly?*

Interesting: *Will the reader find my work interesting?*

Nice Sentence Flow: *Do the sentences flow one into the next?*

Naturally you won't be able to remember each item on the checklist when you actually proofread and revise your test essay, but if you use this checklist each time you proofread your essays as you prepare for the test, you will become accustomed to the components of the checklist. Have it handy each time you write and revise your work.

> **TIP**
>
> It may be helpful for you to know that the first letter of each keyword in the checklist in the "Proofreading Checklist" sidebar spells the words "Bonus Spin." If you remember this phrase, you will recall what you need to check as you proofread your essay.

Let's use the "Bonus Spin" proofreading checklist in Table 4.1 to assess whether our essay fits the criteria discussed.

TABLE 4.1 Proofreading Checklist

Question	Answer
Is my essay convincing to the reader?	*Yes, this essay gives a good argument for the teen center.*
Do I stay on topic?	*Yes, the topic (the new teen center) is discussed throughout, and we do not talk about anything else in this essay.*
Is my writing legible?	*Remember that your handwriting must be legible. If you are accustomed to using a computer for your writing, you will want to take care with your handwriting and ensure that it is readable.*
Are my points and opinions clear to the reader?	*Yes, the points are well described here and should be clear to the reader.*
Are all words spelled correctly?	*The words in our sample essay are spelled correctly. If you are not sure of a word's spelling, decide whether you want to use it or whether you want to use a synonym. Don't take long to decide, though. Remember that points are generally not deducted for spelling, but you won't want to hand in an essay riddled with spelling errors if you can help it.*
Have I transitioned from one idea to the next and from one viewpoint to the next?	*Yes, the transitions here are clear. Remember to move from one idea to the next by linking your ideas.*
Are all sentences punctuated correctly?	*Yes, the sentences here seem to be punctuated as they should be.*
Will the reader find my work interesting?	*Yes, most readers will be able to identify with the problems described in this essay and find it to be interesting.*
Do the sentences flow one into the next?	*Yes, the sentences here go together. Read your own writing to make sure all sentences blend together.*

After you have gone through the entire checklist, you may want to add words and revise some punctuation, or even change or add a couple of sentences to your essay. You may or may not be able to do that. Before deciding anything, you will want to check how much time you have remaining and then decide whether you will need to completely copy your draft onto another sheet of paper. Unless you are a very quick writer, you will want to avoid this time-consuming task at all costs.

If you do end up copying it, take care to ensure that your handwriting is legible and that you don't leave anything out. Remember that in a pinch, if you are unable to copy your revised essay in time, you will always have your original draft to hand in if you absolutely must.

TIP

If you do some any time left over, it's a good idea to use it to read your essay one more time and make sure you are completely happy with it.

Sample Prompt

The following is an example of a sample prompt:

> The city where you live is considering converting an old and unused movie theater into a teen center. The new teen center would have pool tables, Ping-Pong tables, arcade games, and a concession stand and would be designed to keep the city's teens off the streets and out of trouble at night.
>
> Many residents of the city are not happy with the idea. These people say that teens will get into even more trouble in the teen center, or that there will be insufficient supervision because no city employees will want to work the late hours required. They also say it will cost too much money to renovate the movie theater, and they wonder aloud where this money will come from. Many parents say that teens should be hanging out at the city's basketball complex, or that they should be at home studying.
>
> In your opinion, should the city convert the old movie theater into a teen center?
>
> In your essay, take a position on this question. You may write about either one of the two points of view given, or you may offer a different solution. Use specific reasons and examples to support your position.

Now that you have read the paragraph that introduces the issue, spend a few moments just digesting what you read and thinking about what you are being asked in the essay prompt. You may want to underline some parts of the paragraph so that you can refer to them later. Here are some areas that you may find particularly important and that you may want to recall as you write your essay:

TIP

Don't take the time to underline if it is not already something that you are comfortable doing. It is ultimately meant to be a time saver, not a time zapper.

The city where you live is considering converting an old and unused <u>movie theater into a teen center</u>. The new teen center would have <u>pool tables, Ping-Pong tables, arcade games, and a concession stand</u> and would be designed to keep the city's teens off the streets and out of trouble at night.

Many residents of the city are not happy with the idea. These people say that the teens will get into <u>even more trouble in the teen center</u>, or that there will be <u>insufficient supervision</u> because no city employees will want to work the late hours required. They also say it will <u>cost too much money to renovate</u> the movie theater, and they wonder aloud where this money will come from. Many parents say that teens should be hanging out at the city's <u>basketball complex</u>, or that <u>they should be at home</u>, studying.

In your opinion, should the city convert the old movie theater into a teen center?

In your essay, take a position on this question. You may write about either one of the two points of view given, or you may offer a different solution. Use specific reasons and examples to support your position.

How Your Essay Is Scored

At this point, you may be wondering how your essay will be scored and what those scores will mean. Well, let me start by saying that the ACT writing test is the only part of the ACT that is scored manually, that is, by real people. The other ACT test subject areas are scored quickly and efficiently by a computer scanning system, but each ACT essay is individually read and assessed independently by two different scorers. Yes, unbelievable as it may sound, each and every ACT writing test essay is read by at least two professional scorers.

Each scorer will read your essay completely and independently and will use strict guidelines to assign it a score from 1 to 6. (See the sidebar, "What Do the Scores Mean?" for a detailed explanation of the scoring rationale.) A score of 6 applies to an "outstanding" essay, and a score of 1 is used to indicate a "very poor" essay.

TIP

The scores 4, 5, 6 are generally considered to be fitting for students who are prepared to do college-level writing and are the scores most colleges will be looking for.

The two test scorers add their scores together, for a possible total score of 12. If the two scorers' individual ratings for an essay disagree by more than one point, a third reader scores your essay and resolves the matter. Your actual essay is made available to the colleges and universities you stipulated on your original ACT registration if they choose to read it.

What Do the Scores Mean?

A score of 6: Essays receiving this score show that the student is able to respond effectively to the writing task.

A score of 5: Essays receiving this score show that the student is competent in responding to the writing prompt. There are usually a few errors in an essay scored with a "5."

A score of 4: Essays receiving this score show that the student has adequately answered the writing prompt.

A score of 3: Essays receiving this score show that the student is still developing writing skills.

A score of 2: Essays receiving this score are inconsistent in their presentation and demonstrate weak skills.

A score of 1: Essays receiving this score demonstrate weak writing skills.

No Score: Essays receiving this score are blank, off topic, or illegible.

You can read the entire explanation of what scores mean on the ACT website at www.actstudent.org.

Essay scorers are mainly looking for a well-constructed essay. Grammar, punctuation, and spelling are important here, but perhaps not as important as a well-thought-out piece of writing. This means you should not waste any time wondering whether a word is spelled correctly or a comma is correctly placed. Do your best work and spend the bulk of your time ensuring that your essay is the best and most complete that you can write.

Now that you have some solid tips about putting together a good essay quickly, you will need to practice these one more time. We'll do that next.

Practice, Practice, Practice: The Best Way to Improve Your Essay Writing

Even if you are already a good writer, in the weeks prior to the ACT writing test you will need plenty of practice in working with the writing process in this new way: very quickly and efficiently. You have seen how each step of the process is condensed into a very short amount of time. You probably realize now that to write a good essay, you will need to consider the topic, think about and jot down ideas and viewpoints, and then write a good-quality essay faster than you are probably used to writing anything. You need to become especially comfortable with the brainstorming and prewriting processes so that you can concentrate the bulk of your time on the actual drafting portion of the essay.

Just as with anything else you want to become very good at, the more time you are able to devote to practicing essay writing, the better acquainted and more proficient with the process you will be. You will need to become accustomed to writing about a variety of topics, some of which you may find trickier to work with than others.

Remember: For a successful essay in this part of the test, you will need to keep your prewriting—that is, the brainstorming and listing part of your essay writing—to less than 5 of the 30 minutes allotted to complete the essay. Keep that in mind as you practice your writing in the days and weeks prior to your test date.

TIP

As you practice your essay writing, make sure you do not attempt to lengthen your written work by restating the same idea you have already written about. Pay attention to this as you read: Good writers never repeat a point; rather, they offer details to explain it.

Set aside definite time slots within your day to practice your writing. As you began working with this book, you were asked to create a practice schedule for your ACT preparation. You may want to revise that now, depending on how much extra time you think you will need to get your essay writing where you want it to be for the test. It's possible that your essay writing is already fine and that you don't have to change your preparation time schedule at all. But keep the option open to devote more time to practicing writing than you originally planned if it is necessary.

Here are some practice exercises to work through in the days and weeks ahead.

Practice Finding Opposing Viewpoints

Draw a line down the middle of your paper and practice writing opposing viewpoints for one or two of the sample topic sentences after this paragraph. Do one or two more at your next practice session. For each, first read the statement, and then choose what each opposing viewpoint should be. List them and then fill in each side of the chart. Time yourself and attempt to take close to 5 minutes for each. Keep your prewriting scrap papers in a place where you will be able to work with them again when you write introductory sentences.

Here are some sample writing prompts:

- ▶ High school should begin at noon and end at 6:00 p.m. each day.
- ▶ Bicycle riders should be legally required to wear a helmet.
- ▶ Passengers in a car should not have to wear seatbelts if they don't want to.
- ▶ Car insurance rates for high school students should not be tied to their grade point average.
- ▶ Cell phones and driving are not a good mix.
- ▶ All textbooks should become e-books in the next decade.
- ▶ All forms of gambling should be legalized.
- ▶ All citizens of the United States should be required to perform some type of community service.
- ▶ Employers should be permitted to monitor their employees' email accounts.
- ▶ Smoking should be outlawed in this country.

Tables 4.2 through 4.11 list some possible pro and con viewpoints that you may have written down for the sample topics in the preceding list. You may have thought of other ideas, but keep in mind that you should aim for at least three ideas in each column. If you can't think of a third idea, remember: Don't waste time. Just move on.

TABLE 4.2   High school should begin at noon and end at 6:00 p.m. each day.

Should Begin	Should Not Begin
Teens need the extra sleep.	The school day is fine as it is.
Teens' natural wakeup time is late morning.	Not all teens like to sleep through the morning.
Many teens work at night.	Some of the teachers would not agree to this timeframe.

TABLE 4.3   Bicycle riders should be legally required to wear a helmet.

Helmets Should Be Required	Helmets Should Not Be Required
Injuries to the head can be very serious.	People can do what they want with their own bodies.
Some people don't realize how easy it is to fall off a bicycle.	Some people may not be able to afford the price of a helmet.
In case of an accident, people will never be sorry that they had a helmet to protect them.	Government should not be involved with citizens' personal safety.

TABLE 4.4   Passengers in a car should not have to wear seatbelts if they don't want to.

Seatbelts Required	Seatbelts Not Required
There is less chance of death or serious injury.	It's a person's own business whether he or she wants to take a chance.
It is the law in all states of our country.	Some people are uncomfortable with seatbelts on.
In an accident, you could be thrown from the vehicle and cause someone else injury.	Some professional people don't want their clothing to become wrinkled by seatbelts.

TABLE 4.5   Car insurance rates for high school students should not be tied to their grade point average.

Should Be Tied to GPA	Should Not Be Tied to GPA
Students who do well in school are probably careful drivers.	Some students try hard in school but still don't get a high GPA.
Good students should be rewarded for their hard work.	There is probably no correlation between GPA and how well a teen can drive a car.
This may make some students work harder in school.	Parents often pay car insurance rates anyway. The discount is not always rewarding students.

TABLE 4.6   Cell phones and driving are not a good mix.

Are a Good Mix	Are Not a Good Mix
Some calls can't wait.	Phone calls can be a dangerous distraction while driving.
Most people can drive and talk at the same time.	If a call is very important, a driver can pull over to the side of the road.
If people are very careful they can drive and use their cell phone.	All cell phones have voice mail and calls can be returned at a later time.

TABLE 4.7   All textbooks should become e-books in the next decade.

Should Become E-books	Should Not Become E-books
Students wouldn't be carrying heavy textbooks.	Not every student has a computer.
The cost would probably go down if books didn't have to be published on paper.	Not all students like to read their text on a computer screen.
Students would have all of their books with them at all times.	It's difficult to take notes or highlight on a computer.

TABLE 4.8   All forms of gambling should be legalized.

Legalize Gambling	Don't Legalize Gambling
Some people really enjoy it.	The word *all* sounds dangerous.
It's a great source of revenue for some cities.	Some forms of gambling, such as betting on sports events, seem unethical.
Most people can handle how much money they will spend on gambling.	Some people have a serious gambling problem.

TABLE 4.9   All citizens of the United States should be required to perform some type of community service.

Should Be Required	Should Not Be Required
It would make all communities better places to live.	People who don't want to do this should not be required to.
Everyone can do some sort of service if they are given ideas and opportunities.	Some people just don't have time to do it.
People would feel good about themselves.	The community service setup is fine the way it is now.

TABLE 4.10   Employers should be permitted to monitor their employees' email accounts.

Should Be Permitted	Should Not Be Permitted
Employees should have nothing to hide.	Employers should not care what their employees are talking about in their emails.
This might make some employees concentrate more on work.	People should still be entitled to their privacy, even in a work email account.
As long as employees know about the practice, they shouldn't mind.	A level of trust should exist between employer and employee, without monitoring emails.

TABLE 4.11   Smoking should be outlawed in this country.

Should Be Outlawed	Should Not Be Outlawed
It is dangerous to everyone, even the nonsmoker.	It's people's private business whether they want to smoke.
It's a habit that people should be forced to break.	Government should not be permitted to become involved with smoking.
It would cut lung cancer deaths considerably.	Tobacco companies would find themselves in trouble financially.

Practice Writing Introductions

After you feel you have had plenty of practice thinking of opposing viewpoints and brainstorming ideas, you will want to practice writing introductory sentences. When you are satisfied that you are able to quickly determine viewpoints when given a writing prompt, practice writing an introduction for each sample prompt you just worked with. You will want to do a few of these at a time. Attempt to take just a couple of minutes— just as on the actual test—to come up with good introductions for your essays. Remember to restate the original topic in some way in your introduction.

The following list contains completed introductions that map to the topics in Tables 4.2 through 4.11. Yours won't match exactly, but it should be a good beginning to an essay discussing the viewpoints.

High school should begin at noon and end at 6:00 p.m. each day.

For many students, 8:00 a.m. is the worst time of their day. By beginning the school day later, it is a sure bet that all high school students will be more wide awake and more productive. Ultimately, they will learn more.

Bicycle riders should be legally required to wear a helmet.

It's difficult to argue with the facts. It can be dangerous to ride a bicycle. A collision with a car, a tree, or even a pedestrian can cause a bike rider to fall to the ground. Injuries to the head can be extremely serious.

Passengers in a car should not have to wear seatbelts if they don't want to.

Some people find seatbelts to be a constraint. They argue that the likelihood of getting involved in a car accident is slim and that a seatbelt doesn't offer all that much protection.

Car insurance rates for high school students should be tied to their grade point average.

High school students may think twice about both their driving and their school work if it hits them in the wallet. Car insurance rates should be directly tied to the quality of work a student does in school, that is, to his or her grade point average.

Cell phones and driving are not a good mix.

Many people believe they are able to do two, three, or even four things at the same time. These multitaskers, as they sometimes call themselves, are not always as clever as they think they are, especially when they are behind the wheel of a car.

All textbooks should become e-books in the next decade.

With all of the changes the technology era has brought us, it is a wonder worth discussing that most students from first grade to college are still seen regularly lugging a huge backpack of books.

All forms of gambling should be legalized.

Some people find gambling to be a fun way to spend their extra money. For at least as many people, though, gambling is a way they consistently lose the money that they need to live—and they are not able to stop themselves.

All citizens of the United States should be required to perform some type of community service.

Probably everyone who is a citizen of our country would agree that the United States is one of the best places in the world to live and that they would not want to live anywhere else. They appreciate everything that their freedom permits, so they should not complain about giving something back to the community where they live, to their state, or to their country as a whole.

Employers should be permitted to monitor their employees' email accounts.

Sometimes employees forget that the goods and services they use at work are not theirs; they belong to the company or business. Their employer should be able to read through files, look through desktops, and monitor their employees' email accounts.

Smoking should be outlawed in this country.

Although smoking has been proven to be a dangerous and often deadly habit, some people are still hooked. For generations to come, some smokers will choose to keep smoking or will be unable to stop. Outlawing smoking seems to be a drastic step.

Challenge Exercises

Two sample writing prompts appear in the next two sections. Try one now and compare your response to the following one. Think about ways your essay works well and how you could improve it. Then try the second sample.

TIP

To keep close track of time as you work on these exercises, actually write down your beginning time and what time it will be a half hour from that time. Keep this in a conspicuous place as you work on your essay. On the actual test day, the times will probably be written on a board in front of the room. If they are not, or if you don't want to look up during the test, write the test beginning and end times on your scrap paper. Don't forget to pace yourself and glance at the times as you work.

As you work on each sample essay, work under typical test conditions, that is, with a minimum of distractions, with a timer set for 30 minutes, and without using any reference or research assistance. As advised earlier in this chapter, don't use a computer to write your answers; you will want to use the pen-and-paper requirements that you will encounter on the actual test.

Read the example that follows and work through the prewriting, drafting, revising, and publishing phases of the writing process to come up with your complete essay.

Challenge Exercise #1

Students at a local university are protesting a new freshman requirement this school year. The university has said that all first-year students are required to attend classes and may not skip any regularly scheduled class without a valid excuse.

Some students are upset about this new regulation. Until now, class attendance was mainly on a voluntary basis, with students strongly advised but not required to attend each meeting of their classes.

Should college freshmen be required to attend class? Give reasons to support your viewpoint.

Challenge Exercise #2

You and a friend are discussing a history class you are taking. You are learning about the causes of the Vietnam War and about other U.S. history in the late twentieth century. Your friend wonders aloud why this material is even being taught in school. He thinks time is wasted learning about events that occurred in our country in the past. He would rather learn about ways to make the United States and the entire world a happier and safer place to life.

Is learning about history a waste of time? Give reasons to support your opinion.

Challenge Exercise Essay Responses

Challenge Exercise Response #1

After reading the prompt, you should have immediately decided what the opposing viewpoints would be and then created a table. Probable headings for this sample essay are: *Required to Attend Class, Not Required to Attend Class*. The top of your prewriting/brainstorming chart would look like this:

Required to Attend Class	Not Required to Attend Class

Now fill in examples of each viewpoint. Your viewpoints may be similar to those shown here:

Required to Attend Class	Not Required to Attend Class
Students pay money to be in each class, so they should be attending.	Students can often read the textbook and learn most of the material.
Instructors say things in class that are not in the textbook.	Students can often put their time to better use by studying rather than attending class.
Students should be taking notes and really learning the subject from the expert.	Students can get notes from a friend and will learn just as much as they would by being in the class.

Now create the introductory sentences of the essay. For this essay, introductions such as the following work well:

One option for an introduction:

Attendance at college classes should be mandatory for freshmen. College students, especially freshmen, are often overwhelmed by the volume and scope of the work they are presented with. Although these students have some independence, they should not be free to do whatever they want.

Another option:

College classes are created and written so that students learn the information necessary to move on to the next class in a sequence. Although some of the material is included in the textbook, not all of it is. Attendance at college classes should be mandatory for freshmen.

A third option:

Some students find going to class to be a waste of time. They find that the instructors discuss only the material found in the textbook. The students think they could be studying, reading, or working on assignments. Attendance at college classes should never be mandatory for any students.

Now you have the goods to draft the essay. Here are examples of essays from each viewpoint. See how these compare to the essay you have written:

Required to Attend Class

College classes are created and written so that students learn the information necessary to move on to the next class in a sequence. Although some of the material is included in the textbook, not all of it is. Attendance at college classes should be mandatory for freshmen.

College students, especially freshmen, should be required to attend each class session of the classes for which they are registered. They (or usually, their parents) have paid tuition costs to be in each of these classes. Most likely their parents aren't aware that they are not attending class, and would be shocked to find out that they are spending time elsewhere.

Instructors don't always lecture about the material covered in the textbook. Important topics are often only discussed in class. Therefore, students should spend their time sitting in class and listening to the lectures and discussions that are a part of the class time. Students should want to be taking their own notes and really learning the course material so that they will master it and be able to move on to the next class with ease.

Perhaps instructors need to take attendance in their classes and adjust students' grades accordingly. Although this might be thought of as "high school stuff," students need a reason to come to class, and when attendance is reflected in their grades, they will think twice about skipping class.

Not Required to Attend Class

Some students find going to class to be a waste of time. They find that the instructors discuss only the material found in the textbook. The students think they could be studying, reading, or working on assignments. Attendance at college classes should be never be mandatory for any students. Students should be given an option.

Students should not be required to attend class. They are old enough and mature enough to be away at school by themselves, so they should be able to know when it is necessary for them to go to class. In many classes, simply reading the textbook is adequate to understand the material that is taught in class. No new concepts are discussed. Students are then free to work on other assignments, to read, or to do what they want. They don't have to be in class unless they feel it is the best use of their time. In many cases, students can hook up with a friend to get notes. They can attend class a couple of days a week and the friend can go to class the other days. In this way, each student is able to maximize his or her time.

Ultimately, students should be able to do what they want as far as class attendance is concerned. If instructors want to incorporate class attendance into a grade, that is their option. But students may find that attending class is not the best use of their time and may not mind that their grade may be adversely affected.

Challenge Exercise Response #2

First figure out two points of view that your essay can take. For example: *History Is a Waste of Time, History Is Not a Waste of Time, It's Worthwhile to Learn About History, It's Not Worthwhile to Learn About History*. The top of your prewriting/brainstorming chart would look like this:

Worthwhile to Learn History	Not Worthwhile to Learn History

Now fill in examples of each viewpoint:

Worthwhile to Learn History	Not Worthwhile to Learn History
Students need to know how our country came to be.	We should concentrate on the present and not waste time on the past.
"Those who don't study history are doomed to repeat its mistakes."	There are no lessons to be learned from events of long ago.
History is inspiring and tells a compelling story.	There is so little time to learn anyway. Why not spend it on what is happening now?

Now the introductory sentences of the essay are created. For this essay, introductions such as the following work well:

One option for an introduction:

What could be more interesting than the history of our country—the United States of America? What could be more important for us to know? As George Santayana once said, "Those who don't study history are doomed to repeat its mistakes."

Another option:

Studying history is time well spent. Students can come to realize that we actually have little influence over particular events that occur in our country.

A third option:

There seems to be no reason to spend valuable classroom time studying history. Knowing about what happened a long time ago doesn't help in business, in relationships, or in life in general.

Use your introduction as your starting point to write the essay. Here is a sample essay from each point of view:

Worthwhile to Study History

What could be more interesting than the history of our country—the United States of America? What could be more important for us to know? As George Santayana once said, "Those who don't study history are doomed to repeat its mistakes." That's why it is so important for students to learn about the history of their own country and the countries of the rest of the world. Our country has a rich history that is still being written. It is full of joy and sadness, but mainly it tells the story of the growth cycle our country experienced since it first came to be.

Students need to know and should want to know how our country has evolved since it was first discovered and colonized. It is naïve to think that the United States is just here, without taking its past trials and tribulations into account. It's crucial to know the causes of the world wars, why we got involved in the Vietnam War, how slavery was abolished, what types of human rights issues were brought to light at different times in our country's development, and other social and political issues in the past in order to understand what our country is all about. Just as knowing a good friend's prior history helps us understand what makes that person tick, knowing our country's history helps us understand why some of our policies are in place and how some laws came to be.

It's not only that, though. History is interesting to learn about. It is often inspiring and it tells a story. If history teachers strive to make the material in their classes both compelling and relevant to their students, it is certain that most students will be hooked on the subject. Being aware of and understanding the important story of our country helps us be informed citizens of our country.

Not Worthwhile to Study History

There seems to be no reason for students to spend valuable classroom time studying history. Many students yawn through these classes and probably sense that knowing about what happened a long time ago doesn't help in business, in relationships, or in life in general. There is certainly no place for American history in our education system, yet it is taught as a regular class by most schools in our country.

There are a set number of time periods in our too-short school day. Time needs to be spent on learning about the subjects that really matter to success in life, subjects such as reading, grammar, mathematics, and writing. There is no place in a standard school day for students to be learning about what happened long ago. It really doesn't matter anymore. What matters is now, the present, this year, today.

If students find the statesmen, wars, social issues, and other topics of long ago to be of personal interest, there are enough books on these subjects for them to do their own independent reading. They don't have to look any further than their school or public library in town. Anyone can become an expert on any historical subject they want to without the schools being involved at all. Other students who don't care about this old and passé stuff should not be forced to sit through lectures about Thomas Jefferson, the Dust Bowl, the Great Depression, draft dodging, and women's liberation. None of these means anything to life today and most students yawn just thinking about them. Further, there don't seem to be any jobs in today's world where knowledge of U.S. history is necessary. Perhaps the only job where it matters is the job of high school history teacher. But that position should probably be done away with. The money and time can be better spent doing something more contemporary—working with technology or solving the problems of today.

CHAPTER FIVE

The Mathematics Test

There are 60 questions to assess your knowledge of math on the ACT Mathematics test. You have one minute to complete each question. That's right—you have one hour to complete this portion of the test. The questions on the test are designed to be easy to understand and compute quickly. If you know what to expect on the math test, you will have no trouble finishing in the time allotted and doing well on this subject area.

Although the ACT tests your understanding of a wide range of math topics, 40% of the questions you'll see are straightforward problems that require a basic calculation or the application of a concept you probably learned in your first algebra course in high school.

In this chapter, we'll cover the topics introduced in Pre-Algebra and Algebra I courses, which become the foundation for advanced algebra and trigonometry. We'll also give you some powerful strategies that can make you a smarter test-taker. Before we can discuss the more advanced problems that fall within this category, we'll need to lay some groundwork. You need to be familiar with the different types of numbers you may see, as well as with how to perform the four basic math operations with all these numbers.

To complete our discussions of the basics of mathematics, we will define the fundamental notations and properties of algebra. We will also look at number pattern questions and will complete our roundup of elementary algebra by summarizing the skills required to solve problems involving algebraic expressions and equations.

The Basic Structure of the Mathematics Test

Like the other subject areas on the test, the directions for the mathematics test will not change from those that are shown here. Take the time now to read and consider the directions. Then on test day, you won't spend any of your time reading them.

Directions: Solve each of the problems below. Fill in the correct oval on your answer sheet that corresponds to the correct answer.

Make sure that you don't take too much time with those problems that you consider to be difficult. Instead, solve as many as you are able and then use the remainder of the time to go back to those questions you have left.

You may use a calculator on the test. Please keep in mind that all of the following can be assumed, unless stated otherwise on the test:

1. Figures are not necessarily drawn to scale.

2. All geometric figures lie on a plane.

3. When the word *line* is used, it denotes a straight line.

4. When the word *average* is used, it means arithmetic mean.

How to Do Your Best on the Math Test

Aside from practicing for and being prepared for the types of questions you will find on the test, there are some strategies you can use to test smarter on the ACT Mathematics test.

▶ Make sure you first respond to all of the test questions that you definitely know how to answer. On your first pass-through of the test, don't be afraid to skip problems that you know you will have to spend substantial time working on. Mark these by circling the test number in your test booklet and then come back to each of them later.

▶ When you read a problem that contains large numbers, think of a way to create an easier version of the same problem. Simply make up the same problem with smaller numbers. If you can solve the smaller problem, the same method will work on the larger problem.

▶ Look for patterns. Patterns can help you make predictions without grueling calculations.

▶ Identify the information you've been given and what you are asked for. Are you working with factors or multiples? Sometimes just identifying the pieces of the problem can help you see the connection to what you're asked for.

▶ Give the problem a label. Is it a problem about primes or is it an arithmetic sequence? Sometimes just knowing the type of problem you're thinking about can help you draw conclusions.

▶ Sometimes a problem just gives you too much information. Eliminate any distracting information that is not essential to the problem. To do so, you can highlight relevant parts of a diagram or cross out needless information.

▶ Restate intimidating problems using your own words. For example, the question stem "What is the y-coordinate for a point on a line defined by the equation $y = 3x + 3$ if the x-coordinate is 10?" may be restated this way: Given $y = 3x + 3$, what is y if you plug in 10 for x?

▶ If you don't know how to solve an abstract problem with lots of letters, make up the same problem using made-up numbers. Whatever strategy you use with numbers should be applied to the letters as well.

▶ Remember that the answer to every problem is right in front of you, literally. Sometimes the fastest way to get the correct answer is to plug in the choices given and see which one works.

▶ Use the process of elimination to increase the odds of selecting the correct answer. Devise your own personal system for clearly marking choices that *cannot* be correct. For example, marking over wrong answer choices with an x in the test booklet can clarify the choices that you should choose from. An educated guess is more likely to increase your score.

▶ If you are one of the many students who struggle with time on the math section, it will be especially important that you practice pacing yourself. When all else fails, it is okay to guess; remember that the ACT does not have a penalty for guessing, so you should never leave a question blank.

Although the test itself is not overtly divided into the sections shown in the bulleted list that follows, the content that the test covers overall does fall into these categories. Thus, to aid you in your studying, the chapter will be divided in the following manner:

▶ Pre-Algebra/Elementary Algebra

▶ Intermediate Algebra/Coordinate Geometry

▶ Plane Geometry/Trigonometry

Pre-Algebra and Elementary Algebra

This section discusses numbers, operations, and algebraic expressions. It's likely that you'll find most of this chapter's components to be a review of the concepts from your recent math classes, but take the time to ensure that you have a clear understanding of everything discussed.

NOTE

Depending on the amount of preparation time you have, you may want to work through the math sections in this chapter in small chunks. That means taking a section at a time until you are familiar with how to work with those types of problems.

Understanding and Working with Different Number Types

Although you may not be asked to identify the set of irrational numbers on the ACT test, being able to distinguish among the different types of numbers may provide insight into how to solve a problem or help you eliminate some answer choices. Question items will definitely require you to understand concepts such as absolute value and the relationship between positive and negative numbers, and may require that you represent these items abstractly with variables.

Just like anything else, numbers can be grouped by their unique characteristics. If you think of cars in this way, you realize that there are many ways to group cars:

▶ Two-door cars

▶ Four-door cars

▶ Sports cars

▶ Red cars

▶ White cars

▶ Foreign cars

▶ Used cars

- ▸ Brand-new cars

- ▸ Classic cars

- ▸ Fuel-efficient cars

- ▸ Small cars

Many cars will fall into more than one of the listed categories, and there are many other categories that are not even listed.

Numbers work the same way. They can be sorted by rules that describe their unique characteristics. Like cars, numbers can fall into more than one category. These are numbers you would use for counting. The set of whole numbers is the set of counting numbers with the addition of zero. Table 5.1 gives a complete list of the types of numbers, how they are defined, and some examples.

TABLE 5.1 Types of Numbers

Type of Number	Definition	Example
Natural numbers (also called *counting numbers*)	These include the positive numbers that are used for counting. Zero is not included when listing the natural numbers.	$\{1, 2, 3, 4, 5...\}$
Whole numbers	These include the positive counting numbers AND zero.	$\{0, 1, 2, 3, 4, 5...\}$
Integers	These include zero, the positive whole numbers, and their opposites.	$\{-3, -2, -1, 0, 1, 2, 3\}$
Rational numbers	Any number that can be represented as a fraction of two integers. These include repeating decimals.	$\{\frac{2}{3}, 1.92, \sqrt{9}, -3, 14, 0.66666\overline{6}...\}$
Irrational numbers	Any number that cannot be expressed as a fraction of two integers.	$\pi, \sqrt{2}, \sqrt{3}$
Real numbers	All preceding sets fall within this set.	$\pi, \sqrt{2}, \sqrt{4}, 0, -1, \frac{-1}{3}$
Imaginary numbers	These numbers express the square root of negative numbers. You may encounter imaginary numbers when solving for the roots of a quadratic.	$\sqrt{-4} = \sqrt{-}$ $1 \cdot \sqrt{4} = 2i$
Complex numbers	Numbers in the form $a + bi$, where a is the real component and bi is the imaginary component. Every number can be expressed as a complex number.	$2 + 4i, 2 + i\sqrt{5}, 8(8 + 0i)$

> **TIP**
>
> The ACT may refer to a "real number line," which is simply a number line that includes all types of numbers.

> **TIP**
>
> Remember that fractions may never have 0 in the denominator. An expression such as this would be *undefined*. Remember also that zero is neither negative nor positive.

EXAM ALERT

You might be asked to set up an expression that is described as being positive. This translates to the math expression >0.

Operations with Positive and Negative Numbers

Numbers are used to represent ideas. For example, you may have three one-dollar bills. We can use the number 3 to express this idea. But you may also owe someone three one-dollar bills. We use negative numbers to convey this concept, in this case –3. Think of the symbol "–" as meaning "the opposite of." You may see a word problem on the test that uses the phrase "the opposite of a number." This phrase actually means –*n*, where *n* represents a number. Don't let the wording confuse you.

Numbers that are expressed as positive or negative are called *signed numbers*. If a number has no sign, it is always assumed to be positive. Note that the ACT requires that you be able to simplify and evaluate expressions containing signed numbers. Look at the expressions in Table 5.2 and pay close attention to how they are simplified.

TABLE 5.2 Simplifying Expressions That Include Negative Signs

Expression	Simplification	Explanation
$\{-(-4)\}$ $-\{-(-3)\}$	4 -3	An even number of negative signs occurring before a number results in a positive number. An odd number of negative signs results in a negative number.
		Two negative signs appearing before a number form a positive number.
$-\left(\frac{3+5}{8-x}\right)$	$\left(\frac{-8}{8-x}\right)$	You can think of this negative sign as negative 1. The resulting expression is $(-1)\left(\frac{3+5}{8-x}\right)$
-3^2	-9	Do not include the sign when raising a number to a power unless the number and sign are enclosed in parentheses.
$(-3)^2$	9	Everything inside the parentheses gets squared.
$1-(3+2x)=$	$2-2x$	You can change the operation to addition as long as you change the sign of the expression that follows to its opposite. $1+-(3+2x)=1-3-2x$
b^2-4a, if $b=-2$ and $a=-1$	$(-2)^2-4(-1)=0$	Use parentheses when replacing variables with negatives.

TIP

Many students find expressions such as –3² to be confusing. They wonder why the answer is not positive 9, since there is a negative sign before the number. (Negative times negative equals positive.) The problem should be read this way: "Negative, three squared;" not "negative three, squared." Unless the signed number is in parentheses, don't include the sign when you work with the exponent.

Understanding Mathematical Operations

You will need to be able to perform all operations, addition and subtraction as well as multiplication and division, with signed numbers. Later in this chapter, you will read about the order of operations. Let's discuss and review each mathematical operation that you will be required to perform on the test.

Addition

For most students, the trickiest addition scenario involves adding together two or more positive and negative numbers.

To add numbers containing different signs, take the difference between the numbers' values and then take the sign of the larger one. For example, 3 + (–10) is –7. To solve, we took the difference between 10 and 3 (7) and the sign of the larger number (–).

For instance, what would be the results of the following equations?

$$–11 + (–3) = -14$$
$$5 + (–8) = -3$$
$$–4 + (–4) = -8$$
$$9 + (–11) = -2$$

The answer to the first problem in the preceding list would be –11 + (–3) = –14. The signs for both numbers are both negative, and we are being asked to add them together: 11 + 3 = 14. The total is negative, since we are working with negative numbers.

The answer to the next one would be 5 + (–8) = –3. We subtract the smaller number from the larger one (8 – 5 = 3) and then take the sign from the larger number (–).

The answer to the third one would be –4 + (–4) = –8. The signs for both numbers are negative, and we are being asked to add them together: 4 + 4 = 8. The total is negative, since we are working with negative numbers.

The answer to the last one would be 9 + (–11) = –2. We subtract the smaller number from the larger one (11 – 9 = 2) and then take the sign from the larger number (–).

TIP

If you have to combine a long sequence of signed numbers, first convert subtraction operations into the addition of the opposite number. Next, in order to reduce your chances of making an arithmetic error, combine all positive numbers and then combine all negative numbers. In this way, the lengthy problem is reduced to one positive combined with one negative.

For example, the problem 5 + –3 – 6 + 2 – 3 + –4 expressed only in terms of addition is 5 + –3 + –6 + 2 + –3 + –4. Combining all positives and negatives results in 7 + –16, which is –9.

Sometimes it's difficult to know whether a "–" symbol is a negative sign or a subtraction sign. To simplify the process, follow these steps:

1. Assume all signs belong to the number directly behind them.

2. Enclose numbers with their signs in parentheses.

3. Insert plus signs where necessary.

Here is the first example of applying the preceding list of steps:

$$-3 + -5 -3 -2 -2 =$$
$$(-3) + (-5) + (-3) + (-2) + (-2) = -15$$

Let's walk through another problem:

$$(-4 + (-9 + (+3) -4 + -2 =$$

Now, let's walk through the steps:

1. Enclose numbers with their signs in parentheses, like so:

$$(-4) + (-9) + (+3) + (-4) + (-2) =$$

2. Enclose positive numbers in parentheses, like so:

$$(-19) + (+3) = -16$$

3. Add together numbers with like signs:

$$(-4) + (-9) + (-4) + (-2) \text{ and } (+3)$$

4. Because the numbers have unlike signs, subtract the smaller number from the larger number and take the sign of the larger number.

Working with Integers

Working with numbers with negative and positive signs can often be tricky and confusing. Coming up with an answer containing the incorrect sign is an incorrect answer. Review and practice the concept below.

$$5 + -8 -2 + 9 -4 + -1 + 8 =$$

Correct answer:

Enclose numbers with their signs in parentheses:

$$(+5) + (-8) + (-2) + (+9) + (-4) + (-1) + (+8) =$$

Enclose positive numbers in parentheses:

$$22 + (-15) = 7$$

Add together numbers with like signs:

$$(+5) + (+9) + (+8) \text{ and } (-8) + (-2) + (-1)$$

Because the numbers have unlike signs, subtract the smaller number from the larger number and take the sign of the larger number.

The correct answer is 11.

Subtraction

Subtracting numbers with negative signs—for example, –3 – (–4)—can often be confusing. By turning the subtraction into addition, though, the problem can often be solved with less frustration. Turning subtraction into addition means changing the subtraction sign to an addition sign and then changing the sign of the following number to its opposite.

As an example of this technique, consider this equation: –3 – (–4). We would need to change the subtraction sign to an addition sign. The equation becomes –3 + (–4). We'd then change the negative 4 to a positive 4, like so: –3 + (4). Then we would perform the operation. The answer is 1.

> **TIP**
> If you change the subtraction sign to an addition sign in a problem, you must also change the sign of the number that follows.

Working with Subtracting Negative Numbers

Practice subtracting negatives using the following examples.

1. –2 – (–5) =
2. 6 – (–4) =
3. 10 – (–1) =
4. –65 – (–5) =
5. –231 – (–57) =

Correct answers:

1. –2 – (–5) becomes –2 + (5). The answer is 3.
2. 6 – (–4) becomes 6 + (4). The answer is 10.
3. 10 – (–1) becomes 10 + (1). The answer is 11.
4. –65 – (–5) becomes –65 + (5). The answer is –60.
5. –231 – (–57) becomes –231 + (57). The answer is 174.

Multiplication and Division

When working with signed numbers, two like signs yield a positive number, whereas two unlike signs yield a negative number. Thus, a positive number times a positive number or $\frac{positive}{positive}$ = a positive number. For example, $3 \times 7 = 21$.

Consider also that a negative number times a negative number or $\frac{negative}{negative}$ = a positive number. For example, $\frac{-21}{-3} = 7$. In addition, a negative number times a positive number or $\frac{negative}{positive}$ = a negative number (the opposite is also true: a positive number times a negative number = a negative number). For example, $\frac{-21}{7} = -3$.

Working with Multiplying Negative Numbers

Practice multiplying negatives with the following examples.

1. $16 \times 22 =$

2. $-16 \times (-22) =$

3. $-16 \times 22 =$

4. $22 \times (-16) =$

Correct answers:

1. $16 \times 22 = 352$

   (A positive number times a positive number equals a positive number.)

2. $-16 \times -22 = 352$

   (A negative number times a negative number equals a positive number.)

3. $-16 \times 22 = -352$

   (A negative number times a positive number equals a negative number.)

4. $22 \times -16 = -352$

   (A positive number times a negative number equals a negative number.)

In multiplication operations, an even number of negative signs results in a positive number, and an odd number of negative signs results in a negative number. You can sometimes use this fact to eliminate answer choices without doing any calculations. Consider the following problem:

Find x^8 if $x = -4$.

A. -1.0737×10^9

B. -6.5536×10^4

C. -1.088×10^3

D. 6.5536×10^4

E. 1.0737×10^9

By definition, x raised to the eighth power is x multiplied eight times. If -4 is multiplied eight times, the result is a positive number. Knowing this allows you to eliminate right away all answers except D and E. The correct answer is D, a positive number. You will review scientific notation in the section below.

Absolute Value

The absolute value of a real number is its numerical value when it is stripped of its sign. In other words, the absolute value of a number is its magnitude or size, so it is always a positive number. For example, $|3 = 3$, but $|-3 = 3$. Note that a negative sign in front of the absolute value produces a negative result, as follows: $-|-3 = -3$.

You may also take the absolute value of an expression. In this case, you complete all operations first and then take the absolute value of the final answer. For example, |3 + –17 = 14 becomes 3 + –17 = –14. The absolute value of –14 is 14.

Working with Absolute Value

Practice working with absolute value using the following examples.

1. |15 – (–17)

2. |2 + (–9)

3. |–3 + (–16)

Correct answers:

1. |15 – (–17)

   15 + (17) = 32. The absolute value of 32 is 32.

2. |2 + (–9)

   Subtract and take the sign of the larger number: 9 – 2 = 7, –7

   The absolute value of –7 is 7.

3. |–3 + (–16)

   Add the numbers together: –19.

   The absolute value of –19 is 19.

An absolute value test question might ask you to graph the absolute value of an inequality on a number line. Consider this question: "Graph | x ≤2." The 2 in the inequality means there will be two points of interest, 2 and –2. These two points break the number line into three regions. You can plug in points from each region to see which ones keep the statement true. Use a black line to cover all points in the correct range. Remember to use a closed circle when a point is included and an open circle when a point is not included. See Figure 5.1 for the graph of the answer.

-3 -2 -1 0 1 2 3   **FIGURE 5.1**   The graph of | x ≤2.

TIP

The absolute value of 0 is 0.

The absolute value of a number is its size, or its distance from 0 on a number line. You will need to keep this concept in mind when you encounter an equation that contains a variable inside the absolute value sign. Consider the following:

$$|(x – 2) = 1$$

The absolute value of either 1 or –1 equals 1.

Consider both scenarios: $x - 2 = 1$

$x - 2 = -1$

$x = 3 \quad x = 1$

The solutions are 1 and 3.

To practice, find the solution to the following problems:

Problem 1: $|x - 3| = 2x + 5$

First, rewrite the inequalities with both a positive and a negative answer:

$x - 3 = 2x + 5$

$x - 3 = -(2x + 5)$

Now solve each: $x - 3 = 2x + 5$

$-8 = x$

$x - 3 = -(2x + 5)$

$3x = -2$

$x = -\dfrac{2}{3}$

Problem 2: $|x + 4| = -3x - 1$

To solve, first rewrite the equations with both a positive and a negative answer:

$x + 4 = -3x - 1$

$x + 4 = -(-3x - 1)$

Then solve each:

$x + 4 = -3x - 1$

$4x = -3$

$x = -\dfrac{3}{4}$

$x + 4 = -(-3x - 1)$

$x + 4 = 3x + 1$

$3 = 2x$

$x = \dfrac{3}{2}$

Scientific Notation

You may see numbers expressed in scientific notation on the test. Scientific notation is based on powers of the base number 10. It is used to express very large and very small numbers in such a way that they can be worked with easily. Generally numbers written in scientific notation look like this:

$n \times 10x$ where n = a number greater than 1 but less than 10, and x = exponent of 10.

Read through the steps to write numbers greater than 10 in scientific notation. Here the number 67198 is used as an example.

1. To express numbers greater than 10 in scientific notation, first determine where the decimal is located. Move it to the left or the right so that there is only one nonzero digit to its left.

   67198

2. The decimal is here: 67198. When the decimal is moved so that there is only one nonzero digit to its left, the resulting number is expressed like this:

   6.7198

3. The placement of the decimal makes up the n part of the scientific notation expression. Count the number of places that you moved the decimal. That number of positions will equal x in the general expression ($10x$).

4. Multiply the results to get the standard form:

   6.7198×10^4

5. For numbers less than one, follow the same procedure, but move the decimal to the RIGHT. The number of positions that we had to move it to the right will be equal to $-x$, a negative exponent.

You may be required to perform operations with numbers expressed in scientific notation. If you encounter this type of problem, simply follow the rules of multiplying and dividing with exponents. For example, $1.8 \times 10 - 8$ multiplied by 1.2×105 is $(1.8 \cdot 1.2) \times 10(-8 + 5)$, or $2.16 \times 10 - 3$.

Properties

Although you have probably used many mathematical properties throughout your math studies, the distributive and the reciprocal properties are the most likely to appear on the test. This part of the chapter goes into these properties in detail.

The Distributive Property

The most common use of the distributive property is the distribution of multiplication over addition. The distributive property says that when a number is multiplied by the sum of two other numbers, the first number can be distributed to both of those two numbers and multiplied by each of them separately. Here's the distributive property in symbols:

$a \times (b + c) = a \times b + a \times c$

Consider the following equation:

$3(x - y) = 3x - 3y$

The 3 can be distributed, or multiplied by both values within the parentheses, the x and the y.

Note that the most common error students make occurs in a problem like this one:

$3x - 4(x + y)$

Students commonly make errors in problems like this one because they don't distribute the negative sign when they distribute the "4." To solve this problem correctly, first think of it as

$3x + -4(x + y)$

The negative sign stays with the number 4 while it is being distributed among the values in the parentheses. Now you can distribute -4 with x and y and get the following:

$3x + -4x + -4y$

Combining like terms then results in this:

$-1x + -4y$

At this point, you can simplify the equation:

$3x - 4(x + y) = 3x + -4(x + y)$

$3x + -4(x + y) = 3x + -4x + -4y$

$3x + -4x + -4y = -1x + -4y$

Working with Distributive Property

Practice now with these examples of this type of distributive property problems. Then compare your answers with the correct responses that follow.

1. $4y - 14(2x + 2y)$
2. $7x - 5(2x + 8y)$
3. $3x - 4(3x - 2y)$
4. $x - 6(-2x + 4y)$
5. $9x - 2(8x + 4y)$

Correct answers:

1. $4y - 14(2x + 2y)$

    First, add the addition sign so that there is no confusion while distributing:

    $4y + -14(2x + 2y)$

    Now distribute the 14:

    $4y - 28x - 28y$

    Combine like terms:

    $-28x - 24y$

2. $7x - 5(2x + 8y)$

First, add the addition sign so that there is no confusion while distributing:

$7x - 5(2x + 8y)$

Now distribute the 5:

$7x - 10x - 40y$

Combine like terms:

$-3x - 40y$

3. $3x - 4(3x - 2y)$

First, add the addition sign so that there is no confusion while distributing:

$3x + -4(3x - 2y)$

Now distribute the 4:

$3x - 12x + 8y$

Combine like terms:

$-9x + 8y$

4. $x - 6(-2x + 4y)$

First, add the addition sign so that there is no confusion while distributing:

$x + -6(-2x + 4y)$

Now distribute the 6:

$x + 12x - 24y$

Combine like terms:

$13x - 24y$

5. $9x - 2(8x + 4y)$

First, add the addition sign so there is no confusion while distributing:

$9x + -2(8x + 4y)$

Now distribute the 2:

$9x - 16x - 8y$

Combine like terms:

$7x - 8y$

The Reciprocal Property

A number expressed as an exponent can also be expressed in terms of its reciprocal. The reciprocal of a number raised to the exponent y is that number raised to the exponent $-y$.

Numbers with exponents have their reciprocals formed in this way:

$$x^a = \frac{1}{x^{-a}}$$

$$x^{-a} = \frac{1}{x^a}$$

$$3^{-3} = \frac{1}{3^3} = \frac{1}{27}$$

$$4^2 = \frac{1}{4^{-2}} = \frac{1}{(\frac{1}{16})} = 16$$

A reciprocal is the inverted form of the original. The reciprocal property states that a number multiplied by its reciprocal is always 1. For example, 4, which is $\frac{4}{1}$, has the reciprocal $\frac{1}{4}$. If a number is negative, its reciprocal will also be negative. Thus, $\frac{-1}{5}$ is the reciprocal of -5.

Roots and Powers

Both powers and roots are based on the idea of multiplying a number by itself a certain number of times. As you know, for each operation in mathematics, there is an inverse, or opposite, operation. These operations "undo" each other. Roots and powers are inverse operations. For example, if we raise the number 3 by a power of 3, we get 9. If we take the square root of 9, we undo that squaring operation.

You'll need to be comfortable working with square roots in an assortment of ways.

Working with Roots

You have worked extensively with square roots, but keep in mind that there are higher-order roots as well.

TIP

A square root symbol is called a *radical*.

For example, if you are asked to find the third root of a number, this means you are looking for the number that, when multiplied by itself three times, produces the number under the *radical*. Therefore, $3\sqrt{27}$ is 3 because $3 \times 3 \times 3$ is 27.

You'll need to be able to complete all four operations with expressions that involve square roots. Adding and subtracting radicals is similar to adding and subtracting polynomials; that is, you can add and subtract those with like terms.

So you can add $\sqrt{3} + 4\sqrt{3}$ because the 3 under the radical is the same. This adds up to $1\sqrt{3} + 4\sqrt{3} = 5\sqrt{3}$.

You cannot add $2\sqrt{3} + 2\sqrt{6}$, though. The numbers under the radicals, in this case the 3 and the 6, are not the same.

Pay close attention to terms that initially seem as though they can't be simplified, but upon closer inspection are actually quite simple to work with:

$$\sqrt{9} - \sqrt{4} = 3 - 2, \text{ or } 1$$

Terms with radicals can be simplified by working with the numbers under the radical. For example, consider the problem $\sqrt{108}$. Express the number under the radical as the multiplication of its prime factors.

Every pair of factors can be simplified outside the radical. For example, $\sqrt{108}$ can be expressed as $\sqrt{(2 \times 2 \times 3 \times 3 \times 3)}$. The answer is $2 \times 3 \times \sqrt{3}$, or $6\sqrt{3}$.

Consider the problem: $2\sqrt{3} + \sqrt{27}$.

You might need to simplify square roots in order to get the portion under the radical to be the same, as follows:

$$2\sqrt{3} + \sqrt{27} \text{ becomes } 2\sqrt{3} + 3\sqrt{3}, \text{ which equals } 5\sqrt{3}$$

Certain conditions must be true before you add or subtract radical expressions. However, despite what number appears under the radical, simply multiply or divide it, like so:

$$\sqrt{3} \times \sqrt{7} = \sqrt{21}$$

and

$$\frac{\sqrt{8}}{\sqrt{4}} = \sqrt{\left(\frac{8}{4}\right)} = 2$$

Working with Roots

Practice working with square roots with the questions below.

1. $\sqrt{8} \times \sqrt{9} =$
2. $\sqrt{\frac{12}{4}} =$
3. $\frac{\sqrt{8}}{\sqrt{2}} =$
4. $\sqrt{5} \times \sqrt{8} =$

Correct answers:

1. $\sqrt{8} \times \sqrt{9} = \sqrt{72}$
2. $\frac{12}{\sqrt{4}} = \sqrt{\left(\frac{12}{4}\right)} = 3$
3. $\frac{8}{\sqrt{2}} = \sqrt{\left(\frac{8}{2}\right)} = 4$
4. $\sqrt{5} \times \sqrt{8} = \sqrt{40}$

As you work with these equations, remember that roots can be expressed as fractions. For example, $\sqrt{16}$ is also $16^{\frac{1}{2}}$ and $\sqrt{32}$ is also $32^{\frac{1}{5}}$. Some problems might require you to express roots as fractions in order to simplify. In other cases, you can work out the problem without the fractional exponent, but it's important that you recognize that the answer is expressed this way.

Solving Equations with Expressions under Square Root Symbols

A *radical expression* is an equation in which one or more of the variables appear under a radical. The overall strategy in this type of equation is to isolate the radical and then square both sides. Look at the following example:

$\sqrt{(x-2)} - 3 = 5$ (Add 3 to both sides.)

$\sqrt{(x-2)} = 8$ (Square both sides.)

x – 2 = 64 (Add 2 to both sides.)

x = 66

Now check the solution in the original equation:

$\sqrt{(66-2)} - 3 = 5$

$\sqrt{64 - 3} = 5$

8 – 3 = 5 (Check.)

TIP

Squaring both sides of an equation can generate false solutions. Whenever you use this strategy, you must always check the solution in the original equation.

Working with Radical Expressions

Practice working with radical expressions with the questions below.

1. $\sqrt{(x + 4)} + 6 = 10$

2. $\sqrt{(x + 5)} + 3 = 5$

Correct answers:

1. $\sqrt{(x + 4)} + 6 = 10$

   x = 12

   $\sqrt{(x + 4)} = 4$ (To get rid of the 6 in the first half of the equation, subtract 6 from both sides.)

   x + 4 = 16 (To get rid of the radical, square both sides.)

   x = 12 (To get rid of the 4, subtract 4 from both sides.)

   Remember, make sure you check to ensure that this answer works in the original problem.

   $\sqrt{(12 + 4)} + 6 = 10$

   $\sqrt{(16)} + 6 = 10$

   4 + 6 = 10

   10 = 10

2. $\sqrt{(x + 5)} + 3 = 5$

   $x = 95$

   $\sqrt{(x + 5)} = 10$ (To get rid of the 10 in the first half of the equation, subtract 10 from both sides.)

   $x + 5 = 100$ (To get rid of the radical, square both sides.)

   $x = 95$ (To get rid of the 5, subtract 5 from both sides.)

   Remember, make sure you check to ensure that this answer works in the original problem.

   $\sqrt{(95 + 5)} + 10 = 20$

   $\sqrt{(100)} + 10 = 20$

   $10 + 10 = 20$

   $20 = 20$

Bases and Exponents

Exponents are another way to write multiplication. The small number at the top right of another number is an exponent. Table 5.3 summarizes the rules for exponents.

TABLE 5.3   The Rules for Exponents

Operation Rule	Example	Rule Applied	Result
Multiplying (bases must be the same)	$a^5\, a^3$	Add the exponents.	a^8
Dividing (bases must be the same)	$\dfrac{a^8}{a^3}$	Create the subtraction: top exponent minus bottom exponent.	a^5
Zero exponent	a^0	Anything raised to the zero power is 1.	1
Power raised to a power	$(a^3)^5$	Multiply exponents.	a^{15}
Product or quotient raised to a power	$(a^2 b)^3$ $\left(\dfrac{a^2}{b^3}\right)^3$	Distribute the exponent to everything inside the parentheses.	$a^6\, b^3$ $\dfrac{a^6}{b^9}$

TIP

In the expression 2^5, 2 is the *base* and ^{5} is the *exponent*.

The exponent tells how many times the base should be multiplied. In the following example, it shows that the base is being raised to the fifth power, or multiplied five times:

$$2 \times 2 \times 2 \times 2 \times 2 = 32$$

Conversely, $\sqrt{32}$ asks for a number that, when multiplied five times, results in 32. We say the fifth root of 32 is 2.

In the example $(-3)^5$, the -3 in its entirety is being raised to the fifth power, or multiplied five times:

$$(-3)\,(-3)\,(-3)\,(-3)\,(-3) = -243$$

On the test, you will need to be able to use the rules of both roots and powers in more complicated types of expressions and equations.

For example, consider this question:

If $x^2 = 81$ and $y^2 = 16$, what are all of the possible solutions for $x + y$?

  A. 5, 13

  B. –5, –13

  C. 5, –5, 13, –13

  D. –5, 5

  E. –13, 13

At first glance, you might think that there is only one solution to $x + y$:

  9 + 4, or 13

However, the correct response here is C. Why? Well, to answer that question, it is important to remember that negative numbers must be considered as a possible solution when a term is squared. Keeping this in mind, you can see that there are two solutions for x:

  $-9 \times -9 = 81$ and $9 \times 9 = 81$

There are also two solutions for y:

  $-4 \times -4 = 16$ and $4 \times 4 = 16$

So $x + y$ could equal any of the following:

  9 + 4 = 13
  –9 + 4 = –5
  9 – 4 = 5
  –9 – 4 = –13

So, $x + y$ might result in 13, –13, 5, or –5.

Working with Exponents

Practice working with exponents by completing the question below.

If $x^2 = 64$ and $y^2 = 100$, what are all of the possible solutions for $x + y$?

   A. 18, −18

   B. 18, 2

   C. 18, 2, −2

   D. −2, 2, −18, 18

   E. −2, −18

Correct answer:

There are two answers for each square root equation. For $x^2 = 64$, $x = 8$ and $x = -8$. Similarly, $y^2 = 100$ has the solutions $y = 10$ and $y = -10$. So possible answers here are:

$10 + 8 = 18$

$10 - 8 = 2$

$-10 - 8 = -18$

$-10 + 8 = -2$

The correct response is D.

Exponents and Different Bases

You may be asked to solve a problem involving exponents that initially seems impossible because the bases are different. For example, consider the problem $(2y)(4) = 8^3$.

To solve a problem like this, first see if you can express the numbers you have been given in a way that makes the bases the same. Similar to finding a common denominator, you will look for a common base. In the types of problems you will encounter on the ACT test, you will likely have to know how to find this commonality.

In this problem, if you express everything with the base 2, you get this: $(2^y)(2^2) = (2^3)^3$. Realize that you are not changing any numbers here—you are simply expressing some of them in a different way, like so:

$$(2^y)(2^2) = (2^3)^3$$

simplifies to

$$2y + 2 = 29$$

Therefore, $y + 2 = 9$, so $y = 7$.

Working with Exponents with Different Bases

Practice working with exponents expressed with different bases by completing the question below.

$(3^y)(9) = 27^3$

Correct answer:

See if there's a way to convert the numbers so that they have a common base. In this case, we can see that they can all have a base 3:

$(3^y)(3^2) = (3^3)^3$

Now simplify:

$3^{y+2} = 3^9$

$y + 2 = 9$

Negative Exponents

We define a^{-x} as $\frac{1}{a^x}$. An easy way to remember this is to recall that "−" means "the opposite of," or that the base is on the wrong side of the fraction line. The exponent becomes positive when it drifts underneath the fraction line.

> **TIP**
>
> When you are presented with a base raised to a negative power, you can change the base to a positive power by relocating the base and changing the power to the denominator of the fraction.

For example, $8a^{-3}$ (which is actually $8a^{-3}/1$) becomes $\frac{8}{a^3}$ and $\frac{a^{-3}b^2}{c^{-5}}$ becomes $\frac{b^2c^5}{a^3}$.

Factors and Multiples

You will be asked questions on the test that assess your understanding of how numbers relate to each other. These questions may ask you to identify a pattern or the greatest common factor (GCF) of two numbers. The questions might be relatively straightforward or a bit convoluted. This section will help you decipher the relationships.

> **TIP**
>
> As you go through this part of the chapter, remember that the greatest common factor is the largest integer that is a factor of both (or all) numbers. In addition, the greatest common factor of two numbers with variables is the product of the GCF of the numerical coefficients and the highest point of every variable that is a factor of each variable.
>
> For example, the greatest common factor of $10x^2y^6$ and $20\ x^3y^2$ is $10\ x^2y^2$. You know this is the case because 10 is the largest number that is a factor of 10 and 20, and x^2y^2 are the highest points of the variables shown.

Factor Versus Multiple

The terms *factor* and *multiple* are easily confused, and some questions on the test will contain distracters that assume that confusion.

Remember that factors are numbers which when multiplied together, give a certain number; for example, 3 and 4 are some factors of 12. Remember this by telling yourself to "factor the number down" when you see the word *factor*. On the other hand, a multiple is a product of a certain number with any other whole number, so 24, 36, 48 are some multiples of 12. Remember this by thinking of the word *multiply*.

For example, the factors of 24 are:

1 and 24

2 and 12

3 and 8

4 and 6

We can list all of the factors of 24 together as 1, 2, 3, 4, 6, 8, 12, 24.

Here's another example: To test whether 5 is a factor of 36, see if 5 divides into 36 evenly, with no remainder. Because the division produces a remainder of 1, 5 is not a factor of 36.

TIP

The more quick divisibility checks you know, the less work you will have to do to factor numbers. Keep in mind that a number is divisible by:

2 if the ones digit is even

3 if the sum of the digits is divisible by 3

4 if the tens and ones digits form a number divisible by 4

5 if the number ends in a 5 or a 0

6 if the number is divisible by 2 and 3

9 if the sum of the digits is divisible by 9

10 if the ones digit is 0

Multiples of 5 are 5, 10, 15, 20, and so on. There are an infinite number of multiples for each number, so listing them all is not important. Just remember that as you work to solve a problem, you may need to decide quickly whether a particular number is a factor or a multiple of some other number.

To assess whether 144 is a multiple of 36, see if 36 divides into 144 evenly, with no remainder. Because 36 goes into 144 exactly four times with no remainder, that means that 144 is a multiple of 36.

Prime Numbers

Many number pattern questions involve prime numbers. A *prime number* is any counting number greater than 1 whose only factors are 1 and the number itself. Some prime numbers are 2, 7, 13, and 17.

Recognizing prime numbers permits you to write numbers in terms of their prime factorization, that is, breaking the number down to its prime factors. Every number can be written as the product of prime numbers.

TIP

A prime number has only two factors: 1 and itself.
A composite number has more than two factors.

TIP

0 and 1 are neither prime nor composite numbers. 0 has an infinite number of factors and 1 only has 1 as a factor.

To find a number's prime factors, it is easiest to create a factor tree. For example, assume you have to factor the number 270. To do this, begin by choosing any two factors. For example:

2 and 135

The factor tree in Figure 5.2 shows the process of breaking each factor down into its own factors until a prime number is reached. You will note that each branch of the tree ends when a prime number is reached. If you circle the prime factors as they appear as branches on the tree, it's easy to keep track of where you are in the tree.

After you have completed the tree, simply gather up all of the factors that you have circled:

2, 5, 3, 3, 3

reorder them in numerical sequence:

2, 3, 3, 3, 5

and then add the exponent:

$2 \times 3^3 \times 5$

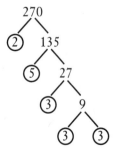

$2 \times 3^3 \times 5$ **FIGURE 5.2**   A prime factor tree for the number 270.

Let's look at another sample question: How many prime numbers fall between 0 and 21? To answer this question, you need to know that the most efficient method you can use to determine the number of primes within a range of numbers is to follow these steps:

1. List numbers greater than 1 within the range given:

   (in this case 2, 3, 4, 5, 6, 7, 8, 9, 10, 11, 12, 13, 14, 15, 16, 17, 18, 19, 20).

2. Cross out all the even numbers *except 2 itself*, because they have 2 as a factor.

3. Cross out all numbers that are multiples of 3, *except 3 itself*.

4. Cross out any numbers that are a multiple of 5, *except 5 itself*.

The remaining numbers are primes. In our problem, the primes are 2, 3, 5, 7, 11, 13, 17, and 19. Thus, there are eight primes between 0 and 21.

Now that you know about prime numbers, let's talk about relatively prime numbers.

Two numbers are considered to be relatively prime if they have no common divisors greater than one. So 11 and 13 are relatively prime numbers, but 12 and 14 are not.

Consider 28 and 45:

$$28 = 2 \times 2 \times 7$$
$$45 = 3 \times 5 \times 3$$

These numbers have no prime factors in common, so they are relatively prime.

Let's try two more:

▶ Are 16 and 52 relatively prime? You can probably see right away that since both numbers are even, they are both divisible by 2. To answer the question, you'll just need to know that. No, 16 and 52 are not relatively prime numbers.

▶ Are $53x^3$ and $22x$ relatively prime? Here you can see that both numbers have at least an x in common. The numbers are not relatively prime, as they have at least x as a factor.

Greatest Common Factor and Least Common Multiple

You might encounter a word problem that requires you to find a *greatest common factor (GCF)* or a *least common multiple (LCM)*. Thus, we'll cover them in this part of the chapter.

Greatest Common Factor (GCF)

The GCF is the largest factor that two or more numbers share. It is used whenever fractions are to be reduced to their lowest terms.

To find the GCF, do the following:

1. Write the prime factorization of both numbers. You may want to use a factor tree to work with large numbers.

2. Circle the factors that both numbers share.

3. Multiply together the factors that the numbers share.

For example, the prime factorizations of 12 and 36 are

$12 = 3 \times 2 \times 2$

$36 = 3 \times 3 \times 2 \times 2$

You would circle the 2, 2, and 3 because both share these factors, and multiply these three numbers together. You would end up with a GCF of $2 \times 2 \times 3$, or 12.

Working with GCF

Practice working with greatest common factor by completing the questions below.

1. Find the GCF of 14 and 49.

2. What is the greatest integer that is a factor of both 3×10^3 and 6×10^5?

3. What is the greatest integer that is a factor of both 5×10^2 and 2×10^3?

Correct answers:

1. Do your calculations:

   $14 = 2 \times 7$

   $49 = 7 \times 7$

   Circle the 7. Since it is the only factor, we know that the GCF is 7.

2. You might initially be wary of the large numbers in this problem. But if you stop to think about what you're being asked, this is really just a GCF problem. Regardless of whether big or small numbers are used, the method of finding the solution is the same.

   First factor $3 \times 10^3 = 3 \times 10 \times 10 \times 10$.

   Now factor $6 \times 10^5 = 3 \times 2 \times 10 \times 10 \times 10 \times 10 \times 10$.

   Circle the factors that the numbers have in common.

   The GCF is the numbers you have circled—the factors they have in common: $3 \times 10 \times 10 \times 10$.

3. Here's what you do:

   First factor 5×10^2 : $5 \times 10 \times 10$

   Now factor 2×10^3 : $2 \times 10 \times 10 \times 10$

   Circle the factors they have in common: 10×10

   The GCF is 10×10, or 100

Least Common Multiple (LCM)

The least common multiple (LCM) of two numbers is the smallest number (not zero) that is a multiple of both. You use the LCM whenever you have to find a common denominator between two fractions.

To find the LCM of two numbers, first list the multiples of the larger number. List the multiples of the smaller number. When you find one that is also a multiple of the smaller number, you have the LCM.

Consider the numbers 9 and 12. The first four multiples of 9 are 9, 18, 27, and 36. The first three multiples of 12 are 12, 24, and 36, and the number 36 is the smallest number that is a multiple of both 9 and 12 because it's the first multiple of 12 that is divisible by 9. Thus, the least common multiple of 9 and 12 is 36.

TIP

When finding least common multiple, don't forget that you are looking for a *common multiple* that is the *smallest*.

Another way to find the LCM is to find the prime factorization of the numbers, like so:

LCM $(9, 12) = x$

$9 = (3, 3)$

$12 = (2, 2, 3)$

Now cross out the factors that are common to both. In this case, it is one of the 3s. You are left with 2, 2, 3, 3. Then multiply the factors together $(2, 2, 3, 3) = 36$. Thus, 36 is the LCM of 9 and 12.

Working with LCM

Practice working with the least common multiple by completing the question below.

Find the LCM of 14 and 45.

Correct answer:

LCM $(14, 45) = x$

$14 = (2, 7)$

$45 = (3, 3, 5)$

Since none of the factors here is a duplicate, none has to be crossed out. Multiply the factors:

$2 \times 3 \times 3 \times 5 \times 7 = 630$

630 is the LCM of 14 and 45.

Divisibility

Divisibility refers to whether there is a remainder when a division problem is solved. To illustrate, we can state that 18 is divisible by 3 because when we divide 18 by 3, there is no remainder. We could have predicted there would be no remainder because 3 is a factor of 18.

You might be asked a question specifically about remainders. For example, consider the sample question:

Which of these does *not* have a remainder?

A. 15 / 6

B. 17 / 7

C. 19 / 4

D. 51 / 3

E. 39 / 2

Notice the word *not* within the question. You may want to circle it because it is easily forgotten as you work through problems. You need to remember that you want the choice that has no remainder—no whole number left over after the division.

You don't necessarily have to do all of the division to find the correct answer here. For example, you can eliminate answers B and C right away because they are prime numbers. They are therefore divisible only by 1 and themselves. You know that these numbers will have remainders when they are divided.

You can quickly eliminate answer E because it is an odd number; therefore, it will not be divisible by 2. When 39 is divided by 2, there will be a remainder.

You are left with A and D. You can either quickly divide these to find the answer, or recognize that 51 can be divided evenly by 3 (when you add together the digits 5 and 1, you get 6, which is divisible by 3, so the entire number then is divisible by 3).

By the process of elimination, then, only answer D does not have a remainder. Thus, answer D is correct.

Working with Divisibilty

Practice working with divisibility by completing the question below. Numbers that are divisible by 4 and 5 are also divisible by what number?

A. 9

B. 12

C. 16

D. 20

E. 25

Correct answer:

This question might leave you feeling as though you don't have enough information, but stop to consider the information given. If a number is divisible by 4, then 4 is a factor of that number. If a number is also divisible by 5, then 5 is a factor of that number.

Any number that has 4 and 5 as factors also has 20 as a factor. If 20 is a factor of the number, the number is divisible by 20.

The answer is D, 20.

Arithmetic and Geometric Sequences

There are two types of sequences that you are likely to encounter on the test. These are discussed briefly below.

Arithmetic Sequence

You will probably see just one arithmetic sequence question and one geometric sequence question on the math test. When you encounter these questions, remember that a *sequence* is a group of numbers arranged in order. That being said, an *arithmetic sequence* is formed by choosing a first term and then adding a constant amount to each succeeding term.

TIP

An *arithmetic sequence* is a sequence (finite or infinite) of real numbers in which each term is the preceding term plus a constant.

So, if you are given a first term of 7 and are told the common difference (constant amount) is 3, it's easy to find the fourth term. The fourth term is $7 + 3 + 3 + 3$, which is 16. But what if you are asked to find the 40th term? Well, you would start by using the following formula to keep from writing out 40 terms:

nth term = *first term* + (*number of terms* – 1) (*constant amount*)

Arithmetic sequence short formula: $n = a1 + (n - 1)d$

So to find the 40th term:

40th term = *first term* (7) + *number of terms* – 1 (40 – 1) times *constant amount* (3)

$7 + 39 (3)$

$7 + 117$

40th term = 124

Working with Sequences

Practice working with arithmetic and geometric sequences by completing the questions below.

1. A manufacturing plant that produces kitty litter is able to increase production by 4 lbs. every day. If the plant started by producing 500 lbs. a day, how much can it produce at the end of 10 weeks?

2. A hockey player has been able to increase his goal attempts by 3 each game this season. If he started with 6 goal attempts per game, how many attempts will he have at the end of the 12-game season?

3. 4, __, __, 28

What numbers must be in the blanks so that the difference between consecutive numbers is the same?

    A. 12, 20

    B. 8, 22

    C. 10, 24

    D. 11, 17

Correct answers:

1. To solve this arithmetic sequence problem, first label the problem and then restate it in your own words. You can restate it as follows: The first term is 500. The constant amount is 4. Because 10 weeks is 70 days, what is the 70th term?

70th term = 500 + (69)(4)

70th term = 500 + 276

Production on the 70th day = 776 lbs.

2. As with the problem above, first label it and then restate it in your own words: The first term is 6. The constant amount is 3. (In arithmetic sequence, the terms *constant amount* and *common difference* mean the same thing.) We are looking for the 12th term.

12th term = 6 + 11(3)

12th term = 6 + 33

12th term = 39 goal attempts

3. This is an arithmetic question with a twist. For this problem, it may be quickest for you to plug in answer choices until you find the choice that works. The alternative is to recognize 4 as a_1. Then, express 28 as the fourth term using the formula, like this: 28 = 4 + (3)d. Solving for d tells you the constant amount is 8. The second term must be 12 and the third must be 20.

Geometric Sequence

You might also see a *geometric sequence* question on the test. This type of sequence is formed by beginning with a number and then multiplying each succeeding term by a common factor.

The formula for working with a geometric sequence is as follows:

nth term = (*first term*)(*common factor*)$^{(number\ of\ terms\ -\ 1)}$

Geometric sequence short version: $n = a_1 \cdot r^{n-1}$

TIP

A geometric sequence is a sequence of real numbers where each term is the preceding term multiplied by a constant number (the common ratio).

Let's look at some examples. The following is a geometric sequence because each number is multiplied by 5.

2, 10, 50, 250, 1250…

This is also a geometric sequence:

8, 16, 32, 64, 128…

The sequence starts with 8 and has a common factor, or common ratio, of 2: 8, 8·2, 8·2·2, etc.

Now consider the following problem: A ball is dropped from a height of 50 inches. If it always rebounds 1/5 of the distance it fell, how far does it fall on its seventh fall?

You should recognize that this problem involves a succession of numbers, each being multiplied by 1/5, which means that it is a geometric sequence. To solve the problem, first you will need to restate the problem as follows: The first term is 50. What is the seventh term if the common factor is (1/5)? The ball's second fall is the amount it rebounded after the first fall, 50·(1/5).

Thus, the following information about the seventh fall holds true:

The seventh fall = $50 \cdot (1/5)^6$

The seventh fall = $50 \cdot (6.4 \times 10^{-5})$

The seventh fall = 0.0032 inches

You might find it easier to make a chart to solve such a problem. In this way, you can systematically figure out each fall. For example:

Fall 1	Fall 2	Fall 3	Fall 4	Fall 5	Fall 6	Fall 7
50	1/5(50) or 10	1/5(10) or 2	1/5(2) or 0.4	1/5(0.4) or 0.08	1/5(0.08) or 0.016	1/5(0.016) or 0.0032

Working with Problems Involving Sequencing

Practice working with word problems involving sequencing by completing the question below.

There are 300 pounds of trash at a temporary landfill. Each day, the amount of trash increases by 10%. What is the likely amount of trash that will be at the landfill at the end of three days?

A. 330 lbs.

B. 333 lbs.

C. 360 lbs.

D. 363 lbs.

E. 390 lbs.

Correct answer:

The correct answer is D. To solve this problem, you will first want to rewrite it: The first term is 300. What is the third term if the constant factor is .10? It's probably easiest to solve this problem by creating a chart and multiplying each day's amount by the constant .10 and then adding it to the preceding day, like so:

Day	Trash in Pounds
1	300
2	330
3	363

Fractions, Decimals, and Percents

Throughout the math test, you will find questions involving fractions, decimals, and percents. Take some time to review the basics of working with adding, subtracting, multiplying, and dividing fractions and decimals, and working with percents. If you haven't worked with these in a while, you may be rusty about the rules and operations.

Fractions and Operations

A *fraction* shows the relationship between a part and a whole. In the fraction $\frac{2}{3}$, we are actually saying "two parts of a three-part whole." In this fraction, the number 2 is the numerator, and the number 3 is the denominator.

TIP

The top number of a fraction is the *numerator*. It tells how many parts there are. The bottom number of a fraction is the *denominator*. It tells how many parts the whole has been divided into.

Table 5.4 reviews the rules for performing operations with fractions. Take some time to remind yourself of how to perform each operation, so you don't have to think about it when you are asked on the test.

Table 5.4 Operations with Fractions

Operation	Problem	Procedure	Answer
Adding and subtracting	$\frac{2}{8} + \frac{3}{5}$	Whether you're adding or subtracting, the denominators must be the same. If they're different, determine the common denominator by using the LCM. Then multiply the top and bottom of each fraction by the same number to express both with the common denominator. Combine the numerators according to the operation, but do not change the denominator.	The LCM of 5 and 8 is 40. Express each with the common denominator 40. $\frac{2}{8} \times \frac{5}{5} = \frac{10}{40}$ $\frac{3}{5} \times \frac{8}{8} = \frac{24}{40}$ $\frac{10}{40} + \frac{24}{40} = \frac{34}{40}$ $\frac{34}{40} = \frac{17}{20}$

(continues)

Table 5.4 *Continued*

Operation	Problem	Procedure	Answer
Multiplying	$\frac{2}{8} \times \frac{3}{5}$	Multiply the numerators, then multiply the denominators.	$\frac{6}{40} = \frac{3}{20}$
Dividing	$\frac{2}{8} \div \frac{3}{5}$	Flip and multiply. Always flip the second fraction, or the fraction on the bottom if its in stacked form.	$\frac{2}{8} \times \frac{5}{3}$ $\frac{10}{24} = \frac{5}{12}$

Working with Fractions

You may feel that you need to review working with fractions. Solve these review questions.

1. 6/7 + 3/5 =

2. 3/4 + 11/12 =

3. 1 3/18 + 16 1/9 =

4. 5 5/6 + 11 1/8 =

5. 3 2/3 + 3 2/5 =

6. 4 3/10 − 1/3 =

7. 6 − 2 4/7 =

8. 15 9/10 − 5/8 =

9. 1 1/2 − 2/3 =

10. 12 1/9 − 3 2/9 =

11. 6/7 × 3/5 =

12. 3/4 × 11/12 =

13. 1 3/18 × 1 1/9 =

14. 5 5/6 × 2 1/8 =

15. 3 2/3 × 3 2/5 =

Correct answers:

1. 6/7 + 3/5 = 32/35

2. 3/4 + 11/12 = 1 2/3 (change the denominators to 12, solve, then reduce to lowest terms)

3. 1 3/18 + 16 1/9 = 17 5/18

4. 5 5/6 + 11 1/8 = 16 23/24

5. 3 2/3 + 3 2/5 = 3 14/15

6. 4 3/10 − 1/3 = 2 29/30

7. $6 - 2\ 4/7 = 3\ 3/7$

8. $15\ 9/10 - 5/8 = 15\ 9/40$

9. $1\ 1/2 - 2/3 = 5/6$

10. $12\ 1/9 - 3\ 2/9 = 8\ 8/9$

11. $6/7 \times 3/5 = 18/35$

12. $3/4 \times 11/12 = -33/48$

13. $1\ 3/18 \times 1\ 1/9 = -1\ 8/27$

14. $5\ 5/6 \times 2\ 1/8 = 12\ 19/48$

15. $3\ 2/3 \times 3\ 2/5 = -12\ 7/15$

Working with Word Problems

Practice working with word problems involving fractions by completing the question below.

If Jan walks $2\frac{3}{4}$ miles today and $5\frac{1}{3}$ miles tomorrow, how far has she walked?

Correct answer:

To solve this problem, add the mixed numbers as in these steps:

Combine the integers:

$2 + 5 = 7$

Combine the fractional parts. To do so, you may need to find a common denominator:

$\frac{3}{4} = \frac{9}{12}$ and $\frac{1}{3} = \frac{4}{12}$, so combined the result is $\frac{13}{12}$.

Add $\frac{13}{12}$, which is 1, and $\frac{1}{12}$, and then add 7 to get $8\frac{1}{12}$ miles.

The answer is $8\frac{1}{12}$ miles.

Fraction Word Problems

Word problems on the test will be designed to test your understanding of how fractions represent ideas. Use these three steps to sort out fraction word problems you encounter:

1. Draw a picture if you need to.

2. Identify the whole (the denominator).

3. Identify the part or parts (the numerator).

Let's walk through a scenario: A group of 834 children attends a local fair about bike safety. Of these, $\frac{2}{3}$ say their parents have already talked to them about bike safety, and $\frac{1}{2}$ of those already own a bike helmet. How many children at the fair already own a bike helmet?

You start by telling yourself that the **whole** in this question is all 834 children who attend the fair. A part of the whole, $\frac{2}{3}$ of 834 ($\frac{2}{3} \times 834 = 556$), know about bike safety. This part, the 556 kids who know about bike safety, is then divided into two groups. Out of 556 kids, a part, $\frac{1}{2}$ of the 556 ($1/2 \times 556$), already own a bike helmet. This last calculation tells you 278 kids of the total group of 834 own bike helmets.

Figure 5.3 shows this problem in graphical form.

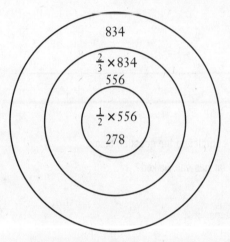

FIGURE 5.3   Pictures can help you think about fraction word problems.

Working with Fraction Word Problems

Practice working with fraction word problems by completing the questions below.

1. A total of 950 cars are on Hal's Used Car Lot. Of these, 1/5 will be sold this week. Of the remainder, 1/2 will need to be moved to the lot on the other side of the town. How many cars will remain at Hal's Used Car Lot?

    A. 95

    B. 190

    C. 380

    D. 475

    E. 760

2. Mike is working for a catering company this summer. Tonight 225 people will be attending a dinner. Of these people, 1/3 requested chicken for dinner and 1/5 asked for a vegetarian meal. How many people are having roast beef, the main dinner choice?

    F. 45

    G. 75

    H. 90

    J. 105

    K. 205

Correct answers:

1. The correct answer is C.

   First identify the whole. In this problem, the whole is 950. The part is 1/5. Multiply 950 either by 1/5 or by .20 to find out how many cars were sold this week.

   950 × .20 = 190 cars sold

   Now you will need to subtract 190 from 950 to see how many cars are on the lot now—the new whole that you will be working with.

   950 − 190 = 760 cars remain on the Lot.

   Half of these cars will be taken across town. Divide 760 by 1/2 to determine how many cars remain at Hal's Used Car lot:

   760/2 = 380 cars are left on Hal's lot.

2. The correct answer is J.

   First, identify the whole. In this problem, the whole is 225. Now identify the part. This problem has two parts, and the first is 1/3. Divide 225 by 1/3 to find out how many people requested a chicken dinner. The result is 75. Now divide 225 by 1/5 to find out how many people requested a vegetarian dinner. The result is 45.

   Add together the chicken and vegetarian dinner people (75 + 45) to find how many people did not order the beef dinner. The result is 120.

   Subtract this number from the whole (225) to find out how many people requested the roast beef dinner.

   The correct answer is 105.

Solving Equations Containing Fractions

The most efficient strategy for solving an equation that contains fractions is to find the least common multiple (LCM of the denominators) and then multiply every term on both sides of the equation by the LCM.

Look at the following:

$$\frac{(x-5)}{3} + \frac{(x-2)}{2} = 3 \text{ (The LCM of 3 and 2 is 6.)}$$

$$6 \cdot \frac{(x-5)}{3} + \frac{(x-2)}{2} = 3 \cdot 6$$

$$2(x-5) + 3(x-2) = 18$$

By multiplying every term on both sides of the equation by the LCM, 6, the equation is cleared of fractions. To finish solving, distribute and then isolate the variable. Finally, check the solution in the original equation.

Working with Equations Containing Fractions

Practice working with equations containing fractions by completing the questions below.

1. Solve: $\dfrac{(x+7)}{6} + \dfrac{(x-3)}{4} = 10$

   A. 5

   B. 12

   C. 15

   D. 20

   E. 23

2. Solve: $\dfrac{(x-6)}{9} + \dfrac{(x+3)}{2} = 4$

   F. 6 1/11

   G. 7

   H. 7 2/11

   J. 15

   K. 79

Correct answers:

1. The correct answer is E.

   $$\dfrac{(x+7)}{6} + \dfrac{(x-3)}{4} = 10$$

   Find the LCM, which is 12. Multiply every term on both sides of the equation by 12.

   $$12 \cdot \dfrac{(x+7)}{6} + \dfrac{(x-3)}{3} = 10 \cdot 12$$

   Solve for x:

   $$2(x+7) + 3(x-3) = 120$$

   $$2x + 14 + 3x - 9 = 120$$

   $$5x - 5 = 120$$

   $$5x = 115$$

   $$x = 23$$

2. The correct answer is H.

   $$\dfrac{(x-6)}{9} + \dfrac{(x+3)}{2} = 4$$

   Find the LCM, which is 18. Multiply every term on both sides of the equation by 18.

   $$18 \cdot \dfrac{(x-6)}{9} + \dfrac{(x+3)}{2} = 4 \cdot 18$$

   Solve for x:

   $$2(x-6) + 9(x+3) = 64$$

   $$2x - 12 + 9x + 27 = 64$$

$11x - 15 = 64$

$11x = 79$

$x = 79/11$

$x = 7\ 2/11$

TIP

Clearing fractions with cancellation can only be done with an equation that has an equals sign. Don't clear fractions when you see a "greater than" or "less than" sign.

Converting Fractions to Decimals

You may be asked to compare fractions that have different denominators. To do this, you can choose to find a common denominator and then assess which fraction is greater. In some cases, however, it may be quicker to convert each fraction to a decimal. To do this, divide the top number (the numerator) by the bottom number (the denominator) using your calculator. For example, 3/5 is 0.6. You can then compare the two decimals and assess which is greater.

Working with Converting Fractions to Decimals

Compare these fractions by changing each to a decimal:

1. 5/6 and 33/92
2. 4/9 and 11/13
3. 3/8 and 7/25
4. 9/11 and 4/5
5. 16/19 and 14/17

Correct answers:

1. 5/6 and 33/92 = .83333 and .3586: 5/6 is greater.
2. 4/9 and 11/13 = .4444 and .8461: 11/13 is greater.
3. 3/8 and 7/25 = .375 and .28: 3/8 is greater.
4. 9/11 and 4/5 = .8181 and .80: 9/11 is greater.
5. 16/19 and 14/17 = .8421 and .8235: 16/19 is greater.

TIP

Fractions that have 0 in the numerator (for example, 0/3) can be replaced with 0. If a fraction has a 0 in the denominator (for example, 3/0), the expression is undefined.

TIP

If you solve a problem but don't see your answer choice listed, check to see whether your answer can be expressed in a different form. For example, 1 3/5 can be expressed as 8/5 or 1.6.

Repeating Decimals

You can look at a fraction as a division problem. Sometimes the division can result in a repeating decimal, which is a digit or group of digits that repeat. To show this, a bar is placed over the digit or digits that repeat. For example, 0.3333... is represented by $0.\overline{3}$.

Consider this type of test question: Given the repeating decimal $0.0031\overline{543}$, where *543* is repeating, find the 40th digit. This problem will easily consume more than your rationed one minute of time if you take the typical approach of writing out all the digits. Instead, look for a pattern. In this example, after the first four digits, a pattern begins such that the 5 occurs at every third place. You know the 8th digit has to be 5. Counting by threes, you will find that the 8th, 11th, 14th, and every subsequent 3rd digit is also 5. The pattern predicts that the 38th digit is 5. Therefore, the 40th digit must be 3.

Percents

Like fractions, percents describe how a part relates to a whole. But in the case of a percent, the whole is always 100. This makes percents efficient to work with. The symbol % means "out of one hundred." Think of percents as a handy way to write fractions with a denominator of 100. For example, 50/100 is 50%. 25/100 is 25%.

A percent can also be converted to a decimal or fraction. Consider the following:

25% = 25/100 = .25
10% = 10/100 = .10
75% = 75/100 = .75

TIP

x% *of* a given number actually means *x*% multiplied by that number.

Knowing how to express percents in a different format can help you solve a problem more quickly. You may find a question on the test that asks you to calculate a percent of a whole. You can choose how you want to represent the percent. Sometimes $x/100$ is better; in other cases, you might choose to use a decimal. For example:

25% of $124.64

looks like this:

= .25 × $124.64
= $31.16
$31.16 = 25% × $124.64

Let's try another one. For instance, you may be asked to solve for any part of this general equation:

10.2 is x% of 50

To solve this, create an equation and then isolate x:

$10.2 = x\% \times 50$

$10.2/50 = x\%$

$0.204 = x\%$

$0.204 \times 100 = x/100 \times 100$

$20.4 = x$

The answer is 20.4%.

An element that might make these problems tricky is if the information is presented in a word problem. If that's the case, simply identify the pieces of information you are given: the part, the whole, and the percent.

You may also need to set up a proportion to solve percent problems like this: What number is 75% of 16? To solve the problem, you set up your proportion like this:

part/whole = percent/100

part/16 = 75/100

Then cross-multiply to get your answer.

$1200 = 100x$

$12 = x$

12 is 75% of 16.

Working with Percents

Practice working with percents by completing the question below.

3 is what percent of 4?

Correct answer:

part/whole = percent/100

3/4 = percent/100

$300 = 4x$

$75 = x$

3 is 75% of 4.

Percent Increase and Decrease

You may be asked on the test to find a percent increase or decrease when you are given two amounts, or you might be asked to increase or decrease another number by a certain percent. Here's the general rule to find percent change:

$$\text{percent change} = \frac{\text{amount of change}}{\text{original amount} \times 100\%}$$

Consider this problem: If taco output decreased from 23 to 8 on each manufacturing machine, what is the percent of decrease?

Find the change: 23 − 8 = 15

Use the rule: 15/23 = amount of change/original amount.

Simplify: 0.652

Express as a percent: $0.652 \times 100\%$

Answer: 65.2% decrease.

Working with Percent Increase and Decrease

Try these percent decrease problems, and then compare your answers to the correct responses below.

1. The school population in Baker City decreased from 560 to 524 this year. What is the percent decrease?

   A. 3.6%

   B. 7%

   C. 36%

   D. 70%

   E. 93%

2. Car production at one plant decreased from 16,500 to 14,000 last year. What is the percent decrease in production?

   F. 9%

   G. 15%

   H. 36%

   J. 75%

   K. 91%

Correct answers:

1. The correct answer is B.

   The school population in Baker City decreased from 560 to 524 this year. What is the percent decrease?

   First find the change: 560 − 524 = 36

   Now divide the amount of change by the original amount: 36 / 500. The answer is .07. Express this as a percent: 7%

2. The correct answer is F.

   Car production at one plant decreased from 16,500 to 14,000 last year. What is the percent decrease in production?

   First find the change: 16500 − 14000 = 1500

   Now divide the amount of the change by the original amount: 1500 / 16500. The answer is .09. Express this as a percent: 9%

Finding a Number Increased by a Percent

There may be a problem on the test asking you to find the result when a number is increased by a certain percent. For example, consider this question: If DVD player sales began at 200 per day and then increased by 40%, how many DVD players are currently being sold daily?

You could set up this problem like this:

200 + 200(40%) = new number of DVD players being sold

200 + 200 (.4)

200 + 80 = new number

280 = current daily sales

There is a quicker way to solve this problem, though. If you think of the current sales as 100% of the old, plus 40% more, the new sales are 140% of the old number. This logic can be set up as follows:

$200 \times 140\%$ = new number

200×1.4 = new number

280 = current daily sales

or set up a proportion:

percent / 100 = increase (or decrease) / original amount

40 / 100 = x / 200

$100x = 8000$

$x = 80$

Now consider this question: What is 15 increased by 30%? The most efficient way to calculate a percent increase is to add 100% to the percent you are given. Express the figure first as a decimal and then multiply the decimal by the number to get the increased number. The math involved looks like this:

$130\% \times 15$, to get 1.3×15

When 15 is increased by 30%, the new number is 19.5.

Working with Increasing by Percent

Practice increasing amounts by a percent by completing the questions below.

1. School pizza sales began at 320 slices per lunch period and have increased by 30% this year. How many slices are being sold now?

    A. 96

    B. 192

    C. 224

    D. 320

    E. 416

2. The price of Mack's home began at $78,000 and has increased 12% in the two years he has lived there. What is it worth now?

   F. $9,360

   G. $18,720

   H. $68,640

   J. $78,000

   K. $87,360

Correct answers:

1. The correct answer is E.

   To solve this problem, you may want to set up a proportion:

   percent / 100 = increase (or decrease) / original amount

   30% / 100 = x / 320

   x = 96

   Now add this to the original amount: 320 + 96 = 416

2. The correct answer is K.

   Set up a proportion:

   percent / 100 = increase (or decrease) / original amount

   12 / 100 = x / 78000

   x = 9360

   Make sure you add this figure to the original amount! 78,000 + 9,360= 87,360

Finding a Number Decreased by a Percent

There are different ways to solve a problem that involves a number decreased by a percent. Let's look at the following question: If the original number of exploding balloons, 180, is decreased by 45%, how many exploding balloons are there now? By reading the question, you know that 100% is being decreased by 45%. This means 55% of the balloons remain. Here's how to set up the problem:

$180 \times 55\%$ = new lower amount

$180 \times 0.55 = 99$

The new decreased amount is 99 balloons.

Now take a look at this question: After a 15% increase, the amoeba population is 345. What was the original amount? To answer this question, first set up an equation:

The entire original, plus 15% more, results in 115%. You know that $1.15 \times x = 345$.

Solving for x equals 300.

Working with Decreasing by a Percent

Practice decreasing numbers by a percent by completing the questions below.

1. After a 25% increase, taxes are now $625 annually. What was the original tax amount?

   A. $125.00

   B. $250.00

   C. $500.00

   D. $625.00

   E. $800.00

2. After a 25% increase in prices, candy bars are now $1.25. What was the original price?

   F. $ .75

   G. $ .95

   H. $ .99

   J. $1.00

   K. $1.20

Correct answers:

1. The correct answer is C.

   The entire original, plus 25% more, results in 125%. You know that $1.25 \times x = 625$.

   625 / 1.25 = 500

   The original tax amount was $500.

2. The correct answer is J.

   The entire original, plus 25% more, results in 125%. You know that $1.25 \times x = 1.25$.

   1.25 / 1.25 = 1

   The original price was $1.00.

Multiple Percent Increase and Decrease

Observing the pattern that results when you substitute simple numbers can often save you time. You can apply the changes in the question to the number 100, which makes for easy percent calculations, to determine the net effect. Consider this question: If the price of border collies increased 15% the first year and 25% the second year, what was the total percent increase after 2 years? You would solve this problem like this:

$100 \times 115\% = 115$ (first year)

$115 \times 125\% = 143.75$ (second year)

$\frac{43.75}{100} \times 100\% = 43.75\%$

The amount of net increase is 43.75%.

Working with Multiple Percent Increase and Decrease

Practice working with situations where there is more than one percent increase or decrease by completing the questions below.

1. If the price of oil increased 8% one year and 11% the next year, what was the total increase after two years?

   A. 11%

   B. 19%

   C. 19.88%

   D. 108%

   E. 119.88%

2. The dry cleaner raised his price 5% last year and plans to raise it 7% next month. What will be the total increase?

   F. 5%

   G. 5.35%

   H. 9%

   J. 12%

   K. 12.35%

Correct answers:

1. The correct answer is C.

   $100 \times 108\% = 108$ (first year)

   $108 \times 111\% = 119.88$ (second year)

   $\frac{19.88}{100} \times 100\% = 19.88\%$

2. The correct answer is K.

   $100 \times 105\% = 105$ (first increase)

   $105 \times 107\% = 112.35$ (second increase)

   $\frac{12.35}{100} \times 100\% = 12.35\%$

Rate Problems

It's very likely that you'll encounter a rate problem on the math test. These problems will probably use one of the three equations below:

▶ Distance = Rate × Time

▶ $\text{Rate}_{first} \times \text{Time}_{first} + \text{Rate}_{second} \times \text{Time}_{second} = \text{Jobs Accomplished}$

▶ Rate × Time × Number of Workers = Jobs Accomplished

Consider the following question: Dharma drives roundtrip from her home to a small town in South Dakota. She completes the 300-mile trip in 6 hours. If she decides to drive 10 miles an hour faster on the return trip, how much time can she save?

To decipher this problem, draw a chart with information from both speed scenarios, like the one in Figure 5.4.

Distance = Rate × Time

Trip up	300	can calculate	6
Trip back	300	R + 10	?

FIGURE 5.4 Organizing information in a chart can clarify rate problems.

Because Dharma drives roundtrip, you know that the second trip is also 300 miles. It's easier to see when the chart is filled in that it's possible to calculate Dharma's original rate. Solving for R in the equation

$$300 \text{ miles} = R \times 6 \text{ hours}$$

means R must be 50 miles/hour. If she increases her speed by 10 mph, her rate on the return trip must be 50 mph + 10, or 60 mph. Now, solve for T in the second equation, where the new R is plugged in:

$$300 = 60 \text{ miles/hour} \times T$$

T is 5 hours. However, do not choose 5 for your answer! The question asks how much time she will save, so compare 6 hours and 5 hours to see that Dharma will save 1 hour. Therefore, the answer is 1 hour.

Functions

A *function* maps a set of input values to set of output values in such a way that each input value produces only one output value. A function must do the following:

▶ Contain one variable, x.

▶ Produce only one output value for any replacement value of x.

For example, $y = x + 3$ is a function. For any replacement value of x, there is only one y.

The notation we use for functions replaces the y with $f(x)$, $g(x)$, or $h(x)$. The notation $f(x) = x^2 - 2$ reads "f of x equals x squared minus two." As you work on these types of problems, remember that functions have both a domain and a range. The *domain* is the set of acceptable replacement values for x. The *range* is the set of possible outcomes for $f(x)$.

> **TIP**
>
> If you find that you confuse the difference between *domain* and *range*, remember two cousins, DIX and ROY. DIX stands for domain, input, and *x* values, whereas ROY stands for range, output, and *y* values.

> **TIP**
>
> We cannot use replacement values for x that require taking the square root of a negative number or division by 0. Replacement values that would result in either must be excluded from the domain. For example, if $f(x) = \sqrt{(8 - x)}$, then we must exclude a value such as 9 that would require taking the square root of a negative number. Therefore, the domain of this function is any real number where $x \le 8$.

The math test may require you to evaluate a function for a specific value of *x* and to combine functions. Evaluating a function is essentially the same as evaluating an expression. In the functional notation, the number inside the parentheses gives the replacement value for *x*. Compare the following:

$$f(-2) = x^2 - 2 \qquad \text{Evaluate } x^2 - 2 \text{ if } x = -2$$
$$= (-2)^2 - 2 \qquad\qquad\qquad = (-2)^2 - 2$$
$$= 4 - 2 \qquad\qquad\qquad\qquad = 4 - 2$$
$$= 2 \qquad\qquad\qquad\qquad\qquad = 2$$

You might also see a more advanced problem such as this: If $f(x) = 3x + 3$, find $f(\frac{a + 3}{3})$. To solve this problem, replace every instance of *x* with $(\frac{a + 3}{3})$.

$$f(\frac{a + 3}{3}) = 3 \cdot \{(\frac{a + 3}{3}) + 3$$
$$= (a + 3) + 3$$
$$= a + 6$$

You also need to know how to combine functions. You can add, subtract, multiply, divide, and find the composition of functions. Refer to Table 5.5 to see how to perform the four basic operations with two distinct functions, given the following:

$$f(x) = x + 3 \text{ and } g(x) = x^2 + 2$$

TABLE 5.5   Adding, Subtracting, Multiplying, and Dividing with Fractions

Operation	Explanation	Result
Find $(f + g)(x)$	To add the functions, combine like terms.	$= x^2 + x + 5$
Find $(f - g)(x)$	To subtract $g(x)$ from $f(x)$, subtract like terms.	$= x + 3 - (x^2 + 2)$ $= -x^2 + x + 1$
Find $(fg)(x)$	To multiply functions, multiply their expressions.	$= (x + 3) \cdot (x^2 + 2)$ $= x^3 + 3x^2 + 3x + 6$
Find $(f / g)(x)$	To express this as a quotient, place the first function's expression in the numerator and the second function's in the denominator.	$= (\frac{x + 3}{x^2 + 2})$

Note that when you find the composition of two functions, one function's expression serves as the input for the other function. There are two notations for composition: $f[g(x)]$ and $(f \circ g)(x)$. In both the notations given, $g(x)$ serves as the input for $f(x)$.

If we use the preceding functions, $f(x) = x + 3$ and $g(x) = x^2 + 2$, we can find both $(f \circ g)(x)$ and $(g \circ f)(x)$. To find $(f \circ g)(x)$, replace every x in $f(x)$ with the expression of $g(x)$, $(x^2 + 2)$:

$$(f \circ g)(x) = (x^2 + 2) + 3$$

To find $(g \circ f)(x)$, replace every x in $g(x)$ with the expression of $f(x)$, $x + 3$. Then simplify:

$$(g \circ f)(x) = (x + 3)^2 + 2$$
$$= (x + 3)(x + 3) + 2$$
$$= x^2 + 6x + 9 + 2$$
$$= x^2 + 6x + 11$$

Notice that $(f \circ g)(x)$ is not the same as $(g \circ f)(x)$.

Probability

You may encounter problems related to determining the possible outcomes of a particular situation. These will require that you predict the number of ways an event may occur given a particular number of choices.

Probability questions involve determining the likelihood that an event will occur by setting up the ratio of desired outcomes to possible outcomes. Probability is defined so that the probability of any event must be 0, 1, or a value between 0 and 1.

Fundamental Counting Principle

If a customer purchasing a sandwich can choose between three different types of bread, three different cheeses, and five kinds of sauce, how many possible sandwiches can be made? Use the *fundamental counting principle* to solve these types of problems. This principle states that if one event can occur in m ways and a second event can occur in n ways, then the total number of ways for the two events to occur is $m \times n$. If we apply this to our sandwich question, the first event, choosing bread, can occur in three ways; the second event, choosing cheese, can occur in three ways; and the third event, choosing sauce, can occur among five ways. Multiplying $3 \times 3 \times 5$, we see that 45 different sandwiches can be made.

Permutations and Combinations

Permutation and combination problems ask about items that can be arranged or selected. They are simply a more abstract application of the counting principle. Students have a tendency to confuse these two words. When you calculate a *permutation*, order is important; all arrangements are included. When you calculate a *combination*, on the other hand, order is not important, and an extra calculation is required to eliminate arrangements that repeat.

To find a combination, first calculate the permutation and then divide by the permutation of the number of items you're choosing in order to eliminate repetition. Of course, the ACT question will not have a sentence that tells you whether order is important. You have to look at the context of the problem to make that call.

For any permutation or combination problem, use the following approach:

▶ Determine whether order is important.

▶ Apply the counting principle.

▶ If order is not important, divide by the permutation of the number of items being chosen to eliminate repetition.

Working with Permutation

Let's look at a permutation question to see how the counting principle applies:

In a city baseball tournament, nine different teams show up to compete. If there will be an award for first, second, third, and fourth place, how many ways can the teams place?

Order is definitely important in this context.

Apply the counting principle to solve the problem. There are nine choices for first place. But for second place, one team has already been assigned to a spot, so there are only eight choices. For third place, there are only seven teams left to assign. And by the time we get to fourth place, there are only six teams to choose from. When you multiply $9 \times 8 \times 7 \times 6$, you get 3,024. The answer is that there are 3,024 ways that the teams may place.

Working with Order and Combination

Now, let's look at a combination question:

You get to choose five beads to go with a bracelet-making kit as part of a craft store promotion. If the store provides 25 different beads for you to choose from, how many different ways can you choose?

First, determine whether order is important in this context. In this problem, it does not matter which bead you choose first because they will all wind up in the same bag.

Second, apply the counting principle. Given that you have five opportunities to choose a bead, figure out how many choices you have for each event. The first time you choose a bead, there are 25 to choose from. The second time you choose, there are only 24 to choose from. Continuing this logic leads to multiplying $25 \times 24 \times 23 \times 22 \times 21$.

Because order is not important, you must divide by the permutation of five items in order to eliminate repetition. The number of ways you can choose five items is $5 \times 4 \times 3 \times 2 \times 1$, or 120.

The final answer is the number of ways to choose 5 out of 25 divided by the number of ways to choose 5:

$$= \frac{(25 \times 24 \times 23 \times 22 \times 21)}{(5 \times 4 \times 3 \times 2 \times 1)}$$

$$= \frac{6,375,600}{120}$$

$$= 53,130$$

You may choose to use formulas to solve permutation and combination problems; however, this requires extra memorization. The formulas for each follow:

Permutation:

$$_nP_r = \frac{n!}{(n-r)!}$$

Combination:

$$_nC_r = \frac{n!}{(n-r)!\,r!}$$

Here, r is the number of items selected, and n is the number of items to choose from.

Probability Rules

Here are the four main rules you should consider when working through probability questions:

- ▸ The probability of an outcome equals the number of desired outcomes divided by the number of possible outcomes.

- ▸ The probability of an outcome is always between 0 and 1, inclusive.

- ▸ If one event or another must occur, the probability of one outcome plus the probability of the other outcome is 1.

- ▸ To find the probability of successive independent events, multiply the probability of each event. *Independent* events do not affect each other's outcomes.

Consider the following question: If a marble is chosen randomly from a box that contains seven rainbow marbles, five clear marbles, and nine black marbles, what is the probability that the marble will *not* be black?

First, consider that it is certain that the marble chosen either is black or is not black. This means the probability of the marble being black and the probability of the marble *not* being black add to 1. You can find the probability that the marble will be black and then subtract from 1 to get the probability that the marble will *not* be black:

Probability the marble will be black: $\frac{9}{21}$

Probability the marble will *not* be black: $1 - \frac{9}{21}$

Probability the marble will *not* be black: $\frac{12}{21}$

Working with Probability

Practice working with probability by completing the questions below.

1. Tex earned 85, 78, 90, and 88 points on four different tests. How many points does he need to earn on the fifth test, if each of the tests is worth 100 points, in order to average 88 for all five tests?

   A. 85.25

   B. 85.8

   C. 88

   D. 99

   E. 100

2. Which value of x satisfies the following equation?

   $-2(x + 4) = 3(x - 2)$

   F. -2

   G. -2/5

   H. 6/5

   J. 14/5

   K. 2

3. If 18 baskets cost $99.00, what is the cost of three baskets?

   A. $2.00

   B. $5.50

   C. $6.00

   D. $16.50

   E. $33.00

Correct answers:

1. The correct answer is D. The sum of the four scores earned so far is 341. The definition of average leads to the following equation:

   $$\frac{341 + x}{5} = 88$$

   Solving for x leads to $341 + x = 88 \cdot 5$ and $x = 440 - 341$. Therefore, the answer is 99. You might also use common sense to determine that the answer should be 99. Of the four test scores, three are 88 or lower. One score is substantially lower. Only a score much higher than 88 can produce an average of 88.

2. The correct answer is G. First, simplify both sides by distributing. The result is $-2x - 8 = 3x - 6$. Isolate the variable by combining x terms on one side and constant terms on the other side to get $-2 = 5x$. Dividing both sides by 5 gives the answer $-2/5$.

3. The correct answer is D. You can set up a proportion to solve this problem as follows:

   $$\frac{18}{\$99.00} = \frac{3}{\$x}$$

   Cross-multiplying produces $18 \cdot \$x = 3 \cdot \$99$. Dividing both sides by 18 to isolate x results in $\$x = \frac{\$297}{18}$. The answer is $16.50.

Ratio, Proportion, Mean, Median, Mode

A *ratio* is a comparison. On this portion of the test, it is likely that the ratios you will see are expressed as fractions. For example, if the ratio of boys to girls in a school is 5 to 3, this can be expressed as

$$\frac{5 \text{ boys}}{3 \text{ girls}}$$

If the ratio of girls to boys in a school is 3 to 5, this can be expressed as

$$\frac{3 \text{ girls}}{5 \text{ boys}}$$

The order in which items appear in a ratio is important. Whichever word comes first in the statement will come first in the ratio. Note also that two ratios that are equal form a *proportion*. The easiest ratio questions are word problems that require you to set up a proportion. Consider the following problem: A scale drawing showing the new dimensions of a kitchen is 7"/10". If you know the longer side of the kitchen is 20", how long is the shorter side?

TIP

You may see that the language varies directly or varies inversely on the test. If x varies directly with y, the resulting equation is $x = k \cdot y$, where k is some constant. The equation implies that as x grows larger, y grows larger. If x varies inversely with y, the resulting equation is $x = \frac{k}{y}$ This equation implies that as x gets larger, y gets smaller.

We can set up a proportion to solve this problem. A common mistake is to put the numbers in the incorrect places when building a proportion. To prevent this, mark a corresponding letter to show what each number represents, as done here with *short* and *long*. To solve the proportion, cross-multiply:

$$\frac{7" \text{ short}}{10" \text{ long}} = \frac{x' \text{ short}}{20' \text{ long}}$$

$7 \times 20 = 10 \times x$ (Cross-multiply.)

$140 = 10x$ (Solve for x.)

$14 = x$

Now consider this example: A class is made up of 8 girls and 11 boys. If the teacher wants to create a larger class of 38 students with the same ratio of boys and girls, how many girls should she include?

NOTE

An exam question might give you the quantity of two parts that make up a whole but then expect you to use ratios of one of the parts compared to the whole.

In this case, the question asks about girls. If there are 19 students in the original class (boys + girls), the original ratio of girls to the class is 8/19. The resulting proportion is this:

8 girls/19 class = x girls/38 class

Because x must be 16, that many girls should be in the new class.

Working with Ratio and Proportion

Practice working with ratio and proportion by completing the questions below.

1. In a forest area, the ratio of raccoons to squirrels is 16 to 9. How many of 300 of these small animals are squirrels?

   A. 12

   B. 34

   C. 78

   D. 108

   E. 192

2. In a certain teacher's drivers ed class, the ratio of passing students to nonpassing students is 7 to 5. How many of 48 recent drivers ed students didn't pass?

   F. 12

   G. 20

   H. 28

   J. 36

   K. 41

Correct answers:

1. The correct answer is D.

   The ratio tells us that of every (16 + 9) 25 small animals, 9 are squirrels. So the ratio of squirrels to the total is 9/25.

   Set up a proportion to multiply 9/25 × the total 300/1.

   There are 108 squirrels.

2. The correct answer is G.

   The ratio tells us that of every (7 + 5) 12 students in the class, 5 did not pass. So 5/12 of the students did not pass.

   Set up a proportion to multiply 5/12 × the total 48/1.

   The result is that 20 students failed.

Mean, Median, and Mode—An Overview

You might be asked to interpret data (for example, temperatures from a particular area, test scores, rate of speed) by finding the mean, the median, or the mode. In simple terms, these are defined as follows:

- ▶ **Mean**—The average
- ▶ **Median**—The value in the middle of a set of numbers when the numbers are written in order from least to greatest
- ▶ **Mode**—The value occurring most frequently in a set of numbers

NOTE

If there are two numbers in the middle of a number set, find the median by dividing them by two. For example, in the set (2, 3, 4, 5, 6, 7) both 4 and 5 are in the middle. The median is 4 1/2 or 4.5.

NOTE

There can be more than one mode in a set of numbers. For example, in the set (23, 44, 33, 33, 44, 27) the modes are 33 and 44, both of which appear twice.

Working with Mean, Median, and Mode

Practice working with mean, median, and mode by completing the question below.

In a particular class of 15 students, the years each student has attended the school vary greatly: (3, 5, 2, 2, 15, 15, 2, 13, 9, 9, 1, 3, 6, 4, 14). Find the mean, median, and mode of this set.

First, order the number set from least to greatest:

(1, 2, 2, 2, 3, 3, 4, 5, 6, 7, 9, 9, 13, 14, 14, 15, 15)

MEAN: To find the mean, add all the numbers together and divide by the total number of students (15). 105 / 15 = 7.

The mean (average) is 7 years.

MEDIAN: This is the number appearing in the middle. Since there are 15 numbers listed, the median will be the average of the seventh and eighth numbers.

7th number = 4

8th number = 5

Median = $\frac{(4 + 6)}{2}$ = 5 years.

MODE: To find the mode, identify the value that occurs most frequently in the set.

In this set, the number 2 appears four times, so 2 years is the mode.

Solving Problems Involving Finding the Mean

The formula for finding the mean is as follows:

$$\frac{\text{sum of the numbers}}{\text{total numbers in the set}}$$

For example, assume that you have scored the following grades on science tests worth 100 points in the first quarter: 85, 99, 81, 75, and 93. What is the mean of these scores? The *mean* of these test scores is (85 + 99 + 81 + 75 + 93) / 5, which simplifies to 86.6.

Now consider this question: Sandra is walking to school. If she walks the first 10 miles at 5 mph and the second 10 miles at 8mph, what is her average speed? If a question asks for the overall average, the answer is not the average of the averages. Instead, find the total distance and the total time, because

rate = distance / time

In this case, applying the formula results in a time of 2 hours for the first portion and $1\frac{1}{4}$ hours for the second portion. The total distance is 20 miles and the total time is $3\frac{1}{4}$ hours. The answer is 20 miles / $3\frac{1}{4}$ hours, or $6\frac{2}{13}$ mph.

Working with Problems Involving Finding the Mean

Practice working with finding the mean by completing the question below.

A driver goes 120 miles. For the first 30 miles, he drives 60 mph. For the next 90 miles, he drives 30 mph. What is his average speed for the trip?

A. 34.28 mph

B. 45.30 mph

C. 50 mph

D. 60.42 mph

E. 70 mph

Correct answer:

The correct answer is A.

To solve, first find the distance for each segment of the trip:

Rate = distance / time

60 / 1 = 30 / x

x = 1/2 hour for the first part of the trip

Rate = distance / time

30 / 1 = 90 / x

x = 3 hours for the second part of the trip

The total distance is 120 miles and the total time is 3 1/2 hours. The answer is 120 miles / 3 1/2 hours, or 34.28 mph.

Solving Problems Involving Finding the Median

The *median* is the value in the middle of the data set after the set has been arranged in order from least to greatest. For instance, in the set {1, 2, 3, 4, 5} the median is the number 3. It is in the middle of the set.

TIP

The word *median* may cause you to think of the grassy section that divides some four-lane highways. This may help you remember what the word means in math: a statistical median—the value in the middle of a data set when the numbers are arranged from least to greatest.

Here's how to find the median in a set of data:

1. Order the data from least to greatest (smallest to largest number).

2. Determine the number (or numbers) directly in the middle of the set. Ensure that there is an equal number of values on either side.

3. If there are two numbers in the middle, find their average. (Add them together and divide by 2.)

TIP

A data set with an odd number of items will have one middle value.
A data set with an even number of items will have two middle values.

Consider the following set of data made up of history test scores: {88, 77, 65, 85, 93, 85, 97, 100}. Assume that you have been asked to find the median. To do this, first arrange the scores in ascending (smallest to largest) order. Be careful as you do this. If you accidentally forget to copy each score, your data will change significantly:

65, 77, 85, 85, 88, 93, 97, 100

The scores in the middle are 85 and 88; so the median is the average of 85 and 88, which is 86.5.

Working with Problems Involving Finding the Median

Practice working with finding the median by completing the questions below.

1. What is the median of the following measurements of windows in a dollhouse?

   (2", 2.5", 1.5", 3", .05", 2.5", 1")

   A. 1"

   B. 1.5"

   C. 2"

   D. 2.5"

   E. 3"

2. What is the median of this set of data?

(2/3, 4/7, 1 1/2, 1/2, 3/4, 1 1/2, 1/2, 2/3)

F. 2/3

G. 4/7

H. 1 1/2

J. 3/4

K. 1/2

Correct answers:

1. The correct answer is C.

(2", 2.5", 1.5", 3", .05", 2.5", 1")

First order the data from least to greatest:

(.05", 1", 1.5", 2", 2.5", 2.5", 3")

There are seven items in the set, so the fourth item is the median.

2. The correct answer is F.

(2/3, 4/7, 1 1/2, 1/2, 3/4, 1 1/2, 1/2, 2/3)

First order the data from least to greatest:

You will have to do some calculations to see whether 2/3 or 4/7 is the smaller of the two fractions. Either convert both to decimals or find a common denominator.

(1/2, 4/7, 2/3, 2/3, 3/4, 1 1/2, 1 1/2)

Now count the number of items in the data set (7).

The median is the fourth item: 2/3

Solving Problems Involving Finding the Mode

You find the *mode* of a data set by determining the most frequent value—that is, the number that appears more than any other. To find the mode, you would do the following:

1. Arrange the numbers in the set in order by size.

2. Determine the number of instances of each numerical value. The numerical value that has the greatest number of instances is the *mode*. Note that there may be more than one mode when two or more numbers have an equal number of instances, and a mode does not exist if no number has more than one instance.

Consider the following data set of history test scores: {88, 77, 65, 85, 93, 85, 97, 100}. To find the mode, first arrange the data set in order: {65, 77, 85, 85, 88, 93, 97, 100}. Once these are in order, it's easy to see that the most frequently occurring value is 85. Thus, the mode of this data set is 85.

> **TIP**
>
> Don't try to find the mode by just glancing at the data set. You can easily miss an instance of a variable and come up with the wrong mode.

Working with Problems Involving Finding the Mode

Practice working with finding the mode by completing the questions below.

1. What is the mode in this data set? (2", 2.5", 1.5", 3", .05", 2.5", 1")

    A. no mode

    B. 1.5"

    C. 2"

    D. 2.5"

    E. 3"

2. What is the mode in this data set? (2/3, 4/7, 1 1/2, 1/2, 3/4, 1 1/2, 1/2, 2/3)

    F. 2/3 and 1/2

    G. 2/3 and 1 1/2

    H. 1/2 and 1 1/2

    J. 1 1/2

    K. no mode

Correct answers:

1. The correct answer is D.

    First order the data from least to greatest:

    (.05", 1", 1.5", 2", 2.5", 2.5", 3")

    You can see that there are two instances of the variable 2.5". This is the mode.

2. The correct answer is G.

    First order the data from least to greatest:

    (1/2, 1/2, 4/7, 2/3, 2/3, 3/4, 1 1/2, 1 1/2)

    You can see that there are two instances of the variables 1/2, 2/3, and 1 1/2. There are three modes for this set of data.

Algebraic Expressions

When ideas are expressed in mathematical terms, the result is an algebraic expression. Algebraic expressions can contain both numbers and letters. Algebraic expressions can take several forms. Here are some examples:

▶ xst

▶ y

▶ $(6 + 3a)$

▶ x^2

▶ xy

▶ $7a \,/\, y$

▶ z

The math test will ask you to evaluate and simplify algebraic expressions. You will learn how to do just that in this part of the chapter.

Order of Operations

When you're facing a lengthy expression containing a variety of operations and symbols of inclusion, it is important that you perform the operations in the correct order. When performing multiple operations within an equation, it is important to follow this order. Using any other order can create an incorrect answer. Thus, you should use these steps when working with order of operations:

1. First, do what is within the parentheses (if any).

2. Next, work with any exponents that may be present in the equation.

3. Now go from left to right and perform multiplication and division as needed.

4. Next, do addition and subtraction from left to right within the equation.

To test yourself, consider the following problem:

$$2^2 - 3 \times (5 - 2)^2 + 2 \div 2$$

If you use the correct order of operations, your equation should simplify as follows:

$$2^2 - 3 \times (3)^2 + 2 \div 2$$
$$4 - 3 \times 9 + 2 \div 2$$
$$4 - 27 + 1 = -22$$

Working with Operations

Check your understanding of operations by working through the following problems.

1. How would this equation be simplified?

   $$3^3 - 4 \times (4)^2 + 2(2y)$$

   A. $-55 + 4y$

   B. $64 + 2y$

   C. $37 + 4y$

   D. $-37 + 4y$

   E. $55 + 4y$

2. How would this equation be simplified?

$6y - 3 (4 + y) + 6$

F. $2y + 6$

G. $9y - 6$

H. $2 (y - 3)$

J. $3y - 6$

K. $15y$

Correct answers:

1. The correct answer is D.

$3^3 - 4 \times (4)^2 + 2(2y)$

Parentheses: $3^3 - 4 \times (16 + 4y)$

Exponent: $27 - 4 \times (16 + 4y)$

Multiplication and division: $27 - 64 + 4y$

Addition and subtraction: $37 + 4y$

2. The correct answer is G.

$6y - 3 (4 + y) + 6$

Parentheses: $6y - 12 + 3y + 6$

Exponent: none here

Multiplication and division: none here

Addition and subtraction: $9y - 6$

Evaluating Expressions

Evaluating algebraic expressions means doing what is directed within the parentheses. These types of problems are similar to following a recipe because you work on it step by step and in a precise order.

When plugging in replacement values, always enclose the value being inserted with parentheses. Forgetting to include parentheses as you work to solve the problem can cause confusion with positive and negative numbers.

Consider this problem: The formula that relates the Fahrenheit and Celsius temperature scales is $F = \frac{9}{5C} + 32$, where F is degrees Fahrenheit and C is degrees Celsius. What is the temperature in Fahrenheit if the temperature in Celsius is 45°?

The problem directs you to replace C with 45°. Plug in 45° and then work out the answer by performing the operations given, being sure to apply the rules of the order of operations:

$$F = \frac{9}{5(45)} + 32$$
$$= 81 + 13$$
$$= 113°$$

Here's another example: Tickets to the fair are \$5.75 for adults and \$3.50 for children. Buses pay a fee of \$9.50 to park in the fair parking lot. A class of 15 children and 6 adults will arrive at the fair in three buses today. Calculate the bill the class will be charged. Note that tax on each ticket is 3%.

6 (\$5.75) + 15 (\$3.50) =

\$34.50 + \$52.50 = \$87.00

\$87.00 × 3% = \$2.61

\$87.00 + \$2.61 = \$89.61

Bus fee: \$9.50 × 3 = \$28.50

Total bill: \$89.61 + \$28.50 = \$118.11

Adding and Subtracting Like Terms

Like terms have the same variables in the same form, but not necessarily in the same order. *3a* and *5a* are like terms, for example, and so are *5xy/b* and *3xy/b*.

Notice the two parts to each of the preceding sets of terms: the number in front, called the *coefficient*, and the variables. To add or subtract like terms, you add or subtract their coefficients.

Consider these two examples:

$3x + 5x + -10x = (3 + 5 + -10)x = -2x$

$4p/ry - 3p/yr = (4 - 3)p/ry$

And this example as well:

$(2x^2 + 5x + 3) + (5x^2 + 5)$

$= (2 + 5)x^2 + 5x + (3 + 5)$

$= 7x^2 + 5x + 8$

If multiplied terms are listed in different orders, you may write the terms in your answer in any order.

Now try this example:

Simplify the following:

$(2x^2 + 5x + 3) - (3x^2 + 5)$

Make sure you distribute the negative before combining like terms. You can insert a 1 after the minus sign to help you remember to do so. Given

$(2x^2 + 5x + 3) - 1(3x^2 + 5)$

you can simplify to

$2x^2 + 5x + 3 - 3x^2 - 5$

The answer is $-1x^2 + 5x - 2$.

Working with Simplifying Equations

Practice working with simplifying equations by completing the questions below.

1. How can this equation be simplified?

   $(6x^2 + 9x - 1) - 2(3x + x^2)$

   A. $4x^2 + 3x - 1$

   B. $7x^2 + 1$

   C. $4x^2 - 3x - 1$

   D. $7x^2 - 1$

   E. $8x^2 + 3x - 1$

2. How can this equation be simplified?

   $(6x^2 + 4xy + 2) - y(x + 3)$

   F. $6x^2 - 3xy - 3y + 2$

   G. $3x^2 + 3xy - 3y + 2$

   H. $3x^2 - 3xy - 3y + 2$

   J. $6x^2 + 3xy - 3y + 2$

   K. $6x^2 + 3xy - 3y - 2$

Correct answers:

1. The correct answer is C.

   $(6x^2 + 9x - 1) - 2(3x + x^2)$

   First multiply the −2 by the variables in the parentheses:

   $(6x^2 + 9x - 1) - 6x - 2x^2)$

   Combine like terms:

   $6x^2 + 9x - 1 - 6x - 2x^2$

   $4x^2 - 3x - 1)$

2. The correct answer is J.

   $(6x^2 + 4xy + 2) - y(x + 3)$

   First multiply the −y by the variables in the parentheses. Remember that the −y is actually −1y.

   $6x^2 + 4xy + 2 - yx - 3y$

   Combine like terms:

   $6x^2 + 3xy - 3y + 2$

Multiplying Expressions with Variables

Whenever you multiply expressions that contain both numbers and variables, you must multiply the variables and the numbers separately: number times number and variable times variable. Multiplying variables often requires you to apply the rules of exponents.

Here are two examples:

$$3a \times 5a = (3 \times 5)(a \times a) = 15a^2$$

$$3xy \times 4rsy/x = (3 \times 4)(xy \times rsy/x) = 12rsy^2$$

> **TIP**
>
> Apply the distributive property to variables in the same way you do with numbers—for instance, $a(b + c) = ab + ac$.

Multiplying Polynomials $(a + b)(x + y)$

Polynomial is the name given to any term or sum of terms meeting the following criteria:

- All variables have whole number exponents.

- No variable appears in the denominator.

So $6x^2 - 8x + 5xy + 3$ is a polynomial, but $1/6x^2 + 5$ is NOT a polynomial.

The easiest way to multiply polynomials is to use the FOIL method. *FOIL* is an acronym that provides the order in which you must multiply terms in a polynomial. The letters stand for First, Outer, Inner, Last.

To get a feel for using FOIL, multiply the following polynomial:
$(3x + 2) \times (2x \times 6)$

> *First terms*: Multiply together the first terms in each set of parentheses. In this case: $3x \times 2x = 6x^2$
>
> *Outer terms*: Now multiply the outer terms. The first and last terms shown here are considered to be the outer terms: $3x \times (6) = 18x$
>
> *Inner terms*: Now multiply together the inner terms. The two inside terms here are considered the inner terms: $2 \times 2x = 4x$
>
> *Last terms*: The last terms are the last ones in each set of parentheses: $2 \times (6) = 12$
>
> Now combine like terms: $6x^2 + 18x + 4x + 12$.
>
> The answer is $6x^2 + - 22x + 12$.

Let's try another one: Simplify $(3x + 2)^2$. Do not square each individual term. This problem simplifies to $(3x + 2) \times (3x + 2)$. You can then use the FOIL method to solve it:

> First: $(3x \times 3x) = 9x^2$
>
> Outer: $3x \times 2 = 6x$
>
> Inner: $2 \times 3x = 6x$
>
> Last: $2 \times 2 = 4$
>
> Now combine like terms $(9x^2 + 6x + 6x + 4)$ to get $9x^2 + 12x + 4$.

Working with Multiplying Polynomials

Practice working with these types of expressions by completing the questions below.

1. How would this polynomial be multiplied?

   $(4x + 4)(2x - 7)$

   A. $8x^2 + 36x + 28$

   B. $8x^2 + 20x + 28$

   C. $8x^2 - 20x - 28$

   D. $8x^2 + 8x + 28$

   E. $8x^2 - 20x - 28$

2. How would this polynomial be multiplied?

   $(4x - 3y)(6x - 4)$

   F. $24x^2 - 16x - 18xy + 12y$

   G. $24x^2 + 16x - 18xy + 12y$

   H. $24x^2 - 16x + 18xy + 12y$

   J. $24x^2 - 16x - 18xy - 12y$

   K. $24x^2 - 16x + 18xy + 12y$

Correct answers:

1. The correct answer is C.

   Use the FOIL method: $(4x + 4)(2x - 7)$.

   First: $(4x \times 2x) = 8x^2$

   Outer: $(4x \times -7) = -28x$

   Inner: $(4 \times 2x) = 8x$

   Last: $(4 \times -7) = -28$

   Combine like terms: $8x^2 - 28x + 8x - 28 = 8x^2 - 20x - 28$

2. The correct answer is F.

   $(4x - 3y)(6x - 4)$

   First: $(4x \times 6x) = 24x^2$

   Outer: $(4x \times -4) = -16x$

   Inner: $(-3y \times 6x) = -18xy$

   Last: $(-3y - 4) = 12y$

   Combine like terms: $24x^2 - 16x - 18xy + 12y$

Factoring Algebraic Expressions

Just as 8 can be separated into its factors, 2, 4, and 8, algebraic expressions can be separated into factors. You can think of factoring as "undoing multiplication."

Factoring Out a Common Term

The first step in factoring any polynomial is to look for the greatest common factor (GCF) in each term. Keep in mind that not all polynomials have a common factor. However, if you can factor out a common term, go through the following steps:

1. Identify the GCF that is contained in *every* term.

2. Write the GCF outside a set of parentheses to denote that this is the term being factored out.

3. Divide each term in the polynomial by the GCF. Write the remaining terms inside the parentheses.

4. You can check your result by multiplying the factors back out using the distributive property.

Look at this equation: $15x^4 + 3x^2 + 12x$. Your first step is to identify the GCF. In this case, 3 is the largest number that 15, 3, and 12 can be divided by, and each variable can also be divided by $1x$. Thus, the GCF is $3x$, and the equation is written like this:

$$3x (5x^3 + x + 4)$$

You would then divide each term by the GCF.

Working with Factoring Algebraic Expressions

Practice factoring algebraic expressions by completing the questions below.

1. How can the following problem be factored?

   $25xy + 5x - 10$

   A. $5x (5xy + x + 2)$

   B. $x (25y + 5 - 10)$

   C. $5 (5xy - x - 2)$

   D. $5x (5xy - x + 2)$

   E. $5 (5xy + x - 2)$

2. How can the following problem be factored?

   $6xy^2 - 3x^2 y + x$

   F. $x (6y^2 - 3xy + 1)$

   G. $3 (2xy^2 - x2y + x)$

   H. $3x (2y^2 - 3xy + 1)$

   J. $x (6y^2 + 3xy + 1)$

   K. $x (6y^2 - 3xy)$

Correct answers:

1. The correct answer is E.

   Look at each variable to see that the greatest common factor is 5. None of the letters can be included in the GCF here, mainly because 10 doesn't have any letters included with it.

   Factor the 5 from each number to get the correct answer.

2. The correct answer is F.

   When you look at each part of this polynomial, you can see that only the x is a factor of all. Factor the x from each part of the polynomial to get the correct answer.

Factoring $x^2 + bx + c$

There is a specific strategy for factoring expressions in this format: $x^2 + bx + c$. Pay attention to the sign of c. If c is positive, its factors must be of the same sign. If c is negative, its factors must be of opposite signs.

Use the following steps to reduce this process to filling in the blanks:

1. Set up parentheses ( )( ).

2. Find the two magic numbers that add up to b, but whose product is c.

3. Write factors as $(x + \text{unknown number})(x + \text{unknown number})$.

Let's apply the steps to factor the following: $x^3 - x^2 - 12x$.

   First, factor out the GCF:

   $x(x^2 - x - 12)$

   Now, examine factors of 12:

   (12, 1, 6, 2, 4, 3)

   $x(\quad)(\quad)$

   −4 and 3 add up to −1, and they multiply to −12.

   $2x(x - 4)(x + 3)$

TIP

Remember that if you find yourself stumped on these types of problems, you can always begin to plug in each answer choice and see if you can come up with the correct response that way. One of the answer choices has to be correct.

Working with Factoring Equations

Practice working with these types of equations by completing the questions below.

1. How can the following equation be factored?

    $x^2 - 10x + 24$

    A. $(x + 6)\,(x + 4)$

    B. $(-x - 6)\,(x + 4)$

    C. $(x - 6)\,(x + 4)$

    D. $(x - 6)\,(x - 4)$

    E. $(x + 6)\,(x - 4)$

2. How can the following equation be factored?

    $x^2 - 14x - 51$

    F. $(x - 17)\,(x - 3)$

    G. $(x + 17)\,(x + 3)$

    H. $(x + 17)\,(x - 3)$

    J. $(x - 17)\,(x + 3)$

    K. $(x - 17)\,(-x + 3)$

Correct answers:

1. The correct answer is D.

    $x^2 - 10x + 24$

    First, see if there is a GCF to factor out. There isn't one here.

    Now, examine factors of 24:

    (2, 12, 6, 4, 3, 8)

    Think about which factors, when added together or subtracted, will produce a −10. You can probably see that it is the 6 and 4. Nothing else will work here.

    $(x - 6)\,(x - 4)$

    −6 and −4 add up to −10 and they multiply to +24.

2. The correct answer is J.

    $x^2 - 14x - 51$

    First, see if there is a GCF to factor out. There isn't one here.

    Now, examine factors of 51:

    (3, 17)

    Fortunately, there are only two factors and you can see that with the plus and minus signs correctly placed, we can form the −14x that is needed in the center of the equation.

    $(x - 17)\,(x + 3)$

    −17 and 3 add up to −14, and they multiply to −51.

The Difference of Two Squares

The difference of two squares is a common pattern in factoring that can save you a lot of time. The rule is as follows:

$$(a^2 - b^2) = (a + b) \times (a - b)$$

Consider $9x^2 - 16y^2$. When the square root of 9 and 16 is each factored out, this can be rewritten as $([3x]^2 - [4y]^2)$. The new expression easily factors into $(3x + 4y)(3x - 4y)$.

> **TIP**
>
> If you come across a complicated expression such as $(x^2 + x - 20) / (x^2 - x + 12)$, you might find a solution faster if you simplify by factoring. The expression factors to $[(x + 5)(x - 4)] / [(x + 3)(x - 4)]$, which simplifies to $(x + 5) / (x + 3)$ because the $(x - 4)$ terms cancel each other out. You will find that this is much easier to work with.

Working with Expressions Containing Squares

Practice factoring these types of expressions by completing the questions below.

1. How can the following expression be factored?

   $9x^2 - 16y^2$

   A. $(3x + 4y)(3x + 4y)$

   B. $(3x - 4y)(3x + 4y)$

   C. $(3x - 4y)(3x - 4y)$

   D. $(3x^2 - 4y)(3x + 4y)$

   E. $(3x^2 + 4y)(3x + 4y)$

2. How can the following expression be factored?

   $25x^2 - 100y2$

   F. $(5x - 10y)(5x + 10y)$

   G. $(5x - 10y)(5x - 10y)$

   H. $(5x^2 - 10y)(5x + 10y)$

   J. $(5x^2 - 10y)(5x - 10y)$

   K. $(5x^2 + 10y)(5x + 10y)$

Correct answers:

1. The correct answer is B.

   $9x^2 - 16y^2$

   It is important to remember the rule when solving these types of equations:

   $(a^2 - b^2) = (a + b) \times (a - b)$

   $(9x^2 - 16y^2) = (3x + 4y)(3x - 4y)$

2. The correct answer is F.

   $25x^2 - 100y2$

   It is important to remember the rule when solving these types of equations:

   $(a^2 - b^2) = (a + b) \times (a - b)$

   $(25x^2 - 100y2) = (5x - 10y)(5x + 10y)$

Solving Linear Equations

Think of an equation like a perfectly balanced scale. The quantities on both sides of the equation may not always look the same, but they have the same value, so the equation itself is balanced. Conversely, if you add an item to one side of a balanced scale without adding the same item to the other side, the scale will no longer be in balance. The same is true with equations: What you do to one side of an equation, you must do to the other side.

> **TIP**
>
> *Isolating* the variable means to maneuver the variable so that it is by itself on one side of the equals sign.

When solving for a variable, the goal is always to isolate the variable. Isolating the variable means to get it by itself on its own side of the equation. Both of the following manipulations are permitted while solving for a variable:

- Adding or subtracting the same quantity from both sides
- Multiplying or dividing both sides by the same quantity

The five steps to solving a linear equation are as follows:

1. Eliminate parentheses by distributing.

2. Simplify each side by adding all like terms.

3. Isolate the variable by getting all terms that contain the variable to the same side and then combining them.

4. Get all constant terms to the other side and then combine them.

5. Solve for the variable.

> **TIP**
>
> If an equation contains fractions or decimals, you might want to multiply every term in the equation by a number that would cause them to become integers. In that way, they will be easier to work with.

Apply the steps in Figure 5.5 to solve for x:

$$4(x - 3) + 2.5 = 2x + - 3(x + 2)$$

Eliminated parentheses

$$4x - 12 + 2.5 = 2x - 3x - 6$$

Simplified each side

$$4x - 9.5 = -1x - 6$$
$$+1x \qquad +1x$$

Got X terms together

$$5x - 9.5 = -6$$
$$+9.5 \quad +9.5$$

Moved constants to other side

$$5x = 3.5$$

Solved for X

$$x = \frac{3.5}{5}$$

$$x = 0.7$$

FIGURE 5.5 Follow these steps to solve a linear equation.

Solving for a Variable in Terms of Other Variables

When you are asked to solve an equation for one variable using other variables instead of numbers, the goal is still the same: Isolate the variable you are solving for. To do that, treat all the other variables as numbers and then use the same procedure.

For practice, solve for *h* in the following problem, as shown in Figure 5.6:

$$A = 1/2h(b_1 + b_2)$$

$$2 \cdot [A] = \left[\frac{1}{2}h(b_1 + b_2)\right] \cdot 2$$

$$\frac{[2A]}{(b_1 + b_2)} = \frac{\left[h(b_1 + b_2)\right]}{(b_1 + b_2)}$$

$$\frac{2A}{(b_1 + b_2)} = h$$

FIGURE 5.6 Solving for a variable in terms of other variables.

Because you are asked to solve for h, you need to isolate h. Treat all the other variables as if they are numbers.

Solving Systems of Linear Equations

Sometimes you might see a question that asks you to consider two or three linear equations at once. These "system of equations" problems ask you to find the solution that makes all given equations true. For our purposes, we will work with three methods for solving a system of equations:

▶ Substitution

▶ Elimination

▶ Graphing

First, we'll look at a problem designed to test your understanding of simultaneous equations. Here's the problem: Given $y = 2x + 3$ and $y = 3x + 4$, what is the coordinate pair that describes the point of intersection of these two linear equations? This question is really asking whether you are aware that the point of intersection is x and y—what we typically call the *solution*. The solution to this problem is easily found using substitution. Substituting for y gives the following:

$$2x + 3 = 3x + 4$$
$$-1 = 1x, \text{ so } x = -1$$

To find y, plug x into either original equation:

$$y = 2x + 3$$
$$y = 2(-1) + 3$$
$$y = 1$$

The point of intersection is $(-1,1)$.

Working with Linear Equations

Practice working with systems of linear equations by completing the questions below.

1. Given $y = 12x + 3$ and $y = 2x + 2$, what is the coordinate pair that describes the point of intersection of these two linear equations?

   A. (9, 1/2)

   B. (5, 63)

   C. (1/2, 9)

   D. (63, 5)

   E. (2, 25)

2. Given $y = 4x - 7$ and $y = 3x + 2$, what is the coordinate pair that describes the point of intersection of these two linear equations?

> **F.** (2, 5)
>
> **G.** (29, 9)
>
> **H.** (9, 3)
>
> **J.** (9, 29)
>
> **K.** (25, 9)

Correct answers:

1. The correct answer is C.

   $y = 12x + 3$ and $y = 2x + 2$

   Substituting for y gives the following:

   $12x + 3 = 2x + 2$

   $10x = 5$

   $x = 1/2$

   Substitute the x value into one side of the equation:

   $12(1/2) + 3 = 9$

   (1/2, 9)

2. The correct answer is J.

   $y = 4x - 7$ and $y = 3x + 2$

   Substituting for y gives the following:

   $4x - 7 = 3x + 2$

   $x = 9$

   Substitute the x value into one side of the equation:

   $4(9) - 7 = 29$

   (9, 29)

TIP

A useful strategy for solving math questions is to restate the question in your own words. For example, if a question asks, "What is the coordinate pair that describes the point of intersection of two linear equations?" you can translate this to "Find the x and y that make both equations true."

TIP

When a question asks for the point of intersection of two linear equations, it's asking you to find the solution, the (x,y) that makes both equations true.

The object of the elimination process is to manipulate each equation so that when you add them all together, the result is an equation that contains only one variable. The following problem is a good candidate for the *elimination* method. Solve the system of equations, as illustrated in Figure 5.7:

$$2x + 2y = 11$$
$$3x + 4y = 18$$

$$-3\,(2x + 2y = 11)$$
$$2\,(3x + 4y = 18)$$

$$-6x - 6y = -66$$
$$6x + 8y = 36$$

$$2y = -30$$
$$y = -15$$

FIGURE 5.7   To find x, plug y back into either original equation.

TIP

Make sure you select the answer that is being asked for. This sounds too obvious to mention, but it's actually one of the most common math errors on this test. If you solve a system of equations, it may sometimes be easier to find y first. That's great unless the question asks for x and you forget to plug y into the equation to find x!

Not all systems of equations have solutions. Parallel lines (linear equations with the same slope) have no solution because they never intersect. On the other hand, equations that are actually the same line have an infinite number of solutions.

Note also that you might be asked to find the solution to a set of inequalities. To do so, graph the inequalities in the coordinate plane by graphing the line and then shading the region that contains a point that makes the inequality true. The part of the graph that contains the overlap of the shadings is the solution set. Remember to use a dotted line for < and > and a solid line for ≥ and ≤.

Solving Operations with Matrices

Matrices don't often appear on the ACT test, but you may get one question about them. Matrices can be used to solve systems of equations. We can compactly represent the coefficients of the variables in the equations $2x + 2y = 11$ and $3x + 4y = 18$ as a matrix, as follows:

$$\begin{bmatrix} 2 & 2 \\ 3 & 4 \end{bmatrix}$$

TIP

A *matrix* is a rectangular array of numbers or variables arranged in rows and columns. The array is enclosed in brackets, and the numbers or variables individually are referred to as *elements*. A matrix is described by the number of rows times the number of columns.

To add and subtract matrices, the matrices must be of the same dimensions so that corresponding elements can be combined, as shown in Figure 5.8.

$$\begin{bmatrix} -5 & 0 \\ 4 & 2 \end{bmatrix} + \begin{bmatrix} 6 & -3 \\ 2 & 3 \end{bmatrix} = \begin{bmatrix} 1 & -3 \\ 6 & 5 \end{bmatrix}$$

FIGURE 5.8 Add corresponding elements when adding matrices.

Figure 5.9 shows an impossible problem because the first matrix is 2×2 but the second is 2×1. You need to be able to identify impossible problems because you won't be able to solve these matrices.

$$\begin{bmatrix} 5 & 0 \\ 4 & 2 \end{bmatrix} - \begin{bmatrix} -4 \\ 1 \end{bmatrix} =$$

FIGURE 5.9 The operation cannot be performed because the matrices do not have rows and columns that match in size.

Solving Inequalities and Inequalities with Absolute Values

Linear inequalities look like linear equations except for the $\geq$, $\leq$, $\geq$, or $\leq$ symbol that replaces the = symbol. When you are asked to solve an inequality, you are asked to find all the values of the variable that make the inequality true. Each of these values is a solution, and together they are called the *solution set*.

The steps necessary to solve linear equations are the same steps you use to solve linear inequalities. The only exception is that you must remember to reverse the direction of the inequality sign if you multiply or divide by a negative.

TIP

Be sure to reverse the direction of the inequality sign if you multiply or divide by a negative number.

Look at the following example:

$$14 - 7x \geq 10x - 3$$

Your first step is to subtract $10x$ from both sides:

$$14 - 17x \geq -3$$

Then, subtract 14 from both sides:

$-17x \geq -17$

Last, divide both sides by –17 and flip the sign:

$x \leq 1$

The solution set is given as $\{x \mid x \leq 1\}$ (the vertical line reads "such that").

Figure 5.10 shows a graph of the solution set.

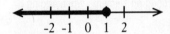
-2 -1 0 1 2

FIGURE 5.10   The solution set to the inequality is graphed on the number line.

TIP

When graphing solution sets on a number line, remember to use a closed circle to include a value. Use an open circle to exclude a value.

Inequalities can also contain absolute value notation. It's helpful to remember the two general patterns for $\leq$ and $\geq$. That is, if $|x \leq c$, then $-c \leq - \leq c$ and the corresponding graph is a single line segment on the number line between $-c$ and c inclusive. If $|x \geq c$, then $x \leq -c$ and $x \geq c$ and the corresponding graph is two rays extending infinitely in opposite directions, as shown in Figure 5.11. The patterns also hold true for $<$ and $>$.

-c   c

-c   c

FIGURE 5.11   When you graph an inequality that contains absolute value notation, you'll see one of the solution sets.

Working with Absolute Values in Inequalities

Practice working with inequalities with absolute values by completing the question below.

Solve and then graph the solution:

$|(3x + 1) < 4$

Correct answer:

Applying the pattern, you can rewrite as follows:

$-4 < 3x + 1 < 4$

To isolate x, subtract 1 from each part:

$-5 < 3x < 3$

To isolate x, divide each part by 3:

$-5/3 < x < 1$

The solution set is $\{x \mid -5/3 < x < 1\}$, and the graph is shown in Figure 5.12.

FIGURE 5.12 The solution to $|(3x + 1)| < 4$ is graphed on the number line.

Intermediate Algebra and Coordinate Graphing

Expect to see logarithms and exponential equations among these advanced equation problems. You'll also need to be able to find the roots of quadratic equations. Factoring quadratics, completing the square, and applying the quadratic formula should all be in your repertoire. You may also be asked to find the solution to a set of simultaneous equations. Although you don't have to use matrices to solve a set of equations, you will need to know how to complete basic operations with them.

Expect to see problems derived from coordinate geometry: the graphs of lines, circles, parabolas, ellipses, and piecewise functions. You'll also need to know more generally how changing a graph affects the equation of the graph.

Intermediate Algebra

You'll be solving an assortment of equations for a variable in these types of test questions.

Solving Quadratics

A *quadratic function* is a function that can be written in the form $f(x) = ax^2 + bx + c$. Simply put, it's an equation that contains an x^2 term. When you graph this function, its shape is a parabola. We say a quadratic is in standard form when we see $ax^2 + bx + c = 0$.

When you are asked to find the solution of a quadratic, you are asked to find the x values that result in a y value of zero. The solutions of a quadratic can be real or imaginary numbers. If the solutions are real numbers, they are also the x-coordinates of the x-intercepts of the graph of the quadratic function.

> **TIP**
>
> There are several ways the test makers may ask you about the solutions of a quadratic. They may use the phrase "find the zeros of the function" or "find the roots of the equation." You can translate this to "find the x values that result in a y value of 0."

You can use three methods to find the solutions of a quadratic on the test. You may be able to factor, you may be able to complete the square, or you may simply plug an answer choice into the quadratic formula.

> **TIP**
>
> The quadratic formula is $\dfrac{-b \pm \sqrt{b^2 - 4ac}}{2a}$. To use the formula, put the quadratic in standard form first: $ax^2 + bx + c = 0$.

> **TIP**
>
> The ACT test might give you a question that states the solutions of a quadratic and then asks you to select the corresponding quadratic. Remember that if a quadratic has the solutions $x = a$ and $x = b$, then the factors must be $(x - a)(x - b)$ because $x - a = 0$ gives $x = a$, and $x - b = 0$ gives $x = b$. By multiplying the factors $(x - a)(x - b)$ with the first, outer, inner, and last (FOIL) method, you return the quadratic $x^2 - ax - bx + ab$.

Because the quadratic formula is straightforward, we'll walk through an example using factoring. Examine the following question: Solve: $x^2 + 2x - 8 = 0$

Recall that when directions in a problem such as this state "solve," your task is to find the x values that make the equation true. Thus, you should first check to see whether the equation factors. In this case, the equation factors as follows:

$$x^2 + 2x - 8 = 0$$
$$(x + 4)(x - 2) = 0$$
$$(x + 4) = 0, \; (x - 2) = 0$$
$$x = -4, \; x = 2$$

The solutions are 2 and –4.

> **TIP**
>
> If you encounter a problem that asks for the solution to a quadratic, remember that the correct answer is right in front of you among the answer choices. The fastest path to a solution may be to plug in answer choices to see which choice makes the equation true.

> **TIP**
>
> An ACT test question may ask you to predict what kind of solutions a quadratic will have. You can use the discriminant, $b^2 - 4ac$, a fancy name for part of the quadratic formula, to predict what the answers will look like. If $b^2 - 4ac = 0$, then there is one real number solution. If $b^2 - 4ac$ is positive, there are two real number solutions. If $b^2 - 4ac$ is negative, there are two imaginary solutions.

> **TIP**
>
> You might need to use imaginary numbers when calculating with the quadratic formula. If you encounter this situation you need to recall that $\sqrt{-1} = i^2$ and $i^2 = -1$.

Solving Exponential Equations

An exponential function is any function in the form $f(x) = a^x$, where a is a positive number and not equal to 1. When $f(x)$ is replaced with a value, the result is an exponential equation. Consider the following problem: Solve: $2^{3x+4} = 32$. You can express 32 as a power of 2 in order to get like bases. Then, because the bases are the same, the exponents can be set equal to each other, like so:

$$2^{3x+4} = 2^5$$
$$3x + 4 = 5$$
$$x = \frac{1}{3}$$

> **TIP**
>
> Recall that if $a^x = a^y$, then $x = y$.

> **TIP**
>
> Whenever you encounter a variable as an exponent, you have two possible strategies for solving. First, try to express terms with like bases so that exponents can be set equal. Second, take the logarithm of both sides so that the exponent becomes a multiplied term according to the power rule of logarithms. Logarithms are discussed in the next section.

Working with Logarithms

When you see the word *logarithm*, you should immediately think *exponent*. Logarithms are the inverse functions of exponential functions. The rare logarithm questions that you might see on the ACT will probably center on understanding the definition of a logarithm.

A logarithm gives you some basic information. It shows that some base raised to an exponent gives a certain value. The information is always given in the following format: $\log_b n = y$. This format means $b_y = n$. The notation reads, "the log of n to the base b equals y." There is a special stipulation that the base has to be a positive number and not equal to 1. The values of n must also be positive.

> **TIP**
>
> When a logarithm notation does not indicate a base, the base is assumed to be 10. When the notation *ln* is used, the base is assumed to be e.

Consider the following question: Solve: $\log_x 81 = 2$. According to the definition, you can express the equation in exponential form as $x^2 = 81$. The solution is 9 because $9^2 = 81$. Notice that -9 is not a possible solution because the base must be a positive number.

If $\log_x 144 = 12$, you know that $x^2 = 12$. The solution is 12 because $12^2 = 144$. (Remember that the base must be positive, so –12 is not a possible solution here.) The use of this easier expression ($x = 12$) to solve a problem is what you will need to know if you do encounter the rare logarithm problem on the ACT.

Coordinate Graphing

About 15% of the ACT falls within the realm of coordinate geometry. You should expect to see about nine coordinate geometry questions. These questions encompass all aspects of graphs in the coordinate plane. You should be familiar with the graphs of lines, circles, parabolas, ellipses, and piecewise functions. Note, however, that if parabolas, circles, and ellipses make your head spin, you can console yourself with the knowledge that you probably won't see more than one such question on the test.

TIP

The *coordinate plane* is defined by the x- and y-axes. Every point in the plane is described by a coordinate pair, (x,y). The intersection of the axes is called the *origin* and is located at (0,0).

You'll encounter questions involving points, lines, and graphing lines on the test.

Graphing Lines

To graph a line you need either a point that falls on the line and the slope of the line, or two points that fall on the line. The equation of a line in slope-intercept form is $y = mx + b$, where m is the slope of the line and b is the y-intercept. The slope of a line defines its steepness and is the ratio of the change along the y-axis to the change along the x-axis.

TIP

To calculate the slope, m, of a line, use any two points (x_1, y_1) and (x_2, y_2) that fall on the line, and plug them into the following:

$$m = \frac{\text{rise}}{\text{run}} = \frac{y^2 - y^1}{x^2 - x^1}$$

To prevent the common error of placing the change in x in the top portion of the ratio, recall the phrase, "y flies high!"

TIP

Slopes can be positive or negative. Positive slopes correspond to lines that seem to be falling forward. Negative slopes correspond to lines that seem to be falling backward.

The ACT frequently uses the terms *y-intercept* and *x-intercept* in coordinate geometry question stems. The y-intercept of a line is where the line crosses the y-axis. To find the y-intercept, let x be 0, then solve for y. Note also that the x-intercept of a line is where the line crosses the x-axis. To find the x-intercept, let y be 0, then solve for x.

> **TIP**
>
> If you are given a linear equation such as $3x + 4y = 4$, you can re-express it in slope-intercept form to quickly find the slope and y-intercept. Moving x to the other side results in $4y = -3x + 4$. Dividing all terms by 4 gives the desired form $y = -3 / 4x + 1$. Now, you can see that the slope, m, is $-3/4$ and the y-intercept is $(0,1)$.

> **TIP**
>
> A horizontal line has slope 0. For example, $y = 3$ has slope 0. A vertical line has a slope that is not defined. For example, $x = 2$ has a slope that is not defined.

Parallel and Perpendicular Lines

Parallel lines never intersect. Two lines are parallel if they have the same slope. For example, $y = -3x + 1$ and $y = -3x - 5$ are parallel lines because both have the slope -3. Perpendicular lines intersect to form right angles. The slopes of perpendicular lines are opposite reciprocals of each other. For example, $y = 1/3x + 5$ and $y = -3x + 2$ are perpendicular lines because the slope -3 is the opposite reciprocal of $1/3$.

> **TIP**
>
> The product of the slopes of perpendicular lines is -1.

> **EXAM ALERT**
>
> It is common to see an ACT question that asks for the equation of a line that is parallel or perpendicular to some given line and passes through a given point. Translate this question in your own words to something like, "Given a slope and a point, can I write $y = mx + b$?" The problem is now reduced to filling in the blanks: $y = \_\_\_\_\,x + \_\_\_\_$. For example, if you are told that a line is perpendicular to the line $y = 2/3x + 2$, that's just math-speak that tells you the slope of the line you're concerned with is $-3/2$. So $y = -3/2x + b$. Given that the line passes through the point $(1,2)$, plug in these coordinates for x and y, then solve for b.
>
> Thus, $y = -3/2x + b$ becomes $(2) = -3/2(1) + b$. Solving for b, $2 + 3/2 = b$. Combining, $b = 7/2$. Therefore, the resulting equation is $y = -3/2x + 7/2$.

Finding the Distance Between Two Points

You can always use the Pythagorean theorem to find the distance between two points. We'll demonstrate with this typical ACT question: Find the distance between $(2,3)$ and $(1,-2)$. Taking the time to create a quick sketch may actually be helpful in this problem. Figure 5.13 shows how to create a triangle that represents the difference in x's and the difference in y's.

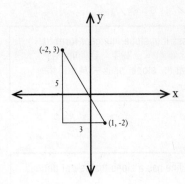

FIGURE 5.13   You can use the Pythagorean theorem or the distance formula to find the distance between two points.

Using the Pythagorean theorem, we get $5^2 + 3^2 = h^2$. Therefore, $34 = h^2$. Taking the square root of both sides gives the result $h = \sqrt{34}$. The distance between the points is $\sqrt{34}$.

TIP

Alternatively, you can find the distance between two points by using the distance formula,

$$d = \sqrt{(x_2 - x_1)^2 + (y_2 - y_1)^2}.$$

Graphing Circles

The equation for a circle centered at (h,k) of radius r is $(x - h)^2 + (y - k)^2 = r^2$. Consider the following question: If a circle is tangent to the x-axis at 4 and tangent to the y-axis at 4, what is the equation of the circle?

Figure 5.14 shows that the circle must be centered at (4,4) and have a radius of 4. The equation is therefore $(x - 4)^2 + (y - 4)^2 = 16$.

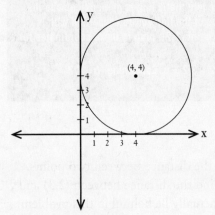

FIGURE 5.14   The equation of this circle is $(x - 4)^2 + (y - 4)^2 = 16$.

Graphing Parabolas

The graph of a quadratic function, $f(x) = ax^2 + bx + c$, is a parabola. A parabola has a vertex and an axis of symmetry. The *vertex* is the point at which the graph turns and is the maximum or minimum value of $f(x)$. The *axis of symmetry* is the imaginary line about which the parabola is symmetrical and is located at $x = -b/2a$. Whether a parabola opens upward or downward is determined by a, the coefficient of the x^2 term. If $a > 0$, it opens upward. If $a < 0$, it opens downward.

TIP

When $f(x) = ax^2 + bx + c$, the expression $-b/2a$ gives the x-coordinate of the line of symmetry of the parabola. The vertex of a parabola is $(-b/2a, f(-b/2a))$.

Figure 5.15 shows the graph of $f(x) = -3x^2 - 30x - 66$.

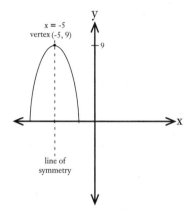

FIGURE 5.15 The graph of $f(x) = -3x^2 - 30x - 66$ is a parabola.

Graphing Ellipses

The graph of an equation in the form $x^2/a^2 + y^2/b^2 = 1$ is a horizontal ellipse. An ellipse has a longer axis (called the major axis) that contains the foci and a shorter axis (called the minor axis). The vertices of the ellipse are (a,0), (–a,0), (0,b), and (0,–b). The length of the major axis is $2a$, and the length of the minor axis is $2b$. The graph of $x^2/25 + y^2/9 = 1$ is shown in Figure 5.16.

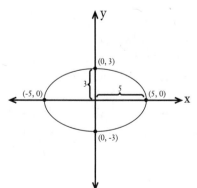

FIGURE 5.16 The graph of $x^2/25 + y^2/9 = 1$ is an ellipse.

Graph Transformations

Any general function can be shifted horizontally or vertically, or made narrower or wider. This is called a *transformation*. You can successfully answer a question about the transformation of a graph on the ACT without being familiar with the original graph. To do so, you need to know how the following changes to equations affect their graphs, given some function $y = f(x)$:

▶ The graph of $y = f(x) + c$ is the original graph shifted up c units.

▶ The graph of $y = f(x) - c$ is the original graph shifted down c units.

▶ The graph of $y = f(x - c)$ is the original graph shifted to the right c units.

▶ The graph of $y = f(x + c)$ is the original graph shifted to the left c units.

▶ The graph of $y = cf(x)$ is narrower if $|c| \geq 1$ and wider if $0 \leq |c| \leq 1$.

Piecewise Functions

Sometimes functions are defined in pieces with different formulas listed for different domains. For example, if you examine the function's graph shown in Figure 5.17, you should be able to determine the domain and range of the piecewise function and write the equation for the function.

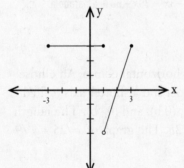

FIGURE 5.17 You'll need to be able to interpret the graph of a piecewise function.

To do so, first determine the pieces of the domain by looking at where the graph changes along the x-axis. The first line runs between -3 and 1 on the x-axis, so the domain is expressed $-3 \leq x \leq 1$. The second line runs between 1 and 3 on the x-axis, 1 not included. This domain is expressed $1 < x \leq 3$. Next, determine what equation will generate the lines in each domain. The first line is $f(x) = 3$. You can use the slope and a point to generate the second equation. The second equation is $f(x) = 3x - 6$. Putting it all together in piecewise format, you get the following:

$$f(x) = \begin{cases} 3 & \text{(for } -3 \leq x \leq 1) \\ 3x - 6 & \text{(for } 1 < x \leq 3) \end{cases}$$

Working with Graphing

Practice working with the variety of ways to graph lines and interpret quadratic equations by completing the questions below.

1. Which of the following quadratic equations has solutions $x = -a$ and $x = 3b$?

    A. $x^2 - 3ab = 0$

    B. $x^2 - 2abx - 3ab = 0$

    C. $x^2 + (a + 3b) + 3ab = 0$

    D. $x^2 + (3b - a) - 3ab = 0$

    E. $x^2 - (3b - a) - 3ab = 0$

2. Find the distance between $(-1,-3)$ and $(4,5)$.

    F. $\sqrt{5}$

    G. $\sqrt{13}$

    H. $2\sqrt{10}$

    J. $\sqrt{89}$

    K. 13

3. What is the point of intersection of $y = 2x + 3$ and $2x + 2y = 4$?

    A. $x = -1/3$

    B. $(-1/3, 7/3)$

    C. $(7/3, -1/3)$

    D. $y = 7/3$

    E. $(1,2)$

Correct Answers:

1. The correct answer is E. If the solutions are $x = -a$ and $x = 3b$, then the factors are $(x + a)$ and $(x - 3b)$. Multiplying the factors results in the original quadratic equation. Using the FOIL method you get $x^2 + ax - 3bx - 3ab$. Factoring $a - x$ out of the two middle terms produces the answer $x^2 - (3b - a) - 3ab = 0$.

2. The correct answer is J. The easiest way to approach this problem is to set up a right triangle whose legs are the distance between the x's and the y's. It is equally valid to use the distance formula, $d = \sqrt{(x_2 - x_1)^2 + (y_2 - y_1)^2}$, but it will not be supplied on the test. The triangle you create should have a leg whose length is 5, the difference of the x-coordinates, and a leg whose length is 8, the difference between the y-coordinates. Plugging this into the Pythagorean theorem gives $5^2 + 8^2 = d^2$. Calculating further results in $89 = d^2$, so $d = \sqrt{89}$. The distance between the points is $\sqrt{89}$.

3. The correct answer is B. The point of intersection of two lines is the same as the solution you get when you solve simultaneously. Rephrase this question as: "Find the (x,y) that make both equations true statements." To do this, use substitution or elimination to solve simultaneously. To use elimination, put the two equations in the same order: $y = 2x + 3$ becomes $-2x + y = 3$ and is easily added to $2x + 2y = 4$. The result is $3y = 7$, so $y = 7/3$. You can stop working here if you recognize that B is the only answer that lists a coordinate point with 7/3 as y. To find the x-coordinate, you can replace y with 7/3 in either original equation and solve for x. Doing so gives $7/3 = 2x + 3$. Solving, you get $7/3 - 3 = 2x$, so x is $-1/3$. The answer is $(-1/3, 7/3)$.

Plane Geometry/Trigonometry

The key to answering geometry and trigonometry questions correctly is making connections. Geometry rules and trigonometry definitions are not difficult, and if a problem requires a complicated formula, such as the law of cosines, the test makers will give it to you. However, if you don't know how to apply the rules or formulas to a scenario, you may get discouraged quickly.

Expect to see around 14 plane geometry and four trigonometry questions. Remember, there are 60 questions on the math test, so about 25% are plane geometry questions and only 7% are trigonometry questions. Some are presented as story questions with no figures. Others are accompanied by diagrams with dimensions and ask for a specific calculation. Regardless of the type of question, you should be prepared to understand geometry notation, demonstrate knowledge of basic definitions and formulas, and draw conclusions about the connections between concepts.

> **TIP**
>
> The directions at the beginning of the math test give three items that are directly related to plane geometry problems. Read them now, not the day of the test:
>
> 1. Figures are not necessarily drawn to scale.
> 2. All geometric figures lie on a plane.
> 3. When the word *line* is used, it denotes a straight line.

Plane Geometry

Plane geometry encompasses geometry notation, angles, parallel lines, and transversals, as well as triangles and the Pythagorean theorem, circles, polygons and quadrilaterals, and other figures. As you read and review, keep in mind that although you should know the basic formulas shown here, any more involved ones will be provided on the test.

Geometry Notation

You have to understand the language of geometry to accurately interpret geometry questions. You must know the meaning of typical notations on diagrams and be able to translate the markings used to denote different constructs.

We'll break down Figure 5.18 to review notions and markings.

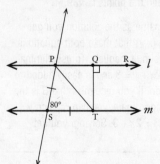

FIGURE 5.18   Parallel lines.

Figure 5.18 shows points P, Q, S, and T. Points are denoted with a single capital letter.

Lines are named with two points that fall on the line, or sometimes with a lowercase letter. In Figure 5.18, line l can also be named line $\overleftrightarrow{PQ}$ or line $\overleftrightarrow{QP}$. Lines extend without end in two opposite directions.

Line segments are also named with two points. Line segment $\overline{ST}$ lies on line m. We can also name it line segment $\overline{TS}$. A line segment consists of two endpoints and all the points in between.

A ray extends indefinitely from an endpoint. The order of the letters of a ray's name is significant. The first letter indicates the endpoint from which the ray extends infinitely. Ray $\overrightarrow{ST}$ extends infinitely to the right, whereas ray $\overrightarrow{TS}$ extends infinitely to the left.

The angle whose measure is 80° has the name ∠TSP. This angle can also be named ∠PST. An angle is the figure formed by two rays with a common endpoint. The common endpoint is the vertex. Notice in both names the vertex is the middle letter. Sometimes an angle is named only with its vertex. This angle can be named ∠S.

The triangle that contains the 80° angle can be named several ways: ΔPTS, ΔTSP, and ΔSPT. Notice the vertices are listed in the order in which they occur. Triangles have three sides and three angles.

TIP

As you might have noted in the discussion of the parts of a triangle, "vertices" is the plural of "vertex."

The tick marks on line segments $\overline{PS}$ and $\overline{ST}$ indicate that the segments are congruent. Congruent segments have equal lengths. Also, angle Q has a special symbol that looks like part of a box. This right angle symbol indicates the angle is 90°. Overall, know that PQTS is a quadrilateral in the figure. Vertices must be named in the order in which they occur. However, the name may start with any vertex. A quadrilateral is a four-sided figure.

Essential Geometry Terms

Before we discuss further concepts in geometry, we need to lay the groundwork of essential vocabulary:

▸ **Perimeter**—The sum of the lengths of the sides of any polygon. To figure out how much fence you need to go around a yard, you must find the perimeter of the yard.

▸ **Area**—The number of square units it takes to completely cover a two-dimensional closed figure. To lay carpet in a room, you must know the area of a room.

▸ **Intersection**—The point at which two lines cross.

▸ **Polygon**—A closed figure with line segments as sides. Line segments intersect at vertices.

- **Congruent shapes**—Shapes that have the same shape and equal dimensions.

- **Diagonal**—A line segment, other than a side, that joins two vertices of a polygon.

- **Interior angles**—Angles located inside a polygon.

- **Exterior angles**—Angles formed by extending the side of a polygon at a vertex. These angles fall outside the polygon.

- **Midpoint**—The midpoint of a segment divides a segment into two equal lengths. The midpoint of a line segment that extends from (x,y) to (x_1,y_1) is $(\frac{x + x_1}{2}, \frac{y + y_1}{2})$.

- **Parallel lines**—Parallel lines or segments do not intersect. Parallel lines have the same slope.

- **Perpendicular lines**—Perpendicular lines or segments intersect to form right angles.

> **TIP**
>
> It is common to encounter a perimeter problem in which you are told that all sides of a shape are either horizontal or vertical. This information is important because not all the lengths of the sides will be given. In these problems, use the opposite sides of the shape to fill in the missing dimensions before finding the perimeter.

Types of Angles

Knowing the attributes of the angles in a problem may be the key to unraveling the problem. Review the angles in Figure 5.19 and be sure you are familiar with the special characteristics of each one.

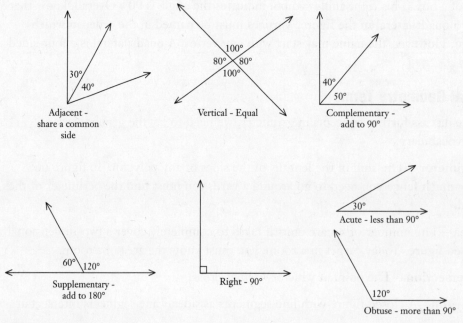

FIGURE 5.19 Types of angles.

Frequently, ACT questions require you to use several angle definitions at once. For example, to solve the problem shown in Figure 5.20, you must find the value of x. This requires you to see that adjacent angles whose outer sides form a line add to 180° and that the angles of a triangle must sum to 180°. Then you must also see that vertical angles are equal.

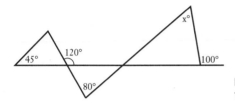

FIGURE 5.20 A plane geometry question that requires you to find the value of x.

Parallel Lines and Transversals

A special situation is created when a line or line segment crosses two parallel lines or line segments. Figure 5.21 shows the angles created in this situation.

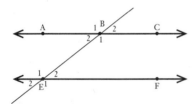

FIGURE 5.21 A line crossing two parallel lines.

> **TIP**
>
> When a line crosses two parallel lines, all the obtuse angles are equal and all the acute angles are equal.

> **TIP**
>
> Frequently, a problem using this scenario might not be drawn in such an obvious way. Two lines may cut the parallel lines, rather than the one shown here. Or, the line that cuts the parallel lines might be part of a shape, such as a triangle. If you encounter a problem like this, determine the information in the diagram that is relevant. Use your pencil to darken the relevant parts. It also might be helpful to extend a line.

Triangles

You'll see triangles in plane geometry questions and in trigonometry questions. As you work on these questions, remember that the shortest side of a triangle is always opposite the smallest angle, and the longest side is always opposite the largest angle.

The formula for the area of a triangle is $b \times h/2$. Remember, the base and height must be perpendicular sides of the triangle. The sum of the angles in a triangle is always 180°.

Similar Triangles

Similar triangles have the same shape. You can identify a pair of similar triangles because they have equal angles. For all similar triangles, the lengths of their corresponding sides are proportional. This means that the ratio of the shortest sides is equal to the ratio of the longest sides, which is equal to the ratio of the mid-length sides. In Figure 5.22, we don't have to be told the triangles are similar. We know they are because both have a right angle and both share a vertical angle, so all their angles must be equal. We can solve for x using proportions. Consider that hyp/hyp = $5/10 = 4/x$ = leg/leg. Therefore, $x = 8$. It's also true that hyp/leg = $5/4 = 10/x$ = hyp/leg.

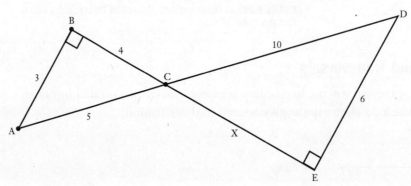

$$\frac{5}{10} = \frac{4}{x} = \frac{3}{6}$$

FIGURE 5.22 Similar triangles.

TIP

Be sure you create the ratios with corresponding sides.

EXAM ALERT

Sometimes a question that requires you to use similar triangles actually asks for the perimeter of a figure. Be sure you answer the question and do not choose a distracter.

30°–60°–90° Triangle

Any time you see a 30°–60°–90° triangle, as in Figure 5.23, you can find the lengths of its sides because all 30°–60°–90° triangles have sides that form the ratio $\frac{1}{2}$, $\sqrt{3}$, 2. For this triangle, the length of the smallest leg × 4 always gives the length of the hypotenuse.

TIP

To remember corresponding angles and sides in a 30°–60°–90° triangle, use the size of the angles and sides. The sides arranged from least to greatest are $\frac{1}{2}$, $\sqrt{3}$, 2. The smallest side, $\frac{1}{2}$, is opposite the smallest angle, 30°. The largest side, 2, is opposite the largest angle, 90°.

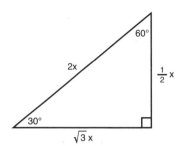

FIGURE 5.23   A 30°–60°–90° triangle.

45°–45°–90° Triangle

Anytime you see a 45°–45°–90° triangle, as in Figure 5.24, you can find the lengths of its sides because all 45°–45°–90° triangles have sides that form the ratio 1, 1, √2. For this triangle, the length of the leg × √2 always gives the length of the hypotenuse.

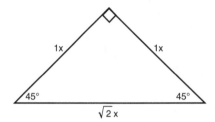

FIGURE 5.24   A 45°–45°–90° triangle.

TIP

To remember corresponding angles and sides in a 45°–45°–90° triangle, recall the saying, "rootnuse." The √2 should always correspond to the hypotenuse.

EXAM ALERT

If you recognize the 45°–45°–90° triangle or the 30°–60°–90° triangle, you can save a lot of time using their ratios instead of the Pythagorean theorem.

Isosceles Triangles and Equilateral Triangles

Equilateral triangles have equal sides and equal angles. The ACT may use tick marks to show the equal angles or the equal sides. If either is shown, the triangle must be an equilateral. Because the sum of a triangle's angles is always 180°, equilaterals always have 60° angles.

Isosceles triangles have two equal sides. The angles opposite those sides are also equal. The ACT may use tick marks (see Figure 5.26) to show the equal angles or equal sides. If either is shown, the triangle must be an isosceles.

TIP

If you encounter a problem that asks for the measure of an angle of a triangle and you don't seem to have enough information, check to see if the triangle is an equilateral or an isosceles.

Pythagorean Theorem and Pythagorean Triples

You can use the *Pythagorean theorem* to solve for the lengths of the sides of any right triangle. The Pythagorean theorem states the following for any right triangle:

$$\text{leg}^2 + \text{leg}^2 = \text{hypotenuse}^2, \text{ or } a^2 + b^2 = c^2$$

In every right triangle, the hypotenuse is the side opposite the 90° angle. The other two sides are "legs" and can be plugged in for either a or b. For Figure 5.25, we can use this theorem to find the length of the hypotenuse, c, as shown in the code that follows the figure:

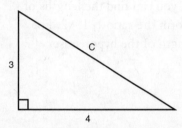

FIGURE 5.25 A right triangle.

$$3^2 + 4^2 = c^2$$
$$9 + 16 = c^2$$
$$25 = c^2$$
$$5 = c$$

> **TIP**
>
> You might encounter a problem that provides the length of a leg and the hypotenuse. In this case, be careful that you plug the lengths into the correct spots in the equation.

Smart test-takers are always on the lookout for ways to save time. Pythagorean triples are common lengths of sides of right triangles and can save you quite a bit of time. If you are given two sides of a right triangle, Pythagorean triples allow you to figure out the third side of the triangle without any calculation. Here are the triples:

▶ 3, 4, 5, and any multiple such as 6, 8, 10

▶ 5, 12, 13, and any multiple such as 10, 24, 26

> **TIP**
>
> If a right triangle has lengths of 3 and 5, without any calculation you know the third side has a length of 4.

Polygons and Quadrilaterals

A *polygon* is a closed figure made up of line segments. The points of intersection of the sides of the polygon are called its *vertices*. Two examples of polygons are triangles and hexagons. Some questions on the ACT focus on the diagonals of polygons. Recall that a diagonal is a line segment, other than a side, that connects two vertices on a polygon. You can draw one diagonal from a vertex in a square. But you can draw three diagonals from a vertex in a hexagon. Other questions present a regular polygon, which is valuable information. Regular polygons have equal angles and equal sides, as demonstrated in Figure 5.26.

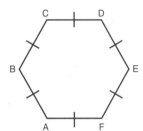

FIGURE 5.26 A regular polygon.

> **EXAM ALERT**
>
> Observing the pattern in a problem with small numbers and then applying the pattern to an ACT question with big numbers is a powerful strategy. If a question asks for the total number of diagonals that can be drawn in a figure with 10 vertices, look for a pattern by observing the number of diagonals in smaller figures. For example, by observing a four-sided figure, which has one diagonal from one vertex, and a five-sided figure, which has two diagonals from one vertex, you can express the number of diagonals drawn from one vertex as $n - 3$. In this case, "n" represents the number of sides, which is the same as the number of vertices. Because you must consider diagonals drawn from every vertex, the expression becomes $n \times (n - 3)$. However, as stated, this expression counts every diagonal twice. If you count a diagonal named $\overline{OD}$, you do not need to count the diagonal $\overline{DO}$. To account for this repetition, the expression becomes $\frac{n \times (n - 3)}{2}$. This general expression allows you to find the number of diagonals in a figure with any number of sides.

> **TIP**
>
> To find the sum of the measures of the interior angles of a polygon, divide the polygon into triangles by drawing lines from one vertex to the other vertices. Count the triangles and multiply by 180°.

> **TIP**
>
> The sum of the exterior angles of a polygon is always 360°. A polygon has two exterior angles at every vertex. The exterior angles are formed by extending the sides of the polygon at a vertex. The exterior angle is formed by an extended side and an actual side of the polygon.

One specific type of polygon is a quadrilateral. *Quad* means four, so it's not surprising that a quadrilateral is a four-sided figure. You need to know the attributes of the quadrilaterals that are frequently found on the ACT, which are listed in Table 5.6.

TABLE 5.6   Quadrilaterals You Need to Know

Name	Defined By	Area Formula	Figure
Trapezoid	One pair of parallel sides.	height × sum of parallel sides / 2	
Parallelogram	Both pairs of opposite sides are parallel.	base × height	
Rectangle	Parallelogram with 90° angles and opposite sides of equal length. One diagonal.	base × height	

TIP

For all parallelograms, opposite angles are congruent and consecutive angles are supplementary.

TIP

For any square, the length of the diagonal is √2 × the side length.

Parts of a Circle

Recall that a circle is the locus of all points in a plane equidistant from a center point. ACT question stems use appropriate terminology to describe the parts of circles. Use Figure 5.27 to review the following special terms:

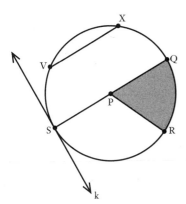

FIGURE 5.27 Parts of circles.

▸ $\overline{VX}$ is a chord. A chord is a line segment that connects any two points on a circle.

▸ $\overline{PQ}$ is a radius. A radius is a line segment that connects the center of a circle to any point on the circle.

▸ $\overline{SQ}$ is a diameter. A diameter is a chord that passes through the center of a circle.

▸ $\overset{\frown}{QR}$ is an arc. An arc is two points on the circle and all the points between them.

▸ Sector PRQ is a sector. A sector is bound by a central angle and an arc.

▸ k is a line tangent to the circle. A tangent line touches the circle at exactly one point.

▸ ∠QPR is a central angle. A central angle is an angle whose vertex is the center of the circle.

TIP

The degree measure of an arc is the same as the degree measure of the central angle that forms the arc. In Figure 5.27, the measure of ∠QPR is equal to the measure of $\overset{\frown}{QR}$.

TIP

Two tangent segments from a point outside a circle are equal.

Note that on the test, you must be able to calculate both the circumference and the area of a circle. The circumference is the distance around the circle. Both formulas are shown here:

Circumference = $2r\pi$

Area = πr^2

TIP

Expect to see an area question that requires some problem solving to figure out the circle's radius. For example, a question might give the dimensions of a rectangle that is inscribed in a circle. To calculate the radius of the circle, you can calculate the diagonal of the rectangle and then take half of it.

> **TIP**
>
> You might encounter a question that combines the concepts of area and probability. For example, if a question shows a figure of a target and asks for the probability of hitting the bull's-eye (inner circle), you can form a ratio of the area of the bull's-eye compared to the area of the entire target.

> **TIP**
>
> You can use a proportion to find the area of a sector if you know the area of a circle, like so:
>
> Degree of central arc of sector / 360° = area of sector / area of circle

> **TIP**
>
> You can use a proportion to find the length of an arc if you know the circumference of a circle, like so:
>
> Degree of arc / 360° = length of arc / circumference

Right Solids

We'll limit our discussion of solids to the types you're likely to see on the ACT—right solids. A right solid is one in which the bases are perpendicular to the surface. You're probably already familiar with a right cylinder. A right cylinder is described by two circular bases and a height that is perpendicular to those bases. A right circular cone is described by a circular base connected to a single point. Although the segments that connect the base and the point are slanted, the height of the cone is still perpendicular to the base. If a right circular cone has a polygon like a triangle or rectangle for a base instead of a circle, the solid is called a *pyramid*. These figures are shown in Figure 5.28.

Cylinder   Cone   Pyramid   **FIGURE 5.28** Right solids.

> **TIP**
>
> If a right cylinder has bases that are polygons instead of circles, the solid is called a *prism*.

Volume

Volume is defined as the number of cubic units that fill a solid. Finding the volume of a cube is easy; the formula is length × width × height. But finding the volume of a solid with a more complicated base may seem difficult. It's simple to find the volume of any right solid, except cones and pyramids, if you remember the formula: area of base × height. Using this general formula, the volume of the cylinder in Figure 5.28 is $\pi r^2 \times$ height.

The main exception to this general rule is the volume of right solids that connect to a point, such as pyramids and cones. To calculate the volume of these solids, use the following formula:

$$\frac{(\text{area of the base} \times \text{height})}{3}$$

> **TIP**
>
> A sphere is a solid that looks like a ball. The radius of a sphere is the distance from the center to any point on the surface. The volume of a sphere is $4/3 \pi r 3$.

> **TIP**
>
> The general formula for the volume of a right solid, excepting cones and pyramids, follows: area of base × height.

> **EXAM ALERT**
>
> **An ACT volume question may present a right solid that has a combination of shapes as a base. Answer this question by finding the area of the base. Then, apply the formula volume = area of base × height.**

> **TIP**
>
> A common error is to forget to divide by 3 when finding the volume of pyramids and cones. To prevent this error, remember that you must divide the product of the area of the base and height of pointy solids by 3.

Surface Area

Surface area is the sum of the areas of the faces of a solid. An ACT question may present a story problem that describes a scenario that requires you to calculate surface area. For example, a question might present a diagram such as the one in Figure 5.29 and then ask you to find the amount of material needed to create or wrap the diagram.

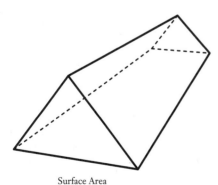

Surface Area

FIGURE 5.29   A prism.

The surface area of the diagram shown in Figure 5.29 is calculated as follows: area of bottom rectangle + areas of two side rectangles + areas of two end triangles.

> **TIP**
>
> You can find the surface area of a cylinder by adding the areas of the two circular bases to the area of the cylindrical surface. The area of the cylindrical surface is the height of the cylinder × the circumference of the circle.

Symmetry

If a shape is symmetric, then there is some line, called the *line of symmetry*, along which the shape can be folded so that the two halves coincide exactly. We can apply this concept to figures on the coordinate plane. Graphs can be symmetric about the x-axis, the y-axis, or even the origin. Symmetry, as it relates to graphs, is summarized in the following list:

- **Symmetric with respect to the x-axis**—When a graph can be folded along the axis and the result is that the two halves of the graph coincide, the graph is symmetric with respect to the x-axis. To test for this symmetry algebraically, replace y with $-y$ in an equation. If the replacement yields the same result, the graph is symmetrical about the x-axis.

- **Symmetric with respect to the y-axis**—When a graph can be folded along the y-axis and the result is that the two halves of the graph coincide, the graph is symmetric with respect to the y-axis. To test for this symmetry algebraically, replace x with $-x$ in an equation. If the replacement yields the same result, the graph is symmetrical about the y-axis.

- **Symmetric with respect to the origin**—When a graph can be rotated some number of degrees about the origin so that the result coincides with the original graph, the graph is symmetric with respect to the origin. To test for this symmetry algebraically, replace x with $-x$ and y with $-y$ in an equation. If the replacements yield the same result, the graph is symmetric about the origin. The graph in Figure 5.30 is symmetric with respect to the origin. If you rotate this graph 180° about the origin, the result coincides with the original.

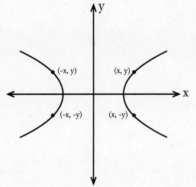

FIGURE 5.30 This graph is symmetric with respect to the origin.

Basic Trigonometric Functions

Expect to see four trigonometry questions on the ACT. Although most students think of trigonometry as more difficult material, ACT questions on this material tend to be straightforward. To be successful on these questions you must know how sine, cosine, and tangent and their reciprocals are defined for acute angles. You must also be able to find the sine, cosine, and tangent of larger angles using related angles. Finally, you should be able to map the graphs of cosine and functions to their equations and solve for θ in trigonometric equations.

Acute Angles

Sine, cosine, and tangent are ratios that occur in a right triangle. Every right triangle has a right angle and two acute angles. The definitions of sine, cosine, and tangent are true for both acute angles. We'll use Figure 5.31 to demonstrate these ratios.

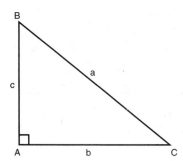

FIGURE 5.31   Sine, cosine, and tangent ratios defined for acute angles.

- Sin $\angle B = \dfrac{\text{length of opposite side}}{\text{length of hypotenuse}} = \dfrac{b}{a}$

- Cos $\angle B = \dfrac{\text{length of adjacent side}}{\text{length of hypotenuse}} = \dfrac{c}{a}$

- Tan $\angle B = \dfrac{\text{length of opposite}}{\text{length of adjacent}} = \dfrac{b}{c}$

Reciprocal Functions

The *reciprocal functions* are defined as the reciprocals of sine, cosine, and tangent. We'll demonstrate these ratios using the angles of Figure 5.31:

- Cosecant $\angle B$ = 1 / sin $\angle B$ = hypotenuse / opposite = $\frac{a}{b}$

- Secant $\angle B$ = 1 / cos $\angle B$ = hypotenuse / adjacent = $\frac{a}{c}$

- Cotangent $\angle B$ = 1 / tan $\angle B$ = adjacent / opposite = $\frac{c}{b}$

Other Angles

If an angle is larger than 90°, we use a *related angle* to find the sine, cosine, and tangent values. The related angle is the positive acute angle formed by dropping a perpendicular to the x-axis. We can use the concept of a related angle along with the unit circle to create a model that makes it straightforward to find the sine, cosine, or tangent of any angle. The unit circle has its center at the origin and has a radius of length 1. Because the radius of the circle is 1, the hypotenuse of any triangle is 1. Therefore, sinθ is the length of the vertical leg of the triangle and cosθ is the length of the horizontal leg. Notice that the (x,y) coordinates of the point on the circle are the lengths of the legs of the triangle. Therefore, *x* of (x,y) is cosine and *y* is sine. We'll walk through an example using the unit circle in Figure 5.32.

To find the sine of 225°, measure the angle counterclockwise from the x-axis. Dropping a perpendicular to the x-axis above forms the related angle, which is 45°. Notice this forms a 45°–45°–90° triangle. The vertical leg of this triangle is therefore $\frac{\sqrt{2}}{2}$. Note that this is a negative value. Therefore, the sine of 225° is $-\frac{\sqrt{2}}{2}$.

Notice that the quadrant that the related angle falls in determines the sign, positive or negative, of the cosine or sine value. Sine is negative in the third and fourth quadrants. Cosine is negative in the second and third quadrants.

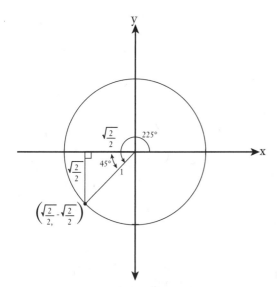

FIGURE 5.32 Using a related angle to find the sine of 225°.

Cosθ and Sinθ Graphs

Cosθ and sinθ are repeating curves that travel an equal distance above and below some center line. You may see the graph of either cosθ or sinθ on the ACT. Both are graphed on an x-axis marked with degrees of θ and a y-axis marked with numbers. The graph of cosine looks exactly like sine, except that the cosine curve has been shifted horizontally so that cos 0° is equal to a value of 1.

Both graphs are described by the following:

▸ **Center line**—The center line is the x-axis or some shift up or down from the x-axis. In $y = 3 + 2\cos\theta$, the x-axis is shifted up 3.

▸ **Amplitude**—The amplitude is how far the curve goes above and below the x-axis. In $y = -2 + 3\sin\theta$, the amplitude is 3. The curve deviates 3 units above and below the x-axis.

▸ **Period**—The period is how frequently the curve repeats. In $y = 3 + 4\cos2\theta$, 2 shows the period is not 360° but 180° because the variable is changing twice as fast.

▸ **Phase shift**—The phase shift represents any horizontal shift to the right or left. In $y = 3 + 4\cos(\theta + 90°)$, the curve has been shifted to the left 90°.

TIP

If sinθ or cosθ is multiplied by a negative, the entire curve flips upside down.

Let's look at an example. We'll examine the curve in Figure 5.33 and map out its equation.

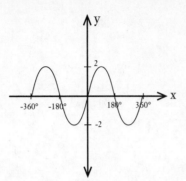

FIGURE 5.33   Sine wave.

At 0°, the function value is 0, so we'll express this graph as sinθ. There is no horizontal shift, so nothing is added to the sinθ. So far we have $y = \sin\theta$. The amplitude is 2 because the graph travels 2 units above and below the center line. Now we have $y = 2\sin\theta$. This graph takes 360° to complete one cycle, so the variable θ is not changed by any multiplier. We know this graph has not been shifted horizontally because the sin curve crosses the origin at θ = 0°. The equation of the curve in Figure 5.33 is $y = 2\sin\theta$.

You might see graphs expressed as a function of radians instead of degrees. *Radians* are another measure of angles. An arc whose length is one radius has a central angle whose measure is 1 radian. The central angle of a full circle is 2π radians.

TIP

The ACT expects you to be able to solve trig problems using either degrees or radians. If you recall the following conversion factor, you can convert the problem into the measure that you are more comfortable with. The measure of a circle is 360° or 2π radians, so the conversion factor is either 360° / 2π or 2π / 360°. You may also recall that the measure of half a circle is 180° or π radians. These measures can also be placed in ratio form and used as a conversion factor.

TIP

You might see other trigonometry identities on the exam, such as $\sin^2\theta + \cos^2\theta = 1$. Sometimes you might need to use the identities to show that two expressions are equal. Although there is no set procedure for proving two trig expressions are true, a good strategy is to look for forms on either side of the equation in which a substitution, or a series of substitutions, transforms the equation into two equal quantities.

TIP

To solve for the missing parts of any triangle, you might choose to use the law of sines or the law of cosines. If a triangle is labeled such that angles are named with capitals and opposite sides of those angles are labeled with the same lowercase letter, it's less complicated to remember the following laws correctly. Although the ACT will probably give you the law, you'll have to apply it correctly. The law of sines states that $a / \sin A = b / \sin B = c / \sin C$. The law of cosines states $m^2 = a^2 + b^2 - 2ab\cos M$, where M and m represent an angle (<u>M</u>) and the side (<u>m</u>) opposite that angle.

Trigonometric Equations

Some equations contain both trigonometric identities and numbers. For example, $\sin\theta = \frac{1}{\sqrt{2}}$ such that $0° \leq \theta \leq 360°$. To solve this equation, you must find the angle, the replacement of theta, whose sin is $\frac{1}{\sqrt{2}}$. Drawing a picture is helpful for organizing the information in this problem (see Figure 5.34).

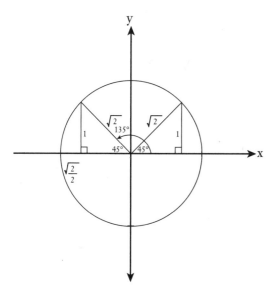

FIGURE 5.34 Possible angles when sin = $\frac{1}{2}$.

The sine ratio is $\frac{\text{opposite}}{\text{hypotenuse}}$, so the triangle you draw in the circle model has a side of 1 opposite the central angle and a hypotenuse of $\sqrt{2}$. A triangle that has sides of this length must be a 45°–45°–90°triangle. An angle that can replace θ is 45°. However, you are asked to consider all angles between 0° and 360°. Sine is also positive in the second quadrant, so 135° is also a value that can replace θ.

TIP

You can use factoring to solve trig equations, but if θ is multiplied by a number, you cannot simplify by dividing both sides of the equation by that number. Given the equation tan 3θ = 1, consider tan x = 1 and then divide your solutions by 3. Recall that 3θ has a domain 3 times that of θ.

Working with Trigonometric Functions

Practice working with trigonometric functions by completing the questions below.

1. The right triangle $\triangle$RST shown here has a hypotenuse 18 feet long. If the sin $\angle$R is the ratio $\frac{3}{4}$, how long is $\overline{\text{TS}}$ in feet?

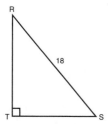

A. 3

B. 6

C. 13.5

D. 15

E. 24

2. The base, $\overline{AB}$, of triangle $\triangle ABC$ is 15 units and 6 units from the center of the circle, point C. What is the circumference of circle C to the nearest tenth of a unit?

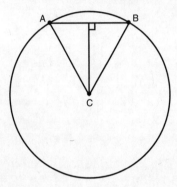

F. 8.0

G. 9.0

H. 9.6

J. 60.3

K. 92.25

3. The (x,y) coordinates in the coordinate plane are given for the vertices of a parallelogram in the following figure. The base of the parallelogram is parallel to the x-axis. What is the area in square units of the parallelogram?

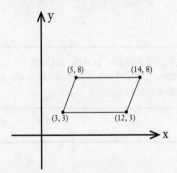

A. 18

B. 22.5

C. 36

D. 45

E. 50

Correct answers:

1. The correct answer is C. Use the definition of the sin of ∠R, which is the ratio of opposite side / hypotenuse, to solve this problem. With the information provided, the resulting ratio is $\frac{3}{4} = x/18$. Solving for x gives 13.5. The length of $\overline{TS}$ is 13.5.

2. The correct answer is J. You can use either right triangle to calculate the radius. Using the Pythagorean theorem results in $(7.5)^2 + 6^2 = r^2$, $r^2 = 92.25$, $r = 9.6$. Plugging 9.6 into the circumference formula gives $2 \cdot (9.6) \cdot \pi$. The circumference is 60.3.

3. The correct answer is D. The area of a parallelogram is the product of the base and height, where the base is perpendicular to the height. The base has a length of 9 and the height has a length of 5. The area is 45 square units.

Sample Exam Prep Questions and Answers

Questions

Use the skills you have reviewed in the previous pages to solve the 10 problems that follow. Compare your answers to the responses.

1. Which of the following quadratic equations has solutions $x = -a$ and $x = 3b$?

   (A.) $x^2 - 3ab = 0$

   (B.) $x^2 - 2abx - 3ab = 0$

   (C.) $x^2 + (a + 3b) + 3ab = 0$

   (D.) $x^2 + (3b - a) - 3ab = 0$

   (E.) $x^2 - (3b - a) - 3ab = 0$

2. Find the distance between $(-1,-3)$, and $(4,5)$.

   (F.) $\sqrt{5}$

   (G.) $\sqrt{13}$

   (H.) $2\sqrt{10}$

   (J.) $\sqrt{89}$

   (K.) 13

3. What is the point of intersection of $y = 2x + 3$ and $2x + 2y = 4$?

   (A.) $x = -1/3$

   (B.) $(-1/3, 7/3)$

   (C.) $(7/3, -1/3)$

   (D.) $y = 7/3$

   (E.) $(1,2)$

4. If $f(x) = x^2 - x - 3$ and $g(x) = x^{1/2}$, what is $f(g(x))$?

   (F.) $x - x^{3/2} - 3x^{1/2}$

   (G.) $x - \sqrt{x} - \sqrt{3}$

   (H.) $x^2 - x - 3 + x^{1/2}$

   (J.) $x - 3$

   (K.) $x - \sqrt{x} - 3$

5. Which of the following represents the solution set of the inequality $|x| \geq 3$ on the real number line?

(A.)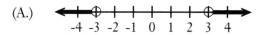

(B.)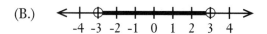

(C.)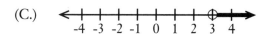

(D.)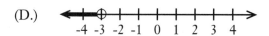

(E.)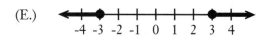

6. A teacher needs to conduct interviews with a representative committee of five students from her class of 32. How many distinct groups of 5 can she select from her class?

   (F.) 6.4

   (G.) 160

   (H.) 16,000

   (J.) 201,376

   (K.) 24,165,120

7. The base, $\overline{AB}$, of triangle $\triangle ABC$ is 15 units and 6 units from the center of the circle, point C. What is the circumference of circle C to the nearest tenth of a unit?

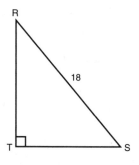

   (A.) 8.0

   (B.) 9.0

   (C.) 9.6

   (D.) 60.3

   (E.) 92.25

8. A sinusoid is shown in the following figure. What is the equation of the sinusoid?

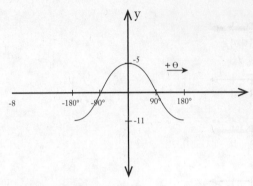

(F.) $y = -8 + 3\cos\theta$

(G.) $y = -8 + 3\sin\theta$

(H.) $y = 3\cos\theta$

(J.) $y = 3\sin\theta$

(K.) $y = -8 + 5\cos\theta$

9. A rectangle is inscribed in the following circle. The rectangle is 9 inches × 12 inches. What is the area of the circle in square inches?

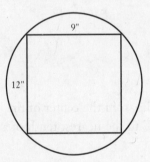

(A.) 7.5π

(B.) 15π

(C.) 36π

(D.) 56.25π

(E.) 225π

10. Consider the functions $y = 2x^2$ and $y = -2x^2$. Which of the following statements are true?

(F.) $y = -2x^2$ is the reflection of $y = 2x^2$ across the y-axis.

(G.) $y = -2x^2$ is the reflection of $y = 2x^2$ across the x-axis.

(H.) $y = -2x^2$ is the translation of $y = 2x^2$ across the x-axis.

(J.) $y = -2x^2$ is narrower than the graph of $y = 2x^2$.

(K.) $y = -2x^2$ is the reflection of $y = 2x^2$ across the origin.

Answers

1. **The correct answer is E.**

   If the solutions are $x = -a$ and $x = 3b$, then the factors are $(x + a)$ and $(x - 3b)$. Multiplying the factors results in the original quadratic equation. Using the FOIL method you get $x^2 + ax - 3bx - 3ab$. Factoring $a - x$ out of the two middle terms produces the answer $x^2 - (3b - a) - 3ab = 0$.

2. **The correct answer is J.**

   The easiest way to approach this problem is to set up a right triangle whose legs are the distance between the x's and the y's. It is equally valid to use the distance formula, $d = \sqrt{(x_2 - x_1)^2 + (y_2 - y_1)^2}$, but this formula will not be supplied on the test. The triangle you create should have a leg whose length is 5, the difference of the x-coordinates, and a leg whose length is 8, the difference between the y-coordinates. Plugging this into the Pythagorean theorem gives $5^2 + 8^2 = d^2$. Calculating further results in $89 = d^2$, so $d = \sqrt{89}$. The distance between the points is $\sqrt{89}$.

3. **The correct answer is B.**

   The point of intersection of two lines is the same as the solution you get when you solve simultaneously. Rephrase this question as: "Find the (x,y) that make both equations true statements." To do this, use substitution or elimination to solve simultaneously. To use elimination, put the two equations in the same order: $y = 2x + 3$ becomes $-2x + y = 3$ and is easily added to $2x + 2y = 4$. The result is $3y = 7$, so $y = 7/3$. You can stop working here if you recognize that B is the only answer that lists a coordinate point with 7/3 as y. To find the x-coordinate, you can replace y with 7/3 in either original equation and solve for x. Doing so gives $7/3 = 2x + 3$. Solving, you get $7/3 - 3 = 2x$, so x is $-1/3$. The answer is $(-1/3, 7/3)$.

4. **The correct answer is K.**

   This question is asking for the composition of two functions. The notation indicates that $g(x)$ is to be used as the input for $f(x)$. The result is $f(x) = (x^{1/2})^2 - x^{1/2} - 3$. Simplifying produces $x - x^{1/2} - 3$. Notice that this answer is not among the choices. However, answer K has an equivalent expression because $x^{1/2}$ is the same as $\sqrt{x}$.

5. **The correct answer is A.**

   The significant points to consider are 3 and -3. When you plug in 3.1 and -3.1, both values make a true statement. Because the symbol is $\geq$, use an open circle in the solution to show that 3 and -3 are not included. Any values bigger than 3 and any values smaller than -3 will make the statement true.

6. **The correct answer is J.**

   Immediately you can identify this question as a combination or permutation. First, determine if order is important. In the context of interviewing, order is not important, so this is a combination question. Find the number of ways to select 5 from 32. The permutation is $32 \times 31 \times 30 \times 29 \times 28$. The calculation gives 24,165,120. This number must be divided by the number of ways to arrange five choices, which is $5 \times 4 \times 3 \times 2 \times 1$, or 120. The division, which eliminates the repeated arrangements, results in 24,165,120/120, or 201,376. You could also have applied the formula for combinations here.

7. **The correct answer is D.**

   You can use either right triangle to calculate the radius. Using the Pythagorean theorem results in $(7.5)^2 + 6^2 = r^2$, $r^2 = 92.25$, $r = 9.6$. Plugging 9.6 into the circumference formula gives $2 \cdot (9.6) \cdot \pi$. The circumference is 60.3.

8. **The correct answer is F.**

   The center line is -8, so the equation should start $y = -8$. The sinusoid peaks at the origin, so this sinusoid can be expressed easily as $\cos \theta$. The amplitude is 3 because the wave rises 3 above and below the center line. Only the equation in answer A includes the information correctly, $y = -8 + 3\cos\theta$.

9. **The correct answer is D.**

   To get the area of the circle, you must first calculate the radius. The diameter of the circle is the diagonal of the rectangle. Use the Pythagorean theorem to calculate the length of the diagonal, $9^2 + 12^2 = d^2$. You might notice that this is a multiple of the triple 3, 4, 5. If $d^2 = 225$, then $d = 15$. If the diameter is 15, then the radius is 7.5. The area is $\pi(7.5)^2$. The result is 56.25π square inches.

10. **The correct answer is G.**

    You know that the sign of the coefficient of the x^2 term indicates which direction a parabola opens. The functions given are identical, except one opens upward and the other opens downward. If you folded the plane along the x-axis, the graphs would coincide. This means $y = 2x^2$ is reflected across the x-axis.

CHAPTER SIX

The Science Reasoning Test

Over the past few years in your high school science classes, you have learned about different scientific concepts and ideas, developed the scientific vocabulary to talk about them, and studied the scientists who have been important to the field. You have probably memorized formulas and definitions and analyzed data from a variety of types of experiments. You may wonder how a 35-minute, 40-question test could possibly encompass all this information, and if it does, how you will ever review for such a test.

The truth is that many students worry unnecessarily about this subject area of the test. There is no need to memorize definitions or formulas. Everything that you need to get the correct answer is included in the passages within the test. The science test deals with interpreting tables, graphs, and passages. Hone your interpretation skills related to these test components, and you will do fine on the science subject area of the ACT.

As you review this chapter, you will realize that the key to doing well on this part of the test is to be able to understand and interpret the reading passages and their accompanying graphs, tables, and passages in an attempt to find the correct answer to each question. You will use a bit of math as you work to answer some of the questions, but you won't be able to use a calculator for this part of the test. That's okay, though—the calculations you will be doing won't be especially tricky.

In this chapter, we'll cover the types of graphs and tables you will see on the test, experimental design, and how to work with opposing viewpoints.

> **NOTE**
>
> Science subject areas covered on the test include biology, chemistry, physics, and earth/space science. The test assumes that students taking it have completed coursework in high school earth science or physical science and a course in biology. Questions on the exam are based on the data and experimental designs presented at the beginning of each passage.

The Basic Structure of the Seven Reading Passages

The science test is arranged into seven reading passages, each one about 100–200 words in length. Typically six of the passages are about specific scientific experiments detailed within the reading. A seventh passage is usually about two scientists taking opposing viewpoints about the same issue.

NOTE

Some students report that the passages are arranged in order of difficulty and that the passage questions are arranged from least to most difficult. However, this pattern does not necessarily hold for every testing instance. An easy question may be offered at the end of a question group, and some passages may be easier for you than others. Don't think about passage or question order. It's usually most efficient to work through the passages in the order they are presented. You should respond to all questions, and take note of questions you are unsure of and want to return to if there is time later.

Like the other subject areas on the test, the directions for the science test will not change from those shown here. Take the time now to read and consider the directions. Then on test day, you won't spend any of your time reading them.

Directions:

Each passage in this test is followed by several questions. After reading the passage, choose the best answer to each question and fill in the corresponding oval on your answer document. You may refer to the passage as often as necessary.

You are NOT permitted to use a calculator on this test.

Following each passage is a set of questions, usually five or six, relating to what you have just read. Each passage contains the same three basic components:

1. The passage text
2. The data presentation (a graph, table, or chart)
3. The actual questions

The following sections will discuss each element in turn.

The Passage Text

Each passage on the ACT Science Reasoning exam begins with an introductory portion that is intended to explain what will follow. You will probably find it most efficient to read through this part relatively quickly as you seek to gain information to begin working on the questions.

TIP

Don't spend too much time reading the introductory portion of the passage. This part of the test is rarely referred to in the questions, despite the fact that it is often quite lengthy.

The amount of time you spend skimming the actual passage should depend on your level of knowledge of the subject area. If it looks unfamiliar, this is a good place to slow down and read carefully.

The Data Section

The data section occurs after the main portion of the passage. Look through these graphs, charts, or diagrams quickly, noting the variables that are being measured and the units being used. Try to figure out how the variables are related. You will find that there is really no way of knowing exactly what you are looking for until you get to the questions.

Note that a variable is a quantity that has a value assigned to it. The science test may refer to independent and dependent variables. We will discuss these two types of variables in this chapter. For now, know that you will need to take a short period of time to really look at the table, graph, or chart that you are given with each passage. Then you will need to answer these questions:

1. What are the variables?

2. How are the variables being measured here?

The Questions Themselves

As mentioned earlier, the science test is composed of seven passages. By dividing the 35-minute testing period into seven blocks of time, you will see that you should allow yourself no more than 5 minutes to work with each passage and its accompanying questions. Your goal should be to try to use less than 5 minutes on at least a few of the passages so that you can bank a few minutes for questions that are particularly tough and time consuming. When you have completed all of the questions, you can go back to those for which you were unsure of the correct response.

TIP

Your watch will be particularly important to you during the science test. Make sure you keep an eye on the time as you work through this area of the ACT.

You will need a good plan to make the best use of your time on the test. Attacking the test in a similar way to the ACT reading test is an excellent strategy. As in the reading test, the answers to all the questions are literally right in front of you. The answers are either within the passage or interpreted from the accompanying tables, charts, and graphs. Here is how the science test is set up.

Read the Passage and Look at the Accompanying Charts

Most of the paragraphs in the science test are set up such that the introductory sentence tells you right away what the passage will be about. For example:

> The following diagram shows the concentration of ions and dissolved gases in the sediment at the bottom of the Pacific Ocean.

You may recognize what you are reading as something that you learned and still recall from a high school science class. Trust that what you read in a passage is correct information. That means that if you already feel you know what the passage is describing, it is not essential for you to read each word about the subject. The passage writers are not trying to trick you here—and if they talk about a theory or law of science, it's the actual one that you have studied in school. Be comfortable knowing that if you want to you can skim the passage if you are already comfortable with the material and concepts it describes.

Next, skim the data section. Don't spend much time trying to figure out exactly what the accompanying charts, tables, and graphs mean right now. You will want to read the heading on each so that you know what it is measuring, but don't spend any time right now closely analyzing these graphics. You don't know what the question is asking yet.

> **TIP**
>
> Jot notes to yourself on the test booklet as necessary. Feel free to mark it up however you wish.

Read the Question Carefully

Questions on this part of the test will fit into one of three types:

- ▶ **Questions that ask you to analyze data**—These data representation questions ask you to read, summarize, estimate, or predict from the data that is provided. You will see a variety of charts, tables, diagrams, and other graphical material that is similar to what you have worked with in science textbooks and journals. The questions here will concentrate on your interpretation of that graphical material. Remember that the answers are right there for you to locate.

- ▶ **Questions that require you to understand how a particular experiment is designed and executed, and ultimately what the experiment proves**—These questions will ask about the design of particular experiments and your interpretation of their results. You will need to understand what the experiment is about to answer these questions accurately.

- ▶ **Questions that ask you to apply, defend, or go against a principle of science**—These are often called "opposing viewpoint" or "conflicting viewpoint" questions and are usually found within the last passage of the test. (See the "Changes in Experiment Design" section, later in this chapter, for more information about this type of question.) The questions here will focus on how you understand or interpret the alternative viewpoints.

> **TIP**
>
> The passage and the accompanying questions appear on either facing pages or the same page, so you will be able to refer to the data with ease when answering the questions.

Before looking at the set of potential answers, try to answer the question on your own. After reading each question, refer to the part of the data or the specific design of the experiment that will help you answer the question. Take time to read fully the part of the passage or graphic that this question addresses. Attempt to come up with an answer to the question, and see whether it appears within the provided choices. If it does, shade in the answer on your answer key and move on. Don't bother considering the other choices. It'll be taking some of your valuable time. Trust yourself.

TIP

Read each question slowly. Understand what it is asking you.

The Specific Structure of the Three Types of Reading Passages

The passages on the test fall into three categories: data representation, research summaries, and opposing viewpoints. *Data representation* passages assess your ability to understand and interpret information on a chart, table, or graph. *Research summary* passages assess your ability to follow the steps and procedures in particular experiments and interpret the results. *Opposing viewpoint* passages present two (or sometimes three) conflicting viewpoints and ask you to answer questions about the conflict, and sometimes how it might be resolved. Table 6.1 shows the number of each type of passage you'll see on the test, as well as the number of questions associated with each passage type.

TABLE 6.1 The Number of Questions and Passages for the Three Types of Passages

Type of Passage	Number of Passages	Number of Questions
Data Representation	3	15
Research Summaries	3	18
Opposing Viewpoints	1	7

TIP

Glance at the questions at the end of the passage to assess how many there are. You can identify the type of passage by the number of questions:

▶ Five questions means a data representation passage.

▶ Six questions means a research summaries passage.

▶ Seven questions means an opposing viewpoints passage.

Data Representation

Graphs are the most efficient way for scientists and researchers to interpret and share the information they collect from their experiments. Most passages that use graphs are not difficult to read if you have some experience reviewing and analyzing graphs prior to the test. This part of the chapter will help you acquire that experience.

Here is what you will need to know to read the tables and charts on the science test.

Recognizing Abbreviations

The graphs and data tables found on the science exam contain not only numbers, but also the units in which the data is measured. These units are often abbreviated. To save time you will want to have a clear understanding of what each abbreviation means and the dimensions they represent.

TIP

Know the terminology of the science test. Become familiar with the vocabulary terms and abbreviations that are common on this test.

For example, density is a measure of the amount of mass per unit volume and can be represented as g/ml for liquids and kg/m^3 for solids.

Problems could also be stated in terms of *specific gravity*, which is the ratio of the density of the liquid in question over the density of water. (The density of pure water at 4°C is 1.00g/ml.)

Most questions on the science test use the metric system as their standard of measurement. Make sure you know what type of measurement is being used to report the data.

Because the metric system uses standard prefixes, you can easily figure out most other metric abbreviations, such as *cl* for *centiliter*. Notice the abbreviations in Tables 6.2 and 6.3. You will find that most are logical and easily deciphered. Don't spend time memorizing these. Read them and think about why each abbreviation is used. Figure out why the abbreviation makes sense. When you run across these on the test, you will easily recall what measures they are.

TABLE 6.2   Metric Unit Abbreviations

Abbreviation	Word
b	bit
B	byte
C	Celsius, Centigrade
cc or cm^2	square centimeter (cm^2 is standard)
cc or cm^3	cubic centimeter (cm^3 is standard)
cm	centimeter
G, GB	gigabyte (GB is standard)
g, gr	gram (g is standard)

TABLE 6.2   *Continued*

Abbreviation	Word
ha	hectare
K	Kelvin
K, KB	kilobyte (KB is standard)
kg	kilogram
kl	kiloliter
km	kilometer
l	liter
m	meter
M, MB	megabyte (MB is standard)
mcg or μg	microgram (μg is standard)
mg	milligram
ml	milliliter
mm	millimeter
MT	metric ton
t, T	metric ton
w, W	watt (W is standard)
kw, kW	kilowatt (kW is standard)
kwh, kWh	kilowatt-hour (kWh is standard)

TABLE 6.3   **English Unit Abbreviations**

Abbreviation	Word
bbl.	barrel
cu.	cubic
doz.	dozen
F., F	Fahrenheit
fl. oz.	fluid ounce
ft.	foot
gal.	gallon
gr.	grain
gr., gro.	gross
in.	inch
k., kt.	karat
k., kt.	knot
lb.	pound
LT, L.T.	long ton
mi.	mile
mph	miles per hour
n.m.	nautical miles
oz.	ounce
pt.	pint

TABLE 6.3 *Continued*

Abbreviation	Word
qt.	quart
sq.	square
rpm	revolutions per minute
T., T	ton
T.	tablespoon in some cookbooks
t.	teaspoon in some cookbooks
tbsp.	tablespoon
tsp.	teaspoon
yd.	yard

Other Common Abbreviations

You likely will see some of these abbreviations within the tables and charts on the science test:

▶ *pH* is a method of expressing the acidity or alkalinity of a solution, based on the concentration of hydrogen ions.

▶ *cal* is short for *calorie*, a quantity of heat energy equal to 4.185 joules. The *Large Calorie* of the nutritionist is a kilocalorie, equal to 1,000 calories.

▶ The single hatch mark (') can stand for a *foot* or a *geographical minute* (a minute of longitude or latitude).

▶ The double hatch mark (") can stand for an *inch* or *a geographical second* (a second of longitude or latitude). So, 5'9" would mean 5 feet, 9 inches. Similarly, 39°31'56" N. would mean 39 degrees, 31 minutes, 56 seconds north.

▶ The Greek letter μ (*mu*) is often used to show the prefix *micro*, especially in scientific publications. For example, μg would be the same as microgram, and μl would be *microliter*. By itself, μ stands for *micron*; mμ means *millimicron*; and μμ means *micromicron* (a millionth of a micron).

▶ The prefix *nano* means *billionth* and is usually represented by the letter *n*, as in *ns* for *nanosecond*.

▶ In standard scientific notation, the word *per* is represented by a forward slash. So, *km/h* is kilometers per hour.

Knowing the Parts of a Graph

There are certain parts of graphs on which you will want to concentrate your attention.

The Title

You will need to figure out right away what the graph is representing. To do so, read the title. For instance, the title of the graph in Figure 6.1 is: "Average Water Temperature in February, Stigmore Lake." We know that the graph will provide water temperatures for dates in February.

Date	Average Temperature for the Week										
2/28											XXX
2/21			XXX								
2/14								XXX			
2/07						XXX					
2/02							XXX				

| 50 | 51 | 52 | 53 | 54 | 55 | 56 | 57 | 58 | 59 | 60 |

Average Water Temperature in February, Stigmore Lake

FIGURE 6.1 Sample graph structure.

The Axes

Make sure you know what the x- and y-axes are measuring on your graph. The x-axis is flat and runs horizontally along the bottom of the graph. The y-axis runs vertically on the graph.

Reading a Graph

When you read a graph, you are looking for trends in the graph data.

NOTE

Science textbooks are a useful resource for reviewing graphs, tables, and charts. Read the summaries at the end of each chapter and answer any question that involves interpreting a graph or data chart.

Journals that discuss general science and biology are also a great place to hone your skills. Many of the current topics in science appearing on the exam will be found in science journals. Do not worry about understanding every part of every article you read. Choose articles that are science related, and pay close attention to the data that is presented. Your science teacher will have some good suggestions about journals to look at and will likely have some back issues for you to borrow for study and review.

A *slope* is the ratio of the rise to the run between any two points on a line. Be prepared for differences in the slopes of graphs you see on the test and in your review. Occasionally, an axis can contain values written in an order that is opposite of what you are accustomed to seeing.

Identifying Trends and Patterns

Some graphs on the exam may take the form of a number of data points scattered across the plot area, but showing some general trend. There isn't always a pattern or a trend to the points on a line, but if you can identify one it will make your problem solving easier. In the following sections, you will learn the principles involved in identifying trends and patterns.

Direct and Inverse Relationships

Some of the data presentation questions on this part of the test will ask about how the relationship between two or maybe even three variables will look when graphed. You might be asked to match the data given in a table with its correct graph. The relationship between the data being measured may be a *direct relationship* or an *inverse relationship*. This is also called a *direct variation* and an *indirect variation*. In this type of table, you will need to find the correct column or row in the data table, scan through the data, and select the graph that most closely matches the data.

TIP

A direct relationship (direct variation) means that both variables vary in the same way: As the x variable increases, the y variable increases, or as the x variable decreases, the y variable decreases.

An inverse relationship (indirect variation) means that both variables vary in the opposite way: As the x variable increases, the y variable decreases, or as the x variable decreases, the y variable increases.

Direct and Indirect Relationship Examples

We'll start with the direct relationship. In this example, you will see that force and acceleration have a direct relationship: A student varies the force applied to a 1kg cart on a low-friction track and measures acceleration (see Table 6.4).

TABLE 6.4 Direct Relationship

Force in Newtons	Acceleration (m/s^2)
0.50	0.45
1.00	0.93
1.50	1.41
2.00	1.87
2.50	2.48
3.00	2.95

TIP

Force is measured in Newtons. One *Newton* is the amount of force required to accelerate a 1kg object by 1 meter per second for each second.

Those who have studied physics will recognize this as an example of Newton's second law: $F = ma$.

The more force that is applied to the cart, the more acceleration will result—a direct relationship. Figure 6.2 shows the direct relationship between force and acceleration. You can see that the lines on this graph move upward and to the right—your clue that the relationships here are direct.

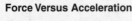
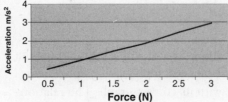

FIGURE 6.2 Direct relationship.

Now we'll move to the indirect relationship: A student applies two Newtons of force to a cart sliding on a low-friction track and varies the mass (see Table 6.5).

TABLE 6.5   Inverse Relationship

Mass (Kg)	Acceleration (m/s²)
0.25	8.22
0.50	4.20
0.75	2.66
1.00	1.97
1.25	1.64
1.50	1.30
1.75	1.11
2.00	1.02

The graph for this inverse relationship should look like Figure 6.3. You can see that the lines move downward and to the right—your clue that this is an inverse relationship.

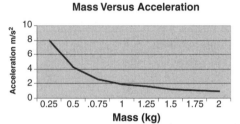

FIGURE 6.3   Inverse relationship.

> **NOTE**
>
> Challenge questions 1–3 at the end of this chapter provide the type of relationship questions you are likely to find on the ACT test.

Extreme Data Points

Extremes are the minimum and maximum points on a table or graph. In Figure 6.4, the extremes are the acceleration rates of 8 m/s/s and 1.5 m/s/s. A question on the test may ask you the maximum speed, minimum concentration, or some other value that will be an extreme data point. These are usually relatively easy to identify on a graph.

Critical Points

Critical points are the values on a graph where change occurs. Sometimes called "points of change," these values can be identified on a graph by looking for areas of dramatic change. Knowing where these critical areas are can help you make generalizations as you evaluate data. If a graph is a straight line and then a point moves above or below the line, you will know that something has occurred at that point, and it is likely that one of the questions accompanying it will somehow ask about it.

In Figure 6.4, you can see that there is a critical point at noon in the nitrogen dioxide value, which is indicated in the legend by NO_2. Something has occurred at this point that has affected this gas.

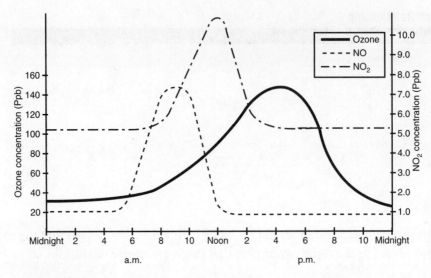

FIGURE 6.4 The concentration of nitric oxide (NO), nitrogen dioxide (NO$_2$), and ozone (O$_3$) during a typical photochemical smog episode.

NOTE

As you read the passages and consider the tables, graphs, and charts included with each, keep in mind that scientists look at a problem in two distinct ways:

▶ *General to specific* (deductive reasoning)

▶ *Specific to general* (inductive reasoning)

Scientists often already know a principle or theory, and they want to see how it applies to something they are studying. This is general-to-specific thinking. For example, the law of inertia states that unless it is acted on by an unbalanced force, an object will maintain a constant velocity. To see what may happen, a scientist may want to apply an upward force to a pebble resting on the ground. This is an example of a general-to-specific way of thinking, often called *deduction* (or deductive reasoning).

On the other hand, there is specific-to-general thinking, or *inductive* reasoning. This involves making predictions (hypotheses) and then setting out to prove or disprove them. For example, if a scientist were to measure 10 seedlings after four days and find that each measured ? inch, she might conclude that all seedlings measure ? inch after four days.

Interpolating and Extrapolating

Some data representation questions will ask you to estimate what value might be found where there is no data. You will need to use a form of estimation to respond to these types of questions.

One type of estimation is called *interpolation*. Interpolation involves the estimation of a value for a function between values that are already known or determined. If done carefully, it is often appropriate to interpolate, to assume that the data points between observed data points follow the same general pattern as what is observed. This is what you will do when the question asks you to guess which value might be found between two existing data points.

For example, look at the data in Table 6.6. Temperature is measured every 2km up to the top of the troposphere, the innermost layer of the Earth's atmosphere. What temperature would you expect to find at an altitude of 13.0km?

TABLE 6.6   Altitude and Temperature in the Troposphere

Altitude (km)	Temperature (°C)
2.0	20
4.0	10
6.0	0
8.0	−10
10.0	−20
12.0	−30
14.0	−40
16.0	−50

The answer is −35°C.

To find the answer, you would read down the "Altitude" column until you find 12.0km. The next higher value is 14.0km; the value you are looking for lies between these two points. Because it appears that the temperature decreases by 10° Celsius for each 2 kilometers of increase in altitude, you should be able to recognize this as a straight-line graph that passes through −35° Celsius at 13.0 kilometers.

Extrapolation is the second type of estimation. It requires you to extend an existing trend further than the existing data, or rather to estimate a value of a function lying *outside* the range of known values. Look again at Table 6.5. If you had to guess, what do you think the temperature would be at an altitude of 18.0km?

The answer is −60°C. This answer is found by extrapolating beyond the limits of the data presented. Again, you should see that this graph is a straight line, and it should pass through −60° Celsius at 18.0km.

Research Summaries

Research summary questions—questions about designing experiments—make up a bit less than half of the 40 questions on the ACT Science Reasoning exam. These types of questions are designed for you to evaluate the data or the design of one or more scientific experiments. The test writers are really trying to assess how much you know about actually doing experiments.

The key to this part of the test is to identify the correct variables and to recognize the limitations of each experiment. A number of twists may be thrown into an experiment or a question, such as changing a procedure or a result. You will need to be sure that you read each question carefully so that you know and understand exactly what is being asked.

The Parts of an Experiment

The scientific method, or scientific process, is considered fundamental to scientific investigation and to the acquisition of new knowledge based on physical evidence. Simply put, it is the correct order in which an experiment is undertaken and performed. You will need to spend some time reviewing the parts of the scientific method now. As you review this section, remember that there is usually, although not always, both an experimental group and a control group in experiments. The experimental group is the group that receives the treatment that an experiment has been designed to test. The control group is treated the same way as the experimental group, except for the procedure that the experiment has been designed to test.

The Six Parts of the Scientific Method

1. **Problem/Purpose:** This part is where the scientific question to be solved is stated. The question is best expressed as an *open-ended* one; that is, a question that is answered with a statement, not just a simple *yes* or *no*.

2. **Research:** In this part, the researchers or scientists investigate what others have already learned about the question. They gather information that will help in performing the experiment.

3. **Hypothesis:** After having thoroughly researched a topic, researchers make an educated guess about what will happen in the experiment. They state their hypothesis in such a way that it can be readily measured. (A *hypothesis* is a statement of a possible explanation for some natural phenomenon.) Scientists then explain how their planned project can demonstrate their purpose.

4. **Procedure:** This part consists of a detailed explanation of how the experiment will be conducted to test the hypothesis.

5. **Analysis:** After the experiment is conducted and assessed, the researchers give a detailed explanation of observations, data, and results. This analysis is essentially a summary of what the experimental data has shown.

6. **Results and Conclusion:** This part is a summary of the results of the experiment and a statement of how the results relate to the hypothesis. If certain results differ from the hypothesis, reasons for this are given here. Often, ideas for further testing are also mentioned here.

To assess an experiment, you will need to know:

▶ Which factor is being varied between the two groups

▶ Which group is the control (if there is a control group in the experiment)

▶ What the results of the experiment show

▶ How the results differ for the control and the experimental groups

The Independent Variable

The *independent variable*, also called the *experimental variable*, is the part of the experiment that the scientist has changed to see how it might affect a different variable. Independent variables can be said to act as a catalyst for the dependent variable.

Figure 6.5 shows the results of a student's investigation of the relationship between the length and period of a pendulum. The *length* of the pendulum is the distance from the center of the pendulum mass (known as the *bob*) to the fixed point where the pendulum is attached. The *period* of a pendulum is the period of time that is required for the pendulum to complete one back-and-forth cycle. The student varied the length of the pendulum and measured the period.

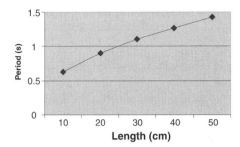

FIGURE 6.5 Length and period of a simple pendulum.

In this example, the length of the pendulum is the independent variable. You can see that changing the length will change the results of the experiment.

> **TIP**
>
> In graphing, the independent variable is usually placed on the x-axis.

The Dependent Variable

The *dependent variable* is the variable in an experiment that changes as a result of changes in the independent variable. In the pendulum experiment example, the dependent variable is the period of the pendulum.

Let's look at another example: To see how varying dosages of a particular drug affect a patient's medical condition, a scientist could look at how symptoms of the condition change when dosages of the drug are increased or decreased. In this case, the drug is the independent variable and the medical condition is the dependent variable. The independent variable (the drug) is being changed. The dependent variable (the medical condition) is affected.

> **TIP**
>
> In graphing, the dependent variable is usually placed on the y-axis.

Using the Scientific Method

Here is how the six parts of the scientific method could be used in a student's experiment. Each component of the process is necessary to the experiment and should be clearly defined. Although you will encounter questions on the test that refer to various parts of the scientific method, these parts won't necessarily be referred to by name.

Strategy for Using the Scientific Method

1. **Problem:** How does temperature affect the size of growing Epsom salt crystals?

2. **Research:** I used library sources and the Internet to try to discover what other people have found out about crystal growth at various temperatures.

3. **Hypothesis:** I predict that, in a 3-hour period, crystals growing in a solution maintained at a temperature of 5°C will attain a larger size than crystals growing in a solution maintained at a temperature of 25°C.

4. **Procedure:** In two identical 400mL beakers, mix 1/2 cup of Epsom salt (magnesium sulfate) with 1/2 cup of 90°C water. Stir for 1 minute and then place one beaker in a refrigerator. Set the other beaker on a counter at room temperature. Wait 3 hours. Set the two beakers side by side. Observe and measure the crystals in the two beakers.

5. **Analysis:** In the solution stored on the counter at room temperature, the largest crystals were less than 1cm in length. In the solution stored in the refrigerator, a crystal mass had grown to a diameter of more than 5cm.

6. **Results and Conclusion:** Epsom salt crystals grew much larger in the cooler environment. The results support my hypothesis. I will now conduct additional experiments (with different starting temperatures, different salt concentrations, and different storage temperatures) to see how my results will change.

Determining Whether the Data Supports a Hypothesis

Some of the questions on the test will offer a possible hypothesis. These questions will ask you to identify experimental data that supports or denies that particular hypothesis. It is likely that the hypothesis will be supported, but you must be especially careful to make sure that the type of data presented is appropriate to answer this question.

For example, you may be presented with information such as this: Biology students surveyed three different streams, from the beginnings of these named streams (the *headwaters*) all the way to where they empty into another body of water (the *mouths*). They were trying to determine the number of different fish species present at each sampling location, as shown in Tables 6.7–6.9.

TABLE 6.7   The Number of Fish Species Present at Nine Sampling Sites in Jump-Off Joe Creek

Kilometers from Source	Number of Fish Species
1.0	3
5.3	6
8.4	7
10.6	8
12.5	9
18.3	13
23.8	8
29.8	5
37.5 (mouth, or end of stream)	4

TABLE 6.8 The Number of Fish Species Present at Nine Sampling Sites in Anchor Creek

Kilometers from Source	Number of Fish Species
0.5	2
3.5	2
7.2	4
10.1	5
12.2	7
17.4	6
21.8	7
23.3	8
27.0 (mouth)	9

TABLE 6.9 The Number of Fish Species Present at Nine Sampling Sites in Clear Creek

Kilometers from Source	Number of Fish Species
0.2	1
2.1	2
4.5	3
7.2	3
9.1	5
11.8	4
14.3	4
15.3	6
18.1 (mouth)	8

After reviewing the tables and figuring out what they measure, you would be presented with a question-and-answer set such as the one shown after this paragraph. Before looking at the answer choices, you should attempt to figure out a response on your own. Think about whether the data in the tables tells you that as you move downstream in the creek, you will find a greater diversity, a wider assortment of fish species. After you have figured out your own answer, see whether it is within the answer choices that you would have been given for this question:

Does the data from these three streams support the hypothesis that, as you move downstream, you will find a greater diversity of fish species?

(A) No, all three streams have fewer fish species near their mouths.

(B) Yes, this is true for all three streams.

(C) This is true for Clear Creek and Anchor Creek, but not for Jump-Off Joe Creek.

(D) This is true for Anchor Creek, but not for Jump-Off Joe Creek and Clear Creek.

If your answer doesn't appear in the choices, quickly see for which creeks the statement is true. Eliminate choices as you are able. In the end, you will see that the results from both Clear Creek and Anchor Creek show an increase in the number of species farther downstream, whereas the number of species in Jump-Off Joe Creek tapers off in the lower reaches. Thus, the answer is C. If you didn't choose C as the correct answer, spend a few minutes reviewing the explanation shown here and the data tables.

The following question-and-answer set also refers to the tables you just reviewed. As with the first question, try to figure out the response before looking at the answer choices:

Do the results of these surveys support the hypothesis that longer streams tend to have more total fish species?

- (F) Yes, Jump-Off Joe Creek was the longest, and it had the greatest number of fish species.

- (G) Yes, longer streams tend to have more total fish species.

- (H) No, this was not true for any of the streams sampled.

- (J) It is not possible to answer this question with the information presented.

The total number of species from each stream is *not* presented in the information given. This is an example of recognizing the limits of the data. Only by comparing the type of species found in each sample with all the samples from each stream would it be possible to determine the *total* number of different species present in each stream. In the end, you should see that the answer is J.

Making Predictions from the Results of an Experiment

You will find test questions asking you to evaluate the results of an experiment, or a series of experiments, and apply them to a similar type of experiment. In many cases, the original experiment is repeated with one variable or procedure altered. To respond to the question, you will need to evaluate how this change affects the experiment. When you encounter these types of questions, always be on the lookout for the words *suppose*, *assume*, and *if*. These words mean that you will need to change something about the experiment or extend the findings to a slightly different circumstance.

For example, suppose that a first study finds that children between the ages of 7 and 9 who watch more than 3 hours of television per day are 10 times more likely to have *attention deficit disorder* (ADD) than children of the same age who watch less than 1 hour of television per day. What might we learn from a second similar study involving children ages 4–6 who watch more than 3 hours of television per day?

Think about how the second study varies from the first one. In the second study, just the age of the children studied is changed. So if the first study is valid, we would expect to see a much higher incidence of ADD among the younger children when we compare them with children of the same age who watch less than 1 hour of television per day.

Challenge question 4 (*Numbers of Fish Species at Various Points Within Four Streams*) at the end of this chapter is a prediction question similar to what you may find on the ACT test.

Ordering Data Sets in Ascending or Descending Order

Some science questions will ask you to order information presented in a data set in either *ascending* or *descending* order.

TIP

Ascending order means the numbers are listed in increasing order (smallest to largest).
Descending order means the numbers are listed in decreasing order (largest to smallest).

For example, given the population data on the following four cities, you might be asked to list them in ascending order based on population. Then you might be asked to list them again, this time in descending order:

London: 7,172,091
Beijing: 5,715,368
Mexico City: 8,605,239
Tokyo: 8,134,683

The proper listing of the cities' population in *ascending* order would be:

Beijing
London
Tokyo
Mexico City

Listed in *descending* order the cities would be:

Mexico City
Tokyo
London
Beijing

Questions on the test are trickier, of course, but you do need to ensure that you know the difference between the two words. For instance, on the test, you may be presented with a passage such as this:

Solubility of Various Types of Salt

A student was studying the effects of temperature on the solubility of three different salts. She slowly heated 100g of water and recorded the temperature and mass of the solute that dissolved.

When the solution would no longer hold more salt, a small amount of precipitate formed at the bottom of the beaker. This indicated that the solution had reached saturation. By heating just enough to dissolve this precipitate, she determined the saturation point for each salt at a number of temperatures (see Figure 6.6).

The graphic shows the highest value (in grams) for each type of salt dissolved in the solution. To determine the saturation value for each substance, we note the highest y-axis (Solubility) value for each salt. To determine the ascending order of these values, we start with the lowest solubility value and proceed upward to the highest solubility value.

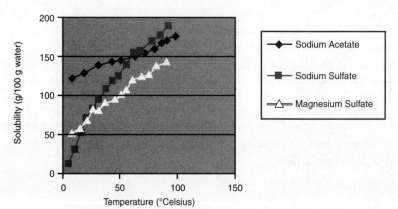

FIGURE 6.6 Saturation point for each type of salt.

After skimming the passage to know what the experiment is about, spend a few seconds looking at Figure 6.6. Then read the question. Think about the answer to the question before reading the answer choices. You already know that the three salts are sodium acetate, sodium sulfate, and magnesium sulfate. In your own mind, order them from the lowest to highest (ascending) solubility. Then, look for the answer that matches your own answer.

At 90°C, what is the ascending order of the solubility of the three salts?

(A) Sodium acetate, sodium sulfate, magnesium sulfate

(B) Sodium sulfate, magnesium sulfate, sodium acetate

(C) Magnesium sulfate, sodium sulfate, sodium acetate

(D) Magnesium sulfate, sodium acetate, sodium sulfate

You should have chosen D as the correct answer. To arrive at this answer, you would need to make sure you read up along the 90°C grid line. Remember that increasing solubility is the order asked for.

Using the same data as the preceding question, answer the following question. As always, before looking at the answer choices, attempt to list the solubility of the four salts on your own. Then refer to the answer choices and see whether your response matches one of these choices:

Suppose that 112g of another salt, such as sodium nitrate, was added to the experiment and it dissolved in 100g of water at 50°C. At this temperature, what would be the solubility of the four salts in descending order (from most to least soluble)?

(F) Magnesium sulfate, sodium sulfate, sodium acetate, sodium nitrate

(G) Magnesium sulfate, sodium nitrate, sodium sulfate, sodium acetate

(H) Sodium acetate, sodium sulfate, sodium nitrate, magnesium sulfate

(J) Sodium sulfate, sodium acetate, sodium nitrate, magnesium sulfate

You should have chosen H as the correct answer. Keep in mind that in this question the order is descending, which means decreasing. To get to the correct answer, start with the most soluble at 50°C and work your way down the 50°C grid line, while including the new data point for sodium nitrate. The main problem here is to find between which two salts the solubility of sodium nitrate will fall. You will see that this ends up being between sodium sulfate and magnesium sulfate.

> **TIP**
>
> Watch for words such as *increasing, decreasing, most, least, ascending,* and *descending* in a problem's question. Identifying these will help you solve the problem more quickly.

Changes in Experiment Design

To test your understanding of an experiment's design, test writers may ask you to explain or interpret specific changes in the design itself. On the test, these "what-if" questions usually have to do with changes to the experimental controls. This means you will need to understand the importance of a control, a reference sample, or any corrections or changes that are made to the raw data.

> **NOTE**
>
> An *experimental control* is the sample to which no changes are made. It is tested with all the experimental procedures included, except for the experimental variable or treatment. When speaking of *experimental controls*, scientists mean that they have made every effort to keep all experimental conditions exactly the same for all trials, samples, or periods of time during the experiment.

For example, in drug-testing experiments there is always a control group in place. Those in this group are given a *placebo* (a pill with no active ingredients) rather than the drug being tested. Those in the control group are not aware they are not being given the actual drug. Scientists use this type of control group to ensure that no other factors, such as psychological factors, are affecting the experiment.

> **NOTE**
>
> Challenge questions 5 and 6 at the end of this chapter provide the type of experiment design questions you are likely to find on the ACT test.

> **TIP**
>
> Don't be confused by complex-looking charts, tables, or graphs. Search for the important piece of information you will need to answer the question.

The test will often present two or three experiments within one passage and ask you to compare the findings. These different experiments allow scientists to verify the conclusions of one experiment with the results from another experiment that arrived at similar conclusions but through a different procedure.

> **NOTE**
>
> Challenge questions 7 and 8 at the end of this chapter provide an example of these types of data comparison.

Opposing Viewpoints

Questions about opposing or conflicting viewpoints are seen by most test takers as perhaps the most difficult part of the ACT Science Reasoning exam. Fortunately, only 7 of the 40 exam questions are of this type. These questions typically appear at the end of the test. Some questions ask you to identify the statement that would best support one of the viewpoints. Other questions ask you to extend the reasoning behind one of the viewpoints to a different situation.

Questions about conflicting viewpoints use the same general format as other types of questions on this exam. An experimental scenario or description of a specific topic is followed by the differing viewpoints from two or more investigators. The questions usually require you to reread each scientist's views carefully.

Questions about conflicting viewpoints may require you to reread the information found in the passage. For this reason, it is important to skim quickly through the passage the first time and jump to the questions as soon as you are able. Then reread carefully the areas that contain information you will need to assess.

> **TIP**
>
> Remember that just as on the reading portion of the test, it is fine to underline parts of the passage that you may want to quickly find later. If it is a timesaver for you, don't hesitate to underline anything on the test.

Typically, the first part of the passage contains information with which both scientists agree. This is the setting or background information, just like the other passages in the science exam. After the first part of the passage, you will read the scientists' or students' unique views. Then, you will need to ask yourself the following questions to interpret the viewpoints of two or more scientists or students:

1. How are their viewpoints similar to or different from each other?

2. What are the strengths and weaknesses of each view?

To answer those questions quickly, it is best to try to put yourself in the position of each scientist. Imagine yourself forming an argument supporting one of their positions. Be careful that you do not use your own opinions or knowledge of the subject in answering these questions.

TIP

Remember that time is limited on this exam. Questions about conflicting viewpoints are a part of the test where you could spend too much time on a small number of questions. Keep in mind that with difficult questions, you should guess, move on, and go back later if there is time.

TIP

When a statement of a principle is given in a passage, assume for your purposes that the principle is an accurate statement of an existing and recognized scientific principle. Don't second-guess whether it is presented the way you learned it in the past. Just accept what the principle says as stated.

Challenge Questions

Temperature and Pressure at Varying Altitudes in Earth's Atmosphere

In Figure 6.7, six atmospheric variables are presented in one diagram. The graph displays temperature on the x-axis and uses five columns of the y-axis for displaying altitude, air density, atmospheric pressure, and the names of atmospheric layers and some cloud types. Note that the temperature *trend* changes from layer to layer.

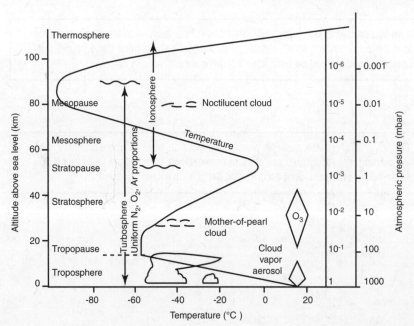

FIGURE 6.7
Atmospheric variables.

1. In Earth's atmosphere's second-lowest layer, the stratosphere, as altitude increases:

    (A) Air temperatures change randomly at various altitudes.

    (B) Air temperatures decrease.

    (C) Air temperatures increase.

    (D) Air temperatures are unaffected by changes in altitude.

2. Throughout all of Earth's atmosphere, as altitude increases:

    (F) Atmospheric pressure remains constant.

    (G) Atmospheric pressure decreases.

    (H) Atmospheric pressure increases.

    (J) Atmospheric pressure is unaffected by changes in altitude.

Earth's crust consists of numerous moving tectonic plates. Along the west coast of South America, the Nazca oceanic crustal plate is descending beneath the South American continental crustal plate. This process is called *subduction*.

The subduction zone is the place where two lithospheric plates come together, one riding over the other. Figures 6.8–6.10 show the data from earthquake foci at the convergent plate boundary along the west coast of South America. The *focus* of an earthquake is the point where the earthquake is actually located, and the *epicenter* is the point on the surface of the Earth that is exactly above the focus. With a quick check of the scattered data, you should see that there is a general trend: The farther east the epicenters are located from the subduction zone, the deeper the earthquakes' foci are located. This trend marks the approximate boundary between the South American continental plate and the Nazca oceanic plate that is subducting beneath it.

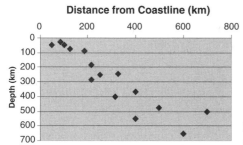

FIGURE 6.8 Earthquake foci along the west coast of South America.

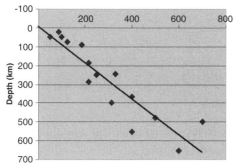

FIGURE 6.9 Earthquake foci along the west coast of South America, showing a trend line (line of best fit).

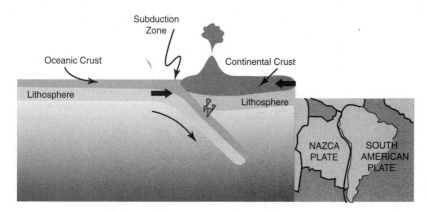

FIGURE 6.10 Meeting of tectonic plates.

3. The most rational assumption from the graph is that:

(A) The depth of the subducted oceanic plate increases as you move westward from the subduction boundary.

(B) The depth of the subducted oceanic plate increases as you move eastward from the subduction boundary.

(C) The depth of the subducted oceanic plate decreases as you move eastward from the subduction boundary.

(D) The depth of the subducted oceanic plate is unrelated to earthquake foci.

Numbers of Fish Species at Various Points Within Four Streams

Recall the biology students who surveyed three different streams for different fish species in Tables 6.7–6.9. Suppose, however, that a fourth stream were surveyed in the same area. This stream is 41km long.

4. In which section would you expect to find the greatest diversity of fish species?

(A) At the headwaters

(B) Halfway between the headwaters and the mouth

(C) At the mouth

(D) At the mouth and the headwaters

Environmental Factors Affecting Tomato Plant Growth

Three experiments were performed to study the environmental factors affecting the size and number of leaves on tomato (*Lycopersicon esculentum*) plants.

Experiment 1: Four groups of 30 tomato seedlings, all 3–4cm tall, were allowed to grow for four weeks, each group at a different humidity level. All the groups were kept at 70°F and received eight hours of sunlight a day. The average widths, lengths, and number of leaves per 1cm of plant stalk are shown in Table 6.10.

TABLE 6.10   Variations in Humidity and Tomato Plant Growth

% Humidity	Average Length (cm)	Average Width (cm)	# of Leaves per 1cm of Plant Stalk
15	5.6	1.6	0.13
35	7.1	1.8	0.25
55	9.8	2.0	0.56
75	14.6	2.6	0.61
95	7.5	1.7	0.52

Experiment 2: Four new groups of 30 seedlings, all 3–4cm tall, were allowed to grow for four weeks, each group receiving different amounts of sunlight at a constant humidity of 50%. All other conditions were the same as in Experiment 1. The results are listed in Table 6.11.

TABLE 6.11 Variations in Sunlight and Tomato Plant Growth

Sunlight (hrs/day)	Average Length (cm)	Average Width (cm)	# of Leaves per 1cm of Plant Stalk
0	5.3	1.5	0.32
3	12.4	2.4	0.59
6	11.2	2.0	0.56
9	8.4	1.8	0.26
12	7.7	1.7	0.19

Experiment 3: Four new groups of 30 seedlings, all 3–4 cm tall, were permitted to grow at a constant humidity of 50% for four weeks at different daytime and nighttime temperatures. All other conditions were the same as in Experiment 1. The results are shown in Table 6.12.

TABLE 6.12 Variations in Temperature and Tomato Plant Growth

Day/Night Temperature (0°F)	Average Length (cm)	Average Width (cm)	# of Leaves per 1cm of Plant Stalk
85/85	6.8	1.5	0.28
85/65	12.3	2.1	0.53
65/85	8.1	1.7	0.33
75/75	7.1	1.9	0.45
65/65	8.3	1.7	0.39

5. Which variable remained constant throughout all the experiments?

   (A) The number of seedling groups

   (B) The percent of humidity

   (C) The daytime temperature

   (D) The nighttime temperature

6. It was assumed in the design of the three experiments that all the tomato seedlings were:

   (F) More than 5cm tall

   (G) Equally capable of producing flowers

   (H) Equally capable of further growth

   (J) Equally capable of germinating

Measuring Tree Water Usage

An *arborist* (a specialist in the care and maintenance of trees) has purchased a treeless, poorly drained land area upon which he would eventually like to build a new home. The arborist wants to use trees to lower the area's groundwater levels. This would help ensure a dry foundation and make the land more aesthetically pleasing.

The arborist conducted experiments at a tree farm to determine the effects of different revegetation strategies on groundwater levels. He wants to compare water usage in different species of deciduous trees growing in different configurations.

Planting trees on cleared land can lower the water table in two ways: by limiting the amount of rainfall that seeps into the ground and by directly using groundwater for *transpiration* (direct evaporation of water from leaves). He conducted experiments to establish the effect of revegetation on groundwater levels and to see which species of trees flourish in swampy conditions.

Experiment 1: The arborist tested different configurations of tree plantings to see how groundwater usage compared (see Table 6.13).

TABLE 6.13   Changes in Groundwater Levels in a One-Year Period in Varying Tree-Planting Strategies

Planting Arrangement	Average Drop in Groundwater Level (cm)
Widely spaced	210
Planted in strips alternating with turf	180
Closely spaced	670

Experiment 2: The arborists measured deciduous hardwood tree seedling growth in waterlogged conditions in a greenhouse. The trees' growth rates were recorded and compared over a one-year period (see Table 6.14).

TABLE 6.14   Relative Growth of Deciduous Hardwood Tree Seedlings Grown in a Greenhouse Under Waterlogged Conditions in a One-Year Period

Species	Growth Rate (% in One Year)
White oak (*Quercus alba*)	85
Sugar maple (*Acer saccharum*)	110
Shagbark hickory (*Carya ovata*)	95
Black walnut (*Juglans nigra*)	80

The arborist concluded that leaf area is the key to reaching maximum water usage. A greater leaf area may be reached by planting trees close together, but once the upper portions of the trees come together to form a large canopy, the number of trees doesn't seem to matter. The arborist concluded that the tree that is healthiest and that can grow the largest canopy is the one that will transpire the most water. Selection of species is therefore critical in maximizing the effect of trees on groundwater levels.

7. To lower the groundwater in the shortest period of time, what should the arborist plant?

   (A) Widely spaced sugar maple trees

   (B) Closely spaced black walnut trees

   (C) Closely spaced sugar maple trees

   (D) Widely spaced black walnut trees

8. Assume that it takes these species 20 years to reach maturity in this type of soil. If the arborist plants a slow-growing species in a widely spaced manner, over the course of the next 20 years, the groundwater level will:

   (F) Not drop as much as with the most rapid method

   (G) Drop rapidly at first and then remain at a constant level

   (H) Drop at a constant rate as the trees mature

   (J) Eventually drop as much as with the most rapid method

Airplane Wings and Lift

The forces that generate lift in airplane wings are numerous and quite complex. Commonly held misconceptions often isolate and oversimplify the forces involved in this complex subject. Here, three students discuss their hypotheses on how the shape of an airplane wing generates lift.

Student 1: The upper surface area of an airplane wing is curved, and the bottom is flat. As the wing is moving, the air that travels up and over the top of the wing has farther to go than the air that only has to travel parallel to the flat underside of the wing. Because both the air going over the wing and the air going under the wing reach the trailing edge of the wing at the same time, the air going over the wing must have greater velocity because it travels a greater distance in the same amount of time. According to Bernoulli's principle, if the velocity of a fluid or a gas is increased, there must be a corresponding drop in pressure. Therefore, pressure is comparatively lower over the top of the wing in comparison with the wing's lower surface. The greater atmospheric pressure below the wing produces a net upward force on the wing. This is what keeps airplanes up in the air.

Student 2: The angle formed by the wing in relation to the air that it moves through is what creates lift. If the front of the wing is higher than the trailing edge, the momentum of the air colliding with the underside of the wing will create lift.

Student 3: Air hitting the leading edge of the wing is deflected up and away from the wing. This creates an area of high pressure at the front edge of the wing. This also creates downward force and an area of lower pressure toward the rear of the wing, which results in upward force. If the area of low pressure at the rear of the wing is larger than the front area of higher pressure, the overall result is an upward force that creates lift.

9. The cross-sectional diagram of an airplane wing shown in Figure 6.11 is consistent with the arguments of which student(s)?

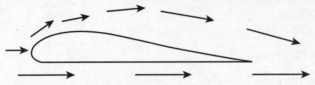

FIGURE 6.11 Cross-sectional view of an airplane wing showing the direction of airflow.

(A) Just student 1

(B) Just student 3

(C) Students 2 and 3

(D) Students 1 and 3

10. Balsa wood gliders (see Figure 6.12) that have their top and bottom wing surfaces completely parallel to each other would be an observation that would strengthen the position of which student(s)?

FIGURE 6.12 A balsa wood glider.

(F) Students 1 and 3

(G) Students 2 and 3

(H) Student 2

(J) Student 3

Challenge Question Answers with Explanations

1. **The correct answer is C.**

   This is an example of a direct relationship question. We see that in the stratosphere, the temperature line indicates higher y-axis values (temperature) as x-axis values (altitude above sea level) increase.

2. **The correct answer is G.**

   This is an example of an inverse relationship question. We see the values for air pressure (given in millibars on the right vertical axis) decreasing as altitude above sea level increases.

3. **The correct answer is B.**

   The scattered data indicates a general trend toward increasing depths of earthquake foci. These increasing foci depths represent the depth of the Nazca oceanic plate as it subducts eastward beneath the South American plate (see Figure 6.10).

4. **The correct answer is B.**

   In scanning the data, you can see that the longest stream has the greatest number of species between the source and the mouth of the stream; whereas in the other two streams, the number of species tends to increase as you move downstream. One possible hypothesis is that longer streams tend to have the greatest diversity of fish species in their middle reaches.

5. **The correct answer is A.**

   The method for each experiment begins with a statement that four groups of 30 tomato seedlings were used. Three of these answer choices list variables that were manipulated.

6. **The correct answer is H.**

   In all three experiments, it is assumed that all the seedlings are equally capable of further growth. Otherwise, one could not be certain that changes in the number of leaves and size were the result of controlled changes in temperature, sunlight, and humidity. Answer F is incorrect because all the seedlings were 3–4cm tall. Also, the seedlings' capability to germinate (answer J) or to produce flowers (answer G) was not mentioned in the experimental description.

7. **The correct answer is C.**

   The sugar maple trees were the fastest-growing species in the greenhouse experiment. Closely spaced trees resulted in the most substantial drop in groundwater levels.

8. **The correct answer is J.**

   The widely spaced trees will eventually grow to form a large canopy. The arborist had concluded that once this occurs, the number of trees doesn't seem to matter.

9. **The correct answer is D.**

The diagram shows air going over the top of the wing. This air must travel a greater distance in the same amount of time as the air traveling underneath the wing. This part of the diagram is consistent with the explanation of student 1. The air traveling over the wing also tends to separate from the top surface of the wing, creating an area of low pressure. This low pressure also creates lift, which agrees with the explanation of student 3.

10. **The correct answer is H.**

The fact that balsa wood gliders are made of flat pieces of wood is consistent with the explanation provided by student 2. A balsa wood glider's flat wings derive lift primarily from the oncoming air meeting the wing at a high angle. In aeronautical terms, this is called the *angle of attack*.

PART II
Practice Exams

FF Fast Facts

Chapter 7 Practice Exam 1

Chapter 8 Answers to Practice Exam 1

Chapter 9 Practice Exam 2

Chapter 10 Answers to Practice Exam 2

Fast Facts

Within each area of the test are certain rules, ideas, and formulas that are important for you to remember. These components are gathered here and arranged by subject area.

For ease of studying, you may want to copy the rules and formulas you don't readily know onto note cards. You can carry the cards with you in the weeks before the test and use them to study and memorize whenever you are able.

Keep in mind that you won't be able to take your note cards into the test site, but you may still want to have them close at hand, even on the morning of the test.

English

1. Use the correct one: *It's = it is*.

2. Singular/plural/possessive: *Players* = plural, *player's* = singular possessive, *players'* = plural possessive.

3. Remember that these words always take a singular verb: *anything, anybody, anyone, either, everything, everybody, everyone, neither, something, somebody, someone, each, nothing, nobody,* and *no one*.

4. Remove the words surrounding *you, me,* and/or *I* to check for correct usage of each word.

5. Skim the passage and underline key phrases.

6. Reread the sentence containing the first underlined word or phrase.

7. Paraphrase what you are being asked in the question.

8. Decide what you think the correct answer could be, and then look at the responses.

9. Use context clues.

10. Work at a consistent pace.

Mathematics

Commit as much of the math information to memory as you are able. You may want to put a pencil check beside the areas you've mastered and work toward a good working knowledge of the other information contained here.

Pre-Algebra and Elementary Algebra

1. Make sure you understand the following number vocabulary:

   ▶ Integers: -2, -1, 0, 1, 2.

   ▶ Odd: -1, -3, 5, 7, 13.

   ▶ Even: 0, 2, -4, 6, 22.

   ▶ Real: 0, -1, π, $\frac{1}{3}$, $\sqrt{2}$.

   ▶ Imaginary: 4i, i2 = -1.

   ▶ Prime: 2, 5, 7, 11. (Note that 0 and 1 are not primes.)

   ▶ Digit: Any symbol between 0 and 9 that holds a place.

   ▶ Consecutive: Numbers that are in a row. For example, 4, 5, 6 and n, $n + 1$, $n + 2$.

   ▶ Divisible: Able to be divided without a remainder.

   ▶ Absolute value: The distance a number is from zero. It is always positive (for example, | - 3 = 3).

2. When multiplying expressions with the same base, add the exponents. When dividing expressions with the same base, subtract the exponents. When raising an expression to another exponent, multiply the exponents.

3. Any expression raised to the zero power is 1.

4. The expression a^{-x} is defined as $\frac{1}{a^x}$.

5. You can use fractional exponents to represent roots. The cube root of 81 can be expressed as $81^{\frac{1}{3}}$.

6. In problems in which bases are different, such as $(2^y)(4) = 8^3$, try to express numbers you are given in a way that results in like bases. For example, $(2^y)(2^2) = (2^3)^3$.

7. You can combine numbers that have the same number under their root symbol just as you add "like terms": $3\sqrt{5} + 4\sqrt{5} = 7\sqrt{5}$. To multiply and divide numbers that have roots, perform the operation on the numbers outside the root symbol and then perform the operation on the numbers inside the symbol. For example, $3\sqrt{8} \times 2\sqrt{1}$ is $6\sqrt{8}$.

8. The distributive property is $a(b + c) = ab + ac$. Remember that $1 - a(b + c) = 1 - ab - ac$.

9. The order of operations is parentheses, exponents and roots, multiplication and division, addition, and subtraction.

10. $\frac{1}{0}$ is undefined. No expression or number can be divided by 0.

11. An arithmetic sequence is formed by adding a constant amount to each succeeding term. The general formula for finding any nth term is: nth term = [(first term) + (number of terms − 1)(constant amount)], or $n = a_1 + (n − 1)d$.

12. A geometric sequence is formed by multiplying each succeeding term by a common factor. The general formula for finding any nth term is: nth term = (first term) × (common factor)$^{(\text{number of terms} - 1)}$, or $n = a_1 × r^{n-1}$.

13. Percent change = $\dfrac{\text{amount of change}}{\text{original amount}} × 100\%$.

14. To find a multiple percent increase or decrease, use simple numbers to observe the general pattern. Apply the changes in the question to the number 100. To find the total percent increase if guitar prices increased 15% the first year and 25% the second year, use the following: 100 × 1.15 = 115 and 115 × 1.25 = 143.75. Therefore, the net increase is 43.75%.

15. If A varies directly with B, then $A = kB$. If A varies inversely as B, then $A = \dfrac{k}{B}$.

16. Mean or average = $\dfrac{\text{sum of the numbers}}{\text{number in the set}}$.

17. To find the median, put the values in ascending order. Determine the value or values in the middle. If there are two numbers in the middle, find their average.

18. Find the mode by determining the most frequent value.

19. The fundamental counting principle demonstrates the following: If a customer ordering a sandwich can order three types of bread, two types of sauce, and four types of meat, then there are 3 × 2 × 4, or 24, possible sandwich combinations.

20. The probability of an outcome = $\dfrac{\text{\# of desired outcomes}}{\text{\# of possible outcomes}}$.

21. The probability of an outcome is always between 0 and 1, inclusive.

22. If a question asks about the probability of an event *not* occurring, you may use the following: The probability that an event won't occur = 1 − the probability the event will occur. This assumes that one or the other must occur.

23. To find the probability of successive independent events, multiply the probability of each event. Independent events do not affect each other's outcomes.

24. Multiply $(a + b)(d + c)$ using the first, outer, inner, last *(FOIL)* method.

25. To factor expressions such as $x^2 + bx + c$, start by factoring out any *greatest common factor (GCF)*. Set up parentheses: ( )( ). Find the two magic numbers that add to b, but whose product is c. Write factors as $(x + \text{magic number})(x + \text{magic number})$. For example, $x^2 + 1x + 6$ factors to $(x + 3)(x − 2)$.

26. The expression $a^2 − b^2$ factors as $(a + b) × (a − b)$.

27. A function maps a set of input values to a set of output values in such a way that each input value produces only one output value. The notation we use for functions replaces the y with $f(x)$, $g(x)$, or $h(x)$.

28. Functions have both a domain and a range. The *domain* is the set of acceptable replacement values for *x*. The *range* is the set of possible outcomes for $f(x)$.

29. You should know these three main equations for rate problems:

   ▶ Distance = Rate × Time

   ▶ $\text{Rate}_{first} \times \text{Time}_{first} + \text{Rate}_{second} \times \text{Time}_{second}$ = Jobs Accomplished

   ▶ Rate × Time × Number of Workers = Jobs Accomplished

Intermediate Algebra and Coordinate Graphing

1. A linear function has the form $y = mx + b$, where *m* is the slope of the line and *b* is the point at which the line crosses the y-axis.

2. A quadratic function, $f(x) = x2 + bx + c$, graphs as a parabola. Its line of symmetry is at $-\dfrac{b}{2a}$.

   You can complete the square to put the quadratic in the form $f(x) = a(x - h)^2 + k$. The vertex is at (h,k). Upward if *a* is positive, downward if *a* is negative.

3. The equation for a circle is $(x - h)^2 + (y - k)^2 = r^2$, where (h,k) is the center and r is the radius.

4. The equation for an ellipse centered at the origin is $\dfrac{x^2}{a^2} + \dfrac{y^2}{b^2} = 1$.

5. Any graph of a function, $y = f(x)$, can be shifted vertically or horizontally:

   ▶ The graph $y = f(x) + a$ is shifted up *a* units, whereas $y = f(x) - a$ is shifted down *a* units.

   ▶ The graph $y = f(x - a)$ is shifted right *a* units, whereas $y = f(x + a)$ is shifted left *a* units.

   ▶ The graph $y = af(x)$ is narrower if $|a \geq 1$, but wider if $0 \leq |a \leq 1$.

6. The quadratic formula is $\dfrac{[-b \pm \sqrt{(b^2 - 4ac)}]}{2a}$.

7. When solving equations that contain $\sqrt{s}$, isolate the $\sqrt{}$ and then square both sides. Always plug the result back into the equation to check your answer.

8. When solving inequalities, you must flip the sign if you multiply or divide both sides by a negative.

9. The distance formula is $d = \sqrt{[(x_2 - x_1)^2 + (y_2 - y_1)^2]}$.

10. To find the slope of a line, *m*, use the following: $\dfrac{y_2 - y_1}{x_2 - x_1}$.

11. Parallel lines have the same slope. However, perpendicular lines have slopes that are opposite reciprocals of each other. The product of the slopes of perpendicular lines is always -1.

12. $y = \log_a x$ means that $a^y = x$ for all $a \geq 0$ and a is not equal to 1.

13. Multiply two matrices only when the number of columns in the first matrix is equal to the number of rows in the second matrix. If the first letter is the number of rows and the second is the number of columns, then an $r \times s$ matrix multiplied with an $s \times t$ matrix results in an $r \times t$ matrix.

Plane Geometry and Trigonometry

1. Vertical angles are equal.

2. Supplementary angles add to 180° and complementary angles add to 90°.

3. When a transversal crosses parallel lines, four equal obtuse angles and four equal acute angles are formed.

4. The three angles of any triangle add up to 180°.

5. The Pythagorean theorem states the following for all right triangles: $\text{leg}^2 + \text{leg}^2 = \text{hypotenuse}^2$.

6. The sides of a 30° - 60° - 90° triangle are in a ratio of $1:\sqrt{3}:2$. Remember that the smallest side, 1, is opposite the smallest angle, 30°. The largest side, 2, is opposite the largest angle, 90°.

7. The sides of a 45°-45°-90° triangle are in a ratio of $1:1:\sqrt{2}$. The different side, $\sqrt{2}$, is opposite the different angle, 90°.

8. The area of a circle is πr^2, and the circumference is $2\pi r$.

9. Use SOHCAHTOA to remember the definitions of sine, cosine, and tangent in a right triangle, as follows:

   ▶ $\text{Sine} = \dfrac{\text{Opposite}}{\text{Hypotenuse}}$

   ▶ $\text{Cosine} = \dfrac{\text{Adjacent}}{\text{Hypotenuse}}$

   ▶ $\text{Tangent} = \dfrac{\text{Opposite}}{\text{Adjacent}}$

10. Secant, cosecant, and cotangent are reciprocals of the basic trig definitions, as follows:

    ▶ $\text{Secant} = \dfrac{1}{\text{Cosine}}$

    ▶ $\text{Cosecant} = \dfrac{1}{\text{Sine}}$

    ▶ $\text{Cotangent} = \dfrac{1}{\text{Tangent}}$

Writing

1. Read the prompt.

2. Create two columns. Write opposing ideas under each.

3. Put an "X" over the column with the most ideas.

4. Write an opening sentence, then an opening paragraph that states your viewpoint.

5. Take one idea from the X'd column and turn this into a topic sentence. Follow the sentence with an explanation that includes ideas and examples that support it.

6. Begin the next paragraph with an opening sentence that uses another of your ideas. Follow it with an explanation that includes ideas and examples that support it. Continue to use this process as you work through all of your ideas in the X'd column.

7. Summarize your thoughts.

8. Look at the time.

9. Reread your work at an appropriate pace, making only necessary changes.

Science

1. Read each passage carefully.

2. Look at each table or figure to see what type of information is being presented.

3. Read each question carefully.

4. Underline the number of the experiment, table, or figure that the question is referring to.

5. Return to the passage and examine the section that the question asks about.

6. Select the answer that best fits the presentation of the data.

7. Double-check to see that the units found in the answer match the units found in the data used to answer the question.

8. Do not spend more than about five minutes on each passage; there are seven passages.

9. Do not spend too much time puzzling over any particular question.

10. Eliminate answers that you know are wrong.

11. Guess as a last resort.

12. Keep track of time.

13. Know these unit abbreviations:

- ▶ kg = kilograms
- ▶ g = grams
- ▶ ppm = parts per million
- ▶ ml = milliliters
- ▶ °C = degrees Celsius
- ▶ m = meters
- ▶ km = kilometers
- ▶ mm = millimeters
- ▶ nm = nanometers
- ▶ °K = degrees Kelvin
- ▶ Hg = mercury
- ▶ J = Joule
- ▶ kJ = kiloJoule

CHAPTER SEVEN

Practice Exam 1

This sample test provides an opportunity for you to simulate what you will experience when you sit for the ACT exam. Ideally, it should be taken under conditions similar to the actual test environment. If you keep to strict test timing, you will be able to get a good picture of how you will do on the ACT Assessment.

Before you begin, ensure that you have scrap paper, the answer sheet included with this book, a calculator, plenty of pencils, and a watch or timer. Do not use research or reference materials as you work on this sample test, or you will get an unrealistic indication of your score.

Move through the test at a good pace and attempt to complete each subject area within the allotted time.

Here's how much time you will be given for each section of the test. As you take the practice test, set a timer for each portion and attempt to follow the test conditions of a quiet room with minimal interruption.

Finished in:

Test	Questions	Time Allotted
44.36 → English	75	45 minutes
Math	60	60 minutes
28 min → Reading	40	35 minutes
30 ml → Science Reasoning	40	35 minutes
Writing (optional)	1 essay	30 minutes
TOTAL TIME		2 hours, 55 minutes (add 30 minutes if you are taking the optional writing test)

In the chapter that follows, you'll find the Answer Key and explanations. Good luck!

ACT English Assessment

The five passages that follow consist of 75 underlined words and phrases in context, and questions about them. Most of these underlined sections contain errors in structure, expression, style, punctuation, or word usage.

The test also includes questions about entire paragraphs and the passage as a whole. These questions are identified by a number in a box.

For each question, select which of the four choices is the best response and darken the appropriate oval on your answer sheet. If you consider the original version to be the best, choose answer A or F: NO CHANGE.

You may wish to read each passage through before answering the questions based on it.

Passage I

[1]

When I think about my favorite experiences in high school, I usually include Mr.

Brown's geometry class on my mental list. I don't think I have ever met any teacher who

was quite as smart, quite as informative, or quite as engaging as he was. Mr. Brown
         (1)
made that year of math never my favorite discipline in school, seem like a pleasure.
                (2)
Who would have predicted that I would actually look forward to the first period of the

school day!

1. ☒ A. NO CHANGE

   ❏ B. quite as smart quite

   ❏ C. quite, as smart quite

   ❏ D. quite as: smart quite

2. ❏ F. NO CHANGE

   ☒ G. math, never my favorite

   ❏ H. math; never my favorite

   ❏ J. math—never my favorite

Question 3 asks about the preceding paragraph as a whole.

The writer intends to add the following sentence to the paragraph in order to provide a more complete opening paragraph.

The last four years have flown by quickly.

In order to accomplish this purpose, it would be most logical to place this sentence:

3. ❑ A. After the first sentence in the paragraph

   ❑ B. Before the first sentence in the paragraph

   ❑ C. After the last sentence in the paragraph

   ❑ D. Before the last sentence in the paragraph

[2]

Prior to each Monday's class, Mr. Brown had the class segregated into learning teams, as

he called them. He configured <u>each teams'</u> desks into a different geometric shape
                                            (4)
first. Then we would have to ascertain what <u>shape our desks are in</u> and then
                                                         (5)
calculate the area of an outline he had drawn on the floor in our area.

<u>We always had fun trying to figure it out before the other groups.</u>
                              (6)

4. ❑ F. NO CHANGE

   ❑ G. each teams

   ❑ H. each team

   ❑ J. each team's

5. ❑ A. NO CHANGE

   ❑ B. shapes our desk are in

   ❑ C. shape our desks were in

   ❑ D. shapes our desks were in

6. ❑ F. NO CHANGE

   ❑ G. Trying to figure it out before the other groups, we always had fun.

   ❑ H. We always had fun, trying to figure it out before the other groups.

   ❑ J. We always had fun trying to figure it out before the other groups figure it out.

[3]

He had novel ways for us to remember how to <u>figure out sine cosine and tangent</u>.
(7)

<u>I still cackle when I think of how the whole class moved outdoors one day.</u>
(8)

<u>We formed a huge human triangle, and then used a long portion of cord, to</u>
(9)

<u>demonstrate what each of those expressions signified.</u>
(9)

7. ❑ A. NO CHANGE

    ❑ B. figure out: sine, cosine, and tangent

    ❑ C. figure out sine cosine, and tangent

    ▣ D. figure out sine, cosine, and tangent

8. ▣ F. NO CHANGE

    ❑ G. When I think of how the whole class moved outdoors, one day I still cackle.

    ❑ H. One day, I still cackle when I think of how the whole class moved outdoors.

    ❑ J. OMIT the underlined portion.

9. ❑ A. NO CHANGE

    ▣ B. We formed a huge human triangle, and then used a long portion of cord to demonstrate what each of those expressions signified.

    ❑ (C.) We formed a huge human triangle and then used a long portion of cord to demonstrate what each of those expressions signified.

    ❑ D. We formed a huge human triangle and then used a long portion of cord, to demonstrate what each of those expressions signified.

[4]

I don't remember what made this all so hilarious, but <u>several students were actually</u>
(10)

<u>on the ground emitting loud guffaws.</u> I can still envision the scene. When the time came
(10)

for the Math Fair in March, I am <u>almost</u> positive that every student entered a
(11)

project even though it was not required. Mr. Brown was proud of all of us, and we

occupied an entire section of the auditorium at the State Finals because 10 of our

projects made it that far. Other schools seemed to have one or maybe two students

representing <u>it</u>.
(12)

10. ❏ F. NO CHANGE

    ❏ G. several students were actually on the ground emitting loud guffaws'.

    ❏ H. several students were actually on the ground emitting loud guffaw's.

    ❏ J. several students were actually on the ground emitting a loud guffaw.

11. ❏ A. NO CHANGE

    ❏ B. Put after *I*

    ❏ C. Put after *positive*

    ❏ D. Put after *student*

12. ❏ F. NO CHANGE

    ❏ G. them

    ❏ H. themselves

    ❏ J. things

[5]

When Mr. Brown's students took the gold, silver, and bronze ribbons, I had known
(13)
that Mr. Brown was beside himself with joy. It's goal seemed to always be to get
(14)
students excited about math. If a student had a fear of math when they began the class,
(15)
I am sure that it was not the case when the class was finished. Mr. Brown retired the

year after he was my geometry teacher. I am privileged that I had him as my instructor.

13. ❏ A. NO CHANGE

    ❏ B. knew

    ❏ C. know

    ❏ D. was knowing

14. ❏ F. NO CHANGE

    ❏ G. Its

    ❏ H. Mr. Browns

    ❏ J. His

15. ⊠ A. NO CHANGE

    ❑ B. beginning the class

    ❑ C. each began the class

    ❑ (D.) he or she began the class

Passage II

[1]

Midland is a small suburban town <u>in need of a face-lift.</u> It might need more extensive
                                    (16)

work, too. <u>Problems with the actual structure of Midland's buildings was becoming</u>
                                    (17)

<u>more and more apparent.</u> Some of them have obvious cracks in the exterior walls that
       (17)

are apparent from the road. The main road entering Midland is potholed and cracked.

The town's park was once beautiful but is now overgrown and littered with debris. Very

few children play here now. <u>The statue of Mayor Midland, a town icon of the 1940s</u>
                                      (18)

<u>is chipped and discolored.</u>
     (18)

16. ⊠ F. NO CHANGE

    ❑ G. who needs a face-lift.

    ❑ H. thats in need of a face-lift.

    ❑ J. needing of a face-lift.

17. ⊠ A. NO CHANGE

    ❑ (B.) Problems with the actual structure of Midland's buildings are becoming
        more and more apparent.

    ❑ C. Problems with the actual structure of Midland's building were becoming
        more and more apparent.

    ❑ D. Problems with the actual structure of Midland's buildings became more and
        more apparent.

18. ⊠ F. NO CHANGE

    ❑ G. A town icon of the 1940s, the statue of Mayor Midland is chipped and
        discolored.

    ❑ H. A town icon of the 1940s, Mayor Midland's statue is chipped and discolored.

    ❑ (J.) The statue of 1940s town icon Mayor Midland is chipped and discolored.

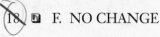
= Marked it Wrong!

[2]

As their driving into the town, visitors might think for a moment that it has actually
                                              (19)
traveled back in time. A five-and-ten-cent store faces a tiny one-room post office. A
      (19)
barber pole sticks out from a small storefront, and Dirks' Barber Shop is painted in black
                                                          (20)
block letters directly on the glass. There are still some hitching post's on either side of
                                                          (21)
Main Street. Older cars dot the parking spaces, and a lone sports car seems out of place.
   (21)

19. ☐ A. NO CHANGE

    ☐ B. As their driving into the town, visitors might think for a moment that they
          have actually traveled back in time.

    ▨ C. As they're driving into the town, visitors might think for a moment they
          have actually traveled back in time.

    ☐ D. As they're driving into the town, visitors might think for a moment it has
          actually traveled back in time.

20. ☐ F. NO CHANGE

    ☐ G. Dirk's Barber Shop

    ☐ H. "Dirk's Barber Shop,"

    ▨ J. "Dirk's Barber Shop"

21. ☐ A. NO CHANGE

    ☐ B. There are still some hitching post's on either side of Main St.

    ☐ C. There are still some hitching post's on either side of main street.

    ▨ D. There are still some hitching posts on either side of Main Street.

[3]

The façade of every store on Main Street have chipped, and peeling, paint. The signage
                                            (22)
for "Mel's Holiday Foods" is devoid now of actual lettering, and the canopy has only

faded block letters. Some of the streetlights which I heard were a gift for Midland from
                      (23)
Mayor Midland's family flicker to the point where they are a nuisance. They would be
          (23)
disappointed to know that these, their memorial gifts was in such a state of disrepair.
                              (24)

22. ❑ F. NO CHANGE

   ❑ G. has chipped, and peeling paint.

   ■ H. has chipped and peeling paint.

   ❑ J. have chipped and peeling paint.

23. ❑ A. NO CHANGE

   ❑ B. Some of the streetlights which I heard were a gift for Midland from Mayor Midland's family, flicker to the point where they are a nuisance.

   ❑ C. Some of the streetlights, which I heard were a gift for Midland from Mayor Midland's family flicker to the point where they are a nuisance.

   ■ D. Some of the streetlights (which I heard were a gift for Midland from Mayor Midland's family) flicker to the point where they are a nuisance.

24. ❑ F. NO CHANGE

   ❑ G. their memorial gifts, was

   ❑ H. their memorial gift were

   ■ J. their memorial gifts, were

[4]

I guess us who live in Midland don't notice the condition of the town. We just except it.
                                        (25)
When I came home after spending a month at my cousin Michael's house in

New Jersey, I was surprised, and almost disappointed in it. I guess I seen the town
                    (26)   (27)
with a new set of eyes. Everything just looked old and sad.

25. ❑ A. NO CHANGE

   ❑ B. I guess we who live in Midland don't notice the condition of the town. We just except it.

   ■ C. I guess we who live in Midland don't notice the condition of the town. We just accept it.

   ❑ D. I guess us who live in Midland don't notice the condition of the town. We just accept it.

26. ❑ F. NO CHANGE

   ❑ G. New Jersey—I was surprised, and almost disappointed in it.

   ❑ H. New Jersey I was surprised, and almost disappointed in Midland.

   ■ J. New Jersey, I was surprised and almost disappointed in Midland.

27. ❑ A. NO CHANGE

    ❑ B. I guess I see the town

    ▣ C. I guess I saw the town

    ❑ D. I guessed I saw the town

[5]

It may seem to outsiders <u>as if no one loves the little town: but we do.</u> I am now
(28)
planning a Town Clean-Up Day for next month. <u>I'll buy paint and get some wood</u>
(29)
<u>lawn mowers and other needed supplies and materials.</u> To make Midland look new and
(29)
pretty again, <u>we will all pitch into make Clean-Up Day a success.</u>
(30)

28. ❑ F. NO CHANGE

    ▣ G. as if no one loves the little town, but we do.

    ❑ H. as if no one loves the little town but we do.

    ❑ J. as if no one loves the little town, but, we do.

29. ❑ A. NO CHANGE

    ❑ B. I'll buy paint, and get some wood, lawn mowers and other needed supplies, and materials.

    ❑ C. I'll buy paint, and get some wood, lawn mowers, and other needed supplies and materials.

    ▣ D. I'll buy paint and get some wood, lawn mowers, and other needed supplies and materials.

30. ❑ F. NO CHANGE

    ❑ G. we will all pitch in, to make Clean-Up Day a success.

    ❑ (H.) we will all pitch in to make Clean-Up Day a success.

    ❑ J. we will all pitch in; to make Clean-Up Day a success.

Passage III

[1]

Ten years ago, after deciding that my exercise routine was greatly in need of a spark,
                (31)
I pulled on my old, flowered, and threadbare bathing suit and headed for my town's

YMCA pool. Many bathing suit's and year's later, I'm definitely regularly in
                                    (32)
the "swim of things."
        (33)

31. ☐ A. NO CHANGE

   ☐ B. After deciding that 10 years ago

   ☐ C. Ten years ago, I, after deciding that

   ☐ D. After 10 years ago deciding that

32. ☐ F. NO CHANGE

   ☐ G. Many bathing suits and year's later,

   ☐ H. Many bathing suit's and years later,

   ☐ J. Many bathing suits and years later,

33. ☐ A. NO CHANGE

   ☐ B. the "swim" of things.

   ☐ C. the swim of "things."

   ☐ D. the swim of things.

[2]

I like many people learned to swim at a young age. It was easy for me to remember
                        (34)
how to swim and stroke efficiently through the water. Surprisingly, what I had

forgotten, though, was that wonderful, euphoric feeling swimmers' experience while
                                                            (35)
buoyant. Indeed, there is nothing quite as perfect as the feeling of cutting through the

cool water with no distractions accept reminding himself not to hit the pool wall
                    (36)
with your head.

34. ❏ F. NO CHANGE

    ❏ G. I, like many people learned to swim at a young age.

    ❏ H. Many people, learned to swim at a young age, like I did.

    ■ J. Like many people, I learned to swim at a young age.

35. ❏ A. NO CHANGE

    ❏ (B.) swimmers experience

    ❏ C. swimmers's experience

    ■ D. swimmer's experience

36. ❏ F. NO CHANGE

    ❏ G. with no distractions except reminding himself

    ❏ H. with no distractions accept reminding yourself

    ■ J. with no distractions except reminding yourself

[3]

There are more tangible benefits to swimming than just that euphoric feeling, though.

Cardiovascular fitness, for instance, is often <u>sighted as one of</u> the best rewards of
(37)
spending time in the water. Indeed, at least 20 minutes of nonstop aquatic movement

can contribute to a healthier and more efficient heart. As with other aerobic exercises,

the HDL cholesterol in the blood is elevated slightly during an aquatic workout,

<u>offering the body increased protection against heart disease.</u> Additionally, because
(38)
the number of calories burned in a 20-minute swimming workout <u>is comparing to</u>
(39)
<u>the same amount of time jogging,</u> the swimmer can list weight control as another
(39)
benefit from the sport. Since I have been swimming regularly, I have found that I can

have the occasional snack and not have it immediately register on the scale the next day.

37. ❏ A. NO CHANGE

    ❏ B. sited, as one of

    ■ C. cited as one of

    ❏ D. sited as one of

38. ☑ F. NO CHANGE

    ❑ G. offering to increase the body's protection against heart disease.

    ❑ H. offering the body increasing protection against heart disease.

    ❑ J. offering the body an increasing protection against heart disease.

39. ❑ A. NO CHANGE

    ☑ B. is comparable to the same amount of time jogging,

    ❑ C. is comparing to the same amount of time jogging,

    ❑ D. is comparable to the same amount of time of jogging,

[4]

Participants don't have to limit their movement in the water to swimming laps.

As entire laps may initially seem daunting, especially for the beginning swimmer.
                                         (40)
Although it is easiest to measure progress if you count the number of laps that you are

able to swim in a certain length of time and then set goals based on that number, those

just getting acclimated to swimming might have to stop frequently and jog in chest-deep

water for a few minutes. So long as the swimmer keeps moving in the water health
                                            (41)
benefits can be realized. Because water provides a minimum amount of stress on the
        (41)
joints, the body is less prone to injury than with other popular types of exercise.

As muscles have to work harder, because of the resistance of the water, they become
                                            (42)
toned and strong. I noticed tangible results within just a few weeks, with my arms and
        (42)
legs appearing more toned and feeling strong.

40. ❑ F. NO CHANGE

    ❑ G. As entire laps may initially seem daunting especially, for the beginning swimmer.

    ❑ H. Entire laps may initially seem daunting, especially, for the beginning swimmer.

    ☑ J. Entire laps may initially seem daunting, especially for the beginning swimmer.

41. ☐ A. NO CHANGE

 ☐ B. So long as the swimmer keeps moving in the water, health benefits can be realized.

 ☐ C. As long as the swimmer keeps moving, in the water health benefits can be realized.

 ☑ D. As long as the swimmer keeps moving in the water, health benefits can be realized.

42. ☑ F. NO CHANGE

 ☐ G. As muscles have to work harder, because of the resistance of the water they become toned and strong.

 ☐ H. As muscles have to work harder because of the resistance of the water, they become toned and strong.

 ☐ J. As muscles have to work harder because of the resistance of the water they become toned and strong.

[5]

<u>With the heart now working more efficienter,</u> those who swim can look for lower
     (43)
blood pressure as being another advantage of the sport. The healthy heart's beating rate

slows down not only after exercise, but also during periods of rest, so that more blood is

pumped per beat.

Although we strive to tune them out, auditory and visual distractions abound when we

are biking, running, walking, playing tennis, and even skiing. Very few forms of exercise

allow one to be happily alone in an otherwise distracting world. For many swimmers,

the exercise affords a level of stress relief unlike other sports. Swimming can be thought

of as the superior sport for those seeking solitude and serenity while attaining an

enhanced level of fitness.

Consider joining me in the pool! You'll be glad you did!

43. ☐ A. NO CHANGE

 ☐ B. With the heart now working efficienter,

 ☐ C. With the heart now working efficiently,

 ☑ D. With the heart now working more efficiently,

[6]

(1)Swimming can be thought of as the superior sport for those seeking solitude and serenity while attaining an enhanced level of fitness. (2)Although we try to tune them out, these distractions are impossible to completely contain. (3)When we are biking, running, walking, playing tennis, and even skiing, auditory and visual distractions abound. (4)That's a big reason swimmers cite their favored form of exercise as a stress reliever unlike any other. [44]

44. Reorder the sentences in the paragraph so that it begins with a topic sentence and the other sentences flow in sequence.

- F. 1, 3, 2, 4
- G. 1, 2, 3, 4
- H. 4, 3, 1, 2
- J. 3, 2, 1, 4

45. The writer of this essay had been asked to write about why swimming is superior to jogging. Has the writer succeeded?

- A. Yes, the author mentions this as the main idea of the essay.
- B. No, the author discusses jogging as being superior to swimming.
- C. No, the author talks about how there are many reasons swimming is an excellent sport.
- D. Yes, the author talks about how calories can be burned during swimming and jogging.

Passage IV

[1]

Many avid readers have their name on the waiting list of public library around the
(46)
country, and they wait patiently for the phone call that tells them that its there turn
 (46)   (47)
to read the next bestseller. They drive to the library and borrow the book, keeping in
          (47)
mind that there is often just a one-week lending period on these high-traffic bestsellers.

Often, they then have to make time to read the book—so that they can complete
                                                      (48)
and return it within that one-week lending period.

46. ❏ F. NO CHANGE

    ❏ G. Many avid readers have their names on the waiting lists of public libraries around the country,

    ❏ H. Many avid readers have their names on the waiting list of public libraries around the country,

    ❏ J. Many avid readers have their name on the waiting lists of public libraries around the country,

47. ❏ A. NO CHANGE

    ❏ B. tells them that it's there turn to read the next bestseller.

    ❏ C. tells them that its their turn to read the next bestseller.

    ❏ D. tells them that it's their turn to read the next bestseller.

48. ❏ F. NO CHANGE

    ❏ G. book, so that they can

    ❏ H. book; so that they can

    ❏ J. book so that they can

[2]

There's an even better way to read all of the books that <u>you're interested in, bestseller,</u>
                                                                              (49)
<u>and older books, hardcovers, and paperbacks.</u> Plus, you can keep the books as long
                    (49)
as you want to, <u>and reading it at</u> your leisure.
                      (50)
It sounds almost too good to be true, but Amazon.com, the giant online marketplace,

has a used-book service <u>that's arguably the best ever dreamed up.</u> You'll have to
                                            (51)
check it out to fully appreciate what they have done at their site.

49. ❏ A. NO CHANGE

    ❏ B. you're interested in: bestsellers, and older books, hardcovers, and paper-
       backs.

    ❏ C. you're interested in; bestsellers, and older books, hardcovers, and paper-
       backs.

    ❏ D. you're interested in—bestsellers and older books, hardcovers and paper-
       backs.

50. ❏ F. NO CHANGE

   ❏ G. and read it at

   ❏ (H.) and read them at

   ❏ J. and reading them at

51. ❏ A. NO CHANGE

   ❏ B. thats arguably the best ever dreamed up.

   ❏ C. thats inarguably the best ever dreamed up.

   ❏ D. that's inarguably the best ever dreamed up.

[3]

First, go to their website (www.amazon.com) and search the title of the next book on

your <u>list of must reads.</u> You'll see that book listed, the purchase price for a
                (52)

brand-new copy of the book, and then, underneath that, the price for the book

<u>in used condition.</u> Prices for used copies of the book are set by individual sellers
      (53)

around the country <u>and reflect what they believe their copy of the book is worth.</u>
                                              (54)

52. ❏ F. NO CHANGE

   ❏ G. list of must-read's.

   ❏ H. list of must-reads.

   ❏ J. list of must read's.

53. ❏ A. NO CHANGE

   ❏ B. if it were in used condition.

   ❏ C. if it was in used condition.

   ❏ D. if it had been in used condition.

54. ❏ F. NO CHANGE

   ❏ (G.) and reflects what they believe their copy of the book is worth.

   ❏ H. and reflecting what they believe their copy of the book was worth.

   ❏ J. and reflected what they believe their copy of the book is worth.

[4]

Deciding which one to purchase, look at the prices and conditions of all of the
(55)
available copies of the book. Some copies of the book may be missing a cover, have
(55)
writing or highlighting on some pages, or have some ripped pages. Depending on what

you'll be using the book for, these types of problems may or may not be important to

you. The book will be sent to you for the price listed, plus a shipping charge. You'll

quickly see that especially popular books have quite a few copies listed, and at first this

may cause confusion. Its your's when you receive the book and you can take your time
(56)
reading it.
(57)
There is an added bonus to this type of used-book sale. After you have read the book,

you can relist it at Amazon.com and sell it in the same way that you bought it. In many

cases, you can sell a book for the same price you I've bought it for and be reimbursed

for shipping expenses from Amazon.

55. ❑ A. NO CHANGE

   ❑ B. Deciding which one to purchase look at the prices and conditions of all of
      the available copies of the book.

   ❑ C. Looking at the prices and conditions of all of the available copies of the
      book decide which one to purchase.

   ❑ D. Look at the prices and conditions of all of the available copies of the book,
      and decide which one to purchase.

56. This sentence would be more effective in this paragraph if it were placed:

   ❑ F. NO CHANGE

   ❑ G. Directly after the first sentence

   ❑ H. As the third sentence

   ❑ J. After the last sentence

57. ❑ A. NO CHANGE

    ❑ B. It's yours when you receive the book and you can take your time reading it.

    ❑ C. When you receive the book it's your's and you can take your time reading it.

    ■ D. When you receive the book, it's yours. You can take your time reading it.

[5]

If you are anxious to get rid of them quick, list your book at a price a few cents
                    (58)
lower than the lowest price that you see. Price it a bit higher if you don't mind sitting

with the book for a period of time. I've listed popular books at competitive prices and
                                                                            (59)
sold them the same day. You can also look through your bookcases at home and list any
        (59)
books that you and your family are simply not interested in anymore. I often buy books
                                                                            (60)
at garage sales, book sales, and clearance tables at bookstores and go home and list them.
                                    (60)
I've bought and sold hundreds of books through Amazon, with only a very rare problem

or hitch.

58. ❑ F. NO CHANGE

    ❑ G. If you are anxious to get rid of it quick,

    ❑ H. If you are anxious to get rid of them quickly,

    ■ J. If you are anxious to get rid of it quickly,

59. ❑ A. NO CHANGE

    ■ B. I've listed popular books at competitive prices, and sold them the same day.

    ❑ C. I've listed popular books at competitive prices and sold it the same day.

    ❑ D. I've listed a popular book at competitive prices and sold them the same day.

60. ■ F. NO CHANGE

    ❑ G. I often buy books at garage sales and book sales and clearance tables at
       bookstores and go home and list them.

    ❑ H. I often buy books at garage sales, book sales, and clearance tables, at book-
       stores and go home and list them.

    ❑ J. I often buy books at: garage sales, book sales, and clearance tables at book-
       stores and go home and list them.

Passage V

[1]

It's entirely possible that many people living in states other than Texas don't realize the accomplishments of one of that state's most famous sons—Sam Houston. Houston was arguably the most important player in the early history of the state of Texas, and the people of Texas still remember him for his bravery. [61]

61. This question refers to the first paragraph above. The writer wants to add a sentence transitioning to the next paragraph. Which sentence below accomplishes this?

   A. Many of them can recite his early history almost by heart.

   B. They have other heroes, too, though.

   C. He died many years ago.

   D. Other states recognize their own heroic citizens.

Born in 1793 in Virginia, Houston's father died suddenly when Sam was just 13.
(62)
Young Sam's mother, Elizabeth, was left with nine children that she took to live on a
(63)
farm near Maryville, Tennessee. The family worked the farm, and Sam became a clerk
(63)
in a general store to help support them. Disenchanted at age 15 with his life, Houston

left his job and family and ran away from home to an Indian reservation near what is

now Dayton, Tennessee.

62. F. NO CHANGE

   G. Sam Houston was born in Virginia in 1793. His father died suddenly when Sam was just 13.

   H. When Sam was just 13, his father, born in 1793 in Virginia died suddenly.

   J. Born in 1793 in Virginia, Houston's father died suddenly. Sam was just 13.

63. A. NO CHANGE

   B. was left with nine children who she took to live on a farm near Maryville, Tennessee.

   C. was left with nine children whom she took to live on a farm near Maryville, Tennessee.

   D. was left with nine children which she took to live on a farm near Maryville, Tennessee.

[2]

He enjoyed their way of life much more than his own, and although he returned home

for a short period of time, Houston eventually moved back and stayed with the tribe.

<u>The Cherokees' of Eastern Tennessee</u> welcomed and adopted Houston, and he
                    (64)

became an official Cherokee with the Indian name *Raven*. This period of his life was the

basis of Houston's lifelong love of the Cherokee Indian.

Although he loved his life with the Cherokee people, after about three years Houston

still had some wanderlust within him and he went back to live with the white man.

<u>By this time he was in debt and realizing the need for educating children in Tennessee.</u>
                          (65)

He opened a private school there, which quickly became very successful. Houston was

able to pay off his debt with his teaching salary. Not completely fulfilled with the

profession of teaching, Houston enlisted in the 39th Infantry of the Army to fight the

Creek Indians. He was seriously injured in the Battle of Horseshoe Bend, sustaining

three possibly mortal wounds. His bravery caught the eye of General Andrew Jackson,

<u>whom took an immediate liking to the Brave Houston.</u>
                    (66)

64. ❑ F. NO CHANGE

   ❑ G. The Cherokees' of eastern Tennessee

   ❑ H. The Cherokees of Eastern Tennessee

   ❑ J. The Cherokees of eastern Tennessee

65. ❑ A. NO CHANGE

   ❑ B. By this time he was in debt and they realized the need for educating children in Tennessee.

   ❑ C. By this time he was in debt and realized the need for educating children in Tennessee.

   ❑ D. Realizing the need for educating children in Tennessee, by this time he was in debt.

66. ❑ F. NO CHANGE

   ❑ G. who took an immediate liking to the Brave Houston.

   ❑ H. whom took an immediate liking to the brave Houston.

   ▣ J. who took an immediate liking to the brave Houston.

[3]

Sam Houston eventually rose to the rank of first lieutenant before leaving the Army
                                    (67)
in 1818 to study law. He was able to establish a law practice in Tennessee within six
    (67)
months, and the popular but quiet man ran for and was elected district attorney soon

thereafter. A few years later, and with Andrew Jackson's continuing strong support,

Houston was elected to Congress and then, by a large margin, won the race for

governor of Tennessee.

Although successful professionally and politically Houston was unhappy in his
              (68)
married life. His wife, Eliza, left him during this time. Sam Houston was distressed
                                 (69)
found himself unable to work effectively and sought the consolation of his friends, the
        (69)
Cherokees. He resigned from politics, and the speaker of the Senate, William Hall,

completed Houston's term as governor of Tennessee. Meanwhile, Houston went to live

with the Cherokees for about five years, eventually moving to Texas.

67. ▣ A. NO CHANGE

   ❑ B. Sam Houston eventually arose to the rank of first lieutenant before leaving the Army in 1818 to study law.

   ❑ C. Sam Houston eventually rised to the rank of first lieutenant before leaving the Army in 1818 to study law.

   ❑ D. Sam Houston eventually was rising to the rank of first lieutenant before leaving the Army in 1818 to study law.

68. ❑ F. NO CHANGE

   ❑ G. Although successful professionally, and politically

   ▣ H. Although successful professionally and politically,

   ❑ J. Although, successful professionally and politically

69. ☐ A. NO CHANGE

 ☐ B. Distressed, Sam Houston found himself unable to work effectively

 ☐ C. Sam Houston distressed, found himself unable to work effectively

 ☐ D. Unable to work effectively, Sam Houston distressed found himself

[4]

Texas is happy to have Houston living there, and elected him as a delegate to the
                                         (70)
Convention of 1833. This was the second convention arranged to discuss problems with
            (70)
Mexico and the constitution that Texas was trying to get Mexico to agree with.

Texas was still a part of Mexico, but the state had come to realize that he wants
                                              (71)
independence. In 1836, they demanded this from Mexico, and positioned Sam Houston
      (71)
as the commander-in-chief of the Texas Army as they fought their civil war.

70. ☐ F. NO CHANGE

 ☐ G. Texas was happy to have Houston living there, and elected him as a delegate
         to the Convention of 1833.

 ☐ H. Texas is happy to have Houston living there, and elected him as a delegate
         to the Convention of 1833.

 ☐ J. Texas was happy to have Houston living here, and elected him as a delegate
         to the Convention of 1833.

71. ☐ A. NO CHANGE

 ☐ B. Texas was still a part of Mexico, but it had come to realize that it wants
         independence.

 ☐ C. Texas was still a part of Mexico, but the state had come to realize that he
         wanted independence.

 ☐ D. Texas was still a part of Mexico, but the state had come to realize that they
         wanted independence.

[5]

(1)A joyful Texas elected Sam Houston president of the now-Republic of Texas. (2)After
a Texas victory at the Battle of San Jacinto, General Santa Anna was captured and he
realized that he would have to give up Texas. (3)Houston successfully led his forces in
many battles against General Antonio Lopez de Santa Anna of Mexico and his troops.
(4)He was released after declaring Texas to be independent of his country.

72. Reorder the sentences in the paragraph above so that it begins with a topic sentence and the other sentences flow in sequence.

☑ Ⓕ 3, 2, 4, 1

❑ G. 4, 3, 2, 1

❑ H. 1, 4, 2, 3

❑ J. 4, 2, 3, 1

[6]

Houston served successive terms from 1838 to 1844, and was always elected by a large

majority. He worked during that time to have Texas admitted to the United States.

<u>Texans became part of the United States in 1845, and the people immediately</u>
                                (73)
<u>elected Sam Houston to the senate.</u> He served from 1845 to 1859.
              (73)

73. ❑ A. NO CHANGE

    ❑ B. Texans became part of the United States in 1845, and the people immediately elected Sam Houston to the Senate.

    ❑ C. Texans became a part of the United States in 1845, and the people immediately elected Sam Houston to the Senate.

    ☑ D. Texas became part of the United States in 1845, and the people immediately elected Sam Houston to the Senate.

By now, Texans were talking about secession from the Union and Houston was completely opposed to the idea. He felt that Texas benefited in many ways by being a part of the United States. In 1859, he used his antisecession campaign to become elected governor of Texas. Two years later, Texas still voted to secede from the United States, with Houston still in strong opposition. By then, he had very few supporters in his quest, and Houston was removed from his position as governor in 1861 when he refused to do anything toward helping Texas break from the Union. This ended Sam Houston's career in politics. He retired with his family to a home that they rented in Huntsville, Texas in 1861, and he died of pneumonia two years later.

Texas remained a part of the United States and the state named a city after Sam Houston. [74]

The following question refers to the entire paragraph above.

74. Which sentence provides the most complete conclusion to this passage?

   ❏ F. He has been forgotten by many people.

   ❏ G. He still has ancestors scattered around the country.

   ❏ H. He had an exciting life.

   ❏ J. There is a statue of Sam Houston today in Statuary Hall in Washington, D.C.

75. What is the main idea of this essay?

   ❏ A. Sam Houston will be remembered forever.

   ❏ B. Sam Houston was a great statesman.

   ❏ C. Sam Houston did what the people wanted.

   ❏ D. Sam Houston had a difficult life.

ACT Reading Assessment

Directions: On this test, you will have 35 minutes to read four passages and answer 40 questions (10 questions pertaining to each passage). Each set of 10 questions appears directly under the passage it refers to. You should select the response that best answers the question. There is no time limit for work on individual passages, so you can move freely between the passages and refer to them as often as you'd like.

Passage I: Prose Fiction

Line   Thursday, June 25. It started out as just a normal and typical day in my life. I am a high school senior, a content although harried high school girl.

        I had a strange experience last year that I still think about quite a bit. It was a late June afternoon, and I had hastily climbed into my dad's car to complete some pressing
(5)   errands. I turned the key to start the car, but the always-trusty automobile would not respond. With Mom at work for another six hours and Dad in Phoenix on business, I found myself immediately stranded and then aggravated. Because Mom was in surgery all day today, it was paramount that I resolve my own problem and not attempt to contact her at what was certainly an inopportune time.

(10)   I sat on the front stoop of my house, sweating in the extreme South Florida humidity, and pondered my situation and options for just a second. My friends were either working or otherwise engaged and would not be able to assist me. I went into the house and scanned the telephone book for either a mechanic or a good idea. Immediately one listing caught my eye: "Mack's Mobile Mechanic Service." I wasted no
(15)   time in ringing Mack right up.

        "Mack" was actually "Joe," and Joe was extremely polite, kind, and eager to please his stranded potential customer: "Let's see, Ma'am. You live in our Zone 2, but heck, I'll just charge you for Zone 1." He quoted me a price for a new battery and told me that they accepted a wide variety of credit cards. I pretended to mull it over for a few
(20)   minutes. "Sounds great," I offered, and Joe told me he'd immediately dispatch his mechanic, Mel, to my address to install the new battery.

        As I waited for Mel to arrive, I found the credit card that I had signing privileges for. I guess Mom and Dad had done that in anticipation of just such an occasion. I pushed the button to open the garage door to outdoors. The late afternoon sky was dark
(25)   and a light rain was just beginning to fall when Mel pulled his truck into my driveway. I grabbed my car keys from the kitchen table and headed outside.

        Tall and lean and bearing a more than passing resemblance to Michael Jordan, Mel requested my car keys and attempted to start the car himself. For a split second, I speculated what I would do if the car decided to turn over for him. I suppose I would have
(30)   turned bright red and apologized profusely. He had no luck either getting the car to respond.

        Mel popped the hood, looked around for a few seconds, then extricated the expired battery. Rain was still just lightly falling. Mel was forthcoming and pleasant, and I was pleased with his seeming efficiency. I still held out hope that I would be able to
(35)   complete at least a few of my errands and meet some friends for a movie.

Mel was moving quickly, so he surprised me by literally stopping in his tracks for a second and bending over to look at the car's radiator. He said something that I was unable to comprehend, so I moved closer to him and the car. Now just two feet from him, I opened my mouth to ask Mel to repeat what he had just said.

(40)   I would not even get one word out of my mouth.

It was at that precise millisecond that an extraordinary bolt of lightning—the biggest, strongest, and most powerful that I have ever been near or even seen—struck my driveway in the narrow two feet between where Mel and I were standing. The bolt hit the driveway with an incredible force, followed by a loud bang that I'm sure was

(45)   heard for miles around. I was thrown with an extreme force directly into the garage. Mel, I learned a few moments later, headed involuntarily for the grass beside the car.

He and I did not utter a sound for about three or four minutes, and the silence was scary as we now stood beside each other in the garage. Eventually, though, our eyes met. "Sandy," Mel slowly said, "we almost lost it there!" I was still unable or perhaps just

(50)   unwilling to speak. We kept looking at each other, and I knew right then that we were in one way now bonded together for life.

Mel admitted to me a few seconds later that the incident was certainly the most frightening that he had ever experienced in his life. I was shaking and not really responding to anything he was saying. Mel wisely stopped the little bit of talking he had

(55)   been doing and then ran over to his truck. Lickity split, he exchanged the old battery with a new one in his truck, wired up the new one, jumped in and started up my car, and prepared an invoice, all in perhaps five minutes' time. "I just want to get out of here," he quietly admitted, as he took the credit card from my hand and asked me the date. "June 25th," I told him, "and don't you forget it!" I signed the charge slip. Again, as before,

(60)   our eyes met, and then he jumped into his truck and was gone. From inside my garage I watched his truck drive quickly away.

Since that day last year, I've conducted my life with a renewed love of just existing, and with an appreciation and interest in those whom I cross paths with. I'm guessing that Mel is doing the same.

1. Based on the information in the passage, the narrator feels close to Mel because he:

   ❑ A. was helping her with the car battery

   ▨ B. shared a near-death experience with her

   ❑ C. actually drove to her home to replace the battery

   ❑ D. was so kind to her

2. The narrator's assertion that "Joe was extremely polite, kind, and eager to please" is based on what detail(s) in the story?

I. his willingness to charge a closer zone's price

II. his kind introduction when he got to her home

III. his offer to send his best mechanic

IV. his suggestion that he accepts credit cards

    ❑ F. I and II

    ❑ G. I and III

    ❑ H. II and III

    ❑ J. I and IV

3. Considering the events of the passage, the narrator's attitude has most nearly changed from:

    ❑ A. despondency to acceptance

    ❑ B. antagonism to redemption

    ❑ C. disappointment to relief

    ❑ D. dynamism to salvation

4. What is probably not true of her motives when the narrator says that "it was paramount that I resolve my own problem and not attempt to contact [her mother] at what was certainly an inopportune time"?

    ❑ F. She was frightened to contact her mother.

    ❑ G. She did not want to make an ill-timed phone call.

    ❑ H. She respected her mother's position.

    ❑ J. She placed emphasis on her independence.

5. How would the narrator have felt if Mel had been successful in starting the car right away?

    ❑ A. relieved

    ❑ B. disconcerted

    ❑ C. embarrassed

    ❑ D. elated

6. All of the following words can be used to describe the narrator EXCEPT:

   ❑ F. able

   ❑ G. coy

   ❑ H. resourceful

   ❑ J. thoughtful

7. Based on the passage, it is reasonable to infer that the narrator:

   ❑ A. had her father's permission to use his car

   ❑ B. had a car but work was being done on it

   ❑ C. was disappointed with her friends' inability to help her

   ❑ D. was typically not as busy as today

8. The details and events in this passage suggest that the narrator:

   ❑ F. is accustomed to doing things on her own

   ❑ G. misses her parents

   ❑ H. wishes her life would slow down

   ❑ J. has always been fearful of lightning

9. It can be inferred that the narrator's friends might be "otherwise engaged" [12] in all of the following ways EXCEPT:

   ❑ A. involved with a family commitment

   ❑ B. cramming for an exam

   ❑ C. tending to a sibling

   ❑ D. enjoying an uneventful afternoon

10. It can be inferred that after the narrator watched Mel pull away she:

    ❑ F. got into the car

    ❑ G. called her friends

    ❑ H. began to cry uncontrollably

    ❑ J. called her mother

Passage II: Social Science

Line   Most American people today can attribute the axiom "Give me liberty, or give me
death" to the great statesman Patrick Henry. Many of those same people, though, don't
have any idea who Patrick Henry was or why he ever uttered those particular words.
They are not aware that Patrick Henry was one of the greatest orators our country has
(5)   ever known and that he was important in our country's earliest history.

        Patrick Henry was born in Virginia in 1736 and was largely educated by his well-
schooled father. Henry decided to go to law school when he was 24 after a failed business left him heavily in debt and in need of another line of work. After he became a
lawyer, it was almost immediately apparent that young Patrick Henry had great talents
(10) as a lecturer, and arguing cases became a perfect way for him to showcase this gift. A
most noted case, the Parson's Cause (a case about a worker's back wages), brought him
particular notoriety, and regardless of their involvement in the particular issue, many
people enjoyed listening to him speak about this case.

        Four years later, Patrick Henry was elected to the House of Burgesses in Virginia
(15) and sped to the role of leader. He realized that his lecturing skills were perhaps his
greatest asset; people gathered to hear him speak and listened to what he said. His
speech discussing his disapproval of the Stamp Act is often thought of as one of his best.

        Henry moved up the political ladder, becoming first a member of the First
Continental Congress, and then for a short time was associated with the Second
(20) Continental Congress. He quickly established himself as an esteemed statesman, and it
was during that time, 1775, that Patrick Henry stood in front of the Virginia Provincial
Convention and urged it to grant the colony the right to bear arms to defend itself
against England. His words, "Give me liberty, or give me death," only served to emphasize his respect and loyalty to those who fought for freedom and are debatably the best-
(25) known words spoken by the great statesman.

        In 1776, Henry was asked to spearhead the writing of the constitution for the
Commonwealth of Virginia. His hard work on this project was rewarded handsomely:
Patrick Henry became governor of that new commonwealth once the charter constitution was ratified. Patrick Henry sank all of his energies into the office of governor,
(30) something of extreme importance since at that time the Revolutionary War was
wreaking havoc on Virginia. He made sure that his army was fed and clothed and had
plenty of weapons and ammunition. Well loved and highly respected by the people, he
served three terms in all as governor.

        In 1788, Patrick Henry was called upon to assist in ratifying the Constitution of
(35) the now-United States. He made no secret of the fact that he was vehemently opposed
to many parts of this important piece of our country's beginnings. Henry stated that he
did not feel that the Constitution truly protected the rights of the individual citizen, nor
of the states. Needless to say, the U.S. Constitution was still approved, and Henry
graciously accepted that decision, although with a caveat: He was directly responsible
(40) for the addition of the Bill of Rights to the Constitution, which addressed those particular areas that Henry found needed more elucidation. He drafted these 10 amendments
to the Constitution, and they were easily ratified.

        Patrick Henry left politics shortly after drafting the Bill of Rights, sensing that he
had completed his mission of getting the new country off to a promising start. In need

(45)   of money, he happily took up his law career once again. By that time, he was renowned
as a public speaker, and his good name made his law business extremely lucrative. Henry
was primarily a criminal lawyer by this time, and many citizens enjoyed sitting in the
courtroom and listening to him argue his cases as a form of recreation. Henry was able
to retire with plentiful assets after working just another six years, settling in his Red Hill
(50)   estate in Virginia.

Citizens and politicians would have nothing of Patrick Henry's attempted retire-
ment, though, and urged him to continue to seek political office. He refused again and
again, saying that he was enjoying the quiet life at the acreage he had worked so hard to
attain. Patrick Henry did not consent to run but was elected governor of Virginia in
(55)   1796, a tribute to the love and respect the country had for him. He refused the office,
which would have marked his sixth term as governor.

A short time later, George Washington urged Patrick Henry to run as candidate
for representative to the Virginia State Legislature, and Henry reluctantly agreed.
Although he won that election, Patrick Henry died before he took office, with a distin-
(60)   guished life in public service as his legacy.

11. Based on the passage, Patrick Henry's feelings about the U.S. Constitution can
most nearly be described as:

❑ A. biased

❑ B. apathetic

❑ C. befuddled

☑ D. vacillating

12. Patrick Henry probably realized early he was a gifted speaker because:

☑ F. Arguing cases was enjoyable for him.

❑ G. He was educated as a lawyer.

❑ H. He was a member of the House of Burgesses.

❑ J. George Washington asked him to run for Virginia State Legislature.

13. According to the passage, Patrick Henry went into law:

☑ A. for financial reasons

❑ B. under parental urging

❑ C. for fame and prestige

❑ D. to become an orator

14. As used in line 46, *lucrative* most nearly means:

    ❏ F. satisfying

    ❏ G. complicated

    ☒ H. profitable

    ❏ J. large

15. Patrick Henry drafted the Bill of Rights for all of the following reasons EXCEPT:

    Ⓐ A. He found weaknesses in the Constitution as it was written.

    ☒ B. His vote to ratify the Constitution was contingent on his doing so.

    ❏ C. He wanted to ensure that the country got off to a good start.

    ❏ D. The people in the new United States were demanding additional rights.

16. According to the passage, which facet of Patrick Henry's life was the most financially successful for him?

    ❏ F. public speaking

    ❏ G. political office

    ☒ H. practicing law

    ❏ J. writing legislation

17. It is likely that Patrick Henry accepted George Washington's suggestion to run for representative to the Virginia State Legislature because:

    ☒ A. He was excited by the idea.

    ❏ B. He was intimidated by George Washington.

    ❏ C. He was paid to run.

    Ⓓ D. He was good friends with Washington.

18. It can be inferred from the passage that Patrick Henry died:

    ❏ F. as an unfulfilled man

    ☒ G   personally satisfied with his legacy

    ❏ H. harboring pessimism regarding the country

    ❏ J. regretting his decision to represent the legislature

19. All of the following words can be used to describe Patrick Henry EXCEPT:

    ❑ A. intellectual

    ❑ B. acrimonious

    ❑ C. renowned

    ❑ D. articulate

20. To emulate the work of Patrick Henry, one would be wise to:

    ❑ F. see a Patrick Henry memorial

    ❑ G. go to law school

    ❑ H. memorize the Bill of Rights

    ❑ J. visit the Red Hill estate

Passage III: Humanities

Line   Hercules is arguably the greatest hero of Greek mythology. Although he was originally designated "Heracules" (sometimes Heracles) by the Greeks, the Romans dubbed him by the derivative "Hercules," and that name has stuck for all time.

    Hercules had a fascinating beginning. His father, Zeus, the king of the gods, was
(5) married to Hera. Hera wanted vengeance because her husband had sired Hercules with the beautiful and young Alcmene, both a princess and a mortal. Hera spent all of her time trying to make the young boy's life miserable by her relentless attempts to take his life. She began her quest very early in the boy's life, sending two serpents to bite and kill the tiny infant. The baby Hercules was able to strangle both of the vipers before they
(10) were able to do him harm.

    Hercules grew up and married Megara, and together they had a family. Hera continued her quest to distress Hercules by sending him into a prolonged phase of madness. During that period, Hercules killed his beloved wife and their children. After a trial at Delphi, the edict stated that Hercules was forced to serve King Eurystheus at
(15) Tiryns for a period of 12 years to repent for his crimes. At the end of that period of time, Hercules would be purified.

    As Hercules' service, King Eurystheus ordered him to perform 12 duties, which were called "labors." His first labor dictated that Hercules kill a lion near the place of his birth, Thebes. Wearing the skin as a trophy, Hercules impressed people all around
(20) that he was able to mortally wound the savage beast.

    Hercules' second labor meant killing the feared serpent Hydra of Lerna. Hydra had various heads, which frustrated Hercules because they were able to regenerate almost instantly after each was cut off. Hercules realized that he was getting nowhere with the dreaded Hydra, so he enlisted the help of his nephew Iolaus, whom he had
(25) brought with him, to burn with fire each neck of the Hydra immediately after each head was cut off. Hercules would cut off a head, and Iolaus would set out to disable it. This worked until they both realized that one particular Hydra head was not to be stopped by

the fire. Hercules buried this head underneath a rock, took his arrows out of his pouch,
and doused them all with Hydra's blood. The poisoned arrows would be invaluable to
(30) Hercules as he pursued his labors, but they would also lead to his undoing.

Hercules was able to capture the giant boar of Erymanthus as his third labor and
the golden-horned stag of Arcadia for his fourth labor. Now over a third of the way
complete with his seemingly insurmountable burdens, Hercules was able to remove a
flock of birds with arrows for feathers from woods near Lake Stymphalus. These birds
(35) had the capability to shoot people with their arrow-feathers, and Hercules successfully
drove them from the populated area. For his sixth labor, Hercules was able to construct
two rivers to flow through King Augeas's stables. These rivers cleaned the stables, and
this labor was the last of the first six labors of Hercules.

The final six labors took him far from his homeland and, once completed, would
(40) grant him immortality.

Hercules had to travel all the way to Crete to perform his seventh labor: to capture
the bull belonging to King Minos. After that success, he herded the human-eating
horses of King Diomedes all the way from Thrace to Eurytheus, feeding the stunned
King Diomedes to them along the way. This meal rendered them unable to eat humans
(45) again.

To complete his ninth labor, Hercules got the belt belonging to the queen of the
Amazons, Hippolyta, as a reward for prevailing in a battle with her. For his tenth labor,
Hercules stole the animals belonging to Geryon, an especially feared monster. He
completed his eleventh duty by stealing the wonderful Golden Apples of Hesperides
(50) from the Tree of Life. He completed his labors by actually going into the feared underworld of the dead and catching the three-headed watchdog Cerberus. He brought the
watchdog to the upperworld.

After successfully completing the 12 assigned labors, Hercules got married again,
this time to the princess Deiaira. When she was threatened and harassed by Nessus,
(55) Hercules shot the perpetrator with one of his poisoned arrows. As Nessus lay dying, he
advised Deiaira that if she were ever to lose Hercules' love, she could put some of
Nessus's blood on Hercules' robe and she would be able to have him back. Eventually
Hercules fell in love with Iola, another princess, and Deiaira remembered the dying
Nessus's advice. She did not know, though, that the blood of Nessus had been poisoned
(60) by the same poisoned arrow that killed him, and Hercules became burned over almost
his entire body when he put the robe on. In terrible agony, he begged to be put onto a
funeral fire to be relieved of his misery. In no time, his body was incinerated and was
taken to the home of the gods, Mount Olympus, where Hercules became a god.

Throughout his life, the mighty Hercules could not be stopped, and in modern
(65) times, his name represents extreme strength.

21. Based on the passage, Hercules' life can be said to have been:

   ☑ A. extraordinary

   ❑ B. insurmountable

   ❑ C. catastrophic

   ❑ D. utopian

22. According to the passage, Hercules lost his wife Megara and family due to:

    ❏ F. a misunderstanding

    ❏ G. an accident

    ❏ H. a natural disaster

    ❏ J. his own actions

23. According to the passage, Hercules had to perform 12 labors so that he would:

    ❏ A. take evil from the land

    ❏ B. impress the king

    ❏ C. repent for his crimes

    ❏ D. prove how strong he was

24. Hercules can be described as all of the following EXCEPT:

    ❏ F. vengeful

    ❏ G. prolific

    ❏ H. clever

    ❏ J. stalwart

25. According to the passage, Hercules showed the people that he had killed the lion by:

    ❏ A. carrying around the lion's head

    ❏ B. wearing the lion's skin

    ❏ C. bringing people to Thebes

    ❏ D. moving on to his next labor

26. Calling someone "Hercules" has what kind of connotation?

    ❏ F. positive

    ❏ G. negative

    ❏ H. neutral

    ❏ J. mixed

27. Inferring from the passage, approximately how long did it take for Hercules to complete each of his labors?

    ❏ A. a day

    ❏ B. a year

    ❏ C. 12 years

    ❏ D. months

28. It can be inferred from the passage that if Hercules had been unable to complete the 12 labors, he likely would have:

   ❏ F. been put to death by the king

   ❏ G. gotten more labors to complete

   ❏ H. been given more time

   ❏ J. turned into a weak animal

29. It can be inferred from the passage that Hercules' wife Deiaira:

   ❏ A. did not intend for harm to be done to her husband

   ❏ B. kept the robe to use in the future

   ❏ C. remarried after Hercules' death

   ❏ D. felt that Hercules got what he deserved

30. According to the passage, why did Hercules think he was immortal?

   ❏ F. He had completed the second six labors.

   ❏ G. He had completed the first six labors.

   ❏ H. He had gone to the underworld of the dead.

   ❏ J. The king had been eaten.

Passage IV: Natural Science

Line

Word origins are oftentimes intriguing to research and think about. A good example is the word *dodo*. People sporadically use the noun in a derogatory sense—to portray a person whom they think to be not particularly sharp. It is a sure bet that these name-callers may not be conscious of the unfortunate origin and true meaning of the
(5) word *dodo*.

Dodo is actually the designation of a now-extinct bird that lived until about 1681 AD. Owing to its time of existence, no photographs and few illustrations are available of the bird. A dodo was thought to have been gray in color and resemble a pigeon, and some historians believe that the dodo was in fact a relative of that particular bird. The dodo
(10) had a great beak with a hook at the end and a tail with an abundance of white feathers.

Possibly because of its inability to fly, or perhaps as the reason for this helplessness, the dodo is thought to have been an overweight species of bird. Some scientists disagree, though, and believe the dodo to have been of a normal weight for its size. This disagreement will never be solved, as the illustrations that exist of the bird show it in a variety of
(15) sizes and shapes.

The dodo lived principally on Mauritius, an atoll off the coast of Africa. The island was a secure environment for the bird—grounded or not, the dodo had few natural predators. As in many other areas at this time in civilization's history, the birds' idyllic

(20)   life abruptly ceased when man moved into the dodo's turf, feral animals in tow. It is thought that some of the explorers who first discovered the birds also surmised that the dodo would make a delectable meal. Man's hunting was another factor that helped lead to the extinction of the dodo bird species. There were substantial slaughters of the dodo. The birds were likely to have been consumed quickly and in large amounts. Likewise,

(25)   feral animals devastated the delicate ecosystem enjoyed for so many years by the dodo. The rabbits, pigs, cats, and other animals imported to the island by the explorers wreaked havoc on the forest there. The dodo was no longer able to find food easily. The birds' delicately formed nests were destroyed by the rapidly reproducing new species of animals. Tragically, these animals found the friendly dodo bird to be easy quarry.

(30)   Make no mistake: The dodo bird was not a dense animal—the human is in many ways less smart. For man to move in and directly cause the extinction of an entire species is indeed tragic. It is hoped that appropriate lessons about fragile ecosystems were learned by this particular extinction.

31. According to the passage, the dodo's demise is chiefly due to:

    A. its inability to fly

    B. the influx of explorers

    C. feral animals

    D. its failure to reproduce quickly enough

32. The noun *dodo* is sometimes used to characterize someone who is:

    F. not very smart

    G. short and stout

    H. clever

    J. argumentative

33. More accurately, the noun *dodo* should be used to describe a person who:

    A. is affected by factors beyond his or her control

    B. fights hard to live

    C. lives in Africa

    D. has had an easy life

34. All of the following are factors leading to the demise of the dodo EXCEPT:

    F. change to the animals' habitat

    G. climate change

    H. hunting by humans

    J. its inability to reproduce quickly enough

35. All of the following words can be used to describe the dodo EXCEPT:

    ❑ A. tragic

    ▣ B. predatory

    ❑ C. extinct

    ❑ D. inadaptable

36. As it is used in line 29, *quarry* most nearly means:

    ❑ F. excavation

    ▣ G. prey

    ❑ H. attackers

    ❑ J. groups

37. The author believes that lessons can be learned from the story of the dodo. What is the main lesson that can be taken from learning about this species' demise?

    ▣ A. Ecosystems are delicate and should be left alone.

    ❑ B. Some species are extinct and will never be back.

    ❑ C. Humans as a species are not very smart.

    ❑ D. The dodo bird was not a stupid animal.

38. The author's tone in this passage is mainly:

    ❑ F. humorous

    ❑ G. poignant

    ❑ H. hostile

    ▣ J. explanatory

39. If you traveled to Mauritius today, it is likely that:

    ❑ A. Few animals would be living in the area.

    ❑ B. Museums would showcase the prized dodo.

    ❑ C. Ancient dodo nests would be preserved in some areas.

    ▣ D. There would be a modern civilization.

40. The author concludes that in many ways the dodos were smarter than humans because:

    ❑ F. The dodos were able to create delicate nests.

    ❑ G. Humans were unable to leave the island.

    ❑ H. The dodos lived in solitude for years.

    ▣ J. Humans were responsible for the extinction of an entire species.

Math Test

60 minutes, 60 questions

Directions: Solve each of the following problems, and then mark the appropriate oval on your answer sheet.

All problems are worth the same number of points, so do not linger over problems that take too much time. Solve as many problems as you can; then return to the problems you did not answer in the time remaining.

You may use a calculator on this test. However, the best way to solve a problem might be without a calculator.

Note that unless otherwise indicated, you should assume the following:

1. Figures may not necessarily be drawn to scale.

2. All geometric figures lie in a plane.

3. The word *line* refers to a straight line.

4. The word *average* refers to arithmetic mean.

1. How can $4\sqrt{3} - \sqrt{48} + 3\sqrt{27}$ be simplified?

$-24 + 3$

27

- A. $6\sqrt{3}$
- B. 9
- C. $9\sqrt{3}$
- D. $15\sqrt{3}$
- E. $18\sqrt{2}$

Do Your Figuring Here.

2. Eloise needs to build a model of a building that is 400 feet tall and 300 feet wide. If she decides the height of her model should be 8 inches, how many inches wide should she make it?

- F. 6
- G. 8
- H. 11
- J. 12
- K. 72

$\dfrac{4}{3} \times \dfrac{8}{6}$

3. The average height of the first 10 people Maria measured was 68 inches. However, the average height of the next 19 people was 65 inches. What was the overall average, in inches, of all the people Maria measured?

68

☐ A. 66

☒ B. 66.03

☐ C. 66.5

☐ D. 67

☐ E. 68.27

Do Your Figuring Here.

133   680

1915

4. On a certain scale drawing, all the dimensions are shown $\frac{1}{16}$ their actual size. If the line that represents a doorway opening on the drawing is $3\frac{1}{4}$ inches, how many feet is the actual door opening?

☐ F. $2\frac{1}{2}$

☐ G. $3\frac{1}{4}$

☐ H. 4

☒ J. $4\frac{1}{3}$

☐ K. 5

$\frac{x}{12} \times \frac{13}{4} \times \frac{16}{1}$ $\frac{208}{4}$ 52

5. The following figure shows the parallelogram ABCD. What is the measure of ∠ADC?

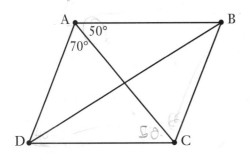

☐ A. 20°

☐ B. 30°

☒ C. 60°

☐ D. 120°

☐ E. 240°

6. A cell phone company charges customers a monthly connection fee of $25. It also charges customers a rate of 10¢ per minute for each minute of cell phone use. Which of the following expressions represents the monthly cost, in dollars, of using a cell phone for *m* minutes?

   ❏ F. $m + 25$

   ❏ G. $25 + 10m$

   ❏ H. $25 \times (0.10) + m$

   ☒ J. $0.1m + 25$

   ❏ K. $(0.10m + 25) \times 30$

Do Your Figuring Here.

25 $10¢$

7. If $f(x) = \dfrac{1}{2x^2} - \dfrac{1}{3x + 7}$, what is $f(-3)$?

   ❏ A. $1\frac{1}{2}$

   ☒ B. $3\frac{1}{2}$

   ❏ C. 5

   ❏ D. $10\frac{1}{2}$

   Ⓔ. $12\frac{1}{2}$

$\dfrac{1}{2(-3)^2} - \dfrac{1}{3(-3)+7}$

$\dfrac{1}{18} + \dfrac{9}{18}$ $\dfrac{10}{18}$ $5/9$

$\dfrac{1}{2(-3)^2} - \dfrac{1}{3(-3)+7}$

-9

$\dfrac{1}{18} - \dfrac{1}{-2}$

$\dfrac{9}{18}$

8. Alicia sold $1,950 worth of product over the last six months. This is 30% more than she sold over the first six months. How much product did Alicia sell in the first six months?

   ❏ F. 585

   ☒ G. $1,365$

   Ⓗ. $1,500$

   ❏ J. $1,893.20$

   ❏ K. $2,535$

$\dfrac{130}{100} X$

$\dfrac{30}{100} \times \dfrac{1950}{1} = \dfrac{\$585}{100}$

$\dfrac{130}{100} \times \dfrac{1500}{1} = \dfrac{195,000}{100}$ $\dfrac{1950}{585}$ $\overline{1365}$

9. In the following figure, $\overline{AB}$ is parallel to $\overline{CD}$. What is the value of x?

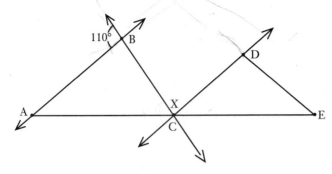

- ❑ A. 20°
- ❑ B. 40°
- ▨ C. 70°
- ❑ D. 90°
- ❑ E. 110°

10. At the local circus, adult tickets sold for $18 and children's tickets sold for $12. If the circus sold 625 tickets for a total of $8,820, how many adult tickets were sold?

- ▨ F. 180
- ❑ G. 220
- ❑ H. 300
- ❑ J. 441
- ❑ K. 490

3960   4860

3240

7938
882   5400
3900

$\dfrac{A}{C}$ $\dfrac{3}{2}$ $\dfrac{2940}{4410}$

300
325

220   3960
405   4860

11. In the following figure, $\overline{AB}$ is the median of trapezoid SRTQ. What is the value of y?

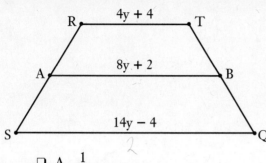

  ❏ A. $\frac{1}{2}$

  ☑ B. 2

  ❏ C. 3

  ❏ D. 5

  ❏ E. This cannot be determined from the information provided.

Do Your Figuring Here.

12. A line passes through the points (2,7) and (–3,2) in the standard (x,y) coordinate plane. What is the y-intercept of the line?

  ❏ F. –13

  ❏ G. –1

  ❏ H. 1

  ☑ J. 5

  ❏ K. 9

13. If $3x - \frac{4}{2} + \frac{9}{10} = \frac{x}{20}$, what is x equal to?

  ❏ A. $-\frac{5}{2}$

  ❏ B. $\frac{22}{31}$

  Ⓒ C. $\frac{22}{29}$

  ❏ D. $\frac{15}{14}$

  ☑ E. 2

2.

14. In the following figure, ∠S is a right angle in ΔRST. $\overline{SQ}$ is the altitude to the hypotenuse $\overline{RT}$. ∠SQT is also a right angle. If $\overline{SQ}$ = 6 units, what is the length, in units, of the hypotenuse $\overline{RT}$?

Do Your Figuring Here.

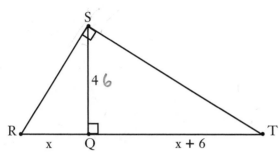

S

4 6

R   Q   T
   x   x + 6

❑ F. 2

▣ G. 4

❑ H. 8

(❑ J.) 10

❑ K. 18

2. 15. What is the slope of any line perpendicular to the line $\frac{4}{3x + 2y} = -14$?

❑ A. $\frac{-3}{2}$

▣ B. $\frac{-3}{4}$

❑ C. $\frac{2}{3}$

❑ D. $\frac{3}{4}$

(❑ E.) $\frac{3}{2}$

16. The opposite of number n is tripled and then added to 24. The result is a positive number. Which of the following choices gives ALL possible values for n?

(❑ F.) All $n < 8$

❑ G. $0 \leq n \leq 7$

❑ H. All $n > 8$

❑ J. All $n \leq 0$

▣ K. 0 only

$-3n$

$-(n)3 + 24 = PN$

$+n+3n \qquad +3n$

_____

$\frac{24}{3} = \frac{3n}{3}$

$8 = n$

17. The French Club is made up of 15 members. All French Club members are going to interview for the French Honor Society; however, the teacher can evaluate groups of only 4 students at a time. How many different combinations of groups of 4 can be formed from the 15 students?

    ❑ A. 24

    ❑ B. 60

    ❑ C. 1,365

    ❑ D. 8,190

    ❑ E. 32,760

Do Your Figuring Here.

18. If the points (5,7) and (–3,–8) lie in the (x,y) coordinate plane, what is the distance between the points?

    ❑ F. $\sqrt{3}$

    ❑ G. 13

    ❑ H. $\sqrt{269}$

    ❑ J. 17

    ❑ K. 25

19. Which of the following expressions is equivalent to $\frac{\sin \theta}{\cos \theta}$?

    ❑ A. $\frac{1}{\cos \theta}$

    ❑ B. $\tan \theta$

    ❑ C. $\frac{1}{\sin \theta}$

    ❑ D. $\frac{1}{\tan \theta}$

    ❑ E. $\sec \theta$

20. Which of the following choices gives a general expression for the total number of diagonals that can be drawn in a convex polygon of N sides?

    ❑ F. $N(N-3)$

    ❑ G. $\frac{N(N-3)}{2}$

    ❑ H. $N-3$

    ❑ J. $\frac{N}{2}$

    ❑ K. $\frac{(N-3)}{2}$

21. When the complement of an angle is tripled, the result is 16° more than the supplement of the angle. What is the measure of the angle?

   ❏ A. −37°

   ❏ B. 12.33°

   (❏ C.) 37°

   ❏ D. 74°

   ❏ E. 90°

22. If $f(x) = x^2 - 3x + 5$ and $g(x) = \sqrt{x}$, what is $(f \circ g)(x)$?

   ❏ F. $x^2 + \sqrt{x} - 3x + 5$

   ❏ G. $x + 5$

   ❏ H. $x - 3x^{1/2} + \sqrt{5}$

   ❏ J. $x - 3x^{1/2} + 5$

   ❏ K. $x^2 - x + 3$

23. A square playground is separated into two sections. If the playground is divided in half by a diagonal whose length is expressed as $4\sqrt{2} \times s$ feet, what is the perimeter of the playground, in feet, expressed in terms of s?

   ❏ A. $4s$

   ❏ B. $2s^2$

   ❏ C. $2s \sqrt{2}$

   ❏ D. $16s^2$

   ❏ E. $16s$

24. How many prime numbers fall between 75 and 100?

   ❏ F. 2

   ❏ G. 4

   ❏ H. 5

   ❏ J. 6

   ❏ K. 7

25. Albi's tuna sales decreased by 15% from 2002 to 2003 and by another 10% from 2003 to 2004. By what percent did his tuna sales decrease from 2002 to 2004?

Do Your Figuring Here.

   ❏ A. 11%

   ❏ B. 12.5%

   ❏ C. 20%

   ☒ D. 23.5%

   ❏ E. 25%

26. In the following figure, a 5-inch-by-5-inch square is inscribed in a circle. What is the circumference of the circle?

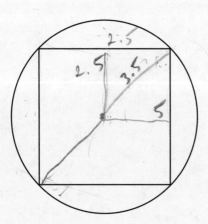

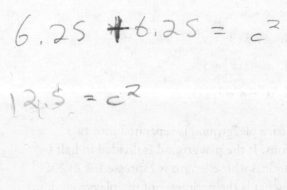

   ❏ F. $\frac{5\sqrt{2}}{2\pi}$ in.

   ❏ G. 5π in.

   ❏ H. $5\pi\sqrt{2}$ in.

   ☒ J. 12.5π in.

   ❏ K. 20π in.

27. An assembly plant was able to manufacture 30 handbags the first day of operation. If the machines were set to increase production each day by 6 handbags, how many handbags had been produced at the end of 31 days?

   ❏ A. 210

   ❏ B. 500

   ❏ C. 681

   ☒ D. 3,720

   ❏ E. 3,813

Do Your Figuring Here.

28. Given the pattern $F^3 + S^3 = (F + S) \times (F^2 - FS + S^2)$, how would $27p^3 x^9 + 8y^6$ be factored?

- [ ] F. $(3px^3 - 2y^2)(9p^2x^6 + 6px^3y^2 + 4y^4)$
- [x] G. $(27 + 8)(p^3x^9 + y^6)$
- [ ] (H.) $(3px^3 + 2y^2)(9p^2x^6 - 6px^3y^2 + 4y^4)$
- [ ] J. $(27p^3x^9 + 8y^6)(729p^6x^{18} - 216p^3x^9y^6 + 64y^{12})$
- [ ] K. The expression cannot be factored.

29. The variable r varies jointly as the square root of d and as y^2, and it varies inversely as x^4. What happens to r when y is doubled, d is quadrupled, and x is halved?

- [ ] A. r is multiplied by $\frac{1}{2}$.
- [ ] B. r is doubled.
- [ ] C. r is multiplied by 16.
- [ ] (D.) r is multiplied by 128.
- [x] E. r becomes undefined.

30. How is $(2x^2 + 5x - 5) - 4(x^2 - 2x + 7)$ simplified?

- [ ] F. $-2x^2 - 3x - 33$
- [ ] G. $6x^2 - 3x + 23$
- [x] H. $-2x^2 + 3x + 2$
- [ ] J. $-2x^2 + 13x - 33$
- [ ] K. $3x^2 + 3x + 2$

31. When you order a new backpack, you can choose from among five colors. You also have a variety of materials from which to choose. The company offers vinyl, leather, and a heavy-blended cotton. Additionally, the company offers to personalize your backpack. Finally, you can choose to have a stain repellent applied. How many different backpacks are available?

- [ ] A. 10
- [ ] B. 12
- [ ] C. 15
- [x] D. 60
- [ ] E. 120

32. What is the product of the following matrices?

$$\begin{bmatrix} 1 & 2 \\ -3 & 0 \\ 5 & 6 \end{bmatrix} \begin{bmatrix} a & c \\ b & d \end{bmatrix}$$

Do Your Figuring Here.

❑ F. Multiplication is not possible.

❑ G. $\begin{bmatrix} a + 2c \\ -3a \\ 5a - 6c \end{bmatrix}$

❑ H. $\begin{bmatrix} a + 2b + c + 2d \\ -3a - 3c \\ 5a - 6b + 5c - 6d \end{bmatrix}$

❑ J. $\begin{bmatrix} a + 2b & c + 2d \\ -3a & -3c \\ 5a - 6b & 5c - 6d \end{bmatrix}$

❑ K. $\begin{bmatrix} 8a & -4d \\ -2b & -4c \end{bmatrix}$

33. How would this expression be simplified?

$-2\sqrt{16\sqrt{2}}$

❑ A. $-2^{13/4}$

❑ B. $-8\sqrt{2}$

❑ C. $-2\sqrt{32}$

❑ D. 2

❑ E. $8\sqrt{2}$

34. The following figure shows two right triangles. If the lengths are given in feet, what is the length, in feet, of S?

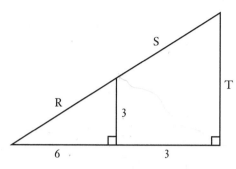

6   3   3

☑ F. $\frac{3\sqrt{5}}{2}$

☑ G. $3\sqrt{5}$

☐ H. $\sqrt{97}$

☐ J. 10

☐ K. 12

35. The following figure is the base of a right solid that is 7 feet high. The base shows two semicircles with centers P and Q. Segments $\overline{NP}$ and $\overline{QR}$ are both 8 inches long. How many 1-inch cubes will this solid hold?

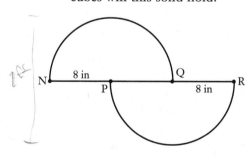

☐ A. 1,406.72

☑ B. 2,813.44

☐ C. 5,626.88

☐ D. 16,880.64

☐ E. 33,761.28

Do Your Figuring Here.

$a^2 + b^2 = c^2$

$36 + 9 =$

$c^2 = 45$

πr^2

$3.14(8)^2$

64π

$\begin{array}{r} 7 \\ \times 12 \\ \hline 84 \end{array}$

36. The initial pressure, temperature, and volume of a quantity of an ideal gas were 6 atmospheres, 520K, and 230 cubic meters, respectively. What would the temperature be, in kelvins, if the pressure were increased to 50 atmospheres and the volume reduced to 200 cubic meters? Note: The gas law for a fixed amount of an ideal gas is expressed here:

$$\frac{P_1 V_1}{T_1} = \frac{P_2 V_2}{T_2}$$

- ❏ F. 3.7×10^1
- ❏ G. 3.768×10^3
- ❏ H. 9.97×10^2
- ❏ J. 2.65×10^3
- ❏ K. 2.65×10^2

37. Given the following equation, what is m?

$$\frac{s}{m} + P = \frac{x}{n}$$

- ❏ A. $m = \frac{sn}{(x + pn)}$
- ❏ B. $m = \left(\frac{n}{x} - \frac{1}{p}\right)s$
- ❏ C. $m = \frac{sn}{pn - x}$
- ❏ D. $m = \frac{sn}{(x - pn)}$
- ❏ E. $m = \frac{-sn}{x + pn}$

Do Your Figuring Here.

38. In a trial, suppose a lawyer wants 2 men and 5 women to make up a special panel. If the 7 panel members are selected at random from a pool of 12 people, which is made up of 5 men and 7 women, what is the probability that the lawyer will *not* get the desired panel?

Do Your Figuring Here.

- ❏ F. $\frac{3}{252}$
- ❏ G. $\frac{3}{12}$
- ❏ H. $\frac{35}{132}$
- ❏ J. $\frac{7}{12}$
- ❏ K. $\frac{97}{132}$

39. Two pipes drain a tank. The first pipe drains the tank in 45 minutes. The second pipe drains the tank in 30 minutes. If the tank is $\frac{7}{9}$ full and the pipes are both draining, how long will it take, in minutes, to empty the tank completely?

- ❏ A. $\frac{7}{45}$
- ❏ B. 14
- ❏ C. 15
- ❏ D. 30
- ❏ E. $58\frac{1}{3}$

40. You throw a ball into the air with an initial velocity of 32 feet per second. The formula that relates the height of the ball, h, to any time, t, is $h = 32t - 16t^2$. How much time, in seconds, does it take for the ball to reach its maximum height?

- ❏ F. −1
- ❏ G. 1
- ❏ H. 2
- ❏ J. 4
- ❏ K. 16

Chapter 7: Practice Exam 1

41. Given the following quadratic formula, what are the values of *b* so that $2x^2 + bx + 4 = 0$ has real roots?

$$\frac{-b \pm \sqrt{b^2 - 4ac}}{2a}$$

- ❑ A. $|b> 4\sqrt{2}$
- ❑ B. $|b \geq 4\sqrt{2}$
- ❑ C. $b \geq 2$
- ❑ D. $b \geq 32$
- ❑ E. $|b \leq 32$

42. Bob is opening a new checking account and can select plan A or plan B. Plan A charges 45¢ for every check Bob writes. On the other hand, plan B charges only 10¢ a check but assigns a monthly fee of $7. Given that Bob wants to pay the minimum amount per month for his checking account, which of the following statements is *not* true?

- ❑ F. If the number of checks per month is less than 19, Bob should choose plan A.
- ❑ G. If the number of checks per month is greater than 20, Bob should choose plan B.
- ❑ H. If the number of checks per month is greater than 18, Bob should choose plan B.
- ❑ J. If the number of checks per month is greater than 21, Bob should choose plan B.
- ❑ K. If the number of checks per month is less than 18, Bob should choose plan A.

Do Your Figuring Here.

43. Square ABCD falls in the first quadrant in the standard (x,y) coordinate plane. If one vertex of the square is at the origin and the length of each side is 6 units, which one or more of the following statements express an equation of the square's diagonals?

　　I. $y = x$

　　II. $y = -x + 6$

　　III. $y = 1$

　　IV. $y = x + 6$

❑ A. II only

☒ B. I and IV

❑ C. III and IV

❑ D. I and II

❑ E. I only

44. Sama received 67, 87, 85, and 79 as marks on her science tests. In her class, in order to qualify for a B, she must earn an average score of 83. What is the minimum score Sama needs on her next test in order to qualify for a B?

❑ F. 99

❑ G. 98

⬚ H. 97

❑ J. 96

❑ K. 95

45. Given $\tan 3\theta - \frac{\sqrt{3}}{3} = 0$ and $0° \le \theta < 360°$, which of the following statements expresses all the possible solutions for theta?

❑ A. 10°, 130°, 250°

☒ B. 10°, 70°

❑ C. 30°, 210°

❑ D. 30°, 390°, 750°, 210°, 570°, 930°

❑ E. 10°, 130°, 250°, 70°, 190°, 310°

46. The volume occupied by a nucleus is approximately 1.0×10^{-15}. If the volume occupied by the negatively charged electrons is approximately 100,000 times larger, which expression represents the approximate volume of a nucleus?

   ❑ F. 1.0×10^{-20}

   ☒ G. 1.0×10^{-10}

   ❑ H. 1.0×10^{-9}

   ❑ J. 1.0×10^{9}

   ❑ K. 1.0×10^{10}

47. In the following figure, the quadrilateral ABCD and the circle are tangent at four points. What is the value of y?

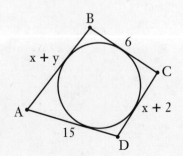

   ❑ A. 4

   ☒ B. 6

   ❑ C. 8

   ❑ D. 9

   ❑ E. 11

48. The equation of a parabola is $f(x) = 2x^2 + 12x + 16$. The graph of a second parabola is exactly the same as the first but shifted 3 units up on the y-axis. Which equation below describes the second parabola?

   ❑ F. $f(x) = 2(x + 3)^2 + 1$

   ☒ G. $f(x) = 3(2x^2 + 12x + 16)$

   ❑ H. $f(x) = x^2 + 6x + 8$

   ❑ J. $f(x) = 2(x + 6)^2 + 1$

   ❑ K. $f(x) = 2x^2 + 1$

Do Your Figuring Here.

49. In the following figure, $\overline{AC}$ is perpendicular to $\overline{DB}$. The (x,y) coordinates of point A, C, and D are given. Point B is the midpoint of $\overline{AC}$. What is the distance between point D and $\overline{AC}$?

Do Your Figuring Here.

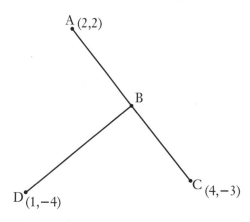

A (2,2)

B

D (1,−4)

C (4,−3)

   ❑ A. $\sqrt{\dfrac{\sqrt{65}}{2}}$

   ❑ B. $\sqrt{2}$

   ❑ C. $\sqrt{37}$

   ❑ D. $\sqrt{46.25}$

   ❑ E. $\sqrt{58}$

50. The slope of a lake bottom drops vertically 16 feet for every 100 feet you travel away from the shore. If you know you are at a place in the lake where the water is 68 feet deep, how far are you, in feet, from the shore?

   ❑ F. 6.25

   ❑ G. 50

   ❑ H. 100

   ❑ J. 425

   ❑ K. 500

51. A painter sits on a platform 8 feet from the ground and adjacent to a building. A 30-foot ladder is leaning against the building, making a 72° angle with the platform. How far up the building, in feet, does the ladder reach?

  ❏ A. 9.27

  ❏ B. 28.53

  ❏ C. 36.53

  ❏ D. 42.5

  ❏ E. 92.33

Do Your Figuring Here.

52. To show that $(\cos x + \sin x)^2 = 1 + \sin 2x$, which of the following identities do you need?

  I. $\cos^2 x - \sin^2 x = \cos 2x$

  II. $2\sin x \cos x = \sin 2x$

  III. $\sin^2 x + \cos^2 x = 1$

  ❏ F. III only

  ❏ G. II only

  ❏ H. I and III

  ❏ J. II and III

  ❏ K. I and II

53. In the following figure, the area of the square is 144 square units. The circles are tangent to the square such that twice the radius of the larger circle added to twice the radius of the smaller circle is equal to the length of one side of the square. If the area of the larger circle is four times that of the smaller circle, what is the area, in square units, of the smaller circle?

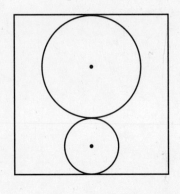

☐ A. 2π

☒ B. 4π

☐ C. 1π

☐ D. $1\sqrt{2}\pi$

☐ E. 12π

Do Your Figuring Here.

54. When you divide $-6 + x^3$ by $x - 2$, the remainder is which of the following?

☐ F. 2

☒ G. $\dfrac{2}{x-2}$

☐ H. $\dfrac{-14}{x-2}$

☐ J. -14

☐ K. $x - 2$

55. If a line passes through the coordinate points (2,3) and (−5,6), what is the x-intercept of the line?

☐ A. $\dfrac{-3}{7}$

☒ B. 3 and $\dfrac{6}{7}$

☐ C. 7 and $\dfrac{2}{3}$

☐ D. $\dfrac{-7}{3}$

☐ E. 9

56. If you have three consecutive odd numbers such that when you double the sum of the first and third, the result is 5 less than 5 times the second, what is the third number?

☐ F. 3

☐ G. 4

☐ H. 6

☒ J. 7

☐ K. 15

$N + N(2) = 5n - 5$

$2n\ 4n =$

$5\ -4n$

$5 = 1n$

$5 = n$

$N,\ N+2,\ N+4$

$N + (N+4)2 = 5N+2 - 5$

$\dfrac{13}{3} = \dfrac{3n}{3}$

$4 . \text{''}$

$N + N+4(2)$

$2n + 4(2) = 5n - 5$

$-2n + 5\qquad -2n + 5$

———————————

$8 = 3n -$

57. In the following figure, central angle BAC is 30°. If circle A has a diameter of 6 units and the triangle formed has a height of 1.5 units, what is the area of the shaded segment in square units?

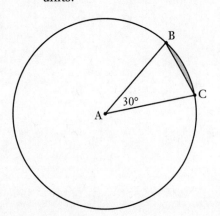

  A. $\frac{3}{4}\pi - 2.25$

  B. $\frac{3}{4}\pi - 4.5$

  C. $3\pi - 2.25$

  D. $3\pi - 4.5$

  E. 6π

58. The graph of the equation $|y = -x$ is symmetric about which of the following?

  I. The origin

  II. The x-axis

  III. The y-axis

  F. II and III

  G. I and II

  H. I only

  J. II only

  K. III only

59. Given the following function, which of the following is a true statement about this function's graph?

$$\begin{cases} y = 3 & \text{if} \quad -\infty < x < 0 \\ y = x & \text{if} \quad 0 \le x \le 2 \\ y = 3 - x & \text{if} \quad 2 < x < \infty \end{cases}$$

- ❏ A. All lines have the same slope.
- ☛ B. There is an open circle and a closed circle on the y-axis.
- ❏ C. The graph of the third piece begins when x is greater than 3.
- ❏ D. To the right of 0, the graph is horizontal.
- ❏ E. The solid circle at $x = 2$ indicates that the graph of the third piece begins when x is greater than 2.

60. In the following figure, triangle $\triangle QRS$ has a right angle and hypotenuse whose length is 8 units. Use similar triangles to find the length of side $\overline{QR}$ in units.

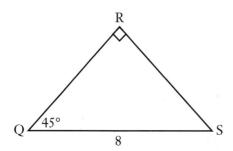

- ❏ F. $2\sqrt{2}$
- ■ G. 4
- ❏ H. $4\sqrt{2}$
- ❏ J. $8\sqrt{2}$
- ❏ K. This cannot be determined from the given information.

Do Your Figuring Here.

Science Reasoning Test

Directions: Read each passage carefully and then read all the questions for each passage. Choose the "best" answer for each question and mark the appropriate oval on the answer sheet. Remember that the Science section is the shortest section of the ACT exam and the smallest part of your grade, so do not spend more time on this section than absolutely necessary.

Passage I, Questions 1–6

Ice core samples from Antarctica can be used as evidence in reconstructing Earth's past climate. Ice core samples are analyzed for isotopes of both oxygen (oxygen-18) and hydrogen (hydrogen-2 or deuterium). The differences in the ratios of the isotopes found in the core samples and the ratios of isotopes found in ocean water allow scientists to determine temperatures from the past. Warmer temperatures will result in a greater proportion of the heavier isotopes being evaporated from the ocean. The evaporated water is deposited as snow that eventually becomes ice, leaving a particular chemical signature in ice core samples. A warmer climate is indicated by larger delta deuterium values.

Variations from current mean temperature from an analysis of the Vostok ice core are plotted in Figure 1. The graph shows a number of complete glacial cycles, each beginning with periods of colder climate and ending with interglacial warm periods. The high points in the graph represent interglacial warm periods. Age is in thousands of years before present (kyr BP).

Figure 2 shows the delta deuterium plotted against the age of the ice core samples taken from Ice Cap C in western Antarctica.

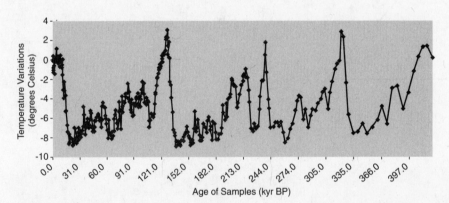

FIGURE 1 Temperature record showing differences from current temperature determined from isotopic variances in ice core sample from Vostok, Antarctica.

Source: Petit, J.R., et al. 2000. Historical isotopic temperature record from the Vostok ice core. In *Trends: A Compendium of Data on Global Change.* Carbon Dioxide Information Analysis Center, Oak Ridge National Laboratory, U.S. Department of Energy, Oak Ridge, TN, USA.

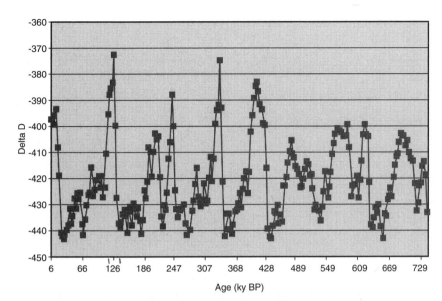

FIGURE 2 Historical delta deuterium values from Dome C Ice Core, Antarctica.

Source: Jouzel, J., et al. 2004. EPICA Dome C Ice Cores Deuterium Data. IGBP PAGES/World Data Center for
Paleoclimatology Data Contribution Series # 2004-038. NOAA/NGDC Paleoclimatology Program, Boulder, CO, USA.

1. How many interglacial periods are shown in Figure 1?

    ❏ A. 3

    ❏ B. 4

    ☒ C. 5

    ❏ D. More than 5

2. According to Figure 1, each glacial period lasts about:

    ❏ F. 10 kyr BP

    ❏ G. 25 kyr BP

    ☒ H. 100 kyr BP

    ❏ J. 200 kyr BP

3. If Figure 1 were used to predict future climate, the next glacial period would:

    ❏ A. begin in 10 kyr

    ❏ B. begin in 50 kyr

    ☒ C. begin in 100 kyr

    ❏ D. have started

4. In Figure 2, the period from 120 kyr BP to 130 kyr BP would have been a period when:

I. Temperatures were colder than present.

II. Temperatures were warmer than present.

III. Deuterium ratios were larger.

IV. Deuterium ratios were smaller.

    ❑ F. II only

    ■ G. II and III

    ❑ H. I and IV

    ❑ J. I and III

5. According to Figure 2, if a delta deuterium value of –410 translates into current mean Antarctic temperature, how many interglacial periods can be seen in the 740 kyr Dome C Ice Core?

    ■ A. 5

    ❑ B. 8

    ❑ C. 9

    ❑ D. 10

6. If greenhouse gases were to increase Antarctica's mean temperature by 3.00° Celsius, delta deuterium values would be:

    ❑ F. between –380 and –360

    ❑ G. between –400 and –380

    ■ H. between –420 and –400

    ❑ J. between –420 and –440

Passage II, Questions 7–11

[1]

Many major metropolitan areas of the world are affected by photochemical smog. The three main ingredients involved are stagnant air, large numbers of commuting automobiles, and sunshine. The daily cycle in cities such as Los Angeles and Houston begins with an increase in the levels of nitric oxide (NO) each morning as a result of the morning rush hour traffic (see Figure 1).

Nitric oxide is the product of a reaction between atmospheric nitrogen (N_2) and oxygen (O_2) that takes place under pressures up to 40 atmospheres and temperatures of 2500° C inside the internal combustion engine of the automobile. The colorless nitric oxide then reacts with more atmospheric oxygen (O₂) to form nitrogen dioxide (NO₂), a brownish gas that gives smog its characteristic color. Nitrogen dioxide is then split by ultraviolet radiation from the sun into NO and a free oxygen atom (O). The free oxygen then reacts with O_2 to form ozone (O_3). Ozone at Earth's surface is a serious human health concern, forming many different harmful chemical compounds. The reactions leading to the formation of ozone are summarized here:

I. $N_2 + O_2 \rightarrow 2\,NO$

II. $2\,NO + O_2 \rightarrow 2\,NO_2$

III. $NO_2 \rightarrow NO + O$

IV. $O_2 + O \rightarrow O_3$

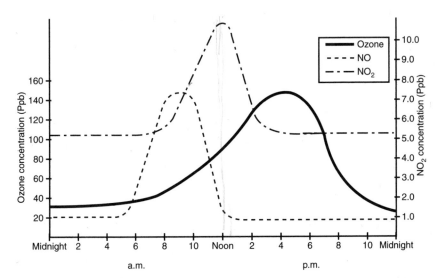

FIGURE 1 The concentrations of nitric oxide (NO), nitrogen dioxide (NO₂), and ozone (O₃) during a typical photochemical smog episode.

7. Which of the equations for the production of ozone listed previously requires the input of energy?

   A. Reactions I and II

   B. Reactions I and III

   C. Reactions II and III

   D. Reactions II and IV

8. If the morning commute took place at 10 a.m., at what time would you expect to see the maximum concentration of nitrogen dioxide?

   F. 1:30 p.m.

   G. 1 p.m.

   H. 12:30 p.m.

   J. 12 p.m.

9. On days when smog is above acceptable safety levels, people should stay indoors:

   ❑ A. from 6 a.m. to noon

   ❑ B. from 10 a.m. to 2 p.m.

   ❑ C. from 2 p.m. to 7 p.m.

   ❑ D. from 6 a.m. to 8 p.m.

10. According to Figure 1 and the reactions presented previously, on cloudy days you would expect:

    ❑ F. less ozone

    ❑ G. clearer skies

    ❑ H. less NO_2

    ❑ J. more NO_2

Nitric oxide (NO) is known to react rapidly with ozone (O_3) to form nitrogen dioxide and elemental oxygen (O_2) via the reaction $NO + O_3 \rightarrow NO_2 + O_2$.

11. Which of the following observations are evidence that this reaction is taking place?

    I. Nitric oxide reaches its maximum during the morning rush hour.

    II. Concentrations of ozone tend to be low along freeways.

    III. Nitrogen dioxide reaches its maximum following the morning commuting hours.

    IV. Nitric oxide concentrations remain low during the afternoon commute.

    ❑ A. Observations I and III

    ❑ B. Observations II and III

    ❑ C. Observations III and IV

    ❑ D. Observations II and IV

Passage III, Questions 12–17

The heat of vaporization for a liquid is the amount of heat per unit of mass that is required to change the liquid into a vapor or gas at the same temperature. The apparatus in Figure 1 was used by a student to measure the heat of vaporization of three liquids: 2-propanol, ethyl alcohol, and methanol. The student conducted six trials for each liquid, maintaining the liquid at the boiling point and collecting the condensed liquid. For each trial, she increased the power output of the immersion heater by using the equation power = current × voltage and then adjusting the current at the rheostat and the voltage at the voltage source. She then recorded the mass of the liquid condensed and the elapsed time and calculated the vaporization rate for each power output (see Tables 1–3). She then plotted the vaporization rate against power output. In the graph in Figure 2, the y-intercept is the amount of heat lost by the calorimeter. By calculating the slope of the plot of the rate of vaporization versus power output and subtracting the y-intercept, she arrived at the heat of vaporization for each of the liquids (see Table 4).

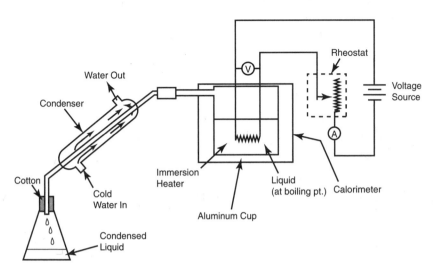

FIGURE 1 Apparatus used to measure the heat of vaporization of liquids.

Table 1   Propanol

Current (Amps)	Voltage (Volts)	Power (Watts)	Time (Seconds)	Mass of Liquid Condensed (Grams)	Rate of Vaporization (1×10^{-3} Grams/Second)
0.51	10.2	5.2	452	3.44	7.63
0.98	10.6	10.4	490	7.84	16.0
1.46	10.4	15.2	478	12.14	25.4
2.10	9.8	20.6	433	14.28	32.8
2.65	10.2	27.0	416	19.97	40.8
2.98	9.6	28.6	428	20.20	47.2

Table 2   Methanol

Current (Amps)	Voltage (Volts)	Power (Watts)	Time (Seconds)	Mass of Liquid Condensed (Grams)	Rate of Vaporization (1×10^{-3} Grams/Second)
0.45	10.0	4.5	520	1.80	3.47
1.12	10.1	11.3	574	3.92	6.92
1.64	10.2	16.7	552	5.74	10.4
2.02	9.9	20.0	536	7.66	14.3
2.55	9.7	24.7	568	10.39	18.3
3.04	9.6	29.2	524	11.00	21.0

Table 3   Ethyl Alcohol

Current (Amps)	Voltage (Volts)	Power (Watts)	Time (Seconds)	Mass of Liquid Condensed (Grams)	Rate of Vaporization (1×10^{-3} Grams/Second)
0.52	9.5	4.9	506	2.33	4.63
1.10	9.8	10.8	531	5.27	9.92
1.48	10.4	15.4	545	8.45	15.5
2.11	10.6	22.4	528	10.66	20.2
2.58	10.2	26.3	516	13.16	25.5
3.16	9.9	31.2	519	16.24	31.3

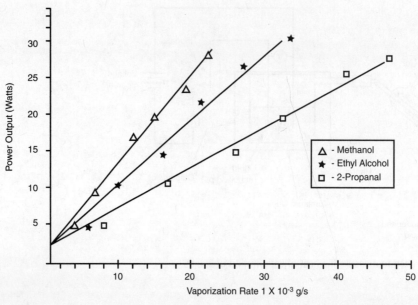

FIGURE 2   Power consumed versus the rate of vaporization for 2-propanol, methanol, and ethyl alcohol.

Table 4   The Heat of Vaporization of 2-Propanol, Methanol, and Ethyl Alcohol

Liquid	Heat of Vaporization (Joules/Gram)
2-propanol	548
Methanol	1,221
Ethyl alcohol	878

12. Which of the following statements accurately identifies the passage of energy through the apparatus in Figure 1?

   ❑ F. Immersion heater → boiling liquid → condensed liquid → air

   ❑ G. Battery → immersion heater → vaporized liquid → condenser water

   ❑ H. Battery → immersion heater → vaporized liquid → condensed liquid

   ❑ J. Battery → immersion heater → boiling liquid → air

13. With a voltage of 20 volts across the immersion heater, what must the current be adjusted to for the power output to equal 5 watts?

   ❑ A. 0.5 amps

   ❑ B. 0.25 amps

   ❑ C. 10.0 amps

   ❑ D. 4.0 amps

14. Before the start of each trial, the liquid was gradually brought to a steady boil. If the student had skipped this step and begun recording data before the liquid had reached the boiling point, which of the following errors would have been introduced into the data?

   ❑ F. The measured rate of vaporization would have been higher.

   ❑ G. The measured rate of vaporization would have been lower.

   ❑ H. The measured rate of vaporization would have been lower and the amount of power consumed would have been less.

   ❑ J. The measured rate of vaporization would have been lower and the amount of power consumed would have been greater.

15. From the information in either Figure 2 or Tables 1–3, list the liquids in order of their rates of vaporization from highest to lowest:

   ❑ A. 2-propanol, ethyl alcohol, methanol

   ❑ B. Methanol, ethyl alcohol, 2-propanol

   ❑ C. 2-propanol, methanol, ethyl alcohol

   ❑ D. Methanol, 2-propanol, ethyl alcohol

16. Using the information in either Table 3 or Figure 2, if ethyl alcohol were heated with a power output of 40 watts, its vaporization rate would be approximately:

   ❑ F. 40 grams/sec

   ❑ G. 20.0×10^{-3} grams/sec

   ❑ H. 40.0×10^{-2} grams/sec

   ❑ J. 40.0×10^{-3} grams/sec

17. Using a slope in Figure 2 as an example, if the heat lost to the calorimeter were less:

    ☐ A. The y-intercept of each line would be closer to the origin and the slope would be less.

    ☐ B. The y-intercept of each line would be farther from the origin and the slope would be less.

    ☐ C. The y-intercept of each line would be closer to the origin and the slope would be greater.

    ☐ D. The y-intercept of each line would be farther from the origin and the slope would be greater.

Passage IV, Questions 18–23

[1]

An *anticline* is a geologic feature that is made up of sedimentary layers of rock that are folded into the shape of an arch or a dome. Because of the differences in the permeability of the various layers of sedimentary rock, anticlines are known to form petroleum traps. In Figure 1, the layer of shale overlying the petroleum deposit acts as an impermeable cap of rock, trapping oil and gas beneath it. In this example, the oil-bearing sedimentary rock is sandstone.

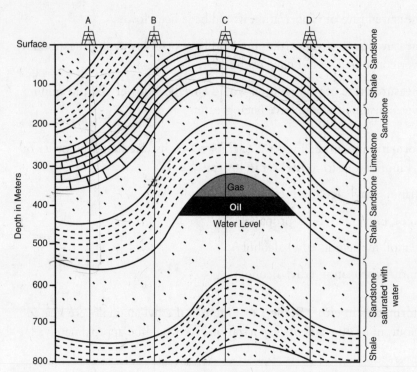

FIGURE 1 A stratigraphic cross-section of the Dry Creek well field. Depths are in meters.

[2]

Twelve kilometers away from Dry Creek, geologists believe they may have found a new anticline petroleum trap in the Potlatch Prairie area. Four exploratory wells are drilled evenly spaced in an east-west line. Data from the wells is shown in Figure 2.

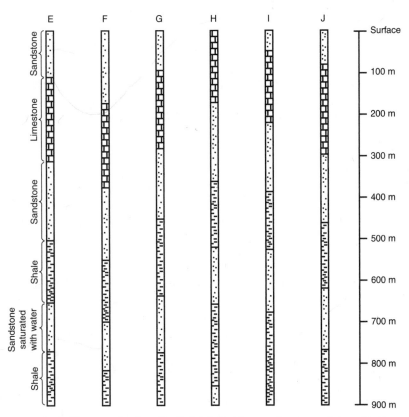

FIGURE 2 Drilling samples from the Potlatch Prairie area showing rock type. Depths are in meters.

18. If Well A was drilled straight down, at what depth would water be first encountered?

   ❑ F. 600m

   ❒ G. 550m

   ❑ H. 450m

   ❑ J. 300m

19. A sample taken from one of the four wells is analyzed and shows a contact between sandstone and shale at 375m and again at 550m. From which well was this sample taken?

   ❑ A. Well A

   ❒ B. Well B

   ❑ C. Well C

   ❑ D. Well D

20. According to Figure 1, the correct order of the densities of oil, natural gas, and water from most to least dense is:

    ❑ F. natural gas, oil, water

    ❑ G. oil, water, natural gas

    ❑ H. water, natural gas, oil

    ☒ J. water, oil, natural gas

21. The principle of superposition states that over time older layers of sedimentary rock are successively covered by younger and younger layers of rock. If you were to walk across the well field in Figure 1 from Well A on the left to Well D on the right, the age of the rock on the surface would become:

    ❑ A. older

    ❑ B. younger

    ☒ C. younger to older and then younger again

    ❑ D. older and then younger

22. Moving from west to east across the Potlatch Prairie area (refer to Figure 2) from Well E to Well J, the layer of contact between an impermeable layer of shale and a layer of sandstone saturated with water:

    ❑ F. becomes deeper

    ❑ G. becomes shallower

    ☒ H. becomes deeper, then shallower, then deeper again

    ❑ J. becomes shallower and then deeper

23. At which location would a new well most likely encounter natural gas at Potlatch Prairie?

    ❑ A. between Wells F and G

    ❑ B. between Wells G and H

    ☒ C. between Wells H and I

    ❑ D. between Wells I and J

Passage V, Questions 24–28

[1]

A scientist is studying a circular strand of DNA known as a *plasmid*. In order to learn more about the structure of plasmid pBR322, the scientist uses restriction enzymes to cut it into restriction fragments, or individual linear fragments cut from the original circular strand of DNA. The resulting fragments are then subjected to gel electrophoresis, a process that uses an electrical field to separate segments of DNA based on their relative sizes. (One thousand base pairs is equal to one kilo-base pair and is abbreviated *kbp*.) Figure 1 shows a photograph of the gel after the DNA was treated with ethidium bromide and illuminated with ultraviolet light. In lane 1, the scientist loaded a DNA ladder, a mixture of DNA segments of known length, and labeled each with its size on the photograph. Table 1 shows the sizes of the DNA fragments from the results of the gel electrophoresis.

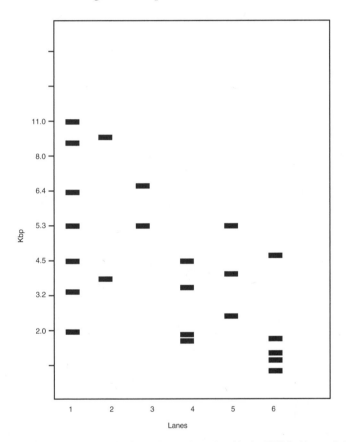

FIGURE 1 Photograph of gel electrophoresis with the DNA ladder and the sizes of each fragment labeled. Units are in kbp.

Table 1   Results of Gel Electrophoresis on Plasmid pBR322 Cut with Restriction Enzymes

Restriction Enzyme	Fragment Size (in kbp)
*Eco*RI	12.1
*Bam*HI	12.1
*Hind*III	3.7, 8.4
*Hae*III	5.2, 6.9
*Eco*RI + *Hind*III	2.7, 3.7, 5.7
*Hind*III + *Hae*III	1.7, 2.0, 3.5, 4.9
*Eco*RI + *Hind*III + *Hae*III	1.1, 1.7, 2.0, 2.4, 4.9

[2]

A second experiment, to test whether the pBR322 plasmid could be used as a way of transferring genes into the bacterium *E. coli*, was conducted. The scientist treated the plasmid DNA with the restriction enzyme *Bam*HI and introduced the gene for kanamycin resistance, *kan^r*, into the plasmid. The pBR322 plasmid contains genes that give *E. coli* resistance to the antibiotics ampicillin and tetracycline. The *Bam*HI recognition site is located in the gene for tetracycline resistance, *tet^r* (see Figure 2). Incorporation of the *kan^r* gene, or any foreign DNA, into the *tet^r* gene would yield bacteria that take up the recombinant plasmid sensitive to tetracycline.

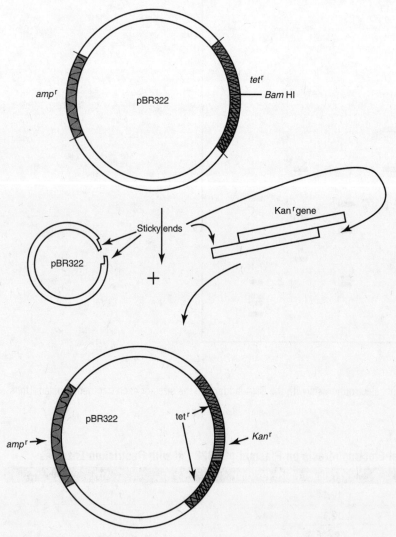

FIGURE 2   Creating recombinant DNA using plasmid pBR322, *Bam*HI, and the gene for kanamycin resistance, *kan^r*.

24. Which of the following tables correctly identifies the restriction enzyme(s) added to lanes 2–6 in the gel shown in Figure 1?

❑ F.

Lane 2	Lane 3	Lane 4	Lane 5	Lane 6
*Hae*III	*Hind*III	*Eco*RI + *Hind*III	*Hind*III + *Hae*III	*Eco*RI + *Hind*III + *Hae*III

❑ G.

Lane 2	Lane 3	Lane 4	Lane 5	Lane 6
*Hind*III	*Hae*III	*Hind*III + *Hae*III	*Eco*RI + *Hind*III	*Eco*RI + *Hind*III + *Hae*III

❑ H.

Lane 2	Lane 3	Lane 4	Lane 5	Lane 6
*Hae*III	*Hind*III	*Hind*III + *Hae*III	*Eco*RI + *Hind*III	*Eco*RI + *Hind*III + *Hae*III

❑ J.

Lane 2	Lane 3	Lane 4	Lane 5	Lane 6
*Hind*III	*Hae*III	*Eco*RI + *Hind*III	*Hind*III + *Hae*III	*Eco*RI + *Hind*III + *Hae*III

25. A restriction map is a drawing of a DNA molecule that shows the relative positions of where each restriction enzyme cuts the DNA strand. Based on the data in Table 1, which of the following restriction maps best represents the relative positions of the recognition sites for *Eco*RI and *Hind*III?

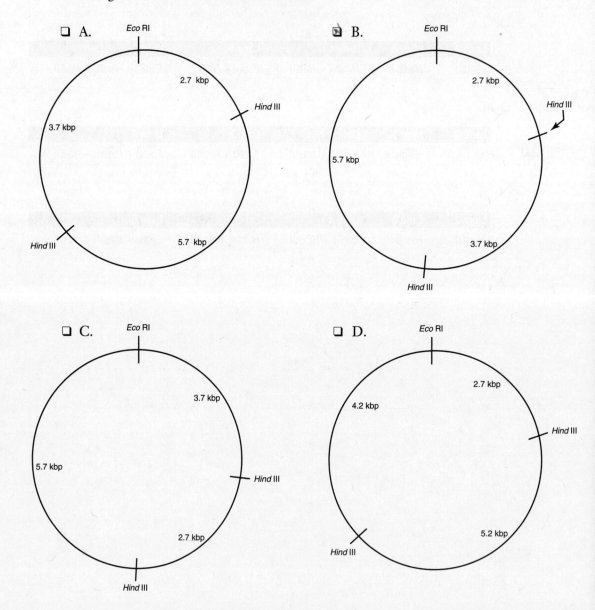

26. Based on the results in Table 1, which of the following diagrams best represents the restriction map for *Hind*III and *Hae*III?

☐ F.

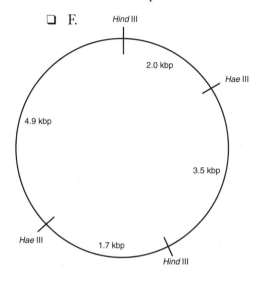

☐ G.

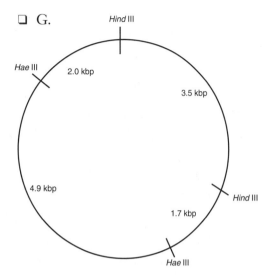

☐ H

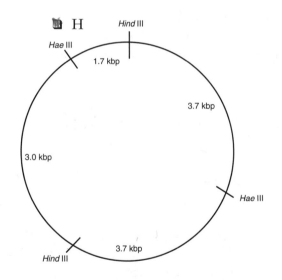

☐ J.

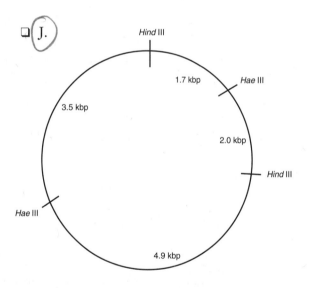

27. In the second experiment, which of the following observations would indicate that *E. coli* has taken up the plasmid pBR332 with the recombinant DNA?

☐ A. All *E. coli* colonies are sensitive to ampicillin.

☐ B. Some of the *E. coli* colonies are resistant to both ampicillin and tetracycline.

☐ C. Some of the *E. coli* colonies are resistant to ampicillin but are sensitive to tetracycline.

☐ D. Some of the *E. coli* colonies are resistant to tetracycline but are sensitive to ampicillin.

28. The scientist used *Hind*III to cut the pBR322 plasmid and inserted fruit fly DNA into the plasmid DNA. Some of the resulting *E. coli* colonies turned out to be sensitive to ampicillin but resistant to tetracycline. Which of the following conclusions can be drawn?

   ❑ F. Both of the restriction sites for *Hind*III lie outside of the *amp^r* gene.

   ❑ G. At least one of the restriction sites for *Hind*III lies within the *amp^r* gene.

   ❑ H. The pBR322 plasmid was not taken up by the *E. coli* bacteria.

   ❑ J. Both of the restriction sites for *Hind*III lie inside the *amp^r* gene.

Passage VI, Questions 29–35

Three students carried out experiments to measure the buoyancy of a metal cube submerged in water. Each used Archimedes' principle, which states that the buoyant force on an object is equal to the weight of the water displaced by the object.

Student 1:

I measured the volume of the cube with calipers. Knowing the density of water, I multiplied the density of water at 4° C by the volume of the cube and arrived at the weight of the water displaced by the cube. According to Archimedes' principle, the buoyant force on the cube is equal to the weight of the water displaced by the cube.

Student 2:

I weighed the cube by suspending it from a balance. Then I weighed the cube in the water. The difference between the weight of the cube in air and the apparent weight in water is equal to the buoyant force on the object. The buoyant force is a result of the difference in pressure on the object. The water at the bottom of the object is under greater pressure than the water at the top of the object, which makes the net force upward.

Student 3:

First, I placed a beaker of water on a balance and adjusted the balance so that it read zero. Then I suspended the cube in the water so that it was submerged. Now what did the scale read? That's right, the buoyant force on the object! If the buoyant force is pushing the cube up, then according to Newton's third law, there must be an equal and opposite force pushing down on the balance. In displacing the water, I have created an action force. The reaction force is the water pushing back on the object.

29. Of the three students, which student *directly* measured the buoyant force?

   ❑ A. Student 1

   ❑ B. Student 2

   ❑ C. Student 3

   ❑ D. None of them

30. Objects that are submerged in air or Earth's atmosphere also experience a buoyant force. Which student's measurement of the buoyant force was not affected by this fact?

   ❏ F. Student 1.

   ❏ G. Student 2.

   ❏ H. Student 3.

   ❏ J. All the students' experiments were affected.

31. Every time you make a measurement, you increase the chance of introducing an error. This argument would support the position of which student(s)?

   ❏ A. Student 1

   ❏ B. Student 2

   ❏ C. Student 3

   ❏ D. Students 1 and 2

32. "The density of water varies with temperature. Let's all use the same room temperature water. That way, we will be able to compare our results." This suggestion likely came from which student?

   ❏ F. Student 1

   ❏ G. Student 2

   ❏ H. Student 3

   ❏ J. Student 2 or 3

33. If a longer string were used to suspend the cube deeper into the water, which of the following statements would reflect the predictions of students 2 and 3?

 I. Student 2 would expect the buoyant force to be greater because the pressure on the object would be greater than near the surface.

 II. Student 3 would expect the buoyant force to be greater because the pressure is greater than near the surface.

 III. Student 2 would expect the buoyant force to be the same because the differences in pressure on the object will be the same.

 IV. Student 3 would expect the buoyant force to be less because the pressure is greater than near the surface.

   ❏ A. I and II

   ❏ B. II and III

   ❏ C. III and IV

   ❏ D. I and IV

34. In the case of floating objects, the procedure of which student(s) could be used to determine the buoyant force?

   ❑ F. Students 1 and 2.

   ☒ G. Students 2 and 3.

   ❑ H. Student 3 only.

   ❑ J. None of the students' procedures could be used to find the buoyant force on a floating object.

35. Students 2 and 3 discuss buoyant force and the shape of floating objects. Which of the following choices correctly matches each student's position?

   I. Student 2: "The shape really doesn't matter; it's how much water is displaced that is important."

   II. Student 3: "As long as the apparent weight is greater than the buoyant force, shape won't make a difference."

   III. Student 2: "Shape is important. The deeper the object extends into the water, the greater the buoyant force will be."

   IV. Student 3: "Shape is not important. Buoyant force is always equal to the weight of the water displaced."

   ❑ A. I only

   ❑ B. I and II

   ❑ C. II and III

   ☒ D III and IV

Passage VII, Questions 36–40

Osmoregulation is a process by which organisms maintain a balance of fluid between their cells and their environment. Paramecia have a higher concentration of solute in their cells than the fresh water where they are found. This means that water is constantly diffusing across their cell membranes. To remove this water, paramecia use contractile vacuoles that expel water out of their cells and back into their environment. Contractile vacuoles are a type of active transport that require energy to transport material against its natural flow.

A student conducts an experiment to determine how contractile vacuole activity in paramecia is related to the solute concentration of their environment. He begins by recording the number of contractile vacuole contractions when the paramecia are in distilled water. He then begins increasing the concentration of the solution by 5 millimoles (mM) of sucrose at a time and recording the time between contractile vacuole contractions. The results of his experiment are shown in Table 1. He then charts the results in a graph, as shown in Figure 1.

Table 1 The Effect of Sucrose Concentrations on Contractile Vacuole Activity of Paramecia

Concentration of Sucrose Solution (mM)	Period Between Contractions (Seconds)	Frequency of Contractions (Contractions/Sec)
0	8.3	0.120
5	8.9	0.113
10	9.7	0.103
15	10.9	0.0917
20	12.5	0.0800
25	14.3	0.0702
30	17.1	0.0585
35	20.2	0.0494
40	27.2	0.0368
45	39.5	0.0253
50	57.8	0.0173

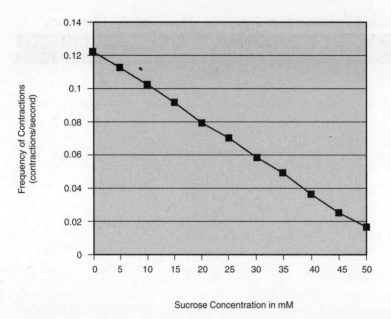

Sucrose Concentration in mM

FIGURE 1 Graph of sucrose concentration versus the frequency of contractile vacuole contractions in paramecia.

36. According to Table 1, for paramecia in pure water, the period of time between each contractile vacuole contraction would be closest to:

✓ F. 8 seconds

❑ G. 9 seconds

❑ H. 10 seconds

❑ J. 50 seconds

37. According to the graph in Figure 1, which of the following statements correctly identifies the relationship between the concentration of the solution and the rate of contractile vacuole contractions?

❑ A. As the concentration of the solution increases, the frequency of contractions increases.

☞ B. As the concentration of the solution increases, the frequency of contractions decreases.

❑ C. As the concentration of the solution decreases, the period between contractions increases.

❑ D. As the concentration of the solution increases, the period between contractions decreases.

38. According to the data in Table 1, which of the following graphs represents a plot of the concentration of the solution versus the period of time between contractions?

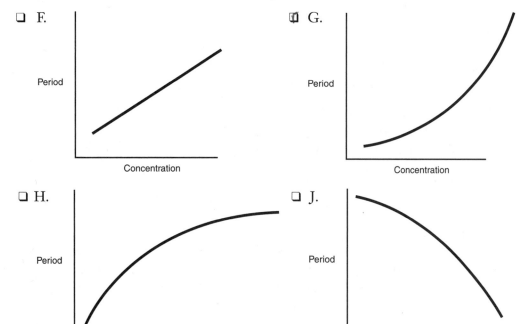

❑ F.

Period

Concentration

☑ G.

Period

Concentration

❑ H.

Period

Concentration

❑ J.

Period

Concentration

39. In Figure 1, at which concentration would the paramecia stop active osmoregulation?

❑ A. 50mM of sucrose

❑ B. 60mM of sucrose

❑ C. 70mM of sucrose

❑ D. 0mM of sucrose

40. If the solute concentration of the solution on the outside of the paramecia were greater than the concentration of the solution inside the paramecia, then:

❑ F. The paramecia would shrink.

☑ G. The paramecia would swell and burst.

❑ H. Contractile vacuole contractions would increase.

❑ J. Contractile vacuole contractions would decrease.

ACT Writing Assessment

Directions: Please write an essay in response to the following topic. During the 30 minutes permitted, develop your thoughts clearly and effectively. Try to include relevant examples and specific evidence to support your point of view. A plain, natural style is best. Your essay's length is up to you, but quality should take precedence over quantity. Be sure to write only on the assigned topic.

You have just read in the newspaper that a big, new shopping mall is being proposed for an area in your town that is approximately a half mile from your home. The mall will have large department stores, a 15-screen movie theater, and an ice skating rink. Your town has had a nice shopping district for more than 50 years, with some stores and restaurants still family-owned. The article you read says that some residents of your town are completely against the mall, and others feel that it will be a boon to the community. In your opinion, is the shopping mall a good idea?

In your essay, take a position on this question. You may write about either one of the two points of view given, or you may present a different point of view on this question. Use specific reasons and examples to support your position.

CHAPTER EIGHT

Answers to Practice Exam 1

English

1. A	26. J	51. A
2. G	27. C	52. H
3. B	28. G	53. A
4. J	29. D	54. G
5. C	30. H	55. D
6. F	31. A	56. F
7. D	32. J	57. D
8. F	33. A	58. J
9. C	34. J	59. A
10. F	35. B	60. F
11. A	36. J	61. A
12. G	37. C	62. G
13. B	38. F	63. C
14. J	39. B	64. J
15. D	40. J	65. C
16. F	41. D	66. J
17. B	42. H	67. A
18. J	43. D	68. H
19. C	44. F	69. B
20. J	45. C	70. G
21. D	46. G	71. D
22. H	47. D	72. F
23. D	48. J	73. D
24. J	49. D	74. J
25. C	50. H	75. B

Question 1

The correct answer is A. The comma lists Mr. Brown's qualities.

Question 2

The correct answer is G. The comma here is segregating a dependent clause.

Question 3

The correct answer is B. The sentence is an introduction to the entire paragraph, so it should correctly be the first, opening sentence.

Question 4

The correct answer is J. *Each* refers to each singular *team*, not all the teams together. Because this is the singular form, you would just add an apostrophe *s* to the word *team*.

Question 5

The correct answer is C. Each group has more than one desk, so the plural form of *desk* is correct and the sentence is written in the past tense. *Were* needs to be used here.

Question 6

The correct answer is F. The sentence is not improved by adding a word or phrase after the noun or rearranging its order.

Question 7

The correct answer is D. The comma is separating the items in a list.

Question 8

The correct answer is F. The sentence is correct as it is. *One day* refers to when the class moved outdoors, not when the narrator cackled. The sentence is necessary because it sets the scene for the next sentence.

Question 9

The correct answer is C. There is no need for commas in this sentence, as there are no clauses that are independent or can be removed or set aside in the sentence.

Question 10

The correct answer is F. An apostrophe is not correct within the word *guffaws*, as it is not being used in the possessive form. Answer H is not correct because "several" students would not produce one "guffaw."

Question 11

The correct answer is A. *Almost* is modifying *positive*, so in this sentence it must appear before the word. If it is placed anywhere else in the beginning of the sentence, it doesn't serve to modify correctly the word it is near.

Question 12

The correct answer is G. The correct pronoun for *other schools* is *them*.

Question 13

The correct answer is B. The sentence is written in the past tense.

Question 14

The correct answer is J. *His* is the pronoun that should follow the antecedent, Mr. Brown, from the sentence directly preceding it.

Question 15

The correct answer is D. The sentence is referring to *a student*, which is one student, so *he or she* must be used.

Question 16

The correct answer is F. The sentence is written correctly as it is.

Question 17

The correct answer is B. The paragraph is written in the present tense, so the original sentence is incorrect. Answer B has the sentence written in the present tense to align with the rest of the paragraph.

Question 18

The correct answer is J. The statue is not a town icon; the mayor was.

Question 19

The correct answer is C. The visitors are those who may think they are traveling back in time, not the town itself. Note the use of the word *their*.

Question 20

The correct answer is J. The quotation marks set off the name of the store. The name of the owner is Dirk, so the shop is Dirk's.

Question 21

The correct answer is D. *Hitching posts* is not a possessive form here and does not need an apostrophe. Also, *Street* should not be abbreviated in a sentence.

Question 22

The correct answer is H. Use the word *façade* and then test *have* and *has* with this word: "façade have" versus "façade has." Commas are not used here because this is not a list.

Question 23

The correct answer is D. The clause is an extra bit of information that is not entirely necessary for the sentence to be correct.

Question 24

The correct answer is J. *Gifts* goes with the verb *were*, but we would not use this plural form of the word with *was*. The comma after *gifts* encloses the entire clause after the word *this*.

Question 25

The correct answer is C. If you take out the beginning of the sentence, "I guess," and just read it as "We who live in Midland," you can see that "Us who live in Midland" is incorrect. The word *except* should be *accept*, meaning "to acknowledge."

Question 26

The correct answer is J. If we use the pronoun *it* in this sentence, it is unclear what we are referring to. There is no reason to put a comma after *surprised*.

Question 27

The correct answer is C. The narrator is speaking in the past tense.

Question 28

The correct answer is G. The colon should not be used here. It is not introducing a list or separating a part of the sentence from the rest.

Question 29

The correct answer is D. The only area where commas are needed is within the list of what the narrator will bring on Clean-Up Day.

Question 30

The correct answer is H. The sentence as it is written is not clear about what will look new and pretty again. Note that the words *into* and *in to* have two different meanings. *Into* means "to go inside," whereas the meaning of "*in to*" must be taken as the two separate words they are.

Question 31

The correct answer is A. The sentence is correct as it is written. Changing the word order confuses the meaning of the sentence.

Question 32

The correct answer is J. The words *suits* and *years* are not in their possessive forms, so they do not need an apostrophe before the *s*.

Question 33

The correct answer is A. The phrase *swim of things* is a play on words of the idiom "swing of things." And to show that it is a special type of wording, it must be set off from the sentence in quotation marks.

Question 34

The correct answer is J. A comma is needed in the original sentence to set off the clause *like many people*. This response sets off the phrase at the beginning of the sentence.

Question 35

The correct answer is B. *Swimmers* is not in the singular or plural possessive form in this sentence, and there is no reason to put the word in quotation marks.

Question 36

The correct answer is J. The words *accept* and *except* should not be confused. The writer is talking to the reader, and the word *yourself* should be used instead of *himself*.

Question 37

The correct answer is C. The other uses of the word *cited* are homonyms.

Question 38

The correct answer is F. The phrase is correct as it is written.

Question 39

The correct answer is B. The word *comparable* means "capable of being compared to," and jogging is what swimming is being compared to.

Question 40

The correct answer is J. The phrase is not a complete sentence.

Question 41

The correct answer is D. The phrase *so long* is not grammatically correct.

Question 42

The correct answer is H. The clause *As muscles have to work harder because of the resistance of the water* explains how they become toned and strong.

Question 43

The correct answer is D. *Efficienter* is not a word, so answers A and B are incorrect. We cannot assume that the heart is working efficiently now, just that it is working more efficiently than before. Therefore, answer C is incorrect.

Question 44

The correct answer is F. Sentence 1 is the topic sentence, and it tells what the paragraph will be about. Sentence 3 further describes the topic sentence, and sentence 2 completes that description. Sentence 4 concludes the paragraph.

Question 45

The correct answer is C. The author does not create the essay according to the parameters of the assignment.

Question 46

The correct answer is G. *Many* implies more than one reader, and *public libraries* have more than one waiting list.

Question 47

The correct answer is D. *It's* is the correct form in this case because it is used in place of *it is*. Also, *their* is the correct form for this sentence.

Question 48

The correct answer is J. The part of the sentence coming after "book" does not need to be separated from the rest of the sentence. It is a part of the main sentence and not a clause that can be thought of as independent from the rest of the sentence.

Question 49

The correct answer is D. The dash (—) is used to separate the two parts of this sentence—the main portion and the examples.

Question 50

The correct answer is H. The sentence is talking about *them*—more than one book.

Question 51

The correct answer is A. The contraction *that's* must be used in this sentence. The word *arguably* means "open to argument."

Question 52

The correct answer is H. The hyphen (-) between the two words joins them together (a book that must be read). The word is in the plural form, not in the possessive form.

Question 53

The correct answer is A. The past, present, and future tenses are not appropriate here. The book is already in used condition and the price of the used book is shown.

Question 54

The correct answer is G. The verb *reflect* must be in agreement with the subject *prices*.

Question 55

The correct answer is D. A comma is required before the coordinating conjunction that separates the two independent clauses.

Question 56

The correct answer is F. This sentence is an introduction, or lead-in, to the rest of this paragraph.

Question 57

The correct answer is D. The organization of this sentence is the easiest for the reader to understand. Review the contraction *it's* and the word *yours* if you are unsure how these are correctly used.

Question 58

The correct answer is J. The sentence is referring to just one book, so *it* (the singular form) must be used. The adverb *quickly* describes how you are trying to get rid of the book.

Question 59

The correct answer is A. The noun (*books*) in the sentence is plural, so the pronoun *them* must be used here.

Question 60

The correct answer is F. The sentence is correct as written.

Question 61

The correct answer is A. As the next paragraph begins discussing Houston's life, this sentence transitions into that information. The other choices do not provide transition; rather, they make a statement that doesn't tie in with the next paragraph.

Question 62

The correct answer is G. The sentence is originally written to imply that Sam Houston's father was born in 1793. The correct answer clarifies the details of the sentence.

Question 63

The correct answer is C. We use *who* or *whom* here because we are talking about people. *Which* is used when we talk about things. Review the uses of these words in the English Assessment section of this book.

Question 64

The correct answer is J. *Eastern* is not a proper noun, and it does not have to be capitalized. The word *Cherokees* is not being used in a possessive form here, so an apostrophe is not used.

Question 65

The correct answer is C. We are talking about one person here, Sam Houston, so *he* and *realized* must be used.

Question 66

The correct answer is J. If necessary, review the use of *who* and *whom* in the English Assessment chapter of this book. *Brave* should not be capitalized here because it is being used only as an adjective to describe Houston and is not a part of his name.

Question 67

The correct answer is A. The sentence is correct as written.

Question 68

The correct answer is H. This is in an introductory phrase and it should be set off with a comma.

Question 69

The correct answer is B. *Distressed* describes how Sam Houston was feeling at this time. The other sample sentence structures are poorly organized.

Question 70

The correct answer is G. This essay is written in the past tense, so the verbs in individual sentences should be in past tense too.

Question 71

The correct answer is D. The pronoun *they* refers to Texans, and the past tense of the verb *want* must be used.

Question 72

The correct answer is F. Sentence 3 is the main idea, sentences 2 and 4 provide supporting details, and sentence 1 summarizes the paragraph.

Question 73

The correct answer is D. The state of Texas, not the people (the Texans), became part of the United States. *Senate* is a proper noun and must be capitalized.

Question 74

The correct answer is J. This sentence tells how the entire country feels about Houston—that he was important enough to merit a statue in Washington, D.C. The other answer choices provide additional details but do not summarize as well.

Question 75

The correct answer is B. The piece discusses Houston's life and how he is forever immortalized in the United States. Reread the first sentence of the piece if you are unsure of why this is the correct answer.

Reading

1. B	15. A	29. A
2. J	16. H	30. F
3. C	17. D	31. B
4. F	18. G	32. F
5. C	19. B	33. A
6. G	20. G	34. G
7. A	21. A	35. B
8. F	22. J	36. G
9. D	23. C	37. A
10. F	24. F	38. J
11. D	25. B	39. D
12. F	26. F	40. J
13. A	27. B	
14. H	28. F	

Question 1

The correct answer is B. Mel and the narrator both shared the experience of almost being struck by lightning.

Question 2

The correct answer is J. Joe didn't actually meet the narrator, so an introduction didn't take place. He didn't offer to send his best mechanic, just *a* mechanic.

Question 3

The correct answer is C. The narrator is disappointed when the car won't start and then relieved by the end of the passage when she is safe and the car is again in working order.

Question 4

The correct answer is F. It is not true that she is frightened to call her mother, more that she wants to handle this on her own.

Question 5

The correct answer is C. The narrator said that she was afraid that the car might actually start for him, and she figured she would be embarrassed and her face would turn "bright red."

Question 6

The correct answer is G. The narrator does not seem to be shy or timid. Instead, she seems to be outgoing and friendly.

Question 7

The correct answer is A. We have no reason to believe that the narrator is using the car without her father's permission. We don't have any clues that she has her own car, but we do know that she is "harried" and that she never expected her friends to be able to help her, so it can be assumed that she is not disappointed by this.

Question 8

The correct answer is F. We know from the passage that the narrator's mother is a doctor and that her father travels, so it can be inferred that the narrator is accustomed to doing things on her own.

Question 9

The correct answer is D. The other answers signify an actual activity the narrator's friends may be undertaking at the time she needs them.

Question 10

The correct answer is F. The narrator mentions that the car is running, so it is probable that she got into it and either completed her errands or turned it off. It is unlikely that she would call either her mother or her friends, as they were both still busy. There is nothing to indicate that the narrator is upset and it is doubtful that she would begin to cry.

Question 11

The correct answer is D. Patrick Henry's feelings about the Constitution were often wavering and undecided, although he did vote for its ratification.

Question 12

The correct answer is F. The passage mentions that Patrick Henry's oratory skills made him a very good lawyer.

Question 13

The correct answer is A. *Lucrative* means "financially rewarding," or "profitable."

Question 14

The correct answer is H. Throughout the passage, Henry's speaking skills seem to be a main reason for his success.

Question 15

The correct answer is A. The passage mentions that Patrick Henry realized that the Constitution needed further detail and was responsible for adding the Bill of Rights. The passage does not discuss the people of the country wanting or demanding additional rights.

Question 16

The correct answer is H. The passage mentions that Henry's law business was "extremely lucrative," and it can be inferred from the reading that his work in government and in political office did not make him rich.

Question 17

The correct answer is D. The passage notes that Patrick Henry "reluctantly agreed" to run, implying that he was not excited about the prospect.

Question 18

The correct answer is G. Patrick Henry led a successful and fulfilling life and likely had no regrets about how he lived it.

Question 19

The correct answer is B. Research the meanings of these words in the dictionary if you are unsure of their meanings.

Question 20

The correct answer is G. To be like Patrick Henry, a career with a law school base would be the likely tack.

Question 21

The correct answer is A. Research the meanings of these words in the dictionary if you are unsure of their meanings.

Question 22

The correct answer is J. Hercules killed his own family after being driven mad by Hera.

Question 23

The correct answer is C. After Hercules killed his wife and children in a fit of madness, the king ordered him to perform the 12 deeds to repent for his crimes.

Question 24

The correct answer is F. *Vengeful* means "unforgiving."

Question 25

The correct answer is B. The skin signified that the lion was dead.

Question 26

The correct answer is F. Hercules was known as a clever and strong hero.

Question 27

The correct answer is B. Hercules was the slave of the king for 12 years and had to perform 12 labors during that time. It is likely that each labor took him approximately a year to complete.

Question 28

The correct answer is F. The labors were serious tasks, and Hercules seemed to have no choice but to complete them.

Question 29

The correct answer is A. The passage mentions that she did not know about the poison and that she was trying to gain Hercules' love back. The other responses cannot be inferred from what is within the passage.

Question 30

The correct answer is F. According to the passage, completing the second half of the labors would render Hercules immortal.

Question 31

The correct answer is B. If the explorers had never arrived on the island, it is possible the dodo would not have died out.

Question 32

The correct answer is F. This is stated in the first paragraph of the passage.

Question 33

The correct answer is A. The dodo did not "fight hard to live," but rather was affected by humans. This was beyond the dodo's control.

Question 34

The correct answer is G. The passage does not mention a change to the climate, but the other factors did contribute to its extinction.

Question 35

The correct answer is B. A predatory animal is one that preys on others. The passage does not mention the dodo as hunting or preying on other animals.

Question 36

The correct answer is G. Something that is quarry is prey. The other animals found the dodo easy to attack.

Question 37

The correct answer is A.

Question 38

The correct answer is J. The author is detailing what happened.

Question 39

The correct answer is D. As there are no remains of the dodo, there could not be anything to showcase in a museum.

Question 40

The correct answer is J. The final paragraph discusses this lesson.

Math

1. C	21. C	41. B
2. F	22. J	42. H
3. B	23. E	43. D
4. J	24. G	44. H
5. C	25. D	45. E
6. J	26. H	46. K
7. E	27. D	47. E
8. H	28. H	48. F
9. C	29. D	49. A
10. G	30. J	50. J
11. B	31. D	51. C
12. J	32. J	52. J
13. C	33. A	53. B
14. J	34. F	54. G
15. E	35. D	55. E
16. F	36. G	56. J
17. C	37. D	57. A
18. J	38. K	58. J
19. B	39. B	59. B
20. G	40. G	60. H

24/60

Question 1

Answer C is correct. To answer this question, you must start by simplifying each individual term. Simplify $\sqrt{48}$ to $4\sqrt{3}$ and simplify $3\sqrt{27}$ to $9\sqrt{3}$. Next, remember that you can add $4\sqrt{3}$ and $9\sqrt{3}$, just as you add the like terms $4x$ and $9x$. Because each term simplifies to a number multiplied with $\sqrt{3}$, all three terms can be combined. The final answer is $9\sqrt{3}$.

Question 2

Answer F is correct. This word problem can be translated easily to a proportion. The first ratio is 400 ft./8 and relates the height of the building to the height of the model. Because you want the width of the building and the width of the model to be related to each other by the same factor as the height, you can set the first ratio equal to the ratio containing the unknown. You wind up with the equation 400 ft./8 in. = 300 ft./x in. When you cross-multiply, you get $400x = 2400$. Solving for x gives the answer 6. Note that you might also set up this proportion as 400 ft./300 ft. = 8 in./x in.

Question 3

Answer B is correct. It is tempting to approach this problem by simply taking the average of 68 in. and 65 in., but this would lead to the wrong answer (answer C). Instead, remember average = sum of values/number of values. You need to find the sum of the heights of all 29 people Maria measured. Then, you can divide the sum by the number of people, 29, to get the correct answer. You can find the sum of the heights of the first 10 people because you know sum of the first 10/10 = 68. The sum of the heights of the first 10 must be 680 in. Using the same strategy, you know the sum of the heights of the next 19 people must be 1,235 in. Adding 680 and 1,235 and then dividing by 29 gives the correct answer, 66.03.

Question 4

Answer J is correct. To solve this problem, note that a scale is just a ratio that tells how a drawing's dimensions are related to actual dimensions. If dimensions on the drawing are 1/16 their actual size, the doorway opening, which is 3 1/4 in. on the drawing, must actually be 16 times larger. To multiply 3 1/4 by 16, put the fraction in improper form, 13/4. The result is 52 inches. Noticing that this value is not among the answer choices might cause you to see that the question asks for the answer to be given in feet. Convert 52 inches to feet to get 4 1/3.

Question 5

Answer C is correct. To answer this question, it's important to know that consecutive angles in parallelograms are supplementary. You know the measure of ∠DAB is 120°. Because ∠ADC and ∠DAB must add to 180°, you can calculate that the measure of ∠ADC must be 60°.

Question 6

Answer J is correct. This question asks you to derive an abstract expression to represent the cost of using a cell phone m minutes. If you don't see how to find the solution, try making up your own number and then use it to calculate the fee. In the expression you develop with your fictional number, replace your number with m. For instance, if I talk 100 minutes, to calculate my monthly fee I'd use this expression: $.10 \times 100 + 25$. The corresponding abstract expression is $0.10m + 25$, or $0.1m + 25$ (answer J).

Question 7

Answer E is correct. Don't be intimidated by the exponents and fractions in this function. Solving this question is as easy as following a recipe. The function tells you exactly what to do with the value of x you are given. You do need to recognize that f(–3) means you should plug the value –3 into the function. To steer clear of a miscalculation, you should replace every x in the function with (–3). The parentheses are essential, especially when there's a negative involved. When you plug in (–3), you get $1/2(–3)^2 – 1/3(–3) + 7$. Simplifying, you get $9/2 + 1 + 7$. The final answer is 12 1/2.

Question 8

Answer H is correct. Solving this question is as easy as finding the discount price of a shirt on sale at the mall. Anytime you are asked to use a percent by which an amount is increased or decreased, you follow the same general formula:

original value + OR – percent × original value = new value

In this question, you can use x to represent the amount Alicia sold in the first six months, the original value. The question gives you the new value: $1,950. Following the formula, you get $x + .30 \times x = 1,950$. Adding like terms, x and $.3x$, you know $1.3x = 1,950$. Solving for x gives the original value, the amount sold in the first six months, as $1,500.

Question 9

Answer C is correct. Start by focusing only on the information in the picture high-lighted by the question. Doing so clarifies that two parallel lines are being cut by a transversal. [lin]BC cuts parallel lines [lin]AB and [lin]CD. Consider other angles that are congruent to ∠X. You should notice that the angle formed by the intersection of [lin]AB and [lin]BC is a corresponding angle. The congruent corresponding angle must be 70° because it is supplementary with the angle whose measure is 110°. (They must add up to 180°.) Therefore, ∠X is 70°.

Question 10

Answer G is correct. There are two ways to approach this problem. The first way, setting up two equations with two unknowns, would make your math teacher proud. You can set up one equation expressing the total number of tickets sold. If we let N_A represent the number of adult tickets and N_C represent the number of children's tickets, the question states $N_A + N_C = 625$. You can set up a second equation expressing the monetary value of the tickets. You know that $N_A \times \$18 + N_C \times \$12 = \$8820$. If you choose the substitution method, you can manipulate the first equation to get $N_C = 625 - N_A$. Substituting this expression for N_C results in the equation $18N_A + 12(625 - N_A) = 8,820$. When you distribute, you get $18N_A + 7,500 - 12N_A = 8.820$. This simplifies to $6N_A = 1,320$. The number of adult tickets sold is 220. The second approach you might take is equally valuable on the ACT. You can plug in answer choices to see which one fits the constraints given in the question. Because answer choices are given in order from least to greatest, it's best to start with a value in the middle (answer choice H). If N_A is 300, then N_C is 625 – 300,325. But $300 \times 18 + 325 \times 12$ is more than 8,820. So, choose the next smaller value (answer choice G). If N_A is 220, then N_C is 405. When you multiply 220×18 and add it to 405×12, you get the correct number, 8,820.

Question 11

Answer B is correct. If you remember that the length of the median of a trapezoid is equal to 1/2 the sum of the lengths of the bases, setting up this problem is a breeze. Using the lengths given in the figure, you get $8y + 2 = 1/2 \times \{(4y + 4) + (14y - 4)\}$. This equation simplifies to $8y + 2 = 1/2\{18y\}$. Solving for y, you find that $y = 2$. To jog your memory, you might think of finding the length of the median as averaging the lengths of the bases.

Question 12

Answer J is correct. First consider that when the equation of a line is expressed as the form $y = mx + b$, b is the y-intercept. To find the equation of this line in slope-intercept form, first calculate the slope, m. The slope is defined as the change in y/change in x. The slope of this line is 7 – 2/2–3, which is 1. Replacing m with the actual slope gives $y = 1x + b$. Next, to isolate b, substitute either coordinate pair for x and y. If you substitute (–3,2), the result is $2 = 1 \times (-3) + b$. This simplifies to $2 = -3 + b$, solving to $b = 5$. The most common error on this type of question is calculating a slope that is the reciprocal of what it should be. Remember that y flies high. Any trick that gets you to put the difference of the y values in the numerator works!

Question 13

Answer C is correct. Nobody likes to solve equations that involve fractions. To solve for x in this problem, start by manipulating this equation to get rid of the fractions. Multiply every term by 20 so that each of the denominators is cancelled out. The new equation is $10(3x - 4) + 2 \times 9 = x$. To simplify, you must distribute the 10 to get $30x - 40 + 18 = x$. Combining like terms gives $29x = 22$. Solving for x gives you 22/29. An alternative way to look at this problem is to recognize that the answer to this question is supplied in one of the answer choices. You can determine which of the choices is correct by plugging in the values to see which one makes a true statement. Choose the fastest way to solve the problem.

Question 14

Answer J is correct. The key to answering this question is being able to recognize the three similar triangles in the following figure. It can be difficult to determine the corresponding sides of the similar triangles without separating the triangles in a quick sketch. After you identify the similar triangles, you can use proportions to find the lengths of the sides. You can solve for x in this problem by setting up a proportion between triangles 2 and 3: $x/4 = 4/x + 6$. To finish, cross-multiply. The resulting equation is $x^2 + 6x = 16$. You can factor this quadratic if you move all variables to the same side. After you have the factors, $(x + 8)(x - 2) = 0$, you can see that x must be 2. A length could not be -8. If x is 2, then the length of $\overline{RT}$ must be 10.

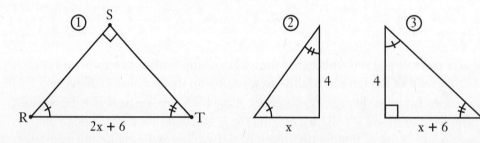

Question 15

Answer E is correct. Remember that the slopes of two perpendicular lines multiply to -1. Given the slope of a line, its perpendicular will be the opposite reciprocal. But to find the perpendicular slope, we must start with the slope of the original line. You can change the equation the question provides into slope-intercept form: $y = mx + b$. When you isolate y, you get $y = -2/3x - 7$. Therefore, the slope of any line perpendicular to this one has a slope that is the opposite reciprocal of $-2/3$. The answer is $3/2$.

Question 16

Answer F is correct. To answer this question, you need to translate words into a math expression: "The opposite of a number tripled and then added to 24" becomes $3(-n) + 24$. "The result is a positive number" means the result is > 0. Zero is not a positive number, so we do not use $\geq$. If $-3n + 24 > 0$, then $-3n > -24$. To solve for n in this inequality, remember that if you divide or multiply by a negative number, you need to flip the inequality symbol. Dividing both sides of the equation by -3 gives you $n < 8$. If you don't know how to solve inequalities, you might try plugging in answer choices to see which one makes a true statement.

Question 17

Answer C is correct. When you read this question, you probably recognized it as either a permutation or a combination question. To determine which one it is, ask yourself if order matters. In the context of this question, the teacher would not interview Bob, Li, Su, and Frank and then interview them again sitting in a different order. Because the order of the students does not matter, this is a combination question. First, find the number of permutations possible choosing 4 from a group of 15. If you visualize choosing a person from the group and having him or her sit in a chair, there are four chairs to fill. For the first chair, there are 15 people from which to choose. For the second chair, there are only 14 people from which to choose because 1 person is already assigned. There are 13 choices for the third chair and 12 choices for the fourth chair. The number of possible choices is $15 \times 14 \times 13 \times 12$, or 32,760. Now, because order doesn't matter, divide out the repetition. Divide by the number of ways you can arrange 4 people: $4 \times 3 \times 2 \times 1$, or 24. The answer is 32,760/24, or 1,365.

Question 18

Answer J is correct. To solve this, consider that you could use the distance formula if you have it memorized, or you could apply the Pythagorean theorem. A quick sketch may help you to see how to use the Pythagorean theorem in this context. The hypotenuse of the triangle is the line segment representing the distance between the two points. One leg of the triangle is the horizontal distance between the two points. Examine the x-coordinates to determine the distance between them on the x-axis. In this problem, the horizontal distance starts at −3 and continues to 5, which means the distance is 8. The other leg of the triangle is the vertical distance between the two points. Examine the y-coordinates to determine the distance between them on the y-axis. In this problem, the vertical distance starts at −8 and continues to 7, which means the distance is 15. Now plug and chug using $a^2 + b^2 = c^2$. Finally, solve for c in the equation $8^2 + 15^2 = c^2$. You find c is 17. Note: You might have saved yourself some work if you recognized the Pythagorean triple 8, 15, 17.

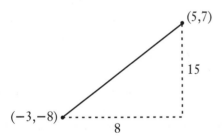

Question 19

Answer B is correct. Start by remembering the basic definitions of $\sin\theta$, $\cos\theta$, and $\tan\theta$. $\sin\theta$ is opp/hyp, $\cos\theta$ is adj/hyp, and $\tan\theta$ is opp/adj. Substituting the basic definitions for cos and sin results in opp/hyp ÷ adj/hyp. When you flip and multiply to simplify this expression, your answer, opp/adj, is equivalent to $\tan\theta$.

Question 20

Answer G is correct. Few students are going to be lucky enough to remember this formula. The alternative is to consider a polygon of a fixed number of sides, maybe six, and see how many diagonals are possible. The following figure shows that three diagonals can be drawn from vertex C to every other vertex except C and the two next to it. Therefore, the number of diagonals that can be drawn from any one vertex is expressed by $(N-3)$, where N is the number of sides. Because you can draw diagonals from any one of the six vertices, you can generalize the number of diagonals as $N(N-3)$. Finally, because the diagonal from $\overline{CD}$ is the same as the diagonal from $\overline{DC}$, our current expression counts every diagonal twice. To fix this, divide by 2. The answer is $N(N-3)/2$.

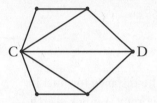

Question 21

Answer C is correct. The key to this question is knowing to express the complement of an angle as $(90-x)$ and the supplement of an angle as $(180-x)$. The word problem then translates to the math equation $3(90-x) = (180-x) + 16$. Distributing, you get $270 - 3x = 180 - x + 16$. Combining like terms results in $74 = 2x$. Solving, you find that $x = 37$.

Question 22

Answer J is correct. This question tests your understanding of the composition of functions. If you think of the two functions as machines that have input and output, this question is asking you to put $g(x)$ into the $f(x)$ machine. To do this, replace every x in $f(x)$ with $\sqrt{x}$. When you simplify $f(x) = (\sqrt{x})^2 - 3(\sqrt{x}) + 5$, you get $f(x) = x - 3\sqrt{x} + 5$. Noting that $\sqrt{x}$ is the same as $x^{1/2}$ leads you to the answer, $x - x^{1/2} + 5$.

Question 23

Answer E is correct. A quick sketch clarifies that this question hinges on finding the length of the side of a square whose diagonal is $4\sqrt{2} \times s$ feet. Your focus is really on one of the isosceles triangles formed by the square's diagonal. You could use the Pythagorean theorem to solve for the length of a side using $x^2 + x^2 = (4\sqrt{2s})^2$. But the fastest way to solve this problem is the mighty 45°-45°-90° triangle. The sides of this special triangle are always related to each other in the same way. Given the hypotenuse, you divide by $\sqrt{2}$ to get the length of a leg. Doing so in this problem means that the length of a leg, or a side of the square, is $4\sqrt{2}\,s/\sqrt{2}$, which is $4s$. The perimeter of the square is $4s$ added four times, which is $16s$.

Question 24

Answer G is correct. Start by remembering that a prime number has only two factors: the number 1 and itself. Because the numbers to consider are between 75 and 100, you have a list of numbers starting with 76 and ending with 99 in which you must identify the primes. All even numbers other than 2 are not primes, so you can immediately eliminate all even numbers in the list. Next, you can eliminate multiples of 3, 5, and 7. This process leaves four numbers—79, 83, 89, and 97. Therefore, the answer is 4.

Question 25

Answer D is correct. This question is more abstract than other percent change questions you may have seen because it doesn't tell you the amounts of tuna Albi sold. One way to simplify this problem is to choose a number—maybe 100 because it's easy to work with—and use it to generalize the percent decrease. If the original is 100, then after the first year it has decreased to 85. After the second year it has decreased to 76.5. The decrease from 100 to 76.5 is 23.5. Finally, $23.5/100 \times 100\%$ is 23.5%. You also can set up an abstract equation in which x represents Albi's tuna sales. Albi's sales in the first year decreased by 15%, which translates to $(x - .15x)$. This amount is then decreased by 10%, which gives $(x - .15x) - 0.1(x - .15)$. This simplifies to $0.765x$. So, the change in value is the original minus the new, which is $1x - 0.765x$, or $0.235x$. Percent decrease is given by change/original $\times 100\%$. In this case, that's $0.235x/1x \times 100\%$, which is 23.5%.

Question 26

Answer H is correct. You know you need the radius or diameter of a circle to find its circumference. If you knew the length of the diagonal of the square, you would have the information to calculate the circumference. Start by finding the length of the diagonal, which is the hypotenuse of the isosceles triangles formed by the square's diagonal. Because the sides of the 45°-45°-90° triangle are always related in the same way, if a leg of the triangle is 5 inches, the diagonal length must be $5\sqrt{2}$ inches. The Pythagorean theorem gives the same result. Circumference is given by $\pi \times$ diameter. Substituting in the diameter length, the answer is $5\pi\sqrt{2}$ in.

Question 27

Answer D is correct. Start by recognizing that this is an arithmetic series. The handbags increase by 6 every day, the common difference, and the question asks for the sum of the terms. The formula to use is $S_n = n/2(a_1 + a_n)$. You want the sum of 31 days of production, so $S_{31} = 31/2(30 + 210)$. Replace a_n with 210 because the last day 210 handbags are produced. You can figure out the number of handbags produced the last day because the first day there were 30, and for 30 days 6 more handbags were added each day, which is $30 + 30 \times 6$. The answer, which is the total number of handbags produced in 31 days, is 3,720. If you don't know the formula for this calculation, try writing out terms to look for a pattern. If you do, you'll notice that the first and last terms add to 240 and the second term combined with the next-to-last term add to 240. You can use this pattern to find the sum of all the terms.

Question 28

Answer H is correct. The easiest way to do this problem is to recognize how the expression fits the pattern of the addition of two cubes. You do have another alternative. You can multiply the answer choices to find the one that gives the unfactored form in the question. The much faster way is to see that the expression in the question can be written as $(3px^3)^3 + (2y^2)^3$. To get the answer, replace every F with the first term, $3px^3$, and replace every S with the second term, $2y^2$.

Question 29

Answer D is correct. To answer this question, set up an equation in which r is equal to $\sqrt{d}$, y^2 is placed in the numerator to reflect direct variation, and x^4 is placed in the denominator to reflect inverse variation. The result is $r = \sqrt{d}y^2/x^4$. Next, replace y with $(2y)$, d with $(4d)$, and x with $1/2\ x$. The expression $r = \sqrt{(4d)}(2y)^2/(1/2x)^4$ simplifies to $128\sqrt{d}y^2/x^4$. Therefore, r is multiplied by 128.

Question 30

Answer J is correct. Start this question by distributing the negative to each term in the second set of parentheses. To prevent an error in this step, change the subtraction to the addition of –4, like this:

$$(2x^2 + 5x - 5) + (-4)(x^2 - 2x + 7)$$

After distributing, the second expression is $(-4x^2 + 8x - 28)$. Combining like terms leads to the answer $-2x^2 + 13x - 33$.

Question 31

Answer D is correct. This is a question in which you must determine the number of possibilities. A tree chart might help you visualize how this works. Five branches represent the five choices of color. Each of these five branches splits into three, representing the three choices of materials. Each of these branches again splits into two, representing the choice to personalize or not. Each of these branches splits into two, to represent the choice to repel stain or not. In all, there are 60 branches. Alternatively, according to the fundamental counting principle, the number of possibilities is given by $5 \times 3 \times 2$.

Question 32

Answer J is correct. This question looks like a lot of work, so look for a clue that might allow you to find the answer in a more creative way. Stop to consider the process of multiplying matrices. The entries in the rows of the first matrix are multiplied by corresponding entries in the columns of the second matrix. Because the number of columns in the first matrix is the same as the number of rows in the second matrix, you know multiplication is possible. Before doing any calculating, examine the answer choices.

Answer G doesn't include any c's or d's. Answer H shows both columns of the second matrix being added together. Answer K does not have enough rows. Regardless of numbers and calculations, only answer J has the correct number of rows and columns.

Question 33

Answer A is correct. To complete this calculation successfully, you must note that $\sqrt{2}$ is nested inside $\sqrt{16}$. Converting the square roots to fractional exponents allows you to continue simplifying. The result is $-2\{16(2^{1/2})\}^{1/2}$. Following the rules of exponents leads to $-2\{16^{1/2}(2^{1/4})\}$. If you express $16^{1/2}$ as $(2^4)^{1/2}$, then all the bases are the same. Then you simplify further and $-2\{2^2(2^{1/4})\}$ becomes $-2^{(1 + 2 + 1/4)}$, which is $-2^{13/4}$.

Question 34

Answer F is correct. To solve this question, you can set up proportions relating the lengths of the sides of similar triangles. Because both triangles have a 90° angle and share an angle, they are similar. You can set a ratio of the hypotenuses equal to a ratio of the bases: $R/R + S = 6/9$. When you cross-multiply, you get $6R + 6S = 9R$. Solving for s leads you to $s = 1/2\ R$. You can find R using the Pythagorean theorem: $6^2 + 3^2 = R^2$. R is $\sqrt{45}$, which simplifies to $3\sqrt{5}$. If $s = 1/2R$, then s must be $3\sqrt{5}/2$.

Question 35

Answer D is correct. This question is really asking you to find the volume of the right solid in cubic inches. The general formula for finding the volume of a right solid is the area of the base multiplied by the height. The fastest way to find the area of this base is to recognize that the area of the two congruent semicircles is the same as the area of one full circle. Plugging the radius, which is 8 inches, into the formula for a circle's area, πr^2, you get 64π in.^{2}. Next, multiply the area by the height. But first convert the length of the height into the appropriate units, inches: 7 feet converts to 84 inches. Finally, multiply 64π in.^{2} by 84 inches to get 16,880.64 in.^{3}.

Question 36

Answer G is correct. To start, substitute the values you are given into the ideal gas law. Doing so results in $(6)(230)/(520) = (50)(200)/T_2$. Next, multiply both sides of the equation by T_2 to move the variable to the numerator: $T_2(6)(230)/(520) = (50)(200)$. Finally, you need to isolate the variable by multiplying both sides by the reciprocal of $(6)(230)/(520)$. $T_2 = (50)(200)(520)/(60)(230)$ kelvins. The calculation results in 3768.115942, which, after rounding, is 3.768×10^3.

Question 37

Answer D is correct. Don't let the letters in this problem intimidate you. The concepts involved are straightforward. Your goal is to isolate m. Multiply every term in the equation on both sides by m to move m into the numerator: $s + mp = xm/n$. Next, manipulate the equation so that all the "m terms" are grouped together: $s = -mp + xm/n$. Now, factor m out of the "m terms" on the right side of the equation: $s = m(x/n - p)$. Finally, to isolate m, divide both sides by $(x/n - p)$ to get $s/(x/n - p) = m$. To further simplify so that the equation matches one of the answer choices, express $(x/n - p)$ as $((x - pn)/n)$. This step allows you to divide $s/((x - pn)/n)$ to get $sn/(x - pn) = m$.

Question 38

Answer K is correct. Consider that if you calculate the probability that the lawyer *will* get the desired panel, you can also find the probability that he will not because the two probabilities must add up to 1. Now your goal is to find the probability that the lawyer will get the desired panel. To do so, you need to know the number of ways the desired outcome can be accomplished and the number of outcomes that are possible. The desired outcome is accomplished when 2 men are chosen from the group of 5 and 5 women are chosen from the group of 7. In this context, order does not matter, so these are combination problems. You need to evaluate $_5C_2$ and $_7C_5$. You can use the formula $_nC_r = n!/r!(n - r)!$ or find the permutations and then divide out the repetition. When you do so, $_5C_2 = 10$ and $_7C_5 = 21$. Because these are independent events, multiply 10 by 21 to get 210. Now you know that the number of ways to achieve the desired outcome is 210. The number of possible outcomes is $_{12}C_7$ because 7 are being chosen from a group of 12 and order doesn't matter: $_{12}C_7 = 792$. The probability that the lawyer will get the panel is 210/792, which reduces to 35/132. The probability that the lawyer will not get the panel is 1 − 35/132, or 97/132.

Question 39

Answer B is correct. If you're confused when you read this problem, try to identify its type. You should be able to deduce that it is a rate problem. When you examine what you are given, you should be able to identify rate 1, rate 2, an unknown time, and a job that needs to be completed. This information fits the general pattern $R_1T_1 + R_2T_2 =$ jobs. However, in this problem, $T_1 = T_2$. When you substitute the values you are given into the equation, you get 1 tank/45 min(T) + 1 tank/30 min(T) = 7/9. Next, solve for T. To do so, multiply every term by the LCM of the denominators—90. The result is $2T + 3T = 70$. Therefore, $T = 70/5$, or 14 minutes.

Question 40

Answer G is correct. One option you have to solve this problem is to plug the times given in the answer choices into the equation to see which one results in the greatest height. On the other hand, knowing a few things about a parabola, the graph of a quadratic, can point you to the correct choice very quickly. With either method, the initial velocity is an unnecessary distracter. Consider that the equation given graphs a parabola.

The point of the ball's maximum height is at the vertex of the parabola. You may remember that, if a quadratic is in standard form, the x-coordinate (in this case, t) of the vertex is $-b/2a$. The equation in standard form is $h = -16t^2 + 32t$, so b is 32 and a is −16. Therefore, the vertex is at $-32/2(-16)$ on the x-axis, which means that the maximum height is at $t = 1$.

Question 41

Answer B is correct. To answer this question, consider that to have real roots, or solutions, $b^2 - 4ac$ must result in a positive number or 0. Because you know the values of a and c, the resulting equation is $b^2 - 32 \geq 0$. Solving for b, you get $b^2 \geq 32$. Taking the square root of both sides results in two solutions for b: $-4\sqrt{2}$ and $4\sqrt{2}$. Because b is squared, any positive or negative number with an absolute value greater than $4\sqrt{2}$ will satisfy the constraint. Put in equation form, this is $|\,b \geq 4\sqrt{2}$.

Question 42

Answer H is correct. On a question like this, you can always evaluate each individual statement. Better still, where the two equations (which represent the two different fee schedules) intersect is the point of interest. The first method is represented by Cost = 0.45 C, and the second method is represented by Cost = 7 + 0.10 C. If you set these equal to each other and solve for C, $0.45C = 7 + 0.10\ C$; therefore, $C = 20$. If there are fewer than 20 checks, A is cheaper. If there are more than 20 checks, B is cheaper. Scanning the options, it is incorrect to say that if the number of checks is greater than 18, plan B is cheaper.

Question 43

Answer D is correct. A quick sketch of the information reveals a square with sides 6 units long on the x- and y-axes. One diagonal passes through the origin and has a positive slope. If it crosses the y-axis at 0, the equation has a y-intercept of 0. The only equation with two variables that fits this description is $y = x$. To find the equation of the other diagonal, use a similar strategy. This diagonal is falling back, so its slope is negative. This line crosses the y-axis at 6, so the y-intercept must be 6. The only equation that fits these constraints is $y = -x + 6$. The answer is I and II. An alternative, but longer, method for answering this question is to figure out the (x,y) coordinates for the square's corners. Then you can use the two points to find the slope and y-intercept of each equation.

Question 44

Answer H is correct. One approach to this question is to use each answer choice to find the smallest choice that results in an average of 83. To speed up this process, add the values you are given, in this case 318, so you are not repeatedly entering them into your calculator. A more focused strategy is to call the unknown value x, set up an equation finding the average of the values set equal to 83, and then solve for x. The equation is 67 + 87 + 85 + 79 + x/5 = 83. This simplifies to 318 + x/5 = 83. To solve, first multiply both sides of the equation by 5 and then subtract 318 from both sides as follows: 318 + x = 415; thus, $x = 97$.

Question 45

Answer E is correct. Before you start calculating this one, you need to remember that the argument 3θ is inviolable, which means you can't divide both sides by 3θ. To isolate θ, move $\sqrt{3}/3$ to the other side of the equation. Proceed as if $\tan\theta = \sqrt{3}/3$. The following figure shows that θ can be 30° or 210°. Now consider that $3\theta = 30°$, which means θ is 10°. Likewise, 3θ is 210°, which means θ is 70°. Because the domain for θ is $0° \leq \theta < 360°$, the domain for 3θ is three times the original: $0° \leq \theta < 1080°$. This means that 10° and 70° are not the only answers because more revolutions are allowed. However, you do not need to find the other angles. Only one answer choice includes 10° and 70° with additional angles. The answer is 10°, 130°, 250°, 70°, 190°, and 310°.

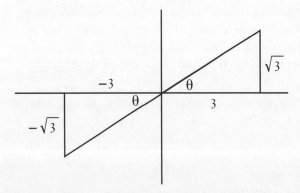

Question 46

Answer K is correct. Do not let the language in this question intimidate you. It is a straightforward scientific notation question. There is more than one way to think about this problem. If the number 1.0×10^{-15} is multiplied by 100,000, it's being multiplied by 10^5. To complete the multiplication, you can think of the number as $(1.0 \times 10^{-15}) \times 10^5$. To simplify, you add the exponents of like bases when they are multiplied. The answer is 1.0×10^{10}.

Question 47

Answer E is correct. The aspect that can make this question difficult is that a lot of information is given in the picture. Look only at point C and the segments extending from it that are tangent to the circle. If two tangents are drawn to a circle from this point, the lengths of the two tangent segments must be equal. You can set up the equation $6 = x + 2$, so x must be 4. Now look at point A. Similarly, $x + y = 15$. Plugging in 4 for x means y must be 11.

Question 48

Answer F is correct. Adding a constant to any $(f)x$ shifts the graph of $(f)x$ up or down by that value. Consider the simplest equation of a parabola: $y = x^2$. When it is shifted 3 units up on the y-axis, the equation becomes $y = x^2 + 3$. Now, adding 3 to the right side of the equation you are given results in $f(x) = 2\,x^2 + 12x + 19$. However, this equation is not listed among the answer choices. It must be in a different form. You can complete the square to put the equation into the form $y = a(x - h)^2 + k$. If you do not have time to do this, you could at least narrow the choices to answers F and J. Completing the square looks like this: $0 = 2\,x^2 + 12x + 19$; thus $-19 = 2(x^2 + 6x + \_\_\_)$. Take 1/2 of 6 and square the answer to get $-19 + 18 = 2(x^2 + 6x + 9)$, which can be written as $1 = 2(x + 3)^2$. The answer is $f(x) = 2(x + 3)^2 + 1$.

Question 49

Answer A is correct. To answer this question, consider that the distance from point D to $\overline{AC}$ is the same as the distance from point D to point B because the two line segments are perpendicular. If you knew the (x,y) coordinates of point B, this problem would be as simple as finding the distance between two points. Oh happy day! Because point B is a midpoint, you can find its coordinates. To do so, add the x-coordinates and divide by 2; then do the same with the y-coordinates: $(2 + 4)/2 = 3$ and $(2 + -3)/2 = -1/2$. Now, find the distance between points B $(3,-1/2)$ and D $(1,-4)$. Using the Pythagorean theorem to find the distance produces the following equations, where the horizontal leg is 2 and the vertical leg is 3 1/2: $2^2 + 3\ 1/2^2 = c^2$; then $4 + 49/4 = c^2$, $65/4 = c^2$, $c = \sqrt{65}/2$.

Question 50

Answer J is correct. This question tells you that for every 100 feet you travel away from the shore, there is a corresponding 16-foot vertical drop. You can set this up as a simple proportion problem. If you let the value you're searching for be x, you can write two ratios comparing the distance from the shore to the vertical drop: $100/16 = x/68$. Cross-multiply to solve for x: $6800 = 16x$. Therefore, $x = 425$. The answer is 425 feet.

Question 51

Answer C is correct. A quick sketch is helpful for this question. Your sketch should reflect a right triangle with the angle opposite the line of the building being 72°. The line below the triangle should indicate a distance of 8 feet. The hypotenuse of the triangle should be labeled 30 feet. You can use the sin identity to find the distance the ladder reaches from the platform to its maximum point on the building. Let x represent the unknown distance. Set up the equation this way: $\sin 72° = x/30$. Then, $x = 30 \times \sin 72°$, so $x = 28.53$. Now, add the additional 8 feet to get the distance the ladder reaches up the building from the ground, which is 36.53 feet.

Question 52

Answer J is correct. The great news about this question is that you have identities listed for you. Your task is only to determine which ones are required. You might be tempted to immediately substitute 1 for $(\cos x + \sin x)^2$. But note that it is $\sin^2 x + \cos^2 x = 1$. The overall strategy in this question is to manipulate both sides of the equation by substituting equivalent identities until the identity on the left is the same as the identity on the right. The substitutions required in this question are as follows:

$(\cos x + \sin x)^2 = 1 + \sin 2x$	Square the term on the left.
$\cos^2 x + 2\sin x \cos x + \sin^2 x = 1 + \sin 2x$	Substitute with identity III on the left.
$1 + 2\sin x \cos x = 1 + \sin 2x$	Substitute with identity II on the left.
$1 + \sin 2x = 1 + \sin 2x$	Because you used identities II and III, answer J is correct.

Question 53

Answer B is correct. Start this question by labeling the figure with the dimensions you know. If the area of the square is 144 square units, the length of a side must be 12 units. The question tells you that twice the radius of the large circle added to twice the radius of the small circle equals 12. You can express this in an equation as $2R + 2r = 12$. The question also tells you $\pi R^2 = 4\pi r^2$. You now have two unknowns, r and R, as well as two equations. You can solve with any method to find both. Using the second equation, isolate R^2: $R^2 = 4\pi r^2 / \pi$. This simplifies to $R^2 = 4r^2$, which means $R = 2r$. If you substitute this back into the first equation, you get $2(2r) + 2r = 12$. Then, $6r = 12$, so $r = 2$. The area of the smaller circle using this radius is 4π.

Question 54

Answer G is correct. This question is a straightforward synthetic division problem. The division process follows the same sequence as the one you use to divide integers. To start, when writing the polynomial include all the 0 terms, such as $0x^2$, and place the terms in descending order. The division is as follows:

$x - 2x^3 + 0x^2 + 0x - 6$

Place the integer 2 over the term you're dividing by to get the remainder, $2/x - 2$.

Question 55

Answer E is correct. To answer this question, consider that the x-intercept is where a line crosses the x-axis. To find this intercept, you need the equation of the line. Use the two points to get the equation of the line in the form $y = mx + b$. Start by finding the slope, which is the change in y over the change in x: $(3 - 6)/2 - -5)$. Now you can write $y = -3/7x + b$. Plug in either coordinate pair to find b. Using $(2,3)$, you get $3 = -3/7(2) + b$. Solving, you get $b = 36/7$. Next, to find the x-intercept, replace y with 0. If $y = -3/7x + 36/7$, then when y is 0, x is 9. The answer is 9.

Question 56

Answer J is correct. Before starting this question, consider that you represent three consecutive odd numbers mathematically with n, $n + 2$, and $n + 4$. First, assume the two quantities described are equal in order to set up the equation. The first quantity is described by adding the first and the third numbers and then doubling the sum, which results in the expression $2(2n + 4)$. The second quantity is described by 5 times the second number, which results in the expression $5(n + 2)$. Now the equation is $2(2n + 4) = 5(n + 2)$. Next, deal with the fact that the quantities are not equal. You are told the first expression is smaller by 5. You can add 5 to that expression so that the quantities are equal: $2(2n + 4) + 5 = 5(n + 2)$. Finally, solve for n. If $4n + 13 = 5n + 10$, then $n = 3$. The question asks for the third number, so the answer is 7.

Question 57

Answer A is correct. Start by finding the area of the sector, the piece of the circle that contains the 30° angle. The sector is 1/12 of the circle because it is 30° out of the full 360°. Therefore, its area will be 1/12 the circle's area. The circle has an area of $\pi \times 9$ square units, so the sector's area is $3/4\pi$. You can find the area of the shaded segment by subtracting the area of the triangle from the area of the sector. To find the area of the triangle, use $(b \times h)/2$, which results in 2.25 square units. Finally, $3/4\pi - 2.25$ is the answer.

Question 58

Answer J is correct. Start by sketching the graph. Your sketch should resemble a V on its side to the left of the y-axis, with the point of the V at the origin. To test for symmetry about the x-axis, visualize folding the graph at the x-axis. If it is symmetrical, the points will coincide. This graph is symmetrical about the x-axis. Next, visualize folding the graph at the y-axis. In this graph, there are no points to the right of the y-axis, so they cannot coincide. This graph is not symmetrical about the y-axis. Next, rotate the image visually 180° about the origin. Again, there are no points to the right of the y-axis to coincide with. This graph is not symmetric about the origin. It is symmetric only about the x-axis. Therefore, answer J (II only) is correct.

Question 59

Answer B is correct. This question tests your understanding of a piecewise function. The graph is broken into pieces according to the domain. Quickly sketching the graph at the different domains will help you examine the answer choices. The following figure shows that answer B is correct: There is an open circle and a closed circle on the y-axis.

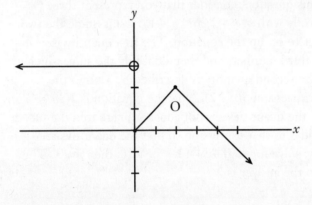

Question 60

Answer H is correct. The question tells you to use similar triangles to find the length of $\overline{QR}$. This means you can use what you know about all 45°-45°-90° triangles. Given the hypotenuse, the length of either side is related by dividing the hypotenuse by $\sqrt{2}$. In this case, $8/\sqrt{2}$ simplifies when you multiply the numerator and denominator by $\sqrt{2}$ to $8\sqrt{2}/2$, or $4\sqrt{2}$. You could also use the Pythagorean theorem to set up the equation $x^2 + x^2 = 8^2$. If the angles are equal, the sides must be as well.

Science Reasoning

1. C	15. A	29. C
2. H	16. J	30. F
3. D	17. A	31. C
4. H	18. G	32. J
5. D	19. B	33. B
6. F	20. J	34. G
7. B	21. D	35. D
8. F	22. H	36. F
9. C	23. C	37. B
10. F	24. G	38. G
11. D	25. B	39. B
12. G	26. J	40. G
13. B	27. C	
14. G	28. G	

Question 1

Answer C is correct. Interglacial periods are represented by the peaks on the line graph in Figure 1. Reading across, you should be able to count five areas when the temperature variations were greater than zero.

Question 2

Answer H is correct. In the line graph in Figure 1, glacial periods are the low areas, ages when the temperatures were below what they are today. Reading across the scale on the x-axis, you can see that the most recent glacial period lasted from about 20 kyr BP (before present) to about 120 kyr BP, which is about 100 kyr. The second, third, and fourth interglacial periods represented on the graph also lasted for about 100 kyr.

Question 3

Answer D is correct. By summarizing the graph in Figure 1, you should be able to see that glacial periods tend to be longer, lasting about 100 kyr, whereas interglacial periods tend to be shorter, each one lasting about 5–10 kyr. The most recent interglacial period, the one we are experiencing today, has already lasted 20 kyr. If the future is anything like the last 420 kyr represented in the graph, we should have already begun a glacial cycle.

Question 4

Answer H is correct. In Figure 2, the period of time from 120 to 130 kyr before the present was a time when deuterium ratios, or delta D values, were smaller. Smaller deuterium ratios are a result of lower temperatures; less heat was available to evaporate the heavier deuterium isotope and less of it was deposited as snow, which became ice in the Antarctic ice cap.

Question 5

Answer D is correct. If a delta D of –410 is the mean Antarctic temperature of today, over the last 740 kyr, there were 10 interglacial periods, or periods when the temperatures were warmer than today.

Question 6

Answer F is correct. By looking at Figure 1, you can see that the interglacial period that occurred 120 kyr before present had a variation of +3.00° from the mean present temperature. In Figure 2, you can also see this same interglacial period as a large peak of about –370 delta D 120 kyr before present. By correlating the two graphs, you should be able to see that +3.00 represents a delta D of between –380 and –360.

Question 7

Answer B is correct. Reaction I is made possible by the high heat and pressure of internal combustion engines, which is an input of energy. No source of energy is given for reaction II, so it can be assumed that it occurs spontaneously. Reaction III requires ultraviolet light from the sun, which is a form of energy. No energy requirement is given for reaction IV. The energy input at reaction I is actually stored and released in reaction II, and the energy of the sun in reaction III is also stored and then released in reaction IV.

Question 8

Answer F is correct. In Figure 1, the highest levels of nitric oxide occur at 8 a.m. Nitrogen dioxide, accumulating as a result of reaction II, peaks three and one-half hours later. If the morning rush hour took place at 10 a.m., a peak in nitrogen dioxide would occur three and one-half hours later, which is 1:30 p.m.

Question 9

Answer C is correct. According to the passage, ozone is a serious health concern. Levels of ozone are highest from 2 p.m. to 7 p.m.

Question 10

Answer F is correct. On cloudy days, less ultraviolet light would penetrate the atmosphere and less free oxygen would be produced from reaction III. With less free oxygen, less ozone would be produced from reaction IV. On cloudy days, with less nitrogen dioxide being consumed in reaction III, more nitrogen dioxide would be present in the atmosphere. Nitrogen dioxide has a brownish color that would make the air smoggier.

Question 11

Answer D is correct. If ozone levels were found to be lower than expected along freeways (Observation II), where nitric oxide concentrations are higher from automobile exhaust, this is evidence that the reaction between nitric oxide and ozone is taking place. This reaction could also explain why there is no peak in nitric oxide concentrations during the afternoon commute (Observation IV): Any available nitric oxide reacts rapidly with abundant ozone, and nitric oxide concentrations remain low. During the morning commute, nitric oxide reaches its maximum (Observation I). This could be seen as evidence that the reaction is *not* taking place because one of the reactants, nitric oxide, is increasing. The increase in nitrogen dioxide following the morning commute (Observation III) is evidence that nitric oxide is being converted into nitrogen dioxide.

Question 12

Answer G is correct. The source of energy in the system is the potential electrical energy stored in the battery. The energy of the battery is converted into heat energy provided by the resistance of the immersion heater. The heat from the immersion heater goes into converting boiling liquid into vaporized liquid. The vapor condenses back into liquid as it is cooled by the cold water in the condenser. The heat from the vaporized liquid flows into the condenser water.

Question 13

Answer B is correct. Using the equation for power, power = current × voltage, and substituting the given values for voltage and power yields the following:

5 watts = current × 20 volts

Dividing both sides of the equation by 20 volts gives 0.25 amps.

Question 14

Answer G is correct. If the liquid was not at a steady boil before the student began to record the time, some of the energy would have gone into changing the temperature of the liquid rather than changing it into vapor. The experiment assumes that all the power used over the measured time period of the experiment was used in changing the liquid into vapor. This would have left the student with a result that less liquid was actually vaporized over the time period, which would have lowered the vaporization rate. The amount of power consumed would not have changed—only the way that it was used.

Question 15

Answer A is correct. By looking over Tables 1–3, you can see that the rates of vaporization over roughly equivalent power levels were greatest for 2-propanol and least for methanol, with ethyl alcohol falling between the two.

Question 16

Answer J is correct. In Table 3, the rate of vaporization of ethyl alcohol increases by about 10.0×10.0^{-3} grams per second for each additional 10 watts of power. At this rate of increase, 40 watts of power would result in a rate of approximately 40.0×10^{-3} grams per second.

Question 17

Answer A is correct. If the calorimeter lost less heat, the y-intercept would move closer to the origin. This would result in a smaller value that would be subtracted from the slope of each line to arrive at the heat of vaporization. With a smaller y-intercept, the slope of each line would also be smaller, meaning that for each power output, greater amounts of liquid would be vaporized.

Question 18

Answer G is correct. Straight down from Well A in Figure 1, the layer of sandstone saturated with water contacts the impermeable shale layer at 550 meters. This would be the depth where Well A would first contact water.

Question 19

Answer B is correct. Well B is the only well that would encounter a sandstone-shale contact at those depths.

Question 20

Answer J is correct. From the stratigraphic cross-section in Figure 1, you can see that in the water-saturated sandstone layer where the natural gas and oil are trapped, the oil is above the water and the natural gas is above the oil. This would indicate that the oil floats on the water and must be less dense than water. The natural gas floats above the oil and therefore must be less dense than oil. The densities from most to least are water, oil, natural gas.

Question 21

Answer D is correct. In the stratigraphic cross-section in Figure 1, some of the younger layers presumably have been eroded away. Moving across the surface from Well A toward Well D, you would at first encounter older layers of rock that were exposed by erosion. Because of the folding of the layers of rock, after passing Well C you would again start encountering younger layers of rock.

Question 22

Answer H is correct. Beginning with the sample from Well E, locate the contact between the impermeable shale and the sandstone saturated with water at about 600 meters deep. In Well F, the contact is at 625 meters, and at Well G it can be seen at about 610 meters. At Well H, this layer can be found at about 500 meters. At Well I, it is at about 520 meters in depth. Finally, at Well J, it is at about 600 meters. The layer of interest becomes deeper, then shallower, and then deeper.

Question 23

Answer C is correct. Correlating the information in the passage and in the figures, you should see that what you are looking for is a petroleum trap. The layer of sandstone saturated with water is of particular interest because it is overlaid by an impermeable layer of shale, which can trap petroleum. Natural gas will likely be found at the shallowest point where it has been forced by the greater densities of water and oil. Samples from Wells H and I represent the two highest points where the contact of sandstone saturated with water and impermeable shale was found. Drilling between Wells H and I would be the best bet for finding natural gas.

Question 24

Answer G is correct. Begin by looking at the photograph of the gel and estimate the lengths of the pieces of DNA in lane 2. Match the lengths with the information in Table 1. You should see that only *Hind*III yields fragments of 3.7 kbp and 8.4 kbp. Now you know that the correct answer is either G or H. Because both of these choices have *Hae*III in lane 3, move to lane 4 and look at the number of segments produced from *Hind*III + *Hae*III and *Eco*RI + *Hind*III. Four segments are produced from *Hind*III + *Hae*III, whereas *Eco*RI + *Hind*III produces three segments. Therefore, lane 4 must be *Hind*III + *Hae*III.

Question 25

Answer B is correct. The easiest way to solve this problem is to look at each figure and picture what it would look like if it had not been cut by *Eco*RI. Add together the two segments that were cut by *Eco*RI, and you should now have two segments that resulted from cutting with *Hind*III only. Checking Table 1, you will see that *Hind*III produces fragments of 3.7 kbp and 8.4 kbp. Look at answer A. If the 3.7 kbp segment and the 2.7 kbp segment are added together, you should have a segment of 6.4 kbp and the other segment would be 5.7 kbp in length. These lengths do not match with 3.7 kbp and 8.4 kbp. In answer B, when the 5.7 kbp segment and the 2.7 kbp segment are added together, you have a segment that is 8.4 kbp and another segment that is 3.7 kbp in length. These lengths match the fragment sizes listed for *Hind*III. Therefore, answer B is the correct choice.

Question 26

Answer J is correct. Look at each diagram and determine the lengths of the fragments that would result if the plasmid were cut by just one of the restriction enzymes. In answer F, if you were to remove *Hae*III from the map and look at the segments that would result from cutting with *Hind*III only, do the resulting segments match the fragment sizes given in Table 1? Adding the 2.0 kbp and 3.5 kbp segments gives you a 5.5 kbp segment. Adding the 4.9 kbp and 1.7 kbp segments gives you a 6.6 kbp segment. Because *Hind*III should result in 3.7 kbp and 8.4 kbp fragments, answer F is incorrect. In the same way, answer G yields fragments of 3.5 kbp and 8.6 kbp, and answer H yields fragments of 7.4 kbp and 4.7 kbp. Answer J yields fragments of 3.7 kbp and 8.4 kbp, which correctly matches the fragment sizes given in Table 1.

Question 27

Answer C is correct. In the recombinant pBR322 plasmid, the *tet*^{r} gene would be inoperative because the *Bam*HI recognition site is within the *tet*^{r} gene. The recombinant plasmid would give *E. coli* bacteria resistance to only ampicillin and not tetracycline.

Question 28

Answer G is correct. If some of the *E. coli* colonies were resistant to tetracycline, they must have taken up the recombinant pBR322 plasmid with the *tet^r* gene. Because the *E. coli* were sensitive to ampicillin, the *amp^r* gene must be inoperative. This means that *Hind*III must have cut the *amp^r* in at least one place, allowing the fruit fly DNA to be inserted, disrupting the DNA sequence, and yielding the *amp^r* gene inoperative.

Question 29

Answer C is correct. Student 1 determined the buoyant force by measuring the volume of the cube and calculating the weight of the water that would be displaced. This is not a direct method of measuring the buoyant force. Student 2 arrived at the buoyant force by subtracting the apparent weight of the cube in water from the weight of the object in air. This method also does not directly measure the buoyant force. Only student 3 directly measured the buoyant force by setting the scale to zero and then measuring the force pushing down on the scale, which must be equal to the buoyant force.

Question 30

Answer F is correct. Student 1 did not measure the weight of the cube in air. Therefore, this measurement would not be affected by the buoyant force of air. Student 2 measured the weight of the cube in air to determine the buoyant force in water, so this measurement would be affected by the buoyant force of air. The measurement of buoyant force made by student 3 would also be affected because, when the cube was lowered into the water in the beaker, the volume of the water with the cube in it would have been greater than the water alone. This increase in volume would have actually decreased the weight of the water on the scale. When the scale was set to zero and the cube was lowered into the water, it can be assumed that the balance was not measuring the weight of the water, only the buoyant force on the cube. The increase in volume of the beaker of water would have had the effect of decreasing the buoyant force measured by the balance.

Question 31

Answer C is correct. Student 3 made only one measurement in determining the buoyant force. Student 1 would have had to make three length measurements to determine the volume of the cube. Student 2 had to make two measurements—the weight of the cube and the apparent weight of the cube in water. The statement supports the position of student 3.

Question 32

Answer J is correct. Student 1 used the density of water at 4° C to determine the weight of the water displaced by the volume of the cube. For this reason, using room temperature water would have complicated the method used by student 1. Students 2 and 3 could have chosen to use whatever temperature water they agreed upon and easily compared results.

Question 33

Answer B is correct. Student 2 stated that the buoyant force is produced by differences in pressure at the top and bottom of the object, which is the same at any depth. This matches statement III. Student 3 believed that the buoyant force could be explained by Newton's third law. The action force is the object displacing the water. The reaction force is the water pushing back on the object. At a greater depth, water is under greater pressure due to the weight of the water pushing down from above. This increased pressure would increase the action force of displacing the water and increase the reaction force, or the buoyant force. Statement II matches what student 3 would expect.

Question 34

Answer G is correct. For an object that is floating, the buoyant force must be equal to the weight of the object. Student 1 never actually weighed the cube, so the buoyant force could not be determined from this procedure. Student 2 weighed the cube in air and then in water and subtracted the apparent weight in water from the weight in air. This procedure could be used, although the apparent weight would be zero and the subtraction would be unnecessary. Student 3 set the scale to zero and then placed the object into the beaker. The increase in weight on the scale would equal both the buoyant force and the weight of the object. So the procedures of students 2 and 3 could be used to determine the buoyant force on floating objects.

Question 35

Answer D is correct. Student 2 believes that the buoyant force is the result of differences in pressure on an object. Forces toward the bottom of an object are greater than the forces at the top, so the overall force is upward. Therefore, if the shape of an object allows it to extend deeper into the water, the greater differences in pressure on the object would produce a greater buoyant force. Student 3 believes that the buoyant force is equal to the force required to displace the water and that the weight of the water is the only thing that influences the buoyant force. The view of student 3 matches statement IV.

Question 36

Answer F is correct. Pure water would be the same as a solution with a concentration of 0 mM. At 0 mM, the time between contractile vacuole contraction cycles found in Table 1 is 8.3 seconds, which is closest to 8 seconds.

Question 37

Answer B is correct. Refer to the graph in Figure 1 of the question. As the concentration of sucrose increases along the x-axis, the frequency of contractions decreases. The slope of the line is negative, indicating an inverse relationship between concentration and frequency. Answers C and D use period as one of the variables, and period is not plotted on the graph. Note that period and frequency are inversely related. If you look at the data in Table 1, you can see that as the concentration of the solution increases, the period of time between contractions increases. This relationship does not match answer C or D. (See Question 38 for more on the relationship between concentration and period.)

Question 38

Answer G is correct. First, identify the two variables you must relate—concentration and the period between contractions. These are found in the first two columns of Table 1. Notice that as the concentration increases, the period between contractions also increases. Most importantly, notice by how much the period increases for each increase of 5mM in concentration. The period does not increase by the same amount each time. The increase in period resulting from an increase in concentration from zero concentration to 5 mM was only 0.6 seconds, whereas the increase in concentration from 45 mM to 50 mM produced an increase of 18.3 seconds. This indicates that the graph of the line relating these two variables is increasing in slope, which is matched by answer G.

Question 39

Answer B is correct. The point when active osmoregulation stops would be the same as the point where the frequency of contractions reaches zero. Extrapolate to the right and estimate the point where the line would intersect the x-axis. A concentration of 60mM would be the best estimate for the point at which the frequency of contractions would equal zero.

Question 40

Answer G is correct. If the solute concentration were greater on the outside of the *Paramecium* cell than on the inside, the net flow of water would be toward the outside of the cell. This would cause the *Paramecium* to lose water and shrink. Also, if no water were entering the cell, there would be no contractile vacuole contractions.

Scoring Your Sample Test

Number of Questions Answered Correctly

Scaled Score	English	Math	Reading	Science
36	75	60	40	40
35	73–74	58–59	38–39	39
34	72	57	37	38
33	71	56	36	37
32	70	55	35	36
31	68–69	53–54	(34) =31	35
30	67	53	33	34
29	65	52	32	33
28	65	50–51	31	33
27	64	48–49	30	32
26	63	45–47	29	32
25	61–62	43–44	27–28	31
24	(58–60) =24	39–42	25–26	29–30
23	56–57	37–38	22–24	28
22	53–55	34–36	21	27
21	50–52	32–33	20	24–26
20	48–49	29–31	19	22–23
19	45–47	26–28	18	(20–21) =19
18	42–44	(22–25) =18	17	18–19
17	39–41	18–21	16	17
16	36–38	16–17	15	16
15	34–35	14–15	14	15
14	32–33	13	12–13	13–14
13	30–31	12	10–11	12
12	28–29	10–11	9	11
11	24–27	9	8	9–10
10	20–23	8	7	8
9	17–19	6–7	6	8
8	13–16	5	5	7
7	11–12	4	5	6
6	9–10	3	4	5
5	7–8	3	4	4
4	6–7	3	3	3
3	4–5	2	2	2
2	1–3	1	1	1
1	0	0	0	0

Use the number of questions you answered correctly in each section to find your approximate ACT scaled score. To estimate your composite (overall) ACT score, add your individual section scores and divide by 4:

English: ___24___

Math: ___18___

Reading: ___31___

Science: ___19___

Composite: ___23___ = F = crappy job Renn.

Although the sample tests in this book aren't official ACT tests, they will provide a close approximation of actual test results if you take each of them under conditions similar to those you'll face when you take the ACT. You can use the Scoring Your Sample Test table to convert your raw score—the number of questions you answered correctly on each test section—into the scaled score that the ACT uses to report your results. Your composite (overall) ACT score is the average of your section scores. Add the scaled section scores and divide by 4 to get the composite score. Remember, this is only an approximation. Many factors affect your actual performance on test day.

Practice Exam 2

This is the second of the two practice exams. For the most accurate assessment of how you will do on the actual ACT Assessment, take this test under test conditions, timing the test as shown in the following table and keeping distractions to a minimum.

As shown in practice exam 1, here's how much time you will be given for each section of the test. As you take the practice test, set a timer for each portion and attempt to follow the test conditions of a quiet room with minimal interruption.

Test	Questions	Time Allotted
English	75	45
Reading	40	35
Math	60	60
Science Reasoning	40	35
Writing (Optional)	1 essay	30
TOTAL TIME		2 hours, 55 minutes (add 30 minutes if you are taking the optional writing test)

In the chapter that follows, you'll find the Answer Key to this test. Good luck!

English Test

The five passages that follow consist of 75 underlined words and phrases in context, and questions about them. Most of these underlined sections contain errors in structure, expression, style, punctuation, or word usage.

The test also includes questions about entire paragraphs and the passage as a whole. These questions are identified by a number in a box.

For each question, select which of the four choices is the best response, and darken the appropriate oval on your answer sheet. If you consider the original version of the text to be the best, choose answer A or F: NO CHANGE.

You may wish to read each passage through before answering the questions based on it.

Passage I

[1]

Relationships. These links are the cornerstone of your business and your personal life.

The stronger that you can make each of your relationships, the more lucrative are the

fruits of the connection for both parties. Indeed, <u>careful nurturing of your relationships</u>
                                                                          (1)
<u>can turn acquaintances into friends prospects into customers and customers into loyal</u>
                                                                          (1)
<u>patrons of your business.</u>
        (1)
Stop right now and think for just a moment of some of the strongest relationships, first

in your personal life and <u>than</u> in your business life. <u>Conjure up a list of those</u>
                              (2)   (3)
<u>connections in your mind that you know to be particularly sounds and that you feel to</u>
                                          (3)
<u>be mutually satisfying.</u>
        (3)

1. ☐ A. NO CHANGE
   ☑ B. careful nurturing of your relationships can turn acquaintances into friends, prospects into customers, and customers into loyal patrons of your business.
   ☐ C. careful nurturing of your relationships can turn acquaintances into friends, prospects into customers, and customers into loyal patrons, of your business.
   ☐ D. careful nurturing of your relationships: can turn acquaintances into friends, prospects into customers, and customers into loyal patrons of your business.

2. ❏ F. NO CHANGE

   ❏ G. than,

   ❏ H. then,

   ◼ J. then

3. ❏ A. NO CHANGE

   ❏ B. Conjure up a list of those connections in your mind that you know to be particularly sound and that you feel to be mutually satisfying.

   ❏ C̸. Conjure up a list, in your mind, of those connections you know to be particularly sound and that you feel to be mutually satisfying.

   ◼ D. In your mind, conjure up a list of those connections you know to be particularly sound and that you feel to be mutually satisfying.

[2]

Now think about why these particularly bonds are so strong and important.

(4)

Certainly these relationships didn't happen overnight. If you take the time to consider

each of these connections on an individual basis, you will likely find a common thread

running through them; that is, for reasons that probably only you will completely

(5)

understand, you have nurtured each of your close relationships to make it what it is

today. You have made a concerted and undoubtedly constant effort to stay in touch with

these particular friends, clients, customers, and potential customers on a consistent basis.

Phone calls, emails, letters, face-to-face meetings; or an assortment of these, all serve

(6)

to continue to keep both sides of your individual connections close and in touch and the

relationships strong.

4. ❏ F. NO CHANGE

   ◼ G. particular bonds are so strong and important.

   ❏ H. bonds are so particularly strong and important.

   ❏ J. bonds are so particular, strong, and important.

5. ❑ A. NO CHANGE

   ❑ B. them that is

   ❑ C. them, that is

   ❑ D. them. That is,

6. ❑ F. NO CHANGE

   ❑ G. meetings or an assortment of these all

   ❑ H. meetings (or an assortment of these) all

   ❑ J. meetings, or, an assortment of these all

[3]

Now stop and think of some of your <u>less close</u> personal and business relationships—
                                       (7)

those customers you don't do much business with, prospects you haven't taken to the

next level, personal connections you have let slide. Although <u>the relationship is</u>
                                                   (8)

important and intriguing to you, it's possible that you communicate with this group only

a few times a year. You haven't transacted much business with them, and your schedule

<u>undoubtedly makes</u> it almost impossible to grow and strengthen these connections to
           (9)

the same mutually satisfying point you enjoy with your closer contacts.

7. ❑ A. NO CHANGE

   ❑ B. less-close

   ❑ C. "less close"

   ❑ D. less, close

8. ❑ F. NO CHANGE

   ❑ G. this relationship is

   ❑ H. that relationship is

   ❑ J. these relationships are

9. ❑ A. NO CHANGE

   ❑ B. undoubtedly make

   ❑ C. doubtingly makes

   ❑ D. doubtingly make

[4]

<u>You wish you often</u> had both the time and the tools necessary to develop and grow
        (10)
this group of contacts, though. You can sense that it is truly opportunity lost, but there

seems to be nothing that you can do about it. You would welcome the chance to tighten

up many of your more casual contacts and wish there were an efficient way to keep

within <u>arms reach</u> of everyone. You'd like to irrigate those relationships that need
        (11)
nourishment as you know each would grow and probably thrive. Further, there's a big

part of you that wishes you were able to cultivate and grow some new personal and

business relationships. Although you already know that your life would be all the richer

with <u>new and mutually fulfilling connections</u>, you have come to the realization that
        (12)
with your hectic lifestyle it is unlikely that any new relationships will be culled this year.

10. ☑ F. NO CHANGE

   ❑ G. Often wishing you

   ❑ H. Wishing often you had

   ❑ J. You often wish

11. ❑ A. NO CHANGE

   ☑ B. arms' reach

   ❑ C. arms-reach

   ❑ D. arm's reach

12. ☑ F. NO CHANGE

   ❑ G. new, and mutually fulfilling connections

   ❑ H. new and mutually, fulfilling connections

   ❑ J. new and, mutually fulfilling connections

[5]

As you are already keenly aware, nurturing customer relationships—even prospective

customer relationships—<u>builds business while nurturing</u> personal relationships
(13)

enhances your life. Although "nurturing" is, in itself, not a new concept, without a clear

plan, nurturing customers can be difficult to execute consistently on a micro, or

individual basis. <u>In the 12 years since our company began, we have successfully</u>
(14)

<u>honed nurturing to a series of deliberate steps and likened it to the practice of farming.</u>
(14)

From planting the seeds to harvesting the crop, we have developed unique concepts of

nurturing and growing your relationships <u>that is</u> far superior to anything used in
(15)

business today—and our measurable results will help you conclude that there is time to

cultivate all of your crops.

13.   ❏ A. NO CHANGE

   ❏ B. builds, business while nurturing

   ▣ C. builds business, while nurturing

   ❏ D. builds business while, nurturing

14.   ❏ F. NO CHANGE

   ❏ G. We have successfully in the 12 years since our company began, honed
nurturing to a series of deliberate steps and likened it to the practice of
farming.

   ❏ H. We have successfully honed nurturing to a series of deliberate steps and
likened it to the practice of farming in the 12 years since our company
began,

   ▣ J. In the 12 years, since our company began, we have successfully honed
nurturing to a series of deliberate steps and likened it to the practice of
farming.

15.   ❏ A. NO CHANGE

   ▣ B. that are

   ❏ C. that was

   ❏ D. that were

Passage II

[1]

In the next decade, many jobs and careers in <u>the STEM (science, technology,</u>
                                                                    (16)
<u>engineering, and math) disciplines</u> will be lacking adequately trained workers. Truth
        (16)
be told, most major industries have been concerned for years that the number of high

school students making <u>a STEM discipline their majors in college</u> is dwindling.
                                            (17)
<u>The government is taking notice too of this declining interest too.</u> Indeed, a
                                    (18)
federally commissioned study by the Rand Corporation last year noted that

"knowledgeable sources… have voiced fears that this [STEM] workforce is aging and

may soon face a dwindling job pool."

16. ▣ F. NO CHANGE

   ❑ G. the science, technology, engineering, and math (STEM) disciplines

   ❑ H. the STEM (science, technology, engineering, and math disciplines)

   ❑ J. the STEM—science, technology, engineering, and math—disciplines

17. ❑ A. NO CHANGE

   ❑ B. STEM disciplines their majors in college

   ▣ C. a STEM discipline their major in college

   ❑ D. a STEM discipline their major in colleges

18. ❑ F. NO CHANGE

   ❑ G. The government is taking notice to this declining interest too.

   ❑ H. The government is taking notice too of this declining interest to.

   ▣ J. The government is taking notice too of this declining interest.

[2]

What's going on? Although it's difficult to pinpoint the exact causes for the seeming

exodus from the STEM disciplines, we do know of a few reasons students are shying

away from these areas. <u>Careers in the STEM fields have long had some stereotypes or</u>
                                                                                    (19)
<u>generalities attached.</u> Students going into science careers, for example, would
      (19)
typically have pre-med as their goal, aspiring to be medical doctors. Other careers in

science were never thought of as particularly popular and there were few role models,

<u>especially for girls', in science fields.</u> Engineering students have long been thought
            (20)
of as both creative and artistic (although engineers themselves are thought of as having

breast-pocket shirt protectors with an ample supply of pens available). Seldom would the

non-doodler express interest in or be recruited to a career in civil engineering.

Technology and math majors have traditionally been thought of as nerds, so those

students who are interested in their social lives probably wouldn't be flaunting their

graphing calculators. <u>In addition, traditionally girls</u> have never thought of entering
                                  (21)
STEM fields in the way boys do. If pre-med wasn't an option, girls would consider

nursing but rarely a career in marine biology, geology, or astronomy.

19. ❑ A. NO CHANGE

    ❑ B. Careers in the STEM fields have long had some "stereotypes" or generalities attached.

    ❑ C. Careers in the STEM fields, have long had some stereotypes or generalities attached.

    ❑ D. Careers in the STEM fields have long had some stereotypes (or generalities) attached.

20. ❑ F. NO CHANGE

    ❑ G. especially for girl's, in science fields

    ❑ H. especially for girls, in science fields

    ❑ J. especially for girls in science fields

21. ❑ Ⓐ. NO CHANGE
   ❑ B. In addition, traditional girls
   ▣ C. Traditionally girls in addition
   ❑ D. In addition traditional girls

[3]

Regardless of the reasons, though, some huge initiatives are attempting to get a handle

on this imminent problem. After intense research, NASA concluded that if they were

successful in interesting even a handful of students early in their school career, they'd

likely have them hooked on space technology for the long term. <u>NASA Explorer</u>
                                                              (22)
<u>Schools is a relatively new program</u> designed to inform and excite elementary grade
        (22)
students in math and science. After a pilot group of 50 schools, 50 new schools are

added to the program each year. Budding NASA scientists and engineers are in the

making, with NASA-sponsored scholarships helping these students pay for college.

To inform more students <u>about which engineering is all about</u>, Project Lead the
                                                      (23)
Way (PLTW), a national nonprofit organization, has developed an engineering program

for middle and high schools. School districts purchase the curriculum and PLTW

rigorously <u>trains teachers: who will implement the program</u> in their schools. Juniors
                            (24)
and seniors who have been part of PLTW in high schools around the country are likely

to be welcomed into the engineering school at the college of their choice upon high

school graduation.

22. ❑ Ⓕ. NO CHANGE
   ❑ Ⓖ. NASA Explorer Schools are a relatively new program
   ▣ H. NASA Explorer Schools are relatively new programs
   ❑ J. NASA Explorer Schools is a relative new program

23. ❏ ~~A.~~ NO CHANGE

    ❏ B. about which engineering is all about

    ❏ C. about what engineering is all about

    ❏ D. about engineering which is all about

24. ❏ F. NO CHANGE

    ❏ G. trains teachers: whom will implement the program

    ❏ H. trains teachers: that will implement the program

    ❏ J. trains teachers who will implement the program

[4]

Also, countless other initiatives are in place. The National Science Foundation, for
                                          (25)
instance, recently awarded a five year-STEM grant to a large community college in Iowa.
                                    (26)
That grant is specifically intended to increase the number of students going into STEM

majors. Byproducts of the grant are STEM academies in high schools, high-interest

summer "bridge" courses to excite non-STEM majors job shadowing, mentoring, and
                                                            (27)
professional development workshops, for teachers, and guidance counselors.
                                    (27)

25. ❏ A. NO CHANGE

    ❏ B. Countless other initiative is in place also

    ❏ C. Countless other initiatives is also are in place.

    ❏ D. Countless other initiatives are also in place.

26. ❏ F. NO CHANGE

    ❏ G. five-year STEM grant

    ❏ H. five year, STEM grant

    ❏ J. five-year-STEM grant

27. ❏ ~~A.~~ NO CHANGE

    ❏ B. excite non-STEM majors, job shadowing, mentoring, and professional
         development workshops. For teachers and guidance counselors.

    ❏ C. excite non-STEM majors, job shadowing, mentoring, and professional
         development workshops for teachers and guidance counselors.

    ❏ D. excite non-STEM majors, job shadowing, mentoring, and professional
         development. Workshops for teachers and guidance counselors.

comeback

[5]

(1) Target those students who do well in math and/or science, but haven't necessarily expressed a strong interest to major in those fields in college. (2) Be aware of and read up on this national problem. (3) What can you do? (4) In summary: become knowledgeable about the types of STEM careers students in your area can pursue.

28. Which of the following sequence of sentences will make the paragraph above most logical?

❑ F. 1, 4, 2, 3

☒ G. 3, 2, 1, 4

❑ H. 3, 1, 4, 2

❑ J. 4, 1, 2, 3

[6]

Arrange for appropriate employers to host a small group of students so that they can

learn more about careers in these fields. Invite professionals in an assortment of jobs in

STEM fields to talk with the students and discuss what they're jobs' entail.
(29)

Keep STEM careers in the forefront of you and your student's minds. If we work
(30)

together, the engineers, scientists, math gurus, and technology experts of tomorrow will

be in training today.

29. ❑ A. NO CHANGE

❑ B. they're jobs

❑ C. their jobs'

☒ D. their jobs

30. ☒ F. NO CHANGE

❑ G. of your and your students' minds.

❑ H. of your and your student's minds.

❑ J. of your and your students' mind.

Passage III

[1]

To this day, General Aung San is thought of as Burma's national hero and his daughter

Aung San Suu Kyi is just as highly regarded. (Burma—the largest country in mainland
                                                                                          (31)

Southeast Asia—is presently called Myanmar. Within the diverse country are 64 indige-
            (31)

nous races, and more than 200 different languages and dialects are spoken there). In
                                                                                              (32)

the years following World War II, Aung San was directly responsible for negotiating

the country's independence from British rule. He had been born in Burma and had

made it his life's work to nonviolently extricate the British from his country so that it

could be a free and democratic nation. The independence wasn't without incident,

though—Aung San never saw the outcome of his labors. The General is assassinated
                                                                                        (33)

just as he is planning Burma's final steps toward independence and its own government.
                            (33)

His daughter, Aung San Suu Kyi, called Daw Suu, was just two years old when her

father died.

31. ❑ A. NO CHANGE

   ❑ B. Burma the largest country in mainland Southeast Asia, is presently called
          Myanmar.

   ☞ C. Burma, the largest country in mainland Southeast Asia is presently called
          Myanmar.

   ❑ D. Burma the largest country, in mainland Southeast Asia, is presently called
          Myanmar.

32. ☞ F. NO CHANGE

   ❑ G. there.). In

   ❑ H. there.) In

   ❑ J. there) In

33. ❏ A. NO CHANGE

   ❏ B. The General is assassinated just as he was planning Burma's final steps toward independence and its own government.

   ❏ C. The General was assassinated just as he is planning Burma's final steps toward independence and its own government.

   ❏ D. The General was assassinated just as he was planning Burma's final steps toward independence and its own government.

[2]

Ma Khin Kyi, the general's widow, was eventually <u>appointed as ambassador to India</u>
                                                                    (34)
and the family moved to New Delhi. Daw Suu was in high school by that time and her

father's nonviolent legacy was never far from her mind. She became fascinated by

Mahatma Gandhi.

(35) General Ne Win had been running the country for years. What began as a plan to

attempt to unite the country saw Ne Win becoming a dictator and people being driven

from their homes by his armies. Journalists were asked to leave and the country was

essentially cut off from the rest of the world. <u>The people of Burma were treated horrible</u>.
                                                                    (36)

34. ❏ F. NO CHANGE

   ❏ G. appointed as Ambassador to India

   ❏ H. appointed Ambassador to India

   ❏ J. appointed as ambassador, to India

35. Which of the following phrases, if inserted at this point, would provide the most effective transition to the next paragraph?

   ❏ A. NO CHANGE

   ❏ B. Regardless,

   ❏ C. Additionally,

   ❏ D. Back in Burma,

36. ❏ ~~F.~~ NO CHANGE

    ❏ G. The peoples of Burma were treated horrible.

    ❏ H. The peoples of Burma were treated horribly.

    ◼ J. The people of Burma were treated horribly.

[3]

<u>Daw Suu now married and living in Britain with her husband and young sons, returned</u>
(37)
to Burma to tend to her ailing mother, who had moved back to her homeland at the

end of her ambassadorship. Daw Suu realized right away that the problems in Burma

were almost insurmountable. Even though Ne Win had eventually resigned from power,

his party, <u>the Burma socialist program party</u> (BSPP), remained in control. The
(38)
angry people, who initially believed that their freedom would be regained, demonstrated

nonstop in the streets for a <u>Democratic System of government</u>. Military leaders
(39)
followed orders to shoot and kill. From her mother's home, Daw Suu attempted to quiet

the demonstrations. The people saw her as hope and listened as she spoke of a free

Burma and an end to violence. The crowds outside her mother's home grew huge,

annoying the BSPP, who harassed and arrested the crowds.

Ma Khin Kyi eventually died and Daw Suu's husband and sons returned to Burma for

the funeral. Her husband had to return to England, but her sons remained with Daw

Suu for a period of time.

37. ❏ ~~A.~~ NO CHANGE

    ❏ B. Daw Suu now married and living in Britain with her husband and young sons, returned

    ❏ C. Daw Suu, now married and living in Britain with her husband, and young sons, returned

    ◼ D. Daw Suu, now married and living in Britain with her husband and young sons, returned

38. ❑ F. NO CHANGE

   ❑ G. the Burma Socialist program party

   ☒ H. the Burma Socialist Program Party

   ❑ J. the Burma Socialist Program party

39. ❑ A. NO CHANGE

   ☒ B. democratic system of government

   ❑ C. Democratic system of government

   ❑ D. Democratic System of Government

[4]

<u>Daw Suu was arrested and forced to stay in her home a day after a ceremony she has</u>
(40)
<u>planned to commemorate her father's death</u>. This day was recognized as Burma's
(40)
national day of remembrance. Armed guards were outside her home constantly, but her

husband was permitted to come and take the boys back with him to England.

<u>Daw Suu begins a hunger strike but the government refuses to listen to her.</u> Her
(41)
sons' visas were cancelled, denying them entry to Burma. Daw Suu was in fear for her

life. <u>Despite no money or no food</u>, she still refused to accept handouts and sold her
(42)
mother's possessions to buy provisions. Her struggle continues to this day.

40. ❑ F. NO CHANGE

   ❑ G. A day after a ceremony she had planned to commemorate her father's death, Daw Suu was arrested and forced to stay in her home

   ❑ H. A day after a ceremony she has planned to commemorate her father's death, Daw Suu was arrested and forced to stay in her home

   ☒ J. Daw Suu was arrested and forced to stay in her home, a day after a ceremony she had planned to commemorate her father's death

41. ❑ A. NO CHANGE

   ❑ B. Daw Suu began a hunger strike but the government refuses to listen to her.

   ❑ C. Daw Suu begins a hunger strike but the government refused to listen to her.

   ☒ D. Daw Suu began a hunger strike, but the government refused to listen to her.

42. ☐ F. NO CHANGE

    ☐ G. Despite money or no food

    ▣ H. Despite having no money or food

    ☐ J. Despite having neither money nor food

[5]

<u>In 1991 Daw Suu was awarded the Nobel Peace Prize for her tireless work for the rights</u>
          (43)

<u>of people of her country</u>. She was not permitted to actually leave and accept the prize;
    (43)

<u>her oldest son Alexander takes her place.</u> Daw Suu used the $1 million prize to set up
       (44)

an education fund in Burma and was eventually released from house arrest because

of a technicality in law. Forever loyal to the people who depended so much on her, she

continued to make speeches against the intolerable form of government in Burma.

Back in England, Daw Suu's husband died of cancer and she felt unable to leave Burma

because she knew she would not regain entrance. <u>Again under house arrest today, Daw</u>
                                     (45)

<u>Suu recently marked her sixtieth birthday there.</u>
    (45)

43. ▣ A. NO CHANGE

    ☐ B. In 1991 Daw Suu was awarded the Nobel Peace Prize. Because of her tireless work for the rights of people of her country

    ☐ C. In 1991 Daw Suu was awarded the Nobel Peace Prize on account for her tireless work on the rights of the people of her country

    ☐ D. In 1991 Daw Suu was awarded the Nobel Peace Prize for her tireless work—for the rights of the people of her country

44. ☐ F. NO CHANGE

    ☐ G. her oldest son Alexander is taking her place.

    ▣ H. her oldest son Alexander took her place.

    ☐ J. her oldest son Alexander had taken her place.

45. ❑ A. NO CHANGE

    ❑ B. Daw Suu is again today under house arrest in Burma and recently marked her sixtieth birthday there.

    🔖 C. Today Daw Suu is again under house arrest in Burma and recently marked her sixtieth birthday there.

    ❑ D. Daw Suu recently marked her sixtieth birthday there, again under house arrest today.

Passage IV

[1]

The problem of adult illiteracy in this country is not waning anytime soon. I recently

worked with a class of adult English language learner (ELL) students. The experience

was an interesting one and I loved working with these people. My class was composed

of students who were complete beginners at learning our language. Some could <u>only say</u>
                                                        (46)

<u>hello or pleased to meet you which</u> they said completely phonetically. <u>Some students' are</u>
       (46)   (47)

intimidated by the placement test that was required of each participant, and it was

difficult to make the students comfortable about it. <u>My attrition rate wasn't too high,</u>
                                                      (48)

<u>and I like to think that was because the students sensed that I truly cared about them.</u>
                                            (48)

I took enormous pride in my students' progress.

46. ❑ F. NO CHANGE

    ❑ G. only say hello, or pleased to meet you, which

    ❑ H. only say 'hello" or "pleased to meet you" which

    🔖 J. only say "hello" or "pleased to meet you," which

47. ❑ A. NO CHANGE

    🔖 B. Some students are

    ❑ C. Some students were

    ❑ D. Some students' were

48. ☑ F. NO CHANGE

    ❑ G. My attrition rate wasn't too high and, I like to think, that was because the students sensed that I truly cared about them.

    ❑ H̸. My attrition rate wasn't too high and I like to think that was because the students sensed, that I truly cared about them.

    ❑ J̸. My attrition rate wasn't too high and, I like to think that was because the students sensed that I truly cared about them.

[2]

Many of these adult learners were attempting to learn English because they had children

in school. They were able to share with me their frustration about not being able to

help <u>their children with schoolwork, not being able to communicate with their</u>
                        (49)

<u>children's friends, and not having other adult friends.</u> I wasn't surprised. It seems
        (49)

sensible to surmise that for most adults coming to a new country with a new language,

it is a struggle. Total immersion into the language is impossible because of the adults'

busy schedule and their family commitments. For some people it is much easier to not

even attempt to learn the new language. It seems possible to get by with limited

English, and it is relatively easy to find and enjoy television and print media in an

immigrant's native language. <u>In many places in our country, big cities especially, this</u>
                              (50)

type of material is widely available. It is easy to think that in the home, families speak

their native tongue almost exclusively with each other. <u>Learning a new language than is</u>
                                    (51)

<u>an uphill climb.</u>
  (51)

49. ☑ A. NO CHANGE

    ❑ B. their children with schoolwork. Not being able to communicate with their children's friends and not having other adult friends.

    ❑ C̸. their children with schoolwork and not being able to communicate with their children's friends and not having other adult friends.

    ❑ D̸. their children: with schoolwork, not being able to communicate with their children's friends, and not having other adult friends.

50. ☑ F. NO CHANGE

 ☐ G. Especially big cities in many places in our country this

 ☐ H. In many places in our country, big cities especially this

 ☐ J. In many places, in our country big cities especially, this

51. ☐ A. NO CHANGE

 ☐ B. Learning a new language, than, is an uphill climb.

 ☐ C. Learning a new language then is an uphill climb.

 ☑ D. Learning a new language, then, is an uphill climb.

[3]

Perhaps there aren't enough of a reward for most immigrants to learn to speak
      (52)
English. The level of literacy that must be attained for the reward of increased wages,

for example, might seem insurmountable to the average immigrant. Although I applaud

and enjoyed those adults for whom I taught, I have heard from other ELL teachers
      (53)
that some of those students are no longer with the program and others, a year later, are

still firmly in the "beginner" class. I do know of one gentleman that emigrated from
      (54)
Sweden because his wife was pursuing her doctoral degree at university here. They have

two young children. His incentive to learn was to keep up with his wife and to talk with

his children, who were learning English at a very fast speed. He is still with the program

and will be a success.

52. ☐ F. NO CHANGE

 ☑ G. Perhaps there isn't enough of a reward

 ☐ H. Perhaps there isn't enough rewards

 ☐ J. Perhaps there aren't enough reward

53. ☐ A. NO CHANGE

 ☑ B. whom I taught,

 ☐ C. for who I taught,

 ☐ D. that I taught,

54. ❑ F. NO CHANGE

    ❑ G. that immigrated

    ❑ H. who emigrated

    ▪ J. who immigrated

[4]

I tend to think that as our schools <u>began tackling literacy</u> with even the youngest
(55)
non-native students, the overall rate of illiteracy will decline in generations to come.

Working with young children is ultimately much more efficient than working with the

busy adult who undoubtedly has a mind full of adult stresses, problems, and concerns.

I'm not sure <u>what is the best way</u> to approach this problem. I would like to think
(56)
that the work we are doing with this rising generation is also going to help eradicate our

serious literacy problem, although <u>as long as families enter</u> our country looking for
(57)
opportunity and a better life, we'll have people of all ages to teach.

55. ❑ A. NO CHANGE

    ❑ B. begin tackling literacy

    ▪ C. began to tackle literacy

    ❑ D. begin literacy tackling

56. ▪ F. NO CHANGE

    ❑ G. whats the best way

    ❑ H. about the best way

    ❑ J. what could be the best way

57. ❑ A. NO CHANGE

    ❑ B. so long as families enter

    ▪ C. despite whether families enter

    ❑ D. however long as families enter

[5]

As part of a class I took part in last year, I became aware of the family literacy centers in

my own city. At first I was surprised that these literacy centers even existed here, as I

had never even <u>drove passed one.</u> The buildings are tucked away in <u>the neighborhood's</u>
          (58)   (59)

across town and those who have no need for their services would never know they exist.

(This caused me to wonder aloud how <u>many whom do need</u> the programs but do not
                                          (60)

live in the neighborhoods served would ever know about them. Certainly there are

plenty of overlooked adults.)

58. ❑ F. NO CHANGE

    ■ G. drove past one.

    ❑ H. driven passed one.

    ❑ J. driven past one.

59. ❑ A. NO CHANGE

    ❑ B. neighborhood's

    ❑ C. the neighborhoods'

    ■ D. neighborhoods

60. ❑ F. NO CHANGE

    ❑ G. many who does need

    ❑ H. many whom does need

    ■ J. many who do need

Passage V

[1]

We all know that water is the healthiest liquid we can possibly drink, but many of us

don't know there is a vast difference <u>in the water available</u> on the market today. Some of
                                        (61)

the bottled <u>water available we buy</u> can harbor all sorts of additives, contaminants,
                  (62)

and bacteria, and can contain a pH level that is far too acidic for a healthy body.

61. ❑ A. NO CHANGE

    ❑ B. in the type of water available

    ▨ C. in the types of water available

    ❑ D. in the waters available

62. ❑ F. NO CHANGE

    ❑ G. available water we buy

    ❑ H. water available we buy

    ▨ J. water we buy

[2]

(1) Our customers agree, and we think that once you try it, you will too. (2) Here at WaterWorks Enterprises we provide to our customers what we consider to be the purest, best tasting, and healthiest water available in the entire country. (3) We searched for the naturally purest water available and with persistence, we found it. (4) Our company, WaterWorks Enterprises, thought we could do better.

63. The sentences in the paragraph above should be correctly ordered as follows:

    ❑ A. 4, 3, 2, 1

    ▨ B. 4, 1, 3, 2

    ❑ C. 2, 4, 1, 3

    ❑ D. 3, 4, 2, 1

[3]

Our secret to truly good water is really no secret at all. We get our water from one of the largest aquifers in the world. Located in <u>Glenn County Michigan</u> this deep
(64)
underground water well is subject to the stringent water testing criteria that Michigan law dictates. <u>The testing on this well are not</u> done annually, or even monthly. Well,
(65)
water testing in Michigan is done constantly and on every batch of water brought up from the well. Naturally, this is quite a bit of extra work, <u>but it is what makes our water</u>
(66)
<u>special you can taste the difference.</u>
(66)

64. ❑ F. NO CHANGE
 ❑ G. Glenn, County Michigan,
 ☑ H. Glenn County, Michigan,
 ❑ J. Glenn County: Michigan,

65. ❑ A. NO CHANGE
 ❑ B. The testings on this well is not
 ❑ C. The testing on this well is not
 ☑ D. The testings on this well are not

66. ❑ F. NO CHANGE
 ❑ G. but it is what makes our water. Special, you can taste the difference.
 ❑ H. but it is what makes our water special. You can taste, the difference.
 ☑ J. but it is what makes our water special. You can taste the difference.

[4]

Indeed, regardless of where it is being shipped, bottled water originating from
  (67)
Michigan must undergo continuous batteries of tests. These include: analysis to detect
                                                    (68)
all varieties of bacteria, traces of chemicals, and toxins, and tests to look for such water

contaminants as uranium, radon, radium, and a host of others. We are thrilled about it
                                                               (69)
that we have never found anything that tainted this water. We do know that the
      (69)
crystallized energized minerals naturally present in this well water are necessary for

energy and good health. We test and monitor the pH level and unlike some other waters

you may buy, no chemical additives are necessary to ensure that the pH balance is

optimum—it is just naturally balanced at 7.2 to 7.4, a level that is perfect for good health.

67. ☑ A. NO CHANGE
 ❑ B. Indeed, irregardless of
 ❑ C. Indeed regardless of
 ❑ D. Indeed irregardless of

68. ❏ F. NO CHANGE

   ❏ G. These include: analyses

   ❏ H. These include analyses

   ☒ J. These include analysis

69. ❏ A. NO CHANGE

   ❏ B. We are thrilled that we have never found anything to taint this water

   ☒ C. We are thrilled that we have never found anything tainting this water

   ❏ D. We have never found anything that tainted this water and we are thrilled

[5]

This water is truly perfect. It is also delicious to drink, and a chilled bottle of our water

will undoubtedly <u>be the cleanest, tasting, best-flavored water</u>, you have ever tried.
                                      (70)

Like our regular customers, you'll find our bottled water to be your drink of choice all

day, every day. The difference will be so apparent that you'll find that other waters

<u>doesn't really taste good</u> to you anymore. Best of all, you'll feel healthier, you'll look
        (71)

healthier, and you'll notice you have more energy. When your friends and coworkers

ask, <u>"What's in the water"?</u> you'll smile as you tell them, "Nothing. Not a thing."
           (72)

70. ❏ F. NO CHANGE

   ☒ G. be the cleanest-tasting, best-flavored water

   ❏ H. be the cleanest tasting best-flavored, water

   ❏ J. be the cleanest tasting best-flavored water

71. ❏ A. NO CHANGE

   ❏ B. really doesn't taste good

   ☒ C. really don't taste good

   ❏ D. don't taste really well

72. ❏ F. NO CHANGE

   ☒ G. "What's in the water?"

   ❏ H. What's in the water?

   ❏ J. "What's in the water."?

[6]

WaterWorks Enterprises is proud to sell this <u>naturally good-flavored water</u> to our
                                             (73)
customers all over the country and we would love for you to join our list of satisfied

customers. To that end, we urge you to read more about WaterWorks, the importance

of pH <u>to your bodies' health</u>, and how you can order and try this water yourself.
       (74)
Go to our WaterWorks Enterprises website now and check out our products. You will

find a complete listing, plus a pricing list and a handy online ordering form. If you'd

rather mail your order or if you don't have Internet access, call one of <u>our sales</u>

<u>representatives</u> today and have a product brochure sent to you. Soon you can be
      (75)
enjoying the taste of real water. Your entire body will thank you for it. Here's to your

natural good health!

73. ☒ A. NO CHANGE
    ❏ B. naturally-good, flavored water
    ❏ C. naturally good, flavored water
    ❏ D. naturally-good-flavored water

74. ❏ F. NO CHANGE
    ❏ G. to your bodies health
    ☒ H. to your body's health
    ❏ J. to your bodys' health

75. ☒ A. NO CHANGE
    ❏ B. our sales' representatives
    ❏ C. our sale's representatives
    ❏ D. our sales representatives'

Reading Test

Directions: On this test, you will have 35 minutes to read four passages and answer 40 questions (10 questions pertaining to each passage). Each set of 10 questions appears directly under the passage it refers to. You should select the response that best answers the question. There is no time limit for work on individual passages, so you can move freely between the passages and refer to them as often as you'd like.

Passage I: Prose Fiction

Line   Twenty-five years ago, I owned and drove an orange MG Midget sports car. I was the coolest 18-year-old in the world back then. I am sure of it.

        In those days, nothing compared with driving east on the Long Island Expressway toward the Hamptons, car top down, my hair tied back. I'd flirt with speeding and then
(5)   slow down to the 60 miles per hour that virtually guaranteed that I would not get the ticket that would send my already high insurance premiums to the point where I could not pay them.

        No one was cooler than I back then. No one, except perhaps for the five or six other orange MG Midget owners whom I would periodically pass in my travels on and
(10)   around Long Island. Sitting low in the dark pit of the tiny car, we drivers would remain faceless, and would greet each other in passing with a quick flash of our vehicle's head-lights. I'd flash once, the oncoming car would respond in kind, and it meant quite simply, "We are members of an exclusive club of orange MG owners, and no one is nearly as terrific as we are." If I had a passenger in the car at the time, it would be even
(15)   more exciting for all of those involved in the encounter ("Oh my goodness, are you in some kind of club?", "Do you know that person?").

        Life was simpler then. I did not even mind stopping at a filling station to gas up the tank. There I would stand, leaning one knee against the car to indicate possession, and I would happily fill up the tank. Then I would dash in to the clerk, and loudly (in
(20)   case there was anyone else around to hear) report that I'd just filled up the orange MG outside. "Which pump?" the clerk would reply in a monotone. I would always have to run back outside and look.

        Things have changed in the ensuing quarter century. I have come back down to earth. I am no longer the coolest gal who has ever driven a tiny car. As a matter of fact,
(25)   back when I was nine months pregnant with my fourth child, my husband, bowing to the decreasing number of seats in our domestic sedan, test-drove a gray-green minivan into our driveway. Seemingly excited, he beckoned me to roll off the couch and look at the "beautiful vehicle" in our driveway. For a split second I thought he was presenting me with an MG, and my heart stopped for a moment as I considered where I'd put the
(30)   infant seat and which child would drive in it first.

        To me, the large beast dubbed "minivan" says, "The driver of this vehicle has a bunch of children and assorted junk in here, and can't fit it all into a normal-size car." There is nothing pretty or even remotely cool about a van, and as I drive around the Midwest where I now live I see thousands of minivans every day. Whereas I used to be
(35)   headlight-flashed because I was so cool, I have quickly learned that if someone, even a

nonvan driver, flashes headlights at me, it is to alert me that there is a police officer or state trooper within 500 yards of my vehicle. This information is not very handy to me, as I rarely speed or call attention to myself.

(40) Whereas my orange MG Midget used to have a gas tank the size of the half-gallon pitcher I now make powdered drink mix in, the van has a gas tank the size of our bathtub. I shove the gas nozzle in and quickly walk away as I mentally list all of the errands I have to complete on my Saturday off from work. I pay by swiping my credit card at the pump, and shudder at the thought of announcing to anyone that I have filled up the big, ugly minivan outside. No, I remain anonymous when I do that kind of dirty

(45) work.

They're classics now—orange MG Midgets. Very occasionally I'll see one in a parking lot or on the road. I am sure that there will be a time again when I drive a car that makes me feel happy and cool. I am guessing, though, that it will probably be about the same time that the word *cool* comes back into style.

1. Based on the information in the passage, it can be inferred that the narrator is:
   - A. a teenage boy
   - B. an adult male
   - C. a teenage girl
   - D. an adult female

2. As used in Line 4, the phrase "flirt with speeding" most nearly means:
   - F. flirt with drivers while driving fast
   - G. speed a bit but drive at a normal rate of speed
   - H. drive down the highway at top speed
   - J. wink while driving fast

3. By the end of the passage, the narrator's attitude can best be described as:
   - A. resigned
   - B. apprehensive
   - C. emblematic
   - D. despondent

4. Which is the best statement about the narrator's attitude about filling the MG and minivan gas tanks?
   - F. An MG takes just a moment to fill.
   - G. A minivan costs too much to fill.
   - H. An MG is more fun to fill.
   - J. A minivan never seems to run out of gas.

5. All of the words below can be used to describe the narrator as a teen EXCEPT:

   ❏ A. proud

   ❏ B. diffident

   ❏ C. devoted

   ❏ D. optimistic

6. According to the essay, the narrator would admit now that:

   ❏ F. Four children is too many.

   ❏ G. Self-image changes as life changes.

   ❏ H. It's foolish to love a car.

   ❏ J. The MG was not that terrific a car.

7. As used in Line 21, the word "monotone" most nearly means:

   ❏ A. lackluster

   ❏ B. colorful

   ❏ C. remarkable

   ❏ D. inspired

8. "Headlight flashing" among MG drivers seems to mean:

   ❏ F. There is a police officer somewhere close.

   ❏ G. "Hello, fellow orange MG Midget driver."

   ❏ H. "Meet me at the next light."

   ❏ J. "Would you like to go on a date?"

9. According to the passage, life for the narrator is now:

   ❏ A. simpler than life back then

   ❏ B. more complicated than life then

   ❏ C. about the same as life was then

   ❏ D. there is no way to know from the passage

10. In the passage, the minivan is likened by the narrator to:

    ❏ F. a gas guzzler

    ❏ G. a beautiful vehicle

    ❏ H. a bus

    ❏ J. a large beast

Passage II: Social Science

Adapted from New Scientist news service

Line   Conventional wisdom has long held that the first settlers arrived on isolated Easter
Island in about 800 AD. Easter Island, a once-lush triangular island in the South Pacific
nearest to Tahiti and Chile, is actually more than 2,000 miles from either of those
regions. When early people arrived on the island centuries ago, these settlers flattened
(5)   the once-lush and plentiful forests there to construct homes and to build the enormous
stone statues that are still closely linked to Easter Island's identity.

       The island was named "Easter Island" by Admiral Roggeveen in 1722, and there
has always been some disagreement about which group of settlers actually arrived at the
island first—a Peruvian or a Polynesian group. The explorer Thor Heyerdahl suggested
(10)   that the enormous statues had to have been built by people of Peruvian descent, as the
works mimicked ancient Incan stonework. Conversely, archaeological support tends to
suggest that the island was first discovered and settled by the Polynesian people in about
1200 AD. These settlers, it is thought by some, created the statues in a quest to incorporate their own culture to the island, to include music, crafts, dance, rock and wood carv-
(15)   ings, and the Rongorongo script, the written language of the Polynesian people.

       Despite the early origins of the island, one concept has rarely been disputed. The
settlers to the island overforested the area and eventually rendered it barren. When
Admiral Roggeveen arrived there, he found starving people and no trees remaining.

       Recent news in the archaeological world suggests that the first settlers arrived at
(20)   the island much later than once believed. Radiocarbon dating of wood found at a new
excavation on the island seems to prove that the first settlers didn't arrive on Easter
Island until 1200 AD. That new excavation site, a beach known as Anakena, is regarded
as the particular spot early settlers would have likely landed.

       Terry Hunt, an archaeologist at the University of Hawaii at Manoa, and Carl Lipo
(25)   of California State University at Long Beach used radiocarbon dating to evaluate
samples taken from Anakena. The scientists realized that long-held assumptions were
incorrect and that humans had come to the island closer to the year 1200 AD, about 400
years after what had been believed.

       "I got those results back and I was skeptical," says Hunt. "I thought, something's
(30)   wrong with these." Further scrutiny and testing of the samples only served to reinforce
the later year. Hunt and Lipo reevaluated evidence that had been previously dated and
came to the conclusion that the 1200 AD date was undoubtedly the correct one.

       Scientists have further inferred that for the island to have been deforested so
completely, the early settlers had to have begun razing the atoll almost immediately after
(35)   their arrival. It would seem that the Polynesians were determined to make their mark on
the island by beginning work on their huge statues and stone heads almost right away.
"There isn't a period of ecological stability," says Hunt. "There was almost immediate
impact. It's isn't a two-part story anymore. There's really just one chapter."

       The Easter Island settlement question isn't necessarily answered, though. Patrick
(40)   Kirch, an archaeologist at the University of California at Berkeley, finds that it makes
more sense that the Polynesian settlers would have arrived at around 900 AD, as they
have been previously shown to arrive on the islands of Mangareva, Henderson, and

Pitcairn—the nearest neighboring islands to Easter Island—shortly thereafter. Kirch believes that the earlier arrival years are still valid despite the testing done by Hunt and (45) Lipo. Kirch wonders whether the samples the scientists tested were actually representative of the entire island and whether there are older and more appropriate sites that could have yielded different dating results.

Scientists may never be able to be completely sure of the time of the first arrival of settlers to Easter Island. They will agree that Easter Island represents an enormous and (50) tragic human calamity to the makeup of a once-vital island. The former lush island became barren mainly because of human naiveté.

To come to a consensus about settlers' arrival, Kirch suggests further testing and dating from a number of additional excavations on the island. "Then we may be able to say we have the answer," says Kirch.

11. The main idea of this passage is:

   ❑ A. Easter Island was devastated by early settlers.

   ❑ B. There is some confusion about whether Polynesians or Peruvians arrived at the island first.

   ■ C. Scientists are unsure when settlers first came to Easter Island.

   ❑ D. Easter Island is isolated from most populated areas.

12. It can be inferred from the passage that presently Easter Island is:

   ■ F. uninhabitable

   ❑ G. thriving

   ❑ H. revitalized

   ❑ J. excavated

13. The confusion about when settlers arrived at the island most likely:

   ❑ A. stems from flawed radiocarbon dating equipment

   ❑ B. has to do with the area from which samples have been excavated

   ■ C. is due to fraudulent scientific claims

   ❑ D. involves mishandling of data

14. The early settlers would have been likely to land on Easter Island at Anakena because:

   ❑ F. It was very close to both Tahiti and Chile.

   ❑ G. They had heard about the area from others.

   ❑ H. It was abundant with fish and wildlife.

   ■ J. It was a beach area and provided a natural entry point.

15. As used in Line 33, deforested most nearly means:

    ❏ A. replanted

    ❏ B. populated

    ❏ C. overgrown

    ▉ D. blighted

16. It can be inferred from the passage that the island of Mangareva:

    ❏ F. is barren

    ❏ G. has ancient Incan stonework

    ▉ H. shows signs of Polynesian influence

    ❏ J. is overpopulated

17. "It isn't a two-part story anymore. There's really just one chapter," most nearly means:

    ▉ A. The scientists are close to knowing which group to blame for the devastation to the island.

    ❏ B. Peruvian settlers began their work immediately upon arrival.

    ❏ C. Polynesian settlers began their work immediately upon arrival.

    ❏ D. The island can be saved if work begins soon.

18. Today, Easter Island can best be described using the adjective:

    ▉ F. opulent

    ❏ G. teeming

    ❏ H. dynamic

    ❏ J. austere

19. According to the passage, the statues of Easter Island:

    ❏ A. are no longer prominent

    ▉ B. are still identified with the island

    ❏ C. are an inconsequential aspect of its history

    ❏ D. provide valuable information about when the island was settled

20. Visitors to Easter Island today would likely find:

    ❏ F. lush green areas and tall trees

    ❏ G. an abundance of wildlife

    ❏ H. ancestors of the early settlers

    ▉ J. little plant or animal life

Passage III: Humanities

Many triathletes who are new to the sport find that once they have competed in an event or two they've been "bitten by the bug." They quickly become enamored with the feeling of physical and mental accomplishment unique to triathlons and they eagerly await the next event. Their goal as they train is to attempt to better many of their
(5) running, swimming, and biking techniques and placement times from their previous race, and re-create that euphoric but physically drained feeling.

To that end, these athletes step up their training, accelerate their workouts, and pay close attention to methodology in all three sports. Is that all that's necessary, though? What do accomplished triathletes do to improve their races?
(10) Veteran triathletes would probably agree that certain tips could be considered very helpful for those training for the triple-sport competitions (swimming, biking, running) that make triathlons by turns physically difficult and mentally stimulating.

First, triathletes-in-training need to set goals for the short, intermediate, and long terms. A short-term goal may be to transition out of your wetsuit in a smooth and
(15) timely manner as you move from the swimming to the biking leg of the competition. This is usually a time of high anxiety as swimmers leave the water and run to their bikes. An intermediate goal may be to train aggressively to complete the swim leg in a predetermined amount of time. An example of a long-term goal might be to qualify for the Hawaii IronMan or other elite triathlon competition at some time in the future. It is
(20) probably most helpful for athletes to think of their personal goals in these areas and then write these in a training log, a notebook where they can be referred to and amended constantly. Spend time at the end of each week planning workouts for the week ahead and note them in this training log. The log will help athletes see progress and plan training as they work consistently to realize their goals.
(25) Triathletes greatly benefit from implementing "bricks" into their training routine. A brick is a training session where the athlete will first work through a rigorous bike workout and then immediately go for a run. If the athlete usually does a two-hour bike ride, he or she should ride for an hour and a half and then run for the final half hour. The brick is designed for the athlete to become accustomed to running directly off a
(30) bike workout. He or she will immediately notice the distinct, tight feeling in the legs when jumping off a bike and immediately beginning to run. Indeed, the legs often feel as though they are made of concrete and are quite stiff. If they start running now with slow strides until they get their familiar running legs back, they will become accustomed to this type of transition. By doing bricks once every other week, the athlete will become
(35) adept at getting into the running stride quickly.

The training triathlete should also practice transitions. Getting into and out of the wetsuit, bike shoes, and running shoes efficiently can make a big difference in race time, especially in shorter triathlons. Some athletes will race without socks to save transition time, but this is often a matter of personal preference. To save time, many triathletes
(40) keep their bike shoes clipped onto their bike's pedals. In that way, they can simply jump onto the bike, start to pedal, and slip their feet into the shoes after they have accumulated some speed.

One overlooked training tip is allowing for a day of no training once a week. All training triathletes should plan into their schedules a day for their body to rest.

(45) Although it is difficult for triathletes to pause during their training, a rest is necessary to give the body the chance to rest and rebuild muscles. Similarly, if they make every fourth or fifth week an easy training week and listen to the body, they will know right away if it feels run down. They can then take workouts easy for a day to help recover and prevent sickness and injury. No athlete wants to train only to sit out because of a

(50) pulled muscle or other injury. They do need to keep in mind that triathlons are intended to be fun!

21. As used in Line 2, "bitten by the bug" most nearly means:
   - ❑ A. hurt by the sport
   - ▣ B. enjoying the sport
   - ❑ C. uncomfortable with the sport
   - ❑ D. buying everything related to the sport

22. According to the passage, the goal of most triathletes is:
   - ❑ F. to win their event
   - ❑ G. to best the best
   - ▣ H. to better their times
   - ❑ J. to complete a race

23. Veteran triathletes are most likely those who:
   - ❑ A. fought in a war
   - ❑ B. are close to retiring from the sport
   - ❑ C. are the oldest ones racing
   - ▣ D. have competed previously

24. According to the passage, the order of events in a triathlon is:
   - ▣ F. swim, bike, run
   - ❑ G. run, bike, swim
   - ❑ H. swim, run, bike
   - ❑ J. run, swim, bike

25. According to the passage, completing the swimming leg can be stressful because the triathlete:
   - ❑ A. has to get ready to run
   - ❑ B. may be unsure of what to do next
   - ▣ C. must remove his or her wetsuit
   - ❑ D. has to locate bike shoes

26. Triathletes should take a day off so that they:
    - ❑ F. can handle personal affairs
    - ❑ G. can recover from injuries
    - ❑ H. can work on their training log
    - ❏ J. can allow the body to rest

27. It can be inferred from the passage that a long-term goal for a triathlete could be:
    - ❑ A. smooth transitions
    - ❑ B. efficient training sessions
    - ❏ C. a national competition
    - ❑ D. recognition in the sport

28. "Bricking" is primarily used by triathletes to practice transitioning from:
    - ❑ F. swimming to biking
    - ❏ G. biking to running
    - ❑ H. running to biking
    - ❑ J. swimming to running

29. According to the passage, one effective way to prevent sickness and injury is to:
    - ❏ A. make every fourth or fifth week an easy training week
    - ❑ B. get plenty of sleep while training
    - ❑ C. eat healthy foods
    - ❑ D. drink plenty of water throughout training sessions

30. What is NOT a reason a training log would typically be used by a triathlete?
    - ❑ F. for planning workouts
    - ❑ G. for assessing progress
    - ❑ H. for amending goals
    - ❏ J. for sharing with colleagues

Passage IV: Natural Science

Line   Thought of as one of the most significant Greek astronomers and geographers of
his time, mathematician Claudius Ptolemy promulgated the geocentric premise in a
structure that prevailed for 1,400 years. The geocentric model presents and attempts to
absolutely prove the early Greeks' assertion that the Earth is the center of the universe,
(5)   with the sun, moon, planets, and stars orbiting spherically around the Earth. At this
point in time, the planets were thought to be Mercury, Mars, Venus, and Jupiter.

        Ptolemy lived and worked in Egypt. The bulk of his most important work can be
dated to the time between the years 127 AD and 141 AD. Scant information is known of
Ptolemy's life, and there are no acknowledged descriptions of his physical appearance or
(10)   even his family background. By analyzing his name, Claudius Ptolemy, researchers cite
the Roman "Claudius" as evidence of that heritage and they believe he was born in
Egypt, most likely of Greek parents.

        Ptolemy is best known for his fascinating undertaking, the *Almagest*. This
mammoth thesis encompasses 13 volumes and is inarguably Ptolemy's most important
(15)   effort. The *Almagest* carefully details Ptolemy's geocentric theory by painstakingly
describing and sketching out his vision of the workings of the universe. Ptolemy outlines
how he has proven that the Earth remains in one fixed place in the universe as the other
components of the cosmos rotate in a clockwise direction around it. This idea, the Earth
as the center of the universe, was originally conceived by Aristotle. Ptolemy's writings
(20)   on the subject became known as the Ptolemaic system.

        In the *Almagest*, Ptolemy talks about epicycles, very small circles on which the
planets orbit. The center of the epicycle moves along in a larger circle known as a
deferent. Ptolemy explained retrograde as the clockwise orbital revolution of the planets
(which is contrary to the direction of most celestial bodies). He implemented epicycles
(25)   in his models to make retrograde more visible. In this way scientists could observe that
the combination of counterclockwise motion, epicycles, and deferent combines to create
the motion of retrograde.

        Ptolemy developed those mathematical formulas necessary to calculate and prove
his theory and in the *Almagest* provides his theorems and proof about the spherical daily
(30)   movements of each planet. Ptolemy devised original trigonometric formulas and theories to prove some of his ideas, developing his own proof for functions having to do with
the chords of a circle. After confirming mathematically Hipparchus's ideas about the
length of a day, Ptolemy was able to extrapolate the theory of the sun's movement (an
entire volume in the *Almagest* is just about the sun). These calculations also enabled
(35)   Ptolemy to predict the planets' positions at various times of day. In the *Almagest*,
Ptolemy presents his ideas about how he can mathematically prove the entire geocentric
theory. The formulas he developed are similar in structure to our current formulas for
finding $sin \, (a + b)$ in a circle.

        In a poll of ancient Greek mathematicians, most would agree that Ptolemy's radical
(40)   work has produced more debate than any other. Differing viewpoints about Ptolemy
ultimately portray him in varied ways, some postulating that he was an expert mathematician and others believing Ptolemy to have actually tarnished the reputation of the
profession that was his life's work.

Chapter 9: Practice Exam 2

The theories presented in the *Almagest* held for lifetimes—until Copernicus
(45)   offered the then-revolutionary heliocentric theory in the mid-1500s. Galileo continued
this work. The heliocentric theory, the sun as the center of the universe, was initially
and for years a shocking thought and remained a great source of controversy among
scientists and the Catholic Church. Indeed, the Catholic Church called the heliocentric
theory a "hypothesis," a word that at that time meant that it was an unproven theory.
(50)   There was a ban on teaching the theory and those who subscribed to the heliocentric
theory were called heretics. Galileo eventually stood trial for his theory.
    The heliocentric theory began to be accepted in small steps, with the idea that the
Earth was not the center of the universe becoming more widely accepted in the eigh-
teenth and nineteenth centuries. The Catholic Church eventually accepted the theory
(55)   because the Bible refers to the sun being in motion and the Earth standing still. Over
time the theory gained universal acceptance and superseded what Ptolemy had taken so
much time to prove.

31. As used in Line 2, *promulgated* most nearly means:

    ❏ A. revised

    ❏ B. derived

    ▣ C. made known

    ❏ D. concealed

32. The passage asserts that the *Almagest*:

    ❏ F. was one of a series of Ptolemy's works

    ▣ G. contained controversial ideas

    ❏ H. is insignificant as compared with other theories

    ❏ J. is largely forgotten by modern astronomers

33. The main point of the first paragraph is:

    ▣ A. Ptolemy is known for his work on the geocentric theory.

    ❏ B. Views during this time were in sharp contrast to Ptolemy's.

    ❏ C. Ptolemy spent years attempting to disprove the early Greeks' theory.

    ❏ D. Five planets were discovered after Ptolemy's time.

34. As defined in the passage, the geocentric theory is:

    ❏ F. planets rotating clockwise around the sun

    ❏ G. planets rotating counterclockwise around the sun

    ▣ H. planets rotating clockwise around the Earth

    ❏ J. planets rotating counterclockwise around the Earth

35. The Catholic Church ultimately accepted the heliocentric theory to be true because:

    ❏ A. It was proven beyond doubt.

    ❏ B. People were leaving the church.

    ❏ C. Galileo became more respected by church elders.

    ☑ D. The Bible makes mention of a similar scenario.

36. As used in Line 51, *heretic* most nearly means someone who:

    ❏ F. teaches about the heliocentric theory

    ❏ G. believes a hypothesis

    ☑ H. goes against church teaching

    ❏ J. believes unaccepted theories

37. According to the passage, how can retrograde best be described?

    ❏ A. the movement of celestial bodies

    ❏ B. very small circles on which the planets orbit

    ❏ C. the larger circle of the epicycle's path

    ☑ D. the clockwise orbital revolution of the planets

38. It can be inferred from the passage that only five planets are mentioned because:

    ❏ F. The other four planets did not orbit.

    ☑ G. The other four planets had not been discovered.

    ❏ H. The other four planets were thought to be inconsequential.

    ❏ J. The other four planets were assumed to be of a different solar system.

39. One enduring contemporary facet of Ptolemy's work is:

    ☑ A. his trigonometric formulas

    ❏ B. the geocentric theory

    ❏ C. the heliocentric theory

    ❏ D. his calculations about the length of a day

40. Ptolemy can be described by all of these adjectives EXCEPT:

    ☑ F. indomitable

    ❏ G. imprudent

    ❏ H. inquisitive

    ❏ J. steadfast

Math Test

60 minutes, 60 questions

Directions: Solve each of the following problems and then mark the appropriate oval on your answer sheet.

All problems are worth the same number of points, so do not linger over problems that take too much time. Solve as many problems as you can, then return to the problems you did not answer in the time remaining.

You may use a calculator on this test. However, the best way to solve a problem may be without a calculator.

Note that unless otherwise indicated, you should assume the following:

1. Figures may not necessarily be drawn to scale.

2. All geometric figures lie in a plane.

3. The word *line* refers to a straight line.

4. The word *average* refers to arithmetic mean.

1. In the right triangle shown below, how long is side AB?

Do Your Figuring Here.

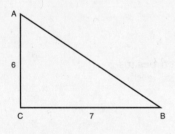

   ❏ A. 5

   ❏ B. √13

   ❏ C. √85

   ❏ D. 26

   ❏ E. 42

2. Mary needs to build a model to scale of a building that is 450 feet tall and 180 feet wide. If she decides the height of her model should be 5 inches, how many inches wide should she make it?

   ❏ F. 2

   ❏ G. 2.5

   ❏ H. 3

   ❏ J. 3.5

   ❏ K. 4

3. Darren received grades of 93, 86, and 87 on his first three history tests. If Darren wants to attain an average of 90, what grade will he have to receive on his next history test?

❏ A. 90

❏ B. 91

❏ C. 92

❏ D. 93

❏ E. 94

Do Your Figuring Here.

4. If the legs of a right triangle measure 9 feet and 12 feet, what is the length, in feet, of the hypotenuse?

❏ F. $\sqrt{22}$

❏ G. $\sqrt{15}$

❏ H. 15

❏ J. 22

❏ K. 24

5. The vehicles in the dealership's car lot include three vans, four pickup trucks, and five sedans. How many different showroom displays of three different vehicles, each consisting of a van, a pickup truck, and a sedan, can be formed from this group of vehicles?

❏ A. 9

❏ B. 12

❏ C. 17

❏ D. 60

❏ E. 75

6. If $3x - y = 7$ and $x + y = 5$, what is the value of x?

❏ F. −6

❏ G. 2

❏ H. 3

❏ J. 7

❏ K. 12

7. If $x = -3$, then $3x^2 - 4x - 3 =$

    ❏ A. −42

    ❏ B. 0

    ❏ C. 12

    ❏ D. 36

    ❏ E. 42

8. $\sqrt{4 + 36} =$

    ❏ F. $\sqrt{8}$

    ❏ G. $\sqrt{40}$

    ❏ H. 8

    ❏ J. 10

    ❏ K. 40

9. $5.256 \div .003 =$

    ❏ A. .1752

    ❏ B. 1.752

    ❏ C. 17.52

    ❏ D. 175.2

    ❏ E. 1752

10. Terry pulled his trailer 260 miles in 5 hours. If he continues at this same rate of speed, what will be his total miles traveled 2 hours from now?

    ❏ F. 52

    ❏ G. 104

    ❏ H. 312

    ❏ J. 364

    ❏ K. 400

Do Your Figuring Here.

11. What is the slope of a line that passes through the points (4, –1) and (–2, 8)?

  ❏ A. $-\dfrac{3}{2}$

  ❏ B. $-\dfrac{2}{3}$

  ❏ C. 3

  ❏ D. $\dfrac{2}{3}$

  ❏ E. $\dfrac{3}{2}$

12. What is the length, in feet, of the hypotenuse of a right triangle with legs that measure 15 and 20 feet?

  ❏ F. 5

  ❏ G. 22

  ❏ H. 25

  ❏ J. $\sqrt{35}$

  ❏ K. $\sqrt{300}$

13. If $x^2 + 4x = 12$, what are all possible values for x?

  ❏ A. only –3 and 4

  ❏ B. only –6 and 2

  ❏ C. only –2 and 6

  ❏ D. only 2 and –4

  ❏ E. only 2

14. A right triangle has sides that measure 2, $2\sqrt{3}$, and 4. What is the cosine of the smallest angle of this triangle?

  ❏ F. $4/\sqrt{3}$

  ❏ G. $3\sqrt{}/2$

  ❏ H. 2

  ❏ J. $\sqrt{2}$

  ❏ K. $\dfrac{1}{4}$

Do Your Figuring Here.

15. On Marty's first six tests, he has an average of 65. After his next test, his average is 66. What was his score on the seventh test?

   ❑ A. 66

   ❑ B. 67

   ❑ C. 68

   ❑ D. 72

   ❑ E. 76

Do Your Figuring Here.

16. A garden club meeting attracts 30 new members. If 9 of those new members are also new to the city, what percent of the new members are new to the city?

   ❑ F. 1%

   ❑ G. 3%

   ❑ H. 9%

   ❑ J. 30%

   ❑ K. 33%

17. Mandy is 2 years younger than Donald. If x represents Donald's age right now, in terms of x what was Mandy's age 3 years ago?

   ❑ A. $x - 2$

   ❑ B. $x - 3$

   ❑ C. $x - 4$

   ❑ D. $x - 5$

   ❑ E. $x - 6$

18. In the figure below, what is the perimeter (in centimeters)?

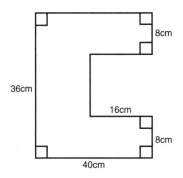

- ❏ F. 108
- ❏ G. 148
- ❏ H. 152
- ❏ J. 160
- ❏ K. 184

19. Eddie has a bag of marbles. There are 10 blue marbles, 8 red marbles, 8 clear marbles, and 2 gold marbles. Eddie pulls out a blue marble and does not put it back in the bag. If he pulls out another marble without looking, what is the probability that he will pull out another blue marble?

- ❏ A. $\frac{1}{10}$
- ❏ B. $\frac{1}{9}$
- ❏ C. $\frac{10}{27}$
- ❏ D. $\frac{5}{14}$
- ❏ E. $\frac{1}{3}$

Do Your Figuring Here.

20. In the figure below, ∠A is a right angle. $\overline{AB}$ is 3 feet long and $\overline{BC}$ is 5 feet long. If ∠C is θ, what is the value of cos θ?

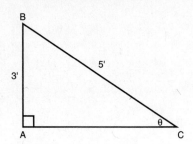

   ❑ F. $\dfrac{3}{4}$

   ❑ G. $\dfrac{3}{5}$

   ❑ H. $\dfrac{4}{5}$

   ❑ J. 4

   ❑ K. 5

21. If $3x - y = 10$ and $x + y = 5$, what is the value of x?

   ❑ A. $1\dfrac{1}{4}$

   ❑ B. 4

   ❑ C. $4\dfrac{1}{2}$

   ❑ D. $-\dfrac{1}{4}$

   ❑ E. -4

22. Dale is 8 years older than Will. Twelve years ago, Will was x years old. How old is Dale now?

   ❑ F. $x + 8$

   ❑ G. $x - 8$

   ❑ H. $x - 20$

   ❑ J. $x + 12$

   ❑ K. $x + 20$

23. In the following figure, the measure of ∠A is 60°. If the measure of ∠C is one-third the measure of ∠A, what is the measure of ∠B?

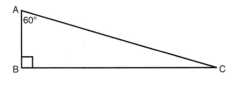

- ❏ A. 20°
- ❏ B. 30°
- ❏ C. 90°
- ❏ D. 100°
- ❏ E. 120 °

24. Andrea has n stars. Lisa has 7 more stars than Andrea and Thomas has 2 stars less than Lisa. How many stars do the three students have in total?

- ❏ F. $3n + 4$
- ❏ G. $3 (n + 4)$
- ❏ H. $n + 5$
- ❏ J. $2n + 5$
- ❏ K. $2 (n + 5)$

25. The perimeter of a square is 4 feet. The length of each side of the square is increased so that the square's area doubles in size. What is the perimeter of the square now?

- ❏ A. $\sqrt{2}$
- ❏ B. 2
- ❏ C. $2\sqrt{2}$
- ❏ D. 4
- ❏ E. $4\sqrt{2}$

Do Your Figuring Here.

26. Which of the following equations is represented by the following figure?

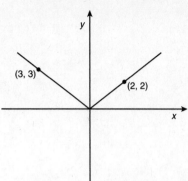

(3, 3) (2, 2)

❑ F. $y = x$

❑ G. $-y = x$

❑ H. $y = |x|$

❑ J. $|y| = |x|^2$

❑ K. $|y| = -x$

27. Pat bought a fishing pole that was on sale for 35% off. He also saved $5 with a coupon he found in the newspaper. The original price of the fishing pole was $75.99. What did Pat pay?

❑ A. $26.59

❑ B. $31.59

❑ C. $50.39

❑ D. $45.39

❑ E. $70.99

28. What is the mean of the following: $3n + 4$, $n + 3$, $2n + 3$?

❑ F. $2n + 5$

❑ G. $3n + 5) \div 3$

❑ H. $6n$

❑ J. $2n - 5$

❑ K. $2n - 5 \div 3$

29. What is the slope of a line that passes through the points (–3, 5) and (4, 7)?

   ❏ A. $\frac{2}{7}$

   ❏ B. $\frac{7}{2}$

   ❏ C. $\frac{1}{2}$

   ❏ D. $-\frac{3}{4}$

   ❏ E. $\frac{3}{4}$

30. The measure of a central angle of a sector of a circle is 60°. If the radius is 6, what is the area of the sector?

   ❏ F. 6π

   ❏ G. 9π

   ❏ H. 10π

   ❏ J. 12π

   ❏ K. 15π

31. $6\sqrt{8} + \sqrt{32} =$

   ❏ A. $6\sqrt{40}$

   ❏ B. $8\sqrt{6}$

   ❏ C. $8\sqrt{8}$

   ❏ D. $12\sqrt{8}$

   ❏ E. 12

32. In an isosceles triangle, the measure of the vertex angle is 50°. What is the measure in degrees of each base angle?

   ❏ F. 40°

   ❏ G. 55°

   ❏ H. 60°

   ❏ J. 65°

   ❏ K. 75°

Do Your Figuring Here.

33. The expression $\sin x + \frac{\cos^2 x}{\sin x}$ is equal to which of the following?

    ❑ A. $\frac{1}{\cos x}$

    ❑ B. $\sin x$

    ❑ C. $\cos x$?

    ❑ D. $\frac{1}{\sin x}$

    ❑ E. 1

Do Your Figuring Here.

34. If one of the roots of the equation $x^2 + kx - 10 = 0$ is 5, what is the value of k?

    ❑ F. $\frac{1}{3}$

    ❑ G. -3

    ❑ H. 0

    ❑ J. 3

    ❑ K. 5

35. Which set shown below could be possible lengths of the sides of a triangle?

    ❑ A. $\{2, 6, 14\}$

    ❑ B. $\{2, 12, 14\}$

    ❑ C. $\{1, 6, 14\}$

    ❑ D. $\{12, 6, 14\}$

    ❑ E. $\{2, 11, 14\}$

36. In rhombus ABCD, side AB = $5x + 3$ and side BC = $2x + 6$. What is the value of x?

    ❑ F. $\frac{1}{2}$

    ❑ G. 1

    ❑ H. $\frac{1}{2}$

    ❑ J. 2

    ❑ K. $2\frac{1}{2}$

37. What are the factors of $3y^2 + 4y - 4$?

   ❏ A. $(3y + 2)(y - 2)$

   ❏ B. $(3y - 2)(y - 2)$

   ❏ C. $(3y + 2)(3y + 2)$

   ❏ D. $(3y - 2)(y + 2)$

   ❏ E. $(3y + 2)(3y - 2)$

38. If the diameter of a circle is 10, what is the length of the circle's circumference?

   ❏ F. 5π

   ❏ G. 10π

   ❏ H. 20π

   ❏ J. 50π

   ❏ K. 100π

39. In the following figure, lines A and B are parallel. What is the value of x?

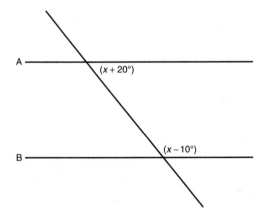

   ❏ A. 50

   ❏ B. 85

   ❏ C. 100

   ❏ D. 110

   ❏ E. 170

Do Your Figuring Here.

40. If 4% of a number is 20, what is the number?

  ❑ F. 50

  ❑ G. 80

  ❑ H. 100

  ❑ J. 500

  ❑ K. 800

Do Your Figuring Here.

41. The perimeter of an equilateral triangle is 24. What is the area of the triangle?

  ❑ A. 8

  ❑ B. 2√3

  ❑ C. 4√3

  ❑ D. 8√3

  ❑ E. 24

42. In the triangle shown below, the value of tanθ is $\frac{4}{3}$. What is the value of AC?

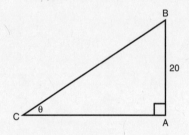

  ❑ F. 12

  ❑ G. 15

  ❑ H. 18

  ❑ J. 22

  ❑ K. 24

43. If the circumference of a circle is π centimeters, what is the radius of the circle in centimeters?

  ❑ A. $\frac{1}{2}$

  ❑ B. 1

  ❑ C. $1\frac{1}{2}$

  ❑ D. 2

  ❑ E. $\frac{\pi}{2}$

44. $4x^2 \times 3x^3 =$

   ❑ F. $7x^5$

   ❑ G. $12x^5$

   ❑ H. $12x^2x^3$

   ❑ J. $12x^6$

   ❑ K. $12x$

Do Your Figuring Here.

45. On $\overline{AB}$, which measures 20 feet, point C is the midpoint. What is the length of $\overline{CB}$ in feet?

   ❑ A. 5

   ❑ B. $5\frac{1}{2}$

   ❑ C. 10

   ❑ D. $10\frac{1}{2}$

   ❑ E. $\sqrt{20}$

46. Penny can drive to upstate New York in 6 hours. What percent of the trip has she completed in x hours?

   ❑ F. $\frac{1}{6}\%$

   ❑ G. $6x\%$

   ❑ H. 6%

   ❑ J. $\frac{100x}{6}\%$

   ❑ K. $\frac{6}{x}\%$

47. In the following spinner, the numbered sections are all of equal size. What is the probability that the next spin will yield an even number?

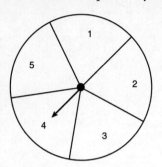

Do Your Figuring Here.

- ❏ A. $\frac{1}{5}$
- ❏ B. $\frac{2}{5}$
- ❏ C. $\frac{3}{5}$
- ❏ D. $\frac{4}{5}$
- ❏ E. 1

48. The value of $(3.5 \times 10^5)^2$ is equal to which of the following?

- ❏ F. 3.5×10^7
- ❏ G. 3.5×10^{10}
- ❏ H. 7×10^7
- ❏ J. 12.25×10^7
- ❏ K. 12.25×10^{10}

49. What is the x-intercept of a line with the equation

$(y - 4) = \frac{1}{2}(x + 4)$?

- ❏ A. 1
- ❏ B. 2
- ❏ C. 4
- ❏ D. 5
- ❏ E. 6

50. What is the value of x in the proportion $\frac{2}{5} = \frac{6}{x}$?

   ❑ F. $\frac{1}{2}$

   ❑ G. $2\frac{2}{5}$

   ❑ H. 3

   ❑ J. 7

   ❑ K. 15

Do Your Figuring Here.

51. At the cafeteria sundae buffet today, there are three kinds of ice cream and five different types of topping. How many one-topping sundaes is it possible to make?

   ❑ A. 3

   ❑ B. 5

   ❑ C. 8

   ❑ D. 12

   ❑ E. 15

52. In parallelogram ABCD below, $\overline{EC}$ = 18, $\overline{EB}$ = 21, and $\overline{AE} = 3x - 6$. What does x equal?

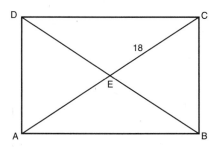

   ❑ F. 2

   ❑ G. 4

   ❑ H. 6

   ❑ J. 8

   ❑ K. 12

53. In a 3/4/5 triangle, what is the value of the sine of the larger of the two acute angles?

   ❑ A. $\frac{3}{4}$

   ❑ B. $\frac{3}{5}$

   ❑ C. $\frac{4}{3}$

   ❑ D. $\frac{5}{3}$

   ❑ E. $\frac{4}{5}$

Do Your Figuring Here.

54. If one of the roots of the equation $x^2 + tx - 10 = 0$ is 5, what is the value of t?

   ❑ F. -3

   ❑ G. 3

   ❑ H. -5

   ❑ J. -15

   ❑ K. 15

55. Which fraction has the greatest value?

   $\frac{3}{7}, \frac{2}{3}, \frac{5}{9}, \frac{6}{11}, \frac{1}{2}$

   ❑ A. $\frac{3}{7}$

   ❑ B. $\frac{2}{3}$

   ❑ C. $\frac{5}{9}$

   ❑ D. $\frac{6}{11}$

   ❑ E. $\frac{1}{2}$

56. Tina has $1,000 in her savings account. If her yearly interest from the account is $50, what is the annual interest rate?

   ❑ F. 2%

   ❑ G. 5%

   ❑ H. 10%

   ❑ J. 15%

   ❑ K. 20%

57. Two trains leave Park Court train station at 9 a.m. They are traveling in opposite directions. Train A is traveling at an average speed of 60 mph. After 3 hours, the trains are 255 miles apart. What is the average speed of Train B, in mph?

   ❑ A. 10

   ❑ B. 15

   ❑ C. 20

   ❑ D. 25

   ❑ E. 30

58. Using the data in the table, calculate the median.

Score	Frequency
60	5
70	5
80	7

   ❑ F. 60

   ❑ G. 65

   ❑ H. 70

   ❑ J. 75

   ❑ K. 80

59. If the cost of a gift is to be equally divided among 11 team members, each would pay $15. If they are able to find 9 more people to pay for the gift, what will each pay?

   ❑ A. $8

   ❑ B. $8.10

   ❑ C. $8.25

   ❑ D. $8.35

   ❑ E. $8.40

60. What is the absolute value of the product of both solutions for x in the equation $2x^2 - 3x - 2 = 0$?

   ❑ F. $-\frac{1}{2}$

   ❑ G. -1

   ❑ H. 0

   ❑ J. 1

   ❑ K. -1

Science Reasoning Test

Directions: Read each passage carefully, and then read all the questions for each passage. Choose the "best" answer for each question and mark the appropriate oval on the answer sheet. Remember that the Science section is the shortest section of the ACT exam and the smallest part of your grade, so do not spend more time on this section than absolutely necessary.

Passage I (Questions 1–5)

It is common knowledge that plants grow better when their caretaker talks to them for at least one hour a day. Some believe the human's release of CO_2 (carbon dioxide) helps in the plant's respiration process. Others say the vibrations caused by sound waves stimulate the plant's photosynthesis process. Researchers designed an experiment to test this tale. Five groups of 100 *Lycopersicon esculentum L.* (tomato) seedlings were placed in five growing chambers, and the seedlings in each chamber were subjected to different types of audio stimulation for one hour a day for one month. The seedlings all received the same amount of sunlight, water, and plant-growing compound. At the end of the trial period, the height of each plant and the number of tomatoes grown were measured. The results are shown in Table 1.

Table 1

Chamber	Type of Stimulation	Average Height of Each Plant (feet)	# of Tomatoes Grown per Chamber (total)
1	None	2	157
2	Kind Human Talking	2.7	162
3	Mean Human Talking	3.5	178
4	Talk Radio	2.1	158
5	Contemporary Music	2.5	161

1. According to the information presented in the passage, which of the following hypotheses would researchers be valid in making?

   ❑ A. There is no correlation between audio stimulation and growth in *Lycopersicon esculentum L.* seedlings.

   ❑ B. *Lycopersicon esculentum L.* seedlings that were subjected to contemporary music grew larger than seedlings subjected to any other type of audio stimulation.

   ❑ C. *Lycopersicon esculentum L.* seedlings subjected to mean human talking bear tomatoes viable for human consumption.

   ❑ D. *Lycopersicon esculentum L.* seedlings grow best when subjected to mean human talking while growing.

2. Which of the following can researchers infer helps plants grow taller, based on the results?

    ❑ F. a human's release of CO_2 (carbon dioxide)

    ❑ G. sunlight

    ❑ H. water

    ❑ J. the growing compound used in the experiment

3. According to the table, how many tomatoes were grown in the chamber that was subjected to mean human talking?

    ❑ A. 157

    ❑ B. 162

    ❑ C. 178

    ❑ D. 161

4. Based on the passage, what was assumed in the design of the experiment?

    ❑ F. The talk radio station would have more commercials than the contemporary music station.

    ❑ G. *Lycopersicon esculentum L.* plants subjected to no audio stimulation would grow at least 1 foot tall.

    ❑ H. *Lycopersicon esculentum L.* seedlings were all capable of further growth and have the capability to bear fruit.

    ❑ J. Plants subject to contemporary music grew larger than plants subjected to talk radio.

5. If researchers wanted to continue testing the theory that plants grow better when subjected to CO_2 (carbon dioxide) released from a human, which experiment can they try next?

    ❑ A. Researchers should vary the amount of sunlight given to each chamber.

    ❑ B. Instead of using tomato plants, researchers should use green bean stalks.

    ❑ C. Double the number of seedlings in each chamber.

    ❑ D. Use male and female and children and adult voices in each chamber.

Passage II (Questions 6–12)

Earthquakes remain one of the most destructive and mysterious natural disasters. Earthquakes occur when any of the Earth's massive tectonic plates either push together or slide past each other. Some earthquakes are associated with periods of volcanic activity and are caused by the movement of magma in the Earth's mantle. Other earthquakes are associated with the collapse of mines or caverns. Earthquakes are measured using the Richter scale, wherein the most devastating earthquakes have a magnitude near 10. While the causes of earthquakes are fairly well researched, researchers debate whether one can effectively predict when and where an earthquake will occur. Two scientists discuss the topics below.

Scientist 1

One can predict the timing and location of an earthquake by studying the history of the Earth. Just as the planet's weather patterns change every few centuries, so do the Earth's massive tectonic plates. By studying the history of earthquakes and the location of their epicenters, researchers can predict with amazing accuracy when and where a tectonic plate will shift, thus causing an earthquake. Earthquake magnitude and timing depend on a number of factors, including the size of the fault between tectonic plates and the amount of stress built up between two abutting plates. Particularly in the Pacific Rim, since the Atlantic Ocean continues to expand at a constant rate, researchers can determine how often plates in the area will shift. Since we know these plates will continue to shift, we can expect a massive earthquake at least once every decade. More should be done to study the history of these large quakes to protect life and property in the future.

Scientist 2

The Earth is an ever-changing and evolving structure, and its exact changes continue to elude researchers. Thus, earthquakes cannot be predicted using historical research. The Earth itself provides clues for when an earthquake will hit. Researchers must rely on seismographs to measure the Earth's shifting, giving researchers a good handle on the amount of stress on tectonic plates in an earthquake-prone region. An earthquake will occur when the stress builds to cataclysmic levels. Additionally, animals native to an earthquake belt can sense the stress that builds between plates and will begin to act abnormally before an earthquake hits. By continually monitoring Mother Nature through seismographs and observations, researchers can predict when and where the world's next large quake will occur.

6. Based on the passage, on which point do the two scientists agree?

   ❏ F. Earthquakes can be predicted by studying the history of past quakes.

   ❏ G. Earthquakes can be predicted by measuring the amount of seismic activity in an earthquake belt.

   ❏ H. Earthquakes can be predicted.

   ❏ J. Earthquakes are a completely mysterious phenomenon.

7. According to Scientist 2, researchers predict earthquakes by:

   A. looking to the Earth itself for clues

   ❑ B. studying the history of earthquakes

   ❑ C. measuring the distance that the Atlantic Ocean expands each year

   ❑ D. measuring the lunar cycle and the ocean's tides

8. An earthquake with a Richter scale magnitude of 8.6 hit a coastal city exactly 10 years to the day after a 7.8 magnitude quake hit the same city. The recent quake followed a series of small tremors over the course of several weeks. How would each scientist likely respond to the latest quake?

   F. Scientist 1 would argue that the quake was expected because the Earth's tectonic plates shifted based on a historical schedule, and Scientist 2 would argue that the quake was expected because of the smaller tremors that had been occurring.

   ❑ G. Scientist 1 would argue that the smaller tremors before the large earthquake should have been a good predictor of the larger quake, and Scientist 2 would argue that the larger quake should have been predicted because the Atlantic Ocean is expanding at a constant rate.

   ❑ H. Both scientists would argue that the earthquake could not have been predicted.

   ❑ J. Both scientists would agree that the smaller tremors could have helped predict the larger quake.

9. In order to better predict when and where earthquakes will occur, Scientist 1 would likely support:

   A. studying the history of past earthquakes

   ❑ B. measuring how much the Atlantic Ocean moves each year

   ❑ C. using animals to predict an earthquake

   ❑ D. further studying the causes of an earthquake

10. There is a direct correlation between the amount of seismic activity that occurs in an area weeks before a large earthquake hits and that earthquake's magnitude. This statement, if true, would best support the view of:

    ❑ F. Scientist 1

    ❑ G. Scientist 2

    H. both scientists

    ❑ J. neither scientist

11. According to the passage, earthquakes are caused by:

  🔖 A. stress in the Earth's tectonic plates building to cataclysmic levels

  ❏ B. animals in an earthquake-prone area acting abnormally

  ❏ C. the Earth's weather patterns

  ❏ D. the Earth's tectonic plates either pushing together or sliding past each other

12. If a recent scientific study showed that the Earth's tectonic plates will continue shifting in the same pattern as the past two centuries, this discovery would support the viewpoint of:

  🔖 F. Scientist 1

  ❏ G. Scientist 2

  ❏ H. both scientists

  ❏ J. neither scientist

Passage III (Questions 13–17)

Sounds are measured by decibels (dB). The higher the decibel measurement, the louder the sound is to a human. Humans can hear sounds up to 194 decibels; however, pain is experienced at around 120 decibels. Without ear protection, sounds over 135 decibels can result in permanent hearing loss. Sustained exposure to sounds greater than 90 decibels can result in some hearing loss. Humans can perceive changes in sound in 5-decibel increments. Table 1 illustrates some common noises and their decibel levels at various distances.

Table 1

Sound	Distance (ft)	Decibels (dB)	Human Response
Jet engine	150	150	Could cause permanent hearing loss
		145	
		140	
		135	
Air raid siren	100	130	Human experiences pain
Pneumatic (jack) hammer	50	125	
Night club	n/a	120	
Radio music with amplifier	n/a	115	Sustained exposure may result in hearing loss
Power saw	50	110	
Jet engine	2,000	105	
Loud shout	50	100	
Train horn	100	95	
Heavy traffic	50	90	
Power drill	50	85	

Sound	Distance (ft)	Decibels (dB)	Human Response
Telephone dial tone	n/a	80	
		75	
		70	
		65	
Conversation	1	60	
Light traffic	50	55	
Quiet office	n/a	50	
		45	
		40	
		35	
Whisper	15	30	
Library	n/a	25	
Leaves rustling	15	20	
		15	
		10	
		5	
		0	Lowest sound heard by humans

13. According to Table 1, which of the following is loudest?

□ A. a power drill at 50 feet

■ B. a power saw at 50 feet

□ C. a jet engine at 2,000 feet

□ D. leaves rustling at 15 feet

14. All of the following are listed in proper order, from quietest to loudest, EXCEPT:

□ F. leaves rustling at 15 feet, library, whisper at 15 feet, and quiet office

□ G. light traffic at 50 feet, conversation, telephone dial tone, and power drill at 50 feet

□ H. heavy traffic at 50 feet, train horn at 100 feet, loud shout at 50 feet, and jet engine at 2,000 feet

■ J. jet engine at 2,000 feet, night club, jet engine at 150 feet, air raid siren at 100 feet

15. According to Table 1, the loudest sound is:

□ A. a jet engine at 2,000 feet

■ B. a jet engine at 150 feet

□ C. leaves rustling at 15 feet

□ D. an air raid siren at 100 feet

16. Based on the decibel measurements for a jet engine 2,000 and 150 feet away, which of the following hypotheses can one make?

    ◼ F. The closer a human is to the source of a sound, the louder the sound.

    ❏ G. The farther a human is from the source of the sound, the louder the sound.

    ❏ H. An air raid siren is always louder than a jet engine.

    ❏ J. An air raid siren is always quieter than a jet engine.

17. According to the passage, what is a human's response to attending a night club?

    ❏ A. temporary hearing loss

    ❏ B. permanent hearing loss

    ◼ C. pain

    ❏ D. none

Passage IV (Questions 18–23)

Sleep is a rest period during which breathing and heart rate slow down, allowing a human's body to rejuvenate its nervous system. Without sleep, humans become irritable and are less successful at completing everyday tasks from balancing a checkbook to driving a car to working in an office. There are four distinct sleep cycles. In the first, humans are conscious and aware of their surroundings. In the second, called "shallow orthodox sleep," humans are asleep but aware of their surroundings. In the third stage, called "deep orthodox sleep," humans are no longer aware of their surroundings. During this stage, the body's repair process reaches its peak. The final stage of sleep, called "REM"—for rapid eye movement—is evidenced by the fact that a human's eyes move back and forth behind shut eyelids. During this cycle, brain activity increases and humans dream. On average, the sleep cycle repeats itself every 90 minutes. Scientists recommend humans get 8 hours of sleep a night, although some people require more sleep to function normally. Others can function perfectly normally on less sleep. To determine how humans perform routine tasks based on the amount of sleep they receive, a series of experiments were performed.

Experiment 1

Researchers assembled a group of 100 healthy adults without any diagnosed sleep problems. For the first night, the group slept for just 1 hour. Throughout the study, the sleep time was increased by 1 hour each night. Throughout the entire trial, the sleep time was consecutive. At the end of the sleep period each night, researchers had the group shoot 10 basketball free throws, and the percentage of shots made was tracked and averaged. The results are shown in Chart 1 below.

Chart 1

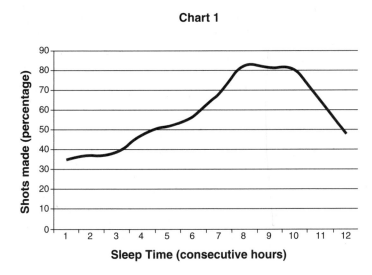

Experiment 2

The same group was assembled as in Experiment 1. This experiment was conducted the same as in Experiment 1, only after every 1 hour of sleep, the group was awakened and kept up for 30 minutes before being allowed to sleep again. The results are show in Chart 2 below.

Chart 2

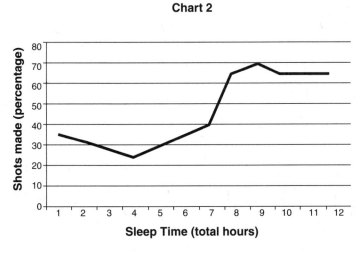

18. According to the data from Chart 1, what percentage of free throws did the group make when it received 9 hours of sleep?

❑ F. 70%

■ G. 81%

❑ H. 65%

❑ J. 85%

19. Researchers want to estimate what percentage of free throws the group will make if it receives 14 hours of interrupted sleep. According to the information in Chart 2, researchers would be correct in predicting:

    A. 65%

    B. 80%

    C. 35%

    D. 22%

20. Based on the data in the two experiments, what hypothesis can researchers make?

    F. There is not enough information to make a valid hypothesis.

    G. All of the members of the group were professional basketball players.

    H. Humans perform routine tasks better when they receive consecutive sleep.

    J. Humans perform routine tasks better when their sleep is interrupted.

21. Suppose researchers wanted to continue their experiment. Which experiment should they logically perform next?

    A. Perform the same experiment without any sleep.

    B. Have the group alphabetize a list of names and measure their accuracy.

    C. Have each member sleep until they wake up naturally, tracking both the number of hours they slept and the percentage of free throws made.

    D. Give the group sleeping pills before its members are allowed to sleep.

22. According to the information presented in Chart 1, humans perform routine tasks best when they:

    F. receive between 8 and 10 hours of sleep a night

    G. receive less than 8 hours of sleep a night

    H. interrupt their sleep every hour

    J. receive more than 12 hours of sleep

23. According to Chart 2, what percentage of free throws did the group make when it got 4 hours of total sleep?

    A. 25

    B. 35

    C. 65

    D. 47

Passage V (Questions 24–29)

Radiation occurs when an element's atoms break up into simpler atoms, thus releasing energy. There are three main types of radiation: alpha, beta, and gamma. Alpha radiation travels at about 5 percent of the speed of light, and its particles cannot pass through a single sheet of paper. Beta radiation particles can travel as fast as light and can penetrate paper but not aluminum (Al). Gamma radiation is similar to the radiation used in a doctor's office to take an X-ray. Gamma rays almost always travel at the speed of light and are usually stopped only by lead (Pb). They can pass effectively through paper and aluminum. The type of radiation emitted depends on the radioactive isotope that is decaying. Scientists performed a series of experiments to determine the type of radiation emitted from a number of isotopes.

Experiment 1

Scientists assembled a group of known radioactive isotopes (radioisotopes) and measured whether their radiation particles could pass through a sheet of paper.

Experiment 2

Scientists used the same radioisotopes as in Experiment 1, only they tested whether their radiation particles could pass through a sheet of aluminum.

Experiment 3

Scientists used the same radioisotopes as in the first two experiments; however, scientists tested whether their radiation particles could pass through a sheet of lead.

The results from all three experiments are shown in Table 1.

Table 1

Isotope	Half-life	Experiment 1 Pass through paper?	Experiment 2 Pass through aluminum (Al)?	Experiment 3 Pass through iron (Pb)?	Result
Polonium^{210}	138 days	No	No	No	Alpha
Strontium^{90}	28.5 years	Yes	No	No	Beta
Thallium^{204}	3.78 years	Yes	No	No	Beta
Cadmium^{109}	453 days	Yes	Yes	No	Gamma
Barium^{133}	10.7 years	Yes	Yes	No	Gamma
Cobalt^{57}	270 days	Yes	Yes	No	Gamma
Manganese^{54}	312 days	Yes	Yes	No	Gamma
Sodium^{22}	2.6 years	Yes	Yes	No	Gamma
Zinc^{65}	244 days	Yes	Yes	No	Gamma

24. According to the information from the passage and the table, which of the following radioisotopes emits only alpha radiation particles?

   ☒ F. Polonium^{210}

   ❑ G. Cadmium^{109}

   ❑ H. Cobalt^{57}

   ❑ J. Sodium^{22}

25. The half-life is the time that it takes for half of an element's initial number of nuclei to decay. According to the table, which of the following elements will take longest for half of its nuclei to decay?

   ❑ A. Zinc^{65}

   ❑ B. Manganese^{54}

   ❑ C. Barium^{133}

   ☒ D. Strontium^{90}

26. The three experiments were similar in that they:

   ☒ F. used the same radioisotopes

   ❑ G. showed that all radioisotopes released gamma radiation

   ❑ H. measured the stability of each isotope

   ❑ J. measured the mass of each isotope

27. All of the following radioisotopes release gamma radiation EXCEPT:

   ❑ A. Cobalt^{57}

   ❑ B. Manganese^{54}

   ☒ C. Thallium^{204}

   ❑ D. Zinc^{65}

For the next two questions, consider the following:

Suppose scientists recently discovered a new element. The element has a half-life of 29 years, and its radiation particles can pass through paper, but not aluminum (Al) or iron (Pb).

28. Which type of radiation does this element emit?

   ❑ F. alpha radiation

   ☒ G. beta radiation

   ❑ H. gamma radiation

   ❑ J. This element is not radioactive.

29. The new element behaves most similarly to:

    ■ A. Strontium^{90}

    ❏ B. Polonium^{210}

    ❏ C. Manganese^{54}

    ❏ D. Cadmium^{109}

Passage VI (Questions 30–34)

A pulley is a simple machine that uses a wheel and axle to change the direction of a force. Diagram 1 (below) shows how a pulley is used:

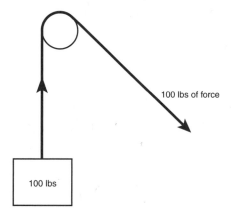

100 lbs of force

100 lbs

DIAGRAM 1

A single pulley changes the direction of a force and provides a mechanical advantage of 1. To lift a block x feet, x feet of rope must be pulled through the pulley. A double pulley system requires less force, providing a mechanical advantage of 2. However, the system requires more rope. Since the rope must pass through two pulleys, $2x$ feet of rope must be pulled to lift the block x feet. Diagram 2 shows how a double pulley system works:

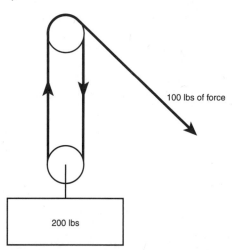

100 lbs of force

200 lbs

DIAGRAM 2

With a mechanical advantage of 2, only n pounds of force must be used to lift a $2n$-pound block. Chart 1 below shows the mechanical advantage and number of pulleys used for systems of up to seven pulleys.

Chart 1

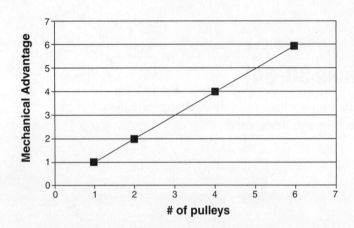

30. According to the information in the passage and Chart 1, what is the mechanical advantage provided by four pulleys?

    ❏ F. 1

    ❏ G. 2

    ✒ H. 4

    ❏ J. 6

31. Which of the following was ignored when calculating mechanical advantage?

    ✒ A. the materials of which the pulleys were made

    ❏ B. the weight of the pulleys and rope

    ❏ C. whether a human or a machine is pulling the other end of the rope

    ❏ D. The resulting mechanical advantage is always equal to the number of pulleys used.

32. If a man can exert 200 pounds of force, and he has a pulley system using six pulleys, based on the information in the passage, what is the largest load the man could lift?

    ❏ F. 200 pounds (lbs)

    ❏ G. 600 pounds (lbs)

    ✒ H. 1,200 pounds (lbs)

    ❏ J. cannot be determined from the information given

33. According to Chart 1, what is the mechanical advantage when moving a load using no pulleys?

   ☐ A. -1

   ◼ B. 0

   ☐ C. 1

   ☐ D. 2

34. Suppose a man can exert 100 pounds of force. Can he move a 200-pound package using a system of pulleys?

   ☐ F. Yes, the man needs to use only one pulley.

   ◼ G. Yes, but the man needs a system with at least two pulleys.

   ☐ H. No, the man exerts enough force to move the box himself.

   ☐ J. No, the man exerts too much force to use a pulley.

Passage VII (Questions 35–40)

The Beaufort scale is named for British admiral Sir Francis Beaufort. It is an internationally recognized scale for describing wind speeds measured 33 feet above the ground. Table 1 outlines the scale.

Table 1

Beaufort Scale	Description	Speed (mph)	Characteristic
0	Calm	<1	Smoke billows up
1	Light air	1–3	Smoke blown by wind
2	Light breeze	4–7	Humans feel wind
3	Gentle breeze	8–12	Extends flag
4	Moderate breeze	13–18	Raises dust
5	Fresh breeze	19–24	Small trees sway
6	Strong breeze	25–31	Umbrellas become difficult to use
7	Moderate gale	32–38	Walking into wind is difficult
8	Fresh gale	39–46	Twigs broken off trees
9	Strong gale	47–54	Roof damage
10	Whole gale	55–63	Trees uprooted/considerable structural damage
11	Storm	64–73	Widespread damage
12–17	Hurricane	>74	Violent destruction

A high school physics class designed prototypes for two wind blockers that can be used in hurricane-prone areas to lessen the destruction of homes and property. One blocker is made of canvas and is strung up near the roof of a home. The blocker is designed to allow wind to pass through it, while slowing it down in the process. The other blocker is a metal blocker used to deflect the wind from hitting a home. The class designed a series of experiments to test the usability and viability of each blocker in the market-place.

Experiment 1

The class designed a series of models to re-create a landscaped home in a hurricane-prone area. The class equipped the model with the canvas prototype. The class simulated wind speeds and observed the resulting destruction. The results were recorded.

Experiment 2

The same experiment was conducted as in Experiment 1, except the metal prototype was used. The results for both experiments are shown in Diagram 1 below.

Diagram 1

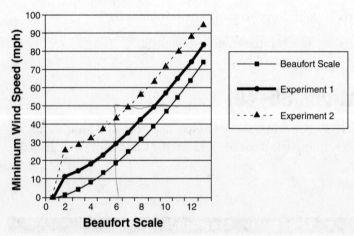

35. According to Diagram 1, if a wind speed of 50 mph measures a 6 on the Beaufort scale, which blocker is the class using?

    ❏ A. none

    ❏ B. canvas

    ▨ C. metal

    ❏ D. plastic

36. According to the passage and Diagram 1, what would be the result of a 40-mph wind using the canvas blocker?

    ▨ F. Walking into the wind would be difficult.

    ❏ G. Smoke would be blown by the wind.

    ❏ H. widespread damage

    ❏ J. violent damage

37. According to Table 1, a wind between 55 mph and 63 mph is described as what?

    ❏ A. hurricane

    ❏ B. storm

    ☒ C. whole gale

    ❏ D. strong gale

38. Experiment 1 and Experiment 2 differed in that:

    ❏ F. Experiment 1 tested the Beaufort scale.

    ❏ G. Experiment 2 did not use a blocker.

    ❏ H. Experiment 1 used models to re-create a landscaped home.

    ☒ J. Experiment 1 used a canvas blocker, and Experiment 2 used a metal blocker.

39. Based on the results in the passage and Diagram 1, which of the following hypotheses can the students make?

    ☒ A. Blockers are effective in decreasing destruction caused by heavy winds.

    ❏ B. The Beaufort scale can be used only at sea.

    ❏ C. Blockers did not have any impact on destruction caused by heavy winds.

    ❏ D. The metal used in Experiment 2 was too brittle to be used in a real-world situation.

40. According to Table 1 and Diagram 1, what is the Beaufort scale measurement and wind description for a 20-mph wind?

    ❏ F. 3, gentle breeze

    ❏ G. 1, light air

    ☒ H. 5, fresh breeze

    ❏ J. 6, strong breeze

Finished with 7 min to go!

Writing Test

Directions: Please write an essay in response to the following topic. During the 30 minutes permitted, develop your thoughts clearly and effectively. Try to include relevant examples and specific evidence to support your point of view. A plain, natural style is best. Your essay's length is up to you, but quality should take precedence over quantity. Be sure to write only on the assigned topic.

You have just found out that the college you plan to attend next year assigns freshmen students who are planning to live in the dormitories a roommate. The school does not permit students to choose or request someone to room with.

Your high school friend is going to a different school next year. If she wants to, she is permitted to place a request citing whom she wishes to room with. She thinks this is a better system.

What do you think?

CHAPTER TEN

Answers to Practice Exam 2

26/75

49/75 correct

English

1. B	26. G	51. C
2. J	27. C	52. G
3. D	28. G	53. B
4. G	29. D	54. J
5. A	30. G	55. B
6. H	31. A	56. H
7. B	32. H	57. A
8. J	33. D	58. J
9. A	34. F	59. D
10. J	35. D	60. J
11. D	36. J	61. C
12. F	37. D	62. J
13. C	38. H	63. A
14. F	39. B	64. H
15. B	40. G	65. C
16. G	41. D	66. J
17. C	42. J	67. A
18. J	43. A	68. H
19. A	44. H	69. C
20. H	45. C	70. G
21. A	46. J	71. C
22. F	47. C	72. G
23. C	48. F	73. A
24. J	49. A	74. H
25. D	50. F	75. A

Question 1

The correct answer is B. The commas here serve to separate the descriptions of relationships.

Question 2

The correct answer is J. *Than* is used after an adjective when comparing two things. A comma is not used here as the phrase that follows is not a clause requiring one.

Question 3

The correct answer is D. Read the sentence carefully to see that the image being conjured up is in the reader's mind. "In your mind" is not enclosed by commas because it explains where the image is to be conjured up.

Question 4

The correct answer is G. In this phrase, *particular* is an adjective modifying *bonds*, and not an adverb (*particularly*).

Question 5

The correct answer is A. The semicolon is used to separate two closely related independent clauses.

Question 6

The correct answer is H. The parentheses are needed to enclose the phrase, which is necessary in the sentence but not as important as the rest of the sentence.

Question 7

The correct answer is B. The hyphen is being used to join the words *less* and *close* to form an adjective describing both *personal* and *business relationships*.

Question 8

The correct answer is J. The paragraph is discussing more than one relationship, so the words must be in plural form here.

Question 9

The correct answer is A. Since *make* refers to *your schedule*, it should be plural here (*schedule makes*, not *schedule make*).

Question 10

The correct answer is J. Using the other responses creates a sentence fragment.

Question 11

The correct answer is D. The phrase refers to the reach of one arm, so the singular form of the word takes the possessive form here.

Question 12

The correct answer is F. A comma is not used here at all.

Question 13

The correct answer is C. A comma is being used here because "while" is being used as a conjunction between two independent clauses.

Question 14

The correct answer is F. The sentence should begin with the introductory phrase and it needs to be set apart from the rest of the sentence by a comma.

Question 15

The correct answer is B. The plural present tense must be used to keep consistent with the rest of the sentence.

Question 16

The correct answer is G. The explanation of the acronym should come before it.

Question 17

The correct answer is C. Check this answer by making the sentence easier: "Hundreds of high school students make English their major in college."

Question 18

The correct answer is J. The sentence states that the government also is taking interest.

Question 19

The correct answer is A. *Generalities* further explains *stereotypes*.

Question 20

The correct answer is H. *Girls* is used in the plural form here and "in science fields" is a clause modifying "role models."

Question 21

The correct answer is A. "In addition" is nonessential here and should be separated from the rest of the sentence by a comma. *Traditionally* describes the actions girls took, not the girls themselves, and is correct here.

Question 22

The correct answer is F. NASA Explorer Schools is a program and the phrase is treated as singular.

Question 23

The correct answer is C. The sentence talks about what engineering is all about.

Question 24

The correct answer is J. Since teachers are people, *who* is used. As the word *who* in the subjective case, it is correct. *Whom* is the objective form of this word.

Question 25

The correct answer is D. *Initiatives* is plural, so *are*, not *is*, is used, and it should correctly come directly after *initiatives*.

Question 26

The correct answer is G. The hyphen is needed to join *five* and *year* to show that it is a "five-year grant," but hyphens are not used anywhere else in this phrase.

Question 27

The correct answer is C. Commas are used here to separate each of the items in a list.

Question 28

The correct answer is G. The paragraph should begin with the introductory sentence and end with the sentence that summarizes the paragraph.

Question 29

The correct answer is D. *Jobs* is in the plural form. *Their* is possessive, not the contraction for *they are* (they're).

Question 30

The correct answer is G. "Your" and "your students'" both modify "minds" here, and *students* is in the plural possessive form.

Question 31

The correct answer is A. The clause "the largest country in mainland Southeast Asia" more fully describes Burma and is an appositive. It can be set off correctly with commas or dashes, as it is here.

Question 32

The correct answer is H. The period is necessary and is placed within the parentheses.

Question 33

The correct answer is D. The paragraph is written in the past tense.

Question 34

The correct answer is F. Titles are capitalized only when they come before the person's name, as in "Ambassador Wilson," so in this case it is not capitalized and there is no need for the comma.

Question 35

The correct answer is D. The phrase takes the reader back to the subject of the ensuing paragraph.

Question 36

The correct answer is J. *Horribly* is an adverb and *horrible* is an adjective. The sentence discusses how the people (an irregular plural) "were treated," so the adverbial form is correct.

Question 37

The correct answer is D. The phrase in commas further explains Daw Suu and can be removed from the sentence without changing the sentence's meaning.

Question 38

The correct answer is H. All of the initial letters of the party's name should be capitalized here.

Question 39

The correct answer is B. None of these words should be capitalized because they are not being used as proper nouns.

Question 40

The correct answer is G. The paragraph is written in the past tense and the sentence is organized more logically when it begins with the introductory clause.

Question 41

The correct answer is D. The passage is in the past tense.

Question 42

The correct answer is J. The phrase says that she has neither money nor food.

Question 43

The correct answer is A. "On account of" is not appropriate here and the work she did for the prize was for all the people of Burma.

Question 44

The correct answer is H. The sentence is in the past tense.

Question 45

The correct answer is C. *Today* means "in the present day" here and can't directly modify any of the nouns in the sentence.

Question 46

The correct answer is J. The words said by the students belong in quotes and a comma separates "pleased to meet you" from the rest of the sentence.

Question 47

The correct answer is C. *Students* is in the plural form and the sentence is in the past tense.

Question 48

The correct answer is F. This sentence does not need any commas.

Question 49

The correct answer is A. The commas here are needed to separate each of the phrases listed.

Question 50

The correct answer is F. The commas here are around an appositive.

Question 51

The correct answer is C. There is no need for commas in this sentence.

Question 52

The correct answer is G. The verb *isn't* is singular, as is *enough of a reward*.

Question 53

The correct answer is B. The students weren't taught "for" anything, they were simply taught. "For whom" is not appropriate here. "Whom" refers to people and is used instead of "that."

Question 54

The correct answer is J. Since the gentleman is a person, *who* is correct here. *Immigrate* means to come into a country.

Question 55

The correct answer is B. This phrase is in the future tense.

Question 56

The correct answer is H. The other choices are not grammatically correct.

Question 57

The correct answer is A. The sentence is correct as it is, and the other choices are not grammatically correct and are not used in standard English.

Question 58

The correct answer is J. *Driven* is correct here as it is the past tense. *Passed* means the past tense of the verb *pass*; the word here is the preposition *past*.

Question 59

The correct answer is D. The plural form of *neighborhoods*, not the possessive, is needed here. *The* is not needed before *neighborhoods*.

Question 60

The correct answer is J. *Who* is used here because it is the subject of the verb. *Does* is not correct, as *many* is considered to be plural.

Question 61

The correct answer is C. *Types* must be used here to show that more than one type of water is being discussed.

Question 62

The correct answer is J. "Available water" is redundant here.

Question 63

The correct answer is A.

Question 64

The correct answer is H. The name of the county is separated from the state name by a comma. There is a comma after Michigan because this is an introductory phrase.

Question 65

The correct answer is C. Well testing is singular, and *testings* is not appropriate.

Question 66

The correct answer is J. This is a run-on sentence and should be made into two sentences to be correct.

Question 67

The correct answer is A. *Irregardless* is not grammatically correct, so these responses can be dismissed. *Regardless* is being used as an introductory phrase, so a comma is needed after it.

Question 68

The correct answer is H. More than one analysis is going on, so the plural form of the word must be used. The colon is not necessary in this sentence.

Question 69

The correct answer is C. *Tainting* is used here as the sentence is in the present tense—something *is not tainting* the water.

Question 70

The correct answer is G. The comma is needed to separate the two characteristics of the water, but nothing else in this phrase.

Question 71

The correct answer is C. Substitute *they* for waters if there is confusion here. *Waters* is plural, so *don't* is correct here. "Really good" is a slang phrase that is not grammatically correct.

Question 72

The correct answer is G. The entire question plus question mark must appear in the quotes.

Question 73

The correct answer is A. The passage tells us that the water has a good flavor and that it's natural. Careful placement of hyphens ensures that it does not say "flavored" water. Adverbs ending in -*ly* are not joined with adjectives with a hyphen.

Question 74

The correct answer is H. The singular possessive is used here.

Question 75

The correct answer is A. The phrase "sales representative" is a type of job and is not in the possessive form.

Reading

1. D	15. D	29. A
2. G	16. H	30. J
3. A	17. C	31. C
4. H	18. J	32. G
5. B	19. B	33. A
6. G	20. J	34. H
7. A	21. B	35. D
8. G	22. H	36. H
9. B	23. D	37. D
10. J	24. F	38. G
11. C	25. C	39. A
12. F	26. J	40. G
13. B	27. C	
14. J	28. G	

wrong

36/40 correct!

Question 1

The correct answer is D. The passage mentions that the narrator is looking back 25 years, to her 18-year-old self.

Question 2

The correct answer is G. The passage says that the narrator slows down to avoid getting a ticket.

Question 3

The correct answer is A. The narrator mentions that in the future she may again have a sports car of her own.

Question 4

The correct answer is H. The narrator discusses how she enjoys stopping to fill up the MG's gas tank.

Question 5

The correct answer is B. The narrator's actions can't be taken as shy, or diffident.

Question 6

The correct answer is G. The narrator makes light of her changed self-image after 25 years.

Question 7

The correct answer is A. It can be inferred that the clerk is bored by the narrator and does not even notice the sports car parked outside.

Question 8

The correct answer is G. The narrator talks about the fraternity of MG Midget drivers.

Question 9

The correct answer is B. The narrator mention how she makes a mental list of what she needs to do each day.

Question 10

The correct answer is J. The passage makes reference to the van as a beast.

Question 11

The correct answer is C. The passage discusses the recent news about carbon dating of a newly excavated area, which disputes long-held beliefs about early settlers.

Question 12

The correct answer is F. According to the passage, the island is barren and can't be inhabited.

Question 13

The correct answer is B. The passage discusses the idea that the area from which samples are excavated determines the age of the samples. Finding the correct area is crucial to finding the settlement period.

Question 14

The correct answer is J. The passage mentions that it is a beach area, making it a logical landing place for early settlers arriving by sea.

Question 15

The correct answer is D. It is believed that the area was made barren, stripped of trees, by the early settlers.

Question 16

The correct answer is H. The passage tells how Polynesian settlers arrived on that island in 900 AD.

Question 17

The correct answer is C. The passage discusses how the Polynesian settlers most likely began their statue building immediately upon their arrival on the island.

Question 18

The correct answer is J. The island is bare.

Question 19

The correct answer is B. The passage states that the statues are still present on the island and are closely linked to Easter Island's identity.

Question 20

The correct answer is J. The passage discusses how the island is largely barren.

Question 21

The correct answer is B. Context clues in the passage suggest that those who are bitten by the bug love the sport.

Question 22

The correct answer is H. The passage mentions that triathletes train to better their previous recorded time.

Question 23

The correct answer is D. It can be inferred from the passage that veteran athletes have taken part in a previous competition.

Question 24

The correct answer is F. This information is inferred from the passage.

Question 25

The correct answer is C. The passage discusses how swimmers practice taking off the wetsuit because it is a difficult transition.

Question 26

The correct answer is J. The passage mentions that taking a day off is a training tip that is not taken advantage of by enough athletes.

Question 27

The correct answer is C. The passage discusses that a triathlete might want to work toward taking part in a national triathlon.

Question 28

The correct answer is G. The passage talks about how this leg of the triathlon is a difficult one, so bricking should be used in training.

Question 29

The correct answer is A. This information is presented in the passage.

Question 30

The correct answer is J. Training logs are primarily personal journals.

Question 31

The correct answer is C. The context clues in the passage tell us that the theory was proven by Ptolemy and written about in a widely known work.

Question 32

The correct answer is G. The passage mentions that some scientists, researchers, and astronomers were not in agreement with Ptolemy's ideas.

Question 33

The correct answer is A. The introductory paragraph provides an overview of Ptolemy's work. The other responses provide details that are discussed in subsequent paragraphs.

Question 34

The correct answer is H. The passage discusses how the geocentric theory said that the Earth was the center of the universe with the planets rotating clockwise around it.

Question 35

The correct answer is D. The passage mentions that over time the theory became more widely accepted by the church because the Bible referred to the sun being in motion and the Earth standing still.

Question 36

The correct answer is H. A heretic is a person who goes against church teaching.

Question 37

The correct answer is D. The passage describes retrograde as this type of rotation.

Question 38

The correct answer is G. The passage mentions that the planets were thought to be just the five listed.

Question 39

The correct answer is A. Ptolemy's trigonometric formulas are still in use today.

Question 40

The correct answer is G. An imprudent person is irresponsible or rash, which doesn't describe Ptolemy.

Math

1. C	21. A	41. D
2. F	22. K	42. G
3. E	23. D	43. A
4. H	24. G	44. G
5. D	25. E	45. C
6. H	26. H	46. J
7. D	27. D	47. B
8. G	28. G	48. K
9. E	29. A	49. E
10. J	30. F	50. K
11. A	31. C	51. E
12. H	32. J	52. J
13. B	33. D	53. E
14. G	34. G	54. F
15. D	35. D	55. B
16. J	36. G	56. G
17. D	37. D	57. D
18. K	38. G	58. H
19. E	39. B	59. C
20. H	40. J	60. J

Question 1

The correct answer is C. Apply the Pythagorean theorem $c = \sqrt{a^2 + b^2}$ with a and b as the two short sides and c as the hypotenuse. The equation becomes thus:

$$c = \sqrt{6^2 + 7^2}$$

$$c = \sqrt{36 + 49}$$

$$c = \sqrt{85}.$$

Question 2

The correct answer is F. Mary is dividing the height and the length by 90 to create her model.

Question 3

The correct answer is E. To find the average, take the sum of all of the test scores and divide it by the number of tests:

$$90 = 93 + 86 + 87 + \frac{x}{4}$$

If you cross-multiply, you will get:

$$360 = 266 + x$$

$$x = 94$$

Question 4

The correct answer is H. To solve, use the Pythagorean theorem $a^2 + b^2 = c^2$:

$$9^2 + 12^2 = c^2$$

$$81 + 144 = 225$$

$$\sqrt{225} = 15$$

Question 5

The correct answer is D. Multiply the number of choices for each spot: 3 vans $\times$ 4 pickup trucks $\times$ 5 sedans = 60.

Question 6

The correct answer is H. To solve, find the solution for y and then plug it into the equation to find x. Change the second equation to $y = 5 - x$. Now insert the value for y into the first equation:

$3x - (5 - x) = 7$

$3x - 5 + x = 7$

$4x - 5 = 7$

$4x = 12$

$x = 3$

Question 7

The correct answer is D. To solve, watch signs and plug -3 in for x:

$[3 \times (-3^2)] - 4(-3) - 3$

$(3 \times 9) + 12 - 3$

$27 + 12 - 3 = 36$

Question 8

The correct answer is G. The numbers under the square root sign must first be added together and then the square root taken.

Question 9

The correct answer is E. This problem can be most easily solved by using your calculator.

Question 10

The correct answer is J. To find the rate he traveled, divide the distance by the amount of time he took. In this case, divide 260 by 5 to get 52. He traveled 52 mph for the 5 hours. Now multiply 52 mph by the remaining 2 hours, to get 104 miles. Add the 104 to the original figure of 260 to get the total miles traveled.

Question 11

The correct answer is A. The formula for slope is $\frac{y^2 - y^1}{x^2 - x^1}$. Therefore, the answer is:

$\frac{8 - (-1)}{-2 - 4}$

$\frac{9}{-6}$

$\frac{-3}{2}$

Question 12

The correct answer is H. You can use the Pythagorean theorem to solve this problem, but a quicker way to find the answer is to notice that this is a 3/4/5 right triangle, and you can see that the legs have been multiplied by 5. The third leg = 25.

Question 13

The correct answer is B. Factoring the equation is a fine way to solve the problem, but the most efficient way to solve this is to plug all of the answers into the equation and see which ones do not work. Eliminate those answers and -6 and 2 are the only values that work.

Question 14

The correct answer is G. To solve, draw the triangle described. Solve by using the SOHCAHTOA calculations, remembering that the longest side is the hypotenuse and the smallest angle is the angle opposite the shortest triangle leg (2). The cosine of the angle is the adjacent leg divided by the hypotenuse, 2 $\sqrt{4}$. Reduce this to $\sqrt{3}/2$.

Question 15

The correct answer is D. The average of the first six tests is 65, so we multiply 6×65 to find their total (390). If his average after seven tests is 66, we find the total by multiplying 7×66 (462). We subtract to find the score on the seventh test (72).

Question 16

The correct answer is J. Divide the part (9) by the whole (30) and multiply the result by 100 to find the percent.

Question 17

The correct answer is D. If Donald is x years old, then Mandy is $(x - 2)$ years old. Three years ago Mandy was $(x - 2) - 3 = x - 5$ years old.

Question 18

The correct answer is K. To solve, first find the length of the unknown side. You know the right side (x) must be equal to 36 cm because the angles forming it are right angles. You can calculate that side then as $36 = 8 + 8 + x$. $x = 20$. Adding the sides gives you $36 + 40 + 40 + 8 + 8 + 20 + 16 + 16 = 184$.

Question 19

The correct answer is E. There are originally 28 marbles in the bag, with 10 blue ones. Eddie removes one blue marble immediately, making the bag total 27 marbles, 9 of which are blue. The probability of Eddie pulling a blue marble next is $\frac{9}{27}$, which reduces to $\frac{1}{3}$.

Question 20

The correct answer is H. To solve, use the SOHCAHTOA formula, so cosine = adjacent over hypotenuse. This is a 3/4/5 right triangle, so cosine $\theta = \frac{4}{5}$.

Question 21

The correct answer is A. Solve for x by using the second equation ($x + y = 5$) to find that $x = 5 - y$. Now plug $5 - y$ into the first equation for x to get:

$3(5 - y) - y = 10$

$15 - 4y = 10$

$5 = 4y$

$y = 1\frac{1}{4}$.

Question 22

The correct answer is K. First find Will's age. If he was x years old 12 years ago, then he is now $x + 12$. Dale is 8 years older than Will, so he is $x + 12 + 8$, or $x + 20$.

Question 23

The correct answer is D. <C = 20° (one-third of <A). The angles of a triangle add up to 180° so <B = 100°.

Question 24

The correct answer is G. Write Lisa's stars as $n + 7$ and Thomas' stars as $n + (7 - 2) = n + 5$. Add them all together: $n + (n + 7) + (n + 5) = 3n + 12$. Factor this to $3(n + 4)$.

Question 25

The correct answer is E. If the perimeter of a square is 4 feet, then each side measures 1 foot. The area of the square is 1 square foot (one side, squared). When the area of the square doubles, it becomes 2 square feet. Each side would be the square root of the area, $\sqrt{2}$ square feet. Now we have the new length of each side of the square. To find the perimeter, add all sides, so $4\sqrt{2}$ is the perimeter.

Question 26

The correct answer is H. If you substitute each of the coordinates shown (2, 2), (0,0), (-3, 3) into the answers given, you will see that just $y = /x/$ works for all ordered pairs.

Question 27

The correct answer is D. Multiply 75.99 times 35%, then subtract the $5. This is the savings. Now subtract the amount saved from the original figure of $75.99.

Question 28

The correct answer is G. To find the mean (the average), add the numbers together and divide by 3.

Question 29

The correct answer is A. To find slope (m), use the formula $\frac{y_2 - y_1}{x_2 - x_1}$:

$$m = \frac{7 - 5}{4 - (-3)} = \frac{2}{7}$$

Question 30

The correct answer is F. To find the area of the sector, create the proportion: area of sector/area of circle $= \frac{\text{central angle}}{360°}$.

$$\frac{x}{\pi r^2} = \frac{60°}{360}$$

$$\frac{x}{36\pi} = \frac{1}{6}$$

$$6x = 36\pi$$

$$x = 6\pi$$

Question 31

The correct answer is C. To solve, recall that when adding radicals, the number in the square root must be the same. Change $\sqrt{32}$ to $\sqrt{4}\sqrt{8}$. Then add: $6\sqrt{} + 2\sqrt{8} = 8\sqrt{8}$.

Question 32

The correct answer is J. Recall that an isosceles triangle has both two equal sides and two equal angles. Subtract 50° from 180° to get 130°. The two remaining angles must be equal, so divide 130 by 2 to get 65°.

Question 33

The correct answer is D. To solve, first find a common denominator so that the fractions can be added. The common denominator is sin x.

sin x/1 times sin x/sin x + cos²x/sin x = sin²x/sin x + cos²x/sin x

= sin²x + cos²x /sin x. Remember that sin²x + cos²x = 1. So sin²x + cos²x /sin x = 1/sin x.

Question 34

The correct answer is G. To solve, substitute the known root for the value of x and solve the equation:

$(5 \times 5) + 5k - 10 = 0$

$15 + 5k = 0$

$(15 - 15) + 5k = 0 - 15$

$5k = -15$

$k = -3$

Question 35

The correct answer is D. Recall that the sum of the lengths of two sides of a triangle must exceed the third side's length. If the sides are added together, only choice D is higher than the third side, 14.

Question 36

The correct answer is G. Recall that the sides of a rhombus have equal length.

$5x + 3 = 2x + 6$

$3x = 3$

$x = 1$

Question 37

The correct answer is D. If this question seems difficult to solve, try using the FOIL method on each answer choice.

Question 38

The correct answer is G. To find the circumference, use the formula $2\pi r$:

$\pi d = 10\pi$

Question 39

The correct answer is B. Recall that the interior angles on the same side of a transversal are supplementary angles. They equal 180°:

$x + 20 + x - 10 = 180$

$2x + 10 = 180$

$2x = 170$

$x = 85$

Question 40

The correct answer is J. Set this up as a proportion to solve:

$\frac{20}{x} = \frac{4}{100}$

$2000 = 4x$

$x = 500$

Question 41

The correct answer is D. First, find the side of the triangle. With a perimeter of 24, each side is $\frac{24}{3}$, or 8. The area is found by using the formula (s = side, A = area):

$A = \frac{s^2}{8\sqrt{3}}$

$A = \frac{8^2}{8\sqrt{3}} = 8\sqrt{3}$

Question 42

The correct answer is G. The formula for $\tan\theta = \dfrac{\text{opposite side to angle}\theta}{\text{adjacent side to angle}\theta}$:

$\frac{4}{3} = \frac{20}{x}$

$4x = 60$

$x = 15$

Question 43

The correct answer is A. The circumference (C) is $\pi = 2\pi r$. Solve for r, canceling out the π on both sides of the equation and divide by 2:

$r = \frac{1}{2}$

Question 44

The correct answer is G. Multiply numbers and add exponents.

Question 45

The correct answer is C. To find the midpoint, divide the line segment by 2. Each segment is equal to 10.

Question 46

The correct answer is J. To find percent, divide the portion of the trip by the whole trip and multiply by 100:

$$(\frac{x}{6})100 = \frac{100x}{6}\%$$

Question 47

The correct answer is B. To find probability, use the formula

$$\frac{\text{number of possible successful spins}}{\text{number of possibilities}}:$$

$$\frac{2}{5}$$

Question 48

The correct answer is K:

$$(3.5 \times 10^5)^2 = (3.5 \times 10^5)(3.5 \times 10^5)$$

$$12.25 \times 10^{10}$$

Question 49

The correct answer is E. To find the slope, use the formula y = mx + b, where m equals the slope and b equals the y-intercept:

$$(y-4) = \frac{1}{2}(x + 4)$$

$$2y-8 = x + 4$$

$$2y = x + 12$$

$$y = \frac{1}{2}x + 6$$

The slope $= \frac{1}{2}$, and the y-intercept = 6.

Question 50

The correct answer is K. By cross-multiplying the numbers, we get:

$2x = 30$

$x = 15$

Question 51

The correct answer is E. To solve, multiply together the two variables: $5 \times 3 = 15$.

Question 52

The correct answer is J. Recall that the diagonals of a parallelogram bisect each other, so $\overline{AE} = \overline{EC}$:

$3x - 6 = 18$

$3x = 24$

$x = 8$

Question 53

The correct answer is E. As a 3/4/5 triangle is a right triangle, the larger acute angle falls opposite the larger side. To find the sine of this angle:

$$\sin s = \frac{\text{side opposite angle}}{\text{hypotenuse}} = \frac{4}{5}$$

Question 54

The correct answer is F. Substitute 5 into the equation for the value of x and solve the equation:

$5^2 + 5t - 10 = 0$

$15 + 5t = 0$

$5t = -15$

$t = -3$

Question 55

The correct answer is B. Change each fraction to a decimal to find the greatest value.

Question 56

The correct answer is G. Use the formula $\frac{\text{amount of interest}}{\text{amount invested}} \times 100$:

$$\frac{50}{1000} \times 100 = 5\%$$

Question 57

The correct answer is D. Recall that distance = rate × time. Find the rate of Train A: 60 (3) = 180. Now add $180 + 3r = 255$ to find Train B's rate:

$3r = 75$

$r = 25$

Question 58

The correct answer is H. If the numbers are all written in a set {60, 60, 60, 60, 60, 70, 70, 70, 70, 70, 80, 80, 80, 80, 80, 80, 80}, the *median* (the number falling in the center of the set) is 70.

Question 59

The correct answer is C:

$\frac{x}{11} = 15$

$x = 165$

$\frac{165}{20} = \$8.25$

Question 60

The correct answer is J:

$2x^2 - 3x - 2 = 0$

$(2x + 1)(x - 2) = 0$

$2x + 1 = 0, x = -\frac{1}{2}$

$x - 2 = 0$

$x = 2$

$| (-\frac{1}{2}) (2)$

$/-1/ = 1$

Science

1. D	15. B	29. A
2. F	16. F	30. H
3. C	17. C	31. B
4. H	18. G	32. H
5. D	19. A	33. B
6. H	20. H	34. G
7. A	21. C	35. C
8. F	22. F	36. F
9. A	23. A	37. C
10. G	24. F	38. J
11. D	25. D	39. A
12. F	26. F	40. H
13. B	27. C	
14. J	28. G	

4 wrong
36 correct!

Question 1

The correct answer is D. *Lycopersicon esculentum L.* seedlings subjected to mean human talking grew largest and bore the most fruit.

Question 2

The correct answer is F. The results show that kind human talking and mean human talking yielded the largest plants, which also bore the most fruit, thus a human's release of carbon dioxide may help plants grow. The passage also mentions that sunlight, water, and growing compound are held consistent in all five chambers, so these should have no impact on the results.

Question 3

The correct answer is C. This is based on the results in the table.

Question 4

The correct answer is H. The experiment and its results will be valid only if all of the plants have an equal chance of further growth.

Question 5

The correct answer is D. The results show a human's release of carbon dioxide has an impact on how tall *Lycopersicon esculentum L.* seedlings grow. The next logical experiment should test whether different humans have an impact on the level of carbon dioxide the plants receive.

Question 6

The correct answer is H. Both scientists agree that earthquakes can be predicted; they disagree on how to predict them.

Question 7

The correct answer is A. Scientist 2's passage states that the Earth itself provides clues on when an earthquake will hit.

Question 8

The correct answer is F. Each scientist discusses this in his respective passage.

Question 9

The correct answer is A. Scientist 1 argues that earthquakes can be predicted using historical research.

Question 10

The correct answer is G. Scientist 2 argues that the Earth itself provides clues, including the amount of shifting between plates, as to when a large earthquake will hit.

Question 11

The correct answer is D. The background paragraph explains this.

Question 12

The correct answer is F. Scientist 1 argues that earthquakes can be predicted using historical research.

Question 13

The correct answer is B. This is based on information in the table.

Question 14

The correct answer is J.

Question 15

The correct answer is B. A jet engine 150 feet away measures 150 decibels, meaning that it is the loudest sound.

Question 16

The correct answer is F. A jet engine 150 feet away measures 150 decibels, whereas a jet engine 2,000 feet away measures only 105 decibels.

Question 17

The correct answer is C. This is based on the "Human Response" column of the table.

Question 18

The correct answer is G.

Question 19

The correct answer is A. The chart remains steady at 65% of free throws made at 10, 11, and 12 hours of sleep. Assume this trend will continue.

Question 20

The correct answer is H. In most cases, a higher percentage of shots were made in experiment 1, which tracked consecutive hours of sleep.

Question 21

The correct answer is C. The experiment wished to test how humans perform routine tasks based on the amount of sleep they received. This is the next logical step to that experiment.

Question 22

The correct answer is F. The group performed the task best when it received between 8 and 10 hours of sleep.

Question 23

The correct answer is A. This is based on data in the passage.

Question 24

The correct answer is F. The table shows that radiation from Polonium^{210} could not pass through paper, which the background information says is a characteristic of an alpha particle.

Question 25

The correct answer is D. The passage shows that the half-life of Strontium^{90} is 28.5 years.

Question 26

The correct answer is F. This is based on the background information in each experiment.

Question 27

The correct answer is C. Thallium^{204} releases beta radiation.

Question 28

The correct answer is G. Since the element's radioactive particles pass through paper, but not aluminum, they are beta particles.

Question 29

The correct answer is A. The half-life and radiation emitted are similar to those of Strontium^{90}.

Question 30

The correct answer is H. This is based on information in Chart 1.

Question 31

The correct answer is B. The pulleys will add weight to the system, thus decreasing the size of the actual load that can be moved.

Question 32

The correct answer is H. The mechanical advantage will be 6. If the man can exert 200 pounds (lbs) of force, he can move a 1,200-pound package.

Question 33

The correct answer is B. Assume the line on the chart continues going downward to the origin.

Question 34

The correct answer is G. This is based on the information found in Diagram 2.

Question 35

The correct answer is C. According to Diagram 1, the data points to Experiment 2, the one where the metal blocker was used.

Question 36

The correct answer is F. Diagram 1 shows that a 40-mph wind in Experiment 1 registered a 7 on the Beaufort scale. According to Table 1, this would result in difficulty walking.

Question 37

The correct answer is C. Table 1 shows that whole gale winds occur between 55 mph and 63 mph.

Question 38

The correct answer is J. This is based on the background information on each experiment.

Question 39

The correct answer is A. In both experiments, the blockers were effective in increasing the minimum wind speeds required to measure another point on the Beaufort scale.

Question 40

The correct answer is H. This is based on either Table 1 or Diagram 1.

Scoring Your Sample Test

Number of Questions Answered Correctly

↙ 26.8

Scaled Score	English	Math	Reading	Science
36	75	60	40	40
35	73–74	58–59	38–39	39
34	72	57	37	38
33	71	56	(36)	37
32	70	55	35	(36)
31	68–69	53–54	34	35
30	67	53	33	34
29	65	52	32	33
28	65	50–51	31	33
27	64	48–49	30	32
26	63	45–47	29	32
25	61–62	(43–44)	27–28	31
24	58–60	39–42	25–26	29–30
23	56–57	37–38	22–24	28
22	53–55	34–36	21	27
21	50–52	32–33	20	24–26
20	(48–49)	29–31	19	22–23
19	45–47	26–28	18	20–21
18	42–44	22–25	17	18–19
17	39–41	18–21	16	17
16	36–38	16–17	15	16
15	34–35	14–15	14	15
14	32–33	13	12–13	13–14
13	30–31	12	10–11	12
12	28–29	10–11	9	11
11	24–27	9	8	9–10
10	20–23	8	7	8
9	17–19	6–7	6	8
8	13–16	5	5	7
7	11–12	4	5	6
6	9–10	3	4	5
5	7–8	3	4	4
4	6–7	3	3	3
3	4–5	2	2	2
2	1–3	1	1	1
1	0	0	0	0

Use the number of questions you answered correctly in each section to find your approximate ACT scaled score. To estimate your composite (overall) ACT score, add your individual section scores and divide by 4:

Read Questions more carefully

English: _____ 20 _____

Math: _____ 25 _____   ← *Just keep working at it*

Reading: _____ 33 _____   ← *so close!*

skip to the questions

Science: _____ 32 _____

Composite: _____ 27.5 _____ ← *need a 28!*

Although the sample test in this book isn't an official ACT test, it will provide a close approximation of actual test results if you take it under conditions similar to those you'll face when you take the ACT. You can use the Scoring Your Sample Test table to convert your raw score—the number of questions you answered correctly on each test section—into the scaled score that the ACT uses to report your results. Your composite (overall) ACT score is the average of your section scores. Add the scaled section scores and divide by 4 to get the composite score. Remember, this is only an approximation. Many factors affect your actual performance on test day.

PART III
Appendixes

Appendix A Glossary

Appendix B Additional Resources

Glossary

A

absolute value   The absolute value of a number is its size. For example, |-3 is 3 because -3 is 3 units from 0. Absolute value is always positive.

acceleration   Any change in motion from a state of uniform motion in a straight line or a position at rest. The units are meters per second squared (m/s^2 or m/s/s). Time appears twice because it is a rate of a rate: change in speed/time.

acceleration due to gravitational force   Objects in free fall (no air resistance) at the surface of the Earth will fall with an acceleration equal to $9.8 \ m/s^2$. Acceleration due to gravitational force is represented with the symbol g.

acute angle   An angle that has a measure less than 90°.

adjacent angles   Angles that share a common ray.

adjective   A word that modifies a noun or a pronoun.

adverb   A word that modifies a verb, adjective, or other adverb.

alleles   Different forms of a gene.

amino acids   The building blocks of proteins. There are 20 essential amino acids. The sequence of amino acids determines protein structure and function.

amplitude   The maximum distance above and below the x axis in the graphs of sine and cosine.

angle   Two rays that begin at a common point and form an angle.

antecedent   The word or phrase to which a pronoun refers.

apostrophe   A mark of punctuation that is (1) used to show where letters have been left out of a contraction, and (2) added to a noun to show possession.

arc   An arc is part of a circle. It consists of two points on the circle and all points in between them.

area   The number of square units it takes to completely cover a closed figure.

arithmetic sequence   A sequence that has a common difference between terms. The sequence is formed by adding the same constant amount to the first term and each succeeding term that follows.

atmospheric pressure   The amount of force per unit area. Commonly measured in millimeters of mercury. Atmospheric pressure at sea level will support a column of mercury that is 760 millimeters high. As the symbol for mercury is Hg, 1 atmosphere is equal to 760 mm Hg. Alternatively, pressure can be measured in Newtons per square meter or Pascals (1 N/m^2 = 1 Pa). As altitude increases, there is less atmosphere above you, and the atmospheric pressure decreases.

B

base   When a number or term is raised to a power, the base is the lower number or term that gets multiplied a specified number of times. In $x3$, x is the base.

base pair   Two nitrogenous bases bonded together in the DNA molecule. The DNA molecule is made of four different nitrogenous bases: adenine, cytosine, guanine, and thymine. Adenine bonds with thymine, and cytosine bonds with guanine. The sequence of base pairs in the DNA molecule is the basis of heredity.

Bernoulli's principle   States that the pressure in a fluid or a gas decreases when the velocity of the fluid increases.

biomass   The total amount of living tissue present within a given trophic level.

Boyle's law   States that the pressure and volume of a gas at constant temperature are inversely proportional to each other. Also, for any sample of a gas at constant temperature, pressure multiplied by volume remains constant: $P_1 V_1 = P_2 V_2$.

buoyant force   The upward force on a submerged or partially submerged object. Equal to the weight of the water displaced by the object.

C

calorimeter   Any apparatus that measures the heat released from a substance.

central angle   An angle whose vertex is at a circle's center.

Charles's law   States that at constant pressure, the volume of a gas is directly proportional to its temperature. Also, at constant pressure, volume multiplied by temperature remains constant: $V_1 T_1 = V_2 T_2$.

chord   A line segment that connects two points on a circle.

circle   The set of all points in a plane that are equidistant from a center point. The standard form for the equation of a circle is $(x–h)^2 + (y–k)^2$, where (h, k) is the center of the circle and r is the radius of the circle.

circumference   The distance around a circle. The circumference is given by the formula $2\pi r$, where r is the length of the radius of the circle.

codon A sequence of three nucleotides found in the messenger RNA molecule during translation that codes for a single amino acid.

colon A mark of punctuation following a clause that can stand by itself. It separates that clause from the list that follows it.

colorimeter A device that measures the absorption of different wavelengths of light.

combination An arrangement of a set of objects in which order is not important. You can use the fundamental counting principle to find the number of possible arrangements of a set of ordered objects, then divide by the factorial of the number of objects being selected to eliminate the effect of order.

comma A mark of punctuation that can be used (1) to separate a phrase that further explains the word the phrase is talking about, (2) to set off added information that can be removed from the sentence, (3) with a conjunction to join two independent clauses (the clauses before and after the comma tell us a complete thought), (4) to set off an introductory phrase in a sentence, (5) to set off a list of adjectives or nouns, and (6) to enclose the name of a person you are writing directly about or talking directly to.

complementary angles Complementary angles add to 90°.

completing the square A method that may be used to find the zeros of any quadratic function. By isolating the terms with variables on one side and then adding a constant to each side so that the variable terms can be written as the square of a binomial, you create an equation that can be solved by taking the square root of both sides.

complex number Numbers in the form $a + bi$, where a is the real component and bi is the imaginary component.

composition When you find the composition of two functions, one function's expression serves as the input for the other. There are two possible notations: $f[g(x)]$ and $f(°g)(x)$. In both notations, $g(x)$ serves as the input for $f(x)$.

concentration The amount of solute dissolved in a solution. Often the number of moles of a solute per liter of solution.

cone A geometric solid whose circular base is joined to its vertex by a curved surface.

congruent Congruent shapes have equal measures and the same shape.

control A trial or series of trials that is conducted to ensure that experimental results are due only to the experimental variable and no bias is introduced by any part of the experimental setup. A control trial maintains the uniform set of conditions found in the experimental trials with the experimental treatment left out.

coordinate plane A two-dimensional representation defined by the intersection of the x-axis and the y-axis.

coordinating conjunction A word (for example, *for, and, nor, but, or, yet, so*) used to connect other words, phrases, and clauses in a sentence.

cosine   In a right triangle, the ratio of the side adjacent to a selected acute angle to the hypotenuse.

cylinder   A geometric solid whose circular bases are joined by a curved surface.

D

Dalton's Law of Partial Pressures   States that the sum of the pressures of each component of a mixture of gases is equal to the pressure of the mixture of gases as a whole ($P_T = p_1 + p_2 + p_3....$)

dash   A mark of punctuation sometimes used to emphasize a part of a sentence that can be segregated from the rest of the sentence.

denominator   The bottom part of a fraction.

density   The mass of an object divided by its volume. Measured in kg/m^3 or g/cm^3.

dependent clause   A clause that cannot stand on its own because it is not a complete thought with a subject and verb.

dependent variable   A variable that depends on the value of an independent variable. By convention, the dependent variable is found on the y-axis of graphs.

diagonal   A line segment, other than a side, that joins two vertices of a polygon.

diameter   A chord that runs through the center of a circle. Its length is always twice the length of the radius.

directly proportional   Two variables are said to be directly proportional when one variable increases and a second related variable also increases, or when one variable decreases and the second variable also decreases.

discriminant   A mathematical expression that predicts what kinds of solutions a quadratic will have. Defined as $b^2 - 4ac$.

distance   The amount of space between two things or points. The base unit is the meter (m). Other commonly used distance units are shown here:

Unit	Symbol	Mathematical Expression
Kilometer	km	1×10^3 meters
Meter	m	Base unit
Centimeter	cm	1×10^{-2} meters
Millimeter	mm	1×10^{-3} meters
Micron	λm	1×10^{-6} meters
Nanometer	nm	1×10^{-9} meters
Angstrom	Å	1×10^{-10} meters

distributive property   States that you can multiply a number outside parentheses with every term or number inside the parentheses in place of simplifying the parentheses first.

divisibility   Capable of being divided, especially with no remainder.

DNA   Deoxyribonucleic acid is the formula for the double-helix molecule, which carries the genetic information for most forms of life. DNA is made up of peptides, which are made up of three parts: a deoxyribose sugar, a phosphate group, and a nitrogenous base.

DNA replication   The creation of new and identical strands of DNA from existing strands of DNA. For cell division to occur, a new copy of DNA must be created so that each daughter cell carries the necessary genetic information.

domain   The set of acceptable input values for a function.

dominance   An organism with a dominant allele present in its genotype will always express the dominant form of the trait in its phenotype. Recessive traits are expressed only when the dominant allele is absent from the genotype. Example: If the allele for tall pea plants is dominant, then a plant that is heterozygous for tall will be tall; a pea plant that is short must be homozygous for the recessive short allele.

drafting   A preliminary form of writing where the focus is on the ideas and less attention is paid to spelling, punctuation, and sentence structure.

E

ecological succession   The predictable progression of change within an ecological community of organisms. Most commonly demonstrated in plant communities through time. Succession begins with a major disturbance followed by the introduction of colonizing species, leading through a progression of characteristic assemblages of species, and ending with a climax community of organisms.

editing   Revising and correcting written work, especially in the area of grammar rules.

electromagnetic spectrum   The spectrum of electromagnetic waves that travel at the speed of light. Visible light is a small part of the electromagnetic spectrum. Ultraviolet radiation has a shorter wavelength than visible light. Infrared radiation has a longer wavelength than visible light.

elimination method   A method used to solve simultaneous equations. The goal is to get one equation that contains only one variable. To do so, any of the equations may be multiplied by a constant so that when the equations are added, one of the variables drops out.

ellipse   A set of points such that the sum of the distances from any point to both foci is always constant. The standard form of an ellipse is $\frac{x^2}{a^2} + \frac{y^2}{b^2} = 1$ or $\frac{x^2}{b^2} + \frac{y^2}{a^2} = 1$.

emigration   The movement of individuals out of a population.

equilateral triangle   A triangle that has sides of equal length.

exclamation mark   A mark of punctuation used to show that a word, phrase, or sentence is emphasized.

exponent When a number or term is being raised to a power, the exponent is the raised number or term and indicates how many times to multiply the base.

exponential function A function of the form $y = a^x$. The base, a, cannot be a negative number, to prevent values of y that are imaginary.

extrapolate To extend a visible trend in the available data.

F

factors Numbers that are multiplied to obtain a product. For example, 3 and 4 are factors of 12.

fiction A story that is not true, but rather made up by an author.

force A push or a pull. Measured in Newtons (N).

frequency The number of times per second something happens. Measured in cycles per second or hertz (Hz).

function Maps a set of input values to a set of output values in such a way that each input value results in exactly one output value. Functions are frequently expressed as $f(x)$, $g(x)$, or $h(x)$.

fundamental counting principle States that if one event can occur m ways and a second event can occur n ways, the total number of ways for the two events to occur is given by $m \times n$.

G

gene A sequence of bases in the DNA molecule that codes for a particular protein.

genotype The genetic make-up of an organism.

geometric sequence A sequence that has a common ratio. The sequence is formed by multiplying the first term and every succeeding term by the same factor.

gravity, or the Law of Universal Gravitation The gravitational force between any two objects is the result of the attraction of their masses. Commonly referred to as the force between an object and the Earth. Also called weight (in Newtons).

greatest common factor (GCF) The biggest factor that two numbers share. The GCF of 16 and 36 is 4.

H

heat The transfer of nonmechanical energy. Given the symbol Q, heat is equal to the mass of a substance times its specific heat capacity times its change in temperature ($Q = mc\lambda T$).

heat of fusion   The amount of heat necessary to change a given amount of solid into liquid.

heat of vaporization   The amount of heat necessary to change a given amount of liquid into vapor.

heterozygous   The genotype of an organism when the alleles for a particular trait are different.

homozygous   The genotype of an organism when the alleles for a particular trait are identical.

hydrostatic pressure   The pressure within a liquid. Hydrostatic pressure increases with increasing depth.

hypotenuse   In a right triangle, the side opposite the 90° angle is the hypotenuse.

I–J

imaginary numbers   Numbers that include the symbol i. By definition, $\sqrt{-1} = i$. The square root of -1 is often encountered when solving a quadratic.

immigration   The movement of individuals into a population.

independent clause   A clause that is a complete thought with a subject and verb.

independent events   Two events are independent if the occurrence of one event does not affect the occurrence of the other event in any way.

independent variable   A variable that causes a change in a dependent variable. The independent variable is the experimental variable, or the variable that is manipulated by the experimenter. By convention, the independent variable is found on the x-axis of graphs.

inequality   A math statement that compares unequal quantities.

inertia   The tendency of mass to resist changes in motion.

inference   The process of deriving logical conclusions from what has been read.

integers   A set of integers contains zero and all other positive and negative numbers that do not have decimal or fractional parts.

interpolate   To estimate a given data point between existing data that displays a visible trend.

inversely proportional   Two variables are said to be inversely proportional when one variable increases and a second related variable decreases.

ion   An atom with a positive or negative charge.

isosceles triangle   A triangle that has two sides of equal length.

isotope   An atom that has the same number of protons but a different number of neutrons. Isotopes of a given element are distinguished by their mass number. For example, carbon-12 and carbon-14 are both isotopes of carbon.

K

kinetic energy   The energy of motion. The kinetic energy is equal to one-half of the mass of a given object in kilograms times the square of its velocity in meters per second ($KE = 1/2\ mv^2$).

L

Law of Cosines   When solving for an unknown measure in a triangle, you can use the Law of Cosines to find the unknown if you do not have the measure of a side and opposite angle as needed in the Law of Sines. The Law of Cosines follows:
$c^2 = a^2 + b^2 - 2ab(\cos C)$. The lowercase letters are side measures, and C represents the measure of the angle opposite side c.

Law of Sines   States the relationships in a triangle between the lengths of the sides and the sines of the angles opposite the sides. It is usually expressed as follows:
$$\frac{a}{\sin A} = \frac{b}{\sin B} = \frac{c}{\sin C}.$$
least common multiple (LCM)   The smallest of the multiples that two numbers have in common. The LCM of 9 and 12 is 36.

line   A set of points that continues infinitely in both directions.

logarithm   Defined by the equation $\log_b A = e$. The equation should be read, "The logarithm of A to the base b equals e."

M

main idea   The topic of a paragraph, essay, or article.

manometer   A device used to measure the pressure of a gas in a closed container.

mass   The amount of matter in an object. Measured in kilograms (kg) or grams (g).

matrix   A rectangular array of numbers or variables. The elements of a matrix are always arranged in rows and columns.

mean (also called average)   The sum of the data set values divided by the number of values in the set.

median   The middle value in a set that has been arranged in ascending order. If there are two values in the middle, the median is their average.

midpoint   A point that divides a segment into two equal lengths.

mode   The most frequent value in a set of data. If no value is repeated, there is no mode. If two values are repeated with equal frequency, there are two modes.

mole   Equal to 6.02×10^{23} particles (Avogadro's number). One mole of a substance has a mass in grams equal to its molecular or formula weight.

molecular weight   The average weight of an atom of a particular element in atomic mass units.

mood   The tone or atmosphere an author creates in a story or poem through attitude, setting, word choices, plot elements, and/or character development.

multiple   The product of a number with any other nonzero whole number. Multiples of 5 are 10, 15, and 20.

N

nonfiction   A piece of writing that is based solely on fact.

noun   A word that names a person, place, or thing.

numerator   The top part of a fraction.

O

obtuse angle   An angle that has a measure more than 90° but less than 180°.

opposing viewpoint   An opinion that is the opposite of the stance you take on a subject or issue.

origin   The point (0,0), where the x-axis and the y-axis meet.

P

parabola   The graph of a quadratic function. If a quadratic equation is given in standard form, $ax^2 + bx + c$, the line of symmetry is found at $\frac{-b}{2a}$.

parallel lines   The slopes of parallel lines are such that the lines never intersect within a plane.

parentheses   Marks of punctuation used to enclose words or phrases that need to appear in a sentence or paragraph, but are not to be emphasized as much as the rest of the sentence or paragraph.

parts per million   The concentration of trace amounts of a substance. Abbreviated as ppm.

percent   A percent is expressed as a ratio whose denominator is 100. The symbol % literally means "per 100."

perimeter   The distance around a closed figure.

period   (1) A mark of punctuation used at the end of a sentence that makes a statement; (2) the number of degrees or radians along the x-axis in which a sine or cosine completes its cycle.

permutation   The arrangement of a set of objects in a particular order. You can use the fundamental counting principle to find the number of possible arrangements of a set of objects.

perpendicular   Lines that intersect in such a way that four right angles are created.

pH scale   The scale that determines whether a substance is acidic, basic, or neutral. The higher the hydronium ion (H_3O^+) concentration, the lower the pH. Seven on the pH scale is neutral. Low pH means the substance is an acid. High pH means it is a base.

phenotype   The outward expression of the genotype of an individual organism.

piecewise functions   Functions represented by several different algebraic expressions that correspond to several different domains.

plasmid   A circular strand of DNA commonly found in bacteria and used in recombinant DNA technology.

plot   The pattern of events in a story.

plural   A noun form used to express that there is more than one of something.

point   In a graph, points are represented by ordered pairs. The first number is the x-coordinate and the second number is the y-coordinate (x,y).

polypeptide   A chain of amino acids bonded together during protein synthesis.

possessive   A noun form that shows ownership.

potential energy   The energy an object possesses because of its position or condition. (The gravitational potential energy of an object is equal to its mass in kilograms times the acceleration due to gravity, 9.8 *m/s²*, times its height in meters [PE = *mgh*]).

power   The amount of work performed per unit time. Usually measured in watts; 1 joule per second is equal to 1 watt.

predator-prey relationship   A relationship in which predators become a dominant form of prey population control.

prime   A counting number greater than 1 whose only factors are 1 and itself. One is not a prime number.

Principle of Square Roots   Given that a squared variable is equal to some constant, the variable has two solutions, one positive and one negative.

probability   The likelihood that a given event will occur as a ratio of favorable outcomes to all possible outcomes.

pronoun   A word used in place of a noun.

proofreading   Reading to look for errors in spelling, grammar, or punctuation.

proportion   States that two ratios are equal in the form of an equation.

pyramid   A geometric solid whose base is a polygon and whose faces are triangles that share a common vertex.

Pythagorean theorem   States that given any right triangle, the following is true: $\text{leg}^2 + \text{leg}^2 = \text{hypotenuse}^2$.

Q

quadrants   The intersection of the x-axis and the y-axis divides the coordinate plane into four quadrants. The first quadrant is in the upper-right corner. The quadrants are labeled counterclockwise from the first quadrant.

quadratic function   A function that can be expressed in the form $f(x) = ax^2 + bx + c$, where a, b, and c are real numbers.

The quadratic formula is used to find the zeros of any quadratic function. The formula follows: $x = \dfrac{-b \pm \sqrt{b^2 - 4ac}}{2a}$.

question mark   A mark of punctuation used at the end of a sentence that asks a question.

quotation marks   A mark of punctuation used to set off material that represents quoted or spoken language.

R

radians   A unit of measure for angles. For any circle, the central angle that corresponds to the arc whose length is one radius is assigned the measure of 1 radian.

radius   The line segment that connects any point on a circle to the center of the circle.

range   (1) The set of possible outcomes for a function; (2) the difference between the largest and smallest number in a set of data.

ratio   A comparison. Ratios are commonly expressed in fraction form, indicating division. If a is compared to b, the implied ratio is $\frac{a}{b}$.

real number set   Includes counting numbers, whole numbers, integers, and rational and irrational numbers.

reciprocal   The reciprocal of a number or expression is the inverted form of the original. A number multiplied by its reciprocal is always 1.

regular polygon   A polygon that has sides of equal length and angles of the same measure.

revising   Changing a draft of written work, usually focusing on content and presentation.

right angle   An angle that measures 90°.

right solid   A solid whose sides meet its base at right angles.

S

salt A substance that dissociates in water, forming a negative ion and a positive ion. A salt can also be the product of an acid-base reaction. Sodium chloride, NaCl, is just one example of a salt.

sector The area enclosed by the rays that make up a central angle and the arc whose endpoints they touch.

semicolon A mark of punctuation used (1) to organize a long and potentially confusing list, or (2) to separate closely related independent clauses that are not joined by a conjunction.

scientific notation Expresses a number as the product of a decimal number and a power of 10.

similar triangles Triangles whose corresponding angles have equal measure. It is also true that the lengths of corresponding sides are proportional.

sine In a right triangle, the ratio of the side opposite a select acute angle to the hypotenuse.

singular A noun form used to express that there is one of something.

sinusoid A curve that resembles the sine curve. The graphs of sine and cosine are sinusoids.

slope The slope of a line is the ratio of the rise to the run between any two points on the line. The slope of a line can be positive or negative. Calculate the slope of any line that passes through (x_1, y_1) and (x_2, y_2) as follows: $\frac{y_2 - y_1}{x_2 - x_1}$.

slope intercept form A linear function can be expressed generally in the slope intercept form as $y = mx + b$, where m represents slope and b represents the y-intercept.

solute The part of a solution that is present in lesser quantity.

solution A homogeneous mixture of two or more substances.

solution (equation) The value that a variable must be in order for the equation to make a true statement.

solvent The part of a solution that is present in greater quantity.

specific heat capacity The amount of heat energy, in joules or calories, required to change 1 gram of a substance by 1° Celsius.

strategy A plan of how something will be done.

style The format a writer uses to write. In creative writing, the style may be unique to the author and reflect his or her personality.

substitution method A method used to solve simultaneous equations. The goal is to get one equation that has only one variable. To do so, the expression for one variable in one equation is substituted for the same variable in a different equation.

supplementary angles   Angles that add to 180°.

supporting details   Details within a piece of writing that back up or emphasize the main idea.

surface area   The sum of the areas of all exposed surfaces of a solid.

symmetry   A figure is symmetric if a line drawn down the middle of the figure results in a mirror image of the two sides.

system of equations   Two or more equations that you consider simultaneously. The solution of a system of equations must be a solution for all equations.

T

tangent   (1) In a right triangle, the ratio of the side opposite the selected acute angle to the side adjacent to the same selected angle: (2) a line within a plane that intersects or touches a circle at only one point.

temperature   The average kinetic energy per molecule of a substance. Measured in degrees Celsius, Kelvin, or Fahrenheit.

Reference	Celsius	Kelvin	Fahrenheit
Absolute zero	−273	0	−459
Freezing point of water	0	273	32
Human body temperature	37	310	98.6
Boiling point of water	100	373	212

time   Measured in seconds (s), hours (hr), months (mo), years (yr), and millions of years (Myr). On graphs, time is always found along the x-axis.

tone   The pitch of a word, phrase, sentence, or paragraph.

transformation   A change made to an original function that results in a new function and corresponding new graph. Transformations may include vertical shifts, horizontal shifts, reflecting about an axis, or a narrowing/widening in shape.

U

undefined   If something is not allowed by math rules, we say it is undefined. Division by zero is undefined.

V

vector   A vector describes a magnitude and a direction. A vector in a plane is a line segment with direction.

velocity   Speed in a given direction.

verb   A word that describes an action.

vertical angles   When two lines intersect, the angles formed that are opposite each other are vertical angles. Vertical angles are always congruent.

viewpoint   An opinion about something.

visible light spectrum   The portion of the electromagnetic spectrum that contains all the visible colors. In order of decreasing wavelength and increasing frequency, the spectral colors are red, orange, yellow, green, blue, indigo, and violet.

volume   (1) The number of cubic units it takes to completely fill a geometric solid; (2) three-dimensional space, or the amount of space occupied by an object. The base unit for measuring the volume of liquids is the liter. Other commonly used volumetric units are shown here:

Measurement	Abbreviation
Liter	L
Milliliter	mL
Cubic meter	m^3
Cubic centimeter	cm^3 or cc
Cubic kilometer	km^3

W

wavelength   The distance between wave crests or similar positions on a wave. The symbol for wavelength is the Greek letter lambda (λ).

work and energy   *Work* is force multiplied by distance. Measured in joules; 1 Newton-meter is equal to 1 joule. *Energy* is needed to perform work and is also measured in joules.

X

x-intercept   The location where a graph crosses the x-axis. Put another way, the x-intercept is the value of x when y is equal to zero.

Y

y-intercept   The location where a graph crosses the y-axis. Put another way, the y-intercept is the value of y when x is equal to zero.

Z

zero factor theorem   States that if two or more factors multiply to zero, at least one of the factors must equal zero.

zeros   The zeros of any polynomial are the x values that cause $f(x)$ to be 0.

Additional Resources

As you prepare for the ACT, you may want to consult other sources. Listed in this appendix are additional resources in each subject area.

English

For additional information and explanation about rules of grammar, punctuation, sentence structure and organization, and other language skills, you may want to read Strunk and White's *The Elements of Style*, or Hopper's *Elements of English*, or look through *The Chicago Manual of Style*.

Hopper, Vincent. *Elements of English*, 5th edition. Hauppauge, New York: Barron's Educational Series (2000).

Strunk, William, Jr., and E. B. White. *The Elements of Style*, 4th edition. White Plains, New York: Longman (2000).

University of Chicago Press. *The Chicago Manual of Style*, 15th edition (2003).

Reading

Reading articles in newspapers such as the *New York Times* and the *Wall Street Journal* will help you increase your fluency and speed. Visit your public library and look for these or for high-quality magazines such as *Atlantic Monthly*, *Harper's*, and *National Geographic*.

Underline details as you read; then after reading an article, jot down on a sheet of paper the answers to these questions: Who, What, Where, When, Why, and How? Refer back to the article for those responses you can't readily recall.

Your English teacher or the media specialist at your school can recommend specific workbooks to increase reading comprehension and speed. One good workbook is *Reading Stories for Comprehension Success*, by Katherine L. Hall.

Hall, Katherine L. *Reading Stories for Comprehension Success*. San Francisco: Jossey-Bass (2000).

Writing

As the test day grows closer, continue to read high-quality writing from magazines, newspapers, and books. Practice writing essays and having your family members, a friend, or a teacher read and comment on your work.

You might want to work with some books specifically devoted to essay writing, such as *Write Better Essays in 20 Minutes a Day* or *Schaum's Quick Guide to Writing Great Essays*. These may be available at your school or local library, and your English teacher may have further recommendations from his or her personal bookshelf that you may be able to borrow for a period of time.

Keep in mind that writing practice is what is essential here. No amount of reading about good writing can make you a good writer—you have to do that on your own. Find time to devote solely to writing, and you will see your essays improve and your essay writing become more automatic.

Write Better Essays in Just 20 Minutes a Day. New York: Learning Express (2006).

McClain, Molly. *Schaum's Quick Guide to Writing Great Essays*. New York: McGraw-Hill Publishing (1998).

Math

The best review for the math ACT test is your high school math textbook. Ask your math teacher to loan you math textbooks from the grade levels in which you may need further review. These will have practice and review sections, as well as in-depth explanations of concepts about which you may need further information.

Bobrow, Jerry. *Cliffs Math Review for Standardized Tests*. Lincoln, Nebraska: Cliffs Notes, Inc. (1985).

Science

To review science concepts for this section of the ACT, it may be most helpful to review science textbooks along with some of the books suggested here. Talk with your science teacher to see whether he or she has textbooks you may borrow and review.

Hewitt, Paul G., John Suchoki, and Leslie Hewitt. *Exploring Conceptual Physical Science*. San Francisco: Addison Wesley (2003).

Miller, Kenneth, R. and Joseph Levine. *Biology*. Upper Saddle River, New Jersey: Prentice Hall (2002).

Bioscience (monthly), Washington DC: The American Institute of Biological Sciences.

Nature (weekly), New York: Nature Publishing Group.

Science (weekly), New York: American Association for the Advancement of Science.

Scientific American (monthly), New York: Scientific American Inc.

General ACT Preparation

ACT Publications, *The Real ACT Prep Guide* (2005).

www.actstudent.org/testprep/index.html (for free sample tests)

Index

NUMBERS

30-60-90 degree triangles, 240
45-45-90 degree triangles, 241

A

abbreviations, science, 266-268, 301
absolute values, 161-163, 225-226, 296
ACT Assessment, 5
    cancellation, 17
    English test
        consistent tone, 72-74
        correct word choice, 73-74
        directions, 24
        expectations, 23-26
        format, 23
        grammar, 46-63
        organization of sentences, 68-70
        paragraph style, 71-72
        passages, 24
        punctuation, 26-45
        sample test questions, 75-79
        sentence structure, 63-68
        sentence style, 71
        strategies, 25
    exam day checklist, 18
    fees, 12
    format overview, 6
    identification, 16-17
    Mathematics test
        basic structure, 153-155
        coordinate graphing, 230-235
        directions, 153
        intermediate algebra, 227-230
        plane geometry, 236-249
        pre-algebra and elementary algebra, 155-226
        sample questions, 256-260

test-taking tips, 154

trigonometry, 249-254

personalized study plan, 9

  schedule setup, 10-11

  study sessions structure, 11

practice exams, 303, 429

  English assessment, 304-326, 385-393, 430-453, 501-508

  Math assessment, 340-361, 400-416, 466-483, 515-525

  Reading assessment, 327-339, 394-399, 454-465, 510-514

  Science Reasoning assessment, 362-383, 417-425, 484-499, 526-530

  scoring, 426-427, 531-532

  Writing assessment, 384, 500

readiness

  ideal candidates, 6-7

  self-assessment, 7-9

Reading test

  content areas, 82-83

  directions, 81-82

  expectations, 81

  order of material, 83

  passage questions, 86-117

  preparation, 83-86

  signal words, 85-86

  time management, 83

registration, 12-13

Science Reasoning test

  challenge questions, 284-291

  reading passages, 261-283

score interpretation, 18-20

special needs accommodations, 13

standards for admission

  Highly Competitive schools, 21

  Less Competitive schools, 21-22

  Moderately Competitive schools, 21

  Most Competitive schools, 20

  Very Competitive schools, 21

test day expectations, 16

test-taking tips, 14-15

Writing test, 119

  challenge exercises, 147-151

  directions, 123-125

  essay scores, 140-141

  practice, 141-146

  preparation, 120-123

  writing process, 125-140

ACT Plus Writing test. See Writing test

ACT Registration, 17

ACT Student website, 19

ACT Test Administration, 17

ACT website, 9

acute angles, 249-250

addition, 158-159, 183

additional information, commas, 31-32

adjectives, 48-49

admission standards

  Highly Competitive schools, 21

  Less Competitive schools, 21-22

  Moderately Competitive schools, 21

  Most Competitive schools, 20

  Very Competitive schools, 21

adverbs, 49-50

algebra (elementary/pre-algebra)

  absolute value, 161-163

  algebraic expressions, 209-220

  arithmetic sequences, 180-181

  bases and exponents, 170-173

  exponents, 170

  factors and multiples, 173-179

  fractions, 183-186

  functions, 197-199

  geometric sequences, 181-183

  linear equations, 220-221

  linear inequalities, 225-226

  matrices, 224-225

  mean, 205-206

  median, 205-208

  mode, 205, 208-209

  operations, 158-161

  powers, 167

  probability, 199-202

  properties, 164-167

  proportion, 203-204

  rate problems, 196-197

  ratio, 203

  roots, 167-170

  rules, 296-298

scientific notation, 163-164

systems of linear equations, 222-224

types of numbers, 155-158

variables in terms of variables, 221-222

algebraic expressions, 209

evaluation, 211-212

factoring, 216

common terms, 216-217

difference of two squares, 219-220

x2 + bx + c format, 217-218

like terms, 212-213

multiplying polynomials, 214-215

multiplying variables, 213

order of operations, 210-211

amplitude (sin and cos graphs), 251

analogies, reading passages (Reading test), 87

analysis (scientific method), 274

angles

acute, 249-250

essays, 130

exterior, 238

geometry notation, 237

interior, 238

related, 250

answers

practice exams

English assessment, 385-393, 501-508

Math assessment, 400-416, 515-525

Reading assessment, 394-399, 510-514

Science Reasoning assessment, 417-425, 526-530

scoring sample tests, 426-427, 531-532

sample questions

English test, 78-79

Mathematics test, 259-260

Reading test, 115-117

antecedent-pronoun agreement, 58-60

anticline, 370

apostrophes (')

contractions, 26

its versus it's, 28

possession, 26-27

your versus you're, 28-29

applications, scientific method, 275-276

arc (circles), 245

area, 237

circle, 299

circles, formula, 245

triangles, 239

arithmetic sequences, 180-181, 297

ascending order, data sets, 279-281

author's point of view, reading passages (Reading test), 88

average, 297

axes

graphs, Science Reasoning test, 269

origin, 230

axis of symmetry (parabola), 232

B - C

bases, 170-171

exponents and different bases, 172-173

negative exponents, 173

billionth (n), 268

body paragraphs, drafting, 133-135

brainstorming (writing process), 127-129

cal (calorie), 268

cancellation, 17

candidates for ACT, 6-7

cause-and-effect relationships, reading passages (reading test), 87

center line (sin and cos graphs), 251

central angles (circles), 245

challenge exercises, writing essays, 147-151

challenge questions, Science Reasoning test, 284-291

character development, reading passages (Reading test), 88

chord (circles), 245

circle equation, 298

circles, 244-246

area, 299

circumference, 245, 299

coordinate graphing, 232

circumference, 245, 299

clauses, separation of with semicolons, 44

coefficient, 212

college admission standards

Highly Competitive schools, 21

Less Competitive schools, 21-22

Moderately Competitive schools, 21

Most Competitive schools, 20

Very Competitive schools, 21

colons (:), 31

lists, 29

setting up quotes, 30

combinations, 200-201

commas (,), 45

additional information, 31-32

enclosing names of persons, 36-37

introductory phrases, 34

joining independent clauses, 32-33

non-essential phrases, 31

series, 34-36

comparisons, reading passages (Reading test), 87

complex numbers, 156

compound subjects, 52-54

conclusion words, reading passages, 85

conclusion/results (scientific method), 274

conclusions, drafting, 135-136

congruent segments, 237

congruent shapes, 238

conjunctions

coordinate, 60-61

subordinate, 61-63

consecutive numbers, 296

consistent tone, English test, 72-74

contact information

ACT Registration, 17

ACT Test Administration, 17

content areas, Reading test, 82-83

contractions, apostrophes, 26

contrast words, reading passages, 85

control group (experiments), 274

conversions, fractions to decimals, 189

coordinate conjunctions, 60-61

coordinate graphing

circles, 232

ellipses, 233

lines, 230

distance between two points, 231-232

parallel and perpendicular, 231

parabolas, 232-233

piecewise functions, 234-235

rules, 298-299

transformations, 234

coordinate pairs, 230

coordinate plane, 230

correct word choice, English test, 73-74

cos graphs, 251-252

cosecant, 299

cosine, 299

cosine ratios, 249

cotangent, 299

counting numbers, 156

critical points (graphs), Science Reasoning test, 271-272

cylinders, surface area, 248

D

dashes (-)

emphasis, 37-38

interruption of a thought, 38

data representation passages, Science Reasoning test

abbreviations, 266-268

graphs, 268-273

data sections, reading passages (Science Reasoning test), 263

data sets, ordering, 279-281

decreasing percentages, 191-195

deductive reasoning, 272

density, 266

dependent variables, 275

descending order, data sets, 279-281

diagonals, 238

diameter (circles), 245

difference of two squares, factoring algebraic expressions, 219-220

digits, 296

direct relationships (graphs), Science Reasoning test, 269-271

direct variation, 269

directions

English test, 24

Mathematics test, 153

Reading test, 81-82

Science Reasoning test, 262

Writing test, 123-125

distance between two points, coordinate graphing, 231-232

distributive property, 164-166, 296

divisibility, 178-179

divisible numbers, 296

division, fractions, 184

domain (functions), 197, 298

double hatch mark, 268

drafting, 130

body paragraphs, 133-135

conclusions, 135-136

introductions, 131-133

E

elementary algebra

absolute value, 161-163

algebraic expressions, 209

evaluation, 211-212

factoring, 216-220

like terms, 212-213

multiplying polynomials, 214-215

multiplying variables, 213

order of operations, 210-211

arithmetic sequences, 180-181

bases and exponents, 170-171

different bases, 172-173

negative exponents, 173

factors and multiples, 173-174

divisibility, 178-179

GCF (greatest common factor), 176-177

LCM (least common multiple), 177-178

prime numbers, 174-176

fractions, 183-184

converting to decimals, 189

equations, 187-189

percentages, 190-196

repeating decimals, 190

word problems, 185-187

functions, 197-199

geometric sequences, 181-183

linear equations, 220-221

linear inequalities, 225-226

matrices, 224-225

mean, 205-206

median, 205-208

mode, 205, 208-209

operations

addition, 158-159

division, 160-161

multiplication, 160-161

subtraction, 160

powers, 167

probability

fundamental counting principle, 199

permutations and combinations, 200-201

rules, 201-202

properties

distributive property, 164-166

reciprocal property, 166-167

proportion, 203-204

rate problems, 196-197

ratio, 203

roots, 167-170

rules, 296-298

scientific notation, 163-164

systems of linear equations, 222-224

types of numbers, 155-158

variables in terms of variables, 221-222

elements, 225

***Elements of English*, 45**

***Elements of Style, The*, 45**

ellipses, coordinate graphing, 233

emphasis, dashes, 37-38

enclosing names of persons, commas, 36-37

English

rules, 295

unit abbreviations, 267-268

English test

consistent tone, 72-74

correct word choice, 73-74

directions, 24

expectations, 23-26

format, 23

grammar
   coordinate conjunctions, 60-61
   parts of speech, 46-50
   pronoun-antecedent agreement, 58-60
   subject-verb agreement, 50-58
   subordinate conjunctions, 61-63
organization of sentences, 68-70
paragraph style, 71-72
passages, 24
practice exams
   answers, 385-393, 501-508
   questions, 304-326, 430-453
punctuation
   apostrophes ('), 26-29
   colons (:), 29-31
   commas (,), 31-37, 45
   dashes (-), 37-38
   exclamation points (!), 38-39
   parentheses (( )), 39-40
   periods (.), 40-41
   question marks (?), 41-42
   quotation marks ("), 42-44
   resources, 45
   semicolons (;), 44-45
readiness self-assessment, 7
sample test questions, 75-79
sentence structures
   fragments, 63-64
   main ideas, 66-68
   run-ons, 64-65
sentence style, 71
strategies, 25
equations
   circles, 298
   factoring, 218
   fractions, 187-189
   linear, 220-224
   rate problems, 196, 298
   simplified, 213
   trigonometry, 253-254
equilateral triangles, 241
essays
   challenge exercises, 147-151
   practice, 141
      finding opposing viewpoints, 142-144
      introductions, 145-146

prewriting essays, 126
   angle, 130
   outlines, 127-128
   viewpoints, 128-129
scoring, 140-141
writing process, 125
   drafting, 130-136
   prewriting, 126-130
   revisions, 136-139
   sample prompt, 139-140
evaluation, algebraic expressions, 211-212
even numbers, 296
exam prep passages (Reading test), 106-111
   correct answers, 115-117
   suggested underlining, 112-114
exam readiness, self-assessment, 8-9
exclamation points (!), 38-39
expectations
   English test, 23-26
   Reading test, 81
   test day, 16
experimental controls, 281
experimental design questions (Science Reasoning test), 281-282
experimental groups, 274
experimental variables, 274-275
experiments
   parts of, 273
      dependent variables, 275
      independent variables, 274-275
      scientific method, 275-276
   predictions based on results, 278
explanations
   Science Reasoning challenge questions, 291
   Writing test directions, 124-125
exponential functions, 229
exponents, 171
   different bases, 172-173
   negative exponents, 173
   rules, 170
expressions
   algebraic, 209
      evaluation, 211-212
      factoring, 216-220
      like terms, 212-213

multiplying polynomials, 214-215

multiplying variables, 213

order of operations, 210-211

positive, 157

radical expressions, 169-170

simplified, 157

undefined, 157

exterior angles, 238

extrapolation, Science Reasoning test, 272-273

extreme data points (graphs), Science Reasoning test, 271

F

factoring, 297

algebraic expressions

common terms, 216-217

difference of two squares, 219-220

x2 + bx + c format, 217-218

equations, 218

expressions, 297

factors, 173

divisibility, 178-179

GCF (greatest common factor), 176-177

LCM (least common multiple), 177-178

prime numbers, 174-176

fees, 12

First terms (FOIL method), 214

FOIL method, 214

foot, 268

force, 270

forming contractions, apostrophes, 26

formulas

area of a circle, 245

area of triangles, 239

circumference, 245

combinations, 201

mean, 206

permutations, 201

quadratic, 228, 298

volume of a solid, 247

forward slash (per), 268

fractional exponents, 296

fractions

addition, 183

converting to decimals, 189

division, 184

equations, 187-189

multiplication, 184

operations, 198

percentages, 190

increases/decreases, 191-195

multiple percent increases/decreases, 195-196

repeating decimals, 190

subtraction, 183

word problems, 185-187

fragments

identification, periods, 41

sentence structure, 63-64

free-writing, 121-123

functions, 197-199, 297

exponential, 229

piecewise, coordinate graphing, 234-235

quadratic, 227-228

reciprocal, 250

fundamental counting principle, 199, 297

G

GCF (greatest common factor), 173, 176-177

general to specific thinking (deductive reasoning), 272

geographical minute, 268

geographical second, 268

geometric sequences, 181-183, 297

geometry, 236

circles, 244-246

notations and markings, 236-237

parallel lines, 239

polygons, 243-244

quadrilaterals, 244

right solids

surface area, 247-248

symmetry, 248-249

volume, 246-247

rules, plane geometry, 299

terms, 237-238

triangles, 239

30-60-90 degree triangles, 240

45-45-90 degree triangles, 241

equilateral triangles, 241

isosceles triangles, 241

Pythagorean theorem, 242

similar triangles, 240

types of angles, 238

grading sample tests. See scoring sample tests, **532**

grammar (English test)

coordinate conjunctions, 60-61

parts of speech

adjectives, 48-49

adverbs, 49-50

nouns, 46

pronouns, 47

verbs, 48

pronoun-antecedent agreement, 58-60

subject-verb agreement, 50

compound subjects, 52-54

problematic situations, 56-58

sentences beginning with phrases/clauses, 54-55

simple subjects, 51-52

subordinate conjunctions, 61-63

graphs, Science Reasoning test

axes, 269

critical points, 271-272

direct and inverse relationships, 269-271

extrapolation, 272-273

extreme data points, 271

identification of trends and patterns, 269

interpolation, 272-273

reading, 269

title, 268

group study, 10

H - I

hexagons, 243

Highly Competitive schools, admission standards, 21

horizontal ellipses, 233

Humanities passages (Reading test), 98

sample passages, 99

sample questions, 100-102

hypotenuse, 242

hypothesis (scientific method), 274-278

ideal test candidates, 6-7

ideas, brainstorming (writing process), 130

identification, 16-17

fragments, periods, 41

trends and patterns, graphs (Science Reasoning test), 269

IEP (Individual Education Plans), 13

imaginary numbers, 156, 296

inches, 268

increasing percentages, 191-194

independent clauses, commas, 32-33

independent events, 201

independent variables, 274-275

indirect variation, 269

inductive reasoning, 272

inequalities, 225-226

inferences, reading passages (Reading test), 88

Inner terms (FOIL method), 214

integers, 156, 296

interior angles, 238

intermediate algebra

exponential functions, 229

logarithms, 229-230

quadratic functions, 227-228

rules, 298-299

interpolation, Science Reasoning test, 272-273

interpretation of scores, 18-20, 140-141

interruption of a thought, dashes, 38

intersection, 237

introductions

drafting, 131-133

essays, practice, 145-146

introductory phrases, commas, 34

inverse relationships (graphs), Science Reasoning test, 269-271

irrational numbers, 156

isolating variables, 220

isosceles triangles, 241

J - K - L

joining independent clauses, commas, 32-33

Large Calorie, 268

Last terms (FOIL method), 214

LCM (least common multiple), 177-178
Less Competitive schools, admission standards, 21-22
like terms, algebraic expressions, 212-213
line of symmetry, 248
line segments, geometry notation, 237
linear approach, writing essays, 131
linear equations, 220-224
linear function, 298
linear inequalities, 225-226
lines
    coordinate graphing, 230-231
    geometry notation, 237
    parallel, 238-239
    perpendicular, 238
    slope, 230
lists
    colons, 29
    organization, semicolons, 44
logarithms, 229-230

M

main ideas
    reading passages, 84-86
    sentence structure, 66-68
major axis (ellipses), 233
markings, geometry, 236-237
mathematics rules
    intermediate algebra and coordinate graphing, 298-299
    plane geometry and trigonometry, 299
    pre-algebra and elementary algebra, 296-298
Mathematics test, 153
    addition, 158-159, 183
    basic structure, 153-155
    coordinate graphing
      circles, 232
      distance between two points, 231-232
      ellipses, 233
      lines, 230-231
      parabolas, 232-233
      piecewise functions, 234-235
      transformations, 234
    directions, 153
    division, fractions, 184

exponents, 170
fractions
    addition, 183
    division, 184
    multiplication, 184
    subtractions, 183
intermediate algebra
    exponential functions, 229
    logarithms, 229-230
    quadratic functions, 227-228
multiplication, 160-161, 184, 213-215
plane geometry
    circles, 244-246
    notations and markings, 236-237
    parallel lines, 239
    polygons, 243-244
    right solids, 246-249
    terms, 237-238
    triangles, 239-242
    types of angles, 238
practice exam
    answers, 400-416, 515-525
    questions, 340-361, 466-483
pre-algebra and elementary algebra
    absolute value, 161-163
    algebraic expressions, 209-220
    arithmetic sequences, 180-181
    bases and exponents, 170-173
    factors and multiples, 173-179
    fractions, 183-196
    functions, 197-199
    geometric sequences, 181-183
    linear equations, 220-221
    linear inequalities, 225-226
    matrices, 224-225
    mean, 205-206
    median, 205-208
    mode, 205, 208-209
    operations, 158-161
    powers, 167
    probability, 199-202
    properties, 164-167
    proportion, 203-204
    rate problems, 196-197
    ratio, 203

roots, 167-170

scientific notation, 163-164

systems of linear equations, 222-224

types of numbers, 155-158

variables in terms of variables, 221-222

readiness self-assessment, 7

sample questions, 256-260

subtraction, 160, 183

test-taking tips, 154

trigonometry

acute angles, 249-250

cos and sin graphs, 251-252

equations, 253-254

related angles, 250

matrices, 224-225

mean, 205-206, 297

median, 205-208, 297

metric system, standard prefixes, 266

micro prefix, 268

midpoint, 238

minor axis (ellipses), 233

mode, 205, 208-209, 297

Moderately Competitive schools, admission standards, 21

Most Competitive schools, admission standards, 20

multiple percent increases/decreases, 195-196, 297

multiples, 173

divisibility, 178-179

GCF (greatest common factor), 176-177

LCM (least common multiple), 177-178

prime numbers, 174-176

multiplication

fractions, 184

operation, 160

expressions with variables, 213

negative numbers, 161

polynomials, 214-215

N

n (billionth), 268

names of persons, enclosing with commas, 36-37

nano prefix, 268

nanosecond (ns), 268

natural numbers, 156

Natural Science passages (Reading test), 102

sample passages, 103

sample questions, 104

negative exponents, 173

negative numbers, 158

multiplication, 161

simplified expressions, 157

subtraction, 160

Newtons, 270

non-essential phrases, commas, 31

notations, geometry, 236-237

nouns, 46

number lines (real), 157

number types, 155-158

number vocabulary, 296

O

odd numbers, 296

operations (mathematical)

addition, 158-159, 183

division, 160-161, 184

exponents, 170

fractions, 198

addition, 183

converting to decimals, 189

division, 184

equations, 187-189

multiplication, 184

percentages, 190-196

repeating decimals, 190

subtraction, 183

word problems, 185-187

matrices, 224-225

multiplication, 160-161, 184

order of, 210-211

subtraction, 160, 183

opposing viewpoints

Science Reasoning test, 282-283

writing essays, 142-144

order combinations, 200

order of operations, 210-211, 296

ordering data sets, 279-281

organization of lists, semicolons, 44

organization of sentences, 68-70

origin (axes), 230

Outer terms (FOIL method), 214

outlines, essays, 127-128

overview of test format, 6

P

parabolas, coordinate graphing, 232-233

paragraphs

    organization of sentences, 69-70

    style, 71-72

parallel lines, 231, 238-239, 298

parallelograms, 244

parentheses (( )), 39-40

parts of a graph

    axes, 269

    title, 268

parts of circles, 244-246

parts of speech

    adjectives, 48-49

    adverbs, 49-50

    nouns, 46

    pronouns, 47

    verbs, 48

passages

    English test, 24, 66-68

    Reading test, 86-88

        Humanities passages, 98-102

        Natural Science passages, 102-104

        Prose Fiction passages, 89-93

        sample exam prep passages/questions, 106-117

        Social Science passages, 93-98

    Science Reasoning test, 261

        data representation, 266-273

        data sections, 263

        opposing viewpoints, 282-283

        questions, 263-265

        research summaries, 273-282

        text, 262

patterns (graphs), Science Reasoning test, 269

per (forward slash), 268

percent changes, 297

percentages, 190

    increases/decreases, 191-195

    multiple percent increases/decreases, 195-196

perimeter (polygons), 237

periods (.), 40

    fragment identification, 41

    sin and cos graphs, 251

permutations, 200-201

perpendicular lines, 231, 238, 298

personalized study plans, 9

    schedule setup, 10-11

    study sessions structure, 11

pH abbreviation, 268

phase shift (sin and cos graphs), 251

piecewise functions, coordinate graphing, 234-235

placebos, 281

PLAN (pre-ACT test), 12

plane geometry

    circles, 244-246

    notations and markings, 236-237

    parallel lines, 239

    polygons, 243-244

    right solids

        surface area, 247-248

        symmetry, 248-249

        volume, 246-247

    rules, 299

    terms, 237-238

    triangles, 239

        30-60-90 degree triangles, 240

        45-45-90 degree triangles, 241

        equilateral triangles, 241

        isosceles triangles, 241

        Pythagorean theorem, 242

        similar triangles, 240

    types of angles, 238

plural possession, 27

point of intersection, 222

points of change, 271

polygons

    perimeter, 237

    quadrilaterals, 244

    vertices, 243

polynomials, algebraic expressions, 214-215
positive expressions, 157
positive numbers, 157-158
possession
apostrophes, 26-27
plural possession, 27
powers, 167
practice
essay writing, 141
finding opposing viewpoints, 142-144
introductions, 145-146
free-writing, 121-123
practice exams, 303, 429
English assessment
answers, 385-393, 501-508
questions, 304-326, 430-453
Math assessment
answers, 400-416, 515-525
questions, 340-361, 466-483
Reading assessment
answers, 394-399, 510-514
questions, 327-339, 454-465
Science Reasoning assessment
answers, 417-425, 526-530
questions, 362-383, 484-499
scoring, 426-427, 531-532
Writing assessment, 384, 500
pre-algebra
absolute value, 161-163
algebraic expressions, 209
evaluation, 211-212
factoring, 216-220
like terms, 212-213
multiplying polynomials, 214-215
multiplying variables, 213
order of operations, 210-211
arithmetic sequences, 180-181
bases and exponents, 170-171
different bases, 172-173
negative exponents, 173
exponents, 170
factors and multiples, 173
divisibility, 178-179
GCF (greatest common factor), 176-177

LCM (least common multiple), 177-178
prime numbers, 174-176
fractions
addition, 183
converting to decimals, 189
division, 184
equations, 187-189
multiplication, 184
percentages, 190-196
repeating decimals, 190
subtractions, 183
word problems, 185-187
functions, 197-199
geometric sequences, 181-183
linear equations, 220-221
linear inequalities, 225-226
matrices, 224-225
mean, 205-206
median, 205-208
mode, 205, 208-209
operations
addition, 158-159
division, 160-161
multiplication, 160-161
subtraction, 160
powers, 167
probability
fundamental counting principle, 199
permutations and combinations, 200-201
rules, 201-202
properties
distributive property, 164-166
reciprocal property, 166-167
proportion, 203-204
rate problems, 196-197
ratio, 203
roots, 167-170
rules, 296-298
scientific notation, 163-164
systems of linear equations, 222-224
types of numbers, 155-158
variables in terms of variables, 221-222
predictions, experimental results, 278

prefixes
micro, 268
nano, 268
preparation
Reading test
reading speed, 83-84
text summarization, 84
time management, 85-86
vocabulary words, 84
Writing test
practicing free-writing, 121-123
reading quality material, 120-121
prepositional phrases, 53
pretests, 9
prewriting essays, 126
angle, 130
outlines, 127-128
viewpoints, 128-129
prime numbers, 174-176, 296
prisms, 246
probability
fundamental counting principle, 199
outcomes, 297
permutations and combinations, 200-201
rules, 201-202
successive independent events, 297
problem/purpose (scientific method), 274
procedure (scientific method), 274
prompts, writing essays, 139-140
pronouns, 47, 58-60
proofreading checklist, essay revisions, 137-138
properties
distributive, 164-166
reciprocal, 166-167
proportion, 203-204
Prose Fiction passages (Reading test), 89
sample passage, 90
sample questions, 91-93
punctuation, English test
apostrophes ('), 26-29
colons (:), 29-31
commas (,), 31-37, 45
dashes (-), 37-38

exclamation points (!), 38-39
parentheses (( )), 39-40
periods (.), 40-41
question marks (?), 41-42
quotation marks ("), 42-44
resources, 45
semicolons (;), 44-45
pyramids, 246
Pythagorean theorem, 231, 242, 299
Pythagorean triples, 242

Q - R

quadratic formula, 298
quadratic functions, 227-228, 298
quadrilaterals, 237, 244
question marks (?), 41-42
questions
Reading test, 106-114
Mathematics test, 256-260
Science Reasoning test, 263-265
quotation marks ("), 30, 42-44

radians, 252
radical expressions, 169-170
radicals, 167-169
radius (circles), 245
range (functions), 197, 298
rate problems, 196-197, 298
ratio, 203
rational numbers, 156
rays, geometry notation, 237
readiness for test
ideal candidates, 6-7
self-assessment
English test, 7
exam readiness, 8-9
Math test, 7
Reading test, 8
Science test, 8
Writing test, 8

reading

graphs, Science Reasoning test, 269

quality materials, Writing test preparation, 120-121

reading passages

English test, 24

Reading test, 86-88

Humanities passages, 98-102

Natural Science passages, 102-104

Prose Fiction passages, 89-93

sample exam prep passages/questions, 106-117

Social Science passages, 93-98

Science Reasoning test, 261

data representation, 266-273

data sections, 263

opposing viewpoints, 282-283

questions, 263-265

research summaries, 273-282

text, 262

Reading test

content areas, 82-83

directions, 81-82

expectations, 81

order of material, 83

passage questions, 86-88

Humanities passages, 98-102

Natural Science passages, 102-104

Prose Fiction passages, 89-93

sample exam prep passages/questions, 106-117

Social Science passages, 93-98

practice exams

answers, 394-399, 510-514

questions, 327-339, 454-465

preparation

reading speed, 83-84

text summarization, 84

time management, 85-86

vocabulary words, 84

readiness self-assessment, 8

signal words

conclusion, 85

contrast, 85

same thought, 86

time management, 83

6, 296

, 161-163

reciprocal functions, 250

reciprocal property, 166-167

rectangles, 244

reflection (symmetry), 249

registration, 12-13

related angles, 250

repeating decimals, 190

research (scientific method), 274

research summaries, Science Reasoning test, 273

dependent variables, 275

experimental design questions, 281-282

independent variables, 274-275

ordering data sets, 279-281

predictions based on experiment results, 278

scientific method, 273-278

resources, English test punctuation, 45

results/conclusion (scientific method), 274

revisions, 136, 138-139

rhetorical skills, 23

right solids

surface area, 247-248

symmetry, 248-249

volume, 246-247

roots

radical expressions, 169-170

radicals, 167-169

rules

English, 295

mathematics

intermediate algebra and coordinate graphing, 298-299

plane geometry and trigonometry, 299

pre-algebra and elementary algebra, 296-298

probability, 201-202

science, 300

writing, 300

run-ons, sentence structure, 64-65

S

same thought words, reading passages, 86

sample questions

English test, 75-79

Mathematics test, 256-260

Reading test, 106-117

schedule setup, personalized study plan, 10-11

science

abbreviations, 266-268, 301

rules, 300

Science Reasoning test, 261

challenge questions, 284-291

practice exam

answers, 417-425, 526-530

questions, 362-383, 484-499

reading passages, 261

data representation, 266-273

data sections, 263

opposing viewpoints, 282-283

questions, 263-265

readiness self-assessment, 8

research summaries, 273-282

text, 262

scientific method, 273-274

application of, 275-276

support for hypothesis, 276-278

scientific notation, 163-164

score interpretation, 18-20

scoring

essays, 140-141

interpretation, 18-20

sample tests, 426-427, 531-532

secant, 299

sector (circles), 245

self-assessments

English test, 7

exam readiness, 8-9

Math test, 7

Reading test, 8

Science test, 8

Writing test, 8

semicolons (;), 44-45

sentences

organization of, 68-70

structures of

fragments, 63-64

main ideas, 66-68

run-ons, 64-65

style, 71

separation of clauses, semicolons, 44

sequences

arithmetic sequences, 180-181

geometric sequences, 181-183

serial commas, 34-36

setting up a schedule, personalized study plan, 10-11

signal words, Reading test

conclusion, 85

contrast, 85

same thought, 86

signed numbers, 157

similar triangles, 240

simple subjects, 50-51

simplified equations, 213

simplified expressions, 157

sin graphs, 251-252

sine, 299

sine ratios, 249

single hatch mark, 268

singular nouns, possession, 27

slope, 230, 269

slope of a line, 298

Social Science passages (Reading test), 93-94

sample passage, 95-96

sample questions, 96-98

SOHCAHTOA acronym, 250, 299

solids (right)

surface area, 247-248

symmetry, 248-249

volume, 246-247

solutions, 222

solution sets, 225

special needs accommodations, 13

specific gravity, 266

specific to general thinking (inductive reasoning), 272

speech, parts of

adjectives, 48-49

adverbs, 49-50

nouns, 46

pronouns, 47

verbs, 48

speed reading, 83-84

spheres, 247

square root symbols, 169-170

standard prefixes (metric system), 266
standard scientific notation, 268
standards for admission
    Highly Competitive schools, 21
    Less Competitive schools, 21-22
    Moderately Competitive schools, 21
    Most Competitive schools, 20
    Very Competitive schools, 21
statement of a principle, 283
strategies
    English test, 25
    test-taking tips, 14-15
structures
    Mathematics test, 153-155
    study sessions, 11
study plans, 9
    schedule setup, 10-11
    study sessions structure, 11
study sessions, structure, 11
subject-verb agreement, 50
    compound subjects, 52-54
    problematic situations, 56-58
    sentences beginning with phrases/clauses, 54-55
    simple subjects, 51
subordinate conjunctions, 61-63
subtraction, 160, 183
summarization of text, Reading test preparation, 84
supplementary angles, 299
surface area, solids, 247-248
symmetry, solids, 248-249
systems of linear equations, 222-224

T

tangent, 299
tangent lines (circles), 245
tangent ratios, 249
terms, geometry, 237-238
test day expectations, 16
tests
    English
        consistent tone, 72-74
        word choice, 73-74

    expectations, 23-26
    format, 23
    grammar, 46-63
    organization of sentences, 68-70
    paragraph style, 71-72
    passages, 24
    practice exam, 304-326, 385-393, 430-453, 501-508
    punctuation, 26-45
    readiness self-assessment, 7
    sample test questions, 75-79
    sentence structure, 63-68
    sentence style, 71
    strategies, 25
Mathematics
    basic structure, 153-155
    coordinate graphing, 230-235
    directions, 153
    intermediate algebra, 227-230
    plane geometry, 236-249
    practice exam, 340-361, 400-416, 466-483, 515-525
    pre-algebra and elementary algebra, 155-226
    readiness self-assessment, 7
    sample questions, 256-260
    test-taking tips, 154
    trigonometry, 249-254
Reading
    content areas, 82-83
    directions, 81-82
    expectations, 81
    order of material, 83
    passage questions, 86-104, 106-117
    practice exam, 327-339, 394-399, 454-465, 510-514
    preparation, 83-86
    readiness self-assessment, 8
    signal words, 85-86
    time management, 83
Science Reasoning
    challenge questions, 284-291
    practice exam, 362-383, 417-425, 484-499, 526-530
    readiness self-assessment, 8
    reading passages, 261-283
scoring sample tests, 426-427, 531-532

test-taking tips, 14-15, 154
Writing, 119
    challenge exercises, 147-151
    directions, 123-125
    essay scores, 140-141
    practice, 141-146
    practice exam, 384, 500
    preparation, 120-123
    readiness self-assessment, 8
    writing process, 125-140
text
    reading passages (Science Reasoning test), 262
    summarization, preparation for Reading test, 84
time management
    preparation for Reading test, 85-86
    Reading test, 83
title (graphs), Science Reasoning test, 268
tone, English test, 72-74
transformations, coordinate graphing, 234
transversals, 239, 299
trapezoids, 244
trends (graphs), Science Reasoning test, 269
triangles
    30-60-90 degree triangles, 240
    45-45-90 degree triangles, 241
    area, 239
    equilateral triangles, 241
    geometry notation, 237
    isosceles triangles, 241
    Pythagorean theorem, 242
    similar triangles, 240
trigonometry
    acute angles, 249-250
    cos and sin graphs, 251-252
    equations, 253-254
    related angles, 250
    rules, 299
types of numbers, 155-158

U - V

undefined expressions, 157
university admission standards
    Highly Competitive schools, 21
    Less Competitive schools, 21-22
    Moderately Competitive schools, 21

    Most Competitive schools, 20
    Very Competitive schools, 21

variables
    algebraic expressions, 213
    in terms of variables, 221-222
    isolating, 220
    Science Reasoning test, 263
verb-subject agreement, 50
    compound subjects, 52-54
    problematic situations, 56-58
    sentences beginning with phrases/clauses, 54-55
    simple subjects, 51
verbs, 48
vertex (parabola), 232
vertical angles, 299
vertices (polygons), 243
Very Competitive schools, admission standards, 21
viewpoints
    essays, 128-129, 142-144
    opposing (Science Reasoning test), 282-283
vocabulary
    number vocabulary, 296
    words, Reading test preparation, 84
volume, solids, 246-247

W

websites
    ACT, 9
    ACT Student, 19
who versus whom, 74
whole numbers, 156
whom versus who, 74
word choice, English test, 73-74
word problems, fractions, 185-187
writing process, 125
    drafting, 130, 136
        body paragraphs, 133-135
        conclusions, 135-136
        introductions, 131-133
    prewriting, 126
        angle, 130
        brainstorming viewpoints, 128-129
        outlining essays, 127-128

revisions, 136, 139
    proofreading checklist, 137-138
rules, 300
sample prompt, 139-140
Writing test, 119
directions, 123-125
practice exam, 384, 500
preparation
    practicing free-writing, 121-123
    reading quality material, 120-121
readiness self-assessment, 8
writing process, 125
    challenge exercises, 147-151
    drafting, 130-136
    essay scores, 140-141
    practice, 141-146
    prewriting, 126-130
    revisions, 136-139
    sample prompt, 139-140

X - Y - Z

x-axis, 269
x-intercept, 230

y-axis, 269
y-intercept, 230

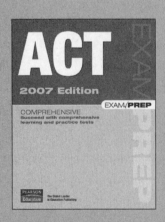